Presidential
Campaigns

Presidential Campaigns

REVISED EDITION

Paul F. Boller, Jr.

New York   Oxford
OXFORD UNIVERSITY PRESS
1996

Oxford University Press

Oxford   New York
Athens   Auckland   Bangkok   Bombay
Calcutta   Cape Town   Dar es Salaam   Delhi
Florence   Hong Kong   Istanbul   Karachi
Kuala Lumpur   Madras   Madrid   Melbourne
Mexico City   Nairobi   Paris   Singapore
Taipei   Tokyo   Toronto

and associated companies in
Berlin   Ibadan

First published in 1984 by Oxford University Press, Inc.,
198 Madison Avenue, New York, NY 10016

First issued as an Oxford University Press paperback, 1985, with a new chapter.

First published as a revised edition, 1996.

Oxford is a registered trademark of Oxford University Press

Library of Congress Cataloging-in-Publication Data
Boller, Paul F.
Presidential campaigns / Paul F. Boller, Jr.—Rev. ed.
p.   cm.
Includes bibliographical references (p.   ) and index.
ISBN 0-19-510716-0—ISBN 0-19-509730-0 (pbk.)
1. Presidents—United States—Election—History—Anecdotes,
facetiae, satire, etc.   2. United States—Politics and government—
Anecdotes, facetiae, satire, etc.   I. Title.
E176.1.B683   1996   324.973—dc20   95-26484

1 3 5 7 9 8 6 4 2

Printed in the United States of America
on acid-free paper

for
John
James, Jr.
John, Jr., and Marina

Preface

Presidential campaigns have been mean and nasty lately, but the fact is they weren't very nice in the old days either. What respectable person today would think of calling one of the candidates for the highest office in the land a carbuncled-faced old drunkard? Or a howling atheist? Or a pickpocket, thief, traitor, lecher, syphilitic, gorilla, crook, anarchist, murderer? Yet such charges were regular features of American presidential contests in the 19th century. And high hats as well as lowbrows indulged in the invective.

In 1800 Abigail Adams lamented that the contest between her husband John and Thomas Jefferson that year had exuded enough venom to "ruin and corrupt the minds and morals of the best people in the world."[1] In 1864 *Harper's Weekly* published a depressingly long list of all the vicious epithets hurled at Abraham Lincoln during his bid for re-election. And in 1884 Lord Bryce, sojourning in the New World, was astonished to find that the Cleveland-Blaine match had come to center on the "copulative habits" of one candidate and the "prevaricative habits" of the other. Bryce was so impressed by the "tempest of invective and calumny which hurtles around the head of a presidential candidate" that he told Britishers they could understand its violence only if they imagined "all the accusations brought against all the 670 seats in the English Parliament" were "concentrated on one man."[2] Historian William S. McFeely is right: campaigns in recent years don't seem so outrageous by comparison.[3]

But presidential campaigns, even at their fiercest, were always more than contests in scurrility. They were also great entertainments. The scurrilousness, in fact, was to some extent part of the fun and the invective at times joyously creative. As early as 1792 the voice of the people, it was said, was "the voice of grog" at election time. From almost the beginning, America's quadrennial confrontation was in part a circus, carnival, vaudeville show, pageant, extravaganza, spectacle, the Greatest Show on Earth. The "great American shindig," one Englishman called it.[4] "Politics," remarked Ronald Reagan in 1966, "is just like show business." Asked what he meant, he explained: "You have a hell of an opening, you coast for a while, you have a hell of a closing."[5] Lord Bryce thought the ballyhoo accompanying presidential canvasses was uniquely (and typically) American.

Some people have deplored the fun and games that go with the quadrennial battles. Writing about the log-cabin–hard-cider campaign of 1840, Carl Schurz lamented that "the immense multitudes gathered at the meetings came to be amused, not to be instructed. They met, not to think and deliberate, but to laugh and shout and sing."[6] But other campaign-watchers gloried in the fun. "When I was a boy presidential campaigns were characterized by a high serious purpose," wrote H. L. Mencken. "But now all that is happily past." Mencken particularly enjoyed nominating conventions. "There is something about a national convention," he wrote, "that makes it as fascinating as a revival or a hanging. . . . One sits through long sessions wishing heartily that all the delegates and alternates were dead and in hell—and then suddenly there comes a show so gaudy and hilarious, so melodramatic and obscene, so unimaginably exhilarating and preposterous that one lives a gorgeous year in an hour."[7] Mencken covered all the conventions from 1900 to 1948 and for his life wouldn't have missed one of them.

But presidential campaigns have always had their serious as well as their silly and scurrilous sides. At times our campaigns have dramatized pressing issues, educated as well as entertained, and presented popular debates as well as variety shows. The issues have ranged all the way from banking (1832), tariffs (1888), and monetary policy (1896) to slavery (1860), foreign policy (1916), and the role of government in coping with economic crisis (1932). Democratic candidate Adlai E. Stevenson thought presidential campaigns provided "a great opportunity to educate and elevate" the electorate and in 1952 and 1956 he did his best to "talk sense" to the American people.[8] But even in the elections in which the hoopla outdid the hortatory, voters usually knew what they were voting for (and against) when they went to the polls. And even in the most momentous campaigns of all, like those in 1860 and 1932, there was frivolity as well as serious discussion throughout. Very early in our history picnics, barbecues, parades, songs, chants, slogans, and rallies became essential parts of presidential campaigns. Even our wartime elections (1864, 1944) had their share of fun-making.

Hundreds of books and articles have been written about American presidential campaigns. Some of them chronicle all the elections from 1789 onward. Many more concentrate on particular elections of special interest and significance. Still more are concerned with customs and procedures—nominating conventions, primaries, voting habits, the

Electoral College, campaign techniques—and pass judgment and propose reforms. The present book tries to do something different. It describes the major thrust of each of the elections from 1789 to 1992 and accompanies them with "campaign highlights"—amusing incidents, significant developments, dramatic happenings, unusual electioneering methods, notable oratory—that help illuminate the candidates and the issues and place the contests in the larger context of American history and culture. Like *Presidential Anecdotes* (1981, 1996), to which it is a sequel, it has been based on diaries, letters, journals, biographies, and autobiographies of the people involved as well as on the work of specialists in campaign history. It has also made use of newspapers, handbills, leaflets, and pamphlets which made their appearance during the quadrennial storms.

Like our Presidents, our presidential campaigns have been multifarious. Some of them have been deadly dull; others have been full of color, suspense, and excitement. I have naturally devoted far more space to the lively encounters than to the pedestrian ones, and the chapters vary considerably in length. I have also bowed to the American passion for contemporaneity by saying more about recent campaigns. There is, unhappily, much that is missing here. The amount of material about our presidential contests is of course prodigious, and the preparation of this book has involved considerable winnowing, pruning, shortening, and excising to bring it down to reasonable length. I regret, among other things, having to say so little about third parties.

Presidential Campaigns, I trust, disproves at least two popular laws of American politics. One of them is Farley's law: that nothing happens between nominating conventions and election day to change the minds of voters. The other is Corwin's law: "if you would succeed in life, you must be as solemn as an ass. All the great monuments on earth have been built to solemn asses." Franklin Roosevelt, a master campaigner, never behaved as if he believed his associate Jim Farley's pronouncement. As for the law formulated by Ohio politician Thomas Corwin during the Gilded Age, there has indeed been a great deal of solemnity attending America's quadrennial encounters but there has also been a great deal of fun.

Paul F. Boller, Jr.

Texas Christian University
Fort Worth, Texas
January 1996

Contents

xii   *Contents*

Presidential Campaigns

★★★★★★★★★★★★★★★★★★★★★★★

CHAPTER ONE

1789
Starting Off: George Washington

The first presidential election in American history was thoroughly un-democratic. There were no primaries, nominating conventions, rival candidates, campaign speeches, or debates on public issues; and the American people didn't even get to vote for their Chief Executive. Yet the election of George Washington as first President of the United States was a perfect expression of the popular will. Rousseau himself couldn't have asked for a more stunning instance of the General Will in action. It was never to be like this again.

Washington, everyone agreed, simply had to be the first President. Even while the Constitution-makers were working on a new framework of government in Philadelphia in 1787, it was taken for granted that the hero of the American Revolution would head any government they succeeded in launching. But the Founding Fathers were not sure the people would choose wisely after Washington passed from the scene, so they devised a clumsy method for selecting Chief Magistrates which they hoped would avoid the weaknesses of popular elections. Each state, according to their plan, would choose several presidential electors and then the electors, collectively known as the Electoral College, would vote for two people, with the one receiving the most votes becoming President and the one with the next most becoming Vice-President. States could choose their electors any way they pleased and each state had as many electors as Senators and Representatives.

Everyone knew the Electoral College would pick Washington for first place with the hearty approval of the people. But Washington, who was fifty-six, had mixed feelings about the honor. He was enjoying retirement at Mount Vernon and wondered whether he was up to the job of heading the young nation's new government. At the same time he liked the U.S. Constitution and was anxious to help get things off to a good start. "We cannot, sir, do without you," a Maryland official wrote him. Alexander Hamilton told him he was convinced that "every public and personal consideration will demand from you an acquiescence in what will *certainly* be the unanimous wish of your country."[1] In the end Washington gave way and received all 69 votes in the Electoral College on February 4, 1789. John Adams became Vice-President but got only 34 votes. That was because some of the electors (chosen on January 4 in some states by state legislatures and in others by popular votes) cast one of their two votes for someone besides Adams to be sure he got fewer votes than the "American Fabius."

Washington's journey to New York for the first inauguration on April 30 was one prolonged ovation. Everywhere he went he was greeted with feasts, flags, parades, toasts, songs, orations, cheers, handshakes, gun salutes, bells, bonfires, and triumphal arches. "Well, he deserves it all," exclaimed people wherever he went.[2] Adams was in a less festive mood. "My country," he told his wife Abigail, "has in its wisdom contrived for me the most insignificant office that ever the invention of man contrived or his imagination conceived."[3] But a Baltimore newspaper regarded inauguration day as a momentous event: "Perhaps that day has exhibited what has never happened before in any part of the globe; above three millions of people, scattered over a country of vast extent, of opposite habits and different manners, all fixing their hopes on the same man, and unanimously voting for him only, without the intervention of force, artifice, plan, or concert."[4]

☆ ☆ ☆

Mr. President

Just before Washington took his oath of office, Congress took up the question of titles for the Chief Magistrate. There were several suggestions: "His Excellency," "Elective Majesty," "His Serene Highness," "Elective Highness," and "His Highness, the President of the United States and Protector of the Rights of the Same." At a dinner party about this time Speaker of the House Frederick A. Muhlenberg of Pennsylvania discussed the subject with Washington and a stout Pennsylvania Congressman named Henry Wyncoop. "Well, General Muhlenberg," said Washington, "what do you think of the title of High Mightiness?" "Why, General," laughed Muhlenberg, "if we were certain that the office would always be held by men as large as yourself or my friend Wyncoop, it would be appropriate enough; but if by chance a President as small as my opposite neighbor should be elected, it would be ridiculous." Washington apparently didn't find the remark funny, but everyone else burst into laughter. In the end Congress adopted a plain title: "Mr. President." For second place someone suggested "His Superfluous Excellency," but Adams was sworn in as "Vice-President."[5]

★ ★ ★ ★ ★ · ★ ★ ★ ★ ★ ★ ★ ★ ★ ★ ★ ★ ★ ★

CHAPTER TWO

1792
Washington Again

Long before his first term was over, George Washington was contemplating retirement. He even asked his old friend James Madison to help him prepare a valedictory statement. Madison tried hard to dissuade him. Washington's refusal to run for re-election, he said, "would give a surprise and shock to the public mind."[1] But Washington was persistent. His health was poor, he said, and his memory declining. And it was about time, he thought, for the young republic to show the monarchies of the world that it could change leaders peacefully. Madison wasn't convinced; nor was anyone else to whom Washington confided his intentions. It was the one thing that his Secretary of State, Thomas Jefferson, and Secretary of the Treasury, Alexander Hamilton, agreed on.

Hamilton and Jefferson had little in common but their red hair. Hamilton was an economic nationalist who wanted to promote the interests of the nation's merchants, bankers, and manufacturers, while Jefferson favored the agrarian classes and leaned toward laissez-faire and states' rights. Hamilton, too, was a self-made man who enjoyed the company of the well-to-do, and the aristocratic Jefferson couldn't help looking down on him as something of an *arriviste*. As Treasury head, Hamilton sponsored measures—funding the national debt, taking over the states' debts, establishing a national bank—that helped the commercial classes of the Northeast but did nothing for Jefferson's beloved farmers and planters. He also took great liberties with the Constitution, Jefferson thought, finding authorization for his bank and even for bounties for manufacturing in some of the vague clauses appearing in that document.

Jefferson became alarmed. It began to look as though Hamilton and his supporters in Congress were trying to establish a "consolidated" government, even a monarchy, that would swallow up the liberties of both the states and individuals, and Washington didn't seem to realize what was going on. Hamilton, moreover, had a stout champion in John Fenno, editor of the influential *Gazette of the United States,* while his critics had no journalistic outlet. To expose the "aristocratical and monarchical" designs of the Hamiltonians, therefore, and to fight Fenno, Jefferson brought Philip Freneau, Republican poet, to the capital and helped him establish the *National Gazette,* a bi-weekly. In no time at all the two papers were engaged in acrimonious exchanges dramatizing the split on policy between Washington's two leading Cabinet members. The Fenno-Freneau frenzy fascinated the public.

Washington was disturbed by both the rift between Hamilton and Jefferson and the rancorous newspaper war raging in the nation's capital. He tried without success to bring his two Cabinet members together. The "spirit of party," as he called it, was another reason for his retirement, but everyone else regarded it as an added reason for his continuing in office. And when, by his silence, he indicated his willingness to serve another term, both the "Federalists" (as the Hamiltonians called themselves) and the "Republicans" (as the Jeffersonians were beginning to call themselves) gave him their warm support.

In 1792, as in 1789, Washington was the unanimous choice of the presidential electors. John Adams, as before, came in a poor second. The electors gave him 77 votes and cast fifty for Governor George Clinton of New York, a devout Republican. "Damn 'em," Adams is alleged to have cried when he heard the news, "damn 'em, damn 'em! You see that an elective government will not do." But he agreed to become "Daddy Vice," as he called it, again, and looked forward to better things in the future.[2]

☆   ☆   ☆

Voice of Grog

When Washington ran for the Virginia House of Burgesses in 1758, he saw to it that the 391 voters and their friends received 160 gallons of rum, beer, and cider on election day. This was called "swilling the planters with bumbo." The swilling was still going on in 1792. "At an election in a certain States," reported the *Gazette of the United States* in November, "a bystander observing the particular situation of a great number of the electors, who had been regaled at the expense of one of the candidates, remarked on the occasion, *That the Voice of the People, was the Voice of Grog.*"[3]

★ ★

CHAPTER THREE

1796
Federalist Succession:
John Adams

By 1796 Washington had had enough. The "spirit of party," which had upset him in 1792, became rampant and rancorous during his second administration; and he was beginning himself to be a prime target of the anti-Hamiltonians. In his Farewell Address, released to the press in September, the first President warned against party strife; he also cautioned the American people against "excessive partiality for one foreign nation and excessive dislike of another." But no one paid any attention (then or now). The development of political parties, which the Constitution-makers had not anticipated, continued apace; and the preference of Jeffersonian Republicans for France and of Hamiltonian Federalists for Britain remained firm and unwavering. The parties continued to disagree violently over domestic and foreign policies alike.

Washington's valedictory attracted both praise and protest. The Federalists hailed it as a reservoir of wisdom and circulated it as a campaign document. But the Republicans spurned it as unabashedly Hamiltonian in outlook. William Duane thought Washington's Farewell "fraught with incalculable evils to your country" and exclaimed: "Would to God you had retired to a private station four years ago. . . ."[1] Benjamin Franklin Bache, Franklin's grandson ("Lightning Rod, Junior"), was even more disdainful. "If ever a nation was debauched by a man," he wrote in the *Aurora*, a Republican paper he and Duane edited in Philadelphia, "the American nation has been debauched by Washington."[2] Bache was especially grieved by Washington's neutrality policy in the war that broke out in 1793 between Britain and America's old Revolutionary ally France. He also thought Jay's Treaty, which Washington sponsored in 1795 to keep the peace with England, was a sell-out: it completely ignored British violations of American neutral rights at sea and her impressment of American sailors into the Royal Navy.

"Washington's Farewell Address," remarked Fisher Ames, Federalist stalwart, was "a signal, like dropping a hat, for the party racers to start."[3] With Washington out of the way, the two fledgling political parties leaped into action. Since 1792 they had acquired the rudiments of organization; and though there were still no formal nominating sessions, party leaders in and outside Congress did meet informally to agree on candidates for the coming contest. Vice-President John Adams, Washington's "heir apparent," was the logical choice for the Federalists; and to capture electoral votes in the South they added Thomas Pinckney, South Carolina diplomat who had concluded an advantageous treaty with Spain in 1795, to the ticket. The Republicans naturally designated Jefferson for first place and picked Senator Aaron Burr of New York as his running mate in order to pick up votes in the North. Elections for presidential electors took place in November; and, as in 1789 and 1792, they were chosen by legislatures in some states and by popular votes in others. For that reason it was both possible and desirable for the Federalists and the Republicans to conduct campaigns for their candidates.

The first real presidential contest in American history turned out to be exuberantly venomous. On both sides handbills, pamphlets, and articles in party newspapers denounced, disparaged, damned, decried, denigrated, and declaimed. There were plenty of issues. For the Federalists there was Jefferson's sympathy for the French Revolution despite the guillotine and the Terror; and there was also his religious heterodoxy. The Republicans had Adams's lack of faith in the people to harp on as well as his preference for high-toned government. Late in October, to the embarrassment of the Republicans, Pierre Adet, French minister to the United States, publicly denounced the Federalists' foreign policy and said French-American relations would improve with Jefferson as President. The Republicans hastily disavowed Adet's action, but the Federalists indignantly called it "an outrageous attempt on the dignity of an independent nation" and claimed it proved Jefferson was the tool of a foreign power.[4]

Adams and Jefferson themselves remained on good terms during the contest and neither deigned to take an active part in it. But their followers throughout the land filled the air with charges and countercharges. It was perhaps surprising, and certainly gratifying, that it all ended peacefully enough. In 1796, as in later elections, there was a great gap between rhetoric and reality. Adams was more of a republican and Jefferson less of a democrat than either friend or foe was willing to acknowledge. Yet the Republicans called Adams "an avowed friend of monarchy" who plotted to make his sons "Seigneurs or Lords of this country."[5] And the Federalists called Jefferson an atheist, anarchist, demagogue, coward, mountebank, trickster, and Franco-maniac, and said his followers were "cut-throats who walk in rags and sleep amidst filth and vermin."[6]

Adams, now sixty-one, won the shouting match, but not by much. He came out on top with 71 votes to Jefferson's 68, Pinckney's 59, and Burr's 30. Some disappointed Republicans taunted him with the cry, "President by three votes!"[7] But Jefferson cheerfully accepted second place under Adams, who, he said, "has always been my senior." The "second office . . . is honorable and easy," he added; "the first is but splendid misery."[8] It didn't take Adams long to find that out.

☆ ☆ ☆

Act, Not Think

The Constitution-framers expected presidential electors to exercise independent judgment when they cast their votes, but the rise of the two-party system changed all that. In February 1797, one of the two Federalist electors from Pennsylvania bolted the Federalist ticket to which he had been pledged and cast his vote in the Electoral College for Jefferson. "What!" cried an angry Federalist, writing to the *Gazette of the United States,* "Do I chuse Samuel Miles to determine for me whether John Adams or Thomas Jefferson shall be President? No! I chuse him to *act,* not to think!"[9]

CHAPTER FOUR

1800
Republican Takeover:
Jefferson's Revolution

John Adams's Presidency was tumultuous. By 1800 a torrent of what he called "squibs, scoffs, and sarcasms" was descending on him.[1] The Republicans continued to doubt his commitment to republican institutions, deplored the drift toward war with France, and blasted the Alien and Sedition Acts which he sponsored in 1798 to stifle critics of his administration. But the High Federalists (or Hamiltonians) liked him as little as the Republicans did. They thought he was an appeaser. When he sent a peace mission to France in 1799 after the disgraceful "XYZ Affair" of 1797, Hamilton and his supporters decided the President was hopeless. They rumbled and grumbled—and moaned and groaned—about Mr. X, Mr. Y, and Mr. Z. That was the way Adams had referred to the three French agents who tried to bribe American diplomats in Paris when he reported the incident to Congress.

As the 1800 election approached, Federalist leaders swallowed hard and, when Washington, shortly before his death, refused to run for a third term, they selected Adams again and put South Carolina's Charles Cotesworth Pinckney, brother of Adams's running mate in 1796, on the ticket with him. Pinckney was famous for having cried, "not a sixpence," when Monsieurs X, Y, and Z tried to bribe him. After the Federalists had made their choices, Republican leaders designated Thomas Jefferson and Aaron Burr as their candidates for a second time. And then Alexander Hamilton leaped into action.

Hamilton had come to loathe Adams. Not only did he oppose the President's efforts at conciliation with France; he also resented Adams's refusal to defer to him as leader of the Federalist party. He finally decided that Adams was even worse than Jefferson. "If we must have an enemy at the head of the Government," he exclaimed, "let it be one whom we can oppose, and for whom we are not responsible, who will not involve our party in the disgrace of his foolish and bad measures."[2] Far better than Jefferson, though, was the Federalist vice-presidential candidate. Hamilton hoped that General Pinckney would draw more electoral votes in the South than Adams and that if New England electors gave the two men equal votes the South Carolinian would take first place in the Electoral College. He took a trip to New England to further his plan. He also wrote a long letter blistering Adams's domestic and foreign policies in order to turn Federalist leaders against the President. " . . . I should be deficient in candor," he wrote, "were I to conceal the conviction, that he does not possess the talents adapted to the *Administration* of Government, and that there are great and intrinsic defects in his character which unfit him for the office of Chief Magistrate." Adams, he said, was petty, mean, egotistic, erratic, eccentric, jealous-natured, and hot-tempered.[3]

Hamilton's letter was not meant for general circulation; he wrote it mainly for Federalists in South Carolina who he hoped would come to prefer Pinckney. Unfortunately for the Federalists, Burr somehow got hold of a copy, turned it over to the press, and soon Republicans everywhere were chortling over *The Public Conduct and Character of John Adams*. Noah Webster responded with a loyal defense of the President and several other Federalist writers did the same. But the damage was done. Republicans made much of Hamilton's "Thunderbolt," as James Madison called it, during the 1800 campaign. For his part, Adams angrily dismissed Hamilton as "an intriguant, the greatest intriguant in the world—a man devoid of every moral principle—a bastard. . . ."[4]

But the Federalists did more than snipe at each other. They also attacked the fifty-seven-year-old Jefferson—Deist, champion of the people, friend of the French Revolution—with savage fury. Their favorite epithet was Jacobin, that is, French radical. For a high-toned people they waved an astonishingly low-level campaign. They charged that Jefferson had cheated his British creditors, obtained his property by fraud, robbed a widow of an estate worth ten thousand pounds, and behaved in a cowardly fashion as Governor of Virginia during the Revolution. Jefferson, wrote one Federalist, was "a mean-spirited, low-lived fellow, the son of a half-breed Indian squaw, sired by a Virginia mulatto father . . . raised wholly on hoe-cake made of coarse-ground Southern corn, bacon and hominy, with an occasional change of fricaseed bullfrog."[5] Queried one Federalist leaflet:

> Can serious and reflecting men look about them and doubt that if Jefferson is elected, and the Jacobins get into authority, that those morals which protect our lives from the knife of the assassin—which guard the chastity of our wives and daughters from seduction and violence—defend our property from plunder and devastation, and shield our religion from contempt and profanation, will not be trampled upon and exploded?[6]

With Jefferson as First Magistrate, warned the *Connecticut Courant,* "Murder, robbery, rape, adultery, and incest will all be openly taught and practiced, the air will be rent with the cries of the distressed, the soil will be soaked with blood, and the nation black with crimes."[7]

In 1800, as in 1796, Jefferson's religion was a primary target. Yale's Congregationalist clergyman-president Timothy Dwight had already set the tone. In a fiery sermon in 1798 he asked why good Americans tolerated such freethinkers as the Jeffersonians. "Is it," he thundered,

> that we may assume the same character, and pursue the same conduct? Is it, that our churches may become temples of reason . . . the Bible cast into a bonfire . . . our children . . . chanting mockeries against God . . . our wives and daughters the victims of legal prostitution; soberly dishonored; speciously polluted; the outcast of delicacy and virtue, and the loathing of God and man . . . our sons the disciples of Voltaire, and the dragoons of Marat. . . ?[8]

John Mason, New York preacher, took up the cry. In *The Voice of Warning to Christians on the Ensuing Election* (1800), he warned that Jefferson was an infidel "who writes against the truths of God's word; who makes not even a profession of Christianity; who is without Sabbaths; without the sanctuary, without so much as a decent external respect for the faith and worship of Christians."[9] And in *Serious Considerations on the Election of a President,* William Linn, another New York minister, lifted quotations from Jefferson's *Notes on Virginia* to shock people and blasted the Vice-President's "open profession of Deism."[10] A writer for the *Connecticut Courant* summed up the case against Jefferson on September 29:

> Look at your houses, your parents, your wives, and your children. Are you prepared to see your dwellings in flames, hoary hairs bathed in blood, female chastity violated, or children writhing on the pike and the halbert? . . . Look at every leading Jacobin as at a ravening wolf, preparing to enter your peaceful fold, and glut his deadly appetite on the vitals of your country. . . . GREAT GOD OF COMPASSION AND JUSTICE, SHIELD MY COUNTRY FROM DESTRUCTION."[11]

But the Republicans did some smearing of their own. They called Adams a fool, hypocrite, criminal, and tyrant, and said that his Presidency was "one continued tempest of *malignant* passions."[12] They also spread the story that he planned to marry one of his sons to one of George III's daughters, start an American dynasty, and reunite the United States and Britain. To this tale they added the story that when Washington heard what Adams was up to he went to him wearing a white uniform and begged him to give up his plan, but that Adams refused. So Washington returned a second time, dressed in black, but was again rebuffed. Finally he donned a Revolutionary uniform, visited the President a third time, and threatened to run him through with a sword. At this point, according to the story, Adams finally agreed to abandon his plan. To the dynasty tale the Republicans added an improbable one about Adams's licentiousness. Adams, they said, sent General Pinckney, his running-mate, to England on a U. S. frigate to procure four pretty girls as mistresses, two for Pinckney and two for the President. "I do declare upon my honor," chuckled Adams when he heard the story, "if this be true General Pinckney has kept them all for himself and cheated me out of my two."[13]

There was, to be sure, some discussion of serious issues in 1800. The Federalists warned that Jefferson's victory would mean dismantling Hamilton's funding system, wrecking the economy, and submitting meekly to French depredations on American commerce. And the Republicans denounced the Federalist party's hawkish policy toward France, its beating of the war drums, and its suppression of domestic dissent. Yet the "spicissitude of black liquor," as Adams called it, was the main feature of America's first—and in some respects worst—vituperative presidential campaign.[14] Abigail Adams lamented that enough "abuse and scandal" was unleashed in 1800 "to ruin and corrupt the minds and morals of the best people in the world."[15]

Things looked promising for the Republicans. In May they won control of the New York legislature, partly because of Burr's great skill in mustering votes in New York City. New York, a crucial state with twelve electoral votes, had supported Adams in 1796; in 1800 the legislature was bound to pick Republican electors. In desperation Hamilton wrote Governor John Jay urging him to call the old Federalist legislature back into session and seek legislation taking choice of electors away from the legislature and giving it to the people voting in districts. He told Jay frankly that "in times like these in which we live, it will not do to be over scrupulous"; the important thing was "to prevent an atheist in religion, and a fanatic in politics, from getting possession of the helm of State." Jay did not bother to answer Hamilton; he simply filed Hamilton's letter away with the notation: "Proposing a measure for party purposes which I think would not become me to adopt."[16]

For a time the Federalists gleefully circulated a story that Jefferson had died. But the Vice-President was very much alive; it was a slave by the same name who had passed away at Monticello. Late in November, as the campaign raged around him, Jefferson went up to Washington, to which the federal government had moved in June, and calmly awaited victory. During November the sixteen states chose their electors, some by popular vote and some by legislative action; and on December 3 the electors cast their votes for President in their respective states. As reports of the voting began trickling into Washington, it became clear that the Republicans had come out on top. "The Jig's Up!" crowed the *Baltimore American*. "Be glad America!" exulted the *Readinger Adler* in Pennsylvania.[17] At parties, festivals, and banquets throughout the land Republicans proclaimed "the reign of terror is past—the dawn of the republican millennium appears in view—and the clouds of aristocracy are passing away as the vapors of the morning."[18] The Federalists began wearing such long faces, joked the Republicans, that barbers had to double their prices for shaving them. When the year reached its end, one Republican writer exuded a warm turn-of-the-century sentiment: "Here ends the 18th Century. The 19th begins with a fine clear morning wind at S. W.; and the political horizon affords as fine a prospect under Jefferson's administration, with returning harmony with France— with the irresistible propagation of the Rights of Man, the eradication of hierarchy, oppression, superstition and tyranny over the world. . . ."[19]

Although not all the returns were in, Jefferson felt confident enough of victory to write Robert R. Livingston on December 14 asking him to become Secretary of Navy in his administration. He also wrote Burr the following day congratulating him on his election as Vice-President and noting that although some of the electors had undoubtedly withheld votes from the New Yorker, he would still probably get at least four or five more votes than Adams. He expressed regret, too, that as Vice-President Burr wouldn't be able to play as active a role in the new administration as Jefferson would like him to. And he mentioned in passing that "several of the high-flying Federalists" were hoping for a tie between him and Burr so they could try for a Federalist President in the House of Representatives. Burr wrote back to say that if the matter came to the House he was sure that Jefferson would get the vote of at least nine states, which was all he needed to win.[20]

By the end of December it was clear that the improbable had happened: not even one of the Republican electors had withheld his second vote from Burr after all and as a consequence there was a tie for first place: 73 votes for Jefferson, 73 for Burr, 65 for Adams, and 64 for Pinckney. This meant that, according to the Constitution, the "high-flying Federalists" were going to have their way: it was now up to the House of Representatives, controlled by lame-duck Federalists, to choose the President. The obvious choice was Jefferson; everyone who had voted in 1800 knew he had been running for first place. But what was obvious wasn't necessarily palatable to die-hard Federalist Congressmen; many of them preferred Burr if only because they disliked Jefferson so much. And Burr did nothing to dissuade them from supporting him for first place, though he did nothing directly to advance his cause.

On February 11, 1801, the House of Representatives met in the unfinished Capitol building in Washington to pick a President. The town was crowded with people; hotels and boarding houses were chock-full and in one place fifty men slept on the floor with their coats as blankets. When the balloting began in the House chamber, every Congressmen but two was present; and one of the two, who was ill, lay in bed in an adjoining committee room and had his ballot brought in for him to sign. Each state had one vote, which was determined by a majority of the state's delegation; but if the delegation was tied the state cast a blank ballot. On the first ballot Jefferson failed to get the nine votes necessary for election; eight states went for him, six for Burr, and the other two were evenly divided and did not vote. So the Congressmen tried again— and again and again. As the balloting continued with no change in the results, many of the Congressmen sent out for nightcaps and pillows and took short naps between ballots in their chairs or on the floor wrapped in coats and shawls. Six more days and thirty-five more votes produced the same outcome. It began to look as though March 4, designated as inaugural day by Congress in 1792, would come and go without Adams's successor being chosen. Outside the Capitol building there were noisy demonstrations for Jefferson. A score of men in a huge sled went shouting through the streets waving a big banner bearing the words, "Jefferson, the Friend of the People."[21]

There were numerous efforts to break the deadlock. Some Federalists approached Burr promising him their support if he agreed to carry on Federalist policies if he became President. Burr resolutely refused to give any such assurances; he held back, though, from bowing out of the contest for first place. But Hamilton, who had helped bring Adams down, now intervened to prevent a Burr victory. He had not really changed his mind about Jefferson; but he held Burr in even lower esteem. He regarded the New Yorker as the "Catiline of America," utterly without principle, public or private, who would employ "the rogues of all parties to overrule the good men of all parties." Jefferson, by contrast, though a "contemptible hypocrite" and "tinctured with fanaticism," at least had some "pretensions to character." "I trust the Federalists will not finally be so mad as to vote for Burr," he wrote New York Senator Gouverneur Morris. "I speak with an intimate and accurate knowledge of character. His elevation can only promote the purposes of the desperate and profligate. If there be a man in the world I ought to hate, it is Jefferson. With Burr I have always been personally well. But the public good must be paramount to every private consideration."[22]

On February 17, six days after the voting had begun, several Federalist Congressmen who had been supporting Burr and failed to get any commitments from him decided to cast blank ballots and end the deadlock. On the thirty-sixth ballot that morning, one Vermont Congressman and four from Maryland abstained from voting and thus gave those states to Jefferson; and Delaware and South Carolina, previously for Burr, cast blank ballots. The outcome: Jefferson won with ten votes to Burr's four. As news of the House's decision spread through the land, exuberant Jeffersonians fired guns, rang bells, and proposed toasts to "Jefferson, the Mammoth of Democracy."[23] But the Federalist *Gazette of the United States* huffily reported that the price of whiskey and gin had risen since Jefferson's election and sniffed: "The bells have been ringing, guns firing, dogs barking, cats mewling, children crying, and Jacobins getting drunk."[24] Jeffersonians had jeered that Adams was "President by three votes" in 1796; Federalists now retaliated by calling Jefferson "President by no votes" because of Federalist abstentions in the House.[25] Later on some of them insisted he had given assurances that "certain points of Federal policy . . . would be observed" if he became President. Jefferson vigorously denied giving any such assurances; but it seems likely that some of his supporters sought to reassure the Federalists about what he would do if he became Chief Executive.[26]

The election of 1796 showed that there could be a peaceful change of Presidents in the new republic; 1800 showed there could be a peaceful change of parties. But it was a narrow squeak. Some ultra-Federalists, blinded by their hatred of Jefferson, talked of prolonging the deadlock in the House of Representatives beyond March 4 and then either calling for a new election or making the President *pro tempore* of the Senate (a Federalist) Adams's successor, or even passing an act making the Chief Justice of the Supreme Court the interim President. When Jefferson heard rumors of such plans, he warned that it would mean civil war. Some of his associates even went so far as to advise Republican states to refuse to submit to a "usurper President" and have the militia ready to march to Washington "for the purpose, not of promoting, but of preventing, revolution, and the shedding of a single drop of blood."[27] To James Monroe, Governor of Virginia, Jefferson himself wrote: "We thought it best to declare openly and firmly, one and all, that the day such an act passed, the Middle States would arm, and that no such usurpation, even for a single day, should be submitted to." The Republicans, he said, were not only determined to resist the "usurpation by arms," but also to call for a convention "to reorganize and amend" the Constitution if the Federalists persisted in their folly.[28]

Jefferson may have exaggerated the peril. The fact that the House deadlock was finally broken on February 17 may be evidence that even if it had continued beyond inauguration day there would still have been a peaceful resolution of the crisis in the end. As Vice-President and thus presiding officer over the Senate, Jefferson would have been able to rule out of order any motion to legislate a President; and, in fact, he had contemplated doing just that if the occasion arose. Still, upsetting the national timetable—the pioneers in American government put great emphasis on exact terms of office and precise dates for oath-taking—might well have had disastrous consequences for the young American political system. After the election, Madison, who had feared the Federalists would resort to force in order to stay in power, expressed enormous relief at the peaceful outcome of the contest; ". . . what a lesson to America and the world," he wrote Jefferson, "is given by the efficacy of the public will, when there is no army to be turned against it."[29] And the *National Intelligencer,* Republican tri-weekly, thought the peaceful settlement of the crisis proved that the "republican system" far surpassed the government of "an hereditary despot or a military usurper."[30] To avoid another situation like the one that faced the nation in 1801, the Twelfth Amendment, requiring the Electoral College to vote separately for President and Vice-President was added to the Constitution in 1804. It was a frank recognition of the existence of political parties in the American system.

Gleeful Republicans called Jefferson's victory "the Triumph of the democratic Representatives in Congress over the tools of the Anglomonarchico Aristocratic faction: the Triumph of the sovereign people over their rebellious servants, and of Human Nature or of Humanity over the accursed Persecutors of the Human Race."[31] Jefferson himself liked to refer to his election as "the revolution of 1800." He claimed too much. His election was by no means a social revolution, though it did mean that a party committed to more popular participation in politics had come into power.

Still, the election of 1800 was an extremely close one. In the Electoral College Adams received only eight fewer votes than Jefferson and if he had taken either New York or South Carolina he would have won the election. By his break with Hamilton and the High Federalists, however, and by his quest for peace with France, Adams had moved a long way from his own party toward Jefferson and the Republicans by the end of his administration. From this point of view, the change of parties in 1801 was less momentous than Jefferson believed it was. The new President admitted as much when he announced in his inaugural address (which Adams deliberately missed): "We are all Republicans; we are all Federalists. If there be any among us who would wish to dissolve this Union, or to change its Republican form, let them stand undisturbed as monuments of the safety with which error of opinion may be tolerated where reason is left free to combat it."[32] After the inauguration Margaret Bayard Smith, wife of the editor of the Jeffersonian *National Intelligencer,* politely poured tea for three Federalist Congressmen.[33] Hamilton himself retired from national politics and Jefferson went on as President to retain many of his old enemy's economic policies.

☆ ☆ ☆

Safe Place

A Federalist lady in a little Connecticut town was so afraid of what would happen to the family Bible if Jefferson became President that she took it to the only Jeffersonian she knew and asked him to keep it for her. The Jeffersonian tried to convince her that her fears about Jefferson were groundless, but she remained unpersuaded. "My good woman," he finally said, "if all the Bibles are to be destroyed, what is the use of bringing yours to me? That will not save it when it is found." "I'm sure it will," insisted the woman. "It will be perfectly safe with you. They'll never think of looking in the house of a Democrat for a Bible."[34]

Loathsome Hag

The "prigarchy" (as Jeffersonians called the Federalists) professed disdain for the "detestable practice of electioneering" and haughtily dismissed the campaign methods developed by Jefferson's followers in the 1790s (parades, barbecues, posters, handbills) as "forensic degladiation." Fisher Ames declared that the "pig sty and politics" were "two scurvy subjects that should be coupled together." Completely overlooking the virulent attacks made by the Federalists on Jefferson, he blamed the vituperative Jeffersonian press for Adams's defeat. In the *Connecticut Courant* (Hartford) for January 5, 1801, a Federalist poet joined Ames in excoriating the press:

> And lo! in meretricious dress,
> Forth comes a strumpet called 'THE PRESS.'
> Whose haggard, unrequested charms
> Rush into every blaggard's arms.
> Ye weak, deluded minds, beware!
> Nought but the outside here is fair!
> Then spurn the offers of her sway
> And kick the loathsome hag away.[35]

Knock-Down Arguments

Looking back on the 1800 election in his old age, a New York Congressman mused: "It was a pleasure to live in those good old days, when a Federalist could knock a Republican down in the streets and not be questioned about it."[36]

★ ★

CHAPTER FIVE

1804
Jefferson's Landslide

The campaign to re-elect Thomas Jefferson in 1804 lacked 1800's drama. Except in parts of New England, where die-hard Federalists still regarded Republicans with loathing, Jefferson's popularity had mounted steadily since he first took office; and everywhere in the country, except in Connecticut, Republicans were rapidly replacing Federalists among the voters.

Jefferson's first term was pleasantly placid. A temporary lull in the war between Britain and France meant that the Republican President, unlike Washington and Adams, didn't have to face any serious challenges to America's neutral rights at sea. With peace came prosperity: a boom in agriculture and foreign trade and a rise in customs receipts for paying the federal government's expenses. With peace and prosperity came lower taxes, a reduction in the national debt, and a cut in military appropriations by one-half. And in April 1803 came the stupendous Louisiana Purchase. By 1804 Jefferson was simply unbeatable.

In February came the first official nominating caucus for President: more than one hundred Republican Congressmen met in Washington on the 25th, renominated Jefferson by acclamation and picked George Clinton, that faithful old Republican from New York, as his running mate. The Federalists held no caucus. Thoroughly demoralized, they simply agreed informally to support Charles C. Pinckney of XYZ fame for President, and Rufus King, New York Senator, for Vice-President. But they blasted the President with a will and a way: made fun of his defense policy, denounced the Louisiana Purchase as unconstitutional, and charged that he made Sally Hemings, an attractive Monticello slave, his concubine and had several children by her. Jefferson's friends denied the last charge, but Jefferson himself remained silent, on the theory that "the man who fears no truth has nothing to fear from lies."

He did, though, indirectly deny the Hemings story in letters to friends and it seems likely it was his nephews, Peter and Samuel Carr, who were really involved with "Black Sal," as the Federalists called her.[1]

Federalist sniping was fruitless. When the electors cast their ballots the ensuing Jeffersonian landslide astonished even the Republicans: 162 votes for Jefferson and only 14 for Pinckney. Even Massachusetts went Republican. Only Connecticut and Delaware (and two Maryland electors) remained true to Federalism. Jefferson was overjoyed. He had succeeded, he thought, in putting the American ship "on her Republican tack." For a French friend he contentedly analyzed the situation. "The two parties which prevailed with so much violence when you were here," he wrote, "are almost wholly melted into one."[2]

Jefferson looked forward to a one-party Republican nation. Though a skillful party leader himself, he still retained the old fear and distrust of the "spirit of party" that had bothered Washington and the Founding Fathers. "The new century opened itself by committing us on a boisterous ocean," he wrote. "But this is now subsidiary, peace is smoothing our paths at home and abroad, and if we are not wanting in the practice of justice and moderation, our tranquillity and property may be preserved, until increasing numbers shall leave us nothing to fear from without." He did not anticipate the choppy seas ahead.[3]

☆　☆　☆

Experiment in Agriculture

As part of his program for economy in government, Jefferson had the army reduced to 3000 men and the navy's frigates retired from active service. To replace the frigates, he sponsored the construction of fifteen little gunboats for coastal defense. By the summer of 1804, Gunboats Number One and Number Two were finished and Number One was sent down to Savannah, Georgia. In September came one of the worst hurricanes ever to hit the coast. Church steeples, trees, and buildings went down before it, stagecoaches were overturned, docks and warehouses destroyed, rice and cotton crops ruined, and Fort Green, off Savannah, was all but blown away. At one point the water was so high, that it was ten feet deeper at low tide than it had ever been at high tide.

When the floods finally receded, Gunboat Number One was found high and dry in a cornfield some eight miles from her moorings. The Federalists had denounced Jefferson's gunboat policy from the beginning; but they now found it a fit object for ridicule. The President, sneered the *Repertory* in Boston, had finally found some use for his gunboat: as a scarecrow in a Georgia field. If the boat stayed planted there, said another wit, it would probably grow into a ship-of-the-line by the time of the next war. And, doubtless, if this "experiment in agriculture" succeeded, Jefferson would probably turn the rice-swamps of Carolina and the tobacco-fields of Virginia into dry-docks and "gun-boat gardens." In Boston, Federalists attending a dinner for vice-presidential candidate Rufus King outdid one another in proposing satirical toasts: "Gun-boat Number One: If our gun-boats are no use upon the water, may they at least be the best upon earth"; "Our Farmers on the Seacoast: May their corn-fields be defended against Gun-Boat Number Three."[4]

★ ★

CHAPTER SIX

1808
Madison and the Dambargo

Early in 1808 thirteen-year-old William Cullen Bryant published a long poem in Boston entitled "The Embargo" containing the following cracks at Thomas Jefferson:

> And thou, the scorn of every patriot's name,
> Thy country's ruin and thy country's shame!
> Go, wretch! Resign the Presidential chair.
> Disclose thy secret measures, foul or fair. . . .
> Go scan, philosophist, thy [Sally's] charms,
> And sink supinely in her sable arms.
> But quit to abler hands, the helm of state,
> Nor image ruin on thy country's fate! [1]

Jefferson, so far as we know, didn't see the young poet's outpourings. But he planned to quit anyway. Like Washington, he thought two terms more than enough. He was eager to retire to study and research at Monticello and wanted his old friend, Secretary of State James Madison, who was fifty-seven, to succeed him as President. A Republican caucus in Congress nominated "little Jemmy" (along with Vice-President George Clinton) in January, as Jefferson wished, but Madison's election was scarcely a shoo-in. He was on the defensive much of the time.

The campaign of 1808 was far livelier than the one four years earlier. Jefferson's second term had suddenly turned tumultuous. In 1803, Britain and France went to war again, resorted to economic warfare, and began disregarding America's neutral rights at sea as in Washington's and Adams's times. Both nations seized American ships trading with the other side; but in addition the British resumed their practice of impressing American sailors into the Royal Navy. After the *Leopard* attacked the *Chesapeake* off the American coast in June 1807, killing and wounding several Americans, Jefferson could have had war. But with him "peace was a passion" and he resorted to "peaceable coercion" instead.[2] In December 1807 he asked Congress to cut off all trade with Europe; his hope was that Britain and France, which depended on American food and raw materials, would be starved into respect for America's trading rights. But the Embargo Act, which Congress passed after a short debate, did not work as Jefferson and Madison had hoped. It seemed to produce no real changes in British and French policy and hurt American farmers, who produced grain for export, and American merchants, particularly those in New England, who prospered from overseas trade. The Embargo Act of 1807, increasingly unpopular and ignored by a growing number of "embargo-breakers," gave the Federalists a new lease on life.

The Great Embargo was one of the main issues of the 1808 campaign. The Federalists charged that it was a plot of Virginians like Jefferson and Madison against the commerce of New England; and since it hurt Britain more than it did France they cited it as another fruit of the "insidious French influence" vitiating Republican foreign policy. There was some heavy-handed humor about it. "The act ought to be called the 'Dambargo,'" cried one Federalist. "Our President," exclaimed another, "delights in the measure because the name hides so well his secret wishes. Read it backward, and you have the phrase, 'O-grab-me.' Divide it into syllables and read backward, and you have the Jeffersonian injunction, 'Go bar 'em.' Transpose the seven letters of the word, and you will have what the embargo will soon produce, 'mob-rage.'"[3]

But the rage was primarily Federalist and engulfed the elite rather than the masses. During 1808 Federalist journals busily churned out satirical poems and angry jokes about the Embargo and tossed off one indignant editorial after another. Early in September the Federalists renominated their 1804 team—Charles C. Pinckney and Rufus King—and stepped up their assaults on the Embargo. "Why is the embargo like sickness?" they asked in a typical squib. "Because it weakens us." "Why is it like hydrophobia?" went another sodden barb. "Because it makes us dread the water." A New York cartoon pictured a huge turtle labeled "O-grab-me" snapping at the backside of an American shipowner. From New Hampshire came a bitter song:

> Our ships all in motion once whitened the ocean;
> They sailed and returned with a cargo.
> Now doomed to decay they are fallen a prey
> To Jefferson, worms and EMBARGO.[4]

From November 4 until December 6 the seventeen states chose their presidential electors in various ways and on December 7 the electors cast their ballots. The results (which Congress formally announced on February 8, 1809) gladdened the hearts of faithful Republicans everywhere: Madison took the election nicely with 122 electoral votes to Pinckney's 47. Pinckney, it is true, won 33 more votes than he did in 1804 (mostly in New England) and the Federalists made some gains in both the Senate and the House. But Madison won the majority of electoral votes in the key states of New York, Pennsylvania, and Virginia, which had for a time seemed in doubt, and the Republicans kept their majority in both houses. Three days before Jefferson left office he signed a bill repealing the Embargo Act. At his friend's inauguration on March 4, he was relaxed, happy, and sociable. The new President, with his mind on foreign affairs, was in a far less cheerful mood.

Hair

Federalists and Republicans differed in dress as well as politics. In Washington, Federalist Congressmen wore long powdered queues and had them dressed every day. Jeffersonians tended to wear short hair, or at least small queues tied up carelessly and requiring little professional attention. One day, when a Federalist was having a shave, his barber suddenly began bemoaning Madison's nomination for President. "Dear me!" he sighed. "Surely this country is doomed to disgrace and shame. What Presidents we might have, sir! Just look at Daggett of Connecticut, and Stockton of New Jersey! What queues they have got, sir!—as big as your wrist, and powdered every day, sir, like real gentlemen, as they are. Such men, sir, would confer dignity upon the chief magistracy. But this little Jim Madison, with a queue no bigger than a pipe-stem! Sir, it is enough to make a man forswear his country!"[5]

French Citizen

During the 1808 campaign, the *Albany Register* suddenly revealed that Jefferson and Madison had been naturalized as citizens of France by the communistic revolutionary assembly there in 1793 and that Madison's letter of acknowledgment, "expressive of his gratitude, his admiration, and his devotion, was transmitted to . . . the bloody Robespierre, who . . . was very much pleased by his civism." The Federalists now had an epithet for Madison: "Frenchman." But the *Baltimore American* scoffed at the idea that "the unsolicited deed of a French National Assembly" was an act of naturalization and pointed out that to make it effective Jefferson and Madison would have had to appear before a

French tribunal to swear allegiance. "INSANITY," was the *National Intelligencer*'s comment on the charge that Madison was a French citizen. The *Intelligencer* was right. It turned out that the French Revolutionary Assembly had conferred honorary citizenship on Washington and Hamilton as well as Madison (and not on Jefferson at all) and had done so a year before Robespierre came into power. In the end even the *Albany Register* admitted it was silly to call Madison a Frenchman.[6]

★ ★

CHAPTER SEVEN

1812
Madison's Wartime Re-election

In 1812 came "Mr. Madison's War"—and Mr. Madison's election to a second term. No President has failed of re-election in wartime. America's first "khaki election" spawned the groups that were always to appear during a war: peace groups castigating the President for taking the country into war and calling for a speedy end to the conflict; harsh critics harping on the President's mismanagement of the war effort and blaming him for reverses on the battlefield; and administration supporters insisting that all good patriots should rally around the flag and help the President bring the conflict to a successful conclusion.

James Madison, now sixty-two, hadn't intended to be a War President; he was no warmonger. But he found he had entered a "hornets' nest" when he became President. Britain's continued interference with American trade and impressment of American sailors into the Royal Navy, while fighting Napoleon, produced increasing demands for strong action by the administration. At the same time the young War Hawks in Congress—men like Kentucky's Henry Clay and South Carolina's John C. Calhoun—were clamoring for war. They wanted to defend America's neutral rights at sea, but they also wanted to drive the British out of Canada and push Spain, now Britain's ally, out of East Florida and add these domains to America's continental empire. The New England merchants who suffered most by British attacks on American shipping strongly opposed the expansionist plans of Congressmen from the South and West; they insisted on keeping the peace despite British high-handedness. But on June 1, Madison finally sent Congress a special message reciting American grievances against Britain and said that Congress must decide whether the United States should use force in defense of her national rights. Congress decided she should. Later that month first the House and then the Senate voted for war.

Madison's nomination for a second term came less than a month before the country went to war. On May 18, over half of the Republican members of Congress met in caucus to endorse the President for re-election and, a little later, Elbridge Gerry, the "Gentleman Democrat" from Massachusetts, a signer of the Declaration of Independence, for second place. In due course Madison received the endorsement of Republicans in the legislatures of eight states and the support of most Republican newspapers in the country. But some Republicans balked. On May 29 a caucus of Republicans in the New York legislature endorsed DeWitt Clinton, mayor of New York, rather than Madison, for President. "It is time to have a change," announced the *Albany Register*.[1]

Clinton was eager to run and thought he had a chance. If he played his cards carefully (and kept a few up his sleeve), he reasoned, perhaps he could attract support from both Republicans opposing the War of 1812 and those calling for a more vigorous prosecution of the war. He might also win a following among Northerners who were tired of the "Virginia dynasty" and Southern Presidents. And maybe he could even win the support of the Federalists, mostly New Englanders, who thought Madison's policies, like Jefferson's, had hurt the Northeast and brought on a needless war with Britain, their favorite country. The Federalists met in New York City in September to discuss "fusion" with the Clintonians. The thought of voting Republican was sickening indeed, but so was the prospect of four more years of "the Little Man in the Palace." After vehement debate, the "Assembly of Notables," as it has been called, voted to endorse Clinton and picked Philadelphia lawyer Jared Ingersoll for Vice-President.

The Clintonians courted both hawks and doves. Their arguments against Madison and for Clinton depended on whether they were addressing War Republicans, Peace Republicans, or Anti-War Federalists. In New England, one Clintonian wrote that the basic issue of the campaign was "Madison and War! or Clinton and Peace" and he turned out a 24-stanza poem comparing "that base wretch . . . who is for WAR" with the candidate who insisted that the "base, outrageous WAR shall cease."[2] But in other parts of the country, the Clintonians presented their candidate as a man who favored vigorous prosecution of the war. Disgusted by all this equivocation and by his own party's opposition to the war, former President John Adams agreed to head the Madison electoral ticket in his Quincy district.

In the end, the Clintonian "coalition" went down to defeat. When the eighteen states now forming the Union cast their ballots late in 1812, they gave Madison a comfortable victory: 128 votes to Clinton's 89. The Federalists were downcast. Though they made some gains in Congress, they were unappeased. They complained that Madison won largely because he took all the electoral votes representing the South's slave population. On January 1, 1813, the *Connecticut Courant* reflected the anguished reaction of New England Federalists to the election's outcome:

The day is past—th' Election's o'er
And Madison is King once more!
Ye demagogues lift up your voice—
Mobs and banditti—all rejoice![3]

Knavery and Resurrection

In the fall of 1812, according to a Federalist tale, in a little town in Maine a Republican farmer named Noble put pressure on Jerry Phillips, one of his hired hands, to vote for Madison. Jerry knew little about politics and had always voted Federalist, but Noble insisted it was important to support the Madison administration in time of war and Jerry finally agreed. "But" said Jerry doubtfully, "ye know, Squire, I've always voted t'other way. When they ask me what for I'm a goin' to vote for Jim Madison, what shall I tell 'em?" "Tell them," said Noble, "that you are bound to vote for the man who will support our navy and stop insurrection." Not long after when Jerry was in the village store he was approached by a Federalist politician who asked him how he intended to vote. "For Jim Madison," said Jerry. "But, Jerry," protested the man, "I thought you were a true patriot." "So I be," insisted Jerry. "Then how can you vote for Madison?" "Because," said Jerry with warmth, "he's the only man that will support the knavery and stop the resurrection!"[4]

★ ★

CHAPTER EIGHT

1816
Monroe: Another Virginia Victory

The election of 1816 was dull as dishwater. There really wasn't much to campaign—or complain—about. The War of 1812, which had begun so ingloriously four years earlier, had ended in Andrew Jackson's stunning defeat of the British in the Battle of New Orleans in January 1815. The United States didn't win the war, but neither did she lose it. The Treaty of Ghent, signed two weeks before Jackson's triumph, ignored all the basic issues that had produced the war, but it did provide for subsequent negotiations over unresolved problems.

Ghent, said Henry Clay, was a "bad treaty"; and John Quincy Adams observed: "We have obtained nothing but peace."[1] But peace was what everybody wanted; and it was accompanied by a tremendous upsurge in national pride throughout the land. The United States hadn't lost anything by the treaty (though the War Hawks didn't get Canada and East Florida) and the American people were eager to celebrate their victories at sea during the conflict and, above all, Jackson's brilliant victory over the British at New Orleans. The war produced America's first great war hero since Washington.

The War of 1812 dealt the Federalist party a fatal blow. The Federalists, particularly in New England, had bitterly denounced "Mr. Madison's War" and refused to support it with men and money. Some of the extremists among them had even talked of secession. After the war the Federalist party, thoroughly discredited, declined into a querulous and disaffected minority with little clout in politics except in a few isolated regions in the country. The Republicans stole most of the Federalist thunder anyway. In 1815 Madison sponsored a national bank for managing the country's finances as well as higher duties on imports to protect America's infant industries from foreign competition. Some Republicans even came to favor federal appropriations for internal improvements. "Our two great parties," remarked John Adams, "have crossed over the valley and taken possession of each other's mountain."[2] Alexander Hamilton would have been astonished. As Jefferson's party federalized, Hamilton's vaporized.

James Monroe, Madison's Secretary of State, who turned fifty-eight in April, was the new Republican heir apparent. He didn't arouse much excitement, but won the Congressional caucus nomination in March and was teamed up with New York Governor Daniel Tompkins, the "Farmer's Boy of Westchester." Once the nominations were made, the outcome of the election was a foregone conclusion. Monroe, observed Rufus King, "had the zealous support of nobody, and he was exempt from the hostility of everybody." The Federalists made no nominations but some of them decided to support King anyway. There was some criticism of the Congressional caucus as a way of selecting candidates and considerable grumbling in the Northeast about the prospect of another Virginia President. But there was no real presidential campaign. Monroe was elected, observed *Niles' Register,* with "less bustle and *national* confusion than belongs to a Westminster election for a member of Parliament in England."[3]

On December 3, the day before electors from nineteen states cast their votes, the *Boston Daily Advertiser* announced resignedly: "We do not know, nor is it very material, for whom the Federal electors will vote."[4] The following day Federalist electors from Massachusetts, Connecticut, and Delaware cast 34 votes for Rufus King, Federalist vice-presidential candidate in 1808 and 1812. Monroe and Tompkins took all of the remaining 183 votes. King's candidacy was unofficial; but he was the last Federalist candidate for President. Long before the Electoral College made its choice King told a friend: "Federalists of our age must be content with the past."[5]

Indiana

Indiana provided the only election excitement in 1816. When Congress met to count the electoral votes, a New York Congressman interrupted proceedings to protest the inclusion of Indiana because the Hoosiers hadn't been in the Union at the time of the election. The Senate then withdrew, and in both houses there was a long debate over whether Indiana had actually been a state after it adopted its constitution but before Congress took it into the Union by a formal act in December. Finally the Senate rejoined the House, the Speaker announced that the House "had not seen it necessary to come to any resolution on the subject," and the count was resumed. Indiana's three votes were counted for Monroe and Tompkins.[6]

★ ★

CHAPTER NINE

1820
Monroe's Quiet Re-election

"The unanimous re-election of Mr. Monroe is morally certain," announced the *National Intelligencer* on October 17, 1820, "as certain as almost any contingent event can be." James Monroe easily won a second term, though his re-election wasn't quite unanimous. The Federalists proposed no candidates this time and there was no serious opposition to Monroe (and his running-mate Daniel Tompkins) among Republicans. The United States was now practically a one-party state and that was fine with Monroe. "Surely our government may go on and prosper without the existence of parties," he declared. "I have always considered their existence as the curse of the country." Like the Founding Fathers, he believed "the existence of parties is not necessary to free government."[1]

The election aroused little interest. "There appears no great excitement in any quarter, concerning the next presidential election," reported the *Ohio Monitor*. "In most of the States the elections occur with great quietness, too great, perhaps, for the general safety of the Republic."[2] Even in states where the people rather than the legislatures chose presidential electors, voting was light. In Richmond, Virginia, only seventeen voters bothered to go to the polls. John Randolph spoke of "the unanimity of indifference, and not of approbation."[3]

Monroe, now sixty-two, won 231 out of the 232 electoral votes cast. The lone dissenter was William Plumer, former Senator and Governor of New Hampshire, who voted for Secretary of State John Quincy Adams. It used to be said that Plumer voted as he did to keep Monroe from getting the unanimous vote of the Electoral College the way Washington did. But Plumer had no way of knowing how the other electors would vote. Besides, he admired Adams. "My acquaintance with Mr. Adams has been long and intimate," he said. "I know he is in every respect qualified for that high trust. Mr. Monroe during the last four years has, in my opinion, conducted, as president, very improperly."[4] Adams was embarrassed by the unexpected vote. But the *Baltimore American* rejoiced that "scarcely a demagogue is found to say *nay*" to Monroe's re-election.[5]

Missouri

In July 1820 Missouri adopted a constitution, but it called for excluding free blacks from the state, and anti-slavery protests forced Congress to keep her out of the Union until August 1821, when she disavowed the exclusion clause. But like Indiana in 1816, Missouri in 1820 cast electoral votes before she formally became part of the Union. This time a Congressional committee recommended that if the new state's votes "shall not essentially change the result of the election," the Speaker of the House should announce what the Electoral College decision would be with Missouri's votes and what it would be without them. Virginia Senator John Randolph denounced the procedure as "irregular and illegal," but Congress adopted it anyway and on February 24, 1821, the President of the Senate announced that the total number of votes for Monroe was 231, "and, if the votes of Missouri were not counted, was 228; that in either case James Monroe had a majority of the whole number of votes given."[6]

CHAPTER TEN

1824
John Quincy Adams
and the "Corrupt Bargain"

The campaign of 1824 began early. Visiting Washington in January 1822, Baltimore publisher Hezekiah Niles was surprised to find "so great a buz about the person who should succeed Monroe."[1] Before long there were seventeen men in the presidential race and "electioneering," noted one reporter, "begins to wax hot." But most of the aspirants turned out to be what a Nashville politician called "Hasbeens," "Cantbees," "Mightbees," and "Wouldabeens."[2] The real contest boiled down to five serious contenders: John Quincy Adams from the Northeast; Henry Clay and Andrew Jackson from the West; William H. Crawford and John C. Calhoun from the Southeast. In 1824 Calhoun dropped out of the race and quickly became the vice-presidential favorite of both the Adams and Jackson supporters.

Monroe himself favored his Secretary of the Treasury, the big, amiable William H. Crawford of Georgia, who had been in public life for many years. So did Thomas Jefferson and James Madison, though neither they nor the President himself made any public commitments. In February 1824 Crawford received the caucus nomination in Washington, but it probably did him more harm than good. Only a third of the Republican members of Congress attended the meeting and Crawford's opponents at once attacked it as undemocratic, dictatorial, unconstitutional, and unrepresentative of the party as a whole. The *Baltimore Morning Chronicle*'s scorn was typical. "The poor little political bird of ominous note and plumage, denominated a CAUCUS, was hatched at Washington on Saturday last," reported the *Chronicle*, right after the meeting. "It is now running around like a pullet, in a forlorn and sickly state. Reader, have you ever seen a chicken directly after it was hatched, creeping about with a bit of egg shell sticking to its back? This is a just representation of this poor forlorn Congressional caucus. The sickly thing is to be fed, cherished, pampered for a week, when it is fondly hoped it will be enabled to cry the name of Crawford, Crawford, Crawford."[3] The other presidential aspirants carefully avoided the caucus pullet. Adams was nominated by the legislatures of most of the New England states, Jackson by the Tennessee legislature and numerous conventions in various parts of the country, and Clay by the Kentucky legislature and several other state legislatures.

Bad luck dogged Crawford's campaign trail from the outset. His caucus nomination became the main issue of the 1824 canvass. Arguments for and against "King Caucus" filled the columns of newspapers and resounded in resolutions passed by state legislatures and local party conventions. But the bent of public opinion was strongly anti-caucus. The caucus, to many people, came to mean arbitrary decisions by a few politicians in Washington in utter disregard of the sentiments of large numbers of people elsewhere. Hezekiah Niles, who fought the caucus in his *Weekly Register,* thought it would be better to have the halls of Congress "converted into common brothels" than used for caucuses.[4] But by the time poor Crawford received his nomination, his health had gone to pieces. He suffered a paralytic stroke in September 1823 and was on his back for nearly eight weeks. He finally went back to work in the Treasury Department with the help of his daughter, but remained feeble. "He walks slowly like a blind man," noted one observer.[5]

Crawford's illness and identification with "King Caucus" boosted the fortunes of his rivals. But they all had strengths of their own. Adams, Monroe's Secretary of State, had served his country with distinction, in Congress and on diplomatic missions, for more than two decades. Many people, including Adams himself, took it for granted he would step into Monroe's shoes in 1825. In the West, however, Adams seemed too much of a New Englander to rouse much enthusiasm. In Kentucky's Congressman Henry Clay Westerners had a favorite son of their own. Speaker of the House for many years, Clay had won fame for his skill as a legislator; he also favored federal appropriations for internal improvements binding the West to other parts of the Union. The "people of the West," said the Kentucky legislators who put his name in nomination, "appeal to the magnanimity of the whole Union, for a favorable consideration of their equal and just claim to a fair participation in the executive government of these states."[6]

Westerners also liked another candidate: Andrew Jackson of Tennessee. Jackson had served in both the House and Senate; but that is not why they liked him. They were thrilled by his military exploits: his crushing of the Creek Indians in 1813; his whipping of the British at New Orleans in 1815; and the vigor with which he pursued Indians in the Seminole War of 1818. His supporters presented him as "the soldier, the statesman, and the honest man; he deliberates, he decides, and he acts; he is calm in deliberation, cautious in decision, efficient in action."[7] Jackson took a lofty position about his candidacy. "The office of chief magistrate . . . ," he wrote in January 1823, "is one of great responsibility. As it should not be sought . . . , so it cannot, with propriety, be declined. . . . My political creed prompts me to leave the affair . . . to the free will of those who have alone the right to decide."[8] Jackson didn't exactly leave it all to the free will of others. He wrote letters, conferred with friends and allies, and permitted his managers to build him up as a man of the people. Though a well-to-do planter by the time he got into politics, he soon became a symbol of the new democracy struggling to be born in the 1820s. In October 1823 some Philadelphians endorsed him because "he has always been a uniform and consistent democrat" and "a friend to the *rights of man* and *universal suffrage.*"[9]

Except for arguments over the caucus, personalities, not issues, dominated the four-sided campaign of 1824. Newspapers glorified the candidates they were backing in extravagant terms and vilified their opponents in abusive language. They made fun of Adams's slovenly dress and "English" wife, called Clay a drunkard and gambler, charged Crawford with malfeasance in office, and accused Jackson of being a murderer for having authorized the execution of mutineers in 1813. If one took all these charges seriously, sighed one politician, he would have to conclude that "our Presidents, Secretaries, Senators, and Representatives, are all traitors and pirates, and the government of this people had been committed to the hands of public robbers."[10]

By the fall of 1824, when the twenty-four states began picking presidential electors, it was clear that Adams and Jackson were the leading candidates. It was also clear, long before Congress assembled in February 1825 to make an official count, that neither had received a majority of the votes cast for President, though Calhoun was elected Vice-President by more than two-thirds of the votes cast. Jackson led the race both in electoral (99) and popular votes (152,901), carrying Pennsylvania, the Carolinas, and most of the West. Adams took New England, most of New York, and a few districts elsewhere, winning 84 electoral and 114,023 popular votes. Crawford ran a poor third with 41 electoral and 46,979 popular votes; and Clay brought up the rear with only 37 electoral votes (though more popular votes than the caucus candidate). By the terms of the Twelfth Amendment, it was now up to the House of Representatives, voting by states, to choose the President from the three highest candidates.

With Clay out of the running, there was a great deal of speculation in Washington as to how the Speaker would use his enormous prestige in the House to influence the voting of his fellow Congressmen. Clay was amused by his sudden popularity with the friends of Adams, Jackson, and Crawford. But he was furious when a Philadelphia newspaper printed an anonymous letter on January 28, charging that he had approached the friends of both Adams and Jackson with offers of his support in return for an appointment as Secretary of State in their administrations. Clay hotly denied the charge; and the Congressional investigation he demanded turned up no evidence for it. But the charge persisted and seemed confirmed when he finally made up his mind whom to support.

There was never any doubt in Clay's mind as to who should become President. Crawford's health ruled him out; so did Jackson's lack of experience, nebulous views on public issues, and reputation as a headstrong military man. ". . . I cannot believe," said Clay, "that killing 2,500 Englishmen at New Orleans qualifies for the various, difficult and complicated duties of the Chief Magistracy."[11] There was really only one choice: Adams. Clay thought Adams was eminently qualified for high office by his talents, energies, and long public service. He also looked on him as less of a threat than Jackson to his own future presidential ambitions. And he knew Adams and he saw eye to eye on the "American System": a program embracing tariffs, a national bank, and federally sponsored internal improvements for binding the different sections of the country together. He decided to do what he could to bring the state delegations into the Adams fold.

On February 9, 1825, the Senate and the House met in joint session, the electoral votes were officially counted, the President of the Senate declared Calhoun elected Vice-President, and then announced that since no one had received a majority of the votes for first place, the House must choose the President from the three candidates who had received the highest number of votes. The Senate retired; and the House, with every member present but one from Virginia, who was ill, proceeded to vote. It took only one ballot: thirteen states declared for Adams, seven for Jackson, and four for Crawford. The Speaker of the House then declared Adams elected President, notified the Senate, and arranged for a committee to inform Adams of his election. In his rather bleak response to the committee, the fifty-seven-year-old Adams said he regretted the impossibility of submitting "the decision of this momentous question" to the people again to obtain "a nearer approach to unanimity."[12]

The Jacksonians were of course no happier with the election than Adams was. They regarded their hero as the real choice of the people. Popular voting, it is true, had been extremely light in states permitting it; and only a few states had listed all four candidates on the ballot. Still, Jackson had won more popular and electoral votes than anyone else, his supporters pointed out, and the House of Representatives had acted wrongly in depriving him of victory. To Jacksonians it seemed as if "King Caucus" had been dethroned only to have the choice of President turned over to a small group of Congressional insiders after all. But the disappointment of Jackson's followers turned to fury three days after the election when Adams announced he was making Clay head of the State Department (a natural stepping-stone to the Presidency). So there had been a "corrupt bargain" between Adams and Clay after all! Cried one Jacksonian newspaper: "Expired at Washington on the 9th of February, of poison administered by the assassin hands of John Quincy Adams, the usurper, and Henry Clay, the virtue, liberty and independence of the United States."[13] "So you see," exploded Jackson to a friend, "the Judas of the West has closed the contract and will receive the thirty pieces of silver. His end will be the same. Was there ever such a bare faced corruption in any country before?"[14]

Jackson spoke hyperbolically. There was nothing really "corrupt" about the Adams-Clay relationship. The two men were in firm agreement on national policies and Adams regarded Clay, with whom he had worked closely as a diplomat, as the best man for the job. But Adams's decision to appoint Clay to his Cabinet, especially as Secretary of State, was a political blunder. It looked as though he was naming his successor; and it looked, too, as if the will of the people, ignored when Clay helped Adams beat Jackson in the House vote, was being further flouted in the administration Adams was putting together. Years later Clay revealed that his friends had told him at the time that "conscious of my own purity of intention," he should accept Adams's offer and that if he refused, "it would be said of me that, after having contributed to the elevation of a President, I thought so ill of him that I would not take the first place under him. . . ."[15] Neither Clay nor his friends seems to have anticipated the violence of the reaction to his acceptance of Adams's offer. Cries of "bargain and sale," "bargain and corruption," and "corrupt bargain" went up everywhere as soon as Adams announced the appointment and were in the air throughout Adams's four years in office.

In October 1825 the Tennessee legislature named Jackson as its choice for 1828. Jackson resigned from the Senate, and headed back to the Hermitage to begin his quest for vindication in the next election. "The people have been cheated . . . ," he fumed. "The corruptions and intrigues at Washington" have "defeated the will of the people."[16] Shortly afterwards he appeared before both houses of the Tennessee legislature and urged an amendment to the Constitution which would put presidential elections in the hands of the people. The campaign of 1828 began in 1825.

☆   ☆   ☆

Writing and Fighting

It's hard to believe: Adams and Jackson once thought well of each other. Adams, in fact, originally wanted Jackson on his ticket. He thought Old

Hickory would add lustre to the Vice-Presidency and that it would "afford an easy and dignified retirement for his old age." The Vice-Presidency, he added, was "a station in which the General could hang no one." For a while supporters of an Adams-Jackson ticket popularized a slogan:

> John Quincy Adams
> Who can write,
> Andrew Jackson
> Who can fight.[17]

Taking the Chair

A few weeks before the House of Representatives was to meet to pick a President, Adams, Jackson, and Clay attended a dinner party in Washington in honor of Lafayette. At the party Clay "was in fine spirits," reported Delaware Congressman Louis McLane, one of the hosts, "and amused himself a little at the expense of the *rivals*." Jackson and Adams were sitting next to each other near the fire with "a vacant chair intervening," and Clay, who was sitting on the opposite side of the room, decided to have a little fun. He suddenly got up, walked over to Adams and Jackson, plunked himself down on the chair between them, and then, "in his inimitably impudent significant manner," according to McLane, cried: "Well, gentlemen, since you are both so near the chair, but neither can occupy it, I will step in between you, and take it myself." Everyone in the room started laughing, but neither Jackson nor Adams saw anything funny about it.[18]

Will of God

When the House of Representatives met on February 9, 1825, to pick a President, it was clear that the vote would be close and that the question of an election on the first ballot turned on the vote of New York. Half of New York's delegation was for Adams and the other half was controlled by Martin Van Buren, a Crawford man who was leading the anti-Adams forces. Van Buren wanted a tie in his delegation on the first ballot; it would prevent New York's vote from being cast and thus forestall Adams's election on the first ballot and possibly ensure his eventual defeat.

One of the votes Van Buren was counting on was that of General Stephen Van Rensselaer, the rich and pious Congressman from the Albany district ("the last of the Patroons") who had assured him he intended to vote for Crawford. The old General went to the Capitol on election day firmly resolved to vote against Adams, but on his arrival he was waylaid by Henry Clay and Daniel Webster; they took him into the Speaker's Room and painted a dismal picture of what would happen to the country if Adams wasn't chosen on the first ballot. Van Rensselaer was deeply upset by the encounter and when Delaware's Louis McLane ran into him afterwards he found him practically in tears. "The election turns on my vote," he told McLane. *"One* vote will give Adams the majority—this is a responsibility I cannot bear. What shall I do?" "Do!" exclaimed McLane impatiently. "Do what honor, what principles direct. General, you are an old man. . . . You want nothing, you have no motive but duty to sway you. Look at me . . . *My vote,* like yours, would turn the scale. But, General, the greater the responsibility, the greater the honor. Let us march boldly in and do our duty." Rejoined Van Rensselaer: "I am resolved. Here is my hand on it."

But Van Rensselaer wasn't really resolved. He was still perplexed when he took his seat in the House Chamber. Profoundly religious, however, he decided to seek divine guidance while waiting to cast his Crawford ballot and bowed his head in prayer. On opening his eyes, he saw a ticket on the floor bearing the name of Adams. Taking this as a Providential sign, he hastily pocketed his Crawford ballot, picked up the Adams ticket, and put it in the box. The result: New York went for Adams, and Adams won the election on the first ballot.[19]

Confrontation

To honor President-elect Adams, President Monroe gave a party in the White House on February 10, and Jackson, with a "large, handsome lady on his arm," was one of the guests. At some point in the evening Adams and Jackson accidentally met in the East Room; the people around them at once stepped back and watched to see what would happen. For a moment or two the two men stared at each other. Then Jackson held out his hand. "How do you do, Mr. Adams?" he said amiably. "I give you my left hand, for the right, as you see, is devoted to the fair. I hope you are very well, sir." Adams shook hands with him and said coldly: "Very well, sir; I hope General Jackson is well!" People were impressed by Jackson's cordiality and Adams's reserve. Having watched the encounter, Louis McLane told his wife that Jackson then went on to congratulate Adams "in quite a manly style. This was carrying the joke too far I think. It shewed superiority over A. for I assure you he could not have done such a thing to be a King."

Everyone in Washington admired Jackson's "manly style" and the way he concealed his bitterness at having been bested by Adams in the House vote. Everywhere he went he was honored. With Adams it was quite otherwise. "He is truly an object of pity," noted Andrew Jackson Donelson, Jackson's secretary. When the Adamses attended the theater one night, the actors, catching sight of them in the audience, began cracking jokes about the House election. Adams received the quips "with death like silence," according to McLane, who was also there. Then someone started singing "The Hunters of Kentucky," a pro-Jackson song commemorating his conduct at New Orleans, and instantly "a universal shout" went up from the audience, followed by "repeated cheerings" for several minutes. "I really feared it would have been difficult to quell it," reported McLane. "It was an awful knell for the President-elect— and he felt it." Then McLane added: "What will he feel, when he hears this shout penetrating every part of the Union? Well may he say, he would not take the office if he could avoid it.[20]

High-Toned Duel

One spin-off of the 1824 election was a duel between Speaker of the House Henry Clay and Senator John Randolph, the eccentric aristocrat from Virginia. In a vituperative speech in the Senate, Randolph accused Clay of forgery; he also attacked the "corrupt bargain" between Adams and Clay and compared them to two villainous characters in Henry Fielding's popular novel *Tom Jones:* "The coalition of Blifil and Black George . . . the combination, unheard of till then, of the puritan with the blackleg." The epithet, blackleg, meaning dishonest gambler, was too much for Clay and he at once challenged Randolph to a duel. Randolph waived his privilege as a Senator and agreed to meet Clay in a forest on the Virginia side of the Potomac above Little Falls Bridge at half past four in the afternoon of April 8, 1826. The weapons were to be pistols, the distance was to be ten paces, and each party was to be attended by his two seconds and a surgeon. There was a law in Virginia against duelling, but Randolph wasn't going to violate it; he told a friend he didn't intend to fire at Clay. ". . . I have determined to receive without returning Clay's fire," he said; "nothing shall induce me to harm a hair of his head; I will not make his wife a widow or his children orphans."

At the appointed hour, Clay and Randolph met, greeted each other politely, and then took their positions: Clay in front of a small stump and Randolph in front of a low gravelly bank. While they were waiting for Clay's second to give the word, the hair-triggered pistol Randolph was trying to adjust suddenly exploded downward by accident. Another pistol was handed to him, the word was given, and an exchange of shots followed. Randolph's bullet struck the stump behind Clay and Clay's knocked up some earth and gravel behind Randolph. Senator Thomas Hart Benton, an observer, then intervened; he offered to mediate the dispute. But Clay waved him away with the cry, "This is child's play," and joined Randolph in insisting on another exchange of shots. In the second exchange, Randolph recieved Clay's fire, which pierced his coat skirt near the hip, then raised his pistol, discharged it in the air, and exclaimed: "I do not fire at you, Mr. Clay," and went over and offered his hand. Clay met him halfway and the two shook hands. "You owe me a coat, Mr. Clay," said Randolph ruefully. "I am glad the debt is not greater," Clay told him. The following Monday they exchanged cards and resumed social relations. Senator Benton said it was "about the last high-toned duel" he ever witnessed.[21]

★ ★

CHAPTER ELEVEN

1828
Jackson vs. Adams

Voters in 1828 regarded the election that year as a momentous event. It wasn't merely a contest between John Quincy Adams and Andrew Jackson; it was a battle over who should rule whom in the young nation. Jackson's supporters saw it as a struggle "between the democracy of the country, on the one hand, and a *lordly purse-proud* aristocracy on the other."[1] For the followers of Adams it was a heroic effort of respectable people to quiet "the howl of raving Democracy."[2] Jackson's victory delighted the masses and dismayed the classes. A "great revolution," both sides agreed, had taken place; henceforth, there was to be more popular participation in American politics.[3]

There were no caucus nominations in 1828. King Caucus was thoroughly discredited four years earlier. Adams was nominated for reelection by state legislatures and special conventions in New England; Treasury Secretary Richard Rush became his running mate. Jackson received his first nomination in October 1825 when the Tennessee legislature warmly recommended him to the people; but before long he was receiving hearty endorsements from conventions and mass meetings in other parts of the country. John C. Calhoun, up for re-election as Vice-President, was picked this time to run with Jackson.

When it came to the issues, everyone knew where Adams stood: he favored the national bank, a protective tariff, and federal appropriations for internal improvements, science, and education. Jackson was evasive about the issues at first. "My real friends," he said, "want no information from me on the subject of internal improvement and manufactories, but what my public acts have afforded, and I never gratify my enemies. Was I now to come forward and reiterate my public opinions on these subjects, I would be charged with electioneering for selfish purposes."[4] In the end, though, he made it clear he intended to "reform the government" by removing officeholders who were incompetent and had received their positions "against the will of the people." He also said he took "a middle and just course" on the tariff and opposed federally sponsored internal improvements, though he favored using surplus federal revenue to help the states build roads and canals.[5]

Adams and Jackson viewed electioneering differently. Adams insisted on sticking to the old custom of remaining (like George Washington) inactive on his own behalf. "If my country wants my services," he said loftily, "she must ask for them."[6] Jackson maintained the customary pose of aloofness in public, but privately plunged energetically into campaign work from the minute he appeared before the Tennessee legislature to acknowledge his nomination and announce his resignation from the Senate. "I am not a politician," he liked to say, but he was, in fact, an organizing genius and one of the shrewdest politicians ever to appear on the American scene.[7] With his charismatic leadership he played a crucial role in developing the new party that began forming around him in 1825 to oppose Adams. He helped revive two-party politics in America after its seeming demise during the Era of Good Feelings.

The Adamsites continued to view parties with distaste and distrust. Like the Founding Fathers, they thought party rivalries destroyed the national consensus and threatened the nation with chaos. The Jacksonians, however, accepted parties as essential to the workings of political democracy and to the safeguarding of liberty. They began developing an opposition party in Congress shortly after Adams's inauguration and went on to establish party organizations in every state in the Union. First called the "Friends of Jackson," the new party eventually took on the name "Democratic-Republican" and, finally, "Democratic." The "Old Republicans" who had supported states-righter William H. Crawford in 1824 joined up shortly after Adams's nationalistic message to Congress in December 1825; Calhoun and his followers came into the Jackson fold soon after. But nothing was left to chance. "To give effect to any principles," Jackson advised, "you must avail yourselves of the physical force of an organized body of men."[8] Before long, central committees were operating in both Washington, D.C., and Nashville, Tennessee, and there were also in each of the states Jackson committees maintaining close relations with the national committees and supervising the Hickory Clubs which were springing up everywhere at the local level.

Scores of able politicians—Martin Van Buren of New York, John Eaton of Tennessee, Thomas Hart Benton of Missouri—joined up to manage the anti-Adams campaign, under Jackson's direction, at the national and state levels; and scores of anti-administration newspapers began appearing in various parts of the country, eager to push Jackson's cause. Jacksonian newspapers played an important part in popularizing

Old Hickory as the "Hero of New Orelans," "the People's Candidate," and "the Farmer of Tennessee," and convincing thousands of voters that Jackson's cause was that of the average American. "What a pleasure it is," exulted one Jacksonian, "to see that party almost unbroken rising in almost every part of the Union to put down the men who would have corrupted and betrayed it."[9]

The Adamsites (or "Coalitionists," as the Adams-Clay people were called) became a party almost in spite of themselves. In time they acquired party organization, began calling themselves "National Republicans," and started fighting back with energy and zeal. But they were never able to match the Jacksonian party for electioneering ingenuity: collecting funds, compiling lists of voters, making up slogans, popularizing political songs, distributing pamphlets and broadsides, and organizing parades, barbecues, dinners, and street rallies for Jackson. When Jackson's "Hurra Boys," as his campaign workers were called, began distributing hickory brooms, hickory canes, and hickory sticks, and planting hickory poles everywhere, Adamsites were confounded. "Planting hickory trees!" they cried. "Odds nuts and drumsticks! What have hickory trees to do with republicanism and the great contest?"[10] Eventually they adopted the oak as a symbol of Adams and had some parades of their own. But they never caught up with their opponents. "Organization is the secret of victory," acknowledged an Adams supporter. "By the want of it we have been overthrown."[11]

In Congress, Jackson's followers, led by Senator John Randolph, harassed President Adams without mercy from almost the day of his inauguration until the day of his defeat. They opposed his proposal for sending delegates to a conference of American republics in Panama, attacked his views on the tariff, denounced his plans for internal improvements, and cited as ominous his suggestion that Congress not "be palsied by the will of its constituents."[12] The "corrupt bargain" with Clay—which the *Rochester Daily Advertiser* called "a triumph of intrigue over the will of the people"—came in for relentless attack both inside and outside Congress; and the Tennessee legislature even suggested impeachment.[13] The Jacksonians also portrayed the President as a reckless spendthrift who lived in "kingly pomp and splendor" in his "presidential palace." When Adams purchased a billiard table and some ivory chessmen with his own funds, they accused him of installing "gaming tables and gambling furniture" in the White House at public expense; and efforts by Adams's friends to set the record straight were fruitless.[14] The Jacksonians also assailed the Puritan New Englander for traveling on Sunday, said he had had premarital relations with his wife, and, in the wildest charge of all, insisted that when he was minister to Russia he had procured a young American girl for Czar Alexander I. Their basic charge, though, was that at heart he was a monarchist like his father ("King John the Second") who despised the people and favored rule by the few over the many. "His habits and principles," said one Jacksonian, "are not congenial with the spirit of our institutions and the notions of a democratic people."[15] When an Adams pamphlet pointed out that Jackson was uneducated and couldn't spell more than one word in four, the Jacksonians retorted that Jackson's natural wisdom and common sense were superior to Adams's book learning and that, fortunately, there were "no Greek quotations" and "no toilsome or painful struggles after eloquence" in him as in the "learned man" in the White House.[16]

The "Friends of Adams" gave as good as they got. To them Jackson seemed preposterous as a presidential possibility. They put him down as ignorant, inexperienced in public affairs, and reckless in his personal behavior. They also questioned the fitness of a "military chieftain" for high office in a republican nation. "You know that he is no jurist, no statesman, no politician," pointed out one of their political handbooks; "that he is destitute of historical, political, or statistical knowledge; that he is unacquainted with the orthography, concord, and government of his language; you know that he is a man of no labor, no patience, no investigation; in short that his whole recommendation is animal fierceness and organic energy. He is wholly unqualified by education, habit and temper for the station of President."[17]

In their eagerness to discredit the "Hero of New Orleans," the backers of Adams, like Jackson's partisans, soon descended into the gutter. Before they got through they had compiled a long list of Old Hickory's sins: adultery, gambling, cock fighting, bigamy, slave-trading, drunkenness, theft, lying, and murder. Their most venomous attack had to do with six militiamen who had been sentenced for desertion and executed, with Jackson's approval, during the Creek War in 1813. Philadelphia editor John Binns got out a "Coffin Handbill" about the incident, portrayed the soldiers as innocent men who had completed their terms of service and merely wanted to go home, and insisted that Jackson had "murdered" them in cold blood. The "Coffin Handbill," which received wide distribution, was enormously effective. Headed by the words, "Some Account of the Bloody Deeds of General Jackson," it was bordered in black, pictured six coffins, one for each militiaman, and singled out one of them, John Harris, for special attention. Harris, according to Binns's fanciful story, was a "Preacher of the Gospel" who had patriotically volunteered for service and then been "shot dead" at Jackson's behest when his tour of duty ended and he wanted to return home. Accompanying the Harris story was a seven-stanza poem, entitled "Mournful Tragedy," lamenting Jackson's bloody deed.[18]

The "Coffin Handbill" moved the Jacksonians to fury. They did their best to publicize what had really happened in 1813. They pointed out that at a time when Jackson was hard-pressed in his encounter with the Indians on the southern border, Harris and the other five militiamen tried to stir up mutiny among the soldiers, broke into a military store-house, stole supplies, burned a bakehouse, and then deserted. When apprehended, moreover, they were given fair trials and their constitutional rights carefully safeguarded. But the Adamsites were not impressed. Even if the "Coffin Handbill" exaggerated things, they insisted, the plain truth was that Jackson was basically a "murderer": he enjoyed killing people. This enraged Isaac Hill, ardent Jacksonian editor of the *New Hampshire Patriot*. "Why don't you tell the whole truth?" he protested. Then he got to the point about his hero. "On the 8th of January, 1815, he murdered in the coldest kind of cold blood above fifteen hundred British soldiers for merely trying to get into New Orleans in search of Booty and Beauty!" Around the country Jacksonian editors enthusiastically reprinted Hill's riposte and Jackson himself had a good chuckle over it.[19]

But Jackson found nothing amusing in the attacks on his family. He was reduced to tears when he came across the following statement in newspapers opposing his election: "General Jackson's mother was a COMMON PROSTITUTE, brought to this country by the British soldiers. She afterward married a MULATTO MAN, with whom she had several children, of which number General JACKSON IS ONE!!!"[20] But he flew into a rage when he read about the assaults on his beloved wife Rachel in Adamsite newspapers and pamphlets. Jackson's marriage had long been a target of his enemies. He had wooed, won, and wed Rachel in 1791 after her first husband, Lewis Robards, had left her to get a divorce. Robards, it turned out had delayed getting the divorce and then sued for divorce on the ground that his wife was living in sin. As soon as the divorce came through, the Jacksons remarried; but malicious stories about Rachel's "adultery" dogged Jackson for the rest of his life. During the 1828 campaign anti-Jackson newspapers revived the old charge of immorality and asked voters: "Ought a convicted adultress and her paramour husband to be placed in the highest offices of this free and Christian land?"[21] When Rachel, whose health was poor, suddenly died in December 1828, Jackson was convinced Adamsite slanders had done her in. "May God Almighty forgive her murderers," he exclaimed at her funeral, "as I know she forgave them. I never can." He never forgave Adams and Clay for not enjoining their followers against bringing Rachel's name into the campaign.[22]

Balloting in the twenty-four states began in September and ran on into November; and, since all but two states now chose presidential electors by popular vote, many people who had never voted before cast ballots this time. "To the Polls!" cried Duff Green in the pages of the *United States Telegraph* on October 20. "To the Polls! The faithful sentinel must not sleep—Let no one stay home—Let every man go to the Polls—Let not a vote be lost—Let each Freeman do his duty; and all will triumph in the success of JACKSON, CALHOUN AND LIB-

ERTY."[23] By early December it was clear that Jackson and Calhoun had triumphed. "Well, for Mr. Jackson's sake, I am glad," sighed Mrs. Jackson when she heard the news; "for my own part," she added dolefully, "I never wished it."[24] A few days later she was dead.

The turnout in 1828 was not overwhelming (around 56 percent of the eligible voters), but it represented three times as many voters as in 1824. Jackson won 647,276 popular and 178 electoral votes to Adams's 508,064 popular and 83 electoral votes. The division was sectional in nature. Adams took New England (except for one vote in Maine), Delaware, New Jersey, 16 of New York's 36 electoral votes, and 6 of Maryland's 11. Jackson won all the rest: the entire West and South, together with Pennsylvania. Calhoun beat Rush for Vice-President by 171 to 83 electoral votes. To Adams supporters the outcome represented the victory of the mob; but to Jackson and his followers it meant the "triumph of the great principles of self government over the intrigues of aristocracy."[25]

When inauguration day arrived Daniel Webster observed with some irritation that people had come five hundred miles to see the sixty-one-year-old Jackson and that they "really seem to think that the country has been rescued from some dreadful danger."[26] To Webster and the other Adamsites, Jackson was of course the great danger and they resolved to throw him out of office four years later.

☆ ☆ ☆

Injudicious

Some people thought Jackson was fuzzy on the issues. He took a "middle and just course" on the tariff and said rates should be "judicious." At this, Clay cried sarcastically: "Well, by —, I am in favor of an *injudicious* tariff!" But Martin Van Buren endorsed Jackson's position in a speech in Albany, New York, calling for a tariff that would be "wise," "just," and "salutary." When he finished his talk, one man in the audience applauded loudly, then stopped, thought for a moment, and in bewilderment asked a friend: "On which side of the Tariff question was it?"[27]

Youthful Indiscretions

To offset a laudatory campaign biography of Jackson by his friend John Eaton, Adamsites got out a thick pamphlet entitled *Reminiscences; or, an Extract from the Catalogue of General Jackson's Youthful Indiscretions between the Age of Twenty-three and Sixty.* In it they listed fourteen fights, duels, brawls, shoot-outs, and free-for-alls in which Old Hickory had been involved before entering presidential politics. His *"intemperate life and character,"* they insisted, rendered him "unfit for the highest civil ap-

pointment within the gift of [the] country." Adams's friends also charged
that Jackson had been involved in Aaron Burr's conspiracy in 1806 to
dismember the Union. Then it turned out that Clay, Adams's Secretary
of State, had been an attorney for Burr at his trial. The matter was
quickly dropped. But not before the Jacksonians triumphantly shouted:
"Henry Clay, a Traitor!"[28]

Tariff of Abominations

During 1828 Jackson's supporters in Congress put together a tariff bill
which helped elect Old Hickory. In drawing up the bill they ignored
New England, which was solid for Adams; they also risked antagoniz-
ing the anti-protectionist South on the assumption that it would never
choose Adams over Jackson. Their main objective was to win Ohio,
Kentucky, and Missouri (which had gone for Adams in 1824), as well
as such important states as Pennsylvania and New York. To please
farmers in those states they placed heavy duties on imported raw materials, especially hemp, flax, molasses, iron, and sail duck. New Englanders screamed; but they didn't matter. Southerners were also incensed; but they were planning to support Jackson in the hope his
administration would reverse things. Some of the Adamsites realized what
the Jacksonians were up to. "I fear this tariff thing," warned one of them;
"by some strange mechanism, it will be changed into a machine for
manufacturing Presidents, instead of broadcloths and bed blankets." He
was right. Despite heavy opposition from New England and the South,
the "tariff of abominations," as its opponents called it, passed Congress
and probably helped Jackson in Indiana, Ohio, Kentucky, Illinois,
Pennsylvania, and New York. It was a shrewd move by Jackson's supporters in Congress.[29]

Evil Weevil

Jackson's campaign managers worked hard to woo the nation's farmers. They portrayed Jackson as a man of the soil who dropped his tools
in the field like Cincinnatus of old to respond to his country's call to
duty in time of crisis. But Adams, they said, was an insufferable snob
who had never worked a day in his life. As long as he remained in the
White House, they warned, his corrupting influence would spread like
a disease over the land. Indeed, they said, an epidemic had already begun. "We are sorry to learn," lamented the *Winchester Virginian*, "that
owing to the ravages committed by [the Hessian Fly], the wheat crop
. . . begins to wear a sickly aspect, and that a general failure of it in
this quarter is to be apprehended. Everything seems to go wrong since
the birth of the present Administration. Contemporaneous with that
event . . . the Weevil first made its appearance; both of which have since
been at work to the no small annoyance of the farmer."[30]

Ebony and Topaz

Adams's public appearances always seemed to play into the hands of the Jacksonians. In October 1827 he went to Baltimore to help celebrate the successful defense of the city against the British attack during the War of 1812. Asked to propose a toast, he cried: "Ebony and Topaz. General Ross's posthumous coat of arms, and the republican militiamen who gave it." His audience was puzzled, so he explained. His allusion, he said, came from Voltaire's *Le Blanc et le noir* (an anti-Christian book, noted the Jacksonians) in which Ebony stood for the spirit of evil (represented by the British General Robert Ross, whose coat of arms received a posthumous addition by the King), and Topaz was the good spirit represented by the American militiamen. When the incident reached the newspapers the Jacksonians had a lot of fun with it. At first, said the *New York Evening Post,* "we supposed it to have been the production of some wicked Jacksonian wag who had undertaken to burlesque the clumsy wit and unwieldy eloquence of the ex-professor." Duff Green said he would make no comment because he wasn't as versed in "Oriental literature" as Adams was. The National Republicans were embarrassed. In a letter to Clay, Charles Hammond wrote: "I wish Mr. Adams' *ebony and topaz* were submerged in the deepest profound of the bathos. You great men have no privilege to commit blunders" like that.[31]

New Orleans Celebration

When the Louisiana legislature invited Jackson to come to New Orleans to celebrate the thirteenth anniversary of his great victory over the British there on January 8, Jackson agreed to go, though he insisted it had nothing to do with the presidential campaign. On December 29, he and his wife boarded the steamer *Pocahontas* at Nashville and began proceeding slowly down the Mississippi toward the Crescent City. While en route they encountered a steamer of faster speed which began zigzagging across the bow of the *Pocahontas.* Jackson finally lost his temper, ordered a rifle, hailed the pilot of the other ship, and told him if he made one more zigzag he'd shoot him. Jackson's aides were upset. A shoot-out, they knew, would play into the hands of Jackson's political enemies. One of them hastened below to tell Mrs. Jackson. "Colonel," said Rachel, "do me the favor to say to the General I wish to speak to him." Jackson at once went down to see her and there was no shooting.

When Jackson got to New Orleans there was a four-day celebration. "We had a harmonious & happy meeting with all our friends & compatriots in arms at New Orleans," he wrote afterwards, "the concourse was unusually great." Jackson did not regard his trip as electioneering but it undoubtedly helped him in the campaign. Time and again he was toasted in New Orleans: "ANDREW JACKSON. His Titles are His Services. His Party the American People."[32]

Spoken To

A farm boy back home from a trip to town to see Jackson boasted that the Hero of New Orleans had spoken to him. His skeptical friends asked what Jackson had said. Said the boy proudly: "He told me to get the hell out of the way!"[33]

Privilege

In a town Jackson was visiting a belligerent Clay man came up to him and cried: "Yes, sir, I want you to understand that I am not going to vote for you." "Sir," said Jackson, looking him straight in the eye, "I have given much of my life to my country, and it was that you might have this privilege!"[34]

ABC

During the campaign anti-Jackson crowds paraded before the Nashville hotel where Jackson was staying waving banners:

> The A
> B
> C
> of Democracy.

> The Adultress
> The Bully
> And the Cuckold

They also sang:

> Oh, Andy! Oh, Andy,
> How many men have you hanged in your life?
> How many weddings make a wife?[35]

Your Candidate

According to a Jacksonian campaign joke, two political foes met and the first man yelled: "Hurrah for Jackson!" shouted the other: "Hurrah for the devil!" "Very well," shot back the first man, "you stick to your candidate, and I'll stick to mine."[36]

No War on Females

To get back at the Adamsites for their attacks on Mrs. Jackson, Duff Green decided to print in the *United States Telegraph* a silly story about Adams's premarital relations with his wife. "Let Mrs. Jackson rejoice," he told Jackson delightedly, "her vindication is complete." But Jackson didn't see it that way. "Female character," he told Green, "should never be introduced or touched unless a continuation of attack should be made against Mrs. Jackson, and then only by way of *Just retaliation* on the known GUILTY. . . . I *never war against females* and it is only the base and cowardly that do." That ended attacks on the President's wife.[37]

The Hunters of Kentucky

One of the most popular songs in 1828 was "The Hunters of Kentucky," written several years before by Samuel Woodworth (author of "The Old Oaken Bucket"), to commemorate Jackson's New Orleans victory over General Pakenham. The Jacksonians distributed thousands of copies of the song, which included the following stanzas:

> You've heard, I s'pose, of New Orleans,
> 'Tis famed for youth and beauty,
> There're girls of every hue, it seems,
> From snowy white to sooty.
> Now Pakenham had made his brags,
> If he that day was lucky,
> He'd have those girls and cotton-bags
> In spite of Old Kentucky.

> But Jackson, he was wide awake,
> And was not scared at trifles,
> For well he knew Kentucky's boys,
> With their death-dealing rifles,
> He led them down to cypress swamp,
> The ground was low and mucky,
> There stood John Bull in martial pomp,
> And here stood old Kentucky.

> Oh! Kentucky, the hunters of Kentucky!
> Oh! Kentucky, the hunters of Kentucky![38]

Mention Modestly

Martin Van Buren, one of Jackson's campaign managers, decided to inject religion into the campaign. He knew that Adams was a Unitarian and he hoped to portray Old Hickory as a more orthodox believer. Writing to New York publisher James A. Hamilton about Old Hickory, he asked: "Does the old gentleman have prayers in his own House? If so, mention it modestly." Hamilton's reply, subsequently published, was more than modest. Jackson, he affirmed, "is a sincere believer in the Christian religion, and performs his devotions regularly with his family in his own House, and in a Presbyterian Church in his neighborhood." Isaac Hill improved on Hamilton. In the *New Hampshire Patriot* he had Jackson saying prayers "every morning and night, also table prayers."

The Jacksonians also publicized a story about Jackson's respect for religion when he was in the army. Once, they said, after he had issued an order forbidding unusual noise in his camp, an officer complained that a group of soldiers had assembled to pray. "Go, then, and join them," Jackson was said to have cried. "God forbid that praying should be an uncommon noise in my camp!"

But Jackson was not a church member. One Sunday, when he was walking with his wife to the little chapel at the Hermitage he had built for her, she asked him to join the church and take communion with her. "My dear," Jackson replied, "if I were to do that now, it would be said, all over the country, that I had done it for the sake of political effect. My enemies would all say so. I can not do it *now*, but I promise you that when once more I am clear of politics I will join the church." After leaving the White House he joined the Presbyterian church.[39]

★ ★

CHAPTER TWELVE

1832
Jackson, Clay, and the Bank War

In July 1832, as the presidential campaign was getting under way, Andrew Jackson vetoed a bill rechartering the Second Bank of the United States (B.U.S.) for twenty more years and Congress was unable to muster enough votes to override his veto. Jackson's vigorously worded veto message delighted his friends and infuriated his enemies. The veto, Maryland Senator Samuel Smith told him, would "cause all the Election to be contested on the principle of Bank or no Bank."[1] Smith was right. The Bank—or "Mammoth Monopoly," as Jackson called it—became the central issue of Jackson's campaign for re-election. For the first time in American history a President took a strong stand on an important social issue and then asked for the approval of the voters at the polls. Jackson had no doubts about the outcome. "The veto works well," he assured a friend a few weeks later, "instead of crushing me as was expected and intended, it will crush the Bank."[2]

Jackson hated "ragg, tagg banks."[3] When he was a land speculator and storekeeper in Tennessee in his younger days, he had run into serious financial difficulties and come to the conclusion that banks were vastly overpaid for their services. The "wretched rag money" they issued was a fraud, he decided; and the credit they extended to people encouraged speculation and indebtedness. "I do not dislike your bank any more than all banks," he told Nicholas Biddle, Philadelphia's genteel B.U.S. President.[4] Old Hickory was a "hard money" man; he thought that specie, i.e., gold and silver, not paper money, should be the medium of exchange in business dealings. When he journeyed from Washington to the Hermitage for a visit a few weeks after his veto message, he insisted on paying for all of his expenses en route in gold. "No more paper-money, you see, fellow-citizens," he announced, "if I can only put down this Nicholas Biddle and his monster bank."[5] His followers referred to gold as "Jackson money," paid wages in gold, called themselves "anti-bank hatters" and "hard-money bakers," put up liberty poles displaying the words "NO BANK! DOWN WITH THE BANK! NO RAG MONEY!" and proposed toasts: "Gold and silver, the only currency recognized by the Constitution!"[6]

It was not Jackson, however, who first brought the Bank into the 1832 campaign. It was Henry Clay. Clay thought he could beat Jackson on the issue. Biddle's headquarters were in Philadelphia and the Bank was popular in Pennsylvania, a key state in any election; there were also many people in Jackson's own party who were friendly to the Bank. By making the B.U.S. an issue in the campaign, Clay reasoned, he might divide the Democratic-Republican party and enable the National Republicans to defeat Jackson's bid for a second term. Biddle had misgivings at first; but he finally agreed to apply for recharter in 1832 even though the Bank's charter did not expire until 1836.

But Clay's plan failed. Jackson's veto message thrilled rather than alienated thousands of Americans. In it, not only did Jackson declare the Bank inefficient, profitable mainly to foreigners, monopolistic, hostile to states' rights, and unconstitutional; he also proclaimed it an instrument of special privilege which favored the rich and well-born at the expense of "the humble members of society—the farmers, mechanics, and laborers—who have neither the time nor the means of securing like favors to themselves."[7] To Biddle, Jackson's appeal to "the Great Unwashed" was a "manifesto of anarchy" and he quickly arranged to distribute 30,000 copies of it to show the voters how silly their President was. But the document helped rather than hurt Jackson. It convinced many voters that the "Jackson cause is the cause of democracy and the people against a corrupt and abandoned aristocracy."[8]

By the time the Bank issue began to rock the nation, the presidential nominations had already been made. To pick candidates the political parties held national nominating conventions for the first time in American history. For the first time, too, there was a third party in the presidential field: the Anti-Masonic party. In September 1831, the Anti-Masons, meeting in Baltimore, convened the very first presidential nominating convention ever held, declared its opposition to secret societies, especially to Freemasons, and picked former Attorney-General William Wirt of Maryland as its candidate. In December the National Republicans also met in Baltimore, with 156 delegates from seventeen states, unanimously chose "Prince Hal" (as Clay was called) for President, picked Biddle's friend John Sergeant of Pennsylvania to run with him, and issued a long address praising Clay's "American System" and faulting the Jackson administration for a long list of sins. In May 1832, the Democratic Republicans (or Democrats, as they were coming to be called) assembled in Baltimore, too, with 334 delegates representing every state but Missouri, and adopted two measures that were to govern their conventions for a century: the unit rule by which the majority of a state's delegation determined the state's vote; and the two-thirds rule for choosing candidates. Jackson had already been nominated by several state legislatures and conventions, so the Baltimore meeting simply concurred in "the repeated nominations which he has received" and went on to select Van Buren as his running mate.[9]

During 1832 Biddle worked hard to retire the President to private life. He subsidized anti-Jackson newspapers, made loans to pro-Bank Congressmen, distributed anti-Jackson speeches, tracts, pamphlets, and journals by the thousands, and even encouraged employers to threaten workers with loss of jobs if they supported Jackson. "I fear the Bank influence more than anything else," said one worried Jacksonian. "I have no doubt that the Bank contributed something close to $100,000 to prevent Jackson's re-election."[10] In their efforts to discredit Old Hickory, the National Republicans spread rumors about his poor health, revived stories about his reckless impetuosity, charged that he traveled on Sunday when he should be in church, and berated him for subscribing to the doctrine that "to the victor belong the spoils" and undertaking an "indiscriminate removal of public officers, for the mere difference of political opinion."[11]

The Jacksonians warned voters against domination by a moneyed aristocracy; for them, B.U.S. President Nicholas Biddle was "Emperor Nicholas," "Czar Nick," or "Old Nick." But the Bankites (as Clay's supporters were called) insisted it was Jackson, not Biddle, who was oppressing the people. Jackson, they said, was a Tyrant, Usurper, Dictator, King Andrew I, King of Kings, who was trampling on the Constitution and the Bill of Rights. With the Bank veto, announced Daniel Webster, Jackson had proposed a "pure despotism" and, like Louis XIV, proclaimed, "I AM THE STATE."[12] One National Republican editor declared that Jackson had "set at utter defiance the will of the people as strongly expressed by their Senators and Representatives," exercised "a power no Monarch in Europe dared attempt," and "proved himself to be the most absolute despot now at the head of any representative government on earth."[13] Screamed one anti-Jackson headline: "THE KING UPON THE THRONE: THE PEOPLE IN THE DUST!!!"[14] To broaden their appeal, the National Republicans made considerable use of cartoons. They pictured Jackson losing his temper at visitors; receiving a crown from Van Buren and a sceptre from the devil; tilting, Don Quixote fashion, at the pillars of the marble bank building in Philadelphia and breaking his lance; and trying, with the help of friends, to force the bank doors open with a battering ram. They also pictured Clay and Jackson as jockeys in a race to the White House with Clay half a length ahead.[15]

But Jackson never doubted the outcome of the race. "Isaac," he told a friend long before the campaign was over, "it'll be a walk. If our fellows didn't raise a finger from now on the thing would be just as well done. In fact, Isaac, it's done now."[16] Clay's supporters may have made effective use of cartoons; but Jackson's friends excelled at organizing torchlight parades, barbecues, glee clubs, and mass meetings at which impassioned orators denounced "the Monster" and urged voters to "stand by the Hero."[17] Visiting the United States at this time, Michel Chevalier, French official, was struck by a Jackson parade he witnessed in New York City. "It was nearly a mile long," he reported. "The democrats marched in good order, to the glare of torches; the banners were more numerous than I had ever seen them in any religious festival; all were in transparency, on account of the darkness. On some were inscribed the names of the democratic societies or sections: *Democratic young men of the ninth* or *eleventh ward;* others bore imprecations against the Bank of the United States; *Nick Biddle* and *Old Nick* here figured largely. Then came portraits of General Jackson afoot and on horseback; there was one of the general, and another in the person of the Tennessee farmer, with the famous hickory cane in his hand. . . . From further than the eye could reach, came marching on the democrats. . . . The democratic procession . . . had its halting-places; it stopped before the houses of the Jackson men to fill the air with cheers, and halted at the doors of the leaders of the Opposition, to give three, six, or nine groans." Chevalier could not help feeling that demonstrations like this "belong to history, they partake of the grand; they are the episodes of a wondrous epic which will bequeath a lasting memory to posterity, that of the coming of democracy."[18] Sometimes there were good Jacksonian turnouts even in Clay's territory. When Jackson passed through Lexington, Kentucky, Clay's home, toward the end of the campaign, a multitude of people streamed down the road for five miles to greet him "with green hickory bushes waving like bright banners in a breeze." Sighed one Ohio supporter of Clay: "There is no withstanding such arguments."[19] It was the hickory-pole campaign all over again.

Long before the returns were all in, it was clear that Jackson, now sixty-five, had won a smashing victory. "The city is lost!" exclaimed a disappointed New York editor. "The returns from the country come in all one way! There is no doubt that Jackson and Van Buren are elected!"[20] Jackson did so well (687,502 popular votes to Clay's 530,189, and 219 electoral votes to Clay's 49) that the anti-Jackson *Vermont Journal* admitted it had "no heart to publish the election returns."[21] Jackson won about 55 percent of the popular votes, Clay won 37 percent, and Wirt, 7 percent. "Who but General Jackson would have had the courage to veto the bill rechartering the Bank of the United States," said one of his followers admiringly, "and who but General Jackson could have withstood the overwhelming influence of that corrupt Aristocracy?"[22]

Jackson, not surprisingly, interpreted his victory as a mandate from the people to proceed against the Bank. He was determined to withhold further government deposits from the Bank and thus eventually bring to an end what he regarded as Biddle's "absolute control over the currency," "control over property," and "control over the people."[23] Jackson took what his enemies regarded as a novel and dangerous view of the Presidency. He regarded himself as the "direct representative of the people" who was obliged to go to bat for them if the other two branches of government disregarded the popular will. His belief that the President derived power from the people who elected him as well as from the Constitution horrified Clay and his followers. "Sir," cried Clay, in a long anti-Jackson speech in the Senate shortly after the election, "I am surprised and alarmed at the new source of executive power which is found in the result of a presidential election. I had supposed that the Constitution and the laws were the sole source of executive authority . . . that the issue of a presidential election was merely to place the Chief Magistrate in the post assigned to him. . . . But it seems that if, prior to an election, certain opinions, no matter how ambiguously put forth by a candidate, are known to the people, those loose opinions, in virtue of the election, incorporate themselves with the Constitution, and afterward are to be regarded and expounded as parts of the instrument."[24] But what Clay regarded as shocking, Jackson thought was natural and normal in a government shaped by majority will. So did thousands of his devoted supporters. "My opinion," sighed William Wirt after the election, "is that he may be President for life if he chooses."[25]

Brawlers

In July 1832, President Jackson had two surgeons remove from his shoulder the bullet he had received in a shoot-it-out with Thomas Hart Benton in Nashville back in 1813. The operation was a simple one and shortly after it was completed Jackson appeared among friends with his arm in a sling and smoking his pipe. The anti-Jackson press was filled with animadversions on the "disgusting affair" in Nashville nineteen years before. This led Jackson's friend Francis P. Blair to dig up a story about a wound Henry Clay had received in a fight. "He was taken to a kind friend's house," wrote Blair in the *Washington Globe*, "he was treated with the utmost tenderness and courtesy by that friend's wife and family, and while enjoying their hospitality he amused himself . . . by winning the money of his kind host." Jackson may have been a brawler in his youth; but Clay, said the Jacksonians, was a gambler and an ingrate as well as brawler.[26]

Out of Order

In a debate about the Bank on July 14, Clay recalled the big fight Senator Benton had once had with Jackson and quoted the Missourian as having said that if Jackson became President, "we must be girded with pistols and dirks to defend ourselves while legislating here." Benton at once denounced Clay's statement as "an atrocious calumny." "What!" cried Clay, "can you look me in the face, sir, and say you never used that language?" "I look, sir," said Benton, "and repeat that it is an atrocious calumny; and I will pin it to him who repeats it here." "Then," said Clay, his face flushed with rage, "I declare before the Senate that you said to me the very words!" "False! False! False!" shouted Benton. Yelled Clay: "I fling back the charge of atrocious calumny upon the Senator from Missouri!" At this point several Senators stepped in between the two men and the Senate presiding officer called them to order. "I apologize to the Senate for the manner in which I have spoken," said Benton, "but not to the Senator from Kentucky." Rejoined Clay: "To the Senate I also offer apology. To the Senator from Missouri, none!"[27]

Whole Hog

Late one night a Kentucky farmer reached the marketplace in Lexington, split a dressed pig into halves, hung them on stout hooks, and, using a bag of meal for a pillow, lay down to sleep in his wagon until dawn. When he awoke, he found half of his pig gone. "I know the sort of man that stole that pork, I do," he yelled to the people gathering in the marketplace. "He was a Clay man!" This angered the people, solidly for Clay, who lived nearby, and they demanded an explanation. "Why," said the farmer, "nobody but a Clay man would have done it; ef he had been a Jackson man he would have gone the whole hog!"[28]

Kiss Him

When Jackson was visiting one town, according to a campaign tale, a proud mother handed a dirty-faced baby up for him to hold. "Here is a beautiful specimen of young American childhood," said Jackson obligingly. "Note the brightness of that eye, the great strength of those limbs, and the sweetness of those lips." Then he handed the baby to his friend John Eaton. "Kiss him, Eaton," he cried, and walked away.[29]

Tariff Crisis

The tariff as well as the Bank agitated the nation in 1832. When Congress passed a protective tariff bill sponsored by Henry Clay in June and Jackson signed it, South Carolina called for a convention to be held in November to take measures to nullify the operation of the tariff within its borders. Jackson, who blamed Calhoun for spreading nullificationist views in his state, made it clear he was going to uphold the tariff law. "Gentlemen," he told his friends, "I never until now believed that Calhoun could poison the minds and pervert the souls of that gallant people. But now I see he has done it. *Of course I shall be re-elected.* It will be my duty, if God spares my life, to enforce the laws of the United States, and *preserve our Federal Union as it is* until the 4th of March, 1837—more than four years hence. I may have to call on my old army of New Orleans to stand by me! They stood by me once when my country was in danger, and I know they will do it again!" Asked if he thought the situation was that serious, Jackson said he feared it was; and when asked what he would do about it, he cried: "Suppress the rebellion, sir; root out the treason, sir, with ruthless hand! Assemble a force sufficient to crush any uprising at any point; assume, as constitutional commander-in-chief, the immediate command and take the field in person, sir! Hang every leader and every false counsellor of that infatuated people, sir, by martial law, irrespective of his name, or political or social position— *the higher, the worse! . . ."* And he added ferociously: "For my part, I declare that I will enforce the laws of the United States if I should have to depopulate the State of traitors and repeople it with a better and wiser race!"

Jackson didn't calm down until he had a mint julep or two. Then he took action: reinforced U.S. troops in federal garrisons in South Carolina and instructed General Winfield Scott to prepare the army for any contingency. In the November election, the Union party, to Jackson's disappointment, went down to defeat in the Palmetto State. Jackson then obtained emergency powers from Congress to enforce the tariff laws. The crisis passed only when a compromise tariff, sponsored by Clay early in 1833, enabled South Carolina to save face and withdraw its nullification ordinance.[30]

CHAPTER THIRTEEN

★ ★

1836
Van Buren's Victory
Over Three Whigs

In February 1835, Andrew Jackson, who had decided against a third term, urged the Democrats to hold a national convention, composed of delegates "fresh from the people," to pick nominees for the election of 1836.[1] He made no secret of his preferences: Vice-President Martin Van Buren of New York, his close friend and associate, for President, and, to balance the ticket, Col. Richard M. Johnson of Kentucky, an old Indian fighter, for Vice-President. There was considerable opposition, especially in the South, to Jackson's choices. Southerners distrusted Van Buren, the smooth New Yorker; but they loathed the Kentucky Colonel who lived with a black woman and had two daughters by her. In the end, though, Jackson, as usual, had his way. The Democrats met in Baltimore in May, unanimously chose Van Buren, fifty-three, as their presidential candidate on the first ballot, and then picked Johnson for Vice-President. Virginia's delegates "hissed most ungraciously" at the choice of Johnson and then walked out of the convention.[2]

To Jackson's enemies the "Van Buren convention" was a farce. It was a "packed office-holders' convention," they charged, as objectionable as the old Congressional caucus.[3] Some states, they pointed out, sent no delegates to Baltimore; other states were vastly over-represented. And from Tennessee itself came not a single delegate "fresh from the people." But a Tennessean who happened to be in town was admitted to the convention and agreed to cast his state's fifteen votes for Van Buren and Johnson. His name was Edmund Rucker and for a time the verb "ruckerize" was used as a synonym for engaging in political skullduggery.[4] Before adjourning, the Baltimore convention issued a lengthy statement of principles that pleased Old Hickory, and Van Buren promised, in his acceptance, "to perfect the work which he has so gloriously begun."[5]

Not everyone thought Jackson's work was glorious. The National Republicans were still fuming over his war against the Bank; and they continued to regard his opposition to high tariffs and internal improvements as injurious to the nation's well-being. Southern states-righters, once friendly to Old Hickory, were now disaffected; the strong stand he had taken against South Carolina's efforts to nullify the tariff laws in 1833 had turned them into implacable anti-Jacksonians. There were others, even in the Democratic party, who thought Jackson was too high-handed and that he was upsetting the constitutional balance between the three branches of government by his actions. And the Anti-Masons, who had run a ticket of their own in 1832, were ready to cast their lot with the anti-Jackson opposition this time. By 1834 various elements opposed to the Jackson administration were coming together into a new party coalition, with supporters in every part of the country, and calling themselves Whigs. The English Whigs of old had fought royal despotism and so had American Whigs during the Revolution. The new Whig party taking shape during Jackson's second administration was dedicated to fighting "King Andrew the First" and welcomed to its ranks all the people who detested Jackson even if they happened to dislike each other too. The Democrats at first dismissed the new grouping of "Federalists, nullifers, and bank men" as an "organized incompatibility" with little real clout.[6] "We have nothing to fear," one Democrat assured Van Buren, "from the combined fragments we have to contend with."[7] But the Whig strategy for 1836 actually had the Jacksonians worried.

The Whigs were too loosely united to hold a national convention in 1836 and agree on a single ticket. Instead, they decided to support favorite sons in various parts of the country with the hope that they could deny Van Buren an electoral victory, force the election into the House of Representatives, as in 1824, and then unite on a Whig President to succeed Jackson. "This disease," as Nicholas Biddle put it, "is to be treated as a local disorder—apply local remedies."[8] Henry Clay, who realized he couldn't defeat Van Buren by himself, supported the favorite-son strategy as the only hope of the Anti-Jacksonians. The Whigs, then, ended with three candidates, all nominated by state legislatures and popular conventions in their respective sections during 1835 and 1836: Massachusetts Senator Daniel Webster, a supporter of Clay's American System and on good terms with the Anti-Masons, could take New England; Tennessee Senator Hugh L. White, a moderate states-righter, would run strong in the South; and Ohio's William Henry Harrison would appeal to the West. But Harrison, War of 1812 general and former territorial governor of Indiana, turned out to be the strongest candidate of the three.

The Whigs were relentless in their attacks on Van Buren. In the Senate, where the "little Magician" was presiding as Vice-President, Henry Clay, with the help of Daniel Webster and John C. Calhoun, did everything he could to embarrass him. The anti-Jackson triumvirate encouraged disorder in the galleries, arranged tie-votes to force him out on a limb where he had to cast the deciding vote, and even called the Sergeant-at-Arms to pursue him when he left the platform without voting. But Van Buren remained imperturbable throughout. "He leaned back his head," noted one reporter, "threw one leg over the other, and sat there as if he were a pleasant sculptured image, destined for that niche of life."[9] The anti-Van Buren press was vitriolic. The *New York American* called him "illiterate, sycophant, and politically corrupt," and the *New York Courier and Enquirer* compared him to "the fox prowling near the barn; the mole burrowing near the ground; the pilot fish who plunges deep in the ocean in one spot and comes up in another to breathe the air."[10]

Van Buren's supporters did all they could to defend their man as a worthy successor to the Hero of New Orleans. They also denigrated the Whig candidates: dismissed Webster as an old Federalist, called White an ingrate who deserted Jackson to further his own selfish ambitions, and pictured Harrison as a failure both as military leader during the War of 1812 and as territorial governor of Indiana. But they also counted heavily on party loyalty, efficient organization, and effective electioneering to carry the day for Van Buren. They set up state and local committees to raise money and distribute campaign material, founded newspapers, and held countless rallies, barbecues, and dinners to further the Van Buren cause. The Whigs, with several candidates in the field, simply couldn't keep up with them. Sighed New York Whig leader Thurlow Weed toward the end: "We are to be cursed with Van Buren for President."[11]

Van Buren won 764,198 popular votes (50.9 percent) and 170 electoral votes, while his three Whig opponents took a grand total of 736,147 popular and 124 electoral votes. "The people are for him," acknowledged William T. Seward, another New York Whig. "Not so much for him as for the principle they suppose he represents. That principle is Democracy." But Harrison, with 584,000 popular and 73 electoral votes, did nicely. Many Whigs agreed with Seward that he should be "a candidate by continuation" for the next presidential contest.[12]

☆   ☆   ☆

Vanburenish

Van Buren's critics made much of his non-commitalism. The word "vanburenish," in fact, was coined to mean evasiveness in politics. In his *Life of Martin Van Buren*, David Crockett, a former Tennessee Congressman who was for White, couldn't find epithets contemptuous enough with which to damn the Democratic candidate: turncoat, noncommitalist, prince of magicians. At six, said Crockett, Van Buren "could actually tell when his book was wrong end upwards; and at twelve, he could read it just as well *upside-down* as *right-side* up, and . . . practiced it both ways, to acquire a shifting knack for business, and a ready turn for doing things more ways than one." Crockett also insisted Van Buren was no man of the people like Jackson but an insufferable snob. He "travels about the country and through the cities in an English coach; has English servants, dressed in uniform—I think they call it livery . . . ; no longer mixes with the sons of little tavern-keepers; forgets all his old companions and friends in the humbler walks of life . . . ; eats in a room by himself; and is so stiff in his gait, and prim in his dress, that he is what the English call a dandy. When he enters the Senate-chamber in the morning he struts and swaggers like a crow in a gutter. He is laced up in corsets, such as women in a town wear, and, if possible, tighter than the best of them. It would be difficult to say, from his personal appearance, whether he was a man or woman, but for his large *red* and *gray* whiskers."[13]

Locofocos

By 1836 the Democrats were being called "Locofocos." It was not a compliment. The name originated in New York and referred to the radical branch of the Democratic party there which opposed banks, paper currency, and monopolies in general, and called for equal rights for all men. When the New York Democrats met in Tammany Hall the night of October 29, 1835, to pick candidates for the state election, the Equal Righters and the conservative Democrats got into a violent argument over nominations. The conservatives finally stalked out of the meeting and blew out the gaslights as they left, leaving the place in darkness. But the Equal Righters had come prepared. They immediately pulled out their "locofoco" matches, lit candles, and went on with the meeting. The next day the *New York Courier and Enquirer* referred to the Equal Righters as "Locofocos," and the name stuck. There were other epithets. A Locofoco chronicler listed some of them: Disorganizers, Intruders, Revolters, Rowdies, Odds and Ends, Sweepings and Remnants, Renegades, Pests, Noisy Brawlers, Political Nuisances, Carbonari, Infidels, Pledge Spouters, Resolution Mongers, Small Fry, Small Lights, Fireflies, Unclean Birds, Jack-o-Lanterns, Scum, Knaves, Cheats, Swindlers, and the Guy Fawkes of politics. But the name, Locofoco, persisted, and many Democrats came to accept it as an honor. But its association with radicalism made it a favorite term for enemies of Jacksonian Democracy.[14]

Rumpsey-Dumpsey Johnson

Whigs supporting General William Henry Harrison made much of the fact that during the War of 1812 he had routed Tecumseh's Indians at Tippecanoe. To counter this, the Democrats put Colonel Richard M.

Johnson of Kentucky on the ticket with Van Buren. It was Johnson, they claimed, who had killed the great Indian chief during the Battle of the Thames in October 1813. While some people wondered whether "a lucky shot, even if it did hit Tecumseh, qualifies a man for Vice President," the Democrats went around singing:

> Rumpsey dumpsey, rumpsey dumpsey,
> Colonel Johnson killed Tecumseh.

But there were skeptics. Some people sang a different tune:

> Rumpsey dumpsey
> Who killed Tecumseh?

Who indeed? No one actually knows. Johnson did lead a charge against Tecumseh's men during the Battle of the Thames and did kill an Indian chief. But there is no evidence that Tecumseh, who was felled during the battle, died at Johnson's hands. But Johnson's friends insisted he had killed Tecumseh, called him "the Hero of the Thames," and distributed a campaign biography commemorating the deed. Richard Emmons, a poet of sorts, wrote a play called "Tecumseh, or the Battle of the Thames, a National Drama in Five Acts," celebrating the deed. Johnson attended one performance and loved it. "I have more friends than ever by the hundreds," he exulted afterward. In campaign speeches he liked to recall the famous episode: "My pistol," he would say, "had one ball and three buckshot in it and the Indian was found to have a ball through his body and three buck-shot in different parts of his breast and head." At this point audiences would yell "Thus Tecumseh fell!"[15]

★ ★

CHAPTER FOURTEEN

1840
Tippecanoe and Tyler Too

The campaign of 1840 was boisterous. To oust Martin Van Buren from the White House and put William Henry Harrison in his place the Whigs pulled out all the stops. "The whole country," observed John Quincy Adams, "is in a state of agitation upon the approaching Presidential election such as was never before witnessed. . . . Not a week has passed within the last few months without a convocation of thousands of people to hear inflamatory harangues against Martin Van Buren and his Administration!" He went on worriedly: "Here is a revolution in the habits and manners of the people. Where will it end? These are party movements, and must in the natural progress of things become antagonistical. . . . Their manifest tendency is to civil war."[1]

The election of 1840 was neither civil war nor revolution; it was mainly fun and games. More people voted that year than in any previous presidential contest. The participation of the average citizen, moreover, in the energetic electioneering—parades, barbecues, rallies, songfests—reached astonishing proportions. During the 1830s, the lowering or abolition of property or tax-paying qualifications for voting in most states meant the gradual democratization of American politics. Presidential contests ceased to be the private preserve of the rich and well-born. They became in part great entertainments in which even people who could not vote joined in on the fun. By 1840 it was necessary for all the presidential aspirants to do what Andrew Jackson had done when he first entered the hustings: bid for the support of the masses. In 1840 the Whigs decided to take a leaf or two from the Jacksonian book and present their candidate as a man of the people and a military hero. Their strategy worked beautifully. As the *Democratic Review* admitted with chagrin after Harrison beat Van Buren in November: "They have at last learned from defeat the art of victory. We have taught them how to conquer us!"[2]

Harrison was an unlikely "people's candidate." Unlike Jackson, who had been born in poverty, the Whig nominee was well-born and college-educated; and he was living on a comfortable farm in North Bend, Ohio, when the Whigs first became interested in him. His military career, compared with Jackson's, was not particularly distinguished. He had, as governor of the Indiana Territory, led the forces that engaged the Shawnee chief, Tecumseh, in battle at Tippecanoe in 1811; but though he beat off the Indians, his men suffered heavy casualties in the encounter. He had been, moreover, merely competent, at best, as commander in the Northwest during the War of 1812. But the Whigs blithely reshaped Harrison's persona. They called him "Old Buckeye" to prove he was just as plain and forthright as "Old Hickory"; and they hailed him as "the Hero of Tippecanoe" to elevate him to the status of "the Hero of New Orleans." In vain did the Democrats point to his unimpressive record. The names, Harrison and Tippecanoe, soon became interchangeable.

To some extent the Whigs stumbled onto their major campaign theme. When they passed over Henry Clay and picked Harrison to run for President at their convention in Harrisburg, Pennsylvania, in December 1839, the *Baltimore Republican* gleefully reported a remark made about the Whig candidate by one of Clay's friends: "Give him a barrel of hard cider and a pension of two thousand a year and, my word for it, he will sit the remainder of his days in a log cabin, by the side of a 'sea-coal' fire and study moral philosophy."[3] Whig leaders quickly turned the sneer into a slogan and began presenting Harrison as the log-cabin–hard-cider candidate who, unlike the high-falutin' Martin Van Buren, was plain, simple, down-to-earth, and very much of, by, and for the people. The Democrats pointed out that it was a Whig, not a Democrat, who had first cast the slur, but the Whigs paid no attention to them. They had decided (as one of them admitted) "that passion and prejudice, properly aroused and directed, would do about as well as principle and reason in a party contest."[4] The log cabin and hard cider soon became the central symbols of their campaign against Van Buren.

The log-cabin–hard-cider campaign had to be seen to be believed. There was no dearth of spectators. Estimates of crowds assembled for Whig rallies ranged from one thousand to one hundred thousand and sometimes were reckoned in terms of acreage covered. Whig parades got longer and longer as the campaign went on: one mile, three miles, ten miles long. And Whig gatherings—replete with speeches, songs, cheers, and hard cider—were almost interminable: two, three, five hours long. Log cabins decorated with coonskins (after the fashion of frontier huts) became ubiquitous: erected at party rallies, drawn along in parades, and stationed in just about every city, town, village, and hamlet in the land. Hard cider was plentiful: the latchstring at the door of the log cabins was always drawn; and there was also sweet cider for the temperate. Slogans, mottoes, nicknames, and catchwords abounded: "The Farmer's President"; "The Hero of Tippecanoe"; "Harrison, Two Dollars a Day and Roast Beef"; and, best of all (since John Tyler of Virginia was Harrison's running mate), "Tippecanoe and Tyler Too!" There were also scores of log-cabin newspapers (Horace Greeley's *The Log Cabin*, a weekly, was the best), log-cabin songbooks, and log-cabin pamphlets and leaflets; and thousands of Tippecanoe badges, Tippecanoe handkerchiefs, and Tippecanoe products (including shaving cream) of all kinds. Whig songs—sung to the tunes of *La Marseillaise, Auld Lang Syne, Yankee Doodle, The Old Oaken Bucket,* and *The Star-Spangled Banner*—were energetic, exuberant, ecstatic, and endless: "The Soldier of Tippecanoe," "The Farmer of North Bend," "The Harrison Cause," "Hurrah for Old Tip," "The Log Cabin Song," "Old Tip and the Log Cabin Boys." At rallies and in parades, Harrison's fans might sing:

> Farewell, dear Van
> You're not our man;
> To guide the ship,
> We'll try old Tip.[5]

Or shout:

> The times are bad, and want curing;
> They are getting past all enduring;
> So let's turn out Martin Van Buren
> And put in old Tippecanoe![6]

The Whigs popularized the expression, keep the ball rolling, in 1840. They actually rolled balls—great, big, huge Harrison balls ten or twelve feet in diameter, made of twine, paper, leather, or tin, and covered with slogans—down the street and from town to town. And as they rolled they chanted:

> What has caused this great commotion, motion, motion,
>   Our country through?
>   It is the ball a-rolling on,
> For Tippecanoe and Tyler too, Tippecanoe and Tyler too.
> And with them we'll beat the little Van, Van, Van;
>   Van is a used-up man,
> And with them we'll beat little Van![7]

There were cartoons as well. One showed Van Buren running down the hill, his hair and coattails streaming in the wind, with a barrel of hard cider rolling after him, and shouting: "Stop that barrel!" Another, entitled "The North Bend Farmer and His Visitors" pictured Harrison with one hand on the plow and another extended in greeting to Van Buren and his aides, saying, "Gentlemen, you seem fatigued. If you will accept the fare of a log cabin, with a Western farmer's cheer, you are welcome. I have no champaigne but can give you a mug of good cider, with some ham and eggs, and good clean beds. I am a plain backwoods-man. I have cleared some land, killed some Indians, and made the Red Coats fly in my time."[8]

When the Democrats met in Baltimore on May 4 to nominate Van Buren for a second term, the Whigs were waiting for them. They had scheduled a National Convention of Young Men for that date and they staged a gigantic parade in the city on the first day to draw attention away from the Van Burenites. "Never before," reported the *Baltimore Patriot*, "was seen such an assemblage of people. . . . It is impossible to convey the slightest idea of the sublime spectacle presented by the procession as it moved through the city." But the editor tried conveying it anyway. "In no country, in no time, never before in the history of man," he reported, "was there a spectacle so full of 'natural glory.' . . . Standing on an eminence commanding a view of the line of the proces-sion in the whole extent of Baltimore Street, you beheld a moving mass of human beings. A thousand banners, burnished by the sun, floating in the breeze, ten thousand handkerchiefs waved by the fair daughters of the city, gave seeming life and motion to the very air. A hundred thousand faces were before you,—age, manhood, youth, and beauty filled every place where a foothold could be got, or any portion of the procession seen. . . . The free men of the land were there,—the fiery son of the South, the substantial citizen of the East, the hardy pioneer of the West, were all there."[9] In the procession were of course the in-evitable log cabins and barrels of cider, as well as brooms with which to "sweep the Augean stables" of Jacksonians. Fumed the Democrats, "In what grave and important discussion are the Whig journals engaged? . . . We speak of the divorce of bank and state; and the Whigs reply with a dissertation on the merits of hard cider. We defend the policy of the Administration; and the Whigs answer 'log cabin,' 'big canoes,' 'go it Tip, Come it Ty.' We urge the re-election of Van Buren because of his honesty, sagacity, statesmanship . . . and the Whigs answer that Harrison is a poor man and lives in a log cabin."[10]

But the Whigs did more than democratize Harrison; they aristocra-tized Van Buren. Before they got through, they had turned the Presi-dent, a dignified and polished but sincerely democratic gentleman, into the effetest of snobs. Congressman Charles Ogle of Pennsylvania led the way. In a speech in Congress in April lasting three days, Ogle lashed out against Van Buren for maintaining a "Royal Establishment" at the nation's expense "as splendid as that of the Caesars, and as richly adorned as the proudest Asiatic mansion." First he surveyed the President's lav-ish garden and grounds; then he entered the President's "palace" and, with rhetorical relish, expanded on "its spacious courts, its gorgeous banqueting halls, its sumptuous drawing rooms, its glittering and daz-zling saloons" and made an inventory of the furnishings, room by room, piece by piece: Ionic columns, marble mantels, gilt eagle cornices, rich-cut glass and gilt chandeliers, gilt eagle-head candelabras, French bronze gilt lamps, gilt framed mirrors of prodigious size, French gilt bronze mantel time-pieces, mahogany gilt-mounted and rosewood pianofortes, mahogany gilt bronze-mounted secretaries, damask, satin, and double silk window curtains, Royal Wilton and Imperial Brussels and Saxon carpets, gilt and satin settees, sofas, bergères, divans, tabourets, and French comfortables, elegant mahogany gilt eagle-mounted French bedsteads, gilt plateaus, gaudy artificial flowers, rich blue and gold bon-bons, tambours, compotiers, ice cream vases, splendid French china vases, olive boats, octagonal bowls, silver tureens, boats and baskets of very rich work, golden goblets, tablespoons, knives and forks. "Is not all this enough to sicken an old-fashioned Democrat?" he cried. "And this is *Van Buren democracy!*" The President's meals were epicurean of course and his toilet well-nigh sybaritic. "And if he is vain enough," Ogle fi-nally concluded, "to spend his money in the purchase of rubies for his neck, diamond rings for his fingers, Brussels lace for his breast, filet gloves for his hands, and fabrique de broderies de bougran à Nancy handkerchiefs for his pocket—if he chooses to lay out hundreds of dol-lars in supplying his toilet with 'Double Extract of Queen Victoria,' Eau de Cologne, . . . Corinthian Oil of Cream . . . , of Eglantine . . . if, I say, Mr. Van Buren sees fit to spend his cash in buying these and other perfumes and cosmetics for his toilet, it can constitute no valid reason for charging the farmers, laborers, and mechanics of the country with bills for HEMMING HIS DISH RAGS, FOR HIS LARDING NEEDLES, LIQUOR STANDS, AND FOREIGN CUT WINE COOLERS."[11]

Ogle's charges produced a sensation in and outside of Congress. Al-though the *Democratic Globe* quite properly labeled his speech an "Om-nibus of Lies," and even a few Whigs acknowledged that Van Buren had spent less on the White House than any other President, the dam-age was done. Ogle's allegations were widely reported and, reprinted in pamphlet form as *The Regal Splendor of the President's Palace,* became one of the major campaign documents of the Whigs. It also inspired one of their favorite songs:

> Let Van from his coolers of silver drink wine,
> And lounge on his cushioned settee;
> Our man on his buckeye bench can recline
> Content with hard cider is he![12]

The picture of Van Buren as a haughty and somewhat effeminate aris-tocrat—"Sweet Sandy Whiskers" was the epithet Thurlow Weed pop-ularized—was indelibly imprinted in the minds of thousands of Amer-icans during the 1840 contest.[13] Coupled with the charge that his policies had produced "hard times"—the Panic of 1837 and the severe depres-sion that followed it—and that he lived in luxury while the masses suf-fered, the Whigs established the image of a selfish and unfeeling Chief Executive that the Democrats were never able to correct.

The Democrats, perhaps mistakenly, decided to concentrate on denigrating Harrison rather than defending Van Buren. They called him senile (he was sixty-eight), said he was both mentally and physically failing, ridiculed his pompous and at times incoherent way of expressing himself, and said he was a crypto-abolitionist who also favored selling white men into slavery. They charged him with "SHOCKING PRO-FANITY," too, and spread rumors that he had cohabited with Indian squaws during his days as a young man on the frontier. They also went to great lengths to prove that he had been anything but a hero at Tippecanoe or anywhere else. The *Rough-Hewer*, a Democratic paper founded to counter Greeley's *Log Cabin*, charged that Harrison had resigned his commission a year before the War of 1812 ended, thus abandoning his country "in the time of her utmost need." Throughout the campaign the Democrats referred to him as "Granny Harrison, the Petticoat General."[14]

The Democrats thought Harrison was a moral as well as a physical coward. When it came to the issues, they said, he was "General Mum." Van Buren's policies as President, they noted, were known to all, but Harrison was implacably tongue-tied on such subjects as abolition, the Bank, and the tariff. "Availability," Senator Thomas Hart Benton taunted, was "the only ability sought by the Whigs."[15] Benton was not exaggerating. The Whigs, as he well knew, were a motley crew of nationalists, states-righters, protectionists, free-traders, pro-Bank, and anti-Bank people drawn from every section of the country; and Harrison's managers could scarcely permit their man to sound off on economic and sectional questions without endangering their shaky coalition. Nicholas Biddle had laid down the rule in 1836; let Harrison "say not one single word about his principles or his creed—," he insisted, "let him say nothing—promise nothing. Let no Committee, no Convention, no town meeting ever extract from him a single word about what he thinks now and will do hereafter. Let the use of pen and ink be wholly forbidden as if he were a mad poet in Bedlam."[16]

Despite Biddle's advice, it was difficult for Harrison to remain still in 1840. "I suffer," he told one of his associates, "from the numerous (and as to the larger portion) most rediculous *[sic]* applications for opinions on almost every subject."[17] When his managers formed a committee to help him frame innocuous responses to mischievous queries, the Democrats sneered at it as a "conscience-keeping committee" and began saying that the Whig candidate was "a man in an iron cage" and "An Old Gentleman in Leading Strings."[18] But Harrison finally decided to take to the stump. He was the first presidential candidate ever to do so and was severely criticized by the Democrats for violating the political proprieties. But in his speeches—at Fort Meigs, Columbus, Cleveland, and elsewhere—he carefully avoided saying anything of substance. He dwelt largely, and lengthily, on his status as "an old soldier and a farmer" and referred people to the record—the ancient record—for his opinions.[19]

The *Democratic Globe* huffily counted eighty-one I's in Harrison's speech at Fort Meigs and sniffed: "What a prodigy of garrulous egotism!"[20] But the crowds loved it all and cheered him on. Meanwhile the log-cabin rallies and hard-cider oratory—what the *Daily Advertiser* called the "buffoonery of 1840"—continued undiminished until it came time to vote.[21]

Harrison's victory was scarcely a surprise. Hard times severely damaged Van Buren's cause, and Whig exuberance roused great expectations for Harrison. As soon as the returns began coming in late in October, it was clear that Tippecanoe was to be the next President. His popular vote, when the balloting ended, was only around 145,000 more than Van Buren's (1,275,612 to 1,130,033); but his electoral triumph was overwhelming (234 votes to 60) and he carried nineteen states to Van Buren's seven. A tiny new party, the Liberty party, attracted only 7,069 votes, mainly in New York and Massachusetts, for its anti-slavery candidate, James Birney of New York; but it was the forerunner of the Free-Soil party of the 1840s and the Republican party of the 1850s.

The Democrats were outraged by the election results. "We have been sung down, lied down, drunk down!" said the *Wheeling Times* indignantly. "Right joyous are we that the campaign of 1840 is closed. Its character and incidents will furnish matter for mortifying reflections for years to come."[22] Overlooking the hickory-pole campaigns the Democrats had once waged for Jackson, Philadelphia's *Public Ledger* sternly lectured its readers on the damage done the nation by Whiggish frivolities. "For two years past," lamented the *Ledger,* "the most ordinary operations of business have been neglected and President-making has become every citizen's chief concern. The result being uncertain, some have been afraid to engage in new enterprises, others have retired from business, others have not dared to prosecute their business with the old vigor. Millions of dollars will now change hands on election bets; millions of days have been taken from useful labor to listen to stump orators, and millions more to build log cabins, erect hickory poles, and march in ridiculous, degrading, mob-creating processions. . . . However high the hopes inspired by the election of General Harrison, they will prove to be delusive."[23]

The Whigs naturally had high hopes. Harrison's victory, they announced, had "redeemed" the nation; it was "the most important event in the political history of a great nation." With the same extravagance that had characterized their campaign talk, they asserted that in elevating Harrison to the Presidency, the American voters had "placed their seal of condemnation upon a band of the most desperate, aspiring and unprincipled demagogues that ever graced the annals of despotism, a band of bold and reckless innovators calling themselves the democracy of the land, at whose head was Martin Van Buren, a monarchist in principle, a tyrant and a despot in practice."[24] John Quincy Adams, as usual, viewed the scene with more detachment. Noting that Harrison's "present popularity is all artificial" and that there was "little confidence in his talents or his firmness," he wrote in his diary: "Harrison came in upon a hurricane; God grant he may not go out upon a wreck."[25] But he went out soon. A month after the inauguration the sixty-eight-year-old General died of pneumonia and Tyler became the first "accidental President." The Whigs were shocked, saddened, and, as states-righter Tyler's predilections became clear, stupefied. Some of them felt like drowning themselves in hard cider.[26]

☆   ☆   ☆

Rhyme, Not Reason

When the Whigs teamed up states-righter Tyler with nationalist Harrison, providing the slogan, "Tippecanoe and Tyler Too," Philip Hone, wealthy New York Whig, who thought adding Tyler to the ticket a big mistake, exclaimed: "There was rhyme, but no reason in it."[27]

Log Cabins and All That

Harrison wasn't exactly born in a log cabin; he grew up in a palatial home in Virginia. But he did own a log cabin for a while. In 1795, when stationed in North Bend, Ohio, as a young lieutenant, he married the daughter of a wealthy farmer, bought some land, and built a five-room log house for his bride. Eventually he added to it and by 1840 it was far from being the rustic hut the Whigs were celebrating. No matter. He went along cheerfully with the log-cabin charade. He told people he would serve, if summoned to high office, but that he preferred staying with his family "in the peace and quiet of our log cabin in the Bend." By this time even the elegant Daniel Webster had to get right with log cabins. He donned plain clothes when he took to the stump for the Whig ticket and confided: "I, sir, have a feeling for log cabins and their inhabitants. I was not myself born in one, but my elder brothers and sisters were." His references to log cabins, according to the *Albany Advertiser,* "suspended for a moment every breath, and brought tears to the eyes of the sternest among his auditors."[28]

Tip and Ty

The West, according to the Whigs, was hot for Harrison and Tyler. "There is not a tree, not a stone in all the West," announced the *Pennsylvanian* on February 28, "that does not own to the Harrison cause. Women name their children Tippecanoe, North Bend, anything that smacks of Harrison. We know a drayman who has called one of his horses Tip and the other Ty, and as he snaps the whip crys out, 'Go it, Tip! come it, Ty!' Harrison and Tyler are everywhere. They are seen in the beams of the western sun. They are heard in every breeze that blows. 'Huzza for Harrison!' shout the urchins as they go home from school. The people are struggling to hold in; they want to vote now." Added a wag: "The hens in the West never lay an egg nowadays but they cackle, 'Tip-tip! Tip-tip! Tyler!'" A young couple in Cincinnati, it was reported, baptized their twins "Harrison" and "Tyler," with the nicknames, "Tip" and "Ty." Another Whig couple named their triplets, William, Henry, and Harrison; the mother, bragged Harrison supporters, "had done the whole Whig ticket!"[29]

The Singing Campaign

During 1840 a flood of musical compositions—waltzes and marches as well as campaign songs—inundated the land. "Some of the songs I shall never forget," moaned a Democratic editor after it was all over. "They rang in my ears wherever I went, morning, noon and night. . . . Men, women and children did nothing but sing. It worried, annoyed, dumbfounded, crushed the Democrats, but there was no use trying to escape. It was a ceaseless torrent of music. . . . If a Democrat tried to speak, argue, or answer anything that was said or done, he was only saluted with a fresh deluge of music." Harrison, remarked Philip Hone, was "sung into the Presidency."

One of the most popular Whig songs, "Should Brave Old Soldiers Be Forgot," mimicked "Auld Lang Syne":

> What tho' the Hero's hard "huge paws"
> Were wont to plow and sow?
> Does that disgrace our sacred cause?
> Does that degrade him? No!
> Whig farmers are our nation's nerve,
> Its bone—its very spine,
> They'll never swerve—they did not swerve
> In days of old lang syne.
>
> No ruffled shirt, no silken hose,
> No airs does Tip display;
> But like "the pith of worth," he goes
> In homespun "hoddin' gray."
> Upon his board there ne'er appeared
> The costly "sparkling wine,"
> But plain hard cider such as cheered
> In days of old lang syne.

There were chants and poems too. One chant went this way:

> Old Tip he wears a homespun coat
> He has no ruffled shirt-wirt-wirt
> But Mat he has the golden plate
> And he's a little squirt-wirt-wirt.

The Whigs squirted tobacco juice through their teeth as they chanted the lines.[30]

Whig Husbands or None

Women couldn't vote, but took an active part in the log-cabin–hard-cider campaign all the same. They wrote political pamphlets, attended conventions, made speeches, proposed "Lady toasts" honoring Harrison, rode in floats, paraded with brooms (to "sweep" the Democrats out of office), sewed banners, prepared food for the "cabin boys," and raised liberty poles with flags proclaiming, "HARRISON, OUR PROTECTOR." "This way of making politicians of their women," complained a Georgia Democrat, "is something new under the sun, but so it is the Whigs go to the strife." Ohio's *Political Tornado* thought that "if the ladies only were entitled to vote, Old Tip would be unanimously elected." Girls in Tennessee wore sashes, announcing, "Whig husbands or none," and elsewhere young ladies refused to marry their suitors until the latter promised to "go for the Protector of the Western home, the Log-Cabin candidate." Sang the Whigs lustily:

> The beautiful girls, God bless their souls, souls, souls,
>   The country through
> Will all, to a man, do all they can
>   For Tip and Tyler too.[31]

Patriotic Whig

One day a bunch of Whigs, headed by Judge Wilson ("Old Jimmy"), editor of the *Steubenville Herald,* arrived in the little town of Salem in the western part of Ohio for a Harrison rally. They were hot, tired, and thirsty and headed for the village tavern, kept by a Democrat named Andrews. "Here, Andrews," cried Old Jimmy, "is a lot of the dryest Whigs you ever saw. I want hard cider for the crowd, with a gourd to drink it from." "Bless your soul, Judge," said Andrews, "I haven't a drop of hard cider in the house." "But," persisted the Judge, "you *must* get us some hard cider, or the convention can't go on." "Well," said Andrews, "I'll do the best I can." He went out to the backyard, found some rainwater in a barrel there, took a few gallons of it, mixed in some vinegar and "forty-rod" whiskey, poured it into a gourd, returned with the stuff, and handed it to the Judge. Old Jimmy joyfully raised the gourd before the crowd and proposed a toast:

> Cold water may do for the Locos,
>   Or a little vinegar stew;
> But give me hard cider and whiskey,
>   And hurrah for Old Tippecanoe!

Then he put the gourd to his lips and was about to take a good swig when the fumes caused him to pause. He smelled the concoction, tasted it, then smelled and tasted again. Finally he shook his head and put it down. "Well, Andrews," he sighed, "this may be good hard cider. But it will take a more patriotic Whig than I am to drink it!" [32]

Nosirrah, Old Tipler

The Democrats had their one-liners too. Asked if they thought Harrison would win, they would reply: "Read his name backwards" ("Nosirrah!") Or they would ask: "Why do the Whigs call their candidate 'Old Tip'?" The answer: "Because he drinks hard cider. 'Old Tipler' is a pretty name for a candidate for the presidency!"

They also had songs of their own. The favorite:

> Hush-a-bye-baby;
> Daddy's a Whig,
> Before he comes home
> Hard cider he'll swig;
> Then he'll be Tipsy
> And over he'll fall;
> Down will come Daddy
> Tip, Tyler and all.[33]

Postmaster

Addressing a meeting in Alexandria, Virginia, a Whig state senator remarked that Van Buren was supported mainly by federal officeholders and that if it weren't for them, Harrison would be elected "by universal acclamation." When a man shouted, "That's not true!" the Senator retorted: "I know that voice; it is the voice of Mr. Moorhead, our postmaster at Pittsburg, and this is another evidence of the truth of my remarks!" [34]

Lincoln's Buckskin

In a debate with Abraham Lincoln, Col. Dick Taylor accused the Whigs of foppery. Lincoln went over, tore open Taylor's coat, and pointed to the ruffled silk shirt and velvet vest Taylor was wearing, as well as his watch chain with gold seals. While Taylor was wearing "ruffled shirts" and "kid gloves," Lincoln told the amused audience, he, Lincoln, was working on a flatboat with "only one pair of breeches" to his name and they were buckskin. "Now," said Lincoln, "if you know the nature of buckskin when wet and dried by the sun, it will shrink . . . and whilst I was growing taller they were becoming shorter, and so much tighter

that they left a blue streak around my legs that can be seen to this day."
He concluded: "If you call this aristocratic, I plead guilty to the charge."[35]

O.K.

Van Buren's lasting legacy may have been the expression, O.K., which
appeared in 1840. Kinderhook, near Albany, was Van Buren's birth-
place, and through the years he had picked up such nicknames as "the
magician of Kinderhook," "your cunning Kinderhook fox," and "the
Kinderhook pony." In the spring of 1840, the Locofoco (radical) Democrats in New York City formed a new organization, the O.K. Club, to
campaign for Van Buren's re-election. On the night of March 27, they
broke into a Whig meeting shouting, "Down with the Whigs, boys, O.K.!"
and their slogan attracted the attention of all the city's newspapers the
next few days. The new term was at first a secret. The Whigs had fun
trying to guess its meaning. Some suggestions: Out of Kash, Out of
Kredit, Out of Karacter, Out of Klothes, Orful Kalamity. But the *New
York Morning Herald* was the most sportive. "THE O.K. CLUB—O.K.
LITERATURE," began the *Herald's* story on March 30. "This gang of
loafers and litterateurs, who broke in upon the Whigs at Masonic Hall
on Friday evening last, and kicked up the row there, are said to number 1,000 bravos. . . . The origin of their name, O.K., is curious and
characteristic. A few years ago, some person accused Amos Kendall to
General Jackson, of being no better than he should be. 'Let me examine the papers,' said the old hero. 'I'll soon tell whether Mr. Kendall is
right or wrong.' The General did so and found every thing right. 'Tie
up them papers,' said the General. They were tied up. 'Mark on them,
"O.K.",' continued the General. O.K. was marked upon them. 'By the
eternal,' said the good old General, taking his pipe from his mouth,
'Amos is *Ole Kurrek* (all correct) and no mistake,' blowing the smoke up
the chimney's cheek. After this the character of Amos was established
on the rock of Gilbraltar. Harvard College, on hearing of this event,
was thrown into extacies, and made the General an LL.D., which he is
to this day."

The *New York Times,* anti-Locofoco, insisted on reversing the initials.
"K.O., KICKED OUT," announced a *Times* headline on April 6. "The
K O system is working admirably. It was first put into operation at Masonic Hall on Friday night, March 27th, where the bullying O K's, who
attempted to disturb and break up a peaceable meeting of citizens were
KICKED OUT." By late May O.K. had become such a popular expression around town that the Locofocos decided to reveal its meaning. The
"very frightful letters O.K.," announced the *New Era,* a Locofoco paper, on May 27, "significant of the birth-place of Martin Van Buren,
Old Kinderhook, is also the rallying word of the Democracy. . . ."

With Van Buren's defeat in November, the Whigs tried to have the last word. "K.K.K.K.K.," proclaimed headlines in Whig newspapers. "KINDERHOOK KANDIDATE KAN'T KOME IT KWITE." By that time, though, the new term, O.K., had swept the entire country and, in the years that followed, it passed into general circulation throughout the world.[36]

Booze

In 1840 the word "booze" became part of the language. During the campaign a Philadelphia distiller by the name of E.C. Booz began putting his whiskey into bottles shaped like log cabins and calling it "Old Cabin Whiskey." Before long, booze and distilled liquor were synonymous.[37]

★ ★

CHAPTER FIFTEEN

1844
Polk and Manifest Destiny

In 1844, for the first time, territorial expansion became the major issue in a presidential campaign. Destiny, it seemed, not Desire, beckoned. For a Puritan nation it was irresistible. It was our "manifest destiny," announced John O'Sullivan, "to overspread and to possess the whole of the continent which Providence has given us for the development of the great experiment of liberty and federative self-government entrusted to us."[1] Where pious Calvinists acknowledged that God's will was ultimately mysterious, devout American expansionists were sure they could read His very thoughts: the good Lord intended the United States to expand westward to the Pacific and absorb the Oregon territory (then in dispute with Britain) and southward to the Rio Grande, adding Texas (over Mexico's protest) to America's continental domain.

In the South, the expansionists talked of the "re-annexation" of Texas. Texas, they insisted, was originally part of the Louisiana Territory, had been unwisely traded to Spain for Florida in 1819, and should be restored to its proper place in the American Union as soon as possible. But "re-annexation" posed some problems. Though Texas, an independent republic since 1836, was clearly anxious to join the Union, there was considerable opposition in the North to adding such a large slave area to the United States. There were fears, too, that "re-annexation" might lead to war with Mexico, which steadfastly refused to recognize Texas independence.

As the presidential contest of 1844 approached, leaders of both the Whig and the Democratic parties hoped to keep the Texas question—which was bound to raise the slavery issue—out of the campaign. Henry Clay, Whig favorite for the presidential nomination, announced his firm opposition to Texas annexation in the foreseeable future; so did Martin Van Buren, who had been recommended for the Democratic nomination by conventions in twelve states. In April 1844, however, President John Tyler, an ardent expansionist, dropped his "Texas bombshell," as it was called, into the campaign: he submitted a treaty of annexation to the Senate, accompanied by Secretary of State John C. Calhoun's vigorous defense of slavery, thus forcing the issue into the open. The Senate turned down the treaty in June; but by then the question of Texas annexation was a burning question throughout the nation.

The Texas question wasn't the only issue of the 1844 campaign but it was a crucial one. Though Clay was nominated by acclamation at the Whig convention which assembled in Baltimore on May 1, he began modifying his position on Texas after his nomination, hoping to attract votes in the South while holding onto the support of anti-slavery Northerners. In the end, his waffling may well have cost him the election by alienating Northerners without placating the South. As for Van Buren, his stand on Texas cost him the Democratic nomination. His Southern supporters were shocked when they read his pronouncement against annexation and began deserting him in droves. By the time the Democratic national convention met in Baltimore on May 27, he had lost much of his support for the nomination.

The Democrats met in Odd Fellows Hall (to the amusement of the Whigs) and after eight stormy trials, turned to James K. Polk of Tennessee, an enthusiastic expansionist, as their candidate. They went on to choose George M. Dallas of Pennsylvania, former minister to Russia, as his running mate; and, before adjourning, adopted a forthright expansionist resolution: "That our title to the whole of the Territory of Oregon is clear and unquestionable; that no portion of the same ought to be ceded to England or any other power, and that the reoccupation of Oregon and the reannexation of Texas at the earliest practicable period, are great American measures, which this convention recommends to the cordial support of the democracy of the Union."[2] Linking Texas with Oregon tended to deflate the slavery issue; it also made expansionism a national rather than a sectional objective. And claiming all of Oregon up to the southern boundary of Alaska (54°40') gave the Democrats a couple of sonorous slogans: "Fifty-four Forty or Fight!" and "All of Oregon or None!"

Polk's nomination excited considerable mirth among the Whigs. They had picked the celebrated Clay (with former New Jersey Senator Theodore Freylinghuysen of New York) to run; but, they asked derisively, "Who is James K. Polk?" Cried a Kentucky Whig, "Great God, what a nomination!" Said a Louisiana Senator in disbelief: "I can hardly believe such a ridiculous thing." Exclaimed Tennessee Congressman: "The idea of Jem Polk being President of the United States!!! We are more disposed to laugh at it here than to treat it seriously." In the forests, said the Whigs, the coons (1840-vintage, presumably) all grinned when they heard of the nomination and ran about singing:

> Ha, ha, ha, what a nominee
> Is Jimmy Polk of Tennessee![3]

But the 48-year-old Polk was not really all that unknown. He had served as Governor of Tennessee, Congressman, and Speaker of the House, and was respected in his party as a hard-working and dedicated Democrat. Clay himself realized Polk was no pushover.

There was, as usual, a lot of *ad hominem* in the campaign. The Whigs harped on Polk's mediocrity. The Democrats insisted that Polk's pedestrianism was preferable to Clay's flashiness. They also assaulted Clay's morals. In a widely circulated leaflet entitled, "Henry Clay's Moral Fitness for the Presidency, Tested by the Decalogue," they announced that the Whig candidate had systematically violated, sin by sin, every one of the Ten Commandments. "The history of Mr. Clay's debaucheries and midnight revelries in Washington," they declared, "is too shocking, too disgusting to appear in public print."[4] Another popular pamphlet, "Twenty-one Reasons Why Clay Should Not Be Elected," gave all the gory details, including Reason Two: "Clay spends his days at the gaming table and his nights in a brothel."[5] Clay's standard, said the Democrats, was "a pistol, a pack of cards, and a brandy-bottle." Proclaimed Democratic banners: "No Duellist!"; "No Gambler!" Warned a Democratic handbill:

> Christian Voters!
> Read, Pause and Reflect!
> Mr. Clay's
> Moral Character[6]

It was impossible for the Whigs to reply in kind. Polk was simply too unimaginative ("Polk the Plodder") for that. They were reduced to concentrating on his lack of qualifications for high office. But Northern Whigs, in a bid for anti-slavery votes, emphasized the Democratic candidate's status as a slave-holder. He was "an *ultra* slaveholder," they insisted, who had recently purchased a large plantation in Mississippi, "*stocked* it with negroes," and "had gone into it *up to his ears.*" They also accused him of having been a slave trader.[7] On August 21, an abolitionist newspaper in Ithaca, New York, published passages from a book entitled *Roorback's Tour through the Southern and Western States in the Year 1836*, describing the encampment in Tennessee of a slave trader who was taking two hundred slaves to market. "Forty of these unfortunate beings," the author was quoted as saying, "had been purchased, I was informed, by the Hon. J. K. Polk, the present speaker of the house of representatives; the mark of the branding iron, with the initials of his name on their shoulders distinguishing them from the rest." The extract turned out to be a fake; it was taken from a recently published travel book which didn't even mention Polk. But the "Roorback forgery," as it was called, appeared in many Whig newspapers in the North

Problem for Whigs: holding the slave & non-slave left of the party together.

before the Democrats were able to expose its spuriousness; and the word "roorback" was for a time used to mean political falsehood.[8]

But Clay was having problems with slavery too. The Liberty party, which had grown steadily since 1840, was running James G. Birney on an anti-slavery platform and threatened to siphon off enough votes of anti-slavery Whigs in the North to put Polk in the White House. To counter the Birney threat, Northern Whigs did everything they could to emphasize Clay's opposition to the annexation of Texas. And even though he was a slaveholder like Polk, they even began presenting him in anti-slavery regions as "*the* Abolitionist Candidate of the North."[9] But Clay had to think of Southern Whigs as well as of anti-slavery people in the North if he was to win and he began modifying his position on Texas to appease the Southerners. But as he warmed to the idea of Texas annexation in public statements he aroused so much hostility among Northern Whigs that he suddenly backtracked. "I am decidedly opposed," he announced late in September, "to the immediate annexation of Texas to the United States."[10] This left everyone confused. But the Democrats got a lot of mileage out of his twists and turns on Texas. A Missouri editor put it this way:

> He wires in and wires out
> And leaves the people still in doubt.
> Whether the snake that made the track,
> Was going South, or coming back.[11]

In the end Clay's equivocations probably alienated Northern voters without helping him much in the South.

When the balloting ended and the votes were counted, it was clear that "dark horse" Polk had bested "Harry of the West" by an extremely close margin. He won only 38,181 more popular votes (1,337,243 to 1,299,062) than Clay did and though he took 170 electoral votes to Clay's 105, his majority in several states was small. After the election Horace Greeley blamed Clay's defeat on the Liberty party (which took 62,300 votes that might have gone to the Whigs), and the *New York Herald* attributed Polk's victory to his stand on Texas.

President Tyler regarded the election as a mandate for Texas and in February 1845 sponsored a joint Congressional resolution admitting the Lone Star Republic to the Union. And after Polk became President he took care of the "re-occupation of Oregon" (in a compromise with Britain at the 49th parallel). Next came the Mexican War (1846–48) and the acquisition of California and New Mexico. Polk was manifestly destiny-ridden.

☆ ☆ ☆

Jackson's Toast

When Van Buren came out against Texas annexation, Polk, who had
been backing the New Yorker, sought out Andrew Jackson to see what
the Democrats should do. Jackson was entertaining some friends when
Polk arrived and, after greeting him, proposed a toast. "Gentlemen,"
he cried, lifting his glass, "a toast to the next President of the United
States!" Polk raised his glass, repeated the toast with the others, then
suddenly stopped, quite embarrassed, and lowered his glass. For Jackson, after a dramatic pause, had added: "To the health of James Knox
Polk!" [12]

Beat Again

Clay was at his home in Ashland when his son returned from Lexington with news of Polk's nomination. According to a later story, never
denied, Clay asked who was going to be his rival and his son told him
to guess. "Matty?" asked Clay. "Cass? Buchanan?" Each time his son said
no, Clay's spirits rose. "Don't tell me they've been such fools as to take
Calhoun or Johnson!" he cried. "No," said his son. "Then who the devil
is it?" said Clay impatiently. "James K. Polk," said his son, thinking his
father would be pleased at the seemingly weak nominee. But Clay got
up, it is said, walked thoughtfully over to the liquor cabinet, filled his
glass, and sighed, "Beat again, by God!" [13]

O'Clay

In New York City the Whigs tried to persuade the Irish they should
pass over Polk for "Patrick O'Clay" in the forthcoming election. [14]

Glorious Opportunity

At a Whig rally in Nashville, S. S. Prentiss of Mississippi gave a four-
hour address that was so powerful his audience asked for an encore.
That night he spoke again and his hatred of Polk and the Democrats
inspired him to such heights of eloquence that when he collapsed, at
the end of the speech, into the arms of Governor James C. Jones, the
latter whispered: "Die, Prentiss, die! You will never have a more glorious opportunity!" [15]

Stricken Down

The reaction to Clay's defeat among his long-time followers was profound. "It was," remarked one observer, "as if the first-born of every

family had been stricken down." Some people wept; others gathered in small groups to discuss in low tones what had happened to their hero; still others went out and beat up a few Democrats. One Kentucky bride and groom, hearing the news, changed their wedding trip from Washington to New Orleans. En route the groom fell ill. The doctor they consulted asked if the young man had suffered any great shock. When the groom mentioned Clay's defeat, the doctor fell into the arms of his patient and they wept together.[16]

Last Presidential Battle

Clay himself was attending a wedding in Lexington when a messenger handed him a paper containing the news from New York of Polk's victory. "He opened the paper," reported a friend, "and as he read the death knell of his political hopes and lifelong ambition, I saw a distinct blue shade begin at the roots of his hair, pass slowly over his face like a cloud and then disappear. He stood for a moment as if frozen. He laid down the paper, and turning to a table, filled a glass with wine, and raising it to his lips with a pleasant smile, said: 'I drink to the health and happiness of all assembled here.' Setting down his glass, he resumed his conversation as if nothing had occurred and was, as usual, the life and light of the company. The contents of the paper were soon known to everyone in the room and a wet blanket fell over our gaiety. We left the wedding party with heavy hearts. Alas! our gallant 'Harry of the West' has fought his last presidential battle." Clay did not say, "I would rather be right than be President," at this time. He made his celebrated remark several years later when championing the controversial Compromise of 1850 in Congress.[17]

Mouse

Despite the ringing campaign slogan, "Fifty-four Forty or Fight," Polk signed a compromise treaty with Britain in 1846, fixing the Oregon boundary at the 49th parallel. Exclaimed Senator Thomas Hart Benton: "Oh, mountain that was delivered of a mouse, thy name shall be Fifty-four Forty!"[18]

★ ★

CHAPTER SIXTEEN

1848
Old Zach and the Michigander

By 1848 slavery was becoming a big issue. Many Americans were beginning to have strong feelings on the subject. Most people agreed that slavery should be left alone in the fifteen states where it already existed, but disagreed violently over whether it should be permitted to expand into new regions. Pro-slavery Southerners insisted that slavery followed the flag and the U.S. Constitution protected it everywhere. But anti-slavery Northerners strongly opposed the advance of slavery into the federal territories; their hope was that a policy of containment would lead eventually to its demise everywhere. Both Democratic and Whig leaders, though, were anxious to bypass the issue; their parties, after all, drew support from voters in every section of the country. But the issue could not be downed. Despite efforts to evade it the slavery question played some part in the 1848 election.

The Democrats were the first to pick candidates. Meeting in Baltimore on May 22, they selected Senator Lewis Cass of Michigan to run for President and coupled him with General William O. Butler, a War of 1812 veteran. Cass, territorial governor of Michigan for many years, was the first Democratic candidate from the Northwest and an advocate of what he called "squatter sovereignty": the right of settlers in the federal territories to decide the slavery question for themselves. But the party platform, to the disappointment of anti-slavery Democrats, took no stand on slavery extension.

At Baltimore the New York delegation split over the platform and the nomination of Cass. The "Hunkers" (conservatives who, it was said, "hunkered" after office) supported the decisions of the convention. The "Barnburners" (anti-slavery men charged with wanting to burn down the barn to get rid of rats) simply couldn't stomach Cass and his squatter-sovereignty doctrine. They walked out of the convention, met with anti-slavery people from other states in June and July, and helped organize the Free-Soil party dedicated to prohibiting slavery in all federal territories. Their candidates were Martin Van Buren and Charles Francis Adams (son of the sixth President) and their slogan was, "Free Soil, Free Speech, Free Labor, and Free Men."

By the time the Free-Soilers picked Van Buren the Whigs had made their choices at a convention in Philadelphia in June: General Zachary Taylor of Louisiana ("Old Rough and Ready"), a Mexican War hero, and Millard Fillmore, former Congressman and now Comptroller of New York. Some Whigs were appalled by the Taylor nomination. Taylor, sixty-four, had never been involved in politics before, knew next to nothing about national issues, and had never even voted. Daniel Webster called him "an illiterate frontier colonel" and warned there were thousands of Whigs "who will not vote for a candidate brought forward only because of his successful fighting in this war against Mexico."[1] But in the end Whig leaders like Webster were reconciled and began promoting Taylor with the voters the way the party had promoted Harrison in 1840. "Old Zach" was in fact a far more distinguished military man than "Old Tippecanoe."

Probably the best speech of the campaign was Abraham Lincoln's in the House of Representatives on July 27. Lincoln, an Illinois Whig, made a virtue out of Taylor's vagueness on the issues. "The people," he said, "say to General Taylor, 'If you are elected, shall we have a national bank?' He answers, 'Your will, gentlemen, not mine.' 'What about the tariff?' 'Say yourselves.' 'Shall our rivers and harbors be improved?' 'Just as you please. If you desire a bank, an alteration of the tariff, internal improvements, any or all, I will not hinder you. If you do not desire them, I will not attempt to force them on you. . . .' " Lincoln went on to tease the Democrats for making so much of Andrew Jackson's name at election time and to ridicule their efforts to portray Cass as a great military hero. He aroused so much mirth in the House that the Democrats finally started shouting: "We give it up!"[2]

Lincoln's teasing was exceptional. Mud-slinging, as usual, dominated the campaign. The Democrats called Taylor a "military autocrat," compared him to Caesar, Cromwell, and Napoleon, and warned he would adopt a bellicose foreign policy if he became President to gratify his lust for martial glory. They also found him conspicuously lacking in other respects: he was Britain's candidate (the London *Times* had praised him), semi-illiterate, a cruel slavemaster, greedy (he had received $168,155.88 in pay and extra allowances, they reckoned, since entering the army in 1808), and too stingy to buy decent clothes. He also swore at his troops. Taylor was distressed by the personal attacks; he complained that the campaign was marked by the "vilest slanders of the most unprincipled demagogues this or any other nation was every cursed with, who have pursued me like bloodhounds."[3]

But the Whigs responded in kind. They found Cass a fountain of evil: he had sponsored legislation in the Northwest "to effect the sale of white vagabonds into slavery"; he had been heavily involved in graft as Superintendant of Indian Affairs (an old charge disproved by a Congressional investigation some years before); he had speculated in real estate while serving as Secretary of War for Jackson and Van Buren; and he was "a sly, artful, intriguing politician," a windbag ("General Gass"), a Michi-gander, and a "pot-bellied, mutton-headed cucumber." One Whig article was headed, "GEN. CASS NOT A TRUTHFUL MAN."[4] But it is safe to say just about everyone was a bit careless with the truth during the campaign.

Thirty states (half slave and half free) participated in the 1848 election; and all the voters (except in Massachusetts) went to the polls on the same day—November 7—in accordance with an act passed by Congress in 1845. Taylor (who may not have voted himself) won by a small majority; he received around 139,000 more popular votes than Cass did (1,360,099 to 1,220,544) and thirty-six more electoral votes (163 to 127), just the electoral vote of New York. But his victory was national, not sectional; eight of the fifteen states he carried were Northern and seven were Southern. Free Soil candidate Van Buren didn't win any states, but he did surprisingly well nonetheless. Although his party had entered the campaign only three months before the election, he won 291,263 votes, around 10 percent of the total. More important: the Free-Soil party held the balance of power in several important Northern states and probably took enough anti-slavery Democratic votes away from Cass, especially in New York, to give the victory to Taylor. The Free-Soilers also elected several men to Congress. Their point of view, it was clear, was beginning to assume some importance in presidential politics.

Once in the White House, Taylor turned out to be a vigorous nationalist; like Jackson, he was basically a Westerner rather than a Southerner. Some people, indeed, called him "a Southern man with Northern principles"; he was opposed to the expansion of slavery into the West and refused to support the Compromise of 1850 which applied "popular sovereignty" to territories taken from Mexico. But on July 4, 1850, the sixty-five-year-old President developed acute gastroenteritis and died a few days later. Millard Fillmore, his successor, strongly supported the Compromise of 1850.

☆   ☆   ☆

Economical Old Zach

In June the Whigs nominated Taylor for President, sent him letter of notification, and awaited his acceptance. They had a long wait. When the letter arrived, collect, at the Baton Rouge post office, Taylor didn't bother to pick it up. He was receiving a lot of unpaid mail at the time and had instructed the postmaster to send it all to the dead-letter office. After a few weeks, when the Whigs found out what had happened, they put another letter in the mail, postage prepaid, and when Taylor received it, he promptly sent off his acceptance. During the campaign the Whigs praised Taylor for his frugality while the Democrats made fun of "economical, comical old Zach."[5]

Turnips

At the Free-Soil party convention in Buffalo in July, some of the delegates had misgivings about Van Buren; they remembered that as President he had pledged himself to veto any bill abolishing slavery in the District of Columbia unless it was approved by Virginia and Maryland. But in a speech on Van Buren's behalf, Barnburner Benjamin Butler tried to convince the delegates that Old Kinderhook was both available and acceptable. He listed Van Buren's fine personal qualities; he also described how absorbed Van Buren became in bucolic pursuits after leaving the White House, and the agility with which he leaped a fence to show visitors a field of sprouting turnips. At this point a delegate interrupted: "Damn his turnips! What are his opinions about the abolition of slavery in the District of Columbia?" "I was just coming to that subject," responded Butler mildly. "Well," said the man, "you can't be a moment too quick coming to it." In the end the convention decided Van Buren was acceptable.[6]

Military Hero

Cass performed creditably as a general during the War of 1812. When General William Hull capitulated to the British at Detroit, he broke his sword rather than surrender it. He also fought bravely under William Henry Harrison during the Battle of the Thames. But Lincoln couldn't resist teasing the "great Michigander" about his military exploits. "By the way, Mr. Speaker," he said in his famous House speech in July 1848,

did you know I am a military hero? Yes, sir; in the days of the Black Hawk war I fought, fled, and came away. Speaking of General Cass's career reminds me of my own. I was not at Stillman's defeat, but I was about as near it as Cass was to Hull's surrender; and, like him, I saw the place very soon afterward. It is quite certain I did not break my sword, for I had none to break; but I bent a musket pretty badly on one occasion. If Cass broke his sword, the idea is he broke it in desperation; I bent the musket by accident. If General Cass went in advance of me in picking huckleberries, I guess I surpassed him in charges upon the wild onions. If he saw any live, fighting Indians, it was more than I did; but I had a good many bloody struggles with the mosquitoes, and although I never fainted from the loss of blood, I can truly say I was often very hungry.[7]

★ ★

CHAPTER SEVENTEEN

1852
Frank Pierce and Old Fuss
and Feathers

It took the Whigs and the Democrats a long time to settle on candidates for the presidential contest of 1852. The Whigs, having won in 1848 with General Zachary Taylor, finally chose another Mexican War hero, General Winfield Scott, as their nominee on the fifty-third ballot and then added William A. Graham, the Secretary of the Navy, to the ticket. The Democrats were a bit quicker: on the forty-ninth ballot they turned to a dark horse, Senator Franklin Pierce of New Hampshire, hardly a national figure, and selected Senator William King of Alabama to run with him. Both parties endorsed the Compromise of 1850, with its notorious Fugitive Slave Act, thus removing slavery, the most burning issue of the day, from the campaign. There remained, then, only personalities. Was Scott truly a pompous ass? Was Pierce really a coward under fire? And what about their war records?

Scott was vulnerable in this kind of campaign. Nicknamed "Fuss 'n Feathers," he was a prima donna in Washington and in the field and loved the parade ground. He was unquestionably able; General-in-Chief of the Army since 1841, he had "conquered a peace" for Polk in 1847 and come out of the Mexican War a hero. But he was extremely rank-conscious, sensitive to his prerogatives, and enamored of fancy uniforms. The Democrats warned of a "Reign of Epaulets" if he became President and dismissed him as a "weak, conceited, foolish, blustering disciple of gunpowder." He "grew up with epaulettes on his shoulders," they sneered, "a canteen on his back, and a breastplate on HIS REAR." The Whigs, they said, might just as well dig up old bones from the battlefield and run them for office.[1]

Pierce, by contrast, according to the Democrats, was a patriotic citizen-soldier. He leaped to the colors when the Mexican War broke out and, as brigadier-general in Scott's army, served with distinction on the battlefield. But the Whigs were not impressed. They took a close look at the record and came up with the revelation that on two occasions (or was it more?) Pierce had fainted in the heat of battle in Mexico. Overlooking the fact that during one battle Pierce had been so badly hurt when his horse fell on some rocks that he passed out afterwards, they nicknamed him "The Fainting General" and asked voters whether they wanted a coward in the White House. One of their prize exhibits was a miniature book, an inch high and a half inch in width, entitled *The Military Services of General Pierce.* Pierce, sneered the *Louisville Journal,* "tumbled from his horse just as he was getting into one fight, . . . fainted and fell in the opening of a second, . . . got sick and had to go to bed on the eve of a third, and . . . came pretty near getting into a fourth, missing it only by about an hour." And so the foolishness went on, day after day, throughout the fall of 1852.[2]

In the end, "GUNPOWDER GLORY," as the Democrats called it, was not enough to carry Scott to victory, the way it had carried Harrison and Taylor. Even Scott's last-minute "nonpolitical" tour of the West, ostensibly to seek a site for a soldiers' home, failed to raise the "drum-and-fife enthusiasm" the Whigs were counting on.[3] With Scott's stunning defeat—he won only four states—the Whig party began its gradual disintegration and disappearance as an independent force in American politics. The figures were cruel: Pierce's 1,601,474 popular (50.9 percent) and 254 electoral votes to Scott's 1,386,580 popular (44 percent) and 42 electoral votes. Most of the Barnburners, including Van Buren, had returned to the Democratic fold and supported Pierce; the Free-Soil Democrats who ran John Hale of New Hampshire on an antislavery ticket polled half as many votes (155,667) as the Free-Soilers had four years earlier; and thousands of Southern Whigs deserted Scott because he did not support the Compromise of 1850 as forthrightly as Pierce did. The voters were not so much rejecting a professional soldier for President in 1852 as endorsing a citizen-soldier who thought the 1850 Compromise would settle America's slavery problem once for all.

☆ ☆ ☆

Spread Durned Thin

When he heard of his nomination, Pierce exclaimed: "You are looking at the most surprised man that ever lived!" He wasn't the only one. In his New Hampshire hometown one man greeted news of the nomination with the exclamation: "Wall, wall, dew tell! Frank Pierce for President! Neow Frank's a good fellow, I admit, and I wish him well, he made a good State's attorney, that's no doubt about that, and he made a far Jedge, thar's no denying that, and nobody kaint complain of him as a Congressman, but when it comes to the hull Yewnited States I dew say that in my jedgment Frank Pierce is a-goin to *spread durned thin.*"[4]

Pierce 'em

"We Polked 'em in '44," went a popular Democratic slogan; "we'll Pierce 'em in '52."[5]

Well-Fought Bottle

The forty-eight-year-old Pierce had a drinking problem, and the Whigs made the most of it. They liked to describe him as "a hero of many a well-fought bottle."[6]

Demonstration

A Whig campaign paper reported that a young man, orating for Scott on the steps of a church, accidentally slipped, rolled down the steps, picked himself up, and announced he had only been showing "how Gen. Pierce fell from his horse" during the Mexican War.[7]

★ ★ ★ ★ ★ ★ ★ ★ ★ ★ ★ ★ ★ ★ ★ ★ ★ ★ ★ ★

CHAPTER EIGHTEEN

1856
Buchanan and Bleeding Kansas

1856 was a year of violence. "We are treading upon a volcano," exclaimed Thomas Hart Benton, "that is liable at any moment to burst forth and overwhelm the nation."[1] Franklin Pierce had promised harmony when he was inaugurated in 1853, but he was doomed to disappointment. Within a few months the seeming calm produced by the Compromise of 1850 was at an end and there was a renewal of the struggle between the North and the South over the question of slavery in the federal territories. Illinois Senator Stephen A. Douglas's Kansas-Nebraska Act (1854) precipitated the new crisis. By the provisions of this Act, the Nebraska Territory was split into two territories, Kansas and Nebraska, the Missouri Compromise line was repealed, and the principle of popular sovereignty was adopted in territories formerly free. The result was "Bleeding Kansas": a bloody struggle, with much loss of life, between free-soilers and pro-slavery settlers for control of Kansas.

The Kansas-Nebraska Act and the civil war in Kansas led directly to the break-up of the two major parties and the formation of a new one. On February 28, 1854, a number of Conscience Whigs, Free-Soilers, and Anti-Slavery Democrats met in Ripon, Wisconsin, to protest the Kansas-Nebraska Act and recommend the organization of a new political party pledged to oppose the further extension of slavery. And on July 6, a giant mass meeting, held in Jackson, Michigan, officially launched the new party, took the name Republican, adopted a platform calling slavery "the great moral, social and political evil" of the day and demanding the repeal of both the Kansas-Nebraska Act and the Fugitive Slave Act and the abolition of slavery in the District of Columbia. By the fall of 1854 the new party was active in all the Western states and in some of the Eastern states. During the following year Republican organizations appeared in most of the Northern states.

The Republican party represented both Northeastern business and Western farming interests. Since it had no Southern support, except in the border states, it was the first major sectional party in the United States. The new party originated in the determination to check the spread of slavery, but economic and political considerations also played an important part in its development. Western farmers supported it because they did not want to have to compete with slaveholders in the Western territories. Eastern businessmen wanted slavery limited in order to prevent the South from acquiring a majority in Congress and blocking the legislation that they desired. The demand for the containment of slavery, in short, appealed to many Northerners who were not abolitionists. The exclusion of slavery from the territories, not the abolition of slavery where it already existed, was the main objective of the new party. Still, many of its members detested chattel slavery.

The Republicans met in Philadelphia on June 17, 1856, for their first nominating convention. "You are here today," announced the chairman in his welcoming address, "to give a direction to a movement which is to decide whether the people of the United States are to be hereafter and forever chained to the present national policy of the extension of slavery."[2] The delegates chose John C. Frémont, the "Pathfinder," famous for his explorations of the Far West, as their candidate. Frémont was a popular hero and his name became part of the party slogan: "Free Soil, Free Speech, Free Men, Frémont." Former Whig Senator William L. Dayton of New Jersey, who had opposed the Compromise of 1850, became the vice-presidential nominee. The Republican platform demanded the immediate admission of Kansas into the Union as a free state, opposed the extension of slavery into the territories, and denounced the Ostend Manifesto (issued by James Buchanan and others) which called for the annexation of Cuba—where slavery was legal—to the United States. The Republicans also called for federal appropriations for internal improvements, including the construction of a railroad to the Pacific.

The Democrats met in Cincinnati on June 2 to select their candidates. The convention passed over both Pierce and Douglas and nominated James Buchanan of Pennsylvania for President and John C. Breckinridge of Kentucky for Vice-President. Buchanan, sixty-five, was the "most available and most unobjectionable" choice.[3] Secretary of State for Polk, he had been minister to England during the fight over the Kansas-Nebraska Act and was far less controversial than either Douglas or Pierce. He had never, said the *Richmond Enquirer* approvingly, "uttered a word which could pain the most sensitive Southern heart."[4] The Democratic platform endorsed the doctrine of popular sovereignty, supported the Kansas-Nebraska Act, and announced that the "party will resist all attempts at renewing, in Congress or out of it, the agitation of the slavery question, under whatever shape or color the attempt be made." It also condemned the "Know-Nothing" movement as contrary to the American "spirit of tolerance and enlightened freedom."[5]

The "Know-Nothing" movement to which the Democrats referred was associated with the American party, another new party, which grew out of a secret society formed in New York in 1849. The American party declared that no alien should be granted American citizenship until he had lived twenty-one years in the United States and that no foreign-born person should be allowed to hold office. The party directed its prejudices against Irish immigrants in particular; it was anti-Catholic as well as anti-foreign. When members of the party were asked about the organization, they were directed to answer, "I don't know," or "I know nothing about it," and soon acquired the name, "Know-Nothings." In 1854 and 1855 the Know-Nothings succeeded in electing a number of governors and Congressmen in several states and even won control of Massachusetts for a time. But the Know-Nothing party did not continue to show any great strength. When its national convention voted to support the Kansas-Nebraska Act in 1855, the party broke into two groups and the anti-Nebraska men left to join the Republican party. The party was considerably weakened by these defections by the time of the election of 1856. Nevertheless it nominated former President Millard Fillmore and Andrew J. Donelson of Tennessee, editor of the *Washington Union,* as its candidates and pledged itself to maintain an indestructible Union, with popular sovereignty in the territories. Its slogan was: "Americans must rule America."[6] Later in the year a national convention composed of remnants of the old Whig party endorsed Millard Fillmore for President.

There was almost as much ballyhoo—torchlight parades, floats, mass meetings, picnics, campaign songs, slogans, fervent oratory, party pamphlets and handouts—as there had been in the log-cabin–hard-cider campaign of 1840. This time, however, there was a real issue: the question of slavery extension. The Democrats called their opponents "Black Republicans" and warned that if Frémont won the election the South would secede and the American Union would fall apart. "If Frémont is elected," cried Governor Wise of Virginia, "there will be a revolution."[7] The Republicans insisted that although there should be no interference with slavery in the South there must be an end, once and for all, to the expansion of slavery into other parts of the United States. Since the Republicans didn't run tickets in the South and the slave states were expected to go for Buchanan, the campaign was concentrated in the North, especially in key states like Pennsylvania. The Republicans organized Rocky Mountain Clubs, Wide Awakes, Freedom Clubs, and (in California) Bear Clubs, excoriated the South as backward and reactionary, and portrayed Buchanan and Fillmore as old fogies. The Democrats shouted, "Buck and Breck," urged voters to "take the Buck by the horns," and warned that Republicanism meant disunion. Businessmen in New York

City, fearing that a Republican victory would disrupt the economy, contributed generously to the Democratic campaign chest. Complained Horace Greeley (who, like many former Whigs, including Abraham Lincoln, was now a Republican): "We Frémonters of this town have not one dollar where the Fillmoreans and Buchaneers have ten each."[8]

The outcome of the election showed that despite the unpopularity of the Kansas-Nebraska Act in the North, the majority of voters still put the preservation of the Union above all other considerations. Buchanan, with 1,838,169 popular votes (45 percent) and 174 electoral votes, carried every Southern state except Maryland. He also carried the free states of Pennsylvania, New Jersey, Indiana, Illinois, and California. Frémont carried the rest of the North with an electoral vote of 114 and 1,341,264 popular votes (30 percent). The Know-Nothings won 874,534 popular votes (25 percent) for Fillmore and carried one state, Maryland, with eight electoral votes. Though the Democrats achieved a comfortable victory, the Republicans showed amazing strength for a new political party; many people regarded it as a "victorious defeat." Exulted poet John Greenleaf Whittier:

> Then sound again the bugles
> Call the muster-roll anew;
> If months have well-nigh won the field,
> What may not four years do?[9]

There was something ominous, however, in the fact that all but a few hundred of Frémont's votes came from the non-slaveholding states. During the campaign the Lower South had made it clear that it would secede from the Union if a purely Northern party won the presidential election.

Bleeding Kansas and Bleeding Sumner

On May 19 and 20, Massachusetts Senator Charles Sumner delivered a long and fervent anti-slavery speech entitled, "The Crime Against Kansas," during the course of which he made critical remarks about several pro-slavery Senators, including Andrew F. Butler of South Carolina. He called Butler the Don Quixote of slavery; he also said Butler "has chosen a mistress to whom he has made his vows, and who, though ugly to others, is always lovely to him; though polluted in the sight of the world, is chaste in his sight. I mean the harlot Slavery." Two days later Butler's cousin, Congressman Preston S. Brooks, walked into the Senate Chamber where Sumner sat writing at his desk and exclaimed: "Mr. Sumner, I have read your speech twice over carefully. It is a libel on South Carolina, and on Mr. Butler, who is a relative of mine. . . ." As Sumner looked up, Brooks began beating him over the head with a stout gutta-percha cane. Blinded by the blood spurting down his face, Sumner wrenched his desk from the floor while struggling to get up, but Brooks kept beating him with the cane until he was almost unconscious. "Don't kill him!" cried elderly Whig Senator John J. Crittenden of Kentucky who heard the noise and came running over to see what was happening. But Brooks continued the assault until his cane shattered into pieces. "I did not intend to kill him," said Brooks, "but I did intend to whip him." By this time two New York Congressmen had rushed up and pulled Brooks away from Sumner and were helping the latter, dazed and tottering, to a room outside the Senate Chamber where he could have his wounds dressed by a physician. Shortly afterwards he was taken home and began his long convalescence in various places in this country and Europe. It was more than three years before he was able to resume his regular duties in the Senate.

The Brooks caning stunned the nation. Northern newspapers, even those unfriendly to Sumner, denounced Brooks's behavior in the strongest terms; and meetings were held and resolutions passed in just about every Northern city to condemn the South Carolina Congressman. The fact that Brooks's attack coincided with a pro-slavery attack on the anti-slavery town of Lawrence in Kansas added to the excitement sweeping the North. In the South, a few people called Brooks's action "unjustifiable, unmanly, ill-timed, ill-advised, cowardly, dastardly," but most Southerners hailed the South Carolinian as a hero. Wherever he went he received lavish praise and sometimes gold-headed canes, inscribed with the words, "Hit him again!" *A Good Deed,"* approved the *Richmond Whig.* "The only regret we feel is, that Mr. Brooks did not employ a horsewhip or a cowhide upon his slanderous back, instead of a cane." A Congressional investigating committee recommended Brooks's expulsion and a majority of the House of Representatives (but not the required two-thirds) voted to expel him. Brooks defended himself in a speech in the House, then resigned, and was promptly re-elected to his seat by his constituents.

"Bleeding Sumner" joined "Bleeding Kansas" as a major campaign issue in 1856. The Republicans printed a million copies of Sumner's speech on Kansas for distribution and made the "Martyr Senator" a party hero. At the Republican convention in June, Sumner received thirty-five votes for Vice-President and would have received even more had he encouraged his supporters. Sumner was unable to stump for the Republican ticket, but he did send letters to be read at Republican rallies reminding people that he was too shattered in health to take part in the campaign. Republican orators made much of the fact that a Southern bully, a typical product of the slavocracy, had brutally attacked a Northern Senator for simply expressing his opinions in the free forum of the U. S. Senate. *The New York Evening Post* put it this way:

> Who, like a caitiff, base and low,
> Came treacherously upon his foe,
> And stunned him with a murderous blow?
>   Preston Brooks!
>
> Who, when his victim senseless lay,
> Cold and inanimate as clay,
> His brutal hand refused to stay,
>   Preston Brooks!

Some Republican Congressmen began arming themselves for self-defense. Others engaged Brooks's partisans in angry debate. In the Senate, Sumner's Massachusetts colleague Henry Wilson denounced the "brutal, murderous, and cowardly assault" and was at once challenged to a duel by Brooks. But Wilson contemptuously refused the challenge; dueling, he said, was "the lingering relic of a barbarous civilization, which the law of the country has branded a crime." In the House, Anson Burlingame of Massachusetts also condemned Brooks, who, he said, "stole into the Senate, that place which had hitherto been held sacred against violence, and smote [Sumner] as Cain smote his brother." "That is false!" cried one South Carolina Congressman. "What!" cried Burlingame, "strike a man when he is pinioned,—when he cannot respond to a blow! Call you that chivalry? In what code of honor did you get your authority for that?" Brooks at once challenged him to a duel. Burlingame accepted the challenge but picked a place in Canada as the meeting place. Brooks then called it off; it wouldn't be safe, he said, for him to travel through the North to get to Canada. Cried the Republicans:

> To Canada Brooks was asked to go,
> To waste a pound of powder or so,
> But he quickly answered, No; No; No.
> For I'm afraid, afraid, afraid,
>   Billy Brooks's afraid.[10]

Eyes Opened

The puppy-dog story told by the Republicans in 1952 was originally a Democratic tale and first appeared in 1856. At a Republican meeting in Clermont, Ohio, that year, it was said, a little boy offered four little dogs for sale to the visitors. "Are these Frémont pups, my son?" someone asked. "Yes, sir," said the boy. "Well, then," said the man, "I'll take these two." A week later the Democrats held a meeting at the same place and the little boy showed up again with his two remaining pups for sale. "My little lad," someone asked him, "what kind of pups are these you have?" "They're Buchanan pups, sir," said the boy. The Republican who had bought the first two overheard the exchange and broke out angrily, "See here, you young rascal, didn't you tell me those pups I bought last week were *Frémont* pups?" "Y-e-s, sir," said the boy; "but these ain't; *they've got their eyes open.*"[11] (By 1952 the pups were Republicans again at the eye-opening.)

Great Horn Spoon

"The pretended Know-Nothing apprehension lest a successor of Julius II should acquire supremacy over the American Union," wrote one critic of the nativists, "is as absurd an anachronism as would be the anticipation of a Carthaginian invasion, or the subjection of the country by mail-clad warriors of a descendant of William of Normandy." Some anti-nativists organized "Say-Nothing," "Do-Nothing," and "Owe-nothing" societies to ridicule the Know-Nothings. They also burlesqued Know-Nothing ceremonies: pictured initiates being seized by a Revolutionary war veteran, whirled around three times, and asked: "Should Uncle Sam's farm, or Brother Jonathan's nation, ever be threatened by the cannibals of the uninhabited regions around the South Pole, or by the Goths and Vandals who drove the Romans into the Mediterranean Sea, will you take up arms, pitchforks, stove pipes, wooden nutmegs, saw logs, and swear by the great horn spoon to lick all creation?"[12]

Nearly Convicted

Many charges were brought against Frémont in 1856, all of them false: that he was a drunkard, a slaveholder, foreign-born, and a crook. But the charge that hurt most was that he was a crypto-Catholic. All sorts of fanciful tales were concocted to prove the allegation: that he crossed himself in a Catholic cathedral in Washington, told a West Point professor he was a Romanist, avowed the doctrine of transubstantiation over a hotel table, refused to accept an Episcopalian prayer book offered him, and promised to favor Catholics if he became President. The Know-Nothings circulated numerous pamphlets on the subject: *Frémont's Romanism Established; Colonel Frémont's Religious History; The Romish Intrigue. Frémont a Catholic; The Authentic Account. Papist or Protestant. Which?* Henry Ward Beecher, eloquent Brooklyn preacher, came to Frémont's defense. Campaigning for the Republicans in New York, he gave the facts: that when Frémont and Jessie Benton fell in love, the latter's father, Thomas Hart Benton, disapproved of the match, so they were secretly married by a priest. "Like a true lover and gallant man," said Beecher, "Frémont said that he did not care who married him so long as it was done quickly and strong. If we had been in Colonel Frémont's place we would have been married if it had required us to walk through a row of priests and bishops as long as from Washington to Rome, ending up with the Pope himself!"

Frémont himself assured anxious inquirers, lay and clerical, that he was a good Episcopalian and that his children had been baptized in that church. But he firmly resisted pressures by Republican leaders to publicly disavow the charge of Catholicism. The main issue of the campaign was freedom, he said, including religious freedom, and under the Constitution there were no religious tests for office-holding. As a result of his silence, however, he was, as William T. Seward put it, "nearly convicted of being a Catholic." Anti-Catholic voters who might have voted Republican supported Fillmore. But, ironically enough, some Catholics thought Frémont was somehow connected with the Know-Nothings and supported the Democrats instead.[13]

Glittering Ubiquities

Some Northern Whigs refused to join the new Republican party because they thought it was a threat to the Union. The sons of both Daniel Webster and Henry Clay denounced the Republicans and came out for Buchanan. The influential Massachusetts Whig Rufus Choate also announced for Buchanan and insisted it was essential "to defeat and dissolve the new geographical party calling itself Republican." Choate assailed the Republican platform for quoting "the glittering and sounding generalities of natural right which make up the Declaration of Independence." "Glittering generalities!" cried Ralph Waldo Emerson when he heard what Choate had said: "Glittering ubiquities, rather!"[14]

Lockjaw

Buchanan kept quiet during the 1856 campaign; he stayed at Wheatland, his country estate near Lancaster, Pennsylvania, and received visitors. "There is a wrong impression about one of the candidates," smirked Republican Thaddeus Stevens in a speech in October. "There is no such person running as James Buchanan. He is dead of lockjaw."[15]

★ ★

CHAPTER NINETEEN

1860
Lincoln and the Sectional Crisis

"The night is departing," James Buchanan told friends right after his election in 1856, "and the roseate and propitious morn now breaking upon us promises a long day of peace and prosperity for our country."[1] Buchanan was convinced he could quiet the agitation over slavery and, by restoring harmony to the nation, become a second George Washington. In his inaugural address on March 4, 1857, he endorsed popular sovereignty in the territories and non-interference with slavery in the South; he also expressed the hope that the whole question of slavery in the territories would be settled by the Supreme Court. Two days later the Supreme Court announced its decision in the Dred Scott case. But instead of settling the slavery controversy, the Dred Scott decision angered the Republicans, split the Democratic party in two, and further exacerbated sectional tensions. For the Court ruled that slavery was legal in all the territories and that neither Congress nor the territorial legislatures had any power to interfere with it.

Southern Democrats were overjoyed by the Dred Scott decision; it supported their views regarding slavery in the territories. But the Republicans were outraged; the ruling ran counter to their main plank: that Congress could and should exclude slavery from the territories. But the Northern Democrats were also dismayed, for the decision utterly destroyed Stephen A. Douglas's doctrine of popular sovereignty. Though Buchanan regarded the Dred Scott decision as "the final settlement" of the slavery question, no one really changed his mind after reading the Court's ruling. Republicans continued to insist that slavery must be checked and urged the Supreme Court to reverse its decision. Douglas and the Northern Democrats went on championing popular sovereignty. And Southern Democrats reiterated their demand, more forcefully than ever, that slavery be protected by federal law in all the territories.

In Kansas, civil war between advocates of freedom and slavery continued its bloody course; and in Congress, where some members went armed, debates were so heated that at times they seemed about to turn into a riot. "By God," cried one Congressman, drawing a pistol on his colleague, "if I can't talk, I can do something else!"[2] Then, in October 1859, militant abolitionist John Brown led his famous raid on the federal arsenal at Harpers Ferry, Virginia, hoping to start a general slave uprising. His capture, trial, and execution turned him into a martyr for Northern abolitionists; in the South, however, his action convinced many people that secession was inevitable.

A few months after Harpers Ferry came the election of 1860. It was the most momentous election in American history. When the Democratic convention met in Charleston, South Carolina, on April 23, the Northern and Southern wings of the party split apart at once. Southern Democrats demanded a platform calling for federal protection of slavery in the territories and a statement that slavery was right and ought to be extended. Cried Ohio Senator George E. Pugh, jumping to his feet: "Gentlemen of the South, you mistake us—you mistake us—we will not do it!"[3] But when the followers of Stephen A. Douglas refused to agree to a pro-slavery platform, delegates from eight Southern states walked out of the convention. "We say, go your way," exclaimed a Mississippi delegate, "and we will go ours." The remaining delegates were unable to muster a two-thirds vote for any candidate, so they adjourned. In June they reassembled in Baltimore and nominated Douglas for President on a popular-sovereignty platform and picked Herschel V. Johnson, former Governor of Georgia, to run with him. About the same time, the Southern Democrats, meeting in the same city, nominated John C. Breckinridge of Kentucky and Joseph Lane of Oregon and adopted a platform demanding federal protection of slavery in the territories. Buchanan threw his support to Breckinridge. So did former Presidents John Tyler and Franklin Pierce.

The Republicans met in a huge box-like structure called the "Wigwam" in Chicago in May and drew up a platform opposing the extension of slavery, denouncing Brown's raid, and upholding the Union. As in 1856, their platform also contained a number of economic proposals designed to attract businessmen in the Northeast and farmers in the West: a protective tariff, the building of a transcontinental railroad, and a homestead act giving free land to settlers. The chief contenders for the Republican nomination were William H. Seward of New York and Abraham Lincoln of Illinois. Seward had long been prominent in national affairs and was far better known than Lincoln, but he had made many political enemies. Furthermore, although a moderate, he had made statements from time to time that made him sound like an outright abolitionist. Lincoln, fifty-one, a newcomer to national politics, had "excited no hates anywhere," was skillful in debate, and, as a self-made man, appealed to plain people in the West.[4] In addition, he came from Illinois, an important state for the Republicans to carry. His friends worked hard for his nomination and finally succeeded in putting him over on the third ballot. The convention chose Hannibal Hamlin, former Democrat from Maine, to run with him.

On May 9, a group calling itself the Constitutional Union party held a nominating convention in Baltimore. Consisting mainly of former Whigs, this party placed single-minded emphasis on the preservation of the Union. In an effort to appeal to both sections, the delegates nominated former Speaker of the House John Bell, a Whig from Tennessee, for the Presidency and Edward Everett of Massachusetts for the Vice-Presidency. Though ridiculed as a "Do Nothing" or "Old Gentleman's" party, the Constitutional Union party was sincerely dedicated to staving off the break-up of the Union. At the convention, according to the *Cincinnati Commercial's* Murat Halstead, "the moment a speaker would say *Constitution; law, Union; American; conservative elements; glorious victory; our fathers; our flag; our country;* or anything of the sort, he had to pause for some time until the general rapture would discharge itself by stamping, clapping hands, rattling canes, etc. I have likened the enthusiasm to that of an Irish audience at an archbishop's lecture."[5] But a New York paper scornfully dismissed the Bell platform as "no North, no South, no East, no West, no Anything."[6]

Lincoln was not on the ballot in the South, and the 1860 campaign resolved itself essentially into two campaigns: Lincoln vs. Douglas in the North, and Bell vs. Breckinridge in the South. Bell's supporters rang bells of all sizes, shapes, and sounds at their rallies, Breckinridge orators warned of the threat to the South posed by a Republican victory, and Douglas men told voters: "We need a statesman, not a rail splitter as President." But the Republicans conducted the most energetic canvass of them all. They sponsored torchlight parades of young men called "Wide Awakes," rail-splitters' battalions, and marches made up of men just as tall as Lincoln (six feet four in stocking feet); they also attacked the Buchanan administration as wasteful and corrupt, extolled "High Old Abe," the "Woodchopper of the West," and urged people: "Vote yourselves a Farm." Lincoln himself decided not to "write or speak anything upon doctrinal points" lest his remarks be distorted by his opponents; but he received a stream of visitors—friends, politicians, office-seekers, reporters, photographers, painters—in Springfield, Illinois, during the campaign.

Douglas went out on the stump. He was the first presidential candidate in American history to make a nationwide tour in person. Not only did he campaign in New England; he also took his campaign to the South, where he urged people to accept the outcome of the election peacefully. "The election of a man to the Presidency by the American people in conformity with the Constitution of the United States," he told

them, *"would not justify any attempt at dissolving this glorious confederacy."*[7]
But many Southerners were implacable. "The South," announced the
Southern Confederacy in Atlanta, Georgia, in August,

> will never permit Abraham Lincoln to be inaugurated President of the
> United States; this is a settled and a sealed fact. It is the determination of
> all parties in the South. Let the consequences be what they may, whether
> the Potomac is crimsoned in human gore, and Pennsylvania Avenue is paved
> ten fathoms deep with mangled bodies, or whether the last vestige of lib-
> erty is swept from the face of the American continent, the South, the loyal
> South, the constitutional South, will never submit to such humiliation and
> degradation as the inauguration of Abraham Lincoln.[8]

Douglas was in Iowa when he heard that Lincoln had carried Pennsylvania and would probably win the election. "Mr. Lincoln is the next
President," he exclaimed. "We must try to save the Union. I will go
South."[9] And he boarded the train, headed south, and gave scores of
speeches from balconies and car platforms upholding the Union.

The split in the Democratic party made Lincoln's victory an almost
foregone conclusion. "THE THING IS DID!" exulted the *Bucyrus Journal* in Ohio. "The Most Glorious Triumph Ever Achieved! Lincoln
Elected! Disunion Rebuked! DOUGLAS NON EST. BRECKINRIDGE
NOWHERE! BELL————————THE COUNTRY SAVED! A Chance
for a Big Yell."[10] But with 1,866,452 votes, Lincoln polled only about
40 percent of the popular vote; his three opponents together won almost a million more votes than he did: Douglas, 1,376,957 (29 percent), Breckinridge, 849,781 (18 percent), and Bell, 588,879 (13 percent). But his electoral victory was substantial: 180 votes to Breckinridge's
72, Bell's 39, and Douglas's 12. Even if the votes of Lincoln's three opponents had been cast for one candidate, he would still have won a decisive majority in the Electoral College because he carried the populous
states of the North and the West.

James Russell Lowell had predicted the election would be a turning
point in American history and he was correct. The electoral vote showed
that the American people had, for the first time, voted along sectional
lines: Lincoln carried 18 free states, Breckinridge, 11 slave states, Bell,
3 border states, and Douglas, Missouri and 3 New Jersey votes. But the
majority of voters undoubtedly favored the preservation of the Union.
Lincoln, Douglas, and Bell all stood for the Union; and Douglas and
Bell outpolled Breckinridge in parts of the South. On December 20,
however, a special convention meeting in Charleston, resolved that "the
Union now subsisting between South Caroline and other States, under
the name of the United States of America, is hereby dissolved."[11] Soon
other states in the South followed South Carolina out of the Union. And
then came America's worst war.

☆ ☆ ☆

Not Much Of Me

When Jesse W. Fell of Bloomington, Illinois, began pushing Lincoln for the Republican nomination, he asked the latter for biographical information. Lincoln sent him a brief sketch of his life with the remark: "There is not much of it, for the reason, I suppose, that there is not much of me." [12]

Rail Splitter

At the Republican state convention in Decatur, Illinois, on May 9, the chairman announced that an old Democrat from Macon County wished to make a contribution to the meeting. At this point John Hanks, Lincoln's cousin, came walking down the aisle carrying two old fence rails with a sign on them announcing: "The Rail Candidate for President in 1860. Two rails from a lot of 3,000 made in 1830 by Thomas Hanks and Abraham Lincoln, whose father was the first pioneer of Macon County." As Hanks proceeded toward the platform shouts went up: "Lincoln! Lincoln! Speech!" A committee then escorted Lincoln to the platform while everyone cheered: "Three times for Honest Abe, our next President!" Then John Hanks instructed Lincoln: "Identify your work!" Said Lincoln candidly: "I cannot say that I split these rails. Where did you get the rails?" "At the farm you improved down on the Sangamon," was the answer. "Well," said Lincoln thoughtfully, "that was a long time ago. It is possible I may have split these rails but I cannot identify them." But the crowd persisted: "Identify your work! Identify your work!" Lincoln decided to join in the fun. "What kind of timber are they?" he asked. "Honey locust and black walnut" he was told. "Well, boys," he said, "I can only say that I have split a great many better-looking ones."

The Decatur convention warmly recommended Lincoln for the Republican nomination and after that the fence-rail story began to spread and was soon taken up by Republican newspapers throughout the North. Horace Greeley's *New York Tribune* even did a feature story on it. From then on Lincoln was known as the "Rail Splitter." At the national convention in Chicago one of the delegates seconding Lincoln's nomination cried: "I arise on behalf of a portion of the delegation from Ohio to put in nomination the man who can split rails and maul Democrats." And after the nomination the Republicans celebrated their candidate's prowess as a rail splitter in countless songs. One of them, sung to the tune of "Uncle Ned," began:

> We've a noble rail splitter, and his name is Honest Abe,
> And he lives in Illinois, as you know;

> And he has all the tools there to carry on his trade,
> And the way he piles them up isn't slow.

Puns proliferated. Lincoln was a rail splitter, cried the Republicans, while Douglas had always split hairs and now had split his party. The *Baltimore Sun* put it to verse:

> Quoth Abe to Steve, "I cannot fail,
> I'm bound to fill that station;
> Long—long ago—I split the rail
>   To fence this mighty nation."
> Quoth Steve, with chuckle hearty,
> "I've split old Jackson's hickory tree,
> The Democratic party."[13]

Self-evident Truths

When the Republicans began adopting their platform on the second day of the convention, there was great applause for the tariff and home-stead planks. Then Ohio abolitionist Joshua Giddings proposed adding the self-evident truths of the Declaration of Independence, beginning with the words, "all men are created equal," to the platform. "When you leave out this truth," he said, "you leave out the party." But his resolution was voted down. "The old man rose," according to reporter Murat Halstead, "and made his way slowly toward the door. A dozen delegates begged him not to go. But he considered everything lost, even honor. . . . The Declaration of Independence had been voted down. He must go!" A little later George W. Curtis, young New York dele-gate, renewed Giddings's proposal. "I have to ask this Convention," he cried, "whether they are prepared to go . . . before the country as vot-ing down the words of the Declaration of Independence. . . . I ask gentlemen to think well before, upon the free prairies of the West, in the summer of 1860, they dare to wince and quail before the men of Philadelphia of 1776—before they dare to shrink from repeating the words that these great men enunciated." Curtis's impassioned plea touched off cries of "No, no," and tremendous applause and the dele-gates voted to include the self-evident truths of the Great Declaration in the platform after all.[14]

Lincoln's Nailers

Lincoln decided to stay in Springfield, Illinois, during the Chicago con-vention. "I am a little too much a candidate to stay home," he ex-plained, "and not quite enough a candidate to go." His managers went to Chicago with only Illinois in the bag, but did everything they could think of to build up support for their man in other state delegations. They hired two Chicagoans, whose shouts, it was said, could be heard above the howling of the most violent tempest on Lake Michigan, to lead the cheers whenever Lincoln's name was mentioned in the convention. They also packed the Wigwam with "Lincoln shouters." When they learned that Seward men had secured a majority of the tickets of admission, they printed and distributed duplicate tickets while the Sewardites were out parading the streets, and when the latter got back they found the convention hall jam-packed with Westerners ready "to shout for Lincoln." Lincoln's men also worked hard to nail down the Indiana and Pennsylvania delegations for their man. "We worked like nailers," said one of them. "We are going to have Indiana for Old Abe, sure," said another just before the balloting. "How did you get it?" someone asked. "By the Lord," he was told, "we promised them everything they asked."

After nailing down Indiana, Lincoln's managers went after Pennsylvania, with fifty-six delegates ready to vote for Simon Cameron, a favorite son, on the first ballot, but open to other candidates after that. As Judge David Davis went into a huddle with the Pennsylvanians, Jesse Dubois telegraphed Lincoln to tell him they could win the Keystone State if they promised Cameron the Treasury Department. "I authorize no bargain," Lincoln wired back, "and will be bound by none." "Damn Lincoln!" exclaimed Dubois. Said Stephen T. Logan: "I am very sure if Lincoln was aware of the necessities—" "Lincoln ain't here," broke in Davis impatiently, "and don't know what we have to meet, so we will go ahead as if we hadn't heard from him, and he must ratify it." About midnight Joseph Medill ran into Judge Davis in a hotel lobby just after he left the Pennsylvania delegation. "How will they vote?" he asked. "Damned if we haven't gotten them," exulted Davis. "How did you get them?" asked Medill. "By paying the price," replied Davis and revealed they had agreed to make Cameron Secretary of the Treasury. Medill expressed some consternation. "Oh, what's the difference," cried Davis airily, "We are after a bigger thing than that; we want the Presidency, and the Treasury is not a great stake to pay for it." A few hours later Lincoln's name was placed in nomination and the "Lincoln shouters" were ready. "Imagine," wrote Halstead, "all the hogs ever slaughtered in Cincinnati giving their death squeals together, a score of big steam whistles going (steam at 16 lbs. per inch), and you conceive something of the same nature." Lincoln reluctantly made Cameron Secretary of War (not Treasury) after the election but he proved so incompetent he had to be replaced in a few months.[15]

Little Woman

When Lincoln received the Republican nomination in Chicago, a friend of his at once wired the news to Springfield: "Abe, we did it. Glory to God!" The telegraph operator in Springfield wrote on a scrap of paper,

"Mr. Lincoln, you are nominated on the third ballot," and gave it to a boy who ran to the office of the *State Journal* where Lincoln was awaiting the news with some friends. Lincoln took the message, read it aloud quietly, and, as his friends started cheering, put it in his vest pocket and said thoughtfully: "There's a little woman down at our house would like to hear this. I'll go down and tell her."[16]

Look Up To

"What's your height?" Lincoln asked Pennsylvania's Judge William D. Kelly, a member of the delegation that came to Springfield to notify him formally of his nomination. "Six feet," responded Kelly, "What is yours, Mr. Lincoln?" "Six feet four," chortled Lincoln. "Then," smiled Kelly, "Pennsylvania bows to Illinois, my dear man. For years," he added, "my heart has been aching for a President that I could look up to, and I have found him at last in the land where we thought there were none but little giants!" Lincoln was amused by the reference to Douglas (the Little Giant).[17]

Everybody Doin' It

Because of the unusual number of candidates in 1860, a little boy, according to a popular joke, asks his pal, " 'S your father goin' to run for President this year?" "Guess so," replies the second boy; "he says he may as well—everybody else is doin' it."[18]

76,000 Rails

Lincoln's rail-splitting came in for considerable ribbing during the campaign. The *Chicago Herald* reported that by the age of eighteen Lincoln averaged 76,000 rails a day. The *New Albany Herald* (Indiana) said that if you put all the rails Lincoln had split together, you could make a ten-foot rail-fence reaching from the North to the South Pole. An Indiana newspaper had fun with the notification ceremony. "The Official Committee arrived in Springfield in dewy evening," went the burlesque, "and went to honest Old Abe's house. Mrs. Honest Old Abe said Honest Abe was out in the woods splitting rails. So the Official Committee went to the woods, where sure enuff they found Honest Old Abe splitting rails with his two boys. It was a grand, a magnificent spectacle. There stood Honest Old Abe in his shirt sleeves, a pair of leather home-made suspenders holding up a pair of home-made pantaloons, the seat of which was neatly patched. 'Mr. Lincoln, Sir you've been nominated, Sir, for the Highest office, Sir.' 'Oh, don't bother me,' said Honest Old Abe, 'I took a stent this mornin' to split three million rails afore night and I don't want to be pestered with no stuff about no conventions till I get my stent done. I've only got two hundred thousand rails to split before sundown. I kin do it if you'll let me alone.' "[19]

Lincoln's Looks

Many newspapers in the North approved the selection of Lincoln as Republican candidate, but some papers were extremely hostile. Complained the *Atlas and Argus* in Albany, New York: "He . . . is not known except as a slang-whanging stump speaker of which all parties are ashamed." The *New York Herald* was even more contemptuous: "The conduct of the Republican party in this nomination is a remarkable indication of the small intellect, growing smaller. They pass over Seward, Chase and Bates, who are statesmen and able men, and they take up a fourth-rate lecturer, who cannot speak good grammar, and who, to raise the wind, delivers his hackneyed, illiterate compositions at $200 apiece. Our readers will recollect that this peripatetic politician visited New York two or three months ago on his financial tour, when, in return for the most unmitigated trash, interlarded with coarse and clumsy jokes, he filled his empty pockets with dollars coined out of Republican fanaticism. If, after he becomes President of the United States, the public finances should fail, he can set out on a lecturing mission through the country, taking Horace Greeley along with him."

The reaction to Lincoln in the South was, to say the least, unfriendly. "A horrid looking wretch he is," said the *Charleston Mercury*, "sooty and scoundrelly in aspect, a cross between the nutmeg dealer, the horse swapper, and the night man, a creature 'fit evidently for petty treason, small stratagems and all sorts of spoils.' He is a lank-sided Yankee of the uncomeliest visage, and of the dirtiest complexion. Faugh! after him what decent white man would be President?" The *Houston Telegraph* also stressed his bad looks. "Lincoln is the leanest, lankest, most ungainly mass of legs and arms and hatchet face ever strung on a single frame. He has most unwarrantably abused the privilege, which all politicians have, of being ugly."

But the *New York Tribune* defended Lincoln. "Truth constrains us to say that 'Honest Abe' is not a handsome man; but he is not so ill-looking as he has been represented. 'Handsome is as handsome does,' however, is a sensible adage." The Douglas Democrats did not of course see it that way. One of their most popular campaign ballads went this way:

> Tell us he's a second Webster,
> Or if better, Henry Clay;
> That he's full of gentle humor,
> Placid as a summer's day.
>
> Tell again about the cord-wood;
> Seven cords or more per day;

> How each night he seeks his closet,
>   There alone to kneel and pray.
>
> Tell us he resembles Jackson,
>   Save he wears a larger boot,
> And is broader 'cross the shoulders,
>   And is taller by a foot.
>
> Any lie you tell, we'll swallow—
>   Swallow any kind of mixture;
> But O don't, we beg and pray you—
>   Don't for land's sake, show his picture.

Albany's *Atlas and Argus* joked about it. "A rough-looking Western hunter," the paper reported, met Lincoln on the prairie, and leveled his musket. "Hold there," cried Lincoln, "you don't mean to shoot me?" "Yes, sir," was the answer; "I've pledged myself if I ever saw a worse-looking man than myself, I would shoot him." "Well," replied Lincoln, "if I look worse than you do, fire away!"

But Dick Yates, a good Lincoln man running for Governor of Illinois, told people at rallies: "Well, if all the ugly men in the United States vote for him, he will surely be elected!"[20]

Have It Nice

After Lincoln's nomination, arrangements were made for Leonard Volk to do a statue of him. Volk dropped by Lincoln's house to make a cast of his hands and asked him to hold a stick or something during the process. Lincoln went to the woodshed and, as Volk later told it, "I heard the saw go, and he soon returned to the dining-room whittling off the end of a piece of broom handle. I remarked to him that he need not whittle off the edges. 'Oh, well,' said he, 'I thought I would like to have it nice.'"[21]

New Clothes

After his nomination Lincoln began receiving gifts, especially wearing apparel, from all over the North. "Well, Mary," he told his wife, 'if nothing else comes out of this scrape, we are going to have some new clothes, are we not?"[22]

Short and Simple Annals

When the *Chicago Tribune*'s John G. Scripps asked Lincoln for information to use in a campaign biography, the latter told him there would be nothing to it but "the short and simple annals of the poor." Lincoln read Scripps's sketch before it was published and noticed that Scripps had reported that he had read Plutarch. When he returned the sketch he told Scripps he hadn't read Plutarch before but since reading the sketch he had read some Plutarch so the statement could be published as accurate. "A scrupulous teller of the truth—," remarked Scripps, "too exact in his notions to suit the atmosphere of Washington as it now is."[23]

Lincoln and Douglas

The Republicans summed it up: "The Long and the Short of the Presidential Canvass: Lincoln and Douglas." And, putting it another way:

> When we put Lincoln in, we shall know what is what;
> When we put Douglas in, we shall know how to squat;
> When we put Breckinridge in, there'll be powder and smoke;
> When we choose Bell and Everett, 'twill be a good joke.

As to slavery: "Lincoln and Hamlin—say you shan't; Breckinridge and Lane—say shall; Douglas and Johnson—say, do as you please; and Bell and Everett—say nothing!" When a Douglas paper accused Lincoln of saying, "damn," the *Sacramento Daily Union* retorted: "Then Lincoln says more than Douglas is worth!" Republican papers also publicized the following:

> Why is Douglas a greater man than Abe Lincoln? Because the former split a party, while the latter only split a rail.
> Jones, did you see that splendid half bust of Mr. Douglas, when you were in New York? Yes; but I've seen a finer one since in Pennsylvania. It was a full bust.
> Lincoln is like a rail; Douglas is the reverse—rail spelled backward (liar).

But the Douglasites essayed the light touch too. The *Cleveland Weekly Plain Dealer* ran a story about "How Jack Became a Democrat." A newly married couple was "snugly ensconced in bed," the story went, when Jack mentioned he was a Republican. His shocked bride can hardly believe it but he assures her he's a "regular out and outer, double dyed and twisted in the wool" Republican. Then, "just double and twist yourself out of bed," she cries. Poor Jack left, but every night he knocked at the bedroom door and his knock went unanswered. Finally at midnight about a week later, loud raps were heard, followed by more raps until the door rattled loudly. "Who's there?" asked the wife, roused from a deep sleep. Came the answer: "The best Democrat you ever did see!"[24]

Steam Engine in Britches

The indefatigable Stephen A. Douglas ("steam engine in britches") offended some people by his campaigning. It was still considered outlandish for presidential candidates to electioneer. Sniffed the *Jonesboro* (Illinois) *Gazette:* "Douglas is going about peddling his opinions as a tin man peddles his wares. The only excuse for him is that since he is a small man, he has a right to be engaged in small business, and small business it is for a candidate for the Presidency to be strolling around the country begging for votes like a town constable." He "demeans himself," the *North Iowan* upbraided him, "as no other candidate ever yet has, who goes about begging, imploring, and beseeching the people to grant him his wish. . . . He should be attended by some Italian, with his hand organ to grind out an accompaniment."

To take off the heat when in the East, Douglas gave out that he was on his way to visit his mother in Clifton Springs, New York, whom he hadn't seen in a long time. But it took a month, and many stop-overs and speeches, to get there and the Republicans showered him with taunts all the way to her town. "A Boy Lost!" exclaimed one Republican hand-bill. "Left Washington, D.C., some time in July, to go home to his mother. He has not yet reached his mother, who is very anxious about him. He has been seen in Philadelphia, New York City, Hartford, Conn., at a clambake in Rhode Island. He has been heard from at Boston, Port-land, Augusta, and Bangor, Me. . . . He is about five feet nothing in height and about the same in diameter the other way. He has a red face, short legs, and a large belly. Answers to the name of Little Giant, talks a great deal, very loud, always about himself. He has an idea that he is a candidate for President." The Republican Campaign Committee issued almost daily handbills, signed, "S.D.'s Mother," appealing for in-formation about "her wandering son." To get to western New York, sneered a New Hampshire paper, Douglas "naturally came to New Haven, Guilford and Hartford on his way, and at the latter place he was 'betrayed' into a speech. Still bent on his maternal pilgrimage, he goes toward Boston. . . . At Worcester, some Judas 'betrayed' him into a speech. At Boston, 'betrayed' again." The *Weekly Illinois Journal* ran "A Plaintive Pome":

> Why did I down to Hartford go?
> 'Twas not my squatter self to show;
> I went to hunt, I told you so,
>   My mother. . . .
>
> At length I hope I shall thee find,
> For thou has been a useful blind,
> That I might often speak my mind,
>   My mother.

In speeches Douglas refused to say anything about the morality of slavery. Asked about it in Bangor, he started talking about popular sov-ereignty. "You are not answering my question, Mr. Douglas," cried his inquirer. "I know all about that; but what is your opinion—is slavery a moral or political evil?" Shouted Douglas: "You may thank me that I do not rebuke you for your impertinence." Seward thought Douglas's attitude hurt him. "Will Judge Douglas ever be President?" someone asked the New Yorker and he replied, "No, sir. No man will ever be President of the United States who spells 'negro' with two g's."[25]

Peeping Through the Fence

In a parade in New York City sponsored by the fusionists (Democrats and Constitutional Unionists), there were several transparencies showing Lincoln and Greeley hobnobbing with blacks and championing amalgamation. One transparency showed Lincoln sitting on a fence with a black man while Greeley stands in front holding the *New York Tribune* and saying, "Vote our ticket—we are not abolitionists until Old Abe is elected." Another had Lincoln on a fence rail, a Negro lurking beneath him, and Greeley waving aside a white man who is saying, "I see the nigger peeping through the fence." The caption: "Lincoln on the fence, the nigger on the fence, the nigger under the fence, the nigger on the wood pile." A third transparency, entitled "Weighed in the Balance," depicted Lincoln sitting on the center of a beam, suspended by a pivot, with a stout black woman on one end and Greeley, who is falling off, on the other. A fourth transparency pictured Lincoln at the head of a ship waving a flag labeled, "Discord," and Greeley at the stern holding the tiller and a copy of the *Tribune*. Between the two sits a thick-lipped black man embracing a white girl, while a fellow black exclaims, "I'se looking at you, Sambo," and Sambo chuckles, "Yah, yah." The ship is labeled, "Steamer *Abe Lincoln*, Captain Greeley." The next scene in the transparency showed the ship touching land and being met by Jonathan who says, "Look here, Old Abe, you can't land that crowd here," while Abe replies, "Why, Jonathan, these are my principles," Greeley cries, "Colored folks have preference of staterooms," and a passenger says, "Free love and free niggers will certainly elect Old Abe if he pilots us safe."[26]

Wide Awakes

The Wide Awakes, a marching club composed of young Republicans, attracted a great deal of attention in 1860. In February, Kentucky Republican Cassius M. Clay was scheduled to speak in Hartford and some of the young men there volunteered to escort him from the railroad station to his quarters in town. They decided to make an occasion out of it. They borrowed torches from the fire department, put on glazed capes to protect their coats from the dripping oil, and marched through the streets in a colorful torchlight parade that delighted the townspeople. After Clay left, they organized a regular company of Wide Awakes, with fifty members, and began meeting regularly for drill. Within a few weeks Wide Awake clubs appeared in other towns in Connecticut and within a few months there were clubs in every Northern state and membership had reached over 400,000. A Wide Awake business quickly developed; soon merchants were advertising: *"Wide Awake Uniforms; Prices Reduced:* Cap, Cape and torch with flags will be furnished at the cost price of $1.15.

The Wide Awakes did many things: escorted speakers, kept order at rallies, canvassed voters, guarded ballot boxes, and distributed campaign material. Above all, they marched and sang songs. In Wide Awake parades, the "officers" carried lanterns and the "privates" held torches. At times the processions involved thousands of young men drawn from several states, all attired in glazed caps and capes and carrying torches. As the Wide Awakes marched, they displayed mottoes and sang campaign songs. Some of their mottoes: "The Pilgrims Did Not Found Our Empire for Slavery"; "Free Soil, Free Speech, and Free Men"; "No More Slave Territories"; "The Union Must Be Preserved—Jackson"; "The Territories Must Be Free to the People". Two of the songs:

> Old Abe Lincoln came out of the wilderness,
>   Out of the wilderness, out of the wilderness,
> Old Abe Lincoln came out of the wilderness
>   Down in Illinois!

> Oh, ain't I glad I joined the Republicans,
> Joined the Republicans, joined the Republicans,
> Ain't I glad I joined the Republicans,
>   Down in Illinois![27]

Stevy Doug

Devoted Republicans made up scores of songs for the 1860 campaign, most of them celebrating their party's identification with freedom and many of them portraying their candidate as a man of the people: "Abe of Illinois," "The People's Nominee," "Hurrah for Abe Lincoln!" On rare occasions there was a touch of humor. One song made something out of the Democratic candidate Douglas's shortness of stature and fondness for drink:

> There was a little man and his name was Stevy Doug,
> To the White House he longed for to go;
> But he hadn't any votes in the whole of the South,
> In the place where his votes ought to grow.
> His legs were short, but his speeches they were long,
> And nothing but himself he could see;
> His principles were weak, but his spirits they were strong,
> For a thirsty little soul was he.[28]

Exception

The Constitutional Union party had the briefest platform: "Resolved: that it is both the part of patriotism and of duty to recognize no political principle other than the Constitution of the country, the Union of the States and the enforcement of the laws." An old fellow, who had been in and out of jail, was asked to support Bell and declared, "I like Bell very much, and I like the Constitution and the Union but damn the enforcement of the laws!"[29]

Whiskers

In mid-October little Grace Bedell of Westfield, New York, saw a picture of Lincoln and told her mother: "I think, mother, that Mr. Lincoln would look better if he wore whiskers, and I mean to write and tell him so." So she wrote Lincoln, told him how old she was and where she lived, said she was a Republican and thought he would make a good President but that he would look better if he grew whiskers. "If you have not time to answer my letter," she concluded, "will you allow your little girl to reply for you?" Lincoln answered on October 19. "My Dear Little Miss: Your very agreeable letter is received," he wrote. "I regret the necessity of saying I have no daughter. I have three sons; one seventeen, one nine and one seven years of age. They, with their mother, constitute my whole family. As to the whiskers, having never worn any, do you not think people would call it a piece of silly affectation if I should begin it now? Your very sincere well-wisher, A. LINCOLN." Months later, on his journey to Washington for the inauguration, Lincoln's train stopped at Westfield, and Lincoln, remembering his little correspondent, mentioned her to former Lieutenant-Governor George Patterson who called out and asked if Grace Bedell was present. She was. The crowd opened a pathway for her and she came up timidly to Lincoln who told her she might see that he had allowed his whiskers to grow at her request. Then, reaching out his long arms, he bent down and kissed her.[30]

Pittomless Bot

One of Mark Twain's favorite campaign stories was about the speech George W. Curtis made for the Republicans in Hartford, Connecticut, the night before the election. In a hurry to catch a train, orator Curtis rushed through his flowery end: "And to-morrow, fellow-citizens, the American people will be called upon to give their verdict, and I believe you, as American freemen, will give that verdict against American slavery. Yes, to-morrow we will go to the polls with freedom's ballot in our hands, trampling slavery's shackles under our feet; and while the Archangel of Liberty looks down approvingly upon us from the throne of Omnipotence, we will consign Stephen A. Douglas to the pittomless bot!" There were loud guffaws in the audience at his slip of the tongue as he rushed out to his waiting carriage.[31]

President of the Universe

Several men were on a train in New England discussing the election, it was reported, when a devout follower of millennialist preacher William Miller interrupted. "Before the election of 1860," he assured them, "the world will have come to an end, and Jesus Christ will be president of the universe." "Sir," said one man firmly, "I'll b-b-bet you t-t-ten dollars New Hampshire w-won't g-g-go for him!"[32]

By Ballot

When Lincoln was in the post office the night before the election, a by-stander asked him how he intended to vote the next day. "For Yates for Governor," he replied. "But for President?" "*How* vote?" he joshed. "By ballot!" When he voted in Springfield the following day, he cut his name from the top of the ballot and then voted the straight Republican ticket for state and local candidates.[33]

CHAPTER TWENTY

1864
Lincoln and the War Crisis

"The country is entering on a new and perilous time," observed Secretary of State William H. Seward in June 1864, "a canvass for the presidency in time of civil war."[1] As the campaign got under way, the prospects for a Union victory were gloomy indeed. Grant was making little·progress in Virginia, Sherman was halted before Atlanta, and the heavy casualties reported from the battlefields shocked and horrified people on the home front. Some people suggested postponing or suspending elections during the crisis; but, as Abraham Lincoln pointed out: "We cannot have free government without elections; and if the rebellion could force us to forgo, or postpone a national election, it might fairly claim to have already conquered and ruined us."[2] Before the year was out the United States went ahead with its voting just as in peacetime. It was the first nation ever to hold a general election during a major war.

The Republicans formed a coalition with Democrats supporting the war, held a National Union convention in Baltimore in June, called for the "utter and complete extirpation of slavery" by means of a constitutional amendment, renominated Lincoln on the first ballot, and picked as his running mate Andrew Johnson of Tennessee, one of the most prominent War Democrats. When delegates from the National Union League dropped by the White House to offer congratulations, Lincoln told them: "I do not allow myself to suppose that either the convention or the League have concluded . . . that I am either the greatest or best man in America, but rather they have concluded it is not best to swap horses while crossing the river, and have further concluded that I am not so poor a horse that they might not make a botch of it in trying to swap."[3]

But there were those in Lincoln's party who were anxious to "swap horses" in midstream. "Mr. Lincoln is already beaten," wailed Horace Greeley. "He cannot be elected. And we must have another ticket to save us from utter overthrow."[4] The Radical Republicans blamed Lincoln for reverses on the battlefield; they also thought he favored a "soft" policy toward the South after the war. Some of them wanted to run Secretary of the Treasury Salmon P. Chase in Lincoln's place; others suggested General Grant, but Grant absolutely refused to be considered. In the end the Radicals settled on the 1856 nominee: General John C. Frémont. Meeting in Cleveland on May 31, they nominated Frémont for President on a platform endorsing "the one-term policy for the Presidency," declaring that "the rebellion must be suppressed by force of arms, and without compromise," and demanding Congressional control of Southern reconstruction and the confiscation of Confederate property. They chose the name, Radical Democracy, for their party.[5]

The Democrats met in Chicago in August, proclaimed the war a failure, demanded an immediate cessation of hostilities, and called for the restoration of the Union by means of a negotiated peace. Their candidate for President was General George B. McClellan, former Commander-in-Chief of Union forces whom Lincoln had dropped in 1862 for having the "slows." McClellan accepted the Democratic nomination but refused to call the war a failure. Said he: "I could not look in the face of my gallant comrades of the army and navy, who have survived so many bloody battles, and tell them that their labors and the sacrifices of so many of our slain and wounded brethren had been in vain; that we had abandoned that Union for which we have so often perilled our lives."[6] McClellan criticized the Republicans for making emancipation one of the goals of the war, but also rebuked Democrats who sought peace at any price. He insisted that *"no peace can be permanent without Union."*[7]

Lincoln's managers were not optimistic about the election. The military situation continued melancholy and Lincoln got all the blame. What historian George Bancroft told his son in 1862 continued to be true in 1864: "The outcry against the conduct of the war is deep and unanimous. All blame Lincoln; all, in all parties. I have not heard one who does not."[8] The *Cincinnati Gazette* suggested that both Lincoln and Frémont withdraw from the race and that the Republicans find someone who "would inspire confidence and infuse a life into our ranks. . . ."[9] Even Thurlow Weed and Henry J. Raymond, strong Lincoln men, began to lose hope. Weed finally told Lincoln his re-election was impossible; and Raymond, chairman of the Republican national executive committee, urged that he make a peace move. But Lincoln was firm; his goal was restoring the Union without slavery and he refused to consider peace terms on any other basis. But when Greeley announced there were Confederate commissioners in Canada willing to talk peace, Lincoln at once delegated the *Tribune* editor to meet with them; and, as he expected, nothing came of Greeley's trip. Lincoln was as distressed by the bloodshed as anyone else; but he would not compromise on the issue of a restored Union without slavery. And Jefferson Davis continued to insist on an independent Confederacy.

The campaign of 1864 was noisy and abusive. The Republicans harped on cowardice, defeatism, lack of patriotism, disloyalty, and even treason among the Democrats. They also held up McClellan's military record to ridicule. For their part, the Democrats emphasized the "ignorance, incompetence, and corruption of Mr. Lincoln's administration" and counted on war weariness to get them votes. "Old Abe removed McClellan," they cried. "We'll now remove Old Abe."[10] Lincoln had been subjected to almost unprecedented abuse in the opposition press ever since becoming President. During his campaign for re-election, however, anti-Lincoln vituperation reached new heights. Of the Lincoln-Johnson ticket the *New York World* sneered: "The age of statesmen is gone; the age of rail splitters and tailors, of buffoons, boors and fanatics has succeeded. . . . In a crisis of the most appalling magnitude requiring statesmanship of the highest order, the country is asked to consider the claims of two ignorant, boorish, third-rate backwoods lawyers for the highest stations in the Government. Such nominations, in such a conjuncture, are an insult to the common sense of the people. God save the Republic!"[11] On September 24, *Harper's* listed some of the "terms applied by the friends of General M'Clellan to the President": Filthy Story-Teller, Despot, Liar, Thief, Braggart, Buffoon, Usurper, Monster, Ignoramus Abe, Old Scoundrel, Perjurer, Robber, Swindler, Tyrant, Fiend, Butcher.[12] Lincoln couldn't help being saddened by the hatred showered on him. "It is a little singular that I, who am not a vindictive man," he mused, "should have always been before the people for election in canvasses marked for their bitterness. . . ."[13] On August 23, Raymond wrote to say that chances of a Republican victory in the fall were exceedingly slim. A little later Lincoln wrote a few lines on a piece of paper, asked his Cabinet members to sign the paper without reading it and then carefully put it away. After the election he showed them what he had written: "It seems exceedingly probable that this administration will not be re-elected. Then it will be my duty to so cooperate with the President-elect as to save the Union between the election and the inauguration, as he will have secured his election on such ground that he cannot possibly save it afterward."[14]

Just about the time Lincoln had reconciled himself to defeat, the military picture began to change. Admiral David G. Farragut captured Mobile Bay, General William T. Sherman took Atlanta and commenced marching through Georgia, Ulysses S. Grant began making progress at Petersburg, and General Philip Sheridan routed Jubal Early's troops from the valleys of Virginia and began his devastation there. "If you want to know who is going to vote for McClellan, mention Atlanta to them," crowed the *Albany Journal.* "The long face and the low muttered growl is sufficient. On the other hand, every Lincoln man bears a face every lineament of which is radiant with joy." [15] The political scene was quickly transformed. Frémont withdrew from the race, Greeley announced he would henceforth "fly the banner" of Lincoln, Chase took to the stump for Lincoln, and Radical Republican leaders who had been chastising Lincoln for his moderate reconstruction plans, began giving him their support. "There is not now, the slightest uncertainty about the re-election of Mr. Lincoln," exclaimed Chase. "The only question is by what popular and electoral majority. God grant that both may be so decisive as to turn every hope of rebellion to despair!" [16]

Lincoln's victory was decisive. On November 8, he won 212 electoral votes (to McClellan's 21) and carried every state but Kentucky, Delaware, and New Jersey. His popular majority was not as sweeping— 2,213,665 votes (55 percent) to 1,802,237 (45 percent)—but it was substantial. Lincoln regarded the outcome of the election as an endorsement of his administration's policies: restoration of the Union with slavery gone forever. McClellan accepted the people's choice with equanimity. "For my country's sake, I deplore the result," he told his brother, "but the people have decided with their eyes wide open." [17] From Grant came a congratulatory telegram: "The election having passed off quickly, no bloodshed or riot throughout the land, is a victory worth more to the country than a battle won." [18] Lincoln himself marveled at "the extraordinary calmness and good order with which the millions of voters met and mingled at the polls" and praised the American people for demonstrating that "a people's government can sustain a national election in the midst of a great civil war." [19]

☆   ☆   ☆

Preferred Disease

In the spring of 1864, a friend told Lincoln nothing could prevent his re-election but Grant's capture of Richmond and then Grant's nomination for President. "Well," Lincoln reflected, "I feel very much like the man who said he didn't want to die particularly, but if he had to die that was precisely the disease he would like to die of." [20]

Jokes

"President Lincoln is a joke incarnate," announced James Gordon Bennett's *New York Herald,* a truculent enemy of Lincoln, in February 1864. "His election was a very sorry joke. The idea that such a man as he should be President of such a country as this is a very ridiculous joke. His debut in Washington society was a joke; for he introduced himself and

Mrs. Lincoln as 'the long and short of the Presidency.' His inaugural address was a joke. . . . His cabinet is and always has been a standing joke. All his state papers are jokes. His letters to our generals, beginning with those to General McClellan, are very cruel jokes. . . . His emancipation proclamation was a solemn joke. . . . His conversation is full of jokes. . . . His title of 'Honest' is a satirical joke. . . . His intrigues to secure a renomination and the hopes he appears to entertain of a re-election are, however, the most laughable jokes of all."[21]

Boots

During the campaign Lincoln received a note from one zealous supporter: "Dear Old Abe—Yesterday I worked hard for you all day and wore out my boots. Please send a new pair by mail."[22]

Lincoln's Daughter

In 1860 Lincoln told the little girl who wanted him to grow whiskers, "I regret the necessity of saying I have no daughter." His enemies said this meant he had one he couldn't acknowledge. His wife, they added, knew about the illegitimate child and that was why she was so emotionally unstable. The spurious story about Lincoln's secret daughter played some part in the 1864 contest.[23]

Lincoln's Song

There were several versions of the story about Lincoln's frivolity on the battlefield, all of them given wide circulation by the Democrats during the 1864 campaign and all of them false. In September 1862, shortly after the battle of Antietam, according to the *New York World,* the *Chicago Times,* and other anti-Lincoln newspapers, the President was driving over the field in an ambulance with Marshal Ward Hill Lamon, General McClellan, and another officer, and observed heavy details of men engaged in burying the dead. When they reached an old stone bridge where the dead were piled the highest, Lincoln suddenly slapped Lamon on the knee and cried: "Come, Lamon, give us that song about 'Picayune Butler'; McClellan has never heard it." "Not now, if you please," McClellan, shuddering, is supposed to have replied. "I would prefer to hear it some other place and time." But Lincoln insisted and Lamon went ahead with the silly song, much to the President's delight. "It would have been indecorous to name Mr. Lincoln the buffoon that he is," proclaimed the *World,* "if he had been merely the Chief Magistrate. But the truth must be told when he is a *Chief Magistrate seeking re-election* . . . The American people are in no mood to re-elect a man to the highest office whose daily language is indecent, and who, riding over the field of Antietam, when thirty thousand of his fellow citizens were yet warm in their freshly-made graves, could slap Marshal Lamon on the knee, and call for the Negro song of 'Picayune Butler.' " "We know the story is incredible," exclaimed New Jersey's *Essex Statesman*, ready to believe anything bad about Lincoln. "The story can't be true of any man fit for any office of trust, or even for a decent society; but the story is every whit true of Abraham Lincoln."

The story was of course every whit untrue and Lamon begged Lincoln to issue a public denial. But Lincoln told Lamon to "let the thing alone." He explained: "If I have not established character enough to give the lie to this charge, I can only say that I am mistaken in my own estimate of myself. In politics, every man must skin his own skunk. These fellows are welcome to the hide of this one. Its body has already given forth its unsavory odor." Lamon went ahead anyway and wrote out a refutation and showed it to Lincoln. "Lamon," said Lincoln after reading it, "your 'explanation' is entirely too belligerent in tone for so grave a matter. There is a heap of 'cussedness' mixed up with your usual amiability, and you are at times too fond of a fight. If I were you, I would simply state the facts as they are. I would give the statement as you have here, without the pepper and salt. Let me try my hand at it." So Lincoln wrote out a statement making it clear that the incident took place sixteen days after Antietam, several miles from the battlefield, and that it was "a little sad song" (as Lamon put it) that Lincoln had requested. "You know, Hill," Lincoln told Lamon, "that this is the truth and the whole truth about that affair; but I dislike to appear as an apologist for an act of my own which I know was right. Keep this paper and we will see about it." But he never got around to making the statement public.[24]

President's Salary

During the campaign the *New York World*, the *Detroit Free Press*, the *Chicago Times*, and other anti-Lincoln newspapers reported that Lincoln drew his salary in gold while insisting that the soldiers be paid in greenbacks. "Abraham Lincoln's salary," went a typical news story, "is legally twenty-five thousand a year. But his legal-tender money, having depreciated to less than half its nominal value, he refuses to take, and demands and receives his pay in gold or gold certificates, while the soldiers of his army have to take their pay in greenbacks. Isn't this patriotic and honest in Old Abe, and ought not he to be re-elected to another four years' hard money for himself, and of largely depreciated money for the people?" The charge had become so widespread by October that F. E. Spinner, United States Treasurer, felt obliged to issue a statement. "The salary of the President," he announced, "is, in accordance with the law paid in warrant drafts on the Treasury of the United States for the amount, less the income tax, which have been sent him regularly monthly. Instead of drawing his money on these drafts, he has been in the habit of leaving it for a long time without interest. In one case all his salary so remained for eleven months. On several occasions I solicited the President to draw what was due him, urging that he was losing largely in interest on the amount due him. He asked me, 'Who gains my loss?' On my answering, 'The United States,' he replied, 'Then as it goes for the good of my country, let it remain. The Treasury needs it more than I do.' " Spinner revealed that by his neglect Lincoln "has lost at least four thousand dollars . . . which he has virtually given to the people of the United States." [25]

Fairly Glowed

During August some Republican leaders who sought to replace Lincoln with another candidate had their eyes on General Grant. When John Eaton, at Lincoln's request, was at Grant's headquarters conferring on military matters, he mentioned the desire of some Republicans to run him for President. At this, Grant pounded the arms of his chair with his fists and cried: "They can't do it! They can't compel me to do it!" When Eaton asked him whether he had told Lincoln that, Grant said he hadn't thought it worthwhile and added: "I consider it as important to the cause that he should be elected, as that the army should be successful in the field." When Eaton told Lincoln what Grant had said, the President "fairly glowed with satisfaction." [26]

Miscegenation

Late in 1863, an anonymous seventy-five-page pamphlet with a strange title appeared in New York City: *Miscegenation: The Theory of the Blending of the Races, Applied to the American White Man and Negro*. The word "miscegenation," meaning race-mixing, was new, but it caught on quickly. The other new word appearing in the pamphlet, "melaleukation," meaning union of white and black, didn't catch on, but that was what the pamphlet was really all about. The pamphlet heartily endorsed both miscegenation and melaleukation. Race-mixing, it declared, invigorated nations. American vitality came, "not from its Anglo-Saxon progenitors, but from all the different nationalities" mingling in the population. But melaleukation, said the pamphlet, would carry the American people to an even higher level of performance. "All that is needed to make us the finest race on earth is to engraft on our stock the negro element." The Republican party was the "party of miscegenation," Lincoln and the abolitionists favored it, and the war to preserve the Union was essentially "a war looking, as its final fruit, to the blending of white and black." The pamphlet contained a long section calling on the New York Irish to overcome their hostility to blacks and intermarry with them as Lincoln wished.

The miscegenation tract created a sensation. It soon appeared in other parts of the country, received extended notices in the daily, weekly, and monthly press, and ended by injecting the issue of miscegenation (formerly called amalgamation) into the campaign of 1864. In Congress, Ohio Democrat Samuel Sullivan Cox quoted from the pamphlet to prove that the Republican party was "moving steadily forward to perfect social equality of black and white" and to the "detestable doctrine of—Miscegenation!" The Democratic press gave generous space to Cox's speech and added strictures of its own to Cox's indictment. In editorials, cartoons, and verse, the Democrats hammered away at the issue, and at rallies people carried placards begging, "Fathers, Save Us from Negro Equality." Advised humorist Petroleum B. Nasby (David R. Locke): "Lern to spell and pronownce Missegenashun. It's a good word."

Leading abolitionists (all of whom received complimentary copies of *Miscegenation*) were a bit puzzled by the tract. Some of them pointed out that melaleukation had been going on for years on Southern plantations outside the bonds of holy matrimony. Others gave cautious assent to the idea of race-mingling. But most abolitionists asserted that while they didn't go out of their way to encourage racial intermarriage, they certainly believed that whites and blacks had a perfect right to intermarry if they so chose. Republican newspapers, however, insisted the pamphlet raised a phony issue and that emancipation did not mean miscegenation.

A few readers were suspicious; they wondered whether *Miscegenation* was a campaign trick. The *Independent,* a Protestant weekly friendly to Lincoln, thought the pamphlet might be "a PIECE OF PLEASANTRY," but it was almost alone in its doubts. The *Independent's* suspicions, however, turned out to be well-founded. On November 1, the *London Morning Herald,* a pro-Southern paper, carried a dispatch from its New York correspondent, with the headline, "THE GREAT HOAX OF THE DAY!" revealing that *Miscegenation* was the work of two New York journalists who wanted to trick the Republicans into making damaging admissions that would hurt them with the voters. Two weeks after the election the *New York World* corroborated the London's paper's exposé; it ran a long story about the "Miscegenation Hoax." But the *World* omitted one vital bit of information: that it was the *World's* managing editor, David Goodman Croly, and one of its reporters, George Wakeman, who had conceived the scheme and carried it into execution.[27]

A Little Longer

After the election, *Harper's Weekly* ran a cartoon showing an extraordinarily tall Lincoln with the caption: "Long Abraham Lincoln A Little Longer."[28]

★ ★

CHAPTER TWENTY-ONE

1868
Grant and Reconstruction

The main issue in 1868 was Reconstruction. Opinions on the subject were varied and violent. Abraham Lincoln wanted to restore the defeated Southern States to the Union as quickly and painlessly as possible and for his leniency won the distrust of Radical Republicans in Congress. After his assassination, his successor, Andrew Johnson, had a brief honeymoon with the Radicals; then there was an explosive falling-out. Johnson and the Radicals in Congress came to disagree bitterly on how the former Confederate states were to be handled.

Johnson thought the President should supervise Reconstruction, while the Radicals insisted that Congress manage it. Johnson favored fairly mild conditions for the readmission of the Southern states into the Union; the Radicals sponsored a harsh program involving military occupation of the South and the building up of the Republican party there with the help of the former slaves. Johnson was willing to extend limited rights to the ex-slaves, but the Radicals demanded full civil rights, including the suffrage, for the freedmen. During 1867 Johnson vetoed one Reconstruction act after another and Congress promptly overrode his vetoes by substantial majorities. In February 1868 the Radicals succeeded in mustering enough votes in the House of Representatives to impeach him for "high crimes and misdemeanors." But when the vote on the charges against him was taken in May, they failed by one vote to win the necessary two-thirds majority needed for conviction. "The country is going to the Devil!" stormed Pennsylvania's Radical Republican Thaddeus Stevens afterward.[1]

On May 20, while the passions aroused by the impeachment trial were still running high, the Republicans met in Chicago, nominated General Ulysses S. Grant (who "saved the Union") on the first ballot and then added the genial Schuyler Colfax of Indiana to the ticket. The Republican platform blistered the Johnson administration, praised Congressional Reconstruction, and called for "equal suffrage to all loyal men in the South," but left the matter of Negro suffrage "in all the loyal states" to the "people in those states." The Democrats, who met in New York on July 4, did a lot of balloting before finally picking Horatio Seymour, former Governor of New York, as their candidate. Seymour was so reluctant to receive the nomination he was called "the Great Decliner." But General Francis P. Blair, who received second place, gladly accepted the honor. He was eager to take to the stump and denounce the Radical Republicans. The Democratic platform condemned Congressional Reconstruction as "unconstitutional, revolutionary, and void," demanded the "immediate restoration of all the states to their rights in the Union under the Constitution," and asked for "the regulation of the elective franchise in the States by their citizens."[2]

The campaign, not surprisingly, centered on the Civil War and Reconstruction. "Scratch a Democrat," cried the *New York Tribune*, "and you'll find a rebel under his skin."[3] During the campaign the Republicans charged that Seymour (a Peace Democrat during the war) had been "a traitor to his government as far as he dared in the agony of rebellion."[4] They also said his health was wretched and there was a streak of insanity in his family. As for Blair, he was a "revolutionist" and a drunkard. His bill for two days in a Connecticut hotel came to ten dollars for room and board and sixty dollars for whiskey and lemons.[5]

The Democrats didn't think Grant, forty-six, precisely a model of sobriety. They referred to him as "Grant the Drunkard," described him as "a soaker behind the door and in the dark," but also claimed he was "drunk in the public streets since the first of January."[6] They also said he was a military despot, had an illegitimate daughter by an Indian woman, and was not overly bright. To the tune of "Captain Jinks of the Horse Marines," they sang:

> I am Captain Grant of the Black Marines
> The stupidest man that ever was seen.[7]

When they got sick of denigrating Grant, they blasted his party for championing Negro suffrage and trying to "Africanize" the South. But some Democrats sought the votes of blacks. In an editorial, "The Colored Voter: A Sober Appeal to His Interest and His Sober Reason," a writer for a Nashville newspaper told the former slaves they owed their freedom to the Democrats and should vote the Seymour-Blair ticket. His curious reasoning: "If your State and her sister Southern states had not seceded from the Union you would not today have been free. . . . If you are indebted to any party or power for your present liberty, you are indebted to the Southern people. . . . In view of these facts which of the two parties has the greatest claim on you for your support? The Democratic Party!"[8]

But most blacks voted Republican. And the black vote was probably crucial to the triumph of the Grant-Colfax ticket in November. Although Grant won 214 electoral votes to Seymour's 80 and carried 26 states to Seymour's 8, his popular majority was only about 310,000 (3,012,833 to 2,703,249). It is apparent that if he had not won the 450,000 to 500,000 votes cast by the freedmen in the Southern states under military occupation, he would not have won his popular majority. The Republicans were fully aware of their dependence on the black vote in 1868. After the election they decided to safeguard Negro suffrage. Within four months the Fifteenth Amendment, providing that the right to vote should not be denied or abridged on account of race, color, or previous condition of servitude, passed both houses of Congress and went to the states. And since the Republicans controlled the majority of state legislatures, three-fourths of the states ratified the amendment within a year.

☆ ☆ ☆

Let Us Have Peace

When a committee called on Grant to notify him of his nomination, he promised to have a letter of acceptance ready the next day. The following morning General Frederick T. Dent, Grant's brother-in-law, went to his office and asked if he had written the letter. "No," said Grant; "I'll do it now." He turned to his desk and commenced writing. When he finished the letter, he gave it to Dent to read. While Dent was reading it, General John A. Rawlins, a close friend, came in and Grant had him read it aloud. Rawlins liked it and told Grant, "All it wants now is your signature." Grant took his pen, wrote "Let us have peace," and signed his name. When Rawlins saw what Grant had added, he cried, "By ---! That clinches it!" Grant's addition became a campaign slogan.[9]

Deaf and Dumb

Before his nomination, Grant had never been interested in politics. The only time he had voted was in 1856, when he supported Buchanan, because "I knew Frémont." And when first asked to be a candidate he said, "I never aspired to but one office in my life. I should like to be mayor of Galena—to build a new sidewalk from my house to the depot." Soon, though, he became interested in the Presidency. But his politics were murky. In January 1868 the *New York Tribune* satirized his political views. "Well, General," the *Tribune* had a Republican ask the Civil War hero, "What do you think will be the effect of negro suffrage, fairly carried out?" And Grant replied: "Have you seen Marshal Brown's pups? They are the finest in the District." But Grant finally identified himself with the Radical Republicans and when Congressman Ben Wade heard about it he was so overjoyed that he threw his hat in the air, hit a chandelier, and broke one of the globes. Sneered the *New York World:* Grant was "at first shy, then he wavered; then he enveloped himself in a thick mystery—and, at last, he has changed his politics."

But while Seymour went on out on the stump, Grant absolutely refused either to campaign or release statements on the issues. Shortly after his nomination, he left Washington for Galena, Illinois, his hometown, and left the conduct of the campaign to his managers. A crowd surrounded him in Jersey City, when he was hurrying to catch a train. "What do you think of the present political prospect?" someone asked him. "I don't think of it at all right this time," returned Grant. "My principal object just now is to catch the train." Jeered a Democratic pamphlet entitled "The Lively Life of U. S. Grant, the Dummy Candidate": Grant "has nothing to say and keeps on saying it day in and day out." The Republicans might have "a deaf and dumb candidate," huffed the *New York World,* but the country couldn't afford "a deaf and dumb President."

But Grant's supporters were anything but deaf and dumb. They sponsored stump speakers everywhere, formed clubs called Tanners (Grant had once been a tanner) to see that the Democrats were properly "tanned," and organized torchlight parades of Union veterans known as Boys in Blue. Grant did take a trip to the West with Generals Sherman and Sheridan that came close to being a campaign tour, but he refused to make any speeches to the crowds that greeted him en route.[10]

Waving the Bloody Shirt

One night in March an Ohioan named A. P. Huggins, who was serving as tax collector and school superintendant in Mississippi, was awakened by some members of the Ku Klux Klan, ordered to leave the state in ten days, and then stripped, given seventy-five lashes, and threatened with death if he disobeyed their order. Huggins reported the incident to the military authorities and an army officer took his blood-stained nightshirt to Washington and gave it to Radical Republican Congressman Benjamin Butler of Massachusetts. A few days later, when Butler was proposing legislation permitting the President to use the army to enforce federal laws in the South, he waved Huggins's gory garment around as he spoke. From 1868 until the end of the century, during presidential contests Republican orators regularly "waved the bloody shirt," that is, blasted the South for starting the Civil War.[11]

★ ★

CHAPTER TWENTY-TWO

1872
Grant and the Liberal
Republicans

Ulysses S. Grant hadn't been President long before a new word entered the English language: "Grantism." It was not a compliment. It meant nepotism, the spoils system, and corruption in high office. Grant was personally honest, but he appointed so many friends and relatives to office that one Senator said the country was suffering from "a dropsical nepotism swollen to elephantiasis."[1] Grant's appointments to his Cabinet and to other positions in the federal government were also misguided; some of his appointees turned out to be hopelessly incompetent and others shockingly corrupt. "It looks at this distance as though the Republican party were going to the dogs . . . ," complained Senator James Grimes of Iowa. "Like all parties that have an undisturbed power for a long time, it has become corrupt, and I believe that it is today the [most] corrupt and debauched political party that has ever existed."[2]

As early as 1870 some of the Republican party's most distinguished members had become disaffected with Grant's administration and were hoping to dump him and his policies in 1872. Calling themselves Liberal Republicans, the reformers in Grant's party demanded a thorough reform of the civil service; they also urged ending Radical Reconstruction and withdrawing all federal troops from the South. Some of them, too, favored a reduction in the high tariff that had lingered from the Civil War. The Liberal Republicans were a varied group. Among them were Charles Francis Adams, Lincoln's minister to England, Carl Schurz, U.S. Senator from Missouri, Salmon P. Chase, Chief Justice of the Supreme Court, and Horace Greeley, celebrated editor of the *New York Tribune*. In January 1872, Missouri liberals led by Carl Schurz held a meeting in Jefferson City, called for an "uprising of honest citizens" against the spoils system, and scheduled a national convention for May 1 in Cincinnati.[3]

The Cincinnati conclave was crowded and clamorous. "A livelier and more variegated omnium gatherum was never assembled," reported the *Louisville Courier-Journal*'s editor Henry Watterson. "There were long-haired and spectacled doctrinaires from New England, spiced by stumpy and short-haired emissaries from New York. . . . There were brisk Westerners from Chicago and St. Louis. . . . There were a few rather overdressed persons from New Orleans . . . and a motley array of Southerners of every sort."[4] The platform, shaped by Schurz, denounced the "notoriously corrupt and unworthy men in places of power" and asked for civil-service reform. It also called for an end to military reconstruction, while endorsing "equal and exact justice for all, of whatever nativity, race, color, or persuasion, religious or political." Since the new party contained both protectionists and free traders, the platform left the tariff question "to the people in their congressional districts and the decision of Congress thereon."[5] There were several excellent choices (including Adams and Chase) for the presidential nomination, but for various reasons, including personal and political jealousies, none of them was able to win a majority of the delegates' votes. On the sixth ballot the convention suddenly stampeded to Horace Greeley; and then chose Governor Benjamin Gratz-Brown of Missouri for second place.

The Greeley choice came as a shock to many people. Greeley, for all his intelligence, sincerity, idealism, and journalistic aplomb, was erratic, crochety, unpredictable, and thoroughly incompetent in the art of politics. About all one could say of him as a candidate was that he was a national celebrity. With his cherubic face, big blue eyes, pilgarlic pate, steel-rimmed glasses, and shuffling gait, he looked more like a character out of a Dickens novel than a presidential hopeful, and he was an easy target for cartoonists and caricaturists. Serious reformers were thunderstruck by the nomination. The *Nation* said it was the biggest disappointment since news of the first battle of Bull Run; Lyman Trumbull feared the nomination would be drowned in a wave of laughter; the *Illinois State Journal* called it a huge joke on the nation; and the *New York Times* declared that if "any one man could send a great nation to the dogs, that man is Mr. Greeley."[6] One reporter thought there had been "too much brains and not enough whiskey" at the Cincinnati convention.[7]

A month after the Greeley nomination, the regular Republicans met in Philadelphia, chose Grant by acclamation for re-election on the first ballot, and adopted a platform paying lip service to civil-service reform and equivocating on the tariff issue, but taking a strong stand in favor of political and civil rights for all citizens in every part of the country. For second place the delegates chose Massachusetts Senator Henry Wilson, "the cobbler of Natick," who was friendly to labor.

When the Democrats held their convention in Baltimore a few weeks later, they were so eager to support "anybody to beat Grant," that in a meeting lasting only six hours they voted to accept both the platform and the candidate of the Liberal Republicans. Some Democrats thought it a grievous error. The choice between Grant and Greeley, moaned Georgia's Alexander Stephens, was a choice between "hemlock and strychnine."[8] Greeley had castigated the Democratic party for years, complained an Indiana Congressman; for the Democrats to support him was like having "the disciples of the Christian religion" abandon their faith to "worship Mahomet as the prophet of God.[9] But the Governor of North Carolina defended fusion. "If the Baltimore Convention puts Greeley in our hymnbook," he said, "we will sing him through if it kills us."[10]

Given the two candidates—a "man of no ideas," as someone put it, versus a "man of too many"—the campaign was predictable.[11] It reduced itself to what the *New York Sun* called "a shower of mud."[12] Republican derision of Greeley—who at one time or another had favored vegetarianism, abolitionism, brown bread, free-thinking, socialism, and spiritualism—was biting and cruel. In *Harper's Weekly*, cartoonist Thomas Nast (who created the elephant as the Republican gonfalen) had a field day with "Honest Old Horace." Picturing the *Tribune* editor as a hopelessly near-sighted and pumpkin-headed clown, he did a savage take-off on Greeley's pamphlet, "What I Know About Farming," in a series of cartoons labeled, "What I Know About Stooping To Conquer," "What I Know About Honesty" (shaking hands with Tammany Boss Tweed), "What I Know About Bailing Out" (a reference to the bail Greeley had helped provide for Jefferson Davis in 1867), "What I Know About Eating My Own Words," "What I Know About Bolting," and "What I Know About Running for the Presidency." In a savage ridicule of Greeley's appeal in his acceptance letter for North and South to "clasp their hands across the bloody chasm," Nast showed Greeley shaking hands with a rebel who had just shot a Union soldier, stretching out his hand to John Wilkes Booth across Lincoln's grave, and turning a defenseless black over to a member of the Ku Klux Klan who has just lynched a black man and knifed a black mother and her child. "I have been assailed so bitterly," wailed Greeley at the end of the campaign, "that I hardly knew whether I was running for the Presidency or the penitentiary."[13] But he hit the road in September (though it was still considered unseemly for presidential candidates to take to the stump) and in a series of impromptu speeches denounced the Republicans for "waving the bloody shirt" and called for a "New Departure," involving conciliation in the Northern treatment of the South. Some observers, previously hostile, were impressed with Greeley's oratory. "THE VOICE OF A STATESMAN," reluctantly conceded the *New York Sun*. "Magnificent Speeches of Dr. Horace Greeley."[14] Others thought Uncle Horace would have done better to keep quiet like Grant. In the politically inept remarks he made from time to time he managed to antagonize both veterans and black voters.

Grant of course received his share of the campaign abuse. All the old charges of 1868 were revived and he was attacked as a crook, drunkard, ignoramus, dictator, swindler, and "utterly depraved horse jockey." But with Greeley in the running, he was unbeatable. With the support of Northern businessmen and bankers, Republican regulars, Union veterans, and blacks (and with the help of Democratic abstainers), Grant won an easy victory in November. He carried 31 states (all but six), took 286 of the 349 electoral votes, and won a popular majority of 763,000 votes over Greeley (3,597,132 to 2,834,125). "I was the worst beaten man who ever ran for high office," said Greeley ruefully after the election.[15] This was an overstatement; he did better than Seymour had done in 1868 and about as well as Clay in 1832, Harrison in 1836, and Van Buren in 1840. But the denouement was dolorous. Shortly before the election his wife died and he confessed to a friend: "I am not dead, but I wish I were." Right after the election he wrote: "Utterly ruined beyond hope, I desire, before the night closes its jaws on me forever, to say that, though my running for President has placed me where I am, it is not the cause of my ruin."[16] Shortly afterwards he was placed in a private sanitorium for mental patients and died there three weeks later. At the electoral counting in February, the Democratic electors gave Greeley's votes to Gartz-Brown and several other Democrats.

☆   ☆   ☆

What's He Doing Here?

Despite "Grantism," the popularity of the Hero of Appomattox was still so great that when one delegate at the Republican convention heard that another delegate wasn't for Grant, he cried in astonishment: "What's he doing here?"[17]

Sing the Tune

Though the Democrats voted to endorse Greeley for President, it was a difficult decision. North Carolina's Robert Vance expressed the feelings of most Democrats when he told the story of an old preacher in whose hymn book a mischievous lad had pasted the song, "Old Grimes is dead, that good old man, we ne'er shall see him more." The preacher, said Vance, opened the book the next day in church, and his eye fell on this "hymn." He blinked, took off his glasses, polished them, read and blinked again, and then said: "Brethren, I have been singing out of this book for forty years; I have never recognized this as a hymn before, but it's here, and I ain't agwine to go back on my book now; so please raise the tune, and we'll sing it through if it kills us!"[18]

Stanley and Livingstone

One humorist said Greeley's nomination even astonished Dr. Livingstone when he returned from five years' isolation in the interior of Africa after his rescue by Henry M. Stanley. Stanley, he said, was filling him in on news of world developments during his absence—the Austro-Prussian War, the execution of Maximilian in Mexico, the Franco-German War, the downfall of Napoleon III, and the rise of the German Empire—and finally mentioned that the Democratic party in the United States had nominated Greeley for President. "Hold on," Livingston broke in instantly. "You have told me stupendous things, and with a confiding simplicity I was swallowing them peacefully down; but there is a limit to all things, and when you tell me that Horace Greeley is become a Democratic candidate I will be hanged if I believe it." [19]

Capital Beaten Candidate

During the campaign Greeley remarked drily: "While there are doubts as to my fitness for president, nobody seems to deny that I would make a capital beaten candidate." [20]

United States vs. Susan B. Anthony

Susan B. Anthony, celebrated suffragette, attended all three conventions—Liberal Republican, Republican, and Democratic—but only the Republicans agreed to include a reference to their "obligations to the loyal women of America" in their platform. It was the first woman's plank in a national platform, and although only a "splinter," Anthony decided to support Grant for President and go out on the stump for the Republican ticket—and for woman suffrage. She also decided to vote, along with several other women, on election day. The Fourteenth Amendment, she told inspectors when registering to vote, guaranteed equal rights for all citizens and that included women and their right to vote.

On November 5 Anthony voted in Rochester, New York. On November 18 she was arrested. She insisted on handcuffs, but the embarrassed marshal declined; she also refused to pay bail, but her lawyer (without consulting her) chivalrously went on her bond. The case of *United States vs. Susan B. Anthony* might have been a landmark had it reached the United States Supreme Court, as Anthony and her lawyers wished. Instead, her trial in a Circuit Court in June 1873 was a farce. Associate Supreme Court Justice Ward Hunt refused to let Anthony testify, permitted testimony she had given after her arrest to be admitted into the record, delivered an opinion he had written before the trial, directed the jury to deliver a verdict of guilty, and refused to let the jury be polled. "Has the prisoner anything to say why sentence shall not be pronounced?" he asked after refusing a motion for a new trial. The prisoner did; she lectured him at length, despite repeated orders to sit down, on his violation of her rights. The judge then fined her $100 and the costs of the prosecution. "May it please your honor," said Anthony firmly, "I will never pay a dollar of your unjust penalty." She never did. The government was glad to drop the case.[21]

★ ★

1876
The Hayes-Tilden Disputed
Election

1876 was America's centennial year. To celebrate one hundred years of national independence the American people flocked to Philadelphia's Centennial Exposition from May to November, staged numerous parties, balls, and tableaux, and purchased untold quantities of centennial buckwheat cakes, soda pop, coffee, cigars, matches, hats, and scarves. They also held the longest, bitterest, and most controversial presidential election in American history. By the end of the year people were wondering whether the election dispute would produce another civil war. There was a fervent centennial prayer: "God save the republic!"[1]

For centennial candidates the Republicans and Democrats both picked governors with reputations for honesty and integrity. The "Old Man," as Grant was called, wanted a third term, but the stench of "Grantism" was still so strong that most Republican wheelhorses categorically ruled him out. James G. Blaine, the "Magnetic Statesman" from Maine, also badly wanted to run, but unsavory connections with the Little Rock and Fort Smith Railroad made him an embarassment to the party too. In the end, the Republicans, meeting in Cincinnati in mid-June, turned to Rutherford B. Hayes, fifty-three, Ohio Governor friendly to civil-service reform, on the seventh ballot, picked New York Congressman William A. Wheeler to go with him, and put together a platform decrying the spoils system and holding public officials "to a rigid responsibility."[2]

The Democrats, meeting in St. Louis late in June, had an obvious choice: Samuel J. Tilden of New York. As District Attorney, Tilden had sent Boss William Tweed and his cronies to jail; and as Governor he had smashed the crooked Canal Ring. Though not every Democrat liked him, they all realized that a "reform campaign without Tilden would be like the play of *Hamlet* with Hamlet left out."[3] The convention nominated him for President on the first ballot, chose Thomas A. Hendricks of Indiana as their vice-presidential nominee, and adopted a platform calling for the end of Reconstruction, civil service reform, and the installation of "honest men" in government.

Hayes and Tilden agreed on major issues: hard money, withdrawing federal troops from the South, and civil-service reform. The Republicans cried, "Hurrah! For Hayes and Honest Ways!" and the Democrats chanted, "Tilden and Reform!" But despite the similarities of the candidates the campaign was acrimonious and at times unseemly. The Democrats had an embarrassment of riches to exploit during the campaign: the scandals of the Grant administration, the hard times following the Panic of 1873, and revelations of corruption in the carpetbag governments remaining in the South. But the Republicans could still count on the Civil War issue; their view was that "not every Democrat was a Rebel, but every Rebel was a Democrat."[4] As freethinker Robert G. Ingersoll, stumping the country for Hayes, put it in what Republicans called the greatest speech of the campaign: "Every man that endeavored to tear the old flag from the heavens that it enriches was a Democrat. Every man that tried to destroy this nation was a Democrat. . . . The man that assassinated Abraham Lincoln was a Democrat. . . . Soldiers, every scar you have on your heroic bodies was given you by a Democrat!"[5]

Republican orators assaulted Tilden with fury. They accused him of evading taxes, praising slavery, making millions as attorney for robber barons like Jim Fisk, coddling corruptionists in New York City's Tammany Hall, and planning to pay off the Confederate debt if he became President. But the Democrats thought up some lies too: that Hayes stole the pay of dead soldiers in his Civil War regiment, cheated Ohio out of vast sums of money while Governor, and shot his mother "in a fit of insanity." Tilden disapproved of smear tactics in political campaigns, but his high-mindedness did him no good. Before the campaign was over he had been called a thief, liar, drunkard, syphilitic, and swindler. The nicknames were nasty: Slippery Sammy, Soapy Sam, Ananias Tilden. One campaign book dismissed him as a criminal, a disgrace to New York State, and "a menace to the United States."[6]

When the mud-slinging ended and the voters registered their choices on November 7, it looked as though Tilden had won. Acknowledged the devoutly Republican *Indianapolis Journal* sorrowfully the following morning: "With the result before us at this writing we see no escape from the conclusion that Tilden and Hendricks are elected. . . . The announcement will carry pain to every loyal heart in the nation, but the inevitable truth may as well be stated."[7] Tilden received a quarter of a million more popular votes than Hayes (about 4,300,000 to 4,036,000) and 184 electoral votes to Hayes's 165, only one short of victory. Twenty electoral votes (South Carolina's 7, Louisiana's 8, Florida's 4, and one of Oregon's 3) were in doubt; Tilden needed only one of them to win while Hayes needed all twenty.

Tilden was sure he had won, and Hayes himself retired election night thinking he had lost. Then Zachariah Chandler, chairman of the Republican national committee, and some of his associates in New York went into action. Not only did they claim Oregon's three votes; they also resolved to secure the votes of South Carolina, Louisiana, and Florida, still under carpetbag rule, for Hayes. To Republican officials in the three carpetbag states they sent telegrams telling them, "Hayes is elected if we have carried South Carolina, Florida, and Louisiana," and asking, "Can you hold your state? Answer at once." The following afternoon Chandler made an audacious public statement: "Hayes has 185 electoral votes and is elected." Soon "visiting statesmen" representing both parties were headed southward to look into the situation. On November 10 President Grant sent more troops into the three states "to preserve peace and good order, and to see that the proper and legal Boards of Canvasses are unmolested in the performance of their duties."[8]

The struggle over the twenty disputed electoral votes lasted from November 8, 1876, until March 2, 1877, and at times threatened to end in violence. Only one of the disputed votes—Oregon's—was clearly Hayes's. In Oregon, a majority of the people had voted Republican; but one of the three electors, J. W. Watts, was declared ineligible because he was a postmaster and the U. S. Constitution forbids federal office-holders from serving as electors. At the prompting of Abram Hewitt, chairman of the Democratic national committee, Oregon's Democratic Governor replaced Watts with a Democrat and sent one Tilden and two Hayes votes to Washington. Meanwhile Watts resigned his job, met with the other Republican electors, and the three of them forwarded three Hayes votes to the national capital. Hewitt admitted that Hayes deserved all three votes; but the Democrats had to claim one of them, he explained, to "offset the palpable frauds" going on in Louisiana, Florida, and South Carolina.[9]

Hewitt was right about the frauds. In all three Southern states the voting had been accompanied by bribery, forgery, violence, intimidation, and ballot-box stuffing. Democrats "bulldozed" or intimidated black voters to keep them away from the polls; Republican officials, backed by federal troops, saw to it that as many blacks as possible voted, sometimes more than once. It is difficult to say who would have won in a free and fair election; but it is probably safe to conclude that the Republicans won a majority in South Carolina and that the Democrats carried both Louisiana and Florida. Soon after the election, agents of both parties, with promises to make and money to spend, appeared on the scene to press their claims. The upshot: two sets of returns, one for Hayes and one for Tilden, were sent to Washington from Louisiana and

South Carolina, and three sets (two for Tilden and one for Hayes) came in from Florida.

It was now up to Congress to decide which sets of returns from the four disputed states were valid. The Constitution states that "the president of the Senate shall, in the presence of the Senate and the House of Representatives, open all certificates, and the votes shall then be counted," but does not outline procedures in case of conflicting returns from any state. The House of Representatives, with a Democratic majority since 1874, balked at letting the president of the Senate, controlled by the Republicans, make the decisions; but the Republican Senate was equally opposed to throwing the final decision about the election into the Democratic House of Representatives. After weeks of acrimonious debate, the two houses finally agreed to set up an Electoral Commission to decide which candidate had won the disputed votes. The Commission was composed of five Senators, five Representatives, and five Supreme Court justices; seven of them were Republicans and seven Democrats. The fifteenth member was to be Justice David Davis, regarded as an independent, but at the last minute he was elected to the U. S. Senate by the Illinois legislature and became ineligible. Justice Joseph Bradley took his place; though a Republican, he was expected to maintain some semblance of nonpartisanship. But he didn't; he ended up voting with his Republican colleagues on every crucial issue. The result was that by a vote of eight to seven, the Electoral Commission awarded all the disputed electoral votes to Hayes, giving him 185 votes to Tilden's 184, and making him President.

Many Democrats, especially in the North, were outraged by the work of the Electoral Commission. The *Cincinnati Enquirer* called it "the monster fraud of the century," the *New York Sun* put black borders on its pages to mourn the demise of democracy, and a Washington paper even suggested doing away with Hayes. "Fraud has triumphed, and triumphed through the treachery of Democrats," cried the *Washington Union,* a Tilden campaign paper. "Honest men or irresolute nature and dull perceptions have assisted, but corruption led the way." [10] In the House of Representatives the Democrats passed a resolution over Republican opposition proclaiming that Tilden had been "duly elected President of the United States"; and in eleven states Democrats began organizing "Tilden-Hendricks Minute-Men" clubs, arming themselves with rifles, and shouting, "On to Washington!" and "Tilden or blood!" [11]

Tilden did not encourage resistance to the Electoral Commission's decision; and Southern Democrats remained on the whole conciliatory. Southern whites knew that Hayes was friendly to them and that in his letter accepting the Republican nomination he had recommended ending military reconstruction. Who knows? Perhaps Southern businessmen, many of them former Whigs, could get more out of a Republican President than out of Tilden, a pennypincher, whose slogan was "Retrenchment and Reform." At a series of secret meetings while the Electoral Commission was still at work, Southern Democratic leaders reached a compromise with Northern Republicans: they agreed to accept the decision of the Electoral Commission in return for pledges that Hayes would pull federal troops out of Louisiana and South Carolina (the two remaining Republican carpetbag governments), appoint at least one Southerner to his Cabinet, and support federal aid to education and internal improvements for the South. The Compromise of 1877, as the informal understanding came to be called, killed all suggestions for a filibuster by the Democrats in Congress and ended the crisis. On the morning of March 2, Senator Thomas W. Ferry of Michigan, the president of the Senate (Vice-President Henry Wilson had died), made the announcement: "Rutherford B. Hayes, having received the majority of the whole number of electoral votes, is duly elected President of the United States for four years commencing on the 4th of March, 1877." [12]

Not all Democrats were reconciled. Some of them contemptuously dismissed Hayes as "Rutherfraud Hayes," "the Fraudulent President," the "Usurper," "the Boss Thief," and "Old 8 to 7." Tilden himself acquiesced in the decision for Hayes, but to the end of his life believed he had been the real winner. In the spring of 1878 the House of Representatives launched an investigation of the election which brought to light flagrant instances of Republican bribery in the South; but revelations that Tilden men had also made bribe offers blunted the committee's findings to some extent.

Meanwhile Hayes buried the bloody shirt: withdrew the last of the federal troops from the South, appointed David M. Key, a Tennessee Democrat, as Postmaster General, appointed many Southern Democrats to local offices, and approved so many appropriations for internal improvements in the South that Northern Republicans began complaining. He was, exulted some Democrats, "the greatest Southerner of the day." [13] Reconstruction came to an end with Hayes. So did federal concern for black civil rights. "The Negro will disappear from the field of national politics," predicted the *Nation*. "Henceforth the nation, as a nation, will have nothing more to do with him." [14]

☆ ☆ ☆

The Plumed Knight

When 1876 opened it looked as though James G. Blaine, the popular Congressman from Maine, had the Republican nomination in the bag. Then his reputation came suddenly under a cloud. As Speaker of the House back in 1869, it was revealed, he had killed a bill that would have deprived an Arkansas railroad of a federal land grant and shortly thereafter received a nice commission from Warren Fisher, Jr., a Boston railroad broker, for handling the railroad's securities. The railroad eventually went bankrupt; but the Union Pacific Railroad had then obligingly stepped in to help Blaine out of his financial difficulties. It was all very curious. Was Blaine behaving the way a Congressman should? Newspapers began demanding a full accounting.

Blaine stoutly denied any wrongdoing. On April 27 he made a speech in the House defending his railroad transactions; his "whole connection" with the Arkansas road, he insisted, had been as "open as the day." But on May 2, a House committee began an investigation; and about this time James Mulligan, a former bookkeeper in Fisher's office, turned up in town with incriminating letters about Blaine's relations with various railroads. Blaine asked to borrow the letters; and when Mulligan, with almost unbelievable naïveté, agreed to hand them over, Blaine firmly refused to return them. Instead, on June 5, he rose dramatically in the House, with the package of letters in his hand, and cried: "I am not afraid to show the letters. Thank God Almighty I am not ashamed to show them." He then held them high. "There is the original package," he announced. "And with some sense of humiliation, with a mortification that I do not pretend to conceal, with a sense of outrage which I think any man in my position would feel, I invite the confidence of 44,000,000 of my countrymen while I read those letters from this desk." He proceeded to read selected extracts from the letters, adding explanatory comments as he went along, and succeeded in convincing the investigating committee that he was above suspicion. "When I think—," he told intimates, "when I think—that there lives in this broad land one single human being who doubts my integrity, I would rather have stayed—" and he let his arm fall, quite overcome with emotion. The following Sunday he fainted on the steps of his church and was taken home unconscious. But he recovered quickly and when the Republican convention opened a few days later he sent his friends there a dispatch announcing he was "entirely convalescent, suffering only from physical weakness."

The "Mulligan letters" probably killed Blaine's chance at nomination. Still, spellbinder Robert G. Ingersoll tossed Blaine's name into the nominating hopper anyway, in what is regarded as one of the greatest nominating speeches of all times. "Like an armed warrior," cried Ingersoll, "like a plumed knight, James G. Blaine marched down the halls of the American Congress and threw his shining lance full and fair against the brazen forehead of every traitor to his country and every maligner of his fair reputation." Ingersoll's description of Blaine as a "Plumed Knight" (which became a nickname) evoked such an enthusiastic response that it looked as though Blaine would win the nomination after all. But Ingersoll's stirring speech was followed by a seconding speech by a Georgia delegate that was so inept it produced laughter, jeers, and cries of "Time! Time! You've said enough!" "Lord bless you," said the Georgian good-naturedly, "I'se got a dozen good points I could make yet." Several other nominations, including Hayes's, followed; and then there was a motion to adjourn. But Blaine's supporters, anxious to ballot while Blaine feeling was still running high, howled it down. By this time it was dark and a Maine delegate asked if the convention hall could be lighted. "I desire to say, for the information of the convention," announced the chairman (no Blaine man, he), "that I am informed that the gas lights of this hall are in such condition that they cannot safely be lighted." A motion to adjourn then carried and Blaine's opponents now had another day to work against him.

Blaine's friends blamed the sudden adjournment for their man's eventual defeat. But probably Mulligan had already done him in. Blaine may have been a "Plumed Knight" to his supporters, but to Thomas Nast (who did a cartoon showing him disrobed and his body covered with tattooed references to various railroad deals) and others he was the "Tattooed Man." [15]

Mark Twain and Hayes

Mark Twain gave Hayes his warm support. Asked to give advice for a Tilden flag-raising, he wrote simply: "Do not raise the flag." At a Republican rally in Hartford, Connecticut, he explained that he was supporting Hayes because he thought there was a chance for civil-service reform if he became President. "Our . . . system, born of General Jackson and the Democratic Party," said the humorist, "is so idiotic, so contemptible, so grotesque, that it would make the very savages of Dahomey jeer and the very gods of solemnity laugh. We will not hire a school teacher who does not know the alphabet. We will not have a man about us in our business life in any walk of it, low or high, unless he has served an apprenticeship and can prove that he is capable of doing the work he offers to do. We even require a plumber to know something *(laughter, and a pause by the speaker)* about his business *(renewed laughter)*, that he shall at least know which side of a pipe is the inside *(roar of laughter)*. But when you come to our civil service we serenely fill great numbers of our minor public offices with ignoramuses. We put the vast business of a Custom-House in the hands of a flathead who does not know a bill of lading from a transit of Venus *(laughter and a pause)* never having heard of them before *(laughter)*. Under a treasury appointment we put oceans of money and accompanying statistics through the hand and brain of an ignorant villager who never before could wrestle with a two weeks wash bill without getting thrown *(great laughter)*. Under our consular system we send creatures all over the world who speak no language but their own, and even when it comes to that, go wading all their days through floods of moods and tenses and flourishing the scalps of mutilated parts of speech. . . ." [16]

Please Remit

The Republicans had more money to spend on campaigning than the
Democrats. Businessmen gave freely to their campaign chest. And Republican officeholders also did their part. Zachariah Chandler, chairman of the Republican national committee, saw to that. He authorized
the sending out of letters to Republican appointees reminding them of
their responsibilities. "Our books," went a typical letter, "show that you
have paid no heed to either of the requests of the committee for funds.
. . . We look to you as one of the Federal beneficiaries to help bear the
burden. Two per cent of your salary is——. Please remit promptly. At
the close of the campaign we shall place a list of those who have not
paid in the hands of the head of the department you are in."[17]

Bradley's Choice

Supreme Court Justice Joseph Bradley was the swing man on the Electoral Commission; he could go either way. The night before the decision on Florida, John G. Stevens, a good Democrat, visited Bradley and
the latter read him the opinion he had just written. As Stevens told
Abram Hewitt shortly afterwards, Bradley intended to uphold the Tilden electors, and, with Florida's votes, Tilden would become President.
But the following day, when the Electoral Commission voted, Bradley
upheld the Republicans in Florida. Stevens and Hewitt were astonished. Sometime "between midnight and sunrise," they decided, Bradley had changed his mind. There were rumors of bribery. "During the
whole of that night," reported the *New York Sun*, "Judge Bradley's house
in Washington was surrounded by the carriages of visitors who came to
see him apparently about the decision of the Electoral Commission. . . .
These visitors included leading Republicans. . . ."

Bradley hotly denied any improper influence. "The whole thing is a
falsehood . . . ," he maintained. "I had no private discussions whatever on the subject at issue with any persons on the Republican side,
and but very few words with any person." As to the opinion he had
read Stevens, Bradley explained: "Whether I wrote one opinion, or
twenty, in my private examination of the subject is of little consequence, and of no concern to anybody." He added that he "wrote and
rewrote the arguments and considerations on both sides . . . sometimes being inclined to one view of the subject, and sometimes to the
other" before making his final decision. Bradley wasn't being entirely
candid. Republican Senator Frederick T. Frelinghuysen of New Jersey
and Secretary of Navy George M. Robeson had dropped by to see him
shortly after Stevens left. And, joined by Mrs. Bradley, they had tried
to persuade him that a Democratic victory would be a disaster for the
nation.

Bradley's Florida vote produced threats on his life and his house had to be placed under guard. Many Democrats were inclined to agree with Senator Lewis V. Bogy of Missouri: "The name of the man who changed his vote upon that commission . . . from Tilden to Hayes, Justice Bradley, will go down to after ages covered with equal shame and disgrace. . . . Never will [his name] be pronounced without a hiss from all good men in this country."[18]

Threats

During the electoral crisis Hayes received many threats on his life. One anonymous letter told him to remember what had happened to Lincoln. One evening, when he was dining with his family, someone fired a bullet through the parlor window which passed through two rooms and lodged itself in the library wall. After that Webb Hayes carried a revolver with him when he accompanied his father on evening strolls. But there were no more incidents.[19]

Undone

After the Electoral Commission picked Hayes as President, Thomas Nast did a cartoon showing the battered and bandaged Republican elephant quoting Pyrrhus: "Another such victory and I am undone."[20]

Unanimous Consent

When Hayes left the White House on March 4, 1881, some people joked: "Mr. Hayes came in by a majority of one and goes out by unanimous consent."[21]

Would Have

During the election crisis, Kentucky Democrat Henry Watterson urged that "a hundred thousand petitioners" and "ten thousand unarmed Kentuckians" go to Washington to see that justice was done. Years later, when he was sitting next to Grant at a dinner party, Watterson told him, "I have a bone to pick with you." "Well, what is it?" asked Grant. "You remember in 1876," said Watterson, "when it was said I was coming to Washington at the head of a regiment, and you said you would hang me if I came." "Oh, no," cried Grant, "I never said that." "I am glad to hear it," smiled Watterson. "I like you better than ever." "But," added Grant drily, "I would, if you had come."[22]

CHAPTER TWENTY-FOUR

★ ★

1880
The Triumph of
"Boatman Jim" Garfield

America's quadrennial contest in 1880 was thoroughly dull. At one point the *New York World* gave more space to the arrival of the "divine Sarah Bernhardt" in America than to the presidential campaign. It was almost as if the United States was trying to compensate for the searing crisis of 1876. Party zealots, to be sure, threw brickbats, slung mud, and rolled in gutters during the campaign, but their invective was for the most part uninspired. And the contesting parties adopted barely indistinguishable platforms, nominated commonplace candidates, and ignored the serious social and economic issues facing the rapidly industrializing nation. At the height of the campaign the golden-tongued freethinker Robert Ingersoll could think of nothing better to say for his beloved Republican party than this: "I believe in a party that believes in good crops; that is glad when a fellow finds a gold mine; that rejoices when there are forty bushels of wheat to the acre. . . . The Democratic Party is a party of famine; it is a good friend of an early frost; it believes in the Colorado beetle and the weevil."[1]

It was Ohio Congressman James A. Garfield, forty-eight, a dark horse, for the Republicans on the thirty-sixth ballot, with Chester A. Arthur, "gentleman boss" from New York City, in second place. This time the Democrats decided to try with a Civil War hero: on the second ballot they picked General Winfield Scott Hancock (after Gettysburg, McClellan had exclaimed, "Hancock was superb"), who knew little about public issues but had been a fair-minded military governor of Texas and Louisiana in 1868. For his running mate they chose William H. English, wealthy Indiana banker, mindful of his money as well as his state's electoral votes. Both parties endorsed civil-service reform, opposed government aid to parochial schools, and objected to Chinese immigration. It remained for the little Greenback-Labor party, which ran General James B. Weaver of Iowa, to make serious proposals for bettering

America's industrial order: a graduated income tax, curtailment of child labor, an eight-hour work day, the regulation of interstate commerce, and a sanitary code for industry.

At the beginning of the campaign the Republicans brought out the bloody shirt again and the Democrats raised a clamor about the "great fraud" of 1876; but these issues soon palled. The campaign then shifted to personalities. The Republicans stressed Garfield's log-cabin birth, his work on the Ohio canal as a boy ("Boatman Jim"), and his rise to eminence in Congress by sobriety and diligence. They also organized Towpath Clubs and arranged for one delegation after another—young people, businessmen, German-Americans, ladies—to call at his home in Mentor, Ohio, and hear his short inspirational talks. A Republican campaign book was filled with Garfield homilies: "Things don't turn up in this world until somebody turns them up"; "If the power to do hard work is not talent, it is the best substitute for it"; "Nine times out of ten the best thing that can happen to a young man is to be tossed overboard and compelled to sink or swim for himself"; "A pound of pluck is worth a ton of luck."[2]

While boosting Garfield the Republicans belittled Hancock. They said his son married a rebel sympathizer, called him a coward (though Grant had praised him during the Civil War), and, in a pamphlet entitled, "A Record of the Statesmanship and Political Achievements of General Winfield Scott Hancock . . . Compiled from the Records," presented readers with seven blank pages. One of Hancock's remarks—"the tariff is a local issue"—evoked large guffaws. Though tariff bills are, in fact, the product of pressures by local interests, *Harper's Weekly* called Hancock's statement "loose, aimless, unintelligent, absurd," and the *Nation* exclaimed: "The General's talk about the tariff is that of a man who knows nothing about it, and who apparently, until he began to talk had never thought about it." In *Harper's,* Thomas Nast pictured the bewildered General on a speaker's platform whispering in someone's ear: "WHO IS TARIFF, AND WHY IS HE FOR REVENUE ONLY?"[3]

But the Democrats had the corruption issue to exploit. Back in 1868 Garfield had received $329 from Credit Mobilier, the Union Pacific Railroad's corrupt holding company, and though he insisted it was a loan, not a bribe, which he had paid off, the Democrats cited it as evidence of corruption and went around chalking the figures, 329, on buildings, sidewalks, doors, and fences (and even, someone averred, "on underclothing and the inside of shoes"). They also reminded voters that as chairman of the House Appropriations Committee he had presented a brief for a pavement contract in Washington and received $5000 for his services. And they made a great deal of the fact that Garfield's running mate, Chester Arthur, was such a notorious spoilsman as head of the New York Custom House that President Hayes had removed him from office.[4]

Democratic efforts were in vain. A fake letter circulated in October associating Garfield with importing cheap labor from China hurt him in California but did not prevent his victory elsewhere. On election day he carried all the Northern and Western states except New Jersey and Nevada and his electoral victory was stunning: 214 to 155. But his popular victory was narrow: 4,454,416 votes to Hancock's 4,444,952, a majority of less than 10,000 out of nine million. Though the campaign was lacklustre the voter turnout was impressive: 78.4 percent of the eligible voters. The return of prosperity after the depression of 1873–79 helped Garfield and so did his party's superb organization and fat campaign chest.

Garfield was not President long. A few months after his inauguration he was assassinated by a disappointed office-seeker, and Chester Arthur became President. "Chet Arthur President of the United States! Good God!" exclaimed one Republican. But the former spoilsman performed creditably in office. He even championed civil-service reform.[5]

The Penny

When Calvin Coolidge was a little boy of eight he asked his father for a penny so he could buy some candy. The father refused. He said a Democrat might be elected President that year and that meant hard times and no pennies to spare. But when Garfield won the election little Calvin got his candy after all.[6]

Threat

A prominent Clevelander drove out to Mentor to warn Garfield of a plot on his life. "Well," sighed Garfield, after hearing the man's story, "if assassination is to play its part in the campaign, and I must be the sacrifice, perhaps it is best. I think I am ready."[7]

Solid South

In 1880 the "Solid South" joined the "bloody shirt" as a Republican campaign issue. When President Hayes withdrew the last of the federal troops from the South in 1877, ending military reconstruction, it was clear there would be no more victories for Republican presidential candidates in the eleven former Confederate states. Southern whites resolved "to vote as they shot" and also to see to it that as few blacks as possible went to the polls to vote for the party that had freed them. Soon Republicans were warning that the "Solid South," with the help of a few Northern states, could win control of the federal government and then arrange to reimburse former Confederates for property damages during the Civil War and provide Confederate veterans with pen-

sions. Hancock issued a statement flatly denying the Democrats favored
such policies, but the Republicans, with Garfield's approval, pressed the
issue anyway.

Republican campaign songs celebrated the Solid South theme. One
of them portrayed Hancock singing a Solid South song to his Southern
brigadiers to the tune of "Yankee Doodle":

> My Brigadiers, let us forget
> Which side it was we fought on,—
> The Union for or Union down,
> For I have quite forgotten.
>
> CHORUS:
> For I a weather (Han)cock am,
> Your favor now imploring
> I turn my tail toward the North
> The solid South adoring.
>
> I see you vote the way you shot,
> For solid South and plunder;
> My men, if you will vote for me
> I'll shoot for you by thunder—CHORUS.
>
> The Northern debt let us forget,
> You want repudiation;
> And eighty thousand soldiers rebs
> We'll pension on the nation.—CHORUS.
>
> My brigadiers, come dry your tears
> I understand your feelings;
> O Brigadiers! for twenty years
> They kept you from the stealings.—CHORUS.

Another song centered on Southern disfranchisement of the blacks:

> Sing a song of shotguns,
> Pocket full of knives
> Four-and-twenty black men,
> Running for their lives,
> When the polls are open,
> Shut the nigger's mouth,
> Isn't that a bully way
> To make a solid South?
>
> Northern sympathizers
> Making speeches chaffy!
> Major-General Hancock
> Eating Rebel taffy;
> English in a quandry
> How to save his dollars
> Along comes a solid South
> And fits them all with collars.[8]

★ ★

CHAPTER TWENTY-FIVE

1884
The Cleveland-Blaine Contest

When the Republicans met in Chicago on June 3, 1884, for their eighth national convention, the Reverend F. M. Bristol delivered the invocation. Not only did he thank the Almighty for the Republican party; he also prayed that "the coming political campaign may be conducted with that decency, intelligence, patriotism and dignity of temper which becomes a free and intelligent people."[1] His prayer went unanswered. The election of 1884, moaned Andrew D. White, was "the vilest" ever waged. "Party contests," lamented the *Nation* on October 23, "have never before reached so low a depth of degradation in this . . . country." "The public is angry and abusive," Henry Adams wrote an English friend. "We are all swearing at each other like demons."[2] Scandal-mongering dominated the campaign, issues were submerged, and voters were finally asked to choose between a candidate who was "delinquent in office but blameless in private life" (James G. Blaine) and one who was "a model of official integrity, but culpable in his personal relations" (Grover Cleveland).[3]

Blaine was the most popular Republican of his generation. When his name was put in nomination at Chicago, the effect was electric. "Whole delegations mounted their chairs," reported the *New York Tribune*, "and led the cheering which instantly spread to the stage and deepened into a roar fully as deep and deafening as the voice of Niagara. The scene was indescribable. The air quivered, the gaslights trembled and the walls fairly shook. The flags were stripped from the gallery and stage and frantically raised, while hats, umbrellas, handkerchiefs and other personal belongings were tossed to and fro like bubbles over the great dancing sea of human heads."[4] But reformers were outraged, not only by Blaine's nomination on the fourth ballot, but also by the choice for second place of General John A. ("Black Eagle") Logan of Illinois, who, like Blaine, was suspected of crooked railroad dealings. Republican liberals, one observer noted, "applauded with the tips of their fingers, held immediately in front of their noses."[5] Charging that Blaine "wallowed in spoils like a rhinoceros in an African pool," reformers bolted the party, held indignant protest meetings in Boston and New York, and announced they would support the Democratic nominee that year if he proved acceptable.[6]

The Democratic nominee—New York's forty-seven-year-old Governor Grover Cleveland—was fully acceptable to reformers in both parties. The *New York World* supported him for four reasons: "1. He is an honest man; 2. He is an honest man; 3. He is an honest man; 4. He is an honest man."[7] As sheriff of Buffalo County and mayor of Buffalo, Cleveland was celebrated for his rugged integrity; and as Governor of New York he came to be known as "Grover the Good." Tammany's Boss Kelly ("Honest John") hated him for bucking the spoils system, but Tammany's hostility was, for reformers, one of Cleveland's strong points. We "love him for the enemies he has made," cried General Edward S. Bragg of Wisconsin when he seconded Cleveland's nomination at the Democratic convention at Chicago in July.[8] To appease the old guard, though, the convention chose Thomas A. Hendricks of Indiana to run with Grover of Buffalo. Right after the Democrats had made their selections, Independent Republicans decided to join up: prominent men like Carl Schurz, Henry Ward Beecher, and Charles Francis Adams, Jr., and influential Republican journals like the *New York Times,* the *Nation,* and *Harper's Weekly.* The *New York Sun* airily dismissed them as "Mugwumps" (an Algonquin Indian word meaning "chief"), a word the *Indianapolis Sentinel* had used in 1872 to describe Independents who thought they were bigger than their party. The *Sun* had its own definitions: "holier-than-thou Pharisees," "big bugs," "swellheads." But the Republican bolters adopted the name with pride; as Mugwumps, they championed civil-service reform, tariff reduction, and simple honesty and efficiency in government. Republican regulars showered them with epithets: "Blackguards," "Soreheads," "Mutineers," "Snakes," "Brawling Pharisees," "Sleek-faced Hypocrites," "Holy Willies," "Dudes," "Goody-Goodies," "Political Hermaphrodites."[9]

Cleveland did little campaigning, preferring to remain hard at work in the Governor's office in Albany; but he did make two brief speeches in October stressing the civil-service issue. Blaine, however, spent six weeks touring the country and making more than four hundred short talks praising protectionism. He loved the platform, was a real spellbinder, and enjoyed damning the Democrats as "rebels" and "free traders" and the Mugwumps as "agents of foreign interests" for backing tariff reduction. But the appearance of James Mulligan on the scene suddenly put him on the defensive. The letters Mulligan had released in 1876 about Blaine's curious railroad connections helped prevent his nomination that year. But now that Blaine had won the nomination, Mulligan, with more letters lifted from the files, seemed bent on doing him in again.

On September 15, the *Boston Journal* published a batch of letters (acquired from Mulligan) written by Blaine to Boston railroad attorney Warren Fisher; and one of them in particular—a letter he had composed for Fisher to sign clearing him of misbehavior in his railroad dealings—placed him in an awkward position. Blaine had sent his self-exonerating letter to the Bostonian on April 16, 1876, along with a covering letter that told Fisher: "The letter is strictly true, is honorable to you and to me, and will stop the mouths of slanderers at once. Regard this letter as strictly confidential." He added that Fisher's signing and releasing the letter he had written for him would be "a favor I shall never forget" and ended: "Kind regards to Mrs. Fisher. Burn this letter!"[10] The eight-year-old letter (which Fisher neither signed nor released) was a godsend to the Democrats. Dubbing Blaine "Slippery Jim" and "Old Mulligan Letters," they reproduced the Blaine letter, distributed it widely as a campaign document, and, at party rallies, encouraged people to chant:

> Burn this letter!
> Burn this letter!
> Burn, burn, oh, burn this letter!
>
> Blaine! Blaine!
> The Continental liar
> From the State of Maine!
> Burn this letter!

The *New York Evening Post* introduced a daily column: "The Blaine Falsehoods Tabulated."[11]

But it was not all smooth sailing for the Democrats. On July 21, the *Buffalo Evening Telegraph* came out with a big headline: "A Terrible Tale: A Dark Chapter in a Public Man's History." The *Telegraph* subtitled its tale, "The Pitiful Story of Maria Halpin and Governor Cleveland's Son," and went on to reveal that as a young man Grover the Good had taken up with a thirty-six-year-old Buffalo widow, had a son by her, and had since provided financial support for the two of them. The *Telegraph* even knew the boy's name: Oscar Folsom Cleveland. Cleveland's friends were stunned by the revelation. But when they approached him, Cleveland admitted the story was basically true (though the *Telegraph* had added a few embellishments); asked how to handle it in the campaign, he said stolidly: "Above all, tell the truth."[12] The Democrats then took the line that the real issue of the campaign was public integrity, not private misconduct. But Cleveland's enemies didn't see it that way. "We do not believe," wrote Charles A. Dana solemnly in the *New York Sun*, "that the

American people will knowingly elect to the Presidency a coarse debauchee who would bring his harlots with him to Washington, and hire lodgings for them convenient to the White House." The *New York Sun* and the *New York Tribune* could scarcely think of words strong enough to convey their contempt for Cleveland: "rake," "libertine," "father of a bastard," "a gross and licentious man," a "moral leper," "a man stained with disgusting infamy," "worse in moral quality than a pickpocket, a sneak thief or a Cherry Street debauchee, a wretch unworthy of respect or confidence."[13]

But Maria's Cleveland had his defenders. The *Nation*'s E.L. Godkin compared the Buffalonian to Benjamin Franklin and Alexander Hamilton—talented but wayward—and insisted Cleveland would make a far better President than a wheeler-dealer like Blaine. And one Mugwump, comparing the privately conventional but politically dishonest Blaine with the publicly trustworthy but privately wayward Cleveland, concluded: "We should therefore elect Mr. Cleveland to the public office which he is so well qualified to fill and remand Mr. Blaine to the private station he is admirably fitted to adorn."[14] The Republicans had fun chanting, "Ma! Ma! Where's my pa?" But after the election the Democrats retorted: "Gone to the White House. Ha! Ha! Ha!" Lord Bryce followed the campaign with wonderment; it seemed to be a contest over "the copulative habits of one and the prevaricative habits of the other."[15]

As November approached, it became clear that the election was going to be close and that New York, with its thirty-six electoral votes, was crucial. The Empire State looked like a toss-up. Cleveland had many Mugwump supporters there; and Tammany, though lukewarm, had no choice but to support him. But Blaine also had hopes for New York; Irish-Americans in New York City (close to half a million) liked him; his mother was Irish Catholic, he was anti-British, he was sympathetic to the Irish cause, and the Republicans had spread rumors that Cleveland was a religious bigot. On the eve of the election the Democrats were running scared in New York and Blaine's supporters were cautiously hopeful. And then, in the final days of the campaign, things turned suddenly sour for the "Plumed Knight."

October 29 was "black Wednesday" for Blaine. Urged by his managers to make an appearance in New York City, he attended a meeting of several hundred pro-Blaine Protestant clergymen that morning in the Fifth Avenue Hotel and heard the Reverend Samuel D. Burchard, a Presbyterian minister, deliver a warm welcoming address that ended with the words: "We are Republicans, and don't propose to leave our party and identify ourselves with the party whose antecedents have been Rum, Romanism, and Rebellion." Blaine somehow missed the bigoted phrase (which James A. Garfield had once used in 1876) and so did most of the people at the meeting. But when the reporter assigned by the Democrats to cover Blaine relayed Burchard's crack at the Catholics to

Democratic headquarters, Maryland Senator Arthur P. Gorman, chairman of the national executive committee, immediately saw its significance. "Surely," he cried, "Blaine met this remark?" "That is the astonishing thing," replied the reporter excitedly. "He made no reference to the words." Said Gorman at once: "This sentence must be in every daily newspaper in the country tomorrow, no matter how, no matter what it costs. Organize for that immediately . . . and it must be kept alive for the rest of the campaign."[16] Within hours the Democrats were spreading handbills quoting Burchard throughout New York City and elsewhere and by the time Blaine got around to disavowing the clergyman it was too late.

Blaine's morning, October 29, may well have cost him thousands of votes among Irish-American voters angered by Burchard's insult to their faith. But the evening of the 29th was equally disastrous. At the invitation of some of New York's wealthiest citizens Blaine attended a lavish fund-raising dinner at the fashionable Delmonico's restaurant, hobnobbed with millionaires like Jay Gould, John Jacob Astor, and Russell Sage, and, though the country was in a depression at the time, had much to say about Republican prosperity in his remarks after dinner. The next morning Joseph Pulitzer's *New York World* had a front-page headline:

THE ROYAL FEAST OF BELSHAZZAR BLAINE AND

THE MONEY KINGS . . .

BLAINE HOBNOBBING WITH THE MIGHTY MONEY KINGS . . .

MILLIONARIES AND MONOPOLISTS SEAL THEIR ALLEGIANCE . . .

LUCULLUS ENJOYS HIMSELF WHILE THE COUNTRY SORROWS . . .

AN OCCASION FOR THE COLLECTION OF A REPUBLICAN CORRUPTION FUND

Accompanying the story was a cartoon showing the "Plumed Knight" dining in luxury with the fat and filthy rich while a starving man and his ragged wife and child beg for crumbs. Thundered the *World:* "From Rum, Romanism and Rebellion, Mr. Blaine proceeded to a merry banquet of the millionaries at Delmonico's, where champagne frothed and brandy sparkled in glasses that glittered like jewels. The clergymen would have been proud of Mr. Blaine, no doubt, if they had seen him in the midst of the mighty winebibbers."[17] It is difficult to say which hurt him more: Burchard or the Belshazzar bash.

On election day Blaine lost New York by 1,149 votes out of more than a million cast and, as a consequence, went down to defeat nationally. The contest was close: Cleveland's popular majority over Blaine's (4,874,986 to 4,851,981) was only around 23,000 out of ten million cast, though he won 219 electoral votes to Blaine's 182. Republicans at first claimed they had won New York; but in a day or two most of them conceded Cleveland's victory. Remembering 1876, however, the Democrats quickly organized a legal committee to ensure an honest count before the Boards of Canvassers in New York and succeeded in proving beyond the shadow of a doubt that Cleveland's victory was genuine. Even the *New York Tribune* (one of the Republican holdouts) finally admitted that "the canvass of the returns has been thorough, careful and honest, and leaves no room for doubt as to the result."[18]

Cleveland's accession to the Presidency meant that the Democrats were finally in power again, for the first time since Buchanan. Some analysts thought Cleveland hadn't really won; it was just that Blaine had, through bad luck, lost. Blaine himself seems to have looked at it this way. After the election he noted ruefully that he had had thousands of Irish votes sewed up in New York to the very end and would have had even more "but for the intolerant and utterly improper remark of Dr. Burchard, which was quoted everywhere to my prejudice and in many places attributed to myself, though it was in the highest degree distasteful and offensive to me." He also told a friend: "I should have carried New York by 10,000 if the weather had been clear on election day and Dr. Burchard had been doing missionary work in Asia Minor or Cochin China."[19]

Cleveland's youthful indiscretion seems to have done him no real harm in Puritan America. After his victory, the Democrats had a new chant:

> Hurray for Maria! Hurray for the kid!
> I voted for Cleveland, and I'm damned glad I did![20]

☆　☆　☆

Misinformed

The elegant New York Senator Roscoe Conkling (whose "turkey gobbler strut" Blaine had once ridiculed) loathed Blaine. When a Republican delegation called to ask whether he was going to campaign for the party's nominee, he snorted: "Gentlemen, you have been misinformed. I have given up criminal law."[21]

Public Trust

After Cleveland's nomination, reporter William H. Hudson was assigned to prepare a campaign document describing Cleveland's achievements as a public official. He went over Cleveland's state papers and public addresses carefully, prepared his manuscript, and then sought a short phrase that he thought would sum up Cleveland's outlook with which to head the document. He was struck by the frequency with which Cleveland had insisted that men in authority were "the people's servants" and held office as trustees of the public. He finally came up with the slogan, "Public Office Is a Public Trust," and showed it to Cleveland. "Where the deuce did I say that?" Cleveland wanted to know. "You've said it a dozen times publicly," Hudson assured him, "but not in those few words." "That's so," said Cleveland reflectively. "That's what I believe. That's what I've said a little better because more fully." "But this has the merit of brevity," persisted Hudson, "and that is what is required here. The question is, will you stand for this form?" "Oh, yes," replied Cleveland. "That's what I believe. I'll stand for it and make it my own." Within a few hours the country was ringing with the phrase, "Public Office Is a Public Trust."[22]

Dirt

Since the Republicans were making so much of Cleveland's involvement with Maria Halpin as a young man, the Democrats tried hard to find out something disreputable about Blaine's private life. They finally came up with the story that he had had premarital relations with his wife. When they showed the material they had dug up to Cleveland, he took it, tore it into little bits, and threw the pieces into the fire. "The other side," he said firmly, "can have a monopoly of all the dirt in this campaign." But the *Indianapolis Sentinel* printed it anyway. "There is hardly an intelligent man in the country," reported the *Sentinel*, "who has not heard that James C. Blaine betrayed the girl whom he married, and then only married her at the muzzle of a shotgun . . . if, after despoiling her, he was too craven to refuse her legal redress, giving legitimacy to her child, until a loaded shotgun stimulated his conscience—then there is a blot on his character more foul, if possible, than any of the countless stains on his political record."

Blaine brought suit against the *Sentinel* (later dropped). He also revealed there had been two marriage ceremonies. On June 30, 1850, he said, when he was a young man living in Kentucky, he had married Harriet Stanwood, but as there was some doubt about the legality of the marriage, the two remarried on March 29, 1851, when they moved to Pennsylvania. Their first child came three months later. Blaine's story struck some Democrats as curious and unconvincing and they demanded concrete proof. But the issue eventually died, partly because Cleveland encouraged his supporters to drop it and partly because the "Mulligan letters" overshadowed it.[23]

Cleveland and the Convict

The Republicans were not satisfied with calling Cleveland a philanderer; they also pictured him as a slacker. During the Civil War, they said, he had escaped the service by sending a convict to fight in his place. The Democrats quickly clarified the record: after drawing lots, Cleveland's two brothers enlisted in the Union army and Cleveland assumed responsibility for supporting his widowed mother. When the draft came, moreover, Cleveland was assistant district attorney and exempt; but he hired a substitute anyway. But the Republicans produced a circular letter signed by two veterans alleging that Cleveland's substitute was a convict. Cleveland wrote back that the man he had hired was a sailor on the Great Lakes without a criminal record of any kind. "If he is alive yet," added Cleveland, "I don't think either of the noble veterans who signed this circular would care to meet him after he read it. . . ." Blaine, it turned out, was not a Civil War veteran either, and the issue was soon dropped.[24]

Tattooed Man

During the Gilded Age one of the chief attractions in Barnum and Bailey's Greatest Show on Earth was a Greek captain who posed in tights, his skin decorated with pictures, as the "Tattooed Man." Thomas Nast had portrayed Blaine as the "Tattooed Man" in 1876; and in 1884 Bernhard Gillam did a series of savage cartoons on the same theme for *Puck,* the satirical weekly. Gillam's cartoons, showing Blaine's plump figure covered with tattooes reading "Mulligan Letters," "Bribery," "Northern Pacific Bonds," "Jingoism," and "Bluster" were enormously effective. In vain the Republicans called attention to the fact that Gillam was an Englishman. The Democrats went around chanting: "Jim! Jim! Tattooed Jim!"[25]

Appendix

Campaign rhymesters had trouble with Cleveland's running mate, Thomas Hendricks, but the *Chicago Herald* finally performed the feat:

> We'll shout for our man and his important appendix!
> We'll whoop'er up lively for Cleveland and Hendricks![26]

Mark Twain as Mugwump

In 1884 Mark Twain joined the Mugwumps in leaving his party and supporting Cleveland. Blaine's skill in lying, he said, had so overwhelmed him that "I don't seem able to lie with any heart, lately." He chided his friend William Dean Howells for his party regularity. "I am persuaded," he said, "that this idea of *consistency*—unchanging allegiance to *party*—has lowered the manhood of the whole *nation*—pulled it down and dragged it in the mud." He was especially scornful of people who turned away from Cleveland because of the Maria Halpin affair. "This present campaign is too delicious for anything," he told Howells. "To see grown men, apparently in their right mind, seriously arguing against a bachelor's fitness for President because he has had private intercourse with a consenting widow! Those grown men know what the bachelor's other alternative was—& tacitly they seem to prefer that to the widow. *Isn't* human nature the most consummate sham & lie that was ever invented?"[27]

Cleveland and the Clergy

Cleveland's candor about his youthful relations with Maria Halpin did not help him with some people. The Reverend Mr. Ball of Buffalo, claiming to speak for a ministerial investigating committee, went in for extravagant extrapolations after the Halpin story came to light. "Investigations," he announced solemnly, "disclose still more proof of debaucheries too horrible to relate and too vile to be readily believed. For many years days devoted to business have been followed by nights of sin. He has lived a bachelor; had no home, *avoiding the restraints of hotel or boarding house life,* lodged in rooms on the third floor in a business block, and made those rooms a harem, foraged outside, also, in the city and surrounding villages; champion libertine, an artful seducer, a foe to virtue, an enemy of the family, a snare to youth and hostile to true womanhood. The Halpin case was not solitary. Women now married and anxious to cover the sins of their youth have been his victims, and are now alarmed lest their relations with him shall be exposed. Some disgraced and broken-hearted victims of his lust now slumber in the grave. Since he has become governor of this great state, he has not abated his lecheries. Abundant rumors implicate him at Albany, and well-authenticated facts convict him at Buffalo." For Ball the election was momentous in 1884: "The issue is evidently not between the two great parties but between the brothel and the family, between decency and indecency, between lust and law."

But Henry Ward Beecher, celebrated Brooklyn preacher, took up for Cleveland. Accusing Blaine of "awhoring after votes," Beecher told a Democratic rally in Manhattan: "If every man in New York tonight who had broken the Seventh Commandment voted for Cleveland, he would be elected by a 200,000 majority." This led the *New York Tribune* to snort that Beecher was issuing an appeal to adulterers to vote Democratic. Cleveland supporter E. L. Godkin published an editorial in the *New York Evening Post* revealing that as a young man in Owensville, Indiana, the sanctimonious Reverend Mr. Ball had lived a dissolute life and been forced to leave town in a hurry after insulting a lady. Unhappily for Godkin, it turned out there were two Reverend Mr. Balls and the one who had been run out of town was not the Buffalo cleric. A libel suit followed and only after many hours in court was Godkin able to escape paying damages for the error he had made in his editorial.[28]

Two Minutes

Blaine's popularity as a politician rested partly on his memory for names. When he was in Lancaster, Ohio, for a speech, a carriage containing three men began approaching him. "I suspect," said his hostess, "that carriage is coming for you, Mr. Blaine." "Yes," he said, "but that is not the point. The point is that there is a man on that front seat whom I have not seen for twenty-seven years, and I have got just two minutes and a half to remember his name in." When the carriage reached him, Blaine jumped from his own carriage, held out his hand, and greeted the man by name.[29]

Foine Day

When it looked as though Cleveland had carried New York and won 219 electoral votes to Blaine's 182, a salute of 219 guns was fired in New York City Hall park. But the man at the gun was told by someone who had come from the *New York Tribune* office that the celebration was premature. "Sure," said the man, "and thin we are firin' for the fun of the thing an' becuz it's a foine day."[30]

Gould and the Apple Tree

The outcome of the 1884 election was in doubt for a few days and there were fears of another crisis like that in 1876. When rumors began circulating that Republican Jay Gould, who controlled the telegraph lines, was delaying and falsifying the returns, a crowd of people rushed to the Western Union building in New York City and began chanting, "We'll hang Jay Gould to a sour apple tree!" From his yacht on the Hudson River, Gould quickly telegraphed his congratulations to Cleveland.[31]

It's Done

After Blaine's defeat, the following lines appeared on a banner displayed in Morristown, New Jersey:

> The World says the Independents did it.
> The Tribune says the Stalwarts did it.
> The Sun says Burchard did it.
> Roosevelt says the soft soap dinner did it.
> We say Blaine's character did it
> BUT WE DON'T CARE WHO DID IT—
> IT'S DONE.[32]

Panic

Cleveland's victory, the first Democratic presidential victory since 1856, was greeted with jubilation in the South. There were victory parades, fireworks, cannon salutes, and hymns of joy everywhere. But Southern blacks panicked; they thought Cleveland's victory meant the restoration of slavery. Some of them began seeking out their former masters and others begged their employers to let them stay on. Cleveland finally issued a statement calling the fear about slavery absurd.[33]

★ ★

CHAPTER TWENTY-SIX

1888
Harrison, Cleveland, and
the Tariff

In 1888 the presidential contest centered on a serious issue: the tariff. President Cleveland injected it into the campaign when he devoted his entire annual message to Congress in December 1887 to lowering the tariff. "What is the use of being elected or re-elected," he said to his advisers, "unless you stand for something?" Tariff reformers were delighted by his speech but Republican leaders predictably called it an "attempt to fasten upon this country the British policy of free foreign trade." Within weeks the Democratic House and the Republican Senate headed for a deadlock on a new tariff bill and soon after the two parties met to pick candidates for the nation's 1888 election.[1]

The Democrats nominated Cleveland for re-election by acclamation in St. Louis early in June, added former Senator Allen G. Thurman of Ohio, a popular but aging and ailing party faithful, to the ticket, and endorsed tariff revision. The Republicans, meeting in Chicago in mid-June, took longer to settle on a candidate. After seven ballots they chose Benjamin Harrison, fifty-four, former Senator from Indiana and a Civil War veteran, and an all-out protectionist, as their standard-bearer. His running mate, Levi Morton, a wealthy New York banker, generous contributor to the Republican war chest, was also a devout protectionist.

As the campaign got under way, Harrison made a hopeful prediction. "We have joined now a contest of great principles," he said, "and . . . the armies which are to fight out this great contest before the American people will encamp upon the high plains of principle, and not in the low swamps of personal defamation or detraction."[2] He was only partly right. Some Republicans called Cleveland the "Beast of Buffalo," said he got drunk all the time, and accused him of beating his wife (he had married Frances Folsom, his twenty-one-year-old ward, in

1886) in fits of drunken rage. The First Lady finally issued a statement saying the charge was a "foolish campaign story without a shadow of foundation." For good measure she added that she wished "the women of our Country no greater blessing than that their homes and lives may be as happy, and their husbands may be as kind, considerate and affectionate as mine."[3] The Democrats tried to get back at Harrison; they said he was a cold fish ("Kid Glove" Harrison), anti-labor, a religious bigot, and favored unrestricted Chinese immigration to keep wages low in America. But for the most part the contestants avoided the "low swamps" and talked about the tariff. There were, though, the usual campaign tricks and plenty of corruption in 1888.

The Republican party, now beginning to be called the G.O.P. ("Grand Old Party"), had several advantages over the Democrats in 1888: better organization, more funds, a candidate willing to take an active part in soliciting votes, and an issue they could easily identify with: Americanism. Harrison's "front porch" campaign in Indianapolis was enormously effective. He received thousands of visitors in his hometown between July and October and made scores of brief speeches, mainly about the tariff, which were widely quoted in newspapers throughout the country. Republican managers also distributed millions of tracts, pamphlets, flyers, and handbills on the tariff and sent many excellent speakers (like Blaine) out on the stump to denounce free trade. To pay for all this they raised more than three million dollars (the biggest campaign fund to date) from industrialists who benefited from high duties on foreign imports. John Wanamaker, Philadelphia merchant, was the chief fund-raiser. Early in the campaign he sent out a circular to leading manufacturers announcing: "We want money and we want it quick." Not long before election day he appealed for more money; and, as he later put it: "We raised the money so quickly that the Democrats never knew anything about it. They had their spies out supposing that we were going to do something, but before they knew what it was we had them beaten."[4] Manufacturers not only came through with the dough; they also warned their employees of wage slashes and even lay-offs if Cleveland won the election.

The Democratic campaign was, by contrast, feeble and fitful. Cleveland refused to campaign himself; he adhered to the traditional view that it was unseemly for presidential candidates to seek votes. He also refused to permit his Cabinet members to go out on the hustings. This meant that his running mate, Allen Thurman, bore the brunt of the battle. The seventy-five-year-old Thurman did the best he could to convince his audiences that the Cleveland administration favored "moderate reductions of tariff duties," not free trade; but he often digressed to mention his personal ailments and once even collapsed on the platform before finishing his remarks.[5]

On November 6, Harrison beat Cleveland in the Electoral College by

233 to 168 votes, but his popular vote (5,439,853) was around 100,000 votes fewer than Cleveland's (5,540,329). Harrison's victory was scarcely a mandate for his tariff views. Cleveland carried the manufacturing states of New Jersey and Connecticut as well as the Solid South and also did well in states like Michigan, Ohio, and California, which were regarded as pro-tariff states. But the Republicans ran a far better campaign than the Democrats did. And they were able to do so partly because their protectionist position enabled them to raise large sums of money among manufacturers. Cleveland took his loss gamely. He was pleased he had forced discussion of the tariff issue. "I don't regret it," he told a friend. "It is better to be defeated battling for an honest principle than to win by a cowardly subterfuge."[6]

☆   ☆   ☆

Murchison Letter

There was much British-baiting in 1888. The Republicans equated tariff revision with free trade and the latter with England and, in a bid for Irish-American votes, accused Cleveland of subservience to the British lion. But the President twisted the British lion's tail too. When accused of taking a soft line with Britain in a dispute over fishing rights in Canadian waters, he sent a message to Congress asking authority for punitive action against Canada that won warm praise in the anti-British press.

Then came the famous "Murchison Letter." Shortly after Cleveland's demand for strong action against Canada, Charles Osgoodby, a California Republican, sent a letter to Sir Lionel Sackville-West, British minister in Washington, asking for advice on how to vote, and signed it "Charles F. Murchison." In his letter Osgoodby pretended to be an American citizen of English birth who had been planning to support Cleveland because he was sound on free trade, friendly to Britain, and hostile to Ireland, while Harrison was a high-tariff man, "a believer in the American side of all questions," and "an enemy to British interests." But, he said, Cleveland's position on the fisheries dispute left him in a quandary. Did it mean Cleveland was at heart anti-British? Or was it a mere election ploy? He was anxious to know, he said, whether Sir Lionel thought he "WOULD DO ENGLAND A SERVICE BY VOTING FOR CLEVELAND AND AGAINST THE REPUBLICAN SYSTEM OF TARIFF." Sir Lionel swallowed Osgoodby's bait hook, line, and sinker. He wrote back to say he thought the Democratic party was "still desirous of maintaining friendly relations with Great Britain" and that Cleveland would eventually "manifest a spirit of conciliation in dealing with the question involved in the message." Osgoodby turned Sir Lionel's reply and his own letter over to Republican headquarters in California and on October 24 they were released to the press.

The "Murchison Letter" made headlines throughout the country, produced bitter exchanges between the Cleveland and the Harrison people, and placed the administration on the defensive. "Bounce him!" screamed the *New York World* of the British minister. Cried magazine publisher A.K. McClure: "Now kick out Lord Sackville with your biggest boot of best leather and you've got 'em. *Hesitation is death.*" Cleveland didn't hesitate for long. The following day he asked the British to recall Sir Lionel and when they refused abruptly dismissed him. But the damage was done. The *Buffalo Express* blasted "the hand-in-glove relations which exist between the Administration and England," and John Sherman, campaigning for Harrison, accused Cleveland of supine Anglophilism and advised his audiences: "They have given Sir Sackville the shake, and now all that remains for you to do is to give Mr. Cleveland the sack." Chanted Republicans:

> West, West, Sackville-West
> He didn't want to go home,
> But Cleveland thought it best.[7]

Steamboat 'Round the Bend

On October 31, the Democrats published a letter dated October 24 which had been mailed to Republican county chairmen in Indiana from Republican National Treasurer Col. W.W. Dudley in New York giving directions on how to handle "floaters" (people who sold their votes) in the Hoosier state. "Divide the voters into blocks of five," read Dudley's instructions, "and put a trusted man with necessary funds in charge of these five, and make him responsible that none get away and that all vote our ticket." Republican National Chairman Matthew S. Quay claimed it was a forgery, Dudley himself brought libel suits (later withdrawn) against newspapers that printed it, and the Republican chairman in Indiana denied Dudley had anything to do with the Hoosier campaign. But the Democrats scoffed at these protestations of innocence and made wide use of the Dudley letter.

Both parties used "floaters," but the Republicans outdid the Democrats in 1888. As election day neared, it looked as though Indiana was swinging to Cleveland. So the Republicans raised $400,000 and assembled an army of more than 20,000 floaters to make the rounds on election day. Freight trains began transporting carloads of men from other states into Indiana just before the election. But some came by water. A little jingle, popular among schoolchildren, emerged:

> Steamboat coming 'round the bend;
> Goodbye, old Grover, goodbye
> Filled up full with Harrison's men;
> Goodbye, old Grover, goodbye!

In the end the Republicans took Indiana by a small plurality.[8]

Providence

A few weeks after the election Matt Quay went to Indianapolis to congratulate Harrison on his victory. Taking his hand, the President-elect, a pious Presbyterian, exulted: "Providence has given us the victory." "Think of the man!" Quay told a Philadelphia journalist a few weeks later. "He ought to know that Providence hadn't a damn thing to do with it." Harrison, he added, would never know how many Republicans "were compelled to approach the gates of the penitentiary to make him President." Quay was miffed by some of Harrison's appointments and may have been exaggerating. Still, Harrison quickly learned that more than Providence had been involved when he began organizing his administration. Before receiving the Republican nomination in June, he had told his managers: "Remember, no bargains, no alliances, no trades. I may like to be President, but if I am to go to the White House, I don't propose to go shackled." But soon after his election he was complaining: "I could not name my own Cabinet. They had sold out every place to pay the election expenses."[9]

★ ★

CHAPTER TWENTY-SEVEN

1892
Cleveland's Return to Power

In 1892's quadrennium Grover Cleveland and Benjamin Harrison went at it again. Neither was popular with party leaders. Harrison was notoriously cold and aloof and Cleveland doggedly independent and bullheaded. "The two candidates were singular persons," observed Henry Adams, "of whom it was the common saying that one of them had no friends; the other only enemies."[1] Robert Ingersoll quipped that "each side would have been glad to defeat the other if it could do so without electing its own candidate."[2]

The Republicans, assembling in Minneapolis on June 7, nominated Harrison on the first ballot, picked Whitelaw Reid, publisher of the *New York Tribune*, as his running mate, and adopted a platform reaffirming their belief in "the American doctrine of protectionism" and attributing "the prosperous condition of our country" to the "wise revenue legislation" of their party.[3] The Democrats, who met later that month in Chicago, also picked their man, Grover of Buffalo, on the first ballot; and, since Cleveland was known for his hard-money views, selected former Congressman Adlai E. Stevenson of Illinois, a soft-money man, to run with him. Their platform contained the usual platitudes, but was vigorous enough when it came to the tariff: it denounced "Republican protection as a fraud, a robbery, of the great majority of the American people for the benefit of the few."[4]

Except for their acceptance letters, filled mostly with conventionalities, Harrison and Cleveland did little themselves to present their opinions to the public. Harrison's wife was seriously ill (she died two weeks before the election), so the President gave no "front porch" speeches as he had in 1888; and Cleveland for the most part avoided making public pronouncements out of respect for Harrison's wife. Cleveland's economic conservatism, especially his attachment to the gold standard, brought him the hearty support of Eastern bankers and merchants; and this time the Democratic party had more money to spend than the Republicans. But there was a dearth of torchlight parades, lengthy processions, and brass bands in 1892. Even the bloody shirt played only a minor role in the contest.

With the People's party, a new organization, the 1892 campaign came alive. The Populist convention in Omaha, Nebraska, on July 4, was fervent and frenetic. "It was a religious revival," reported one observer, "a crusade, a pentecost of politics in which a tongue of flame sat upon every man, and each spoke as the spirit gave him utterance."[5] Ignatius Donnelly's preamble to the Populist platform was angry and impassioned about the plight of the farmer and worker in the new industrial order and the platform itself promised to restore government "to the hands of the plain people." The Populists presented a long list of reforms, including the popular election of Senators, a graduated income tax, antitrust activity, and public ownership of the railroads, but placed special emphasis on inflating the currency by increasing the amount of paper money in circulation and adopting the free and unlimited coinage of silver at a ratio of sixteen ounces of silver to one ounce of gold.[6]

The Populists' proposals for currency expansion, particularly the free-silver plank, roused fiscal conservatives like Cleveland to wrath. They regarded the free silver demand as ignorant, reckless, and threatening to the American economic order. But farmers in the South and the West, the backbone of the Populist movement, were unquestionably suffering from a shortage of money. As the world market for agriculture expanded after the Civil War, there was a steady decline in the prices of wheat, cotton, and other produce which they raised for export. But the farm equipment they depended on remained expensive; and to pay for it they borrowed heavily and mortgaged their land at high interest rates. What they needed, they insisted, was higher prices for their produce and more money to pay off their debts. And this meant breaking the grip of hard-money bankers and big businessmen in the East on the nation's economy and instituting measures for the rapid expansion of the currency. Time and again delegates to the Omaha convention voiced their opposition to the gold standard by singing the "People's Hymn" to the tune of the "Battle Hymn of the Republic" and also chanting:

> All hail the power of the People's name,
> Let autocrats prostrate fall,
> Bring forth the royal diadem
> And crown the people sovereign, all.[7]

James B. Weaver, who had run on the Greenback ticket in 1880, received the Populists' presidential nomination and James G. Field of Virginia the nomination for Vice-President.

One of the Populists' best campaigners was Mary Lease of Kansas.

Not only did she tell farmers to "raise less corn and more hell"; she also declared that "Wall Street owns the country" and that "it is no longer a government of the people, by the people, and for the people, but a government of Wall Street, by Wall Street, and for Wall Street." Lease and Weaver teamed up in campaign trips through the South and West. They usually spoke to different crowds at the same time and after an hour or so "exchanged pulpits," as they put it, and started in again. In many places they drew great audiences, some of which "could only be counted by acres." People were mostly friendly, though on occasion they encountered heckling and egg-, tomato-, and rock-throwing, especially in the South, and sometimes Weaver, according to Mrs. Lease, "was made a regular walking omelet."[8]

During the campaign Populist leaders made a bid for labor support; their platform declared that the interests of "rural and civic labor" were the same and that "their enemies are identical." But urban workers couldn't quite see it that way; their view of farm prices was, not surprisingly, somewhat different from that of the Populists. Still, the labor issue was important in 1892, mainly because of the strike that summer by workers at the Carnegie Steel Company in Homestead, Pennsylvania. To crush the steelworkers's union, Carnegie's general manager Henry Clay Frick proposed a contract slashing wages 22 percent, and when the union rejected it, instituted a lockout, put scabs to work, and hired armed Pinkerton detectives to guard the plant. A pitched battle between strikers and Pinkertons followed, and the Governor of Pennsylvania finally sent national guardsmen to Homestead to restore order. Frick won in the end, but his behavior hurt the G.O.P. badly. Republican faithfuls had always insisted that high tariffs meant high wages; but Frick's action—cutting wages while the steel industry was prospering behind tariff walls—belied their doctrine. The Democrats made the most of the inconsistency and began citing Homestead in their assaults on protectionism. But many Republicans, including Harrison and Reid themselves, were upset by Frick's policies. The labor vote, as they feared, went to Cleveland on election day.

On November 8, Cleveland won a decisive victory in his third race for the Presidency, carrying seven Northern states, including New York, as well as the Solid South, and winning 277 electoral votes to Harrison's 145 and over 380,000 more popular votes than Harrison (5,556,543 to 5,175,582). For the first time since the Civil War, moreover, the Democrats won a majority in both houses of Congress. But the Populists also did surprisingly well for a third party entering the lists for the first time: 1,040,886 popular votes and 22 electoral votes (Colorado, Idaho, Kansas, and Nebraska, plus one vote each from North Dakota and Oregon). In the West, farmers normally Republican voted Populist but in the South they stayed with the Democratic party, mainly because it was the party of white supremacy. The high McKinley tariff probably hurt

Harrison with industrial workers in the East, but the Homestead strike also played its part. In post-election analyses, both Democrats and Republicans agreed that Homestead had hurt Harrison.

Carnegie Steel bigwigs, normally Republican, were reconciled. "I am very sorry for President Harrison," said Frick, "but I cannot see that our interests are going to be affected one way or the other by the change of administration." Andrew Carnegie felt the same way. "Cleveland! Landslide!" he exclaimed after the election. "Well, we have nothing to fear and perhaps it is best. . . . Cleveland is a pretty good fellow." Later on he said: "I fear that Homestead did much to elect Cleveland—very sorry—but no use getting excited."[9]

Fish Lines

While the Democratic convention was going on, Cleveland seems to have had his mind as much on fishing as on the balloting. He received the news from Chicago by special wire in the gun-room in his cottage, Gray Gables, at Buzzards Bay, where he and his wife were entertaining actor Joseph Jefferson and his son Charles. The Jefferson boy kept a tally of the balloting and later wrote: "All were bending over my shoulder watching the figures when the spell was broken by Mr. Cleveland remarking in a startled tone, 'I forgot to dry my lines today.' At the critical moment when New York was about to cast her vote and the danger of a break was greatest, Mr. Cleveland arose and went out to hang up his lines as unconcernedly as though the covention were of no interest to him."[10]

Iceberg

Harrison's "low temperature" alienated party workers. Pennsylvania's Matt Quay had managed Harrison's 1888 campaign skillfully, but wasn't sure he wanted to work for the "White House iceberg" again. When Harrison told him that God had put him where he was, Quay snapped, "Let God re-elect you then," and stomped out of the White House.[11]

News from Gettysburg

When Republican Governor James B. Foraker of Ohio made an impassioned bloody-shirt-waving speech for Harrison, Finley Peter Dunne reported it satirically in the *Chicago Herald.* "Harrison," Dunne reported Foraker as saying, "volunteered and went to the front, Cleveland volunteered to stay at home. . . . The Republican party raised the army without him, got the money to clothe the soldiers without him and won the glorious victories of the war without him. *(Cheers)* . . . I don't believe any Copperhead should be made President of the United States. *(Applause).* I don't believe any man should be elected who would not feel at home in the Grand Army of the Republic. *(Cries of 'That's so!').*" Then, concluded Dunne, "all the people put on their hats and went out to see what news had come from Gettysburg, where a terrible battle is still raging." [12]

Rainier or Tacoma

Adlai E. Stevenson, Cleveland's running mate, proved to be a skillful campaigner, especially in the Northwest. The big issue there was whether the majestic mountain in Washington should be called Rainier or Tacoma and people wanted to know what he thought about it. He solved the problem neatly. In every speech he made from the rear platform of his train he devoted his peroration to discussing the beauty of the mountain and then concluded: "This controversy must be settled, and settled right by the national government. I pledge myself here and now that if elected I will not rest until this glorious mountain is properly named. . . ." At this point he would pull a secret cord to notify the engineer and his remaining words were always drowned out by the scream of whistles and blast of steam as the train moved out of the station. [13]

★ ★

CHAPTER TWENTY-EIGHT

1896
McKinley, Bryan, and Free Silver

The campaign of 1896, the liveliest since the Civil War, centered on the
money question. "Night and day," reported a correspondent for the
London Daily Mail, "in every newspaper, in every café, in every street
car, it is the dollar and the dollar alone, whose fate is discussed."[1] In
the "Battle of the Standards," as it was called, the Republicans upheld
the gold standard while the Democrats went partly Populist and came
out for the free and unlimited coinage of silver at a ratio of sixteen
ounces of silver to one ounce of gold.

But the monetary agitation was symptomatic not systemic. It was the
terrible depression following the Panic of 1893 that produced the great
debate over money. While protectionists continued to insist that high
tariffs created jobs and opened the way to recovery, currency inflation-
ists saw no solution to the crisis so long as there was a shortage of money
in circulation. The monetary debate involved a sectional clash: the
agrarian West and South vs. the urban East. It also involved economic
strife: debtors vs. creditors, hard-pressed farmers vs. prosperous industrialists, the underprivileged many vs. the privileged few. "In form," said
reformer Henry George, "the struggle is on the currency question. But
these are only symbols, and behind them are gathered the world-
opposing forces of aristocratic privilege and democratic freedom."[2]

The monetary question dominated the conventions of both major
parties. When the Republicans met in St. Louis on June 16, some of the
delegates wanted to emphasize the tariff again and soft-pedal the currency issue. But the Easterners insisted on a strong fiscal plank and the
party ended by opposing the free coinage of silver "except by international agreement" and declaring that "the existing gold standard must
be preserved."[3] Some twenty silver Republicans from the West, led by
Colorado's Senator Henry M. Teller, walked out of the convention (while

the band played "Silver Threads among the Gold"), founded the National Silver party, and later gave their support to the Democrats. Once the silverites were gone, it was easy to agree on candidates. On the first ballot William McKinley, Governor of Ohio, long backed for the Presidency by Cleveland industrialist Mark Hanna as "the advance agent of prosperity," won the nomination and was teamed up with Garret A. Hobart, a New Jersey corporation lawyer.

McKinley, fifty-three, had once been a "straddlebug"; he had even supported silver measures when he was in Congress. But he was a devout "Goldbug" by now, and, as sponsor of the high-tariff act of 1890, was identified with Republican protectionism as well. "The money question is the vital thing," a friend told him after the convention. "I am a Tariff man, standing on a Tariff platform," responded McKinley. "This money matter is unduly prominent. In thirty days you won't hear anything about it." But Judge William R. Day of Canton, Ohio, disagreed. "In my opinion," he said, "in thirty days you won't hear of anything else." [4]

Judge Day was right. When the Democrats, meeting in St. Louis on July 16, rudely snubbed President Cleveland and the Gold Democrats and enthusiastically adopted a free-silver plank, it was clear that money, not tariffs, was to dominate the campaign. The candidate, William Jennings Bryan, former Congressman from Nebraska and a passionate silverite, was determined to give the monetary issue primacy. In a debate on the party's currency plank, he delivered one of the most impassioned speeches ever made in a party convention and brought the delegates to their feet howling in ecstasy with his cry toward the end: "We have petitioned, and our petitions have been scorned; we have entreated, and our entreaties have been disregarded; we have begged, and they have mocked when our calamity came. We beg no longer; we entreat no more; we petition no more. We defy them. . . ! Having behind us the producing masses of this nation and the world, supported by the commercial interests, the laboring interests, and the toilers everywhere, we will answer their demand for a gold standard by saying to them: You shall not press down upon the brow of labor this crown of thorns, you shall not crucify mankind upon a cross of gold!" [5]

Bryan's "Cross of Gold" speech touched off a demonstration lasting close to an hour, during which delegates shouted, cheered, and wept, carried Bryan around on their shoulders in triumph, and waved banners on which were scribbled the words, "NO CROWN OF THORNS! NO CROSS OF GOLD!" Gold Democrats were appalled. "For the first time," exclaimed an Eastern delegate, "I can understand the scenes of the French Revolution." [6] The convention chose Bryan (at thirty-six, the youngest man ever nominated for President) on the fifth ballot and, to balance the ticket, picked Arthur Sewall, a rich Maine shipbuilder, for second place. With the silverites in the saddle, the Goldbugs, determined not to be crucified on a cross of silver, angrily walked out of the

Dem Platform
+ Pop.
evander/.

convention, organized the National Democratic party to fight Bryan, and ran John M. Palmer for President. After it was all over someone asked New York's conservative David B. Hill whether he was still a Democrat. "Yes," he sighed, "I am a Democrat still—*very* still." Observed the *New York World:* "The sceptre of political power has passed from the strong certain hands of the East to the feverish, headstrong mob of the West and South."[7]

The Populists were in a quandary. Should they maintain their independence in 1896, thus splitting the silver forces, or should they endorse Bryan, thus jeopardizing their broader objectives? They finally decided to support Bryan. The Democratic platform, after all, contained a number of Populist planks in addition to free silver: supporting tariff reduction, a graduated income tax, and stricter railroad and trust regulations; condemning the use of court injunctions against strikers; and disapproving of the bond issues which Cleveland arranged with J. P. Morgan in 1895 to maintain the nation's gold reserves. As a compromise, the Populists substituted Georgia's Thomas E. Watson for the Democrat's Arthur Sewall as Vice-President, under the impression that the Democrats would accept Watson too. Only after fusion had become official did they learn that the Democrats had no intention of dropping Sewall from the ticket. By then it was too late to back out. Populist faithfuls, who saw their party go down the drain after fusion with the Democrats in 1896, deplored the obsession with silver. "Free silver," said Henry Demarest Lloyd, "is the cow-bird of the Reform movement. It waited until the nest had been built by the sacrifices and labors of others, and then it laid its eggs in it, pushing out the others which lie smashed on the ground. It is now flying around while we are expected to do the incubating."[8]

Mainly because of Bryan, the handsome young Nebraskan with the magnetic voice, the campaign of 1896 was almost continuously exciting. Bryan—"the Silver Knight of the West," "the Great Commoner," "the Peerless One"—took unashamedly to the stump in a quest for votes and when he was charged with lacking dignity he exclaimed: ". . . I would rather have it said that I lacked dignity than . . . that I lack backbone to meet the enemies of the Government who work against its welfare in Wall Street." In Philadelphia he asked: "What other Presidential candidates did they ever charge with lack of dignity?" "Lincoln," said someone in the crowd. "Yes, my friends," said Bryan, "they said it of Lincoln." "Jackson," suggested someone else. "Yes, they said it of Jackson." "And Jefferson," volunteered another Bryanite. "Yes," said Bryan, "and of Jefferson; he was lacking in dignity, too."[9] While bands played "El Capitan," the Democratic marching-song, Bryan went around the country, speaking in little towns as well as big cities and from train platforms as well as in large auditoriums, preaching the gospel of free silver. "Where there is more money in circulation," he said time and again, "there is a better chance for each man to get money than there is when money is scarce." Gold, he insisted, helped only the classes, while free silver helped both the masses and the classes: "There are those who believe that, if you will only legislate to make the well-to-do prosperous, their prosperity will leak through on those below. The Democratic idea, however, has been that if you legislate to make the masses prosperous, their prosperity will find its way up through every class which rests upon them."[10]

Before the campaign was over Bryan had traveled 18,000 miles by train, made more than 600 speeches (sometimes ten or twenty a day), addressed five million people, and talked of many things: farm prices, mortgage rates, the need for credit, and railroad regulation. But he subsumed all of these issues under the super-issue of free silver, made the white metal synonymous with democracy and the people, and identified gold with Wall Street, the special interests, privilege, and plutocracy. Like the "Cross of Gold" speech at the convention, Bryan's campaign speeches were filled with religious imagery and evangelical fervor and aroused many of his listeners to a pitch of passion that dumbfounded when it did not alarm respectable people in the East. "It was a fanaticism like the Crusades," observed Kansas Republican journalist William Allen White, who was both fascinated and repelled. "Indeed, the delusion that was working on the people took the form of religious frenzy. Sacred hymns were torn from their pious tunes to give place to words which deified the cause and made gold—and all its symbols, capital, wealth, plutocracy—diabolical. At night from ten thousand little white schoolhouse windows, lights twinkled back vain hope to the stars. . . . They sang their barbaric songs in unrhythmic jargon, with something of the same mad faith that inspired the martyrs going to the stake. Far into the night the voices rose—women's voice, children's voices, the voices of old men, of youths and of maidens, rose on the ebbing prairie breezes, as the crusaders of the revolution rode home, praising the people's will as though it were God's will, and cursing wealth for its inequity."[11]

The Republicans were savage in their assaults on Bryan. No epithet was too strong to hurl at the Democratic standard-bearer: socialist, anarchist, communist, revolutionary, lunatic, madman, rabble-rouser, thief, traitor, murderer. The *New York Times* called him "an irresponsible, unregulated, ignorant, prejudiced, pathetically honest and enthusiastic crank." The *New York Tribune* referred to him as a "wretched, rattle-pated boy, posing in vapid vanity and mouthing resounding rottenness," and the *Philadelphia Press* dismissed his followers as "hideous and repulsive vipers."[12] A Chicago clergyman even announced that the "Chicago platform was made in Hell," and Theodore Roosevelt contemplated appearing "on the field of battle, sword in hand," in the event of a Bryan victory.[13] But the Republicans did more than mouth maledictions. Under the adroit direction of Mark Hanna, chairman of the

Republican national committee, they amassed ample funds from banks, insurance companies, and industrial corporations, distributed tons of pamphlets, leaflets, banners, posters, and McKinley buttons and sent out hundreds of able speakers to explain to the voters why gold meant stability and prosperity while silver threatened anarchy and economic collapse. Some bankers told farmers their mortgages would be foreclosed if they voted Democratic, and some employers put warning slips in their workers' pay envelopes: "If Bryan is elected, do not come back to work. The plant will be closed." Bryan's grasp of the money question was undoubtedly simplistic; but it is clear that the views of his opponents were equally lacking in sophistication. Their hysteria at the thought of silver matched the Bryanite frenzy at the idea of gold. "The whole currency question," Finley Peter Dunne's comic character Mr. Dooley finally decided, "is a matter of lungs."[14]

McKinley's campaign was quieter than Bryan's but no less energetic. Like Benjamin Harrison in 1888, but on a much larger scale, McKinley carried on a "front-porch" campaign at his home in Canton, Ohio. His manager Mark Hanna arranged for hundreds of delegations—representing farmers, workers, businessmen, veterans, college students, clergymen, lawyers, doctors—to take the train to Canton, deliver complimentary little addresses, which had been carefully cleared beforehand, at McKinley's place, and then listen to brief responses by the Republican candidate, also carefully prepared ahead of time. McKinley's brief speeches were widely reported in the press and some of his remarks became popular campaign material: "Good money never made times hard"; "Our currency today is good—all of it is as good as gold"; "We want good prices and good wages, and when we have them we want them to be paid in good money." In all the Republican campaign literature he sent out Hanna tried to get across the idea that McKinley and gold mono-metallism meant a return to prosperity after the searing depression of the Cleveland years and a boost in employment and wages for the workers. The most popular Republican slogan was "McKinley and the Full Dinner Pail."[15]

Hanna and his associates were alarmed in August; Bryan and the gospel of silver seemed to be sweeping the country. By October they were reassured; a revival of business, followed by rising prices, seemed to be taking the wind out of Bryan's sails. On November 5, almost fourteen million citizens went to the polls, more than ever before, and gave McKinley over 600,000 more popular votes than Bryan (7,111,607 or 50.88 percent to 6,509,052 or 46.77 percent) and 95 more electoral votes (271 to 176). The Republicans also had majorities in both houses of Congress. The sectional cleavage was clear: McKinley carried the industrial North and Middle West as well as several states in the Far West, while Bryan took the Solid South and the Plains and Mountain states. There was also an economic cleavage: McKinley not only captured the votes of the urban middle and upper middle classes; he also did better than Bryan with urban laborers and the most prosperous farmers, neither of whom saw anything to gain from currency inflation. Bryan's strongest supporters were poverty-stricken farmers in the West and the South; but he also attracted many citizens everywhere who were bothered by plutocratic rule in a democratic country and by the social ills that accompanied the industrialization of the economy after the Civil War: sweatshops, slums, child labor, widespread poverty.

By the time of McKinley's inauguration the long depression touched off by the Panic of 1893 was ending and the Republicans could claim to be the party of prosperity. The opening of gold mines in South Africa and elsewhere increased the world's gold supply and ironically brought about the currency inflation for which the silverites had been clamoring. Still, Bryan's message had not been merely monetary; he had dramatized many issues in 1896 that continued to be pressing. Even his opponents—some of them at least—couldn't help being impressed by the gallant fight he had waged against great odds. "The great fight is over," Republican Senator Henry Cabot Lodge's wife wrote Sir Cecil Spring-Rice, the British Ambassador, afterwards, "and a fight conducted by trained and experienced and organized forces, with both hands full of money, with the full power of the press—and of prestige—on the one side; on the other, a disorganized mob at first, out of which there burst into sight, hearing, and force—one man, but such a man! Alone, penniless, without backing, without money, with scarce a paper, without speakers, that man fought such a fight that even those in the East can call him a Crusader, an inspired fanatic—a prophet! It has been marvellous. Hampered by such a following, such a platform . . . he almost won. We acknowledge to 7 millions campaign fund, as against his 300,000. We had during the last week of the campaign 18,000 speakers on the stump. He alone spoke for his party, but speeches which spoke to the intelligence and hearts of the people, and with a capital P. It is over now, but the vote is 7 millions to 6 millions and a half!" [16]

Patent Medicine

At the St. Louis convention McKinley buttons, canes, and posters appeared everywhere. There was even a drink, "the McKinley," consisting mainly of bourbon whiskey. After McKinley's nomination Mark Hanna saw to it that millions of pamphlets, leaflets, and handbills were distributed on his behalf. Said young Theodore Roosevelt in dismay: "He has advertised McKinley as if he were a patent medicine." [17]

No Favors

When the Democratic convention adjourned, one of the big railroad companies offered to transport presidential nominee Bryan back to

Lincoln, Nebraska, in a private Pullman car. "Mr. Bryan," one of his friends told him when the invitation arrived, "you should not accept this offer. You are the Great Commoner, the people's candidate, and it would not do to accept favors from the great railroad corporations." Byran agreed and refused the offer.[18]

No Trapeze Artist

As Bryan's energetic campaign got under way Hanna became worried. "We have got to get McKinley out on the road to meet this thing," he told Myron Herrick, "and I wish you would . . . map out a campaign for him." The two visited McKinley in Canton. "Things are going against us, William," Hanna told him. "You've got to stump or we'll be defeated." McKinley flatly refused. "You know I have the greatest respect for your wishes, Mark," he said, "but I cannot take the stump against that man." He spelled it out: "If I took a whole train, Byran would take a sleeper; if I took a chair car, he would ride a freight train. I can't outdo him, and I am not going to try." He added: "If I should go now it would be an acknowledgment of weakness. Moreover, I might just as well put up a trapeze on my front lawn and compete with some professional athlete as go out speaking against Bryan."[19]

Rabbits' Feet

At the Democratic convention Bryan carried around a rabbit's foot which a Southern delegate had given him. He also kept the one that was thrust into his hand as he left the convention hall after his Cross-of-Gold speech. But after his nomination he received thousands of them. At one town during the campaign he was presented with "the foot of a rabbit killed at midnight, in a churchyard during the dark of the moon," and he exclaimed: "If all the people who have given me rabbits' feet in this campaign will vote for me, there is no possible doubt of my election!"[20]

Choke to Death

A black man working on the wharf in Savannah, according to a story appearing in Republican newspapers, was paid off in silver and put the half-dollar in his mouth to bite it and see whether it was silver or lead. To his dismay it slipped into his throat and stuck about halfway down. In great consternation he sought out a surgeon and asked him to cut it out. "Can't cut that out," said the surgeon, "it's got to stay there. Say, boy," he went on, "are you registered?" "No, sar," said the worker, "I isn't registered." "Well," said the surgeon, "you go and get registered right away, and vote for McKinley, because if Bryan is elected that half dollar will be a dollar and then you'll choke to death."[21]

The Platte

For his eloquence Bryan was commonly known as "The Boy Orator of the Platte." But Senator Joseph Foraker reminded people that in Nebraska the Platte River was "six inches deep and six miles wide at the mouth."[22]

Repeal the Law

A farmer and a blacksmith, according to a popular Republican tale, got into a discussion in a village store in Virginia about the money question. "I'm a Dimmycrat," said the farmer, " 'cos what the country needs is mo' money. The Dimmycrats has promised to help us to that. Stands to sense, sixteen silver dollars is better 'an one gold dollar." "How yo' goin' to git it?" demanded the blacksmith. "Ain't yo' ever heern of the law of supply and demand?" "In cose I has," said the farmer, "but that law won't make no difference. We'll repeal that law jist ez soon ez Bryan's 'lected."[23]

McKinley Filling

A little girl, according to one campaign story, went to the dentist with her mother to have a small cavity in one of her teeth filled. She got into the chair and as the dentist began his work, the mother asked what he was going to use for a filling. "Silver," he said. At that, the girl straightened herself up, pushed the dentist's hand aside, and said with great earnestness: "I will not have my tooth filled with silver. I am for McKinley!"[24]

Campaign Coins

The Republicans circulated toy coins ridiculing the monetary views of the Democrats. One such coin had the words, FREE COINAGE, 16 to 1, inscribed on one side and, FROM SILVER MINES OF BUNCO STATE, on the other. Another campaign coin showed a picture of Bryan and the words, IN GOD WE TRUST . . . FOR THE OTHER 47 CENTS.[25]

Sound Roof

The Sunday School lesson for the day was about Solomon's temple and the teacher explained that the temple was overlaid with sheets of pure gold. A little later the minister tested the children on the lesson. "How was Solomon's temple roofed?" he asked at one point. Exclaimed a big boy: "With sound money!"[26]

Bryan and the College Kids

On the afternoon of September 24, Bryan began speaking to a sympathetic crowd of people on the New Haven green. Suddenly a bunch of Yale students showed up and started heckling him. "I have been so used to talking to young men who earn their own living," cried Bryan, amid catcalls, hisses, groans, and cheers for McKinley, "that I hardly know what language to use to address myself to those who desire to be known, not as the creators of wealth, but as the distributors of wealth which somebody else created." The Yalies tried to drown him out with their college yell, "Brek-ek-ek-ek, Ho-ax, Ho-ax," and finally brought in a brass band that made so much noise Bryan had to abandon his speech. "Do not blame the boys," he said afterward. "You could not expect much more of some of them. Their fathers, some of whom have gotten rich by the oppression of the poor, have threatened their employees with discharge if they vote their convictions." Yale's president expressed regret at the incident, but noted that "boys will be boys, you know."

The anti-Bryan press praised the Yalies. Queried the *New York Sun:* "Has not a crowd in the open air as much right to hiss as to cheer?" But a mass meeting of Cherokee, Creek, Choctaw, and Seminole Indians in Indian Territory took Bryan's side. "Resolved," they declared, "that we contemplate with deep regret the recent insulting treatment of William Jennings Bryan by students of a college in the land of the boasted white man's civilization, and we admonish all Indians who think of sending their sons to Yale that association with such students could but prove hurtful alike to their morals and their progress toward the higher standard of civilization." A little later, when Bryan spoke in Ithaca, New York, he encountered similar hostility from a crowd of Cornell students. But a few students were friendly and tried to get him a fair hearing. Years later, when Bryan was Wilson's Secretary of State, he saw to it that the leader of the friendly Cornell students got a job in the State Department.[27]

Wrecked Distillery

Though Bryan was a teetotaler, he sometimes turned up for speeches "smelling like a wrecked distillery." The story was that he solved the laundry and bathing problem while campaigning by taking his clothes off between stops and rubbing himself with gin to get rid of the odor of perspiration.[28]

Pickpockets for Bryan

The Democrats faced an unexpected problem when pickpockets began joining Bryan's campaign party. Forty or fifty would board his train as the day began, take seats in the smoker, and then get off at each stop and fan out among the people gathered to hear Bryan and go to work. Bryan unwittingly facilitated their work. He was in the habit of asking people who had gold in their pockets to raise their hands and, then, those with silver to raise theirs, in order to make the point that both metals were commonly accepted. The pickpockets would then quietly move in. The problem got so serious that Bryan eventually employed a Pinkerton detective to accompany him.[29]

Bryan and the Alienists

Bryan was the first presidential candidate to attract the attention of professional psychologists (or "alienists," as they were then called). On September 27, the *New York Times* published an editorial entitled "Is Mr. Bryan Crazy?" The *Times* thought he was and as proof presented a list of extravagant statements Bryan had made in the campaign. "No one," said the editors, "can look through it without feeling that these are not adaptations of intelligent reason to intelligent ends." The same issue of the *Times* featured a letter by "an eminent alienist" announcing that an analysis of Bryan's speeches led inescapably to the conclusion that the Democratic candidate was unbalanced and that if he won the election there would be a "a madman in the White House."

The eminent alienist's letter touched off an orgy of polemical psychologizing about Bryan. On September 29 the *Times* published a series of interviews with New York psychologists with the heading, "Is Mr. Bryan a Mattoid?" The next day there were more interviews and a new headline: "Paranoid or Mattoid?" Most of the psychologists interviewed regarded Bryan as mentally unfit, though they could not agree on the technical epithet: megalomania, delirium, mattoid, paranoia querulenta, querulent logorrhoea, graphomania, paranoia reformatoria. Admonished one psychologist: "We must rid our minds of the idea that Mr. Bryan is ordinarily crazy. . . . But I should like to examine him for a degenerate." Another professional thought paranoia was much too good for Bryan. "I do not think," he said solemnly, "that he was ever of large enough calibre to think clearly and consecutively. His mental territory is not sufficiently extensive. A sophomore at City College has a better education. To accuse him of paranoia is to flatter him, inasmuch as a paranoiac may have a large organization, even if perverted."[30]

Front Porch

McKinley's front-porch campaign went over big. Thousands of well-wishers flocked to Canton from all over the country; and since railroads gave low excursion rates, visiting McKinley, it was said, was "cheaper than staying home." By election day some 750,000 people from thirty states in over three hundred delegations had called on him in Canton, Ohio. The leader of each delegation would greet him; then he would mount a chair and make a few remarks about sound money. Sometimes a band would play, "The Honest Little Dollar's Come To Stay." And on occasion delegations of children would chant:

> Governor McKinley, he's our man;
> If we can't vote for him our papas can.

Some visitors sought souvenirs: wood from the fence and porch and blades of grass from the lawn. Before long the lawn and the fence were gone and the porch in a state of collapse. But guests gave as well as got: flowers, food, and clothing by the carload; eagles named McKinley, Republican, and Protection; badges, canes, and flags. Some gifts were special: a strip of jointed tin, sixty feet long, with the names of the Republican candidates on it; a gavel made out of a log taken from a cabin once occupied by Lincoln; the largest plate of galvanized iron ever rolled in the United States; a finely polished stump of a tree from Tennessee. McKinley's staff consumed the food; the Canton zoo took the birds; and the trash heap eventually wound up with the rest.[31]

Dollar Mark

William Randolph Hearst's *New York Journal* was one of the few major newspapers to support Bryan. In the pages of the *Journal*, cartoonist Homer Davenport pictured Mark Hanna, chairman of the Republican national committee, as "Dollar Mark" Hanna: a greedy, bloated plutocrat, surrounded by money bags and covered with dollar signs, who dominated McKinley, a little fellow wearing a Napoleon hat too big for him. According to Hearst (and Davenport), Hanna was the puppetmaster who pulled McKinley's string, the organ-grinder for whom McKinley danced, and the ventriloquist who made dummy McKinley speak. The *Boston Evening Transcript*, another Bryan paper, warned of a new "Hannaverian dynasty."[32]

Sixteen-to-One Threats

To counter *Coin's Financial School*, William H. Harvey's popular free-silver tract, which the Democrats distributed by the thousands, the Republicans circulated about 250 different pamphlets on the money question in various languages—German, French, Italian, Hebrew, as well as English—warning that if Bryan won, industry and agriculture would go under, workers become jobless, and widows and orphans lose all their savings. The "Wholesale Dry Goods Republicans" put it into a song:

> Before Billy Bryan was thought of,
> The taking of orders was fun;
> Then a man used to say, "Send sixteen,"
> But now he says, "Send only one."

To hammer the point home, railroads put notices in pay envelopes warning of a shutdown if Bryan won, bankers promised to extend mortgages for five years at low interest rates if McKinley became President, and one manufacturer began paying his employees in Mexican dollars to show them that a silver dollar was worth only fifty cents. "Men," the head of the Steinway Piano Works warned his employees, "vote as you please, but if Bryan is elected tomorrow the whistle will not blow Wednesday morning." The Indiana Bicycle Works, with 1,500 employees, even shut down right after Bryan's nomination. Explained the company's president: "We cannot risk in further manufacturing until our monetary contest is settled." In New England many firms put up big signs: "This factory will be closed on the morning after the November election if Bryan is elected. If McKinley is elected, employment will go on as usual."[33]

Follow the Leader

Late election night, when it was clear McKinley had won, H. H. Kohlsaat, Republican owner of the *Chicago Times-Herald*, found some businessmen celebrating in a Chicago nightclub. One man, he reported, "started the old boyhood game of 'Follow the Leader.' He was joined by bank presidents, merchants, Chicago's foremost men; they went over sofas, chairs, tables, up-stairs and down-stairs, and wound up with dancing in each other's arms."[34]

★ ★

CHAPTER TWENTY-NINE

1900
The McKinley-Roosevelt Triumph

The campaign of 1900 was to some extent a repeat performance. William McKinley and William Jennings Bryan went at it for a second time, the Republicans trotted out the "full dinner pail" again, and the Democrats, under Bryan's prodding, once more unfurled the banner of free silver. Silver was really a dead issue in 1900. The inflation produced by increased supplies of gold in the world had made it supererogatory. But Bryan continued to believe silver was relevant and forced a sixteen-to-one plank on this party over considerable opposition. Bryan, snorted Thomas B. Reed, "had rather be wrong than President."[1]

But 1900 was not another free-silver campaign. Something new had been added: imperialism. In 1898 the United States had gone to war with Spain over Cuban independence and emerged from it with vast new overseas possessions in the Caribbean and the Pacific. Bryan had patriotically volunteered to fight in that war (he became a colonel but didn't get overseas), but, like many other old-fashioned Americans, he was repelled by the idea of empire and proposed to base his case against McKinley in 1900 on the issue of imperialism. Bryan's timing was off again. The Treaty of Paris, giving the United States the Philippines, was ratified by the U.S. Senate in 1899, with Bryan's backing, and the Great Commoner had difficulty in getting voters excited over a *fait accompli*. But he did his valiant best, as usual, though McKinley didn't even bother to stage another front-porch campaign. The nineteenth century's last presidential campaign was not one of the nation's more rousing contests.

The party conventions—the Republicans in Philadelphia in June and the Democrats in Kansas City in July—were about as forgettable as the campaign itself. Both McKinley and Bryan achieved their nominations on the first ballot, and the Democrats had no difficulty in joining Bryan with that dignified Illinois silverite, Adlai E. Stevenson, who had served as Cleveland's Vice-President from 1893 until 1897. There was a good deal of suspense, however, at the Republican convention over the choice for second place. From the beginning, Theodore Roosevelt was a leading contender. T.R. had made headlines as a "Rough Rider" in Cuba during the Spanish War and had gone on to make a good record as Governor of New York; but neither McKinley nor Mark Hanna (now Ohio Senator but also Republican national chairman again) took to him especially. They thought he was a little too flamboyant and unpredictable; they preferred someone saner and safer. Thomas Platt, New York boss, also found T.R. hard to handle; and, with the help of Pennsylvania's Matt Quay, he was quietly promoting him for the second spot on the ticket, as a way of getting him out of New York. But T.R. did have his zealous backers. The Western delegates were crazy about him. They liked him because he was a good cowboy; and they admired him for his valor in Cuba. Periodically they marched down the aisles crying: "We want Teddy! We want Teddy!"[2]

T.R. disclaimed any interest in the nomination, but obviously enjoyed the ovations, and, though afraid the Vice-Presidency might mean political oblivion, seemed eager to prove he could get nominated if he so desired. Hanna was upset by the Roosevelt boom. "Don't any of you realize," he cried at one point, "that there's only one life between that madman and the Presidency?" Hanna wanted McKinley to throw his support to someone else, but the President stubbornly refused to intervene in the convention's proceedings. In the end T.R. received the vote of every delegate (except his own) and the Republicans were able to come up with a catchy slogan: "William McKinley, a Western man with Eastern ideas; and Theodore Roosevelt, an Eastern man with Western characteristics." Resigned to it all, Hanna told McKinley: "Your *duty* to the country is to *live* for *four* years from next March." But T.R. eventually established cordial relations with the national chairman and assured him: "I am as strong as a bull moose and you can use me to the limit, taking heed of but one thing and that is my throat."[3]

T.R. was as energetic a campaigner as Bryan. He traveled 21,000 miles, spoke in hundreds of towns and cities, and held audiences spellbound. " 'Tis Tiddy alone that's runnin'," exclaimed Mr. Dooley, "an' he ain't a-runnin', he's gallopin'."[4] T.R. felt strongly about the issues. He warned voters that Bryan's victory would mean "fearful misery, fearful disaster at home" and would "paralyze our whole industrial life." As to empire-building, T.R. took an aggressive line. "We are a nation of men, not a nation of weaklings," he announced. "The American people," he said, were "as ready to face their responsibilities in the Orient as they were ready to face them at home." He added that the question was not "whether we shall expand—for we have already expanded—but whether we shall contract."[5]

Bryan, backed by the Silver Republicans again, by some of the Populists, and by a few anti-imperialist organizations, campaigned almost as vigorously as he had in 1896, though with far less hope of victory. At the outset he singled out three issues for emphasis: the money question, the trusts, and imperialism. He soon realized that free silver no longer evoked much interest and moved on to imperialism, making much of the contradiction between democracy and empire and insisting that the Philippines (where Emilio Aguinaldo was leading a rebellion against American rule) be given independence as soon as possible. "I would not exchange the glory of this Republic," he cried, "for the glory of all the empires that have risen and fallen since time began."[6] Toward the end of his campaign Bryan also talked about the overweening power of the trusts in American life; and he linked his three enemies—trusts, gold, and empire—by seeing all three as different devices by which the plutocracy fastened its grip on the nation and kept the democratic masses in subjection. McKinley, of course, saw the three as indispensable means to financial stability, increased productivity, and flourishing trade by which the business classes would keep the dinner pail full for the masses.

On election day the voters chose McKinley and Roosevelt—but not necessarily empire and trusts—over Bryan and Stevenson, giving McKinley 7,219,525 popular and 292 electoral votes, a popular plurality of 860,788 votes, and turning down Bryan's second bid for the Presidency with only 6,358,737 popular and 155 electoral votes. Some Republicans interpreted their victory—the greatest since 1872—as a mandate for McKinley's foreign policy; but it is more likely that the wave of prosperity that swept the country at the turn of the century had far more to do with it. With industrial production and foreign trade flourishing and wages and farm prices on the uptick, McKinley seemed like a real "advance agent of prosperity" to many Americans and they saw no reason not to vote for "Four Years More of the Full Dinner Pail." At one point during the campaign, when a young Bryanite orator begged a Missouri audience to reject imperialism, an old farmer yelled out: "Well, I guess we can stand it, so long as the hogs are 20 cents a hundred."[7]

Tom Platt, for one, was doubly pleased by the election. He looked forward to March 4, 1897, when McKinley would take his oath as President again and T.R. would "take the veil" as Vice-President. T.R. himself told friends he "now expected to be a dignified nonentity for four years."[8] Six months after the inauguration the fifty-eight-year-old McKinley was assassinated by a young anarchist while attending the Pan-American Exposition in Buffalo, New York, and T.R.—"that damned cowboy," as Hanna called him—became Chief Magistrate.

☆   ☆   ☆

Little Willie

Even before McKinley's renomination William Randolph Hearst's *New York Evening Journal* began running a series of cartoons called "Willie and His Papa," portraying the President as Mark Hanna's little boy. In a typical cartoon young Willie, wearing a velvet Lord Fauntleroy suit, sat on the lap of his pot-bellied and bediamonded Papa (who was labeled "the Trusts"), and they were chatting: "Whose little boy is oo?" "I's oor little boy." [9]

Acceptance Hat

Theodore Roosevelt (who John Hay said was "more fun than a goat") disavowed any interest in the vice-presidential nomination. But when he attended the Republican convention he did not wear the kind of straw hat the other delegates did; he wore a broad-brimmed black hat like those the Rough Riders wore in Cuba. "Gentlemen," said one Republican delegate, "that's an acceptance hat." [10]

Had Their Way

After McKinley and Roosevelt were safely nominated, New York Senator Tom Platt told reporters: "I am glad that we had our way. The people, I mean," he quickly corrected himself, "had their way." [11]

Auto-Intoxication

T.R. campaigned with such exuberance that an Iowan cried: "Has he been drinking?" "Oh, no," was the answer, "he needs no whiskey to make him feel that way—he intoxicates himself by his own enthusiasm." [12]

Sleeping with McKinley

At one whistle stop, a Democratic orator announced confidently that Mrs. Bryan would be sleeping in the White House after March 4. "If so," cried a Republican in the crowd, "she'll be sleeping with McKinley!" [13]

★ ★

CHAPTER THIRTY

1904
T.R.'s Smashing Victory

The main issue in 1904 was Theodore Roosevelt. After becoming President upon McKinley's assassination in 1901, T.R. was upset by sneering references to "His Accidency" and anxious to legitimate his tenure in the White House. "I'd rather be elected to that office than have anything tangible of which I know," he told a friend. "But I shall never be elected to it," he added mournfully, thinking of the Old Guard Republicans. "They don't want me."[1]

The forty-five-year-old T.R. need not have worried. The Old Guard would have preferred someone more conventional but had no intention of turning him out. He was the most popular President since Jackson. His "Square Deal"—which included conservation of the nation's natural resources, regulation of the big corporations in the public interest, and friendliness to labor unions—attracted wide support. The Democrats dismissed his administration as "spasmodic, erratic, sensational, spectacular, and arbitrary," but thousands of people loved the T.R. style.[2] They would have enjoyed a lively presidential campaign too. But T.R. stuck loyally to the rule that Presidents don't take to the stump, and his opponent, Judge Alton B. Parker of New York, also refrained from campaigning. The result was a surprisingly colorless contest for one involving the Rough Rider.

The Republicans convened in Chicago on June 23, nominated T.R. on the first ballot, added Senator Charles W. Fairbanks a wealthy conservative from the doubtful state of Indiana, to the ticket, and adopted a platform repeating Republican platitudes about money and tariff and praising T.R.'s policies. In St. Louis the following month, the Democrats had far less consensus. The Eastern delegates—"Reorganizers" or "Safe-and-Saners"—took over, swept two-time loser Bryan and his followers aside, and selected Alton B. Parker, conservative Chief Justice of the New York Court of Appeals, as its presidential candidate. Bryan tried in vain to get a free-silver plank adopted but the platform was silent on the money question. When notified of his nomination, however, Judge Parker announced that he supported the gold standard and if the delegates disapproved he would withdraw. Convention leaders assured him monetarism was not an issue in the campaign.

Until Parker declared for gold he had been so squeamish as a judge about making political pronouncements that he was called "the enigma from New York." The *New York Sun* thought he had all "the salient qualities of a sphere."[3] His running mate, Henry G. Davis of West Virginia, who was even more obscure, was eighty-two years old and hardly known outside of his state ("a reminiscence from West Virginia").[4] But he was a millionaire and was expected to share his largesse with his party. As it turned out he added nothing either to the party's canvass or to its coffers. Not surprisingly, Bryanites and their "Peerless Leader" were unable to work up much steam for their party's ticket.

On October 1, Joseph Pulitzer published an editorial in the *New York World* that stirred up about the only excitement of the campaign. In it, he asked the President why the Bureau of Corporations (an agency in the Department of Commerce and Labor) had done so little regulating since its founding in 1903. And he went on to ask why T.R. had made George B. Cortelyou, head of the Commerce Department, national chairman of the Republican party. Did the corporations "that are pouring money into your campaign chests," Pulitzer wanted to know, "assume that they are buying protection?" He went on to pose a series of questions: "1. how much has the beef trust contributed to Mr. Cortelyou? 2. how much has the paper trust contributed to Mr. Cortelyou? 3. how much has the coal trust contributed to Mr. Cortelyou? 4. how much has the sugar trust contributed to Mr. Cortelyou? 5. how much has the oil trust contributed to Mr. Cortelyou? 6. how much has the tobacco trust contributed to Mr. Cortelyou? 7. how much has the steel trust contributed to Mr. Cortelyou? 8. how much have the national banks contributed to Mr. Cortelyou? 9. how much has the insurance trust contributed to Mr. Cortelyou? 10. how much have the six great railroads contributed to Mr. Cortelyou?"[5] T.R. ignored Pulitzer at first, but when Parker began attacking "Cortelyouism" and talked about "blackmail," he charged into the arena with such fury that the Democrats dropped the issue. "The assertion," T.R. stormed, "that there has been any blackmail, direct or indirect, by Mr. Cortelyou or by me, is a falsehood."[6]

On November 8, T.R. swept to victory in a landslide that astonished even him. "I am stunned," he told his son Kermit, "by the overwhelming victory we have won."[7] Taking every Northern state plus West Virginia and Missouri among the border states, he won 7,628,785 popular votes (57.4 percent) to Parker's 5,084,442 (37.6 percent) and 336 electoral votes to Parker's 140. It was the most decisive victory since Jackson beat Clay in 1832. Poor Parker was the worst-beaten candidate since Horace Greeley in 1872; he was defeated, as humorist Irwin Cobb put it, "by acclamation."[8] T.R. gleefully told his wife: "I am no longer a political accident."[9]

Roosevelt looked forward eagerly to the full term he had earned on his own. "Tomorrow," he cried on inauguration eve, "I shall come into my office in my own right. Then watch out for me!"[10] During his second term he sponsored stricter railroad regulation, a Meat Inspection Act, more conservation measures, and a Pure Food and Drug Act.

☆ ☆ ☆

Concise Impropriety

On May 18, Ion Perdicaris, a wealthy American-born citizen residing in Morocco, was kidnapped by a bandit named Raisuli and held for ransom. President Roosevelt at once rushed warships to Moroccan waters and arranged for Secretary of State John Hay to send a dramatic message to the American consul-general in Tangier: "This Government wants Perdicaris alive or Raisuli dead." By this time the Moroccan government had secured Perdicaris's release and it turned out he was registered in Athens as a Greek subject. But T.R. went ahead anyway and when the words, "Perdicaris alive or Raisuli dead," were read to the Republican convention meeting in Chicago, they roused the delegates to a high pitch of excitement. "It was magnificent—magnificent!" cried New York's Senator Chauncey M. Depew. For a time the Republicans had a rousing slogan: "Perdicaris alive or Raisuli dead!" When the furor died down, Hay wrote amusedly in his diary: "It is curious how a concise impropriety hits the public."[11]

Faults

"And has he no faults, this hero of mine?" asked the author of a laudatory T.R. campaign biography. "Yes," he answered, "he has and I am glad of it, for I want a live man for a friend, not a dead saint. . . ." T.R.'s faults, it turned out, were two. First: "he cannot dance." Second: "I have heard him sing—that he cannot do."[12]

Didn't Stay Bought

Early in October, T.R. became worried about carrying New York and appealed to railroad magnate E. H. Harriman and U. S. Steel head Henry Clay Frick for funds. Harriman gave $50,000 and raised $250,000 more from friends; Frick came through with $100,000. After the election, when T.R. stepped up his program for regulating business and began talking about the "criminal rich" and the "malefactors of great wealth," Harriman and Frick felt betrayed. "He got down on his knees to us," fumed Frick. "We bought the son of a bitch and then he did not stay bought!" T.R. later denied he had sought their aid.[13]

★ ★

CHAPTER THIRTY-ONE

1908
Taft's Big Victory Over Bryan

"What is the *real difference*," asked Joseph Pulitzer in 1908, "between the Democratic and Republican parties?" The Taft-Bryan confrontation that year was scarcely momentous. William Jennings Bryan, no longer obsessed by silver, was championing a variety of reforms designed to humanize America's industrial society. William Howard Taft was more conservative, but he, too, under T.R.'s grooming, was also taking a forward-looking line. And the Republican and Democratic platforms had more in common this time—especially in their critical view of the trusts—than in disagreement. The voters, declared the *Washington Post*, "refuse to go into hysteria in 1908 over the puny little questions that divide the two parties."[1]

The parties may have converged in 1908 but the candidates were scarcely clones. Bryan, mellower than in 1904 but still eager, energetic, and evangelistic, was convinced he could ride to victory on a wave of Progressivism this time. Taft—big, good-natured, basically conservative in temperament—wasn't especially eager to run. His preference was for the bench; but the pressure of his wife and brother, and of T.R. himself, led him into presidential politics and he tried hard to convince himself that this was what he really wanted and enjoyed. At the Republican convention in Chicago in June the mention of T.R.'s name produced a forty-nine-minute demonstration during which the delegates chanted, "Four—four—four years more!" But T.R., who pulled all the convention's strings from Washington, saw to it that "Big Bill" was nominated on the first ballot, joined with conservative Congressman James S. ("Sunny Jim") Sherman of New York for second place, and wedded to a Progressive statement of party principles. It wasn't T.R.'s fault—though Mrs. Taft suspected it might be—that the genial Ohioan got only twenty-nine minutes of applause to the President's forty-nine. Mrs. Taft nervously kept time.[2]

In Denver the following month, Bryan, like Taft, was nominated on the first ballot and, like T.R., shaped his party's Progressive platform and approved the choice for second place: John W. Kern of Indiana, a spellbinder with great popularity in the West. But Bryan did even better than T.R. when it came to demonstrations. The minute his name was mentioned, the delegates began dancing and parading in the aisles, shouting: "Bryan! Bryan! Bryan! Bryan!" Their demonstration, reported William Allen White, was "the greatest ever made in history."[3] It went on for an hour and a half. Bryan's supporters were bent on making it even longer than the one following the Cross-of-Gold speech in 1896 and checked periodically with each other: "Have we gone over the time yet?"[4]

Bryan soon proclaimed the basic issue of the campaign: "Shall the people rule?" The choice in 1908, he said, was between a government devoted to the people's rights and government by privilege. It was an old theme with Bryan; but this time it was not sidetracked into silver and no longer seemed so outlandish. Progressivism—especially when it came to controlling the big trusts—was becoming respectable in middle-class America. Taft, with T.R. at his elbow, took an advanced position on many issues, though Bryan, with his deep-seated Populist predilections, was undoubtedly far more of a reformer. Bryan, the *New York Evening Post* concluded, represented the "great wave of discontent and desire for radical changes, which has swept over a large part of the country."[5]

At the outset neither Bryan nor Taft was anxious to do much campaigning; but after a spiritless beginning the contest began picking up steam as the two of them took to the stump. Bryan continued to be good at it but Taft was clumsy at first. He read lengthy speeches, filled with statistics and references to court decisions, that left audiences listless; and, in his guileless candor, sometimes made tactless remarks in public. In one speech he offended Civil War veterans by alluding to General Grant's bouts with the bottle during his encomium of the Civil War hero. But with T.R.'s coaching he gradually improved and even began enjoying the hustings. "Hit them hard, old man!" T.R. prodded him. And again: "Do not answer Bryan; *attack* him. Don't let him make the issues."[6] Taft did attack; he said Bryan's economic views were "full of sophistries" and would produce "a paralysis of business."[7] Bryan retorted that the Panic of 1907 had occurred under Republican, not Democratic auspices. But he also tried to turn T.R.'s popularity to his own advantage by praising many of the Rough Rider's policies and claiming they were borrowed from him. Yet Bryan and T.R. had one heated exchange. In September, William Randolph Hearst released letters taken from the files of the Standard Oil Company showing secret dealings between several prominent politicians and the great oil trust. One of them was Oklahoma Governor Charles N. Haskell, Bryan's campaign treasurer. Haskell resigned his position, but T.R. accused Bryan of "moral obliquity" for insisting he was innocent until proven guilty.[8]

On November 3 the voters turned down Bryan's third and last bid for the Presidency more emphatically than ever before. Bryan was stunned by the returns; he "could not understand," he told Louis Post, "how we were so badly beaten." Taft won a popular majority of more than a million (7,677,788 to 6,407,982) and 159 more electoral votes than Bryan (321 to 162). "We have beaten them to a frazzle!" exulted T.R.[9] It was the worst of Bryan's three defeats. Despite an increase in the nation's population Bryan received even fewer votes than in 1896.

Baffled by it all, Bryan invited readers of his newspaper *The Commoner* to write in explaining what went wrong. The letters poured in for weeks after the election and he carried them in his paper under the heading, "SOLVING THE MYSTERY OF 1896." But there was really no mystery. Business people naturally preferred Taft; and labor, despite AFL Samuel Gompers's endorsement of Bryan, continued to be lukewarm to the Great Commoner. Taft's close association with T.R. also gave Big Bill a big boost. "Roosevelt has cut enough hay," said some Republicans. "Taft is the man to put it into the barn."[10] So, too, thought T.R. himself, at least for a while. And then he began having doubts.

☆ ☆ ☆

T.A.F.T.

Jokes circulated about the fifty-one-year-old Taft's subserviency to T.R. "That's a splendid phonograph, old man," went one story. "It reproduced the sound of Roosevelt's voice better than I ever thought possible. What make?" "We call it the Taft," was the reply. Another joke had it that T.A.F.T. meant, "Take Advice from Theodore."[11]

Farther and Farther Away

After Bryan's nomination Taft received a telegram from one of his admirers: "Hearty congratulations on your certain election in November. Bryan was nominated for the first time at Chicago, for the second time at Kansas City, and for the third time at Denver. He will be nominated for the fourth time at Salt Lake, for the fifth time at San Francisco, for the sixth time at Honolulu and for the seventh time at Manila, thus getting steadily farther and farther away from the White House."[12]

The Golf Problem

At the outset of the campaign T.R. gave Taft terse advice: "Photographs on horseback, yes, tennis, no, and golf is fatal." But Taft spent a lot of time playing golf. He told reporters that 297 pounds was too much to carry around while campaigning and he was trying to lose twenty-five to thirty pounds on the links. But a man wrote T.R. from Illinois pointing out that "thousands and thousands of laboring people" regarded golf as a "dude's game" and suggested the Republican candidate "cast aside golf and take an axe and cut wood." T.R. thought it was good advice and told Taft he had received hundreds of letters about Taft's golf-playing. "It is just like my tennis," he said. "I never let a photograph of me in tennis costume appear."

But T.R. advised Taft against horseback riding, too, because it was "dangerous for him and cruelty to the horse." One day Taft's horse actually collapsed under him and the search for a sturdier steed received a lot of attention. One man wrote the White House, tongue in cheek: "I have got one so big that I had to build a special stall to keep him in. He's twenty-five hands high (8'4") and weighs three thousand five hundred pounds. I am sending him on free by freight." Taft continued to sneak off to play golf as often as he could, but the reporters covering him, many of whom also played the game, were good about keeping it out of the papers.

Bryan had no golf problem; in fact, he engaged in no sport whatever. "Exercise for its own sake," noted a campaign biography, "is not included in Bryan's schedule of living." The author nailed his point home: "To imagine Mr. Bryan playing tennis is preposterous."[13]

Caught It

After the election Charles Thompson was riding a trolley car near Bryan's place, Fairview, and saw Bryan's young daughter Ruth running to catch it. She made it just in time, dropped into the seat beside him, and panted: "I seem to be the only member of the Bryan family that ever ran for anything and caught it."[14]

Don't Want Me

After his third defeat Bryan liked to tell the story of the drunk who tried three times to get into a private club, was thrown downstairs each time, and on landing in the street after his third attempt, picked himself up, dusted off his clothes, and said thoughtfully: "They can't fool me. Those fellows don't want me in there!"[15]

★ ★

CHAPTER THIRTY-TWO

1912
The High Tide of Progressivism:
Wilson, Roosevelt, and Taft

The campaign of 1912 was one of the liveliest in American history. The Republican party split in two, with the regular Republicans nominating William Howard Taft for a second term and the insurgents organizing a new Progressive party to run Theodore Roosevelt for President. The Democrats had their conservatives and liberals too, but, after many ballots, managed to agree on New Jersey's reform governor, Woodrow Wilson, as their standard-bearer. The three-cornered race kept the country agitated for months.

Personalities were important in 1912: the genial (but now aroused) Taft; the energetic, crusading T.R.; and the moralizing, schoolmasterish Wilson. But so were principles: Taft's conservatism, Roosevelt's Progressivism, and Wilson's liberalism. In speeches accepting their party's nominations, all three recognized that a "new day" had dawned for America and that it was the duty of government to concern itself with the general welfare. Laissez-faire no longer seemed adequate. Even Taft acknowledged that the good old days of unbridled acquisition and social irresponsibility were gone forever. How could the United States possibly be a great world power if large numbers of its citizens were deprived and disaffected?

T.R. dominated the 1912 contest. He had not lost interest in politics when he left the White House in 1909, confident that Taft would continue with his policies. He was still fairly young, his energy and ambition as boundless as ever, and his concern for the country's welfare undiminished. After several months hunting big game in Africa and an ego-boosting tour of Europe, he returned to the United States in June 1910 and received a tremendous welcome in New York City. During the next few months Republican Progressives sought him out and labored to convince him that Taft had sold out to the Old Guard and that he must get into action again.

Roosevelt at first refused to commit himself; after all, he had for-sworn another term in 1908. But he finally decided that the third-term tradition applied to three consecutive terms and that it was permissible for him to run again. "My hat is in the ring!" he announced jubilantly in February 1912. "The fight is on and I am stripped to the buff!"[1] By this time he had outlined his New Nationalism, a program involving so-cial welfare, direct democracy, and federal regulation of business, and had exchanged hot words with Taft over the latter's movement to the right. T.R. charged that his former friend had yielded to "the bosses and to the great privileged interests" and was "disloyal to every canon of ordinary decency;" Taft retorted that those supporting T.R.'s New Nationalism were "destructive radicals," "political emotionalists," and "neurotics."[2]

T.R., still enormously popular, was unquestionably the choice of the Republican rank and file for the G.O.P. nomination. He bested the President in nine state primaries, including Ohio; poor Taft won only one primary. But Republican state conventions all elected delegates committed to the President. When someone suggested the two men withdraw in favor of a compromise candidate, T.R. cried: "I'll name the compromise candidate. He'll be me. I'll name the compromise plat-form. It will be our platform."[3] Taft, whose dander was up, was simi-larly determined to get the nomination for himself. Taft's supporters controlled the party machinery, and when the Republican convention met in Chicago in June they awarded most of the contested seats to the President, nominated him for a second term on the first ballot, and for second place again picked James S. Sherman (who died on October 30 and was replaced by Columbia University president Nicholas Murray Butler). During the proceedings, convention chairman Elihu Root ruled so many insurgent motions out of order that finally one T.R. man in-terrupted for a point of order and cried: "I make the point that the steam roller is exceeding the speed limit!" After that T.R.'s supporters took to shouting, "Toot! too! Toot! too!" and rubbing sheets of sand-paper together every time Root spoke. But when Taft won, they stormed out of the convention, met with T.R. (who had come to Chicago wear-ing a big sombrero), and cheered lustily when he agreed to run on an independent ticket.[4]

Two months later T.R.'s supporters—social workers, reformers, in-tellectuals, feminists, Republican insurgents, disgruntled politicians, and businessmen who favored the New Nationalism—held a convention of their own in Chicago, sang "Onward Christian Soldiers" and the "Battle Hymn of the Republic," organized the Progressive party, and nomi-nated T.R. for President and Senator Hiram Johnson of California for Vice-President. T.R.'s appearance on the platform touched off a tu-multuous demonstration. For fifty-two minutes people shouted, yelled, and waved red bandanas, and when T.R. tried to quiet them, began singing:

> Thou wilt not cower in the dust,
> Roosevelt, O Roosevelt!
> Thy gleaming sword shall never rust
> Roosevelt, O Roosevelt![5]

In the "Confession of Faith" which he made after order was restored, T.R. outlined his Progressive principles, dismissed the Republicans and Democrats as "husks, with no real soul within either, divided on artificial lines, boss-ridden and privilege-controlled," and exclaimed: "I hope we shall win. . . . But win, or lose, we shall not falter. . . . Our cause is based on the eternal principle of righteousness; and even though we who now lead may for the time fail, in the end the cause itself shall triumph. . . . We stand at Armageddon, and we battle for the Lord."[6] The new party drew up a platform (or "Covenant with the People") calling for better working conditions in factories, government aid to agriculture, women's suffrage, the popular election of Senators, a federal income tax, the conservation of natural resources, federal commissions to manage the tariff and regulate the trusts, and a host of other measures designed to further social justice and popular rule. "I'm feeling like a Bull Moose!" T.R. told reporters at one point; and the Progressives adopted the bull moose as their party symbol. Then they went forth to do battle singing, chanting, shouting, and screaming: "Follow! Follow! We will follow Roosevelt! Anywhere, everywhere, we will follow on!"[7]

With the Republicans divided, the Democrats were almost sure of victory if they chose wisely. Though the thrice-defeated William Jennings Bryan was out of the running this time, he played a prominent part in the Democratic convention which met in Baltimore late in June. When the delegates chose the conservative Alton B. Parker (1904 candidate) as temporary chairman, an indignant Bryan sponsored a resolution opposing the nomination of "any candidate for President who is the representative of or under any obligation to J. Pierpont Morgan, Thomas F. Ryan, August Belmont, or any other member of the privilege-hunting and favor-seeking class."[8] And when, after the balloting began, New York's Tammany Hall began voting for Champ Clark of Missouri (Speaker of the House and the favorite of party regulars), Bryan announced he wouldn't support anyone backed by Tammany and persuaded Nebraska's delegation to switch to the fifty-five-year-old Woodrow Wilson. Wilson's nomination didn't come until the forty-sixth ballot and it took more than Bryan to achieve it. But Bryan became an ardent Wilson man, and the New Jersey Governor (a conservative who gradually "Bryanized" his thinking about social issues after entering politics in 1910) felt deeply indebted to the Great Commoner. Under Bryan's influence, the platform adopted by the Democrats was an advanced one. But it differed from the Progressive party "Covenant" by stressing tariff reduction and trust-busting rather than regulatory commissions to handle the problem of monopoly. The Democratic vice-presidential candidate, Thomas Marshall of Indiana, was famous mainly for having declared: "What this country needs is a good five-cent cigar."[9]

Taft bowed out very early in the campaign. "Sometimes," he wrote plaintively in July, "I think I might as well give up so far as being a candidate is concerned. There are so many people in the country who don't like me. Without knowing much about me, they don't like me—apparently on the Dr. Fell principle . . . they don't exactly know the reason, but it is on the principle:

> I don't like you, Dr. Fell,
> The reason why I can not tell,
> But this I know and know full well,
> I don't like you, Dr. Fell.[10]

It wasn't that voters disliked Taft; they simply found his conservatism beside the point in an era of reform. His placid personality, too, was in sharp contrast to T.R.'s vigor and Wilson's earnestness. "I have been told that I ought to do this, ought to do that . . . that I do not keep myself in the headlines," Taft told newsmen in August. "I know it, but I can't do it. I couldn't if I would, and I wouldn't if I could." Except for his address accepting the Republican nomination he made few speeches. But he viewed the Progressive movement as "a religious cult with a fakir at the head of it" and secretly hoped for a Wilson victory.[11] So did many Republican bigwigs, shocked by T.R.'s endorsement of the recall of judicial decisions by popular referendum. Aware that Taft's chances of victory were slim, Big Business contributed only meagerly to the Republican war chest this time around.

With Taft sulking on the sidelines, the 1912 contest turned into a duel; and the contest between T.R. and Wilson held the nation fascinated for weeks on end. T.R. was, as usual, good at coining phrases, getting headlines, and rousing audiences by his moral fervor and vigorous offensive. When Bryan said the Rough Rider had stolen many of his ideas from the Democrats, T.R. retorted: "So I have. That is quite true. I have taken every one of them except those suited for the inmates of lunatic asylums."[12] He also called Taft a "fathead" with the "brains of a guinea pig" and contemptuously dismissed Wilson's program for trust-busting as "rural Toryism."[13]

But Wilson was effective on the campaign trail too—lucid, impassioned, at times witty—and refrained from indulging in personalities. The campaign was still young when he discovered the tariff was a stale issue and began devoting his speeches to the trusts. With the help of Louis Brandeis, brilliant young Boston lawyer, he formulated a program he called the "New Freedom" with which to challenge T.R.'s New Nationalism. T.R. insisted big corporations were here to stay and essential to efficient production but that they must be regulated in the national interest. Wilson warned that regulatory agencies might fall into the hands of the interests they were designed to control and that it was necessary to break up monopolistic organizations and restore freedom of competition so that every ambitious individual might have a chance to rise in life. It was a question, he insisted, of "regulated competition" vs. "regulated monopoly." "Ours is a programme of liberty," he told his audiences; "theirs is a programme of regulation."[14]

On the night of October 14, as T.R. was getting into his car to drive from the hotel to the main auditorium to Milwaukee to speak, a fanatic named John Shrank stepped up, shouted something about a third term, and shot him in the breast. As the crowd converged on the assassin, T.R. cried: "Stand back! Don't hurt the man!" Doctors in Roosevelt's party wanted to rush him to the hospital at once, but he waved them aside. "You just stay where you are!" he cried. "I am going to make this speech and you might as well compose yourself." When they persisted, he cried: "Get an ambulance or a carriage or anything you like at ten o'clock and I'll go to the hospital, but I won't go until I have finished my speech." He then ordered his car to proceed to the auditorium and said fervently: "I will make this speech or die. It is one thing or the other." When he reached the hall, someone announced that he had been shot and as he went out on the platform he "smiled and waved his hand," according to one reporter, "and the men and women stood up on their seats and cried and shouted their sympathy and affection." "It is true," said T.R., almost in a whisper. "I am going to ask you to be very quiet and please excuse me from making a long speech. I'll do the best I can, but there is a bullet in my body." He then took his manuscript from his coat pocket; it was soaked with blood. "It is nothing," he said, as people gasped. "I am not hurt badly. I have a message to deliver and will deliver it as long as there is life in my body." The audience became deathly still as he went on to say: "I have had an A-1 time in life and I am having it now." It was, he said, a very natural thing that weak and vicious minds should be inflamed to acts of violence by the kind of artful mendacity and abuse that have been heaped upon me for the last three months."[15]

Roosevelt went on to talk for an hour and a half about the New Nationalism and was then taken to the hospital. The X-rays revealed that the bullet had fractured his fourth rib and lodged close to his right lung. "It is largely due to the fact that he is a physical marvel that he was not dangerously wounded," observed one of the surgeons. "He is one of the most powerful men I have ever seen laid on an operating table. The bullet lodged in the massive muscles of the chest instead of penetrating the lung."[16] T.R. took a couple of weeks off from campaigning to recuperate; and both Taft and Wilson sent telegrams of sympathy and called a halt to their own activities for the time being. It was just as well. T.R.'s throat was almost gone by this time from incessant speech-making; and Wilson, too, needed respite from the rigorous demands of the hustings.

Wilson's victory on November 5 came as a surprise to no one, certainly not to either T.R. or Taft. Wilson won by a landslide in the Electoral College, carrying forty of the forty-eight states, with 435 votes to T.R.'s 88 (six states) and Taft's meager 8 (two states). But he won only 41.9 percent of the popular votes (6,283,019); T.R.'s 4,119,507 (27.4 percent) and Taft's 3,484,956 (23.2 percent) made it clear that he had needed the split in the Republican party to win. He received fewer popular votes, in fact, than Bryan had won in each of his three tries for the Presidency. But even as a minority winner President Wilson had a clear mandate for reform. The voters had cast more votes for the New Freedom and the New Nationalism than they had for the kind of conservatism that President Taft represented. And they had even given Eugene Debs over 900,000 votes (6 percent of the total), the most any Socialist candidate ever received in a presidential contest. On the local level the Progressives, who concentrated primarily on advancing T.R.'s candidacy, did poorly. The Democrats succeeded in carrying both houses of Congress (and won twenty-one governorships) and it looked as though the President-elect would have clear sailing for his New Freedom after inauguration day.

On the night of the election a group of Princeton students came by to congratulate Wilson on his victory and he remarked thoughtfully: "I myself have no feeling of triumph tonight. I have a feeling of solemn responsibility."[17] T.R., for his part, was realistic about it all. "The fight is over," he declared. "We are beaten. There is only one thing to do and that is to go back to the Republican party. You can't hold a party like the Progressive party together. . . . There are no loaves and fishes."[18] Since the Progressive party was largely a T.R. phenomenon, it did not last long after its defeat in 1912. Some of the Bull Moosers returned quietly to the G.O.P. after the election; others remained loyal to Wilson. But in the Republican party after 1912 the Old Guard was unmistakably in the saddle.

Have Another Cup?

In 1904, T.R. had announced he wouldn't be a candidate for a third term, but, having changed his mind, he issued a clarification in 1912: "My position on the third term is perfectly simple. I said I would not accept a nomination for a third term under any circumstances, meaning of course a third consecutive term. . . ." Elaborated the *Outlook* facetiously: "When a man says at breakfast in the morning, 'No, thank you, I will not take any more coffee,' it does not mean that he will not take any more coffee tomorrow morning, or next week, or next month, or next year." Thereafter any vaudeville comedian could get a big laugh by asking the audience: "Have another cup of coffee?"[19]

Driven into Corner

Before Taft no President had stumped in a primary campaign and no President had ever taken to the stump after his renomination. Before Taft, it was rare for any presidential candidate to seek votes. Greeley in 1872, Bryan in 1896, and, to a limited extent, Blaine in 1884 and Taft in 1908, had stumped the country, but none was President at the time. It was Taft's anger at T.R., who had bitterly criticized his administration, that propelled him to the hustings. He was also disturbed by his former friend's movement to the left. "Whether I win or lose is not the important thing," he told journalist Charles Thompson. "But," he added, eyes blazing, "I am in this fight to perform a great public duty— the duty of keeping Theodore Roosevelt out of the White House."

Taft did poorly in the primaries, compared with T.R., but was determined to win the nomination anyway. "Thompson," he told his journalist-friend a month before the convention, "I expect to be nominated for President, and I want to be. So that I can keep Theodore Roosevelt from wrecking the Republican party." "Seems to me," said Thompson, "he's got pretty far along with that already." "That isn't what I mean," said Taft. "I don't mean wrecking it in an election. I mean warping it away from its purpose and changing its character. I mean changing it to a radical party from a party of moderate liberalism." Taft's conviction that he must accept T.R.'s challenge and fight back was his primary reason for breaking precedent and appealing to the masses for votes. "Even a rat," he explained gloomily, "will fight when driven into a corner."[20]

Onward

At the Bull Moose convention in August, Governor Hiram Johnson marched at the head of the California delegation with a banner reading:

> I want to be a Bull Moose,
> And with the Bull Moose stand
> With Antlers on my forehead
> And a Big Stick in my hand.

Delegates from Michigan got the whole convention parading to the tune of their own song:

> Follow, follow, follow,
> We will follow Roosevelt,
> Anywhere, everywhere,
> We will follow on!

And the New York delegation, headed by Jewish philanthropist Oscar S. Straus, marched through the aisles singing "Onward, Christian Soldiers."[21]

Only Vice

After formally accepting the Democratic nomination for Vice-President, Governor Thomas Marshall of Indiana gave Wilson a book inscribed: "From your only vice, Thomas R. Marshall." Later on he liked to quip: "Once there were two brothers. One ran away to sea, the other was elected Vice-President, and neither of them was heard of again."[22]

See Me Clearly

T.R.'s mother was a Georgian and when the Rough Rider spoke in Atlanta the crowd was at first friendly. But when T.R., who had attacked the Republican party in the North, started in on the Democrats, the crowd turned hostile, started hissing and booing, and threatened to shout him off the platform. Suddenly T.R. sprang up on a table. His movement took everyone by surprise and people stopped heckling to see what he was going to do next. T.R. waited until he could be heard and then, beaming amiably, announced: "I got up here so that you can all see me clearly." He was allowed to finish his speech.[23]

Successful Speech

In informal talks from the rear-end of his train, T.R. got in the habit of repeating remarks that had gone over big the first time he made them. Whenever children flocked together on the railroad tracks he would say, "Children, don't crowd so close to the car; it might back up, and we can't afford to lose any little Bull Mooses, you know." If a woman had a baby in her arms, he would say: "I like babies; I'm in the grandfather class myself, you know." And whenever a Grand Army man appeared in the crowd, he would say: "Comrade, you who wear the button—" and the people always cheered. Finally, after a thirty-day swing around the circle, T.R. headed homeward and told reporters they wouldn't have to hear any more speeches. The reporters began singing, "We're going home, we're going home," and then started imitating T.R.'s voice, manner, and gestures, and tossing off all the stock remarks they had heard so often. Suddenly T.R. emerged from his compartment, saw what was going on, wagged his big forefinger at the reporters, and began mocking himself. "Comrade, you who wear the button," he began, then tore through his "social and industrial justice" paragraph, implored, "children, don't crowd so close to the car, it might back up, and, in his highest falsetto, cried: "We can't afford to lose any little Bull Mooses, you know!" It was not his greatest speech, the reporters agreed, but it was one of his most successful.[24]

Libel

Some people questioned T.R.'s sanity. Dr. Allen McLane Hamilton discussed the subject in the *New York Times*. Dr. Morton Prince wrote a long paper about it. "T.R. would go down in history," declared Prince, an apostle of the New Psychology, "as one of the most illustrious psychological examples of the distortion of conscious mental process through the forces of subconscious wishes." A Chicago real-estate dealer offered to donate $1000 to charity if T.R. were "not proved to be insane."

Alcoholism was another charge. Ever since 1900, T.R.'s enemies had been circulating stories that he was given to drunken rages in public. "Roosevelt's drinking like a fish," a stranger told a reporter covering T.R.'s campaign in Butte, Montana. "I was just talking to one of the reporters who are going around with him, and he tells me that he has just had an interview with Roosevelt fifteen minutes long, and that in those fifteen minutes Roosevelt drank fourteen highballs." When the reporter told one of T.R.'s friends, the latter said, "Did you tell him he was a liar?" "What was the use?" sighed the reporter. "He would only have made it twenty highballs the next time he told the story, and said I was the reporter who told him."

The lies about T.R.'s drinking—he was in fact an extremely light drinker—finally got into print. In a story about T.R., the *Iron Age* asserted that the rough Rider "lies and curses in a most disgusting way. He gets drunk, too, and that not infrequently, and all his intimates know about it." At this point T.R. sued for libel and eventually won.[25]

Silent Movie

During his Western tour, T.R. arranged for his special train to stop at a little station in Arizona so some of the Rough Riders from Spanish-American War days could ride over from their ranches to shake hands with their old commander. The Rough Riders cantered in, some of them from forty miles away, and were waiting for T.R. when his train pulled into the station. As soon as T.R. went into a huddle with his old comrades, the moving-picture man in the party (whom T.R. had christened "Movie") saw a chance to get some good campaign shots, so he yelled over to T.R. that he was going to start cranking the camera. T.R. got the point, grinned, turned to the Rough Riders, arranged them appropriately around him, and began orating. "Throw a little ginger in, Colonel!" shouted "Movie," as he ground away; and T.R., pretending to be giving an impassioned campaign speech, spouted any nonsense that came into his head: "Barnes, Penrose and Smoot—do you remember the charge up San Juan?—Jack Greenway, one of the best men in my regiment—recall of judicial decisions—the man with the muckrake—Alice in Wonderland is a great book—Bob Evans took the fleet into the Pacific—" The Rough Riders listened in astonishment, while T.R. campaign workers, standing behind the camera, almost doubled up in laughter. "That'll be a corker, Colonel," said "Movie" finally, stopping the crank. T.R. then joined the rest of his party in the roars of laughter. "By George!" he gasped, mopping his brow, "I haven't had so much fun in a week!"[26]

Gentlemen in the Boxes

Despite his reputation for austerity, Wilson developed a ready wit during the campaign. At a railroad station, where people mounted the tops of box-cars to hear him speak, he addressed them: "Fellow citizens—Gentlemen in the boxes—."[27]

Tobacco

In a speech at the Monmouth County Fair in Red Bank, New Jersey, on August 30, Wilson drew the picture of a group of men sitting around the stove in a country store chewing tobacco, spitting in a sawdust box, and discussing the affairs of the neighborhood. "Whatever may be said against the chewing of tobacco," he went on to say, "this at least can be said for it, that it gives a man time to think between sentences." A newspaper promptly published that part of the speech with the heading, "Advocates the Chewing of Tobacco," and shortly thereafter tobacco firms began reproducing the newspaper report as part of an advertising campaign. "The whole point of the thing was missed," said Wilson ruefully when he saw what had happened. "I wasn't advocating the chewing of tobacco, but I was advocating thinking between sentences!"[28]

Woody

Taft was known as "Big Bill" and Roosevelt had several nicknames: Teddy, the Rough Rider, the Bull Mooser. Wilson, though, seemed too aloof to most people to win a popular nickname and he rather regretted it. Once, however, when he was addressing a crowd of devoted Democrats in the Middle West, he received tumultuous applause at one point and someone yelled: "That was a good one, Woody!" Wilson beamed and continued with such enthusiasm that the crowd went wild when he finished. Afterward, his face still glowing, he said to reporter Charles Thompson: "Did you hear, Mr. Thompson. They called me Woody!"[29]

★ ★

CHAPTER THIRTY-THREE

1916
Wilson and the Great War

In 1916 the American people hoped for peace and prepared for war. The savage conflict which exploded in Europe in 1914 inevitably involved America's neutral rights at sea and led to clashes with both England (whom most Americans favored) and Germany (whose submarine campaign produced American as well as Allied casualties). After the sinking of the *Lusitania,* with 128 Americans aboard, in May 1915, President Wilson took up "preparedness" and sponsored legislation to expand the nation's military and naval forces and build up its merchant marine. But he began building a welfare as well as a warfare state during his first term, abandoning his own restrictive New Freedom for T.R.'s expansive New Nationalism and sponsoring a series of Progressive measures—trust-regulatory and farm and labor legislation—designed to strengthen the American economy and produce a patriotic citizenry.

Wilson hoped that a strong and united America—what he called "Big America"—would be able to play an important part in world affairs when the Great War (later called the First World War) was over. Wilson didn't intend for foreign affairs to get involved in politics; he wanted to center his campaign for re-election in 1916 on Progressivism and "Americanism" (loyalty to the United States rather than to one's land of ethnic origin). But foreign policy quickly became the major issue. Most Americans, including Wilson himself (but not the bellicose Theodore Roosevelt) were anxious to avoid embroilment in the terrible war overseas.

From the outset, the overwhelming desire for peace dominated the proceedings of the Democratic convention when it met in St. Louis on June 14. In his keynote speech the first day, Martin H. Glynn, former Governor of New York, began talking about "Americanism," as Wilson had wished, but roused little interest among the delegates. But when he said that keeping out of war was the "paramount issue" and began giving examples of how the United States had handled foreign crises without going to war, there was wild applause and the delegates shouted, "Go on! Go on!" At this point Glynn discarded his prepared speech and began discussing Wilson's efforts to preserve American neutrality in some detail. And whenever he gave a specific example the delegates shouted: "What did we do? What did we do?" "We didn't go to war!" Glynn shouted back each time. "This policy . . . ," he went on to say "may not satisfy . . . the fire-eater or the swashbuckler . . . But it does satisfy the mothers of the land, at whose hearth and fireside no jingoistic war has placed an empty chair. It does satisfy the daughters of this land, from whom bluster and brag have sent no husband, no sweetheart and no brother to the mouldering dissolution of the grave."[1]

On the second day of the convention, Senator Ollie James of Kentucky, permanent chairman, continued the peace theme, and William Jennings Bryan did the same when he came to speak. "I agree with the American people," exclaimed Bryan, "in thanking God we have a President who has kept—*who will keep*—us out of war." After Wilson was nominated for re-election on the first ballot and Thomas Marshall chosen again for second place, the Democrats coined one of the most famous slogans in campaign history: "He kept us out of war."[2]

The Republican convention opened in Chicago early in June. T.R. wanted the nomination badly, but his defection in 1912 made him a pariah with party regulars and the Republicans chose Supreme Court Justice Charles Evans Hughes, former Governor of New York and a moderate Progressive, as their candidate on the third ballot. They did, though, pick T.R.'s old Vice-President, Charles W. Fairbanks, for second place and adopt a platform chiding Wilson for his supine foreign policy. The Progressive party held a convention, too, in Chicago, and nominated T.R. for President, but the Rough Rider flatly refused to accept the honor. "Americans are two-party people," he told the dismayed delegates, and, forgetting about the GOP's origin, added: "There is no place for a third party in our politics."[3]

When the Republicans nominated Hughes, T.R. announced: "I'll support Hughes, but not until he declares himself. We must know where he stands on national honor, national defense and all the other great questions before we accept him."[4] T.R. ended by backing Hughes but it was a lukewarm gesture. To friends he referred to the dignified Justice as a "bearded iceberg." For T.R., Wilson was of course far worse: a "damned Presbyterian hypocrite" and a "Byzantine logothete." But he also called Hughes a "whiskered Wilson" and once said the only difference between the two candidates was "a shave."[5] His hawkish pronouncements during the campaign proved to be Hughes's albatross.

Hughes had a tough campaign on his hands. If he took the T.R. line that Wilson was not aggressive enough in defending American rights, he risked alienating large numbers of voters who were anxious to stay out of war. But if he said that Wilson's partiality for England might produce war with Germany, he not only faced estrangement from Republican hawks like T.R. and Senator Henry Cabot Lodge of Massachusetts; he also opened himself up to charges of being pro-German. He was handicapped, too, by the hard, cold fact that in May 1916 Wilson's diplomatic pressure had succeeded in forcing the Germans to suspend their unrestricted submarine campaign, at least for the time being. Hughes tried to escape his dilemma by saying he was for "America first," favored a truly neutral policy which condemned "improper interference with American commerce or with American mails" by both Britain and Germany, and wanted "a flag that protects the American in his lawful rights wherever his legitimate business may take him." But he also equivocated. Sometimes he attacked Wilson for not standing up to the Germans; other times, particularly in German-American areas, he took a softer line. Some people began calling him "Charles Evasive Hughes"; others accused him of being pro-German.[6]

Wilson, who did far less campaigning than Hughes, increasingly warmed to the peace theme. In statement after statement which he put out at "Shadow Lawn," his new summer home at Long Branch along the New Jersey shore, he cited his own efforts to keep the peace without surrendering American rights, and, by linking Hughes with T.R., succeeded in tagging the Republicans as the war party. For a time, Hughes tried to get mileage out of the failures of Wilson's Mexican policy, which, among other things, involved sending American forces into Mexico to pursue bandit Pancho Villa who had raided Columbus, New Mexico. But he roused little support on this issue; he seemed to be recommending armed intervention at the very time when a joint Mexican-American commission had been established to settle the disputes between the two countries. Shifting to domestic policy, Hughes tried to make a major issue of Wilson's labor policy, calling the Adamson Act, an eight-hour law for railroad workers (which Wilson sponsored to avoid a nationwide strike) a "force law" and "labor's goldbrick." But about all he accomplished was to confirm labor leaders like Samuel Gompers in their preference for the President. Wilson decided not to waste time answering Hughes's attacks on his administration. "I am inclined," he told Bernard Baruch, "to follow the course suggested by a friend of mine who says that he has always followed the rule never to murder a man who is committing suicide slowly but surely."[7]

Some people thought Hughes committed suicide in California. The California GOP was bitterly divided between the conservative Old Guard and militant Progressives like Governor Hiram Johnson (T.R.'s running mate in 1912), who was making a bid for a Senate seat in 1916. When Hughes visited California on his Western tour in August, he made the rounds with Republican regulars at his side and seemed to be going out of his way to keep his distance from Johnson and the Progressives.

Hughes was anxious to avoid getting embroiled in an intraparty fight; but his failure to seek Johnson out and cultivate his friendship turned out to be a major error. On August 21 came the famous "forgotten handshake." On that day Hughes stopped at the same hotel in Long Beach where Johnson was staying, but the two never got to meet. When Hughes was back in Los Angeles, he learned what had happened and sent Johnson a friendly note, but by then it was too late. Johnson officially supported Hughes but did nothing to help him in California. Among California Progressives, in fact, the word went out that their preference was for Johnson for the Senate and Wilson for the Presidency. In the end Johnson did very well in his election to the U.S. Senate while Hughes lost the state.

New York Congressman John W. Dwight thought Hughes's chances in California had hinged on a single dollar. Hughes could have carried the state and won the election, he said afterward, if "a man of sense, with a dollar, would have invited Hughes and Johnson to his room when they were both in the same hotel in California. He would have ordered three Scotch whiskies, which would have been seventy-five cents, and that would have left a tip of twenty-five cents for the waiter. . . . That little Scotch would have brought those men together; there would have been mutual understanding and respect and Hughes would have carried California and been elected."[8] It is a dramatic, but simplistic way of looking at it.

As election day approached, the Democrats stepped up their peace campaign; and in "front porch" speeches at "Shadow Lawn," Wilson warned that a Republican victory would mean entry into the European war. "I am not expecting this country to get into war," he declared on October 21. "I know that the way in which we have preserved the peace is objected to, and that certain gentlemen say they would have taken some other way that would inevitably have resulted in war, but I am not expecting this country to get into war, partly because I am not expecting these gentlemen to have a chance to make a mess of it."[9] Democratic campaigners touring the West emphasized keeping out of war and Democratic leaflets and handbills, distributed by the millions, did the same. One pamphlet reminded American mothers that Wilson had "saved their sons and their husbands from unrighteous battlefields" and another summed it all up as follows: "More than all, our country is at peace in a world at war." On November 4 the following full-page advertisement appeared in leading newspapers in various parts of the country:

You Are Working—*Not Fighting!*
Alive and Happy;—*Not cannon Fodder!*
Wilson and Peace with Honor?
or
Hughes with Roosevelt and War?

Roosevelt says we should hang our heads in shame because we are not at *war* with Germany on behalf of Belgium! Roosevelt says that following the sinking of the *Lusitania* he would have foregone diplomacy and seized every ship in our ports flying the German Flag. That would have meant *war!*
Hughes says He and Roosevelt are in Complete Accord

. . . .

The Lesson is Plain:
If You Want WAR, Vote for HUGHES!
If You Want Peace with Honor
VOTE FOR WILSON!
And Continued Prosperity.[10]

When returns began coming in from precincts in the East on election night, November 7, it looked as if Hughes was going to sweep the country. He carried every Eastern state north of the Potomac except New Hampshire and Maryland and also won in several Midwestern states. By midnight he was sure of 254 electoral votes; all he needed to win was twelve more votes and California's thirteen would put him over the top. The *New York Times*, which had backed Wilson, conceded the election to Hughes, and the *New York World* followed suit soon after. Late editions of several newspapers carried big pictures of the Republican candidate with the caption: "THE PRESIDENT-ELECT—CHARLES EVANS HUGHES." Hughes retired that night thinking he had probably won and Wilson thought the same. "Well," said Wilson resignedly, "I will not send Mr. Hughes a telegram of congratulations tonight, for things are not settled. . . . There now seems little hope that we shall not be drawn into the War, though I have done everything I can to keep us out; but my defeat will be taken by Germany as a repudiation of my policy. Many of our own people will so construe it, and will try to force war upon the next Administration."[11] Wilson's forebodings were premature. As returns began trickling in from the West (where communications in some places were very slow), it became clear that the outcome was still very much in doubt. A dramatic—but apochryphal—story has it that in the wee hours of the morning after the election a reporter called Hughes's hotel room in New York City and was told by the valet: "The President has retired." "When he wakes up," the reporter is supposed to have shot back, "tell him he is no longer President."[12]

When all the returns were in at the end of the week, it turned out that Wilson had not only carried California by more than 3800 votes out of a million cast; he also swept almost the entire West as well as the Solid South, winning a popular majority of some 600,000 votes over Hughes. Wilson won 9,129,606 (49.4 percent) popular votes (3,000,000 more than in 1912) to Hughes's 8,538,221 (46.2 percent) and 277 electoral votes to Hughes's 254. It was a remarkable victory. The Democrats had begun the campaign as a minority party taking on a Republican party that had reunited. But Wilson, largely because of his identification with peace and progressive reform, succeeded in winning over Republican farmers in the West as well as working people who had once voted for the "full dinner pail"; he also attracted many former Bull Moosers to his banner. Many socialists, moreover, supported him. "I would rather see Woodrow Wilson elected than Charles Evans Hughes," wrote Max Eastman in *The Masses*, "because Wilson aggressively believes not only in keeping out of war, but in organizing the nations of the world to prevent war. . . ."[13] Because of defections to Wilson, Socialist party candidate Allen Benson did far less well (581,113 votes) than Eugene Debs had done in 1912. Both Robert LaFollette (Progressive Republican Senator from Wisconsin who had supported Wilson) and William Jennings Bryan interpreted Wilson's victory as a vote for peace. The British Ambassador agreed. "The United States does not want to go to war," he reported, "and the elections have clearly shown that the great mass of the Americans desire nothing so much as to keep out of war. It is undoubtedly the cause of the President's re-election.[14] But Germany resumed its unrestricted submarine campaign not long after the election, bringing its relations with the United States to the breaking point.

In March 1917 Woodrow Wilson took his oath of office as President for a second term. In April the United States declared war on Germany. This should have pleased T.R., but it didn't. Because Wilson refused to commission him as an officer to lead a volunteer division to fight in France, his contempt and hatred of the President continued undiminished. It was the one constant in his long and energetic career.

☆ ☆ ☆

Greatest Asset

Mrs. Hughes was the first wife of a presidential candidate to make an extended campaign tour with her husband. She added charm and zest to her husband's campaign and helped keep his spirits high. As she sat at a tiny table in the train pouring grape juice for newsmen, Hughes tenderly waved his hand toward her and said: "Gentlemen—the greatest asset of the Republican Party!"[15]

Straddle

Just before the Democratic convention met, Wilson asked Josephus Daniels, his Secretary of the Navy, why he supported woman suffrage so strongly. "I have two reasons that are convincing," Daniels told him. "What are they?" Wilson wanted to know. "My mother and my wife," said Daniels. Wilson wanted to leave the matter to the states, but only a few states, Daniels reminded him, had given women the ballot, and it was necessary for voting to be uniform in all the states. Despite Daniels's argument, Wilson stuck to his position and dictated the plank adopted by the Democrats in 1916: "We recommend the extension of the franchise to the women of the country by the States upon the same terms as to men." Had it not been for the war in Europe, Wilson's straddle might have cost him votes. But the suffragists looked on him as the peace candidate and tended to overlook the fact that his stand on woman suffrage was not as forthright as Hughes's.[16]

Kicked Higher

Early in the campaign Secretary of the Navy Josephus Daniels succeeded in persuading two celebrities—Thomas A. Edison and Henry Ford—to come out for Wilson. Neither was a Democrat, but they admired Wilson and agreed to write letters on his behalf. Edison's was particularly effective: "They say Wilson has blundered. Perhaps he has, but I notice he usually blunders forward."

Daniels regarded the Edison-Ford endorsements as real vote-getters; but the Democrats needed more than that. They desperately needed money, according to Vance McCormick, chairman of the Democratic national committee, and he told Daniels he had invited the two famous men to meet with him to discuss the campaign. Both had agreed to come provided, "Josephus Daniels will be at the conference." Daniels of course went; and the four men had a splendid lunch together in a fine hotel. After the first course, Edison pointed to a large chandelier, with many globes, hanging in the middle of the room, and said, "Henry, I'll bet you anything you want to bet that I can kick that globe off that chandelier." Ford took him up on the bet. Edison got up, pushed the table to one side, took his stand in the center of the room, and, with his eyes fixed on the globe, made "the highest kick" Daniels "had ever seen a man make and smashed the globe into smithereens." Triumphantly he cried: "Henry, let's see what you can do." Ford took careful aim, but his foot missed the chandelier by a fraction of an inch. Crowed Edison: "You are a younger man than I am, but I can out-kick you!"

During these shenanigans, McCormick nervously waited for Daniels to get to the point of the conference. Daniels eased into it. He told the two celebrities that he had just returned from a campaign trip in the West and that the parts of his speeches that got the warmest response were those in which he quoted their endorsements of Wilson for re-election. But he went on to say that although the outlook for Wilson was good in the West, the campaign was lagging in the East primarily because the Democrats did not have money enough to present Wilson effectively to the voters there. "All this campaign spending is the bunk," said Ford. "I wouldn't give a dollar to any campaign committee." "I think you are quite right, Mr. Ford," said Daniels tactfully. "Most money spent in campaigns is the 'bunk.' It is often used for corrupt purposes, to buy influence and to buy votes. Wilson would not wish to be elected by any such method. I assure you that not one dollar you give will be used for any purpose except for legitimate publicity, which both you and Mr. Edison would approve." But Ford persisted. "I will not give a cent to the campaign fund," he said as they were taking their coffee. But he added: "I sincerely hope that Wilson will be elected and in my own way I will see that the reasons why he ought to be elected are presented in the papers of large circulation in the pivotal states."

Wilson's campaign workers were tremendously disappointed when they heard about how the meeting with Edison and Ford went. "Ford will not do anything," one of them told Daniels. "He was just talking that way to get out of giving you any money." But a few days later several newspapers around the country with large circulations carried a full-page article, signed, "Henry Ford," advocating the election of Wilson. Said Daniels jubilantly: "He had kicked higher than Edison."[17]

Peck's Bad Boy

About a year and a half after Wilson became President, his first wife, Ellen, died, and for some time he was desolate. Then he met Edith Bolling Galt, a forty-two-year-old widow, fell madly in love with her, got engaged, began appearing in public with her, and they were soon married. Some people were shocked; they thought he had taken up with Mrs. Galt too soon after the death of Ellen. Some of Wilson's advisers, in fact, counseled delay until after the election, but Wilson rejected their advice and was married in December 1915.

During 1916 there was a lot of tongue-clucking. Stories circulated that Wilson had started pursuing Mrs. Galt before Ellen died, that the latter had contemplated divorce, and that she had died of a broken heart. But another set of stories linked him with Mrs. Mary Hulbert, the former Mrs. Peck, whom Wilson had befriended some years before and with whom he had carried on a lively correspondence. Wilson's friendship with Mrs. Peck was innocent enough; his first wife had shared in it. But rumor-mongers made a scandal out of it, called Wilson "Peck's bad boy" (a reference to George W. Peck's Bad Boy stories) and said the affair with Mrs. Peck had broken Ellen's heart. They also said Wilson had pushed Ellen downstairs causing injuries that led to her death. One story had it that Mrs. Peck was planning breach-of-promise proceedings against the President, but that Wilson hired Boston lawyer Louis Brandeis to pay her $75,000 to call it off. Brandeis publicly denied the story; he called it a "vile slander." Wilson himself wrote his former Princeton pastor: "I do not know how to deal with the fiendish lies that are being invented and circulated about my personal character, other than to invite those who repeat them to consult anybody who has known me for any length of time. . . . Poison of this sort is hard to find an antidote for." The whispering campaign probably didn't hurt Wilson much; for some people, indeed, it may have made him seem more human. But his managers took it seriously enough to prepare an article about his family life, "Mr. Wilson as Seen by One of His Family Circle," and see that it received wide circulation. After the election Wilson remarked that the campaign had been "one of the most . . . unfair on the part of the Republican opposition that the country has ever seen." [18]

Keep Shirt On

The first returns indicated Hughes was winning, but he refused to take it for granted. When the *New York World* and several other newspapers declared him the winner, reporters begged for a statement. "Wait till the Democrats concede my election," said Hughes firmly, "the newspapers might take it back." Times Square flashed the news of a great Hughes victory to a crowd of 100,000 and an American flag appeared from the roof of Hotel Astor, where Hughes was staying, with two searchlights playing on it. Besides it was a huge electric sign proclaiming "HUGHES," through the night. Delegations from Republican and Union League clubs urged Hughes to appear on the balcony and accept the applause of the milling crowd below, but Hughes held back. "If I have been elected President," he said, "it is because the people of this country think that I'll keep my shirt on in an emergency. I'll start out now by not yielding to this demand when I am not positive that I have been elected." [19]

Immediate Succession

On election night, Wilson was so sure he had lost that he might have issued a concession statement had not his secretary, Joseph Tumulty, dissuaded him from doing so. But, because of the war crisis, he was prepared to turn his office at once over to Hughes when the returns were all in. "I feel that it would be my duty," he wrote Secretary of State Robert Lansing, "to relieve the country of the perils of such a situation at once. The course I have in mind is dependent upon the consent and co-operation of the Vice-President; but, if I could gain his consent to the plan, I would ask your permission to invite Mr. Hughes to become Secretary of State and would then join the Vice-President in resigning, and thus open to Mr. Hughes the immediate succession to the presidency." [20]

Moth-Eaten

Hughes didn't get around to sending Wilson a congratulatory telegram until November 22. "It was," said Wilson, "a little moth-eaten when it got here but quite legible."[21]

Roosevelt's Contribution

T.R. campaigned more for war than for Hughes and induced many voters to pick Wilson as the peace candidate. After the election some New York Democrats who had supported Hughes wired congratulations to T. R. on the election of Wilson, to which, they said, "you contributed more than any other person in America. . . . Wilson ought to give you a Cabinet position, as you elected him, beyond doubt. . . . You made Wilson a million votes."[22]

CHAPTER THIRTY-FOUR

1920
Harding, Nostrums, and Normalcy

The choice in 1920, said the *Nation,* was between Debs and dubs. Debs was Eugene Victor Debs, Socialist party candidate, running for President from Atlanta Penitentiary where the Wilson administration had put him for anti-war speeches during World War I. The "dubs" were Warren G. Harding, running on the Republican ticket, and James M. Cox, the Democratic aspirant. Woodrow Wilson, felled by a stroke in 1919, wanted the election to be a "solemn referendum" on the League of Nations, but it turned out to be a referendum more on the ailing President than on the League. For the American people were seething with discontents: anger over the high cost of living and widespread unemployment, resentment over wartime controls, and disenchantment with Wilson's crusade to make the world safe for American democracy.[1]

The Democrats remained loyal. The platform they drew up at their convention in San Francisco late in June endorsed the League. So did Cox, mildly progressive Governor of Ohio, who received the nod on the forty-fourth ballot. He and his running mate, Franklin D. Roosevelt, Wilson's Assistant Secretary of the Navy, called on the President right after the convention and promised to work for the League. They did just that, too, in their tours of the country in the fall.

The Republicans were so sure of winning they didn't bother to put their best foot forward. After a deadlock between two respectable candidates at their Chicago convention early in June, they settled on a throughgoing mediocrity on the tenth ballot: Warren G. Harding, Ohio Senator and publisher of the *Marion Star.* Harding, fifty-four, was popular, had no political enemies, came from a pivotal state, and, as a small-town, self-made businessman, had an obvious appeal to voters in a nostalgic mood. Some people were appalled by the choice; they called him a "puppet candidate" and a "party hack." But Connecticut Senator Frank

Brandegee put it this way: "There ain't any first-raters this year . . . ; we got a lot of second-raters and Warren Harding is the best of the second-raters."[2]

The Republicans picked Massachusetts Governor Calvin Coolidge to run with Harding. Coolidge's fame rested on the fact that he had broken a police strike in Boston in 1919 and proclaimed: "There is no right to strike against the public safety by anybody, anywhere, anytime." The Republican platform excoriated Wilson and everything he stood for, but, to placate pro-League Republicans, announced that "the Republican party stands for agreement among nations to preserve the peace." During the campaign Harding came out for some kind of "association of nations," but his heart wasn't in it.[3]

Harding's chief contribution to the campaign was a slogan: "Back to Normalcy." In a speech in Boston in May his passion for alliteration had produced the following: "America's present need is not heroics but healing; not nostrums but normalcy; not revolution but restoration . . . not surgery, but serenity." In the manuscript of his speech he had used the word, normality, but it came out, normalty, when he read it. Amused reporters changed it to "normalcy," which sounded better, and thus a slogan was born.[4] The word did, in fact, encapsulate Harding's basic outlook. He did yearn for the "good old times" of the late nineteenth century when the Republicans ran things and when the small-town virtues of simple piety and patriotism seemed to rule the land. Curiously, though, for all his nostalgia, Harding did not himself live by those values. He chewed tobacco, played poker, imbibed whiskey (despite the 18th Amendment, prohibiting alcoholic beverages, added to the Constitution in 1919), and had extra-marital love affairs.

Harding's was mainly a front-porch campaign in Marion, Ohio, where he uttered platitudes and pleasantries to patriotic, professional, and party groups making the pilgrimage to his place. Every so often his managers sent him off with ghost-written speeches for a bit of stumping but he was better in an informal setting. In the middle of one pre-packaged address he stumbled over a passage, paused, and then told his audience frankly: "Well, I never saw this before. I didn't write this speech and don't believe what I just read."[5] Cox did some real campaigning: he traveled 22,000 miles and spoke to two million people in a valiant effort to attract support for Wilson's League. It was all in vain. Just before the election the *Literary Digest* sent out millions of postcards in the first ambitious poll ever taken during a presidential campaign and then predicted an overwhelming Republican victory.

The *Literary Digest* was right (though it was to be egregiously wrong in 1936). "It wasn't a landslide," said Joseph Tumulty of Harding's victory on November 2; "it was an earthquake."[6] The man from Marion won 60.2 percent of the popular votes (16,152,200) to Cox's 9,147,353), a plurality of 7,004,847, breaking all records and surprising even Re-

publican leaders themselves by the magnitude of his victory. Harding's
electoral victory was similarly lopsided; he carried every state outside
of the Solid South, plus Tennessee, and won 404 votes to Cox's 127.
The Republicans also won a majority of 22 seats in the Senate and 167
in the House. But less than half of the eligible voters cast ballots. This
was partly because Harding's victory was such a sure thing that many
people thought it a waste of time to go to the polls. The turnout of
women (enfranchised by the 19th Amendment) was also low; outside
of the West women were not used to voting and in the South they took
little interest in the campaign.

When Champ Clark of Missouri, defeated after twenty-eight years in
Congress, was asked to comment on the election, he spit out one word:
"Wilson!" There was some truth in his explanation. During the campaign the Republicans had popularized two slogans: "Back to Normalcy" and "Down with Wilson!" The *New York World*, disappointed at
Cox's defeat, thought it was the result of "stored up resentment" among
voters "for anything and everything they had found to complain of in
the last eight years." "The country," said the *New York Tribune*, "was weary
of Wilsonism in all its manifestations."[7] But the voting was not all negative. Harding's image—handsome, dignified, amiable, small-townish—
was appealing to many people, and his call for old-fashioned ways of
facing new-fangled perplexities thrilled people who were bewildered by
the urbanizing thrust of postwar American culture. Harding helped elect
himself.

☆ ☆ ☆

Smoke-Filled Room

There was no "smoke-filled room" in Chicago. Had there been one, Republican bosses might well have put together a different ticket. The
convention was largely leaderless and the delegates picked Harding because they liked him. He was second or third on the list for most of
them, but he emerged as an obvious choice to end the deadlock between General Leonard Wood and Illinois Governor Frank Lowden.
The delegates were hot, tired, and eager to wind up their business and
go home. Senate leaders like Lodge were surprised by the way the delegates suddenly began flocking to the Apostle of Normalcy and, after
that, quickly picked Silent Cal for second place, and then adjourned.

But Harry Daugherty, Harding's zealous promoter for the Presidency since 1919, had predicted a smoke-filled room. At least he got
credit for predicting one. In February 1920, a *New York Times* reporter
sought him out for an interview, but Daugherty, who was checking out
of the Waldorf-Astoria Hotel, said he didn't have time to talk. Following him out of his room into the corridor, the *Times* man began putting
words in his mouth. Harding had only a few pledged delegates, didn't

he? Did that mean Daughterty expected to win the nomination for him by backstairs manipulation? Did he think that at some point the weary bosses, gathered in the back room of some hotel, would finally turn to Harding at two in the morning? "Make it two-eleven," said Daughterty calmly, as he stepped into the elevator. The reporter's story the next morning quoted Harding's manager as saying: "I don't expect Senator Harding to be nominated on the first, second, or third ballots, but I think we can afford to take chances that at about eleven minutes after two, Friday morning of the convention, when fifteen or twenty weary men are sitting around a table, someone will say, 'Who will we nominate?' At that decisive time, the friends of Harding will suggest him and we can well afford to abide by the result." The story was subsequently revised to read, "fifteen men, bleary-eyed with lack of sleep and perspiring profusely," and, finally, in the most popular version, to "fifteen men in a smoke-filled room."

Republican big shots at the nominating convention did, in fact, begin to consider Harding as a possibility in the wee hours of the morning. At 2:00 a.m. (not 2:11 a.m.) on Friday, George Harvey and Senator Frank Brandegee sent for the Ohioan and said: "We think you may be nominated tomorrow; before acting, we think you should tell us, on your conscience and before God, whether there is anything that might be brought up against you that would embarass the party, any impediment that might disqualify you or make you inexpedient, either as a candidate or as President." Harding asked for time to think it over and they left him alone. Harding's ruminations in solitude are anybody's guess. Perhaps he contemplated his love affairs. He had been involved with Carrie Phillips, a married woman in his hometown, for years; he had a young mistress, too, Nan Britton, who had borne him a daughter, and was in Chicago at the time. He may also have thought about the rumor that he was partly black; the story had come up in his races for the Senate. If he thought about these things as problems he seems to have brushed them aside, for after about ten minutes he came out of the room and told Harvey there was "nothing, no obstacle" to his candidacy.

After Harding's nomination, someone phoned Senator Boies Penrose, a Harding backer who lay ill in Philadelphia, with the news and added that everybody hoped Harding's "weakness for women" wouldn't be brought up in the campaign. "No worries about that!" said Penrose confidently. "We'll just throw a halo around his handsome head and everything will be all right!" But Republican leaders saw to it that Carrie Phillips and her husband took an expense-paid trip to the Orient to investigate "the raw silk trade" and were out of the country for the duration.

Surprised and pleased by the nomination, Harding is said to have remarked: "I feel like a man who goes in on a pair of eights and comes out with aces full." But Mrs. Harding, aware of his weak heart, exclaimed: "I can see but one word over his head if they make him President, and that word is Tragedy."[8]

Vox

In his column, "Conning Tower," F. P. A. (Franklin P. Adams) put it this way:

> Harding or Cox?
> Harding or Cox?
> You tell us, populi;
> You've got the vox.[9]

Black Like Me?

One day, toward the end of the campaign, Joseph Tumulty, President Wilson's private secretary, rushed over to the White House with a leaflet in his hand and handed it to the President, who was sitting in a wheelchair on the south portico with his wife and having some milk and crackers. "Governor," he cried in great glee, "we've got 'em beat! Here's a paper which has been searched out and is absolutely true, showing Harding has Negro blood in him. This country will never stand for that!" Wilson slowly drank his milk and then said: "Even if that is so, it will never be used with my consent. We cannot go into a man's genealogy; we must base our campaigns on principles, not on back-stairs gossip. That is not only right, but good politics. So I insist you kill any such proposal." Tumulty wilted, Mrs. Wilson wrote later, "like a little boy who has been caught robbing a bird's nest."

Not everyone shared Wilson's scruples. Pamphlets, leaflets, and flyers about Harding's alleged Negro ancestry began appearing on doorsteps, in hotels, and on trains, and some of them contained pictures of the White House with the caption, "Uncle Tom's Cabin?" Racist jokes also circulated. According to one of them, Sambo asks, "Did yo' heah de big news, Ephum? Dey done nomernate Mistah Hahding at Chicago." "Sho!" exclaims Ephraim. "Who'd de white folks nomernate?"

A week before the election some 250,000 copies of "An Open Letter to the Men and Women of America" turned up in the San Francisco post office, containing a genealogical table tracing Harding's bloodline to "a West Indian Negro of French stock" who had lived in Blooming Grove, Ohio, in the early 19th century, and an affidavit stating that Harding "is not a white man; he is not a creole, he is a mestizo. . . . May God save America from international shame and domestic ruin." The Open Letter was signed by W. E. Chancellor, who reporters learned was an economics professor at Wooster College in Ohio with an obsession about race. The college trustees ordered Chancellor to retract his statements and when he refused they fired him.

Harding wanted to issue a public denial of Chancellor's allegations, but Mrs. Harding counseled silence and Republican leaders agreed. As Boise Penrose put it: "We've been having a lot of trouble with the negro vote lately." But the party got out pictures of Harding's Caucasian-looking parents and elaborate genealogies proving his family was lily-white. Daugherty told the press that the Hardings were "a blue-eyed stock from New England and Pennsylvania, the finest pioneer blood, Anglo-Saxon, German, Scotch-Irish, and Dutch." One wag wanted to know why he had overlooked the Scandinavians and neglected the French vote.

The newspapers for the most part killed the story, Cox and the Democratic national committee repudiated it, and the Wilson administration saw to it that Chancellor's pamphlets were barred from the mails. So the tale traveled mainly by word of mouth and seems not to have made much difference in the campaign. At one point a reporter for the *Cincinnati Inquirer* asked Harding point-blank: "Do you have any Negro blood?" "How do I know, Jim?" smiled Harding. "One of my ancestors may have jumped the fence." [10]

★ ★ ★ ★ ★ ★ ★ ★ ★ ★ ★ ★ ★ ★ ★ ★ ★ ★ ★ ★

CHAPTER THIRTY-FIVE

1924
Keeping Cool with Coolidge

In 1924 the voters decided to "Keep Cool with Coolidge." Keeping cool, as far as Calvin Coolidge was concerned, meant conservatism, conventionality, and close-mouthedness. During the campaign, the story goes, a newsman sought him out. "Mr. President," he said, "what do you think about Prohibition?" "No comment," replied Coolidge. "Will you say something about unemployment?" "No," said Coolidge. "Will you tell us your views about the world situation?" persisted the reporter. "No." "About your message to Congress?" "No." The disappointed reporter started to leave, but as he reached the door Coolidge said, "Wait." Hopefully the man turned around and Coolidge cautioned: "Now remember—don't quote me." [1]

For all his taciturnity (and he could be talkative, too, if he so chose), "Silent Cal" was one of the most popular men ever to occupy the White House. He became President when Harding suddenly died of a heart attack in August 1923 and people at once took to his imperturbable style and saw no reason not to keep him in office another four years. True, shocking revelations of corruption under Harding—especially the Teapot Dome scandal, involving the secret leasing of the nation's oil reserves to private parties in return for bribes—came to light shortly after Coolidge took office. But Coolidge was not himself implicated, his reputation for honesty was unclouded, and he saw to it that the guilty (which included several high officials) were brought to justice.

The fifty-one-year-old Coolidge was quickly nominated on the first ballot at the Republican convention in Cleveland in June; one of the seconders said he "never wasted any time, never wasted any words, and never wasted any public money." The vice-presidential nominee, former Budget Director Charles G. Dawes, was, by contrast, known as "Hell 'n Maria" for his rambunctious platform style. The Republican platform, reflecting Coolidge's views, stressed government economy, reducing the national debt, and restricting immigration; it also made a polite bow to Prohibition. The Cleveland convention was the most boring in Republican history. Sessions were at times meagerly attended. The most popular drink was a Keep-Cool-with-Coolidge highball made of raw eggs and fruit juice. Will Rogers suggested the city open up the churches to liven things up a bit.

The Democrats more than made up for Republican lethargy. Meeting in Madison Square Garden in New York amid a heat wave in late June, they split almost at once, with the Eastern, urban, and "wet" (anti-Prohibitionist) wing pitted against the rural and "dry" (Prohibitionist) wing representing the West and the South. About the only thing the delegates all agreed on was Mississippi Senator Pat Harrison's indictment of Republican corruption in his keynote address. The first big fight came over the Ku Klux Klan, an anti-Catholic, anti-Semitic, anti-black, and anti-foreign-born organization which had risen to prominence after World War I, especially in the West and the South. After four days of wrangling, the platform committee decided not to recommend an anti-Klan plank but to propose instead an innocuous statement decrying all attempts to limit constitutional liberties. The committee's majority report touched off a stormy fight in the convention; hundreds of additional policemen had to be rushed to Madison Square Garden to keep order. The aging Bryan argued against using "three little words," Ku Klux Klan, in the platform condemning religious bigotry, not because he approved of the Klan, but because he thought it would magnify the importance of the organization, offend sincere people who were members, and tear the Democratic party apart. To his humiliation he was roundly booed by delegates from the East. After hours of angry exchanges the delegates finally rejected by one vote the proposal to denounce the Klan by name: 542.15 to 541.15. The platform—one of the lengthiest ever drawn up—ended by condemning "any effort to arouse religious or racial dissension." It also made a graceful gesture to Coolidge's predecessor: "Our party stands uncovered at the bier of Warren G. Harding"; but "bier" was changed to "grave" at Bryan's suggestion to avoid offending the Prohibitionists.[2]

With the platform out of the way, the delegates proceeded to enter a nine-day deadlock over the presidential nomination. The anti-Klan forces tended to back Alfred E. Smith, popular Catholic Governor of New York (whom Franklin D. Roosevelt, just returning to public life after his bout with polio, nominated as "the Happy Warrior of the political battlefield"), while those who, like Bryan, wanted to mute the Klan issue, tended to favor California's William G. McAdoo, Wilson's Secretary of the Treasury and son-in-law. In ballot after ballot the delegates remained deadlocked between the two; neither Smith nor McAdoo was able to muster the two-thirds vote needed for the nomination and nei-

ther was willing to withdraw. The convention broke all kinds of dubious records: cast more ballots, heard more speeches, had more demonstrations, fistfights, and committee meetings, and consumed more hot
dogs and soda pop than any other convention in history. "A Ballot a
day keeps the nomination away!" cried one wit; "Half a vote, half a vote
onward, into the jaws of debt, into the mouth of hell, moves the convention," sighed a delegate with a predilection for Tennyson. On the
ninth day of the stalemate Smith and McAdoo released their delegates
and at long last, on the 103rd ballot, the nomination went to John W.
Davis, New York lawyer from West Virginia who had served as Wilson's Solicitor-General and ambassador to Britain. To balance Davis's
conservatism the delegates chose Bryan's brother Charles, Governor of
Nebraska, for second place. "Is it true, or is it a dream?" murmured
one delegate after it was all over.[3]

Depressed by the choice between rock-ribbed Republican Coolidge and
Wall Street lawyer Davis, Progressives in both parties decided to found
a party of their own. They knew they couldn't win, but they hoped to
take enough electoral votes away from Coolidge and Davis to throw the
election into the House of Representatives where they might have a
chance. At their convention in Cleveland in July, 1200 delegates (and
9000 spectators)—farmers, craftsmen, preachers, professors, house-
wives, small businessmen—met to organize a mighty farm-labor party
to "break the power of the private monopolistic system over the economic and political life of the American people," nominated Wisconsin's Progressive Republican Senator Robert M. LaFollette ("Fighting
Bob") for President, and picked Democratic Senator Burton K. Wheeler
of Montana for second place. Conservatives denounced LaFollette as a
dangerous radical, but the Communists, running William Z. Foster for
President, called the Progressive platform "the most reactionary document of the year."[4]

Coolidge was a shoo-in; just about everyone acknowledged that from
the outset. Davis worked hard for his party but failed to puncture Silent Cal's imperturbable calm. The identification of Coolidge with prosperity made his task hopeless. On November 4 the Republicans had a
landslide. Coolidge won 15,725,003 popular votes (54 percent), carried
35 states, and took 382 electoral votes, while Davis garnered only
8,385,586 popular votes (28.8 percent), 12 states, and 136 electoral votes.
LaFollette ran second to Coolidge in several Western states, including
California, but, to his surprise and chagrin, won only 4,826,471 popular (16.5 percent) and 13 electoral votes (Wisconsin's). Coolidge's popular vote exceeded that of Davis and LaFollette combined. "Calvin
Coolidge was the issue," declared the *Boston Transcript* after the election, "and to the President belongs the victory." "In a fat and happy
world, Coolidge is the man of the hour," observed William Allen White.

"Why tempt fate by opposing him?" Supreme Court Justice Oliver Wendell Holmes, Jr., was pleased by the outcome of the election. "While I don't expect anything very astonishing from it," he said, "I don't want anything astonishing."[5]

Good Man

When Republican leaders asked Coolidge to suggest a running mate he said he would let the convention pick him. "It did in 1920," he added, "and it picked a durned good man."[6]

Posterity

When one long-winded speaker at the Republican convention said he was "speaking for the benefit of posterity," Will Rogers told his colleagues in the press gallery, "If he don't get done with that thing pretty soon, they'll be here."[7]

Real Beer

In his keynote address at the Democratic convention Mississippi's Pat Harrison called for a new Paul Revere and the galleries cheered loudly thinking he had said, "What this country needs is real beer."[8]

Visitors

As the Democratic convention dragged on day after day Will Rogers finally complained that New York City had invited the delegates to visit the place, not to live there.[9]

Clouded Crystal Ball

Bryan's opposition to John W. Davis led H.L. Mencken, covering the Democratic convention for the *Baltimore Sun,* to report: "Everything is still uncertain in this convention but one thing. John W. Davis will never be nominated." Minutes later the convention picked Davis. "Why that's incredible!" cried Mencken when he heard the news. "I've already sent off a story that it's impossible." Then he added: "I wonder if those idiots in Baltimore will have sense enough to drop the negative."[10]

Same Face

During the 1924 campaign, Congressman Allen T. Treadway asked Coolidge for a photograph, saying, "I have one, but it was taken when you were Lieutenant Governor." "I don't see what you want another for," snapped Coolidge. "I'm using the same face."[11]

Red-Fellows

When Coolidge posed in Indian regalia while visiting a reservation, Will Rogers wired him: "Politics makes strange red-fellows."[12]

★ ★

CHAPTER THIRTY-SIX

1928
Hoover, Smith, and
the Catholic Issue

In 1928, the two major presidential candidates, Herbert Hoover and Alfred E. Smith, had a great deal in common. They were both self-made men, proud of their rise from obscurity to eminence, and deeply devoted to the system in which they had personally experienced success. But the dissimilarities outweighed the commonalities. Hoover began as a farm boy in Iowa with a Quaker background, worked his way through college, became a mining engineer, acquired great wealth, and achieved fame as organizer of Belgian relief during World War I and as administrator in the Wilson, Harding, and Coolidge administrations. Smith, by contrast, was an Irish Catholic who grew up on the sidewalks of New York, worked as an errand boy on the Lower East Side and as clerk in the Fulton Fish Market, went into politics as a young man, and moved, with the help of Tammany Hall, from the New York Assembly to the governorship of New York, where he gained a reputation for efficiency and social concern.

There were two Americas in 1928's candidates: city and country, East and West, Protestant and Catholic. There were also two styles: Smith, informal, down-to-earth, expansive, wise-cracking; Hoover, austere, reserved, blunt, humorless. "Al," moreover, with his brown derby and big cigar, was a "wet," while the "Great Engineer," with his plain dress and severe manner, was "dry." The stage was set for an exciting—but dirty—presidential campaign.

By the time the Republicans met in Kansas City on June 12 for their quadrennial festivities, it was clear to most delegates: "Who but Hoover?" On the first ballot they put him up for first place and then teamed him up with Senator Charles Curtis from the farm state of Kansas, the first vice-presidential candidate with Indian blood. Hoover, fifty-three, seemed a sure thing; though distrusted by the Old Guard (even Coolidge mordantly referred to him as "the Wunduh Boy"), he had the confidence of the business community. Not only was he an efficiency expert as Commerce Department head; he also showed humanitarian zeal as well as administrative competence once again when he managed relief in 1927 for victims of the Mississippi Valley floodings: "the one tranquil among the raging floods."[1] The platform to go along with Hoover contained no novelties; it attributed the good times to Republican policies and called for more of the same: economy, tax reduction, high tariffs, and full enforcement of the 18th Amendment.

The Democratic platform was less complacent. It charged that Republican rule had left the country with "its industry depressed, its agriculture prostrate" and proposed reforms: tariff revision and farm-relief measures. As for Prohibition, the Democrats pledged the party to "an honest effort" to enforce the 18th Amendment and criticized the Republicans for failing to do just that. The 1928 convention, which met in Houston (to please Southern Democrats) on June 26, was a sharp contrast to 1924's. William McAdoo, spokesman for the rural South and West, had dropped out in 1927 "in the interest of party unity," and the delegates in Houston resolved to submerge their rural-urban, North-South, and wet-dry differences in dedication to the common cause. With McAdoo out of the running, there was only one logical candidate: Al Smith, the enormously popular and successful governor (elected four times) of New York, a key state in any election. Al's friend Franklin Roosevelt nominated him as the "happy warrior" (as in 1924) and the delegates quickly chose him on the first ballot as their standard-bearer. To balance the ticket they picked Senator Joseph G. Robinson of Arkansas, a Protestant Prohibitionist, for second place. One observer summed it all up afterward: "The Democratic donkey with a wet head and wagging a dry tail left Houston."[2] In a telegram to the convention Smith made it clear he favored local option: the right of states to pass legislation permitting light wines and beers if they so desired. For some Democrats the dry Protestant Southerner simply did not compensate for the wet Catholic New Yorker on the ticket.

By 1928 radio had become important for vote-getting. Here Hoover had an advantage. Though he tended to be prolix, ponderous, and pedantic in his speech-writing, he came across as a high-minded statesman in addresses he delivered over the nationwide hook-up. Smith was better in person: breezy, witty, free and easy in interactions with live audiences. In the presence of the mike, however, he seemed to freeze up; and his rasping East Side accent and unusual pronunciations—"radd-ee-o" and "horspital"—repelled the fastidious. But Smith never had much of a chance anyhow. The country was still prosperous for most of the people who voted, and Hoover made the most of it. Said the Great Engineer in his speech accepting the nomination: "We in America today are nearer to the final triumph over poverty than ever before in the history of the land."[3] Hoover stressed the "American system" of free enterprise as the source of prosperity and Republican orators promised a "chicken in every pot and two cars in every garage" with a Hoover victory. Smith tried hard to woo businessmen to his banner. He said they could trust the Democrats, came out for protective tariffs, and chose several wealthy men for top positions on his staff. For his campaign manager he picked the millionaire John J. Raskob, high in the councils of General Motors and du Pont. But there was a catch: Raskob, like Smith himself, was a wet and a Catholic.

Religion didn't decide the election of 1928, but it was a major issue throughout. Even before Smith became a candidate, he had made clear his belief in "the absolute separation" of church and state in America. "I have taken an oath of office nineteen times," he declared. "Each time I swore to defend and maintain the Constitution of the United States. . . . I have never known any conflict between my official duties and my religious beliefs."[4] But the whispers and rumors about his religion were persistent and pernicious: that the Pope had his bags packed ready to move to Washington once Smith won the election; that Protestant marriages would be annulled and Protestant children declared bastards in the event of a Smith victory; that Smith planned to extend Manhattan's new Holland Tunnel under the Atlantic to the basement of the Vatican once he was in the White House. But the anti-Catholic campaign was out in the open too. Many Protestant ministers suspended for the duration the church-state separation they thought they cherished and preached sermons against the Democratic candidate. "If you vote for Al Smith," cried one preacher, "you're voting against Christ and you'll be damned."[5] Anti-Catholic literature dating back to the pre-Civil War Know-Nothing days was revived and circulated in great quantities throughout the country. "A Vote for Al Smith Is a Vote for the Pope," cried Klansmen; a Smith triumph, they said, meant "Rum, Romanism and Ruin."[6] Smith's advisers wanted him to ignore the Catholic hate-mongers on the theory that if he let them alone they would wither on the vine. Smith, though, was so incensed by some of the things said that he insisted on fighting back. But when he went to Oklahoma City to make a major speech about religious intolerance on September 29, he was greeted with fiery KKK crosses en route and with implacable hostility in the auditorium there. The next evening popular evangelist John Roach Straton thrilled thousands of people in the same place with a speech on "Al Smith and the Forces of Hell."

Prohibition was almost as big an issue in 1928 as religion. Indeed, many Protestant drys linked the two. Hoover's position was of course impeccable: he called Prohibition "a great social and economic experiment, noble in motive and far-reaching in purpose," and said it "must be worked out constructively." Smith, disturbed by the crime spawned by Prohibition, favored "fundamental changes in the provisions for national prohibition" and thus aroused the wrath of the Anti-Saloon League, the Women's Christian Temperance Union, and other militant dry groups. Some people called him "Al-coholic" Smith and spread stories about how he was so drunk in public once that he had to be held up by two men. In radio broadcasts evangelist Straton equated Smith with the urban evils of "card playing, cocktail drinking, poodle dogs, divorces, novels, stuffy rooms, dancing, evolution, Clarence Darrow, overeating, nude art, prize-fighting, actors, greyhound racing, and modernism."[7]

Smith's associations with Tammany Hall also hurt him with many people in the South and the West. No matter that other cities and the Republicans themselves had political machines and bosses. Tammany, somehow, symbolized to rural voters all that was bad about big-city politics. It was "not that Governor Smith is a Catholic and a wet which makes him an offense to villagers and town dwellers," pointed out William Allen White, "but because his record shows the kind of President he would make—a Tammany President." White added that "Tammany is Tammany, and Smith is its prophet. . . . The whole Puritan civilization which has built a sturdy, orderly nation is threatened by Smith."[8] During the campaign enthusiastic crowds turned out to hear Smith speak in the East; in the rural areas of the West and South, however, his receptions tended to be cool. A Catholic, a wet, a New Yorker, and a Tammany man, he might as well have come from another planet.

After the election Hoover claimed that he was attacked as much as Smith was and that the anti-Smith and anti-Hoover smears somehow balanced out in the end. He was wrong. Hoover slanders were far fewer and relatively innocuous: that he stole from a Chinaman when in the Far East; that he was an Anglophile ("Sir Herbert"); that he was secretly a British citizen.[9] Hoover's supporters were able to dispose of these charges with ease. Hoover himself stayed mostly above the fray; his pose was that of a man above politics. He refused to debate Smith; in fact, he refrained from even mentioning his name. In his acceptance speech he came out against religious bigotry and a little later dissociated himself from one of the more outrageous attacks on Smith's religion. But for the most part he said or did little to check the anti-Catholic crusade of some of his supporters. He was more concerned about the fact that some of the proposals in the Democratic platform—for farm relief and public power—were horrendously "socialistic."

Hoover's campaign managers were spectacularly successful in portraying him as a man for the times: an efficient engineer in a technological era, a skillful administrator in a corporate age, and a shrewd and far-sighted businessman in an age of increasing productivity. The *New York Herald Tribune* stressed his "precise fusion of engineering and business ability" and the *New York Times*'s Anne O'Hare McCormick noted that in 1928 Americans had a chance to vote for "a great engineer at a time when they believed that the big problems of government are engineering problems." Bruce Barton announced that if Hoover and Smith both applied for jobs in his advertising agency, he would hire the former at once. "I might get more fun out of having Smith around," he said, "but I'd make more money with Hoover." Chortled the *San Francisco Chronicle:* "Wouldn't YOU jump at the chance if you could hire him for YOUR business?" But Hoover was put forth as a great humanitarian as well as a great engineer, administrator, and businessman. He was "America's greatest administrator in human welfare," according to Republican orators; "a specialist in public calamities."[10] What did Smith, a mere politician, have to offer the country in comparison with Hoover's manifold skills and talents?

Hoover swept the nation on November 6. Not only was the popular vote lopsided: 21,392,190 (58 percent) to 15,016,443 (41 percent); so was the electoral vote: 444 to 87. Hoover carried forty states, including Smith's New York, all the border states, and five states in the Solid South. The Republicans also won a huge majority in the House of Representatives. There were some compensations for Smith. With nearly eight million more people casting votes in 1928, Smith won twice as many votes as Davis had four years earlier; in fact, he won almost as many votes as Coolidge had won in 1924. He also carried a dozen of the largest cities, including New York City, Boston, Cleveland, St. Louis, and San Francisco, which the Republicans had won in 1924. Still, his defeat was stunning and he felt it keenly. "Well," he is supposed to have sighed after the returns were in, "the time hasn't come yet when a man can say his beads in the White House." A post-election joke had it that after the election he wired the Pope: "Unpack!"[11]

Smith was convinced that religion had done him in. He was partly right; unquestionably bigotry cost him many votes. So did his wetness and his association with Tammany. But Hoover himself was probably closer to the mark when he said: "General Prosperity was on my side." The Republican party was still the majority party in 1928, the times were still relatively good, and millions of voters believed Republican orators when they identified the GOP with economic advance. "You can't lick this prosperity thing," cried Will Rogers after the election.[12]

One of the Republican slogans was: "Hoover and Happiness or Smith and Soup Houses? Which Shall It Be?" The voters chose Hoover. As it turned out, they got soup houses too.

☆   ☆   ☆

Difference Between Parties

"I have been studying the parties," wrote Will Rogers in 1928, "and here is the difference. Hoover wants all the drys and as many wets as possible. Smith wants all the wets and as many drys as possible. Hoover says

he will relieve the farmer even if he has to call Congress. Smith says he
will relieve the farmer even if he has to appoint a commission. Hoover
says the tariff will be kept up. Smith says the tariff will not be lowered.
Hoover is in favor of prosperity. Smith says he highly endorses prosperity. Hoover wants no votes merely on account of religion. Smith wants
no votes solely on religious grounds. Both would accept Muhammed
votes if offered. . . . If a man could tell the difference between the two
parties, he could make a Sucker out of Solomon."[13]

Hoover and the Babe

One afternoon in September Hoover went to see the New York Yankees play the Washington Senators and before the game started
cameramen persuaded him to pose with the Yankees' Babe Ruth. But
when they went to fetch Ruth he declined. "It's a matter of politics," he
said. The Senators' president Clark Griffith was shocked. "I am at a loss
to explain such conduct," he said. Ruth, after all, had been posing with
celebrities for years. Why the Hoover brush-off? One explanation: Col.
Jacob Ruppert, onetime brewer, owned the Yankees. "If Babe Ruth ever
posed with any Dry," someone observed, "Jake Ruppert'd slap a fine on
him quicker'n you can say 'three strikes.' " Ruth later apologized for his
behavior; he said he had "labored under a misunderstanding" and hoped
Hoover would be "gracious enough at some future time to permit me
to present myself to him." Hoover said he sympathized with Ruth for
"not wanting to hold up the game for mere photographers."[14]

Nine Times

During the 1928 campaign Smith was warmly received in Boston and
one man in the crowd yelled: "I'll vote nine times for you, Al!" "O.K.,
pal," Smith shouted back, "but don't get caught at it!"[15]

Hate

In 1928 Catholic-haters distributed copies of *The Awful Disclosures of Maria
Monk,* a spurious book first circulated in 1836 by the Know-Nothings,
purporting to reveal stories of sexual orgies and murder in a Montreal
nunnery. They also circulated a fake Knights of Columbus oath that
had surfaced periodically since the 1830s, pledging members to "wage
war on Protestants and Masons." In Vermont a leaflet exclaimed: "May
the good Lord and the Southland keep us safe from the rule of the
Wet, Tammany, Roman Catholic Booze Gang." In upstate New York
leaflets warned:

> When the Catholics rule the United States
> And the Jew grows a Christian nose on his face,

> When Pope Pius is head of the Ku-Klux-Klan
> In the land of Uncle Sam
> Then Al Smith will be our president
> And the country not worth a damn.

In Birmingham, Alabama, some citizens met in July to discuss politics. They began by dragging in an effigy of Al Smith. "What shall we do with him?" asked the presiding officer. "Lynch him!" yelled the citizens. A man with a knife at once fell on the dummy's throat, gashed it open, and spattered a red fluid (mercurochrome) around the wound. Then, with howls of joy, people began firing revolver shots into the "corpse," kicking it and spitting at it. Finally they got a rope, noosed it, and dragged it around the hall for a hanging. A length the Klan demonstration came happily to an end.[16]

Sprinklin'

A woman from the East campaigning for Smith in Oklahoma got into a conversation with an old lady in a little town there who was a devout Baptist. "So you be the woman speaker, be you?" said the Oklahoman, "and you're for Smith?" "Yes," said the Easterner. "Well, I ain't," snapped the old woman. "Perhaps if you would let me talk to you," said the Smith woman, "I might change your mind." "No, you couldn't," said the old woman firmly. "Smith's one of them Catholics and they brought in sprinklin'."[17]

Execrable Taste

Snobbery as well as bigotry entered the 1928 campaign. "Can you imagine Mrs. Smith in the White House?" cried Mrs. Florence T. Griswold, Republican national committeewoman, in a speech in Houston. "Can you imagine an aristocratic foreign Ambassador saying to her, 'What a charming gown,' and the reply, 'You said a mouthful!' " There were shrieks of laughter in Mrs. Griswold's audience. In Springfield, Massachusetts, Senator Frederick H. Gillett made the same point talking to a group of Republican women workers. He described the charm, culture, and intelligence of Mrs. Hoover and then said: "Of course, I cannot say very much of Mrs. Smith, because I have never known her, but if the contest was between Mrs. Hoover and Mrs. Smith—" He was interrupted by wild applause. Afterward the *New York Times* flayed him for his "execrable taste."[18]

Roman

At a party in Savannah, Georgia, after his defeat, Smith got to talking with a lady who said she admired him but hadn't voted for him because of his religion. "But," said Smith amiably, "surely you voted for our host, the Mayor of Savannah, and he is a Catholic." "O! yes," said the lady, "I voted for him; but he is an Irish Catholic while you are a Roman Catholic." [19]

★ ★

CHAPTER THIRTY-SEVEN

1932
Roosevelt, Hoover,
and the Great Depression

In 1917, when Herbert Hoover was Food Administrator in the Wilson administration, the word "Hooverize" meant to conserve food for the war effort; in 1932, when Hoover was President, the word "Hooverville" meant a squalid collection of shacks in which the poor and unemployed tried to manage survival.

It was a disastrous comedown for the "Great Engineer." During the 1932 campaign there were bitter jokes about the President. Hoover asked his Secretary of Treasury, according to one of them, to lend him a nickel to buy a soda for a friend, and the latter said: "Here's a dime. Treat them all!" And a Kansas farmer, went another story, declared that Hoover was the greatest engineer in the world, since "he had drained, ditched, and damned the United States in three years." Even ex-President Coolidge was depressed. "This country," he announced, "is not in good condition." [1]

"General Prosperity had been a great ally in the election of 1928," Hoover acknowledged in his *Memoirs;* but "General Depression," he added ruefully, "was a major enemy in 1932." [2] He was quite right. The Great Depression which followed the devastating stock market crash of 1929 was the worst in the nation's history and shattered the President's reputation for administrative skill and humanitarian concern. Hoover was, in fact, the first President to take positive measures to cope with an economic depression; but the action he took—expanding public works and sponsoring the Reconstruction Finance Corporation to lend money to banks, industries, and state and local governments—failed to stem the tide of disaster. By the time Americans launched their thirty-seventh presidential election, industrial production was at a low ebb, unemployment was widespread, and the farmers faced ruin. "Damn Hoover!" exploded a man who bit into an apple and found a worm there. By 1932 millions of people were damning Hoover and the Republican party. When the nominating conventions met in Chicago in June, the Democrats knew they could win if they avoided major errors. And the Republicans realized they faced almost certain defeat. President Hoover, Secretary of State Henry Stimson reported, was "rather blue" about it all.[3]

But Hoover felt obliged to run again to vindicate himself and his policies; and the Republicans could scarcely deny him renomination without admitting failure. The Republican convention was dispirited and dolorous. Though Hoover and his Vice-President, Charles Curtis, were both renominated on first ballots, there were no spontaneous demonstrations, colorful eulogies, or triumphant parades. The delegates didn't even bother to post pictures of the President around the convention hall. The Republican platform praised the administration's anti-depression measures, called for a balanced budget and a protective tariff, and urged repealing the 18th (Prohibition) Amendment and returning the control of the liquor traffic to the states. "Surely it is astonishing," remarked columnist Walter Lippmann, "that in the midst of such great economic distress there should be no rumbling here of social discontent."[4]

With the Democrats it was quite otherwise. The presidential nomination was a great prize this time and the battle to win it in some ways more exciting than the campaign that followed. Franklin D. Roosevelt, two-term Governor of New York, was the front-runner; he had shown vigor and resourcefulness in meeting the economic crisis in New York and his supporters had been carefully gathering support for him for some time. But Alfred E. Smith wanted to try again; and he had the support of party regulars, particularly in the East. John Nance Garner, Speaker of the House, was also popular; he had the backing of the Texas and California delegations and William Randolph Hearst was pushing hard for him in his chain of newspapers across the country. When the delegates began voting in Chicago, at 4:28 a.m. on the morning of July 1, FDR led on the first ballot—with Smith in second place and Garner trailing far behind—but he lacked the necessary two-thirds to win. He gained a few votes on the second and third trials but still not enough to go over the top. The convention adjourned at this point—it was now 9:15 a.m.—and during the next few hours FDR's managers worked frantically trying to line up additional votes.

The Roosevelt men finally made a deal with Garner: if he released his delegates he would receive second place on the ticket. Garner knew he couldn't win first place himself and he was far closer in sympathies to FDR than to Smith. He was also anxious to avoid a deadlock in the convention. "Hell," he said later, "I'll do anything to see the Democrats win one more national election."[5] Hearst, who controlled the California delegation, decided FDR was acceptable (especially since he had repudiated the League of Nations in February) and finally agreed to go along with Garner. That evening, when the name of California was called on the fourth ballot, Smith's old enemy, William McAdoo, went up to the rostrum and cried: "California came here to nominate a President; she did not come here to deadlock this convention or to engage in another disastrous contest like that of 1924. California casts 44 votes for Franklin D. Roosevelt." "Good old McAdoo!" smiled FDR when he heard the news over his radio in Albany.[6] Smith (who had become estranged from Roosevelt after 1928) stubbornly refused to release his delegates so the nomination could be made unanimous; but FDR won on the fourth ballot anyway and the next day Garner was added to the ticket.

"It's a kangaroo ticket," sighed a disappointed Texas politician after Roosevelt's nomination. "Stronger in the hindquarters than in the front."[7] He was not the only person to underestimate Roosevelt. Wrote H. L. Mencken: "Here was a great convention . . . nominating the weakest candidate before it."[8] Walter Lippmann was even more disparaging. He had already dismissed FDR as "an amiable boy scout." The New York Governor, he now wrote, "is no crusader. He is no tribune of the people. He is no enemy of entrenched privilege. He is a pleasant man who, without any important qualifications for the office, would very much like to be President."[9] It was Lippmann's most famous gaffe and FDR was amused (and irked) by it.

The fifty-year-old FDR surprised Lippmann (and a lot of other people) by his verve and vigor; he had a way of doing that. He decided to fly to Chicago to accept the nomination, partly to show that his crippled condition was no handicap and partly to show that he was a man of action. "I have started out on the tasks that lie ahead," he told the delegates when he reached the convention center, "by breaking the absurd tradition that the candidate should remain in professed ignorance of what has happened for weeks until he is formally notified of that event many weeks later. . . . You have nominated me and I know it, and I am here to thank you for the honor. Let it . . . be symbolic that in so doing I broke tradition. Let it be from now on the task of our Party to break foolish traditions." He went on to endorse his party's call for a balanced budget, reduced federal expenditures, repeal of the 18th Amendment, aid to agriculture, federal public works, and relief for the unfortunate; he also emphasized his belief that the federal government had a "continuing responsibility for the broader public welfare." And he roused his audience to cheers with his peroration: "I pledge you, I pledge myself, to a new deal for the American people. Let us all here assembled constitute ourselves prophets of a new order of competence and of courage. This is more than a political campaign; it is a call to arms. Give me your help, not to win votes alone, but to win in this crusade to restore America to its own people." The following day newspapers carried a cartoon by Rollin Kirby showing a farmer looking at an airplane in the sky on which appeared the words NEW DEAL. The name stuck.[10]

Garner was so sure the election was in the bag that he advised: "Sit down—do nothing—and win the election." He did just that himself; he gave only one speech, over the radio, and decided that one speech per campaign was about right.[11] FDR couldn't have disagreed more. He loved campaigning and was a superb barnstormer; he was also anxious to show that he could put up with the rigors of the stump ("Roosevelt the Robust"); he was eager, too, to outline some of his plans for handling the crisis. Roosevelt's "brain trust"—a group of academic advisers headed by political scientist Raymond Moley of Columbia University—helped him with policies and speech-writing; and his campaign manager, the amiable Big Jim Farley, handled the practical details of vote-getting. FDR's energy astonished his associates; he seemed never to tire and his spirits were unflagging. During the campaign he traveled about 13,000 miles by train and made sixteen major addresses, each devoted to a special topic, and many minor ones. At the same time he developed good relations with party regulars (even Smith campaigned for him, though without warmth) and he wooed and won to his cause such distinguished Progressive Republicans as Robert LaFollette, Jr., of Wisconsin and George Norris of Nebraska. "What this country needs," announced Senator Norris, to FDR's delight, "is another Roosevelt in the White House."[12]

Much of what Roosevelt said during the campaign was unexceptionable, even conventional, and at times some of his supporters thought he was talking too much like his opponent, especially when he called for economy in government and a balanced budget. "In Franklin Roosevelt," said one newspaper, "we have another Hoover." One columnist even wrote a satirical piece about "Herbert Roosevelt" and "Franklin Hoover."[13] But FDR also broke new ground in speeches about aid to the farmers, federal development of electrical power, and federal relief. And in his address to the Commonwealth Club in San Francisco on September 23, he presented the basic philosophy underlying the New Deal when he insisted that the federal government must help the business community develop "an economic constitutional order" in which there would be a fairer distribution of wealth and in which every man would be assured the "right to make a comfortable living."[14] California Progressives like Hiram Johnson were delighted by his speech. President Hoover was horrified.

Hoover had not planned any extensive campaigning at first; he felt duty-bound to remain hard at work in the White House in the crisis. But Democratic assaults on the "Hoover depression" roused his wrath and in October he decided to take to the stump (and to the mike) to defend himself. In nine major addresses he insisted that the depression grew out of World War I and originated abroad (and not at home, as FDR maintained) and that the measures he had taken had prevented total collapse: "let no man say it could not have been worse."[15] He reiterated his faith in individual initiative and free enterprise, accused the Democrats in Congress of blocking his efforts to restore the economy, and called FDR's proposals radical and socialistic. He also emphasized the fact that there were signs of recovery appearing in the fall of 1932 and that only fears in the business community over what FDR might do would block an upturn in economic conditions.

Hoover was the last President to write his own speeches. He carefully conceived, organized, and drafted all of them. But they sounded dreary, especially over the radio, compared with FDR's lively offerings. In some cities people booed and even thumbed their noses at the President. FDR was furious at Republican charges he was under the influence of radical foreign notions. "My policy," he cried at one point, "is as radical as American liberty, as radical as the Constitution of the United States." He wanted to make an even stronger response to allegations of un-Americanism; but his advisers convinced him it was wiser not to engage in polemical exchanges. He did, though, say that Hoover's record as President was like that of the Four Horsemen: "Destruction, Delay, Despair and Doubt." But he rarely sounded portentous. His breezy optimism was a sharp contrast to Hoover's dour solemnity. He livened his speeches with catchy phrases and homely tales. In a speech at Columbus, Ohio, on August 20, which went over big, he did an amusing take-off on *Alice in Wonderland* to point up the absurdities of Republican economic policies.[16]

As the campaign proceeded, Hoover became increasingly shrill. He was sincerely convinced that FDR's policies were dangerous and destructive. In his last major speech, in Madison Square Garden on October 31, he not only warned that there would be an increase in unemployment if FDR won the election; he also said that if FDR's proposals for tariff revision were carried out, the "grass will grow in the streets of a hundred cities, a thousand towns; the weeds will overrun the fields of millions of farms. . . ." But his basic point was that the main issue of the campaign was individualism vs. regimentation. "We are told by the opposition that we must have a change," he said, "that we must have a new deal. It is not the change that comes from normal development of national life to which I object, but the proposal to alter the whole foundations of our national life which have been builded through generations of testing and struggle, and of the principles upon which we have builded the nation." (And on which Hoover had builded his administration.) Hoover dismissed the New Deal as un-American. "Indeed," he said on November 5, "this is the same philosophy of government which has poisoned all Europe. They have been the fumes of the witch's cauldron which boiled in Russia and in its attenuated flavor spread over the whole of Europe, and would by many be introduced into the United States in an attempt to secure votes through protest of discontent against emergency conditions."[17]

On November 8, some 40,000,000 people went to the polls and cast a decided vote against Hoover's Old Deal. FDR won over 7,000,000 more popular votes than Hoover: 22,821,857 (57.4 percent) to 15,761,841 (39.7 percent); he also carried 42 of the 48 states and won 472 electoral votes to Hoover's 59. The Democrats also won both houses of Congress by big majorities. The election was not necessarily a mandate for the New Deal; the New Deal was still rather vague in FDR's mind. But it unquestionably represented "a firm desire on the part of the American people," as William Allen White admitted, "to use government as an agency for human welfare."[18] But it was a vote for reform, not revolution. The Socialist party's Norman Thomas won only 882,000 votes in 1932; and the Communist party's William Z. Foster attracted only about 103,000 votes. Some conservatives, in fact, were relieved by the outcome. Said Hoover's Secretary of Commerce Roy Chapin: "The mood of the country was such that . . . perhaps we are lucky that we didn't get a Socialist or Radical instead of Roosevelt."[19]

Happy Days

FDR had been Assistant Secretary of the Navy under Wilson and thought it would be appropriate for the band to play "Anchors Aweigh" after he was nominated for President. But when the band struck up the tune after John E. Mack's nominating speech, Louis Howe and Edward Flynn, hearing it on the radio, thought it sounded terrible. "That sounds like a funeral march," cried Flynn. "Why don't we get something peppy for them to play, like 'Happy Days Are Here Again'?" Howe agreed, they telephoned the convention, and soon delegates were singing what was to become Roosevelt's campaign theme song:

> Happy days are here again!
> The skies above are clear again!
> Let's all sing a song of cheer again—
> Happy days—are—here—a-gain![20]

Bike Ride

H. L. Mencken criticized FDR's "Christian Science smile," but many people thought the Democratic candidate's breezy affability was good for the nation's morale. "Roosevelt smiles and smiles and smiles," said one reporter, "and it doesn't get tiresome. He can smile more than any man in American politics without being insipid." Roosevelt was a great tease, too, and reporters enjoyed exchanging pleasantries with him. From the beginning he had planned to fly to Chicago after his nomination but kept his plans secret. When news of a new trimotored plane at the Albany airport leaked out, reporters began predicting he would fly to Chicago. Asked about it, he laughed and said: "Now, I'll tell you what I am going to do. I'm going to bicycle out to Chicago. I'm going to get one of those quintets—you know, five bicycles in a row. Father will ride in the first seat and manage the handlebars. Jim will ride second, then Elliott, then Franklin, Jr., and then John." He also added Samuel I. Rosenman, close friend and speech-writer, to the party: "Sam will follow—on a tricycle."[21]

Acceptance

When Louis Howe read the acceptance speech FDR had prepared with the help of his "Brain Trust," he was disappointed. He didn't think it was good enough for his hero so he went to work and wrote one of his own. When Roosevelt reached Chicago, Howe met him at the airport and gave him his manuscript as they got in the car to go to the convention center. "I tell you it's all right, Franklin," he assured FDR. "It's much better than the speech you've got now—and you can read it while you're driving down to the convention hall, and get familiar with it." "But, Louis," protested Roosevelt, "you know I can't deliver a speech that I've never done any work on myself, and that I've never even read. It will sound stupid, and it's silly to think I can." But Howe persisted. "All right, Louis," Roosevelt finally yielded, "I'll try to read it over while we are riding down to the convention hall." As the car made its way through the streets of Chicago, FDR waved his hand, tipped his hat, and shouted, "hello" to the crowds gathered to greet him, and glanced at Howe's manuscript on his lap from time to time. By the time he reached the convention center he had decided what to do: substitute the first page of Howe's speech for the first page of his own and then deliver the rest of his speech as planned. When Roosevelt began following his plan, speechwriter Judge Samuel Rosenman was dismayed by the unfamiliar words; but as Roosevelt eased into the speech approved by the Brain Trust he quickly relaxed. FDR's gesture seems to have pleased Howe; at least he never complained about receiving only first-page billing.[22]

Brain Trust

Two groups of advisers helped FDR: politicians like Jim Farley and Edward J. Flynn and professors like Raymond Moley and Rexford Tugwell. Louis Howe was skeptical about the professoriate and one day in a conversation with Roosevelt referred derisively to "your brains trust." A little later Roosevelt used Howe's term when talking to newsmen, a *New York Times* reporter picked it up and used it in a news article the following day, and the name stuck. Eventually the "s" was dropped and "Brain Trust" was used for Roosevelt's advisers even after the original group dissolved. After Roosevelt's election, when a hostile critic made fun of the Brain Trust, Secretary of Interior Harold L. Ickes wanted to know what part of the anatomy he suggested thinking with.[23]

Sent the Army

Not long after Hoover's renomination a "Bonus Expeditionary Force" (B.E.F.) composed of about 20,000 World War I veterans, hit hard by the depression, came to Washington to demand the early payment of the bonus due them in 1945. Hoover refused to meet with B.E.F. representatives and many of the veterans settled down in the city in tar-paper shacks and packing-crate huts. Hoover became alarmed; and on July 28, at his order, General Douglas MacArthur broke up the B.E.F. camp with troops, tanks, and tear gas, and drove the veterans out of town. "A challenge to the authority of the United States Government," announced Hoover, "has been met, swiftly and firmly." Though most newspapers backed Hoover's action, the *Washington News* exclaimed: "If the Army must be called out to make war on unarmed citizens, this is no longer America."

Hoover's assault on the bonus-marchers hurt him in his campaign for re-election. When Vice-President Charles Curtis was speaking in Las Vegas, Nevada, the following month, hecklers began crying: "Why didn't you feed some of those ex-soldiers in Washington?" "I've fed more than you have, you dirty cowards!" shouted Curtis angrily. "I'm not afraid of any of you!" "Hurrah for Roosevelt!" people started yelling. "If you wait for him to be elected," cried Curtis, "you'll be an old man."

After FDR's inauguration, the Bonus Army was back in Washington. Roosevelt asked his wife Eleanor to go out to talk to the veterans and added: "Above all, be sure there is plenty of good coffee. No questions asked. Just let free coffee flow all the time. There is nothing like it to make people feel better and feel welcome." Eleanor Roosevelt went out, talked to the veterans, and led them in singing, "There's a Long, Long Trail." Afterward one of them remarked: "Hoover sent the army. Roosevelt sent his wife."[24]

Exercise Out of a Book

Some of FDR's associates advised against a campaign tour. They knew Republicans were casting doubts on his health and stamina and were afraid that nervous exhaustion or even a slight accident en route might play into their hands. "Well, I'm going anyhow," said FDR firmly when Jim Farley and Charley Michelson told him they thought a western trip was too dangerous. "Why take a chance?" they asked him. "Because I want to," was his reply. "And," he added, "I'm not going to take a doctor along either." And so he went and, superb campaigner that he was, the trip was a great success. Impressed by Roosevelt's vast knowledge of public issues, Charley Michelson, Roosevelt's publicity director, once asked him, "Governor, how on earth did you accumulate so much definite knowledge of so many things?" "Well," Roosevelt replied, "you fellows with two good legs spend your spare time playing golf, or shooting ducks and such things, while I have had to get all my exercise out of a book!"[25]

Married

When FDR became President he surprised people by his firmness and decisiveness. During the campaign, however, he impressed some people as being vague on the issues. Heywood Broun called him "a corkscrew" and Walter Lippmann said he was "an amiable man" and not much more. Years later, one of Eleanor Roosevelt's friends confessed he had voted for Norman Thomas in 1932. "So would I have," she said, "if I had not been married to Franklin."[26]

Signal

A Democratic doggerel commemorated Secretary of the Treasury Andrew ("Andy") Mellon as well as President Hoover:

> Mellon pulled the whistle
> Hoover rang the bell
> Wall St. gave the signal
> And the country went to hell.[27]

Iowa

Even before FDR gave a farm speech in Topeka, Kansas, Senator Thomas P. Gore of Oklahoma wired him: "If every Democrat in Iowa should be put in jail on election day, you would carry President Hoover's native state anyway."[28]

Alternative

After his election, FDR was told by a friend that if he succeeded as President he would go down in history as the greatest American President but if he failed he would live on as the worst one. "If I fail," said Roosevelt solemnly, "I shall be the last one."[29]

★ ★

CHAPTER THIRTY-EIGHT

1936
Roosevelt and the New Deal

"There's one issue in this campaign," FDR told Raymond Moley in the summer of 1936, "It's myself, and people must be either for me or against me." Moley was shocked by the apparent conceit, but the President spoke truly. By 1936 Roosevelt was the center of both passionate adoration and burning hatred. With millions of Americans he was, as Jim Farley remarked, "more popular than the New Deal itself."[1]

The measures Roosevelt sponsored during his first years in the White House did not produce prosperity. But they pulled the country out of the doldrums and saw to it that millions of people were better off than they had been when he first took office. At the same time the New Deal's sharp departure from traditional use and wont produced indignation, alarm, and then outright loathing on the part of reactionaries in both parties. The J. P. Morgans absolutely forbade the mention of FDR's name in their household; and at least one wealthy businessman left the country for the duration. FDR's old friend Alfred E. Smith, once a foe of privilege but now the friend of the fashionable, "took a walk," and began delighting Roosevelt-haters in both parties by his blasts at the New Deal. Charged Smith: "The young brain-trusters caught the Socialists in swimming and they ran away with their clothes."[2]

To unseat Roosevelt the Republicans, meeting in Cleveland early in June, picked Alfred M. Landon, Governor of Kansas, on the first ballot. The Landon choice pleased businessmen: he was an oil man and a fiscal conservative and had balanced his state's budget. But Republican Progressives liked him too: he was a former Bull Mooser who had sponsored New Dealish measures as Governor. He came from a farm state, moreover, and had a chance of winning back Western farmers who had gone for FDR in 1932. Landon's forthright and folksy manner also seemed to be an asset; he was called the "Kansas Lincoln." For second place the Republicans turned to another former Bull Mooser who, unlike Landon, was now deeply conservative: Colonel Frank Knox, publisher of the *Chicago Daily News*. The Republican platform blew hot and cold on the New Deal: flayed the Roosevelt administration for reckless spending, unbalanced budgets, and assaults on free enterprise, but also endorsed federal relief for the unemployed, social security for the elderly, farm credits, and the right of labor to organize and bargain collectively. During the campaign Landon himself reflected the ambivalence of his party toward FDR's handiwork. The New Deal, in short, if not FDR himself, was now the center of political debate.

From start to finish, Franklin Roosevelt—"the Champ"—dominated proceedings of the Democratic convention which met in Philadelphia late in June. The delegates greeted Kentucky Senator Alben Barkley's militant New Deal keynote address with joy and jubilation and, when FDR's name was put in nomination for a second term, "danced and pranced," according to the *New York Times*, "whooped and hollered, marched and capered in a mighty effort to display their enthusiasm for their leader."[3] There were speeches on FDR's behalf by forty-nine men and eight women which took all day to deliver and part of the night (and produced a "sirocco," someone said, "which is believed to have altered the climate of Philadelphia").[4] The convention went on to renominate "Cactus Jack" Garner for second place and adopt a platform promising an expansion of the New Deal. In his acceptance address, FDR thrilled millions who heard him over the radio by his blast against "economic royalists" and his insistence that Americans had a "rendezvous with destiny" in their struggle to "save a great, a precious form of government for ourselves and for the world."[5]

There was an abundance of fringe parties in 1936. The Socialist party ran Norman Thomas again; and the Communist party, the Socialist Labor party, and the Prohibitionist party all put up candidates. Overshadowing them all, however, was the new Union party, a loose collection of anti-New Deal malcontents, containing both radical and reactionary elements. The Union party included followers of Francis Townsend, an elderly California physician with a plan for federal pensions of $200 a month for everyone over sixty; members of the National Union for Social Justice, founded by Father Charles E. Coughlin, Michigan's eloquent (and increasingly intemperate) "Radio Priest," a currency-inflationist who had once backed FDR but was now virulently anti-New Deal as well as anti-Wall Street; and backers of Rev. Gerald L. K. Smith, a spellbinding hate-monger from Louisiana who took upon himself the mantle of Populist Huey Long when the latter was assassinated in 1935.

William Lemke, Republican Congressman from North Dakota, was the Union party's presidential candidate. His supporters called him "Liberty Bill"; his critics pointed out that the Liberty Bell was cracked. Coughlin and Smith, who competed for the limelight, dominated the campaign; they hardly mentioned Lemke in their tours of the country. And instead of stressing the party's platform—which included vague promises of old-age pensions and help for farmers and workers—they concentrated on attacking FDR and the New Deal as Communistic. In a speech in Cleveland in July, Coughlin not only called the President "Franklin Double-Crossing Roosevelt"; he also ripped off his clerical collar and said he was a "liar" and a "betrayer." In New Bedford, Massachusetts, he announced: "As I was instrumental in removing Herbert Hoover from the White House, so help me God, I will be instrumental in taking a Communist from the chair once occupied by Washington."[6] Lemke himself, practically forgotten during the campaign, never resorted to rabble-rousing, but his earnest campaign speeches, mostly about the farmer's plight, lacked excitement and roused little enthusiasm.

When the campaign began, "Alf" Landon faced a tough problem. How could he endorse the New Deal, even in part, without being charged with "Me Tooism" by conservatives? And how could he emphasize his criticisms of the New Deal without alienating the kind of Progressives in both parties he hoped to attract to his cause? Landon ended by trying both approaches. He began his campaign in a benign mood. Though criticizing FDR for his spending policies, he made it clear that he thought well of the President ("a fine and charming gentleman") and shared many of his social objectives.[7] But toward the end of the campaign he began taking a hard line and soon sounded like Herbert Hoover in his denunciations of FDR's "strangling of free enterprise." Two-thirds of the press was for Landon and some newspapers made no effort to conceal their partisanship in news columns as well as editorials. The Hearst papers charged that FDR was surrounded by a "Communist entourage," and the *Chicago Tribune* reported that "Moscow Orders Reds in U.S. To Back Roosevelt" and predicted a Landon defeat would mean "Moscow in the White House." During the campaign the *Tribune* reminded its readers in every issue the number of days left "in which to save your country."[8]

To the consternation of his associates, FDR took it easy at first. He went on a leisurely sailing vacation and then attended a few official conferences where he made non-political remarks. In October, however, he took to the stump and in both personal appearances and radio addresses made it obvious once again that among campaigners he was absolutely without peer. FDR's speeches not only defended specific New Deal programs; they also made two major points: that the American people—farmers, workers, businessmen—were better off in 1936 than they had been in 1932; and that the reforms he sponsored were the true (and only) way to avoid the radical solutions that most Americans shunned. A "true conservative," he reminded his audiences, "corrects injustices to preserve social peace." FDR made fun of Republicans who insisted they could do everything his administration had done but do it more economically and efficiently. "Who is there in America," he cried, "who believes that we can run the risk of turning back our Government to the old leadership which brought it to the brink of 1933?"[9] Everywhere he went FDR attracted huge crowds and tremendous enthusiasm. In Chicago five miles of streets were filled with his admirers, and 100,000 people packed the stadium to hear him speak.

In the final days of the campaign Republican leaders resorted to scare tactics. They began charging that the Social Security Act, scheduled to go into effect on January 1, 1937, was a gigantic swindle. Not only did it mean a "pay reduction" for American workers; it also put "half the working people of America under Federal control." The Republicans of course omitted the fact that the deduction from wages and salaries was to be used to finance old-age pensions and was matched by contributions from employers. Instead, in bulletins posted in factories, they announced: "YOU'RE SENTENCED TO A WEEKLY PAY REDUCTION FOR ALL YOUR WORKING LIFE. YOU'LL HAVE TO SERVE THE SENTENCE UNLESS YOU HELP REVERSE IT NOVEMBER 3." And slips inserted in workers' pay envelopes warned: "Effective January, 1937, we are compelled by a Roosevelt 'New Deal' law to make a 1 per cent deduction from your wages and turn it over to the government. Finally, this may go as high as 4 per cent. You might get this money back . . . but only if Congress decides to make the appropriation for this purpose. There is NO guarantee. Decide before November 3—election day—whether or not you wish to take these chances." In a radio speech on the subject, Republican national chairman John Hamilton announced that workers would have to wear metal dog-tags carrying their social-security numbers; and the Hearst newspapers ran pictures of a man wearing such a tag with the caption "YOU."[10]

FDR was in an angry mood when he defended the Social Security Act in a speech in Madison Square Garden on the eve of the election. He exposed the spurious nature of Republican charges and pointed out that most Republicans in Congress had voted for the social-security legislation. And, to the delight of his audience, he went on to challenge the forces of "selfishness and greed" which were arrayed against him. "Never before in history," he cried, "have these forces been so united against one candidate as they stand today. They are unanimous in their hate for me—and I welcome their hatred. I should like to have it said of my first administration that in it the forces of selfishness and of lust for power met their match. I should like to have it said of my second administration that in it these forces met their master."[11]

Even after Landon stepped up his assaults on the Roosevelt administration, he had little reason to think he could win the election. When a reporter asked him whether he could beat FDR, Landon said candidly: "No chance." Then he begged the reporter to keep his remark out of the papers and the latter obliged.[12] FDR, for his part, never felt

244   *Presidential Campaigns*

he had to run scared. Just before election day he figured he would take 270 electoral votes to Landon's 178. But Jim Farley was more sanguine. "Roosevelt," he said, "will carry every state except Maine and Vermont."[13] He was right on target. On November 3, not only did every state but Maine and Vermont go for FDR, giving him 523 electoral votes to Landon's 8; he also won a popular plurality of more than 11,000,000 votes: 27,751,597 (60.8 percent) to Landon's 16,679,583. The Democrats also made great gains in both houses of Congress. The third parties did poorly: the Socialists won only 187,720 votes for Norman Thomas, and the Communists 80,150 for Earl Browder. The Union party did the best: it won 882,479 votes on election day, far fewer than expected, and then quickly died.

The election was a massive vote of confidence in FDR and his New Deal. In 1932 people voted against Hoover; in 1936 they voted for FDR; farmers in the West and the South, workingmen with varied ethnic backgrounds in the urban centers; middle-class wage-earners; and reform-minded intellectuals. American blacks, too, traditionally Republican, moved in large numbers to the Democratic party in 1936, partly because New Deal relief measures had rescued them from starvation and partly because leading New Dealers, including Eleanor Roosevelt, were openly sympathetic to their aspirations. Landon was buried, said Idaho's Progressive Senator William E. Borah after the election, because the masses of people believed he represented an outmoded philosophy of politics.[14]

☆ ☆ ☆

Landon Bridges

The Republicans considered adding New Hampshire Senator Styles Bridges to their ticket until someone warned that the Democrats might start chanting, "Landon Bridges Falling Down!" With Colonel Knox on the ticket, the Republicans were able to chant: "Off the Rocks with Landon and Knox!"[15]

Hoover Hay

In 1932 Hoover warned that if FDR became President grass would grow in the streets. In 1936 the Democrats threw the warning back in his face. In front of their convention hall in Philadelphia they displayed a mowing machine, a rake, and a farm wagon bearing an empty hay rack, all drawn by sad-eyed mules and carrying signs twitting the Republicans: "Hoover and his party didn't give us the chicken for the pot, nor the two-car garage, and now they renege on the promise of a grass-cutting job"; "The GOP elephant, foodless for three long years, counted on feeding upon Hoover grass. What will the poor beast do now, poor thing?"; "Hay, hay, Hoover!" There were also verses:

Well, Mr. Hoover, here we come,
To do the job you wanted done;
We're all ready to begin to mow,
But where's the grass you said would grow?

The Democratic exhibit went over big. Philadelphia merchants began renting donkeys themselves and walking them about town carrying signs advertising their wares.[16]

Oh, Susanna!

Landon's acceptance ceremony took place in Topeka on July 23 and, since he was the first Kansan to receive the nomination of a major party, the *Wichita Beacon* called it "Kansas' Most Glorious Day." In newspapers, a Topeka optometrist began advertising: "The Eyes of the Nation Are Upon Topeka Today. . . . It Pays To See Accurately." After Landon's acceptance speech, Republicans sang "Oh, Susanna," with new words:

Landon, oh Landon
Will lead to Victory—
With the dear old Constitution,
And it's good enough for me.

During the campaign the Republican slogan was "Life, Liberty, and Landon," and the official emblem was the sunflower, the Kansas state flower. Tiffany's featured a nineteen-petal gold sunflower, set with yellow diamonds, for $815, but there were not many takers. But there were more new words for "Oh, Susanna":

The alphabet we'll always have
But one thing sure is true
With Landon in, the New Deal's out
And that means P.D.Q.
Alf Landon learned a thing or two,
He knows the right solution,
And in the White House he will stay
Within the Constitution.[17]

Outsmarted

In 1936 the United Mine Workers (UMW) voted to endorse FDR, and UMW chief John L. Lewis and two other officials called on the President to give him a check for $250,000. Hoping to develop some influence with the administration, Lewis asked if a photographer could record the historic scene. "No, John," said Roosevelt, beaming, "I don't want your check, much as I appreciate the thought. Just keep it, and I'll call you if and when any small need arises." As the group left the White House Lewis remarked gloomily that they had been "outsmarted," for now, he said, there was no limit to the amount the Democrats could ask for. His companions disagreed; FDR's victory was such a sure thing, they argued, that they would probably save a large part of the $250,000. "You don't know politicians," said Lewis. "They stay under the golden drip from the honey barrel until no drop is left." He was right. There were repeated requests for help from the Democrats as the campaign got under way and soon the UMW's $250,000 was all gone.[18]

Categorical Denial

In a speech in Pittsburgh on October 19, 1932, FDR had called for reduced federal spending, but when his New Deal programs produced heavy spending the Republicans charged he had betrayed his Pittsburgh promises. Roosevelt was bothered by the charge and at the beginning of his 1936 campaign told speechwriter Judge Rosenman: "I'm going to make the first major campaign speech in Pittsburgh at the ball park in exactly the same spot I made that 1932 Pittsburgh speech; and in the speech I want to explain my 1932 statement. See whether you can prepare a draft giving a good and convincing explanation of it." So Rosenman got out a copy of the 1932 address, read it carefully, went to see Roosevelt, and told him that only one kind of explanation was possible. "Fine," said Roosevelt, a bit surprised, but pleased all the same. "What sort of explanation would you make?" "Mr. President," said Rosenman, "the only thing you can say about that 1932 speech is to deny categorically that you ever made it!"[19]

Stretcher

Nothing irritated Socialist leader Norman Thomas more than the charge that FDR had carried out the Socialist platform of 1932. "Roosevelt did not carry out the Socialist platform," he insisted, "unless he carried it out on a stretcher!"[20]

Frightful Five Minutes

When FDR arrived at Franklin Field in Philadelphia to deliver his acceptance address, he spied the eighty-four-year-old poet Edwin Markham ("The Man with the Hoe") in the crowd and waved to him. But as Markham pressed forward to shake hands, someone inadvertently pushed him, he bumped into James Roosevelt, and the latter stumbled against his father. At this point the pressure snapped the steel brace holding FDR's right leg out of position and, to everyone's horror, Roosevelt fell over. A Secret Service man moved fast and caught the President before he hit the ground, but the manuscript of his speech slipped out of his hands and the pages scattered into the crowd. But Roosevelt's bodyguard quickly snapped the brace back to position and helped the President to his feet and the latter exclaimed, "Clean me up." He also told people to keep their feet off "those damned sheets" on the ground. "Okay, let's go," he said, after people had brushed the dirt off his clothes and gathered up the pages of his manuscript. Then, noticing Markham was close to tears, he stopped, smiled, and shook hands with him. A moment later he was on the platform, putting the crumpled pages of his speech together and getting ready to speak to the 100,000 men and women gathered in the stands. Afterwards he confessed that "it was the most frightful five minutes of my life."[21]

S.O.B.

"Mr. Roosevelt," said one workingman, "is the only man we ever had in the White House who would understand that my boss is a son-of-a-bitch."[22]

Stuffed Shirts

Landon once complained to John Hamilton, chairman of the Republican national committee, "Why don't you ever bring workingmen to see me? All I ever see are stuffed-shirt businessmen and bankers."[23]

FDR-Landon Meeting

Roosevelt and Landon were the first candidates to meet during a campaign since Wilson and Taft in 1912. At a conference of governors in Des Moines, Iowa, to discuss the drought, the two men met, shook hands, ate lunch together, and chatted for close to an hour. "Well, Governor," said FDR as they parted, "however this comes out, we'll see more of each other. Either you come to see me or I'll come to see you." "I certainly shall," said Landon. "And, Governor," added FDR, "don't work too hard!" Afterward Republican Senator Arthur Capper of Kansas commented: "Harmony dripped so steadily from each rafter that I fully expected one of the candidates to withdraw."[24]

Observant

"Wherever I have gone in this country," announced Landon in one speech, "I have found Americans." The sentence evoked so much mirth that Landon began cracking down on his speech-writers.[25]

Harvard

In July, FDR attended Harvard University's tercentenary celebration and the students booed him. When he came to speak, the President recalled that at Harvard's 200th anniversary a century before, "many of the alumni of Harvard were sorely troubled by the state of the Union. Andrew Jackson was President. On the 250th anniversary of the founding of Harvard College, alumni were again sorely troubled. Grover Cleveland was President." He paused. Then: "Now, on the 300th anniversary, *I* am President."[26]

On The Payroll

Landon himself refrained from Red-baiting, but Knox charged that "the New Deal candidate has been leading us toward Moscow." And when Landon telephoned at one point to suggest moderating his statements, Knox struck a T.R. pose and told some newsmen: "Boys, I've got another McKinley on my hands." But both Knox and former President Hoover assailed the Democrats in such extravagant terms that it began to look as though it would backfire. One reporter facetiously asked FDR if the two men were on the Democratic payroll. "Strictly off the record," said FDR, mock-seriously, "it is a question of how much longer we can afford to pay them. They have been so successful that they are raising their prices."[27]

Literary Digest Poll

" 'THE DIGEST's PRESIDENTIAL POLL IS ON!" announced the editors of the *Literary Digest* jubilantly on August 22. "Unruffled by the tumult and shouting of the hottest political race in twenty years, more than 1,000 trained workers have swung into their accustomed jobs. . . . THE DIGEST's smooth-running machine moves with the swift precision of thirty years' experience to reduce guess-work to hard fact. . . . Once again, THE DIGEST was asking more than ten million voters— one out of four, representing every county in the United States—*to settle November's election in October.* . . . When the last figure has been totted and checked, if past experience is a criterion, the country will know *to within a fraction of 1 per cent,* the actual popular vote of forty millions."

On September 5, the *Digest* gave the first returns from its postal-card poll: Landon was ahead in four states. The following week Landon was still ahead; and so it continued, week after week, as the *Digest* reported the latest results of its straw vote. On October 17, Landon was ahead in 32 of the 48 states, with FDR leading in only 16. On October 24, Landon was winning 54 percent of the votes and Roosevelt only 40 percent. And on October 31, just before election day, the *Digest* confidently proclaimed Landon the sure winner (370 electoral votes to 161) and quoted what Jim Farley had said about the *Digest* poll in 1932: "The LITERARY DIGEST poll is an achievement of no little magnitude. It is a Poll fairly and correctly conducted."

Landon's abysmal defeat on November 3 left the editors of the *Digest* reeling. "WHAT WENT WRONG WITH THE POLLS?" they cried on November 14. Recalling that they had hit the nail on the head in 1920, 1924, 1928, and 1932, they tried to figure out why, using precisely the same methods, they had failed so dismally in 1936. Possibly it was because they polled automobile owners and people listed in phone books and missed the "lower strata"; or perhaps it was because they had failed to give due weight to different groups and classes in the voting population. Farley's astonishingly accurate forecast, the editors noted, was based on reports from tens of thousands of precinct leaders throughout the country. But the *Digest* had one consolation: FDR wasn't such a hot forecaster either. His last guess was only 360 electoral votes to 171.[28]

Meddlers

Roosevelt's electoral victory was the greatest since Monroe's in 1820. The old adage "As Maine goes, so goes the nation" was revised to "As Maine goes, so goes Vermont." After the election someone hung a sign on a bridge leading from New Hampshire into Maine reading, "YOU ARE NOW LEAVING THE UNITED STATES." Someone suggested FDR balance the budget by selling Maine and Vermont to Canada. FDR liked to joke about the two states he didn't carry. "I knew I should have gone to Maine and Vermont during the campaign," he said, "but Jim Farley wouldn't let me." For a while there was talk about whether the Republican party, like the old Whig party, might fold up and disappear. Wrote one humorist: "If the outcome of this election hasn't taught you Republicans not to meddle in politics, I don't know what will."[29]

CHAPTER THIRTY-NINE

★ ★

1940
Roosevelt, Willkie,
and the War in Europe

1940 was the year of the *Blitzkrieg*. In April the Nazis suddenly invaded Norway and Denmark. In May they overran Holland and Belgium. And in June France fell before the Nazi onslaught. Two days after France signed an armistice with Germany, the Republican convention met in Philadelphia to nominate a President and the following month, as the *Luftwaffe* prepared to launch an air attack on Britain, the Democrats held their nominating convention in Chicago.

Like the election of 1916, the election of 1940 was overshadowed by the war in Europe. Should the United States remain aloof from the conflict overseas? Should she give all aid short of war to the British who were now fighting alone? Or should she enter the war at once to help her beleaguered British friends? Ever since September 1939, when World War II commenced, a great debate had been raging—in newspapers, magazines, over the radio, in Congress, and in the lecture hall—over America's foreign policy; and Americans had divided into doves (anti-interventionists), hawks (interventionists), and what might be called hawkish doves (those favoring all aid to Britain short of war). The 1940 campaign reflected, indeed intensified, the division over foreign policy. Both the Republican and Democratic platforms represented a compromise between hawks and doves: promised to stay out of war but favored aid to nations whose liberty was threatened by aggression.

If the party platforms were similar in some respect, the conventions were not. The Republican convention, which opened on June 29, was filled with suspense. Front-runners for the presidential nomination were New York's celebrated gang-buster, District Attorney Thomas E. Dewey, and Ohio's Senator Robert A. Taft, son of William Howard Taft, and both were acceptable to party regulars. But a newcomer to politics—forty-eight-year-old Wall Street lawyer and utilities executive Wendell L. Willkie—was also attracting a great deal of attention, much to the dismay of the Old Guard. Willkie was something of a maverick; he had been a Democrat until 1939, supported most of the New Deal, openly favored aid to Britain, and was utterly without political experience. But he was bright, lively, forthright, and articulate, and also had a home-spun air about him that appealed to many people. A Willkie "boom" had been in motion months before the convention met; amateur poli-ticians like Russell Davenport, managing editor of *Fortune,* and Oren Root, Jr., young New York lawyer, had been founding Willkie Clubs, circulating Willkie petitions, sponsoring Willkie appearances, and bom-barding delegates to the Republican convention with Willkie letters and telegrams. Influential lords of the press, like *Time*'s Henry L. Luce, and wealthy New York bankers and businessmen were also pushing for a Willkie nomination. But the tousle-haired businessman from Indiana had also developed an ardent following among young men and women who, like Willkie himself, were amateurs in politics.

When the Philadelphia delegates got around to balloting, Dewey and Taft, as expected, took first place. By the fourth ballot, however, Willkie was in the lead. As balloting proceeded, people in the galleries kept up a continual chant: "We want Willkie! We want Willkie!" They finally got him on the sixth ballot after the backers of Dewey and Taft failed to join forces to stop him. "Nothing exactly like it ever happened before in American politics," reported *Newsweek* afterwards. "Willkie had never held public office or even sought it. Virtually a neophyte in politics, he had entered no primaries, made no deals, organized no campaign. . . . His backers were uninitiated volunteers, as strange to the ways of the ward bosses and state chairmen as their hero."[1] To go with Willkie the delegates chose Oregon's Charles L. McNary, Minority Leader in the Senate, a friend of public power, but fairly conservative otherwise. After the nominations were made Willkie appeared before the convention to promise "a crusading, aggressive fighting campaign."[2]

Like the Republicans, the Democrats, meeting in Chicago on July 15, had an exciting convention, too, though the suspense was of a quite dif-ferent sort. The big question was: Would the President run for a third term? FDR was apparently undecided for some time about what to do; in 1939 he gave the green light to several of his associates interested in the 1940 nomination, but did nothing seriously to groom a successor. Had there been no world crisis he probably would have retired to pri-vate life at the end of his second term; but the outbreak of war in Eu-rope in September 1939 led him to keep his options open. By May 1940, when the Nazi hordes overran the Low Countries, he seems finally to have decided to run again; and leading New Dealers and Democratic politicians were pressing him hard to do so. Having decided, FDR shrank from seeking the nomination openly; he wanted the party to "draft" him. But the Roosevelt "draft," like the Willkie "boom," could not be left to chance. It had to be skillfully managed.

Harry Hopkins, one of FDR's closest friends and advisers, was in charge of things at Chicago. In the bathroom of his hotel suite (the only place where he had any privacy) he had a direct telephone line to the White House and kept in close touch with the President throughout the convention. On the second day, Kentucky Senator Alben Barkley, the permanent chairman, gave a lively speech; and the minute he mentioned FDR's name, Chicago Mayor Ed Kelly signaled Thomas F. Garry, the city's Superintendent of Sewers, who was stationed in front of a microphone in a room under the auditorium, and Garry started yelling: "We want Roosevelt! The world wants Roosevelt!" And during the twenty-two minute demonstration for Roosevelt that followed, the "voice from the sewers," as it came to be called, continued thundering out pro-Roosevelt slogans through the loudspeakers in the convention hall. When the demonstration ended, Barkley reported FDR's decision to the delegates: "The President has never had and has not today any desire or purpose to continue in the office of the President, to be a candidate for that office, or to be nominated by the convention for that office. He wishes in all earnestness and sincerity to make it clear that all delegates to this convention are free to vote for any candidate. This is the message I bear to you from the President of the United States." Another noisy demonstration followed and the "voice from the sewers" took up the chant again: "The party wants Roosevelt. . . . Illinois wants Roosevelt. . . . The world needs Roosevelt. . . . Everybody wants Roosevelt!"[3] Soon after, the delegates nominated the President for a third term, not by acclamation, as FDR had wanted, but by an overwhelming majority of the voters on the first ballot.

The vice-presidential nomination produced a crisis. Many of the delegates balked at FDR's choice for his running mate: Secretary of Agriculture Henry A. Wallace, a militant New Dealer, an exponent of aid to Britain, and a promising vote-getter in the farm belt. But Wallace had once been a Republican, some people regarded him as a "mystic," and the delegates resented "dictation" from the White House. When Hopkins reported the resistance to Wallace to the President, the latter's "Dutch" was up. "Well, damn it to hell," he told Hopkins, "they will go for Wallace or I won't run, and you can jolly well tell them so." He even drafted a speech refusing the nomination.[4] But Eleanor Roosevelt flew to Chicago to make a speech on Wallace's behalf, Hopkins and Roosevelt's other managers at the convention worked hard on the delegates, and in the end the convention complied with Roosevelt's wishes and picked Wallace in one ballot.

In a burst of energy Willkie launched his campaign against "the third-term candidate," as he liked to call FDR. "Bring on the Champ!" he cried. Then he went on a speech-making tour of the country during which he covered 34,000 miles by train, visited thirty-four states, and made over five hundred speeches. He made a lot of errors at first: neglected organization, left too much to amateurs, tried to write all of his own speeches, and, after acquiring speech-writers, made so many impromptu talks on his own that he fell far behind schedule and was reduced at times to a hoarse whisper. He made two points at first: that in seeking a third term the President was trying to perpetuate "one-man rule"; and that the New Deal had failed to bring about economic recovery because it stressed the distribution rather than the production of goods. But the third-term issue evoked little response, except among those already resolved to vote against FDR. And the emphasis on productivity lost steam when a war boom, growing out of increased defense spending, produced unmistakable signs of an uptick in employment and production. By early September reporters were asking: "What has happened to Willkie?"[5]

On September 3, Roosevelt stole the show when he announced that he had just issued an executive order turning over to the hard-pressed British fifty or sixty destroyers of World War I vintage in return for long-term leases on British air and sea bases in Newfoundland, Bermuda, and the Caribbean. Willkie, like most Americans, approved the destroyer-bases deal, but deplored the fact that "the President did not deem it necessary in connection with this proposal to secure the approval of Congress or permit public discussion prior to adoption." After a conference with Republican leaders he put it more strongly; it was, he said, "the most arbitrary and dictatorial action ever taken by any President in the history of the United States."[6] But Willkie's reservations about Roosevelt's agreement with Britain were scarcely good campaign material; and another issue he raised—that the Roosevelt administration had neglected the nation's defenses—backfired when the Democrats pointed out that a majority of Republicans in Congress had voted against the administration's defense bills in the late 1930s.

There remained, then, the biggest issue of all: war or peace for America. Though Willkie saw eye to eye with FDR on the need to help Britain even at the risk of war, he was also aware of the burning desire of most Americans to stay out of war and finally decided to make use of it in his bid for votes. Early in October he began warning that if FDR won the election, it would mean "wooden crosses for sons and brothers and sweethearts." He pooh-poohed the administration's promises to stay out of war; if FDR's pledge in 1940 to stay out of war was no better than his pledge in 1932 to balance the budget, warned Willkie, American boys are "already almost on the transports." He even predicted that if FDR were re-elected the United States would be at war by April 1941. "Is there anybody here," he cried in one speech, "who really thinks that the President is sincerely trying to keep us out of war?" And again: "We are being edged toward war by an administration that is alike careless in speech and action." Willkie presented himself as the real peace candidate. "If you elect me President . . . ," he told voters, "no American boys will be sent to the shambles of the European trenches."[7]

Willkie's anti-war appeal quickly caught fire and for the first time his campaign began to pick up steam. "The effects of this," confessed Robert E. Sherwood, one of FDR's speech-writers, "were felt powerfully in the White House during the last week in October. I had to read the letters and telegrams and reports that flooded in and . . . I was amazed and horrified at the evidences of hysteria. . . . Newspapermen . . . reported mounting waves of fear throughout the country, which might easily merge into tidal proportions by election day and sweep Willkie into office."[8] When FDR began his active campaigning with a speech in Philadelphia on October 12, he attempted to meet Willkie's charges head-on. "I am an old campaigner," he told his delighted audience, "and I love a good fight."[9] FDR discussed many issues in his five major campaign speeches: his continued support of New Deal reforms, his efforts to strengthen America's defenses in a world at war, and his commitment to aid Britain as a means of defending the United States itself. But he placed major emphasis, as Willkie was doing, on his determination to keep the United States out of a shooting war. His strongest anti-war statement came in a speech in Boston on October 30. En route to Boston, his advisers, alarmed by Willkie's sudden surge in public-opinion polls, insisted that FDR reiterate his promise to keep the country out of war. "But how often do they expect me to say that?" protested the President. "It's in the Democratic platform and I've repeated it a hundred times." "I know it, Mr. President," said Sherwood, "but they don't seem to have heard you the first time. Evidently you've got to say it again—and again—and again." FDR liked Sherwood's way of putting it and decided to remind voters that he had repeatedly promised to stay out of war. When Judge Samuel Rosenman, another speech adviser, suggested adding the phrase, "except in case of attack," FDR exclaimed: "Of course we'll fight if we're attacked. If somebody attacks us, then it isn't a foreign war, is it? Or do they want me to guarantee that our troops be sent into battle only in the event of another Civil War?" And so his appeal in Boston to the "mothers and fathers" of America was unqualified: "I have said this before, but I shall say it again and again and again: Your boys are not going to be sent into any foreign wars."[10]

There was an unprecedented turnout of voters on November 5, and Roosevelt overwhelmed Willkie at the polls. He carried thirty-eight states (449 electoral votes) to Willkie's ten states (82 electoral votes) and won 54.8 percent of the popular votes: 27,243,466 to 22,304,755. FDR's victory was not as great as in 1936 but it was impressive enough. In a world at war the third-term issue had seemed inconsequential to the majority of voters. What counted, it seemed, was the feeling that in a dangerous world the United States had better not change horses in midstream. In time of peace Willkie might well have won; in time of peace, though, FDR probably wouldn't have run for another term. But the Republicans determined to have the last word. In 1951 they succeeded in getting the 22nd Amendment, prohibiting third terms, added to the U.S. Constitution. Better late, apparently, than never.

☆ ☆ ☆

Town Whore

When Willkie arrived in Philadelphia for the Republican convention he spotted reporters in the railroad station and cried: "Ask me any damn thing in the world and I'll answer it. Nothing is off the record. So shoot. Ask me anything you want." "Where's your staff?" they asked. "I haven't any." "Where are your headquarters?" "Under my hat." "What about talk of a Taft-Dewey coalition to block your nomination?" "It's a lot of bunk." "Will you be nominated?" they finally asked him. "Yes," Willkie assured them. "And if I'm not, the nomination won't be worth having." He started off, but stopped for a moment, and added: "Boys, be sure to put it down that I'm having a swell time." In the lobby of his hotel Willkie ran into his conservative fellow Hoosier, Senator James E. Watson, from Rushville, Mrs. Willkie's hometown. "Jim," said Willkie, "couldn't you be for me?" "No, Wendell," said Watson, a party regular, "you're just not my kind of Republican." "I admit I used to be a Democrat," said Willkie amiably. "Used to be?" snapped Watson. "You're a good Methodist," returned Willkie. "Don't you believe in conversion?" "Yes, Wendell," said Watson, "if the town whore truly repented and wanted to join my church, I'd welcome her. I would greet her personally and lead her up the aisle to the front pew, but I'd be damned if I'd ask her to lead the choir the first night." "Aw, Jim," grinned Willkie, "you just go to hell." [11]

Good Democrat

FDR genuinely liked Willkie and once told a friend: "You know, Willkie would have made a good Democrat. Too bad we lost him." [12]

Any S.O.B.

Hostility to Henry Wallace for second place was strong at the Democratic convention, especially among conservatives. When Governor Rivers of Georgia asked Governor Phillips of Oklahoma what he thought of the Wallace candidacy, the latter said: "Henry's my second choice." "Who's your first choice?" asked Rivers. "Any son of a bitch," replied Phillips, "red, white, black or yellow, that can get the nomination!" [13]

Roosevelt's Words

Willkie seemed to have mixed feelings about FDR's policies and one critic said, "Every time Willkie opens his mouth he puts Roosevelt's words in it," while another taunted: "He agreed with Mr. Roosevelt in the entire program of social reform—and said it was leading to disaster."[14]

Willkie's Boners

"Don't forget, young fellow," Willkie's running mate, Charles McNary, told him, "in politics you'll never be in trouble by not saying too much." But Willkie's off-hand remarks got him in trouble during the campaign. While touring Chicago and its suburbs, he began a speech with the words, "Now that we are in Chicago," and someone shouted, "No, you're in Cicero." "Well," said Willkie quickly, "all right, this is Cicero. To hell with Chicago!" And his remark made headlines in the Chicago papers the next day. In a labor speech in Pittsburgh he made another blunder. After promising to "tie labor into the councils of our government" by appointing an actual labor leader as Secretary of Labor he added: "And it won't be a woman, either." His crack at Secretary of Labor Frances Perkins produced laughter and applause, but FDR, listening to the speech on the radio, caught the blunder. "That was a boner Willkie pulled," FDR told Mrs. Perkins afterwards. "He was all right. He was going good when he said his appointment of a Secretary of Labor would come from labor's ranks. That was legitimate political talk, but why didn't he have sense enough to leave well enough alone? Why did he have to insult every woman in the United States? It will make them mad; it will lose him votes." "You'll be surprised to know, Mr. President," said Perkins, "that I already have about five hundred telegrams and letters from women, expressing irritation, and more than half of them tell me they are Republican women."[15]

Opposing Candidate

FDR's general policy in campaigns was never to mention the name of the opposing candidate. "Call him the gentleman from Indiana," FDR would tell his associates with a smile. "Call him our opponent. Call him anything, but never call him bad names. That creates an unfavorable impression among Americans. And never mention his name. Many people, hundreds of people, just cannot remember names. If they don't hear the opponent's name, that is clear gain for us. They have heard my name so often and so long that it in itself is a political asset, and you can trust them, particularly the Roosevelt haters, to say my name plenty of times. In the end, lots of people go to the polls and look the list of candidates over and make up their minds after they get to the ballot box. I know that sounds feeble-minded, but I know it's true. When they look over the list they vote for people whose names they know. We don't want to do anything to advertise the name of the opposing candidate." [16]

1940 Psalm

A Republican update of the 23rd Psalm circulated widely in 1940. "Roosevelt is my shepherd. I live in want. He maketh me to lie down on park benches, He leadeth me past still factories, He disturbeth my soul. He crooneth me into paths of destruction for His party's sake. Yea, though I walk through the shadow of Depression, I anticipate no recovery, for He is with me, His policies and diplomacies they bewilder me, He prepareth a reduction in my salary, He anointeth my small income with taxes, My expenses runneth over. Surely unemployment and poverty shall follow me all the days of my life, and I shall dwell in a mortgaged house forever." [17]

I Wanna Be a Captain

In 1940 the Air Corps was expanding rapidly and when the President's son Elliott, the operator of radio stations in Texas, volunteered for service, he was commissioned as a captain and became a liaison officer between the Air Corps and the Signal Corps for the procurement of radio equipment. Though Elliott was ineligible for the draft, because of age and poor eyesight and because he had a family to support, there was an immediate outcry among Republicans that the President's son was receiving preferential treatment. After Willkie referred sarcastically to "overnight captains," in a speech in Cleveland, his supporters went into action. They got out buttons, reading, "I Want To Be a Captain, Too," organized "I Want To Be a Captain" clubs throughout the country, and began singing a song written for the occasion: "Elliott, I Wanna Be a Cap'n Too!" On October 14, Elliott submitted his resignation, but it was turned down. Explained his commanding officer: "His services are needed." [18]

Martin, Barton, and Fish

Roosevelt's speech in Madion Square Garden, one of his most successful, echoed Eugene Field's children's poem, "Wynken, Blynken, and Nod." Discussing the votes against defense appropriations by such Republican Congressmen as Joe Martin, Bruce Barton, and Hamilton Fish, FDR pointed out the "perfectly beautiful rhythm" of the names and singsonged, "Martin, Barton, and Fish." The crowd howled with delight and when he repeated the phrase again later in the speech it brought the house down. Two days later, when he mentioned Martin in a speech in Boston, someone in the gallery yelled, "What about Barton and Fish?" The crowd at once took up the chant: "Martin, Barton, and Fish!" Later on Willkie was reported to have sighed: "When I heard the President hang the isolationist votes of Martin, Barton and Fish on me, and get away with it, I knew I was licked." [19]

★★★★★★★★★★★★★★★★★★★★★★★★★

CHAPTER FORTY

1944
Roosevelt's Wartime Mandate

The election of 1944 was the first wartime presidential contest since 1864. Some Americans wondered whether the country could afford the luxury of holding a national election while still engaged in savage fighting all over the globe. There were rumors, in fact, among Franklin Roosevelt's enemies, that the President was planning to suspend elections "for the duration." Early in February a reporter asked Roosevelt at a press conference about reports that the election would be called off. "How?" asked FDR impatiently. "Well, I want you to tell me." "Well, you see," said Roosevelt with a touch of sarcasm, "you have come to the wrong place, because—gosh, all these people haven't read the Constitution. Unfortunately, I have." [1]

The Republicans certainly proceeded as if they expected an election and had a chance to win. Before they held their convention in Chicago late in June, there had been a boom for Pacific war hero General Douglas MacArthur, but he had withdrawn his name; so had Wendell Willkie after a disastrous defeat in the Wisconsin primary. That left Thomas E. Dewey, the efficient young Governor of New York with the fine baritone voice and smooth diction. When he ran for Governor in 1942 he had promised to serve out his four years, so he was careful not to make an active bid for the Republican presidential nomination two years later. But his name appeared on write-ins in state primaries, Republican state conventions elected delegates pledged to him, and when the Chicago conclave met he was the obvious choice. He won all the votes on the first ballot except one (a Wisconsin delegate voted for MacArthur because "I'm a man, not a jellyfish"), and his team-mate, also chosen on the first ballot, was John W. Bricker, conservative Governor of Ohio. The Republican platform accepted most of Roosevelt's policies, domestic and foreign, but promised to manage them better; and, as usual, denounced excessive governmental interference with business. [2]

Dewey took the position that the Roosevelt administration was super-annuated. In his acceptance address, his main point was that the Democrats had "grown old in office," had become "tired and quarrelsome," and that "wrongdoing, bungling and confusion" prevailed in the "vital matters of taxation, price control, rationing, labor relations, man-power. . . ." Dewey also promised that the Republicans would solve the problems of full production and employment which the New Deal had botched by its "curtailment and restriction" of private enterprise. Harold L. Ickes, FDR's acidulous Secretary of the Interior, had made fun of the youthful Dewey in 1940 by saying he had "thrown his diaper into the ring." This time he noted that in capitulating to the New Deal, Dewey had "thrown in the sponge as well." For good measure he also said (borrowing from Alice Roosevelt Longworth) that the New Yorker looked "like the groom on the wedding cake." During the campaign the Republicans got even by linking the Democrats with the Communists.[3]

In 1944 there was little of the uncertainty about FDR's intentions that had puzzled Democrats in 1940. Most people took his renomination for granted and, on July 11, FDR wrote Robert Hannegan, chairman of the Democratic national committee, that "as a good soldier" he would "reluctantly" run again if his party wanted him to, but that he "would not run in the usual partisan sense." On July 20, the Democrats meeting in Chicago voted overwhelmingly on the first ballot to nominate him for a fourth term and then went on to confront the same problem that had almost disrupted their convention four years earlier: choosing FDR's running mate. Vice-President Henry Wallace made an eloquent New Dealish speech seconding FDR's nomination that touched off fervent cries among the delegates: "We want Wallace! We want Wallace!" FDR wanted Wallace too. "I like him and I respect him and he is my personal friend," he said. "For these reasons I personally would vote for his renomination if I were a delegate to the convention." But opposition to Wallace among party conservatives was so vehement that FDR decided to give way.[4]

FDR's preference, after Wallace, seems to have been for James F. Byrnes of South Carolina, one of his top wartime advisers; but labor leaders like Sidney Hillman, chairman of the CIO's Political Action Committee (which contributed generously to FDR's campaign and worked hard to get out the vote), made it clear that Byrnes, a conservative on race and labor issues, was absolutely unacceptable. FDR then settled on Harry Truman, much-liked Senator from Missouri and a loyal New Dealer who had attracted favorable national attention as head of a Senate committee investigating war contracts. Truman was not eager for the nomination; he loved the Senate and regarded the Vice-Presidency as a demotion. But Hannegan and other party leaders worked hard on him and finally FDR himself interceded. In a call to Hannegan FDR asked: "Have you got that fellow lined up yet?" "No," said Hannegan, "he is the contrariest Missouri mule I've ever dealt with." "Well," said FDR, "you tell him, if he wants to break up the Democratic party in the middle of the war, that's his responsibility." "Now what do you say?" Hannegan asked Truman after relaying FDR's message to him. "Well, if that's the situation," said Truman, "I'll have to say yes, but why the hell didn't he tell me in the first place?" Wallace received more votes than Truman on the first ballot, but on the second trial Truman won the nomination. He was called "the new Missouri Compromise."[5]

After Truman was nominated, *New York Times* columnist Arthur Krock reported that FDR had told Hannegan: "Go down and nominate Truman before there's any more trouble. And clear everything with Sidney." Hannegan called the story "an unmitigated lie," but the Republicans pounced on it with glee. "CLEAR EVERYTHING WITH SIDNEY," they insisted, was the Roosevelt line. Dewey, in contrast, they said, would clear everything with Congress and the American people. "It's your country," they cried, "and why let Sidney Hillman run it?" They also linked Hillman, who had praised Russia's heroic resistance to the Nazi invasion, with Earl Browder (who had urged Communists to support FDR this time). "Everything in your government," they warned, "will be cleared with the radical Sidney Hillman and his Communist friend Earl Browder." And they announced: "Sidney Hillman and Earl Browder's Communists have registered. Have you?" They even waxed poetic:

> Clear it with Sidney, you Yanks
> Then offer Joe Stalin your thanks,
> You'll bow to Sid's rule
> No matter how cruel,
> For that's a directive of Frank's.[6]

In his acceptance speech on July 21, FDR reiterated his determination not to campaign "in the usual sense" because of his responsibilities as Commander-in-Chief and he didn't take to the stump until mid-September. Dewey thus dominated the early weeks of the campaign and took a dignified stance at first. He endorsed most of the New Deal's social legislation, refrained from attacking FDR's foreign policy, and accepted American participation in an international organization after the war. His main thrust was the necessity for fresh young blood to replace the "tired old men" encrusted in office since 1933 and provide vigorous leadership in the tasks of peace and reconstruction after the war. After "twelve long years," he said, it was "time for a change," and he presented himself as a model of crisp efficiency by his finely honed (but unexciting) speeches, impeccable garb, cool demeanor, and split-second timing when it came to speeches and press conferences.[7]

But the response was disappointing; independent voters saw no reason to support him, and Republican faithfuls were with him anyway. Another issue—the President's failing health—aroused more interest. So persistent, in fact, were rumors about FDR's inability to survive another term in office that Vice Admiral Ross McIntire, the President's personal physician, felt obliged to issue a statement saying there was "nothing wrong organically with him at all. . . . He's perfectly O.K. . . . The stories that he is in bad health are understandable enough around election time, but they are not true." The Republicans then shifted to a juicier issue: Communism. In 1940 FDR had twitted the Republicans about the fact that they were lined up with the American Communists in their opposition to his policies. But in 1944 the tables were turned. With Russia as America's wartime ally, American Communists were now giving FDR their hearty support and the Republicans tried to make a campaign issue out of it. Republican newspapers and orators—and Dewey himself—talked so much of Communist influence on the Roosevelt administration that FDR came to regard 1944 as "the meanest campaign of his life."[8]

At the beginning of the contest FDR seemed apathetic. "He just doesn't seem to give a damn," said one of his aides worriedly.[9] But late in September he came suddenly alive. Roused to wrath by the attacks on his administration, he decided to make five major speeches to answer his critics and to prove that he could still take it physically. His first speech—to the Teamsters Union in Washington on September 23—was by general agreement among his friends the best campaign speech of his career. "Well, here we are—here we are again—after four years—and what years they have been!" he began with a smile. "You know, I am actually four years older, which is a fact that seems to annoy some people. In fact . . . there are millions of Americans who are more than eleven years older than when we started to clear up the mess that was dumped into our laps in 1933." To the delight of his audience FDR went on to ridicule Republicans who "suddenly discover" every four years, just before election day, that they love labor, after having attacked it "for three years and six months." He recalled how most Republicans had opposed New Deal measures which they now endorsed in their party platform and then one by one took up the charges leveled at him and demolished them all with evident relish.[10]

But the highlight of FDR's Teamsters speech centered on trivia. A few weeks earlier, the Republicans had charged that the President wasted a lot of the taxpayers' money on travel for his dog. Said FDR mockseriously: "These Republican leaders have not been content with attacks—on me, or my wife, or on my sons. No . . . they now include my little dog, Fala. Well, of course, I don't resent attacks, and my family doesn't resent attacks, but Fala *does* resent them. You know—you know—Fala's Scotch, and being a Scottie, as soon as he learned that the Republican fiction writers . . . had concocted a story that I had left him behind on an Aleutian island and had sent a destroyer back to find him—at a cost to the taxpayers of two or three, or eight or twenty million dollars—his Scotch soul was furious. He has not been the same dog since. I am accustomed to hearing malicious falsehoods about myself. . . . But I think I have a right to resent, to object to libellous statements about my dog." FDR was at his very best. Reported *Time:* "He was like a veteran virtuoso playing a piece he has loved for years, who fingers his way through it with a delicate fire, a perfection of tuning and tone, and an assurance that no young player, no matter how gifted, can equal. The President was playing what he loves to play—politics."[11] It was now a race, said one wag, between "Roosevelt's dog and Dewey's goat."[12]

Dewey fought back hard; like the prosecuting attorney he had once been in New York he virtually put the President on trial and arraigned him for a long list of crimes: incompetence, arrogance, inefficiency, fatigue, and senility. But it did him no good. Though pollsters predicted a close election, it turned out on November 7 to be what *Time* called "Franklin Roosevelt in a walkover."[13] The President carried thirty-six states with 432 electoral votes and won over 3,500,000 more popular votes than Dewey: 25,602,504 to 22,006,285. Quipped FDR afterwards: "The first twelve years are the hardest."[14] Observed the *New York Times:*

Franklin D. Roosevelt has been re-elected in a war year as a war President who could promise the country victory in the war and on the basis of victory, a lasting peace. If a majority of the American people were willing to accept the hazardous precedent of a fourth term, it seems clearly because they were convinced that in his extraordinary crisis the Republican party offered them no satisfactory substitute for Mr. Roosevelt's experience in military affairs and foreign policy, and no equally good assurance that under Republican leadership the country could achieve a lasting peace.[15]

On January 20, 1945, FDR took his oath of office as President for the fourth time. On April 12 he died suddenly of a cerebral hemorrhage, and Harry Truman became President.

☆　☆　☆

Don't Let's Be Beastly

In a poem entitled "Don't Let's Be Beastly to America," Britain's *New Statesman and Nation* tried to explain the behavior of the American people in 1944 to its readers:

> If America seems lately
> To be burning for a row,
> It doesn't matter greatly,
> For she's not herself just now.
> Her condition is affecting,
> For she's just come over queer—

Yes, America's expecting,
And her time is drawing near. . . .
We must not attempt to change her,
Nor her indignation rouse,
Till the Dewey little stranger
Has arrived at the White House,
Or till Roosevelt on election
Celebrates victorious morn—
She'll return our tried affection
Once a President is born.[16]

Extenuating Circumstances

To a friend worried about a fourth term, Roosevelt exclaimed: "I hate this fourth term as much as you do—and the third term as well—but I do not worry about it so much as a matter of principle. It would be a mistake, of course, to establish it as a tradition but I think I can well plead extenuating circumstances."[17]

Tired Old Men

On the opening night of the Democratic convention, keynoter Senator Robert Kerr of Oklahoma responded to Dewey's cracks about "tired old men" in the Roosevelt administration. "Shall we," he roared, "discard as a 'tired old man' 59-year-old Admiral Nimitz . . . 62-year-old Admiral Halsey . . . 64-year-old General MacArthur . . . 66-year-old Admiral King . . . 64-year-old General Marshal? No, Mr. Dewey, we know we are winning the war with these 'tired old men,' including the 62-year-old Roosevelt as their Commander-in-Chief."[18]

Half a Horse

Hooting at the don't-change-horses-in-midstream argument for FDR, Dewey observed that when the Democrats replaced Wallace with Truman, they changed one-half of the horse.[19]

Ghouls

During the campaign FDR took a vacation at Bernard Baruch's place in Hob Caw, South Carolina, and banned reporters from the estate. But they came anyway, met with Mike Reilly, Secret Service agent, in nearby Georgetown, and told him they had heard the President had had a heart attack and was in a hospital in either Chicago or Boston. Reilly denied the story but the newsmen refused to believe him. "Will you believe he's here if you see him for yourself?" he finally asked, and when they said they would, he arranged for them to see FDR from a distance the next morning. "He looks tired," said one of them. "He is," retorted Reilly, "and that's why he's on vacation." When Reilly saw FDR a little later the latter asked him: "Mike, didn't you have some newspapermen with you this morning?" "Yes, sir," admitted Reilly. "Did Mr. Baruch know you brought them on his estate?" "No, Mr. President." "What are they here for?" FDR wanted to know. Reilly then told him about the rumors he was dying and how he tried to convince the reporters they were false. But almost immediately he realized he had blundered, for FDR's lips grew thin, his chin came jutting out, his eyes glittered, and, looking at Reilly steadily for a moment, he cried: "Mike, those newspapermen are a bunch of God-damned ghouls." [20]

Pearl Harbor

In 1944 the Japanese attack on Pearl Harbor on December 7, 1941, almost became a campaign issue. Shortly after the conventions some Republicans began charging that the Roosevelt administration knew that an attack was coming and failed to prepare for it. The introduction of Pearl Harbor into the campaign dismayed Army Chief of Staff General George C. Marshall. He was afraid it would lead to the revelation that the United States had broken the secret Japanese diplomatic code before the war and thereby place its continued use in jeopardy. On September 26, he sent Colonel Carter C. Clarke, an intelligence officer, to discuss the matter with Dewey and beg him to keep Pearl Harbor out of the campaign. Dewey told Clarke he already knew that American cryptographers had cracked "certain Japanese codes before Pearl Harbor" and at least twelve Senators also knew about the code-breaking. He also insisted that FDR "knew what was happening before Pearl Harbor, and instead of being re-elected he ought to be impeached." Clarke left without any commitments from Dewey.

But Marshall kept up his pressure on Dewey: by letters, telephone calls, and intermediaries. Not only did he insist FDR knew nothing about the entire operation; he also made it clear that no decoded message singling out Hawaii as the point of attack in 1941 had reached the War Department until it was too late. He went on to reveal that several American victories over the Japanese in the Pacific had rested in part on information obtained from Japanese decoded messages and added: "You will understand . . . the tragic consequences if the political debates regarding Pearl Harbor disclose to the enemy . . . any suspicion of the vital sources of information we now possess."

In the end Dewey yielded. He ordered his aides to assemble everything they had unearthed about Pearl Harbor and "put it away securely and forget it." Late in October Harry Hopkins told FDR about Marshall's action. FDR was surprised, but expressed confidence that Dewey would not make use of vital secret information for political purposes. "My opponent," he told Hopkins, "must be pretty desperate if he is even thinking of using material like this which would be bound to react against him." Not until after the war was information about the code-breaking made public. Roosevelt's supporters blamed the military for being taken by surprise at Pearl Harbor, but Dewey himself—and many Republicans—remained convinced that FDR himself shared in the responsibility for the disaster at Pearl Harbor.[21]

Collywobbles

When FDR was in San Diego in July he suffered from what he called "the collywobbles" and stayed on the train the night before reviewing a Fifth Marine Division exercise. When he saw his son James, on leave from the Navy, in the evening, he said he felt tired but otherwise all right. But suddenly he began groaning and as James ran to his bedside he cried: "Jimmy, I don't know if I can make it. I have horrible pains." His son gripped his hand and said he would call for the doctor, but FDR told him it was probably indigestion and he would feel better if he could stretch out for a few minutes. James helped him out of bed and onto the floor of the railroad car where he lay for about ten minutes. Gradually the color returned to his face and his breathing returned to normal. "Help me up now, Jimmy," he said finally. "I feel better." James helped him into the wheelchair and FDR seemed his old self. But after that his son began having doubts about his wisdom in running for a fourth term despite the assurances of Admiral Ross McIntire, his personal physician in October, that "the President's health is perfectly okay."

Rumors about FDR's health circulated throughout the campaign. At one point a reporter told Dewey point-blank that FDR was a dying man and Dewey had "an absolute duty" to raise the health issue publicly. Dewey had several discussions with his advisers about it. "There wasn't a single night went by we didn't argue that one out . . .," said Dewey adviser Herbert Brownell later. "Some people wanted to go all out, stating that he was on his death bed, and getting all the evidence that we could." In the end Dewey decided to avoid the issue, partly out of fear that it would backfire.[22]

Eternal Hope

The day before the election FDR made a short informal talk at Wappingers Falls, New York, and told the crowd that someone had told him if he ran often enough he might eventually carry Maine and Vermont (the only two states that went Republican in 1936). "Hope springs eternal," he said.[23]

Concession

At 3:16 a.m. after the polls closed Dewey appeared in the half-empty ballroom of his hotel in New York to admit defeat but sent no message of congratulations to FDR. FDR, who heard Dewey's concession over the radio, waited until 4:00 a.m. and then telegraphed Dewey: "I thank you for your statement, which I have heard over the air a few minutes ago." Afterward he told his aide, Bill Hassett: "I still think he is a son of a bitch." Not until three days later did Dewey get around to sending his congratulations, to which FDR responded at once.[24]

★ ★

CHAPTER FORTY-ONE

1948
The Great Truman Surprise

In 1948 the crystal ball was clouded. Most of the experts—pundits, prophets, pollsters, prognosticators—were way off target when they forecast the behavior of the American voters on November 2. In America, politics and certitude may well be immiscible.

Early in September, Elmo Roper reported that Thomas E. Dewey was leading Harry Truman by a margin of 41 to 31 percent and that "no amount of electioneering" could alter the result. Pollsters George Gallup and Archibald Crossley also forecast a substantial Dewey victory. Fifty of the nation's leading political writers picked Dewey as the winner; and a St. Louis betting commissioner called the Republican candidate a fifteen-to-one favorite. "Thomas E. Dewey's election as President is a foregone conclusion," announced Leo Egan in the *New York Times.* Predicted the *Kiplinger News Letter:* "Dewey will be in for eight years—until '57." Just before election day *Life* carried a big picture of Dewey with the caption, "The next President of the United States," and the headline of *Changing Times,* a new weekly, was: "WHAT DEWEY WILL DO."[1]

Expectations of a Republican victory in 1948 were not based entirely on wishful thinking. There was a lot of grumbling that year about a decade and a half of Democratic rule. In the 1946 elections the Republicans won control of Congress with their slogan, "Had enough?" Truman seemed weak and bumbling compared with FDR and, in May, Dr. Gallup reported that only 36 percent of the people thought he was doing a competent job. There were many domestic discontents: high taxes, the rising cost of living, labor strife, and revelations of corruption in Washington. Foreign affairs, too, were stormy. World War II ended, not in peace, but in a Cold War between "capitalism" and "communism." And the Communists—Stalin in Eastern Europe and Mao Zedong in China—seemed to be forging ahead everywhere. Reactionaries charged Truman was "soft" on Communism; radicals castigated him for his "hard" line. And millions of non-ideological voters thought he could have done much better both at home and abroad. "To err is Truman," quipped his critics; "I wonder what Truman would do if he were alive."[2]

For a time Dwight D. Eisenhower, one of World War II's most popular war heroes, seemed to be the great shining hope of leaders in both parties. The Republicans sounded him out early in 1948 and the Democrats in July, but both were firmly rebuffed. With Ike out of the picture a Dewey-Truman confrontation was inevitable. Dewey had done well in the primaries, and Truman was eager to prove he could win on his own. Announced the latter: "I was not brought up to run from a fight."[3]

The Republicans chose Dewey in Philadelphia late in June in a mood of euphoria. Truman was a "gone goose," Congresswoman Clare Boothe Luce told the exuberant delegates; his "time is short" and his "situation is hopeless."[4] The convention (the first ever to be televised) picked California Governor Earl Warren for second place and adopted a platform promising a foreign policy based on "friendly firmness which welcomes cooperation but spurns appeasement" and a domestic policy devoted to "the rooting out of Communism wherever found." Dewey's acceptance speech was dignified and lofty and he seemed to be trying to stand above mere politics.[5]

Truman loved politics. In June he took a "non-political" tour of the nation (which fooled no one) that boosted his spirits. By departing from prepared texts (he was a poor manuscript reader) and speaking off the cuff, he came across as friendly, forthright, and funny and began attracting cheering crowds wherever he went. He took a belligerent line: the Republican Congress was "the worst in my memory" and more interested in "the welfare of the better classes" than in the welfare of ordinary people. "Lay it on, Harry!" cried people in the audience. "I'm going to, I'm going to," responded Truman. "I'm pouring it on and I'm gonna keep pouring it on."[6] The *Washington Star* thought he was acting like a ward heeler, but his audiences loved it. Truman emerged from his tour confident he could win. But when the Democrats met in Philadelphia the following month they were dispirited and unhappy and resigned to backing a loser. After nominating the sixty-four-year-old President on the first ballot they picked Kentucky's Alben W. Barkley, Senate Majority Leader, who had delivered a rip-roaring keynote address, as his running mate. The *New York Post's* advice: "The Party might as well immediately concede the election to Dewey and save the wear and tear of campaigning."[7]

There were defections from the Democratic party on both left and right in 1948. On the left were the Progressives, led by Henry A. Wallace, who held the Truman administration primarily responsible for the Cold War and organized the Progressive Citizens of America in 1947 and the Progressive party in 1948 to promote world peace. At the party's convention in Philadelphia in July, the delegates (pacifists, reformers, New Dealers dissatisfied with Truman, and, inevitably, a sprinkling of American Stalinists) picked Wallace to run for President and Idaho's Democratic Senator Glen Taylor (the "Singing Cowboy") for Vice-President. The Progressive platform rejected the Marshall Plan for European economic recovery and the Truman Doctrine of containment (which at this time involved military and economic aid to Greece and Turkey) and urged negotiations with Russia to end the Cold War. In his acceptance speech Wallace called for the development of "progressive capitalism" in America and a foreign policy centered on the United Nations as the arbiter of international disputes. The Progressive slogan: "One, two, three, four; we don't want another war!"[8]

The revolt on the right, like that on the left, antedated the Democratic party convention and revolved around civil rights. In February, Truman had proposed a series of measures to Congress guaranteeing the rights of black Americans which touched off an angry response among Southern segregationists and threats of independent political action. The Democratic convention brought the civil-rights dispute to a head. When the delegates voted to adopt a statement praising Truman for his "courageous stand" on civil rights and calling on Congress to adopt his recommendations, thirty-five delegates (all of Mississippi's and half of Alabama's) walked out of the convention. A little later the States' Rights Democratic party (which had already been formed) held a convention in Montgomery, Alabama, attended by delegates from thirteen states, nominated South Carolina Governor J. Strom Thurmond for President and Mississippi Governor Fielding Wright for Vice-President. The "Dixiecrats," as the states-rights segregationists were called, hoped the election would be thrown into the House of Representatives where the South could swing the balloting to an opponent of civil-rights legislation.

The secessions from the Democratic party seemed not to faze Harry Truman; nor did he share the despondency of the delegates who had dutifully picked him to run in 1948. In his acceptance speech he startled everyone by his cocksureness. "Senator Barkley and I will win this election," he crowed, "and make these Republicans like it, don't you forget that. We'll do that because they're wrong and we're right." The delegates leaped to their feet in a frenzy of cheering as Truman continued: "The reason is that the people know the Democratic party is the people's party, and the Republican party is the party of special interests and it always has been and always will be." In the most militant acceptance address since Bryan's in 1896, Truman went on to defend the record of his administration and lambaste the Republican-dominated 80th Congress for having done nothing about inflation, the housing shortage, social security, health insurance, and civil rights. Then came his big surprise: "On the twenty-sixth day of July, which out in Missouri they call Turnip Day, I'm going to call that Congress back and I'm going to ask them to pass laws halting rising prices and to meet the housing crisis which they say they're for in their platform. At the same time I shall ask them to act on other vitally needed measures such as aid to education, which they say they're for; a national health program, civil rights legislation, which they say they're for; [and] funds for projects needed . . . to provide public power and cheap electricity . . . ." Pointing out that Congress could do the job in fifteen days if it wanted to, Truman concluded: "What that worst Eightieth Congress does in its special session will be the test. The American people will decide on the record."[9]

To a great extent Truman ran against the 80th Congress rather than Dewey in 1948. When Congress met in special session on July 25, amid angry charges that the President was engaging in "cheap politics," Truman made eight social-welfare recommendations (which Ohio Senator Robert A. Taft called an "omnibus left-wing program") and then gleefully watched the expectable: two weeks of haggling and then adjournment with nothing accomplished.[10] Truman now had a name for the Republican Congress: "the do-nothing Congress." He then embarked on a strenuous campaign—21,928 miles and 275 speeches—lasting from Labor Day until Election Day, utterly convinced he could win the voters to his cause. "I'm going to fight hard," he told Barkley; "I'm going to give them hell." He did just that. He called the 80th Congress "the worst in history," assailed the "gluttons of privilege" dominating the G.O.P., called Republicans "a bunch of old mossbacks" and "bloodsuckers with offices in Wall Street," dismissed the Republican party as "the party of . . . Hoover boom and Hoover depression," and charged that "the notorious 'do-nothing' Republican Eightieth Congress" had "stuck a pitchfork in the farmer's back."[11]

The populistic theme of Truman's campaign would have warmed the heart of Bryan and probably surprised FDR by its bellicosity. "Is the government of the United States going to run in the interest of the people as a whole," he asked, "or in the interest of a small group of privileged big businessmen?" Wherever he spoke he drew large and friendly crowds, at "whistlestops" as well as in major cities, and there were usually cries from the audience, "Give 'em hell, Harry!" His appearances on train platforms were especially popular. "Howja like to meet my family?" he would ask, after a short speech, and then introduce his wife Bess as "the boss" and daughter Margaret as "the boss's boss." But despite the warm response to his "give-'em-hell" speeches, the polls continued to show him far behind Dewey.[12]

For the most part Dewey ignored Truman. He also avoided specific issues as much as possible and concentrated on convincing voters that he was a high-minded, public-spirited, conscientious, and efficient administrator who could bring unity to the country and effectiveness to its foreign policy. His glittering generalities were in sharp contrast to Truman's sizzling particularities. "Ours is a magnificent land," he said in a typical statement. "Don't let anybody frighten you or try to stampede you into believing that America is finished. America's future . . . is still ahead of us." Dewey seemed stuffy to many people; they were jarred by his favorite ejaculations, "Oh, Lord," and "Good gracious," and his way of saying "period" at the end of sentences. He was, people cracked, "the only man they knew who could strut sitting down"; he was "a man you had to get to know to really dislike." The *New Yorker*'s Richard Rovere reported that at rallies "he comes out like a man who has been mounted on casters and given a tremendous shove from behind." [13]

As Truman barnstormed across the country, he made fun of Dewey's "soothing-syrup campaign" and said the unity the Republicans wanted was the kind that benefited the special interests. Goaded by the President's incessant gibes, Dewey finally lost his "cool," accused him of mudslinging, and began talking about Communists in government. He also pointed out that while Truman was President millions of people had been delivered into Soviet slavery after World War II. But Dewey usually refrained from bringing foreign policy into the campaign. He adhered to the policy known as "bi-partisanship" by which both parties informally agreed to remove foreign affairs as a campaign issue. But there was nothing bi-partisan, of course, about Wallace; he made foreign policy the center of his crusade and charged that under Truman "our allies in war" were being treated "as enemies in peace." But Soviet actions in 1948—taking over Czechoslovakia by a coup in February and instituting a blockade of West Berlin in July—took the wind out of Wallace's sails. Truman's response to the Berlin crisis—instituting an airlift to supply the 2,400,000 West Berliners with food and provisions—met with the approval of most Americans. [14]

In the final days of the campaign Dewey took time out to plan his inauguration; after all, the "do-nothing" Congress had made generous appropriations for the occasion. On the day before the election the Gallup poll gave Dewey 49.5 percent and Truman 44.5 percent of the popular votes, and the Crossley poll forecast 49.9 percent for Dewey and 44.8 percent for Truman. And Elmo Roper saw no reason to revise the figures he had reached months before (Dewey, 52.2 percent, and Truman, 37.1 percent): "I stand by my prediction. Dewey is in." But Truman was undaunted. "The smart boys say we can't win," he cried in his final speech in St. Louis. "They tried to bluff us with a propaganda blitz, but we called their bluff, we told the people the truth. And the people are with us. The tide is rolling. All over the country. I have seen it in the people's faces. The people are going to win this election." [15]

Truman won all right. On November 2 he received a plurality of over 2,000,000 popular votes (24,105,812 to 21,970,065) and carried 28 states

(303 electoral votes) to Dewey's 16 (189). The Democrats also captured both houses of Congress. "When you win," Truman told reporters, "you can't say anything. You're just happy." But he couldn't help teasing the savants. In St. Louis, on his way back to Washington, he held high for reporters a copy of the *Chicago Tribune* with that morning's headline, "DEWEY DEFEATS TRUMAN" and for some time afterwards had fun imitating radio commentator H.V. Kaltenborn's staccato-voiced prediction of his defeat election night. When he got back to Washington he found a sign in front of the *Washington Post* building announcing: "Mr. President, we are ready to eat crow whenever you are ready to serve it." The *Post* also invited him to a banquet for "political reporters and editors, including our own, along with pollsters, radio commentators and columnists . . . The main course will consist of breast of tough old crow en glace. (You will eat turkey.)" The Democratic national committee offered to furnish toothpicks since it would take months to get the crow out of the diners' teeth. But Truman politely declined. "The fellow who lost," he said, "feels bad enough without being crowed over." [16]

At least one pollster did some crowing. Wilfred J. Funk, editor of the old *Literary Digest*, which had folded after its preposterous prediction of a Landon victory in 1936, said frankly: "I do not want to seem malicious, but I can't help but get a good chuckle out of this." [17] He also said he wondered whether the word "science" could be applied to poll-taking. The other pollsters—George Gallup, Elmo Roper, Archibald Crossley—acknowledged that poll-taking was still "an infant science" and launched self-study investigations to find out just where they went wrong. In the end they concluded, among other things, that placing too little emphasis on the undecided voter and minimizing last-minute shifts in voters' preferences had led them astray. As for the erring columnists, reporters, and editorial writers, they blamed themselves for having depended too much on the polls and failing to go out into the country to make first-hand investigations of their own to find out what the people were thinking. "We were wrong, all of us," wrote columnist Marquis Childs, "completely and entirely, the commentators, the political editors, the politicians—except for Harry S Truman, and no one believed him. The fatal flaw was the reliance on the public opinion polls." [18]

Historians, with their retrospective wisdom, can see forces at work in 1948 that were not apparent to Truman and his contemporaries. The Dixiecrat defection, it now seems clear, was far less damaging to Truman than it seemed to be at the time. Thurmond won 1,760,125 popular votes, carried four states (South Carolina, Mississippi, Alabama, and Louisiana), and won 39 electoral votes. But the rest of the South stayed solidly Democratic, despite reservations about Truman; and Northern blacks, who had not been absolutely sure about Truman until the Dixiecrat revolt, gave him their overwhelming support. The Progressives (who won a disappointing 1,157,326 votes for Wallace) also probably

helped Truman more than they hurt him. They did deprive him of votes
in New York, Maryland, and Michigan and thus ensured Dewey victories in those states; but they also took the taint of "Communism" away
from him. As Truman moved to the left during the campaign, advanced New Dealers who had been cool to him began deserting Wallace
and returning to the fold; and before long it was obvious that loyal Stalinists, rather than militant New Dealers like Wallace himself, were
coming to dominate the Progressive movement. Reactionaries might accuse Truman of coddling the Communists at home and abroad; but the
very existence of the Progressive party belied the charge. Truman rolled
up large majorities among Catholics who were disturbed by the oppression of their co-religionists in the Stalin-dominated nations of Eastern
Europe. But the total vote was low: only 51.2 percent of the voters went
to the polls in 1948. Dewey thought that "overconfidence" had kept large
numbers of Republicans from bothering to vote on November 2. If so,
he had only himself to blame. The campaign he waged was so dull that,
as New Dealer Paul Porter put it, he "snatched defeat out of the jaws
of victory." Even *Time* admitted Dewey was not "well liked."[19]

When asked about his victory, Truman's first reaction was: "Labor
did it."[20] Labor, it is true, did support Truman loyally in 1948 the way
it had supported Roosevelt. But the farmer was also crucial to Truman's victory. Dewey neglected agriculture during the campaign, while
Truman, stumping in the farm belt, managed to convince farmers that
the Democrats, unlike the Republicans, had their interests at heart.
Truman, in short, earned his victory by the remarkable campaign he
put on; he waged the kind of campaign, according to journalist I. F.
Stone, that FDR would have waged, and he was able to hold together
the old coalition—labor, farmers, the South, blacks, and ethnic minorities—that had given FDR so many triumphs. "You've got to give the
little man credit," said Republican Senator Arthur Vandenberg of
Michigan admiringly. "There he was flat on his back. Everybody had
counted him out but he came up fighting and won the battle. That's
the kind of courage the American people admire."[21]

☆ ☆ ☆

Whistlestops

President Truman's "non-political" trip to California in June, "fur to
get me a degree" at Berkeley, infuriated the Republicans, especially since
his rear-platform appearances en route went over big. Fumed Republican Senator Robert A. Taft of Ohio: "Our gallivanting President is
blackguarding Congress at every whistle-stop in the West." His remark
quickly backfired. Democratic officials telegraphed local officials along
the President's route: "PLEASE WIRE THE DEMOCRATIC NA-
TIONAL COMMITTEE WHETHER YOU AGREE WITH SENA-

TOR TAFT'S DESCRIPTION OF YOUR TOWN AS A QUOTE WHISTLE STOP END QUOTE." They received a flood of indignant responses. From Indiana: "Senator Taft in very poor taste to refer to Gary as quote whistle stop unquote. 135,000 citizens of America's greatest steel city resent this slur." From Idaho: "If Senator Taft referred to Pocatello as a 'whistle-stop,' it is apparent he has not visited progressive Pocatello since the time of his father's 1908 campaign." From Washington: "Seattle is not a whistle stop, but everyone who sees her stops and whistles." Declared the mayor of Eugene, Oregon: "Must have the wrong city." Said the president of the chamber of commerce in Laramie, Wyoming: "Characteristically, Senator Taft is confused." And the mayor of Los Angeles: "The term hardly applies."[22]

Dead Pigeon

Everything went wrong at first at the Democratic convention. There were signs in the auditorium: "WE'RE JUST MILD ABOUT HARRY." When taps sounded for the war dead, the bugles hit several sour notes. When Lawrence Tibbett sang "The Star-Spangled Banner," the organist gave him such a high pitch he sounded as if he were strangling. And when, at Truman's appearance, a flock of doves was released as a symbol of peace, one of them perched on the bald head of Speaker of the House Sam Rayburn of Texas, who was presiding ("Funniest thing in the convention," according to Truman) and another banged into the balcony and flopped dead on the floor ("A dead pigeon," said one delegate, looking up at Truman). But Senator Barkley's rousing keynoter and Truman's fighting acceptance address revived the spirits of the delegates.[23]

Dewey and the Engineer

On October 13, when Dewey was speaking from the rear platform of his train to some people in Beaucoup, Illinois, the train gave a sudden jerk and started backing into the crowd and people began rushing away screaming. No one was hurt; but Dewey exclaimed: "That's the first lunatic I've had for an engineer. He probably should be shot at sunrise, but we'll let him off this time since no one was hurt." Dewey's remark hurt him in the Midwest and the Democrats made the most of it. "We've had wonderful train crews all across the country," announced Truman; they "are all Democrats." He added that Dewey "objects to having engineers back up. He doesn't mention that under that great engineer, Hoover, we backed up into the worst depression in history." Harold Ickes said the engineer had been listening to too many Dewey speeches: "Every speech he listened to sounded as though Dewey was going to turn the clock back to the days of Harding, Coolidge and Hoover. He honestly thought Dewey wanted the train to run backwards too." The engineer himself said, "I think as much of Dewey as I did before, and that's not very much."[24]

Saturday

At one train stop, Dewey said he was glad to see so many children in the crowd and added they should be grateful because he got them a day off from school. Cried one kid: "Today is Saturday!" The crowd roared.[25]

S.O.B.

Dewey's running mate, Earl Warren, was frustrated by Dewey's insistence on a low-key campaign. "I wish," he once muttered, "I could call somebody an S.O.B.!"[26]

Plumbing

Both Truman and Dewey were present at the dedication of New York's Idlewild Airport on July 31. Truman flew in from Washington in the *Independence*. Dewey motored to LaGuardia Field, chartered a plane, and flew the eight miles to Idlewild so he could arrive by plane too. Truman himself seems not to have been as confident of victory at this point as he later claimed to be. At one point he told Dewey in a whisper he hoped the latter would do something about the White House plumbing once he moved in there.[27]

Horsemanship

Campaigning in a little Texas town, Truman noticed a young cowboy showing off his horsemanship in the midst of a crowd gathered around his train and, fearing someone might get hurt, he descended from the platform and grasped the horse's bridle. "Right nice horse you have there, son," he said, pulling the horse's mouth open and studying the teeth. "I see it's eight years old." Then he handed the bridle to a man standing near by and suggested he take the horse out of the crowd. As he returned to his place on the platform the young Texan muttered: "Who'd of thought that the President of the United States would know about horses?"[28]

Dr. Dewey

In a much-liked speech in Pittsburgh, Truman teased Dewey about his high-sounding platitudes and pretended Dewey was a physician and the

United States was a patient having a check-up. "You been bothered much by issues lately?" he had Dr. Dewey ask. "Not bothered, exactly," said the patient. "Of course, we've had a few. We've had the issue of high prices, and housing, and education, and social security, and a few others." "That's too bad," said the doctor. "You shouldn't have so many issues." "Is that right?"cried the patient. "We thought that issues were a sign of political health." "Not at all," said the doctor. "We shouldn't think about issues. What you need is my brand of soothing syrup—I call it unity." Truman then twirled an imaginary mustache and had the doctor edge a little closer to the patient and say: "Say, you don't look so good." "Well," said the patient, "that seems strange to me, Doc. I never felt stronger, never had more money, and never had a brighter future. What is wrong with me?" "I never discuss issues with a patient," said the doctor, "but what you need is a major operation." "Will it be serious, Doc?" "Not very serious. It will just mean taking out the complete works and putting in a Republican administration." But Dr. Truman went on to give a better diagnosis: the patient's trouble lay with the "do-nothing Republican Eightieth Congress."[29]

Overtime

The Republicans had plenty of money to pay for Dewey's train trips and radio broadcasts, but the Democrats were frequently strapped for funds. In Oklahoma City, they discovered there wasn't enough money to pay for getting the Truman train out of the station and had to arrange an emergency collection party on the spot. Sometimes, too, when Truman was on the radio, he was cut off in mid-speech because the time paid for was used up. But several times fund-raiser Louis Johnson allowed the networks to cut Truman off the air before he finished to dramatize the party's financial plight. Once a radio executive told Johnson, "We'll have to cut him off in a minute unless you agree to put up more money." "Go ahead," smiled Johnson, "that will mean another million votes!"

In Chicago, Truman was interrupted so often by applause that it began to look as though he would run over his allotted time. "He's going over," Ken Fry, producer of the show, told publicity man Jack Redding. "How much?" asked Redding. "At least five minutes, maybe more." Redding checked with the CBS executive: "Can we go over?" "I have no choice," said the CBS man. "If you do, you've got to pay." Redding went back to Fry and told him: "Cut him off on a high note." Then he added in a loud voice: "The networks won't let the President of the United States finish his speech!" He was immediately surrounded by a flock of reporters wanting to know: "What goes?" Explained Redding: "The network has a rule that the President cannot run over more than two minutes without paying for a full half hour additional time." Redding's statement brought a story in the newspapers the next day, hundreds of indignant letters to the editor, and thousands of contributions to the Democratic national committee from people throughout the country.[30]

Improbable

In Kansas City, Missouri, a feed-supply company conducted an informal poll: decorated the feed sacks with elephants and donkeys and had farmers register their political preferences by the sacks they chose. By early September, after 20,000 farmers in six Midwestern states had been polled in this way and 54 percent had picked the Democratic sacks, the firm abandoned the survey. "We read the Gallup and Roper polls that were all for Dewey," announced a company official, "and we decided that our results were too improbable."[31]

Red and White Faces

New York Daily Mirror, November 1: "We assume, on the basis of all available evidence, that Governor Dewey will be our next President. . . ."

New York Daily News, October 15: "President Truman appears to be the only American who doesn't think Thomas E. Dewey is going to be elected barring a political earthquake. . . ."

New York Sun, October 4: "The main question is whether Governor Dewey will win by a fair margin or by a landslide."

San Francisco Chronicle, October 29: "It is a Godsend to this country and to the world at large that Harry Truman will get his dismissal notice next Tuesday."

Wall Street Journal, September 24: "A man as close to the presidential chair as Governor Dewey knows very well that some of the things he would like to do, he will not be able to do. . . ."

Marquis Childs, October 21: "A Dewey landslide in popular votes looks a lot less likely than it did a month ago. On the other hand, the Republican majority in the electoral college still promises to be top-heavy."

David Lawrence, November 1: "Governor Dewey will be elected by a substantial majority in the Electoral College."

Drew Pearson, November 1: "Truman put up a courageous fight. . . . But, with Dixiecrats and Wallaceites against him, he cannot possibly win."

Walter Winchell, November 2: "Mr. Truman in a cocky speech the other day said: 'The polltakers and wrong-guesser faces will be red!' The gamblers are betting Mr. Truman's will be white."[32]

Only Way

After the election comedian Groucho Marx declared: "The only way a Republican will get into the White House is to marry Margaret Truman."[33]

Change of Plans

After Truman's victory, Nassau County Republican Women replaced a scheduled talk on "Our New Republican President" with one entitled, "It Pays To Be Ignorant."[34]

Pitching Pennies

After his defeat Dewey vacationed in Arizona. One day he went out behind his hotel, took off his coat, rolled up his sleeves, squatted down in the dust, and began pitching pennies with his two boys. When his wife warned that photographers might catch him in an undignified pose he told her: "Maybe, if I had done this during the campaign, I might have won."[35]

★ ★

CHAPTER FORTY-TWO

1952
The Eisenhower Landslide

In 1952 the Republicans thought they had a sure-fire formula for success: K_1C_2. The Korean War, Corruption, and Communism, they announced, were the crucial issues of the campaign that year.

The Korean War, which began in 1950, was in a stalemate, and the Truman administration, according to the Republicans, denied the military the means to win it. Corruption, moreover, was rife in Washington, they insisted, and the administration was dragging its feet on prosecuting officials involved in graft, bribery, and influence-peddling. And Communism (a hardy perennial) was spreading rapidly, here and abroad, they cried, mainly because the Democrats had been coddling it ever since 1933. Had not the United States "lost" China when the Communists won the civil war there in 1949? And wasn't America's "loss" of that ancient land (and Stalin's takeover of Eastern Europe) due primarily to the fact that Communists and fellow-travelers had infiltrated the State Department under the Democrats and shaped its policies?

In vain the Democrats insisted that "Korea, corruption and communism in government are not really controversial issues" and that "no one is running on a pro-corruption ticket or in favor of treachery."[1] Flourishing their K_1C_2 formula, the Republicans talked of "plunder at home, blunder abroad" and promised to "clean up the mess in Washington" if they got into the White House.[2]

The Republican formula should have been $K_1C_2 + E$, or, better still, $E + K_1C_2$. The GOP had an unbeatable candidate this time: the enormously popular Dwight D. Eisenhower, commander of Allied forces in Europe during World War II, and, after the war, president of Columbia University and commander of NATO forces in Europe. Not all Republicans, though, wanted Ike as their standard-bearer. Old-line Republicans preferred Robert A. Taft ("Mr. Republican"), the conscientious Senator from Ohio, who was conservative on domestic issues and, in foreign policy, wary of excessive American intervention abroad. Ike, at first, was a mystery; for a long time no one knew precisely where he stood on the issues. In 1948, in fact, both the Democrats and the Republicans had sought him as a candidate. But in January 1952 he announced he was a Republican and in June resigned his post as NATO commander to seek the Republican nomination. The sixty-one-year-old Eisenhower turned out to be a moderate: critical of the welfare state but willing to accept most New Deal reforms. In foreign affairs he championed the kind of world leadership for the United States that FDR and Truman had sponsored.

At the Republican convention in Chicago in July, Ike won the presidential nomination on the first ballot (after a bitter dispute between the Taft people and the backers of Ike over the seating of delegates). For his running mate he picked young Senator Richard M. Nixon of California, a "gut fighter" famous for his work as member of the Senate committee which investigated Alger Hiss, State Department official accused of turning secrets over to the Russians. The Republican platform stressed Korea, communism, and corruption, and for the Democratic policy of "containment" proposed to substitute "liberation": a policy directed toward "genuine independence" for all "captive peoples" under Communist rule throughout the world.[3]

On March 2, Truman announced he would not be a candidate for re-election (though he was exempt from the 22nd Amendment's prohibition of third terms) and began looking to Adlai E. Stevenson, Governor of Illinois, as the Democratic nominee. But Stevenson (grandson of Cleveland's Vice-President, 1893–97), who was running for re-election as Governor, was reluctant to challenge a war hero. "I just don't want to be nominated for the Presidency," he said firmly. "I have no ambition to be President. I have no desire for the office, mentally, temperamentally, or physically." "Well," one Democrat wanted to know, "what'll you do if we nominate you anyway?" "Guess I'll have to shoot myself," said Stevenson wryly.[4] But he made a beautiful speech welcoming the Democrats to Chicago late in July, filled with wit, charm, and eloquence, and, as the *New York Times*'s James Reston put it, "talked himself into the leading candidate's role" as a consequence.[5]

But Stevenson held back. "I thought I came here to greet you, not you to greet me," he quipped when the delegates responded to his welcome with shouts of "We want Stevenson!"[6] In the end, however, the Democrats chose him as their candidate on the third ballot and he was the first genuinely drafted presidential candidate since Garfield in 1880. For his running mate the delegates selected John Sparkman, New-Dealish Senator from Alabama. Stevenson's acceptance speech was as impressive as his welcoming address. He asked members of both parties "to debate issues sensibly and soberly," reminded Americans there were no easy decisions in times of trouble, and warned that "sacrifice, patience, and implacable purpose may be our lot for years to come."[7]

Ike's managers were anxious to avoid the "me-tooism" they thought had hurt Willkie in 1940 and Dewey in 1944 and 1948. Their strategy was "Attack! Attack! Attack!"[8] They also decided to aim their efforts at the stay-at-homes rather than independent voters. And they were bent on "packaging" their product with the help and guidance of experts in advertising. At an early briefing they talked so much about "merchandising Eisenhower's frankness, honesty, and integrity," that the Republican candidate became disconsolate. "All they talked about," he told a friend, "was how they could win on my popularity. Nobody said I had a brain in my head." Ike went along with the plan but it bothered him. "To think," he said, shaking his head, "that an old soldier should come to this."[9]

To sell Ike to the voters Republican strategists relied almost as much on television as on personal appearances. Eisenhower commercials were a major feature of the campaign, especially in its later stages. In one commercial, an announcer exclaimed, "Eisenhower answers the nation," and the scene shifted to a man in the street asking, "Mr. Eisenhower, what about the high cost of living?" Eisenhower's reply: "My wife, Mamie, worries about the same thing. I tell her it's our job to change that on November fourth." In another sequence, a citizen remarks: "It was extra tough paying my income tax when I read about the internal revenue tax collectors being fired for dishonesty." Then Ike says: "Well—how many taxpayers were shaken down, I don't know. How many crooks escaped, I don't know. But I'll find out after next January." And in still another commercial, when a man asks which party will lick inflation, Ike says: "Well, instead of asking which party will bring prices down, why not ask which party has put prices up?"[10]

Ike eventually traveled 33,000 miles, mostly by plane, and delivered over two hundred speeches, forty of which were televised. But his early appearances were lacklustre and disappointing to his followers. He took the "middle road" and, although attacking centralized power in Washington, accepted the social gains of the Roosevelt era as "solid floors" on which private enterprise could build a better life for the people. In September, though, he made his peace with Republican right-wingers. A two-hour conference with Senator Taft in New York produced the statement that the two men agreed for the most part on domestic and foreign policies, that they regarded the basic issue of the campaign as "liberty against creeping socialism," and that the Ohio Senator would work for Ike's election. Ike's "Great Crusade," taunted Stevenson, had turned into a "Great Surrender"; Taft "lost the nomination but won the nominee."[11] This was an exaggeration. Ike remained somewhat more liberal than Taft. But he did move increasingly to the right thereafter and began adhering more faithfully to the K_1C_2 formula.

Republican extremists, however, were an embarrassment to Eisenhower. When asked right after his nomination whether he would support smear artists like Senators William Jenner of Indiana and Joseph R. McCarthy of Wisconsin, he said he would endorse all the Republican candidates but wouldn't support "anything that looks . . . like unjust damaging of reputation."[12] But when he was in Indiana in mid-September, he had to appear on the same platform with Jenner (who had called his friend General George C. Marshall a "front man for traitors") and receive his public embraces. Afterward he told a friend, "I felt dirty from the touch of the man," but kept his qualms to himself. When he was in Milwaukee on October 3, he included a vigorous defense of Marshall (whom McCarthy had called a "traitor") in the speech he planned to give: "I know that charges of disloyalty have . . . been leveled against . . . Marshall. I have been privileged for thirty-five years to know General Marshall personally. I know him, as a man and as a soldier, to be dedicated with singular selflessness and the profoundest patriotism to the service of America. And this episode is a sobering lesson in the way freedom must not defend itself." The passage appeared in a press release; but under pressure from Republican leaders in Wisconsin, Ike left it out when he came to deliver the speech. Many of his admirers were dismayed by his knuckling under to the McCarthyites. "Do I need to tell you that I am sick at heart?" cabled Arthur Hays Sulzberger, publisher of the pro-Eisenhower *New York Times.* In a later speech, though, Ike did praise Marshall as one of the "great American patriots."[13]

Ike became increasingly strident as the campaign progressed (he called the Democratic platform "un-American"), but he never took the low road. That was left to Senators Jenner and McCarthy and to Ike's running mate, Richard Nixon. Nixon did not put it as crudely as McCarthy and Jenner did, but he made the same point: the Democrats were "soft" on Communism. He claimed that the Truman administration had "covered up this Communist conspiracy and attempted to halt its exposure" and that Stevenson himself ("Adlai the Appeaser") took a "soft attitude toward the Communist conspiracy at home" and had received "a Ph.D. from Dean Acheson's College of Cowardly Communist Containment" in foreign affairs. "Can such a man," he liked to ask, "be trusted to lead our crusade against communism?" The Communists, he told voters, in both Russia and the United States, wanted a Democratic victory.[14]

But then, suddenly, Nixon found himself on the defensive. On September 18 there was a huge headline in the *New York Post,* "SECRET NIXON FUND," followed by the revelation that "Secret Rich Men's Trust

Fund Keeps Nixon in Style Far Beyond His Salary." Sixty-six wealthy Californians, the *Post* reported, had set up a "slush fund" of over $18,000 for Nixon when he was in the Senate. The news hit the front page of newspapers throughout the country and Republicans panicked while Democrats chortled. Nixon at once called the *Post* story a Communist "smear," but a little later he announced that the fund went to pay for his political expenses and wasn't for his personal use. Taft made a vigorous defense of Nixon, but some Republicans thought he ought to withdraw from the ticket; they wondered how Ike could wage a campaign against corruption if his running mate was under suspicion.[15]

On September 23, at Ike's suggestion, Nixon appeared on television in Hollywood to defend himself. In his speech, which attracted the largest television audience up to that time, Nixon not only defended the fund and made an accounting of his personal finances; he also talked lengthily (and lachrymosely) about his humble beginnings, his rise in life by diligence, determination, hard work, and self-denial, and about the plain and simple style to which he, his wife Pat, and his two little girls, were accustomed to live. He also brought his dog into the picture. "One other thing I probably should tell you," he said, "because if I don't they will probably be saying this about me, too. We did get something, a gift, after the nomination. A man down in Texas heard Pat on the radio mention the fact that our two youngsters would like to have a dog and, believe it or not, the day before we left on this campaign trip we got a message from Union Station in Baltimore, saying they had a package for us. We went down to get it. You know what it was? It was a little cocker spaniel dog, in a crate that had been sent all the way from Texas— black and white, spotted, and our little girl Tricia, the six-year-old, named it Checkers. And you know, the kids, like all kids, loved the dog, and I just want to say this, right now, that regardless of what they say about it, we are going to keep it."[16] Nixon's performance thrilled thousands. An avalanche of letters, cards, and telegrams poured into the Republican national headquarters praising Nixon, and he stayed on the ticket.

One of the highlights of the 1952 campaign was Stevenson's wit. "They tell me I laugh too much," he mused at one point. "I don't see how in hell you could do this job without laughing about it occasionally." He called the Republican platform "a bunch of eels" and declared: "Nobody can stand on it." When a platform on which Ike was standing suddenly collapsed, Stevenson remarked: "I'm glad the General wasn't hurt. But I wasn't surprised that it happened—I've been telling him for two months that nobody could stand on that platform." He also said that if the Republicans "will stop telling lies about us, we will stop telling the truth about them." Ike was irked by Stevenson's quips and in one speech scolded him for making humorous remarks about somber subjects. In response, Stevenson said he now knew what the initials GOP stood for: "Grouchy Old Pessimists." Alluding to Ike's rapprochement with Mc-

Carthy, he also said: "My opponent has been worrying about my funnybone; I'm worrying about his backbone."[17]

But Stevenson combined the light touch with high seriousness. He was resolved to "talk sense to the American people." He pointed out that Republican talk of "liberating" captive peoples from Communist control was either reckless or meaningless and that bombing China to end the Korean stalemate (which General Douglas MacArthur and his Republican supporters proposed) would involve the United States in a terrible land war in Asia and perhaps even touch off World War III. He was eloquent, too, in defending America's Bill of Rights freedoms against the assaults of the McCarthyites. "Because we believe in a free mind," he declared, "we are also fighting those who, in the name of anti-communism, would assail the community of freedom itself. . . . The pillorying of the innocent has caused the wise to stammer and the timid to retreat. I should shudder for this country, if I thought that we, too, must surrender to the sinister figure of the Inquisitor, of the great accuser. . . ."[18]

In a speech in Detroit on October 24, Ike dropped a bombshell: he promised to end the war in Korea if he became President. "The biggest fact about the Korean war," he said, "is this—it was never inevitable, it was never inescapable." As President, he announced, he would give priority to ending the war honorably and would go to Korea himself to facilitate that objective. "I shall make that trip," he declared. "Only in that way could I learn how best to serve the American people in the cause of peace." Ike's statement, "I shall go to Korea," shoved all the other news off the front pages of most newspapers. Though the Democrats dismissed it as a "grandstand gesture," it met with an overwhelmingly favorable response from the American people.[19] Polls which had been giving Ike a slight lead over Stevenson all along now gave him certain victory. "For all practical purposes," wrote one reporter, "the contest ended that night." In retrospect Stevenson (who had himself toyed with but discarded the idea of promising to go to Korea) agreed: ". . . if it hadn't been for that going-to-Korea business, I might have beaten him."[20] Probably not; the people's discontents, especially with the Korean stalemate, were such that the belief that it was "time for a change" (a popular Republican slogan) was deep and widespread in 1952. But the "going-to-Korea business" undoubtedly added to Ike's appeal.

On election day, November 4, it was a massive landslide for Eisenhower. Even the pollsters, who had put Ike comfortably ahead all along, were surprised by the extent of his victory. His plurality was enormous: more than 6,500,000 votes. He won 55.4 percent of the popular votes (33,824,351) and carried 39 states with 442 electoral votes. He was the first Republican since Hoover, moreover, to make inroads in the South (where he had done extensive campaigning), winning Virginia, Tennessee, Texas, and Florida. Stevenson failed to carry a single state outside of the South, won only 27,314,987 popular votes (44.4 percent), and carried only nine states with 89 electoral votes.

The election of 1952 was a hearty vote of confidence in Ike himself rather than in his party. In the Congressional elections the Republicans won a majority of only eight in the House and a tie with the Democrats in the Senate. Eisenhower, wrote columnist Marquis Childs after the election, "was above politics. That was part of his attraction for a people who tend to regard the political process as, at best, a dubious luxury, an expensive kind of game in which we are forever indulging the players. In so many respects he was uncommitted, a clean slate on which each citizen could write his own hopes and aspirations."[21]

After it was all over Stevenson said he felt the way Abraham Lincoln had after losing an election: like the little boy who stubbed his toe in the dark and said "he was too old to cry, but it hurt too much to laugh."[22]

Pardner

It took a military man like Eisenhower a little while to get used to the informalities of democratic politics. When he flew to Kansas City on June 3 to begin his campaign for the nomination, he was met at the airport by Colorado Governor Dan Thornton, a big, jovial man who wore cowboy boots and a ten-gallon hat. When Thornton saw Ike, he rushed over, gave him a hearty slap on the back, and cried, "Howya, pardner!" Ike's eyes blazed for a moment and his back stiffened. Then he relaxed, grinned, reached out his hand, and said: "Howya, Dan?"[23]

No Log Cabin

When a writer approached Stevenson with the idea of doing a campaign biography, the latter exclaimed: "I don't see how you're going to do it. My life has been hopelessly undramatic. I wasn't born in a log cabin. I didn't work my way through school, nor did I rise from rags to riches, and there's no use trying to pretend I did."[24]

Damned Rain

When Stevenson started to speak in Pontiac, Michigan, a storm which had been threatening suddenly broke and the rain began pouring down on about a thousand people huddled together. "I'm not going to talk to you about labor policies," began Stevenson. "I'm not going to talk to you about foreign policies. In fact, I'm not going to talk to you about a thing, because of this damned rain. Good-bye!" The crowd laughed and broke up.[25]

Just a Politician

As a TV make-up man worked on Ike's face, he mused, "What a come-down! I used to be a paratrooper with you in France. Now I just smear this stuff on homely mugs. And you used to be a five-star general, but now you're just a politician!" It was one of Ike's favorite stories.[26]

38th Platitude

Ike's generalities led reporters to call him "the extremely General Eisenhower." *New York Times* columnist James Reston called them "dynamic platitudes." But one reporter noted that when Ike "utters the most obvious platitude, [people] look at that serious face as if they had heard something that ought to be graven on stone and passed on to the third and fourth generation." Once a newspaperman on the Eisenhower train asked, "Where are we now?" Sighed his companion (with the division of Korea in mind): "Crossing the thirty-eighth platitude!"[27]

Eggheads

In their *New York Herald Tribune* column, Joseph and Stewart Alsop first described Stevenson and his aides as "eggheads," probably because of Stevenson's baldness and the intellectual background of his speech advisers. The word had the same kind of pejorative connotations among Republicans as FDR's "Brain Trust" had had years before. Quipped Stevenson: "Eggheads of the world unite; you have nothing to lose but your yolks!" Stevenson's ex-wife, with Betty Macdonald's best-seller *The Egg and I* in mind, playfully announced she was going to write a book called *The Egghead and I.* After Ike became President he put a Latin motto on his desk: *Suaviter in modo fortiter in re.* "That proves I'm an egghead," he told a reporter.[28]

Nixon's Crisis

Nixon's second crisis (as he called it in his book *Six Crises,* published in 1962) strained his relations with Eisenhower to the breaking point.

When Ike first heard of Nixon's secret fund, he expressed confidence in Nixon's integrity, but told a press conference: "Of what avail is it for us to carry on this crusade against this business of what has been going on in Washington if we ourselves aren't as clean as a hound's tooth?" After that he waited a while before getting in touch with his running mate, and when he finally did call him up, he didn't ask him to stay on the ticket; instead, he told him, "you are the one who has to decide what to do." When Nixon said people ought to hear "my side of the story," Ike agreed, and urged him "to go on a nationwide television program" to explain things to the people. "General," Nixon asked, "do you think after the television program that an announcement could then be made one way or another?" "We will have to wait three or four days after the television show," Ike told him, "to see what the effect of the program is." "General," said Nixon testily, "the great trouble here is indecision." And he added: "There comes a time in politics when you have to pee or get off the pot." But Ike refused to give any assurances.

Less than two hours before Nixon was to appear on the air, Thomas E. Dewey called Nixon to tell him that Ike's top advisers had decided that "at the conclusion of the broadcast tonight you should submit your resignation to Eisenhower." Nixon was thunderstruck; he knew it meant the end of his career. When he asked whether this was Eisenhower's desire, Dewey was a bit evasive, though he gave the impression he was speaking for the General. "What," he said finally, "shall I tell him you are going to do?" Nixon coldly told him to listen to his broadcast.

Nixon's telecast may have reduced many people to tears but Eisenhower was not one of them. Watching Nixon on TV in Cleveland with some of his advisers, he jabbed his pencil onto a yellow pad he was holding a couple of times. The first jab came when Nixon suggested all the candidates make complete statements about their finances the way he was doing: "Because, remember, a man who's to be President and a man who's to be Vice President must have the confidence of all the people." Was Ike thinking, as he jabbed, of all the gifts he had received as a war hero, and of the preferential tax treatment Congress gave him when it came to royalties on his book *Crusade in Europe?* The second jab—which broke the pencil point—came when Nixon made it clear he was bypassing Ike when it came to his future. Cried Nixon at the conclusion of his speech: "Wire and write the Republican National Committee whether you think I should stay or whether you think I should get off. And whatever their decision is, I will abide with it." When Nixon finished, Ike told Arther Summerfield, chairman of the Republican national committee, "Well, Arthur, you sure got your money's worth."

Ike tried to stay in command. He told a crowd in Cleveland that Nixon had behaved bravely in a tough situation, but also said he still hadn't made up his mind about Nixon. He then read a telegram he had sent his running mate: "While technically no decision rests with me, you and I know the realities of the situation require a pronouncement which the public considers decisive. My personal decision is going to be based on personal conclusions. I would most appreciate it if you can fly to see me at once. Tomorrow evening I will be at Wheeling, West Virginia." But Nixon balked. Buoyed by the flood of congratulatory telegrams and telephone calls his telecast had elicited, he ignored Ike's request and announced he was continuing his campaign. "Will be in Washington Sunday," he wired Ike, "and will be delighted to confer with you at your convenience any time thereafter." Ike yielded at this point; he gave Nixon his endorsement and Nixon flew to West Virginia. And when Nixon arrived at the airport, Ike ran up to him and said (possibly with a touch of condescension), "Dick, you're my boy!" Some observers thought the two men never really trusted each other after that.[29]

Words

When an aide told Stevenson it cost $60,000 to put one of his speeches on TV, the latter exclaimed: "I wish you hadn't told me. Now, every time I start to put a word on paper, I'll wonder whether it's an expensive ten-dollar word, or a little, unimportant word like 'is' or 'and' that costs only $1.75."[30]

Trinity

During the campaign Congresswoman Clare Boothe Luce predicted Ike would get the woman's vote because he "exemplifies what the fair sex looks for—a combination of father, husband and son."[31]

Zoo

Ike's aide Sherman Adams and his wife voted in New York on election day and then spent the afternoon at the Bronx Zoo. When they returned to the Commodore Hotel that evening to await the returns with Eisenhower, they happened to mention they had just come from the zoo. "Quite a change from a political campaign," someone said. "No, not much," said Mrs. Adams quietly.[32]

The Joys of Campaigning

After the election Stevenson reflected on the demands of campaigning. "You must emerge," he wrote, "bright and bubbling with wisdom and well-being, every morning at eight o'clock just in time for a charming and profound breakfast talk, shake hands with hundreds, often literally thousands of people, make several inspiring 'newsworthy' speeches during the day, confer with political leaders along the way and with your staff all the time, write at every chance, think if possible, read mail and newspapers, talk on the telephone, talk to everybody, dictate, receive delegations, eat, with decorum—and discretion—and ride through city after city on the back of an open car, smiling until your mouth is dehydrated by the wind, waving until the blood runs out of your arm, and then bounce gaily, confidently, masterfully into great howling halls, shaved and all made up for television with the right color shirt and tie—I always forgot—and a manuscript so defaced with chicken tracks and last minute jottings that you couldn't follow it, even if the spotlights weren't blinding, and even if the still photographers didn't shoot you in the eye every time you looked at them. . . . But the real work has just commenced—two or three, sometimes four hours of frenzied writing and editing of the next day's immortal mouthings so you can get something to the stenographers, so they can get something in the mimeograph machines, so they can get something to the reporters, so they can get something to their papers by deadline time. . . . Finally sleep, sweet sleep, steals you away, unless you worry—which I do."[33]

★★★★★★★★★★★★★★★★★★★★★★★★

CHAPTER FORTY-THREE

1956
Another Eisenhower Landslide

In 1956 Dwight D. Eisenhower and Adlai E. Stevenson confronted each other again. But 1956 lacked 1952's sparkle. Both men were well-known now and relied more on television appearances than on old-fashioned barnstorming. Stevenson's chances, too, seemed slim from the beginning. A Gallup poll gave the popular Ike a three-to-two lead over any Democratic candidate.

The Republicans needed Ike. They had lost control of Congress in 1954, while Ike's hold on the people remained firm and unwavering. Under Ike, the Korean War came to an end, "McCarthyism" as a disruptive force declined with the Wisconsin Senator's censure by his colleagues in 1954, and the nation was prospering. One Republican leader, asked what he would do if Ike refused to run again, exclaimed: "When I get to that bridge, I will jump off it!"[1]

Ike originally planned to serve only one term, but as time passed he began toying with the idea of running again. In September 1955, however, he had a heart attack; and though he made a good recovery there were doubts about his intentions. But on March, 1956, he announced that he would accept another nomination, though he acknowledged that a second term would require "a regime of ordered work activity, interspersed with regular amounts of exercise, recreation and rest." Then came an operation for ileitis in June. But again he recovered quickly, said he was "in better shape" than before, and announced he still planned to run. His press secretary, James Hagerty, reported that Ike's decision to run came during his three-week convalescence: "It was then that he faced the sheer, god-awful boredom of not being President."[2] The Republicans, meeting in San Francisco toward the end of August, renominated him by acclamation, adopted a platform citing his accomplishments, and picked Richard M. Nixon again to run with him.

Stevenson, who went on a world tour and then worked hard to build up his party after his defeat in 1952, threw his hat into the ring in November 1955. "I shall be a candidate for the Democratic nomination for President next year," he announced, "which, I suspect, is hardly a surprise."[3] Whether he would have entered the lists had he thought Eisenhower intended to run again it is impossible to say. This time, in any case, there was no draft; he had to work for the nomination. His main challenger was Senator Estes Kefauver of Tennessee; he lost to him in the Minnesota primary and only narrowly defeated him in Florida. But with a big victory over him in California, his nomination was clinched. Kefauver withdrew from the race; and though former President Truman pushed Governor Averell Harriman of New York as a more aggressive candidate, the Democrats picked Stevenson on the first ballot at their national convention in Chicago early in August. To the surprise of party regulars Stevenson then threw the choice of his running mate into the hands of the delegates. "The choice will be yours," he announced. "The profit will be the nation's." Young Senator John F. Kennedy of Massachusetts did enormously well in the balloting; but in the end the delegates chose Kefauver on the second ballot. In an elegant acceptance speech, Stevenson called for a "New America" where "poverty is abolished," "freedom is made real for everybody," and the ancient idea "that men can solve their differences by killing each other" is discarded.[4]

Eisenhower did less campaigning in 1956 than in 1952, partly because of his health and partly because he knew he would win. He emphasized peace, prosperity, and unity in his speeches; he also pointed with pride to the record of his administration: ending the Korean War, launching a gigantic interstate highway system, extending social security, remodeling the defense establishment, freeing the economy of many "repressive controls," and achieving a surplus in the 1956 budget. Ike urged Nixon to campaign "on a higher level than in the past."[5] The latter reminded the President that "You don't win campaigns with a diet of dishwater and milk toast," but agreed not to make "personal attacks on the integrity of our opponents." During the campaign a "new Nixon" seemed to emerge; he campaigned strenuously enough, covering 42,000 miles in all, but refrained from the red-baiting that had been a feature of all his previous campaigns.[6]

Ike seemed an easy winner, but Stevenson put on an energetic campaign anyway. He wanted to contrast his own vigor with Ike's diminished capacity. In a series of speeches he issued five policy papers for a "New America," centering on senior citizens, health, education, natural resources, and economic policy, seeds that later found fruition in John Kennedy's New Frontier and Lyndon Johnson's Great Society. At the same time he placed special emphasis on two immediate proposals: ending the draft and developing a highly trained professional volunteer defense corps in its place; and seeking an agreement with Russia and the other atomic powers to put an end to the testing of nuclear bombs. Ike criticized both proposals as unrealistic, but after his re-election sought a ban on nuclear testing himself, while Nixon, also critical, ended the draft and sponsored a volunteer army after he became President in 1969.[7]

During the final days of the campaign foreign news dominated the headlines. In Hungary, Russian tanks brutally suppressed a revolt in Budapest against Soviet domination in late October. And in Egypt, President Gamal Abdel Nasser's nationalization of the Suez Canal, owned chiefly by British and French stockholders, touched off an invasion of the country by British and French forces, acting in concert with Israel, aimed at getting rid of Nasser and internationalizing the Canal. The United Nations called for an immediate cease-fire in Egypt which Eisenhower joined the Russians in supporting; he insisted that military intervention in Egypt "can scarcely be reconciled with the principles and purposes of the United Nations Charter."[8] Bowing to U. N. pressure, Britain, France, and Israel agreed to withdraw their troops; and a U. N. police contingent was sent into the area to maintain order. Stevenson was extremely critical of U. S. policies in both Eastern Europe and the Middle East; he thought they showed "the total bankruptcy of the administration's foreign policy." The Republican party's "liberation" policy recklessly encouraged uprisings in Eastern Europe, he pointed out, but when they came, the United States could do nothing to help the insurgents without risking war with Russia. And in the Middle East, he observed, Ike's policy ended by alienating three of America's best friends.[9] But Stevenson's criticisms evoked little response. The Middle East crisis, if anything, strengthened Ike's position with the American people. In time of crisis, many people argued, it was dangerous to change Presidents; and Eisenhower, with his vast military and civilian experience, they said, was just the man to be at the helm at this point.

The Middle Eastern crisis may have helped Eisenhower some, but he surely would have won the election without it. By early November he was so sure of victory he decided to do no more campaigning. His triumph on November 6 was overwhelming. He did even better than in 1952. With 35,581,003 popular votes (57.4 percent) to Stevenson's 26,031,322 (42 percent), he won a popular majority of over nine and a half million; he also carried 41 states (457 electoral votes) to Stevenson's seven states (73 electoral votes), all of them in the South. It was the most smashing victory since Roosevelt's victory over Landon in 1936. Ike not only carried six states in the once Solid South; he also carried most of the big Northern cities, normally Democratic, and did well with both labor and the blacks.

After the election Stevenson announced gamely that he was "disappointed but not bruised" and Eisenhower declared that the Republican party, brought up to date under his administration, had triumphed.[10] "Modern Republicanism," he declared, "has now proved itself and America has approved of modern Republicanism. Modern Republicanism looks to the future and this means it will gain constantly new recruits."[11] But Ike was too modest. The election was really another personal triumph for the sixty-six-year-old President. He outran the Republican Congressional ticket by over 6,500,000 votes and the Democrats took control of Congress, 49 to 47 in the Senate and 234 to 201 in the House.

Welcome Back

Ike's heart attack produced several "sick jokes." One had Nixon greeting him jovially in front of the Capitol after he got out of the hospital: "Welcome back, Mr. President, I'll race you to the top of the stairs."[12]

Ridiculous Costume

During the California primary campaign Stevenson donned blue jeans, a denim jacket, cowboy boots, a string necktie, and a ten-gallon hat and rode horseback in a parade at Los Banos before delivering an address. Afterward he told aides to get him "out of this ridiculous costume" and moaned: "*God,* what a man won't do to get public office!"[13]

With a Smile

During the primary campaign a hostile-looking man held up a big Kefauver sign as the bus Stevenson was on passed by. Stevenson gave him a big smile and muttered: "Hello, you son of a bitch!"[14]

Bottle and Jigger

The Republicans met in Chicago in 1952; the Democrats were there in 1956. When a Chicago nightclub owner was asked whether there was any difference between a Republican and a Democratic convention, he said there was: "Democrats pour by the bottle, Republicans pour by the jigger."[15]

Talked Too Long

When Stevenson was campaigning in California a woman asked him where he got his coat of tan: "You been playing golf?" "No," said Stevenson, "I got this tan making outdoor speeches in Florida." "Well," said the woman, "if you got that brown you talked too long."[16]

Hemingway

When someone remarked that Stevenson had a way with words, Ike said testily that if that were the criterion, "we ought to elect Ernest Hemingway."[17]

Between Two Extremes

Commented young comedian Mort Sahl during his act in a San Francisco night club: "Eisenhower stands for 'gradualism.' Stevenson stands for 'moderation.' Between these two extremes, we the people must choose!"[18]

Not Mad at Him

When Stevenson asked a farmer who was critical of Eisenhower's farm policy, "But why aren't people mad at Eisenhower?" the farmer exclaimed: "Oh, no one connects *him* with the Adminstration." Stevenson told the story to his associates to show how hard it was campaigning against the popular General.[19]

Honorary Degree

Because of two-time loser Stevenson's effort to "talk sense to the American people," Bill Wirtz once remarked: "If the Electoral College ever gives an honorary degree, it ought to go to Adlai Stevenson."[20]

★★★★★★★★★★★★★★★★★★★★★★★★★★★★★★

CHAPTER FORTY-FOUR

1960
Kennedy and the New Frontier

In a speech at the annual Alfred E. Smith memorial dinner in New York in 1959, Massachusetts Senator John F. Kennedy reminisced about an election he thought would be of special interest to his audience. "I think it well," he said, "that we recall what happened to a great governor when he became a Presidential nominee. Despite his successful record as governor, despite his plain-spoken voice, the campaign was a debacle. His views were distorted. He carried fewer states than any candidate in his party's history. To top it off, he lost his own state that he had served so well as a governor." At this point Kennedy paused a moment; then he said innocently: "You all know his name and his religion—Alfred M. Landon, Protestant." [1]

Kennedy's leg-pull went over big. He used it again after entering the presidential race. But in 1960, as in 1928, despite his quip, religion entered the campaign. With the Catholic Kennedy confronting the Protestant Vice-President Richard M. Nixon, many citizens voted their religion rather than their politics on November 8. Some Protestant Democrats supported Nixon for religious reasons and some Catholic Democrats who had supported Eisenhower returned to the Democratic fold in 1960 because of religion.

Both Kennedy and Nixon won their nominations on the first ballot. Kennedy came first. When the Democrats assembled in Los Angeles on July 11, he had proven himself as a vote-getter. Not only had he been re-elected to the Senate in 1958 by the largest popular majority in Massachusetts history; he had also bested Minnesota Senator Hubert Humphrey in both the Wisconsin and West Virginia primaries and, in the latter, shown he could do well among Protestant voters. After receiving the nomination, Kennedy, forty-three, chose Senate Majority Leader Lyndon B. Johnson of Texas as his running mate. Some Northern

Democrats were dismayed, thinking JFK had betrayed his liberal principles by picking Johnson, but Kennedy adviser John Kenneth Galbraith told them facetiously: "This is the kind of political expedient Franklin Roosevelt would never have used—except in the case of John Nance Garner."[2] LBJ fought hard for the ticket, turned out to be as liberal as JFK, and, after becoming President, something of a Populist. In his acceptance address, Kennedy talked of a "New Frontier"—new challenges like the exploration of outer space and new ways of coming to grips with the old problems of war, poverty, and ignorance. He wanted to "get the country moving again" and called for "a new generation of leadership—new men to cope with new problems and new opportunities."[3]

The Republicans met in Chicago on July 25 and nominated Nixon at once and chose Henry Cabot Lodge, former Massachusetts Senator and chief U. S. Representative at the United Nations, for second place. Nixon's acceptance wasn't as heady as Kennedy's but just as concerned with moving forward. Like JFK, Nixon promised to build a better America, but stressed Republican methods—reliance on private enterprise and reduced government spending—and contrasted them with Democratic dependence on the federal government. Like Kennedy, though, he placed a great deal of emphasis on keeping ahead of the Russians, in economic as well as military strength. Referring to a recent boast of Soviet Premier Nikita Khrushchev, he declared: "When Mr. Khrushchev says our grandchildren will live under communism, let us say his grandchildren will live in freedom."[4]

In accepting the nomination, Nixon promised to campaign in all fifty states (Alaska and Hawaii had joined the Union in 1959). A knee infection in August, however, landed him in the hospital for two weeks and his advisers urged abandoning the pledge. But he insisted on making up for lost time and before he finished he had put on one of the most grueling campaigns in presidential history. Nixon knew he had to attract the votes of Democrats as well as independents in order to win, for the Republicans were still in a minority, and for that reason he minimized party labels in his speeches and urged voters to pick the better man. He also made much of Kennedy's youth and immaturity and contrasted them with his own wide experience in national and international affairs. "After each of my foreign trips," he boasted, "I have made recommendations which were adopted. . . ." Unhappily for Nixon, about this time when reporters asked the President what major decisions his Vice-President had participated in, Eisenhower, who was tired and anxious to end his press conference, exclaimed, "If you give me a week, I might think of one." The Democrats were delighted.[5]

JFK refused to be intimidated by cracks at his youth. To the Republican slogan, "Experience counts," he retorted that he, too, was experienced. "The Vice-President and I came to Congress in 1946," he pointed out. "I've been there for fourteen years, the same period of time that he has, so that our experience in government is comparable." He also gibed: "Mr. Nixon is experienced, experienced in policies of retreat, defeat, and weakness" which were producing the erosion of America's prestige in the world.[6] America's "decline" under the Republicans, in fact, was the main theme of Kennedy's campaign. Time and again, he emphasized the fact that America's production was lagging, its defenses (particularly in the development of missiles) falling behind Russia's, and its influence with the non-aligned nations falling behind that of the Communists. Nixon hotly denied that America had declined, but to the end of the campaign Kennedy insisted that the election represented "a race between the comfortable and the concerned, a race between those who want to be at anchor and those who want to go forward."[7]

Kennedy could not campaign effectively, however, until he had disposed of the religious issue once for all. On September 12 he agreed to appear before the Ministerial Association of Houston, Texas, to present his views and answer questions posed by the city's Protestant ministers. The position he took at Houston was crystal-clear: he favored absolute separation of church and state, opposed federal aid to parochial schools, opposed sending an ambassador to the Vatican, and put his oath to the Constitution above the dictates of the Church in the realm of politics. "I am not the Catholic candidate for President," he told the assemblage, "I am the Democratic Party's candidate for President who happens also to be a Catholic. I do not speak for my church on public matters, and the Church does not speak for me." Kennedy went so far in this direction that some Catholics complained he was becoming more Protestant than the Protestants. His Houston appearance, which was telecast, reassured many Protestants. "As we say in my part of Texas," cried Speaker of the House Sam Rayburn, "he ate 'em blood raw." But despite the efforts of both parties to keep religion out of the campaign, millions of anti-Catholic tracts, filled with abuse, made the rounds, just as in 1928.[8]

In 1960 came the first television debates between major presidential contestants. At the outset of the campaign Nixon agreed to meet JFK in a series of four debates. Kennedy welcomed the national exposure the encounter provided and he was anxious to show the public he was knowledgeable, mature, and experienced. Nixon, who was proud of his skill as a debater, also hoped to show himself to good advantage. He regarded himself as an expert in foreign affairs and expected to shine in that area. He was eager, in addition, to show people there was a "new Nixon," calm, wise, and statesmanlike, who had long since discarded the mud-slinging of the old days.

Both candidates worked hard studying up for the first debate, which was telecast from Chicago on September 26. The topic, unfortunately for Nixon, was domestic rather than foreign affairs and the cameras were kinder to Kennedy than to Nixon. During the debate Kennedy looked pleasant, relaxed, and self-assured, while Nixon (who had barely recovered from his illness) looked pale, tired, and emaciated, with his customary five o'clock shadow making him look a bit sinister. Kennedy was on the offensive throughout; he listed the shortcomings of the Eisenhower administration and impressed viewers with his factual mastery of a mass of material. Nixon was perforce on the defensive; he concentrated on Kennedy's criticisms and tried to score points by effectively rebutting them one by one. While Nixon, in short, addressed himself mainly to Kennedy, the latter directed his remarks to the television audience and on the whole came off better. Radio listeners had the impression that Nixon did as well as, if not better than, Kennedy in the confrontation; but televiewers, including Nixon's own fans, generally agreed that Kennedy came out ahead in the first debate.

For the next three debates, Nixon concentrated on appearances: put on weight (his doctor encouraged him to devour milkshakes), used makeup, and saw to it that he got more rest before the encounters. Foreign affairs occupied much of the discussion in the later debates and Nixon felt that he did exceptionally well in this area. But there was a falling-off in the television audience after the Chicago meeting; about 70,000,000 people saw the first debate, but fewer than 50,000,000 watched the remaining three. The upshot was that Kennedy gained more than Nixon did by the encounters. Kennedy, wrote the *New York Times*'s James Reston, "is gradually switching roles with Vice President Nixon in these TV debates. He started out, like the Pittsburgh Pirates, as the underdog who wasn't supposed to be able to stay the course with the champ, but is winding up as the character who has more specific information on the tip of his tongue than Mr. Nixon. . . . Mr. Nixon's presentation was general and often emotional; Mr. Kennedy's curt and factual. Mr. Nixon, whose campaign is based on his reputation for the knowledge of the facts and experience, was outpointed on facts. Mr. Kennedy, who was supposed to be the matinee idol lacking experience, seldom generalized, plunged into his answers with factual illustrations and made no appeal to emotion other than the usual Democratic we-take-care-of-the people argument. . . . In sum, Mr. Kennedy gains as these debates go on even if he does no more than stay level with the Vice President."[9]

On October 19, two days before the final debate, the Rev. Martin Luther King, Jr., civil-rights leader, was arrested with fifty-two other blacks for trying to desegregate a restaurant in Atlanta, Georgia, and sentenced to four months in prison. When Kennedy heard the news he at once telephoned Mrs. King to express his concern, and his brother Robert got in touch with the judge involved and secured King's release on bail. Nixon discussed the case with Eisenhower's Attorney-General, decided it would be improper for him to intervene, and remained silent. Kennedy's action understandably met with a warm response among blacks. King's father, also a Protestant minister, told reporters he had planned to vote for Nixon because Kennedy was a Catholic but had changed his mind. "Because this man was willing to wipe the tears from my daughter-in-law's eyes," he said, "I've got a suitcase of votes, and I'm going to take them to Mr. Kennedy and dump them in his lap." Told of King's comment about Catholicism, Kenndy said wryly: "Imagine Martin Luther King having a bigot for a father." Then he added: "Well, we all have fathers, don't we?"[10]

Toward the end of the campaign President Eisenhower leaped into the fray. He spoke for Nixon in the crucial states of Ohio, Pennsylvania, and New York and, with his immense prestige (he could have had a third term had he so desired and the Constitution permitted it), contributed a great deal to Nixon's campaign. Democrats charged that Ike was trying to carry Nixon "piggyback" into the White House. But Harry Truman (lukewarm at first and then enthusiastic about JFK) also got into the act, did his customary Populistic barnstorming, and, at one point, told Southerners if they voted for Nixon they deserved to go to hell. When Nixon strongly protested Truman's language, Kennedy said he would tell the former President "that our side" should "try to refrain from raising the religious issue."[11]

In the middle of October George Gallup predicted a close election, so close, in fact, that he refused to make any forecasts. Several other psephologists concurred in his judgment. Quipped comedian Mort Sahl: "Neither candidate is going to win."[12] But just before election day, political observers began predicting a victory for Kennedy. *Time, Newsweek,* and *U.S. News and World Report* all picked Kennedy as an easy winner; David Lawrence and Samuel Lubell also foresaw a substantial Kennedy victory. They were right about the victory, but wrong about its magnitude. In the early returns on election night, November 8, Kennedy was ahead; but as the hours passed his lead steadily diminished and the outcome wasn't certain for two or three days. In the largest turnout in the nation's history Kennedy ended by winning 34,227,096 popular votes (49.7 percent) and Nixon 34,107,646 (49.5 percent), a plurality of only 119,450. In electoral votes, however, Kennedy's victory was a comfortable one: 303 to 219. It was the closest popular vote since the Harrison-Cleveland contest of 1888, and political commentators fumbled for expressions to describe it: "hairline decision," "victory by a hair's breadth," "dangerously narrow margin." Some Republicans charged irregularities in voting, especially in Illinois and Texas, and *New York Herald Tribune* writer Earl Mazo launched a series of investigatory articles on voting frauds in those states. But Nixon persuaded him to call off the investigation. "Earl," he said, "no one steals the presidency of the United States," and he went on to explain how disruptive, as well as impractical, the demand for a recount would be and how damaging for the United States abroad.[13]

On January 20, 1961, JFK, at forty-three the youngest man ever elected President, and the first Catholic, took his oath of office and launched his activistic administration. After the inauguration Nixon told a Kennedy aide he regretted he hadn't said some of the things Kennedy had said in his inaugural address. "What part?" the aide, surprised, wanted to know. "That part about 'Ask not what your country can do for you, but what you can do for your country'?" "No," said Nixon, "the part that starts, 'I do solemnly swear'."[14]

☆ ☆ ☆

Send Bill to Daddy

Kennedy was irked by charges that his father, Joseph Kennedy, ambassador to England under Roosevelt, was spending lavish funds to promote his son's candidacy, but he could joke about it. He was amused by the skit put on by newsmen at the Gridiron Club dinner in 1958 which portrayed him as singing, "Just Send the Bill to Daddy" (to the tune of "My Heart Belongs to Daddy"). In the speech he gave afterward he claimed to have received a wire from his "generous Daddy" saying: "Dear Jack; Don't buy a single vote more than is necessary—I'll be damned if I'm going to pay for a landslide." He continued the joke after receiving the Democratic nomination. "On this matter of experience," he said in one campaign speech, "I . . . announced earlier this year that if successful I would not consider campaign contributions as a substitute for experience in appointing ambassadors. Ever since I made that statement, I have not received one single cent from my father."[15]

Din-Din

In a speech in Oshkosh, Wisconsin, Kennedy contrasted drab Republican administrations with lively Democratic ones and quoted an old pro-New Deal poem:

> Plodding feet
> Plodding feet
> Tramp—tramp
> The Grand Old Party's
> Breaking camp.
> The blare of bugles, din-din
> The New Deal is moving in.

After his speech the *New York Times*'s Austin Weinstein told him: "You were a little off in that speech tonight." "A little off?" said Kennedy quizzically. "That line of verse," said Weinstein, " 'The blare of bugles, din-din, the New Deal is moving in.' There should be another 'din' in there. 'The blare of bugles, din-din-din.' " Kennedy stared at him for a moment and then went to bed. The next morning, as he was shaving, he told his friend David F. Powers: "Haven't we got enough troubles without that Weinstein complaining because he thinks there ought to be another din? What am I supposed to do? Put it to music and play it for him?"[16]

Difficult Language

Bishop John Wright told Ted Sorensen, JFK's chief aide, that in 1959 Pope John XXIII, who had been studying English, asked him about JFK's chances in 1960. "Very good," Wright told him; and the Pope, recalling the stories circulating during the 1928 campaign, said facetiously: "Do not expect me to run a country with a language as difficult as yours."[17]

If He'd Lost

JFK was worn out after his grueling primary campaign, but his father said: "He would be a lot more tired if he'd lost."[18]

The Man

When Adlai Stevenson (whom some people wanted to run again) arrived in Los Angeles as a member of the Illinois delegation to the Democratic convention, he was amused to see a large woman, obviously pregnant, parading down the street with a big placard inscribed, STEVENSON IS THE MAN.[19]

N.P.

After Kennedy's nomination Ted Reardon, one of his aides, asked him to autograph a copy of his acceptance speech for his son. Kennedy obligingly wrote, "To Timmy, with best personal regards from your old friend John Kennedy," on the first page and underneath it scratched initials that looked like "N.D." Did that mean Notre Dame, a possible school for his son, Ted wanted to know. "Hell, no," said Kennedy. "That's N.P.— Next President."[20]

Disneyland

After losing his bid for first place Lyndon Johnson agreed to be Kennedy's running mate and tried to get his family together to appear on the stage with the Kennedys to present a unified front before the delegates. "We didn't come out here to see Disneyland," he scolded one of his daughters who was late in arriving from a sightseeing tour. "I know," she said, "But we didn't come out here to see you run for Vice President either."[21]

Reynolds

A cocky Irishman from Boston named Pete Reynolds went to Texas to pave the way for Kennedy's appearances there. In El Paso he told some local reporters that JFK didn't need any help from LBJ in Texas. "Kennedy," he said, "is more popular down here than Johnson and he needs us in Texas more than we need him." Reynolds's statement made the front page of the newspapers the next morning and when Kennedy arrived in El Paso late in the afternoon LBJ rushed up to him with a bunch of newspaper clippings in his hand. Kennedy fired Reynolds at once but LBJ remained unappeased. He talked about the man all the way to the hotel, continued talking about him over drinks, and was still talking about him when JFK finally excused himself and went to bed. The next day, when LBJ came to the hotel room for breakfast Kennedy asked him how he was feeling. "I didn't get much sleep last night," said LBJ. "I was too busy thinking about that fellow you brought down here from Boston."[22]

No Mention

When Nixon went to the hospital because of his knee injury, Kennedy suspended his campaign for the time being. "Senator," a reporter finally asked him, "when does the moratorium end on Nixon's hospitalization and your ability to attack him?" "Well," smiled Kennedy, "I said I would not mention him unless I could praise him until he got out of the hospital, and I have not mentioned him."[23]

Put to Music

In one hurried speech Kennedy used the same phrase three times in the same sentence and people began laughing. So did Kennedy. "We are going to put this speech to music," he said, "and make a fortune out of it."[24]

Kitchen Debates

To prove his experience in foreign affairs, Nixon made much of the fact that he had successfully out-argued Soviet Premier Nikita Krushchev in an American kitchen on display at the Moscow World's Fair in 1959. But Kennedy was unintimidated. "Mr. Nixon may be very experienced in kitchen debates," he said. "So are a great many other married men I know."[25]

Lying There

Sometimes, when it was hard to rouse Kennedy at dawn for another day of hard campaigning, Dave Power would cry: "What do you suppose Nixon's doing while you're lying there?"[26]

Lower Voting Age

Every so often Kennedy was greeted by yelling and jumping children and at one stop he said: "If we can lower the voting age to nine, we are going to sweep this state."[27]

Bare-Faced

When Nixon called one of Kennedy's statements a "bare-faced lie," Kennedy retorted: "Having seen him four times close-up and made up, I would not accuse Mr. Nixon of being bare-faced." And in a speech in the Bronx he said: "Nixon, in a high-level or high-road campaign which emphasizes the issues, in the last seven days has called me an economic ignoramus, a Pied Piper, and all the rest. I just confine myself to calling him a Republican!" Then, as the crowd laughed and applauded, he said: "But he says that is really getting low."[28]

Spillman

At a New York dinner Kennedy claimed he had "asked Cardinal Spellman what I should say when people ask me whether I believe the Pope is infallible, and the Cardinal replied, 'I don't know, Senator—all I know is he keeps calling me "Spillman".' "[29]

Deeply Touched

Kennedy's fall campaign schedule included many fund-raising appearances. At one Denver luncheon Kennedy told the audience: "I am grateful to all of you. I could say I am deeply touched, but not as deeply touched as you have been in coming to this luncheon."[30]

Presidential Profanity

When the question of former President Truman's salty language was raised during one of the television debates, Kennedy suggested referring the matter to Mrs. Truman while Nixon solemnly expressed the hope that the next President would express himself more decorously. At a dinner attended by both candidates not long afterwards Kennedy couldn't resist teasing Nixon about what he had said. "One of the inspiring notes that was struck in the last debate," he said in his speech, "was struck by the Vice President in his very moving warning to the children of the nation and the candidates against the use of profanity by Presidents and ex-Presidents when they are on the stump. And I know after fourteen years in Congress with the Vice President that he was very sincere in his views about the use of profanity. But I am told that a prominent Republican said to him yesterday in Jacksonville, Florida, 'Mr. Vice President, that was "a damn fine speech" ' and the Vice President said 'I appreciate the compliment but not the language.' And the Republican went on, 'Yes sir, I liked it so much that I contributed a thousand dollars to your campaign.' And Mr. Nixon replied, 'The hell you say.' " Nixon joined in the roar of laughter.[31]

Names

In discussing foreign affairs, Kennedy liked to point out that nationalist movements around the world used American slogans and names and quoted American, not Russian, statesmen. "There are children in Africa named Thomas Jefferson, George Washington and Abraham Lincoln," he would say, and in Harlem, where Congressman Adam Clayton Powell gave him a rousing introduction, he added, "There may be a couple of them called Adam Clayton Powell." Powell at once leaned over and whispered, "Careful, Jack!"[32]

Dubious Compliment

When New York clergyman Norman Vincent Peale announced that "American culture" was "at stake" in the election and that if a Catholic became President, "I don't say it won't survive, but it won't be what it was," Kennedy responded: "I would like to think he was complimenting me, but I'm not sure he was."[33]

You Fellows

Shortly after a statement issued in his name produced an adverse reaction, Kennedy told his aides: "O.K., if I win this election, I will have won it myself, but if I lose, you fellows will have lost it!"[34]

Better Crowds

When Kennedy went over to talk to Nixon right after the second TV debate, a photographer appeared to take a picture. At this point Nixon began waving his finger at Kennedy the way he had done it in his kitchen debate with Khrushchev. "I thought, here it comes," said Kennedy afterwards, "he is going to tell me how wrong I am about the plight of America—and do you know what he said? 'Senator, I hear you have been getting better crowds than I have in Cleveland.' "[35]

Activities

In a speech stressing private enterprise as the key to economic growth, Nixon, to the amusement of some people, told a Mississippi audience: "I note the tremendous progress of this city. The mayor was telling me in the last twelve years he has been mayor you have had practically a doubling of population. Where has that progress come from? That progress has not come primarily from government, but it has come from the activities of hundreds of thousands of individual Mississippians given an opportunity to develop their own lives."[36]

Herblock Image

During the 1950s, Herbert Block, cartoonist for the *Washington Post,* pictured Nixon with a heavy black beard, dark eyes, hanging jowls, and a ski-jump nose. The caricature upset Nixon so much that he kept the paper out of his house so his children wouldn't see it. "If he lives to be a hundred," said a friend, "he'll never forget that Herblock cartoon of the welcoming committee, and him climbing out of the sewer to greet it, all covered with that stubbly beard of his." In 1960 Nixon was criticized by some people for the "kid-glove" campaign he was waging against Kennedy. "I have to erase the Herblock image first," he explained.[37]

Baby

While campaigning, Kennedy found that voters liked to hear about his expectant wife Jackie. So one day in Eugene, Oregon, he said his wife was absent because she was "otherwise committed," and there was friendly laughter in the crowd. In northern California the next day he said, "My wife has other responsibilities," and the response was even warmer. The following day he announced, "My wife is going to have a boy in November," and it became a standard remark in subsequent speeches. In Los Angeles a reporter asked, "How do you know it's going to be a boy?" "My wife told me," answered Kennedy. She turned out to be right.[38]

Problem

"People keep asking me," Nixon told one audience, "why can't you do something about your face? Well, if I grew a beard they'd say I was trying to look like Lincoln. A mustache might make me look like Dewey. And if I let my hair grow, they'd say I was trying to look like Bobby [Kennedy]." [39]

LBJ Report

As returns were coming in election night, LBJ called to say Texas was close but safe. JFK hung up and told his friends with a smile: "Lyndon says, 'I hear *you're* losing in Ohio but *we're* doing fine in Pennsylvania.' " [40]

CHAPTER FORTY-FIVE

1964
Lyndon Johnson and the Great Society

In 1964 the Republicans offered voters "a choice, not an echo": the ultra-conservative Senator from Arizona, Barry M. Goldwater. "In Your Heart," Goldwaterites chanted, "You Know He's Right." Right about what? About the iniquities of the welfare state and the disgracefulness of a conciliatory foreign policy. "I find that America is fundamentally a Conservative nation," declared Goldwater; the people "yearn for a return to Conservative principles."[1] There was to be no Willkie-Dewey-Nixon "me tooism" this time around.

The Democrats disagreed. They wanted to carry on with the recently assassinated President Kennedy's plans for civil-rights legislation, federal aid to education, and medical care for the elderly. With Lyndon B. Johnson, fifty-six, as their standard-bearer, they stressed "consensus": the acceptance by most Americans of the welfare state at home and coexistence with the Communist powers abroad. Johnson was eager to put Kennedy's New Frontier proposals into effect and build a "Great Society" in which the quality of life would be high for everybody. When the Republicans put up pictures of Goldwater with the slogan, "In Your Heart You Know He Is Right," the Democrats added: "Yes—Extreme Right."

To Extreme Rightists Goldwater was well-nigh a dream candidate. The Arizona Senator linked the welfare state with "softness" on Communism and "crime in the streets" and promised moral as well as economic salvation by a return to the pre-New Deal past. His simplistic stance appalled serious conservatives. "Barry Goldwater is not a conservative at all," exclaimed Walter Lippmann. "He appears to be totally without the essential conservative respect and concern for the social order as a living body. He is a radical reactionary who would, if we are to believe what he says, dismantle the modern state."[2] But Goldwater's admirers—conservative rank-and-file Republicans as well as superpatriots and ultra-rightist ideologues—regarded him as one of the few trustworthy leaders in the nation.

Goldwater himself wasn't especially eager for the Republican nomination and didn't announce his availability until late in 1963. Disarmingly frank on occasion, he admitted freely that he doubted whether he was up to the job of President. "You know," he once remarked, "I haven't really got a first-class brain."[3] Ever since 1961, however, his devoted followers had been flocking to precinct meetings and mobilizing support for him at the grass-roots level throughout the country and on the eve of the Republican convention they had mustered enough delegates to assure his nomination on the first ballot. By the time Republican moderates like Governor Nelson Rockefeller of New York became aware of what was happening it was too late.

From start to finish, the Republican convention, which opened in San Francisco on July 10, was dominated by Goldwaterites. When Rockefeller rose on the convention floor to defend a minority resolution denouncing extremists (whom he called "kooks"), he was shouted down by the angry crowd. "This is still a free country, ladies and gentlemen," cried Rockefeller when he could be heard again, and went on to deplore the venomous attacks the extremists were making on moderates like himself. "These things," he said, "have no place in America. But I can personally testify to their existence. And so can countless others who have also experienced anonymous midnight and early morning telephone calls, unsigned threatening letters, smear and hate literature, strong-arm and goon tactics, bomb threats and bombings, infiltration and take-over of established political organizations by Communist and Nazi methods." Amid shouts, yells, screams, boos, hoots, and hisses, he concluded: "Some of you don't like to hear it, ladies and gentlemen, but it's the truth."[4] Goldwater was of course quickly nominated; and for his running mate he picked William Miller, an obscure upstate New York Congressman, whose views paralleled his own. "One reason I chose Miller," explained Goldwater, "is that he drives Johnson nuts."[5] In his acceptance speech Goldwater uttered one of the most famous lines ever spoken during a presidential campaign: "I would remind you that extremism in the defense of liberty is no vice!" Cried one reporter afterward: "My God! He's going to run as Barry Goldwater!"[6] Middle-of-the-road Republicans were sick at heart.

Lyndon Johnson had been following Republican proceedings with glee. To Johnson the problem was not so much beating Goldwater; it was beating him by a landslide. He was well aware of Goldwater's "Southern strategy": his hopes for carrying the South because of his emphasis on states' rights and refusal to endorse civil-rights legislation. He also knew Goldwater hoped to benefit from the "white backlash" and win the support of Northern whites who were put off by the rise of black militancy and disturbed by riots in the black ghettoes of New York and other Eastern cities in the early 1960s. But Johnson thought he could hold the South and also win support from the traditional New Deal constituency: farmers, labor, blacks, ethnic minorities, and intellectuals. He was counting on a "frontlash" too, that is, support from Republican liberals who simply could not stomach the takeover of their party by extremists on the right.

The Democratic convention, which opened in Atlantic City on August 24, was soporific, compared with the San Francisco conclave. But LBJ, pulling all the strings in Washington, did what he could to liven things up. He kept everybody in suspense about his choice for second place, Minnesota Senator Hubert H. Humphrey, until the last minute. Then he insisted on flying to the convention with Humphrey at his side and making the vice-presidential nomination himself right after the delegates had chosen him for President by acclamation. Johnson's acceptance speech asked for a mandate to continue the late John F. Kennedy's policies and "to supplement the program with the kind of laws that he would have us write." LBJ missed the moving tribute to Kennedy that was a highlight of the convention, but he approved the convention's work. "I've been going to conventions since 1928," he said, with a straight face, "and this one is the best of all."[7]

1964 surely presented choices, not echoes. But despite the vast gulf between LBJ's social views and Goldwater's, the campaign fell far short of the one four years earlier when it came to discussing the issues. The main reason was that the Democrats put Goldwater on the defensive from the outset. All they had to do was to quote him: what he had written in his newspaper columns and books and, most of all, what he had said in casual remarks about the big issues through the years. Goldwater was famous for "shooting from the lip"; he never bothered to tailor his remarks to his audiences and rarely pondered the implications of what he was saying. The result was that he landed himself in a maze of contradictions and gave the impression of being reckless and irresponsible. In Charleston, West Virginia, a depressed area, he assailed the Employment Opportunity Act; in Knoxville, Tennessee, center of a region transformed by the Tennessee Valley Authority, he attacked public power; in St. Petersburg, home of retired people, he suggested that Social Security be made voluntary ("RIGHT CITY," announced the *St. Petersburg Times*, "WRONG SPEECH"); in Memphis, cotton capital of the world, he said cotton subsidies had been "forced on the farmers by Washington"; and in North Dakota he told farmers a decline in price supports for farm goods would be good for them.[8]

When it came to foreign policy, Goldwater seemed even more outrageous: he wanted to break off relations with Russia, get out of the U. N., use "low-yield nuclear bombs," if necessary, to fight the Communists in Vietnam and elsewhere, and said he'd like to "lob one into the men's room of the Kremlin and make sure I hit it." Criticized for his recklessness, he said candidly: "I wanted to educate the American people to lose some of their fear of the word 'nuclear.' When you say 'nuclear,' all the American people see is a mushroom cloud. But for military purposes, it's just enough firepower to get the job done." The Republicans "are giving us a choice," exclaimed James Reston, "but what a choice!"[9]

Goldwater quotes became a major feature of the 1964 campaign. In no other presidential contest was "quotemanship," that is, the deft use of quotations for polemical purposes, as popular as it was in the Johnson-Goldwater campaign. In books, pamphlets, newspaper advertisements, and leaflets, the Democrats regaled voters with Goldwater statements, frequently lifted out of context, to show how ignorant, ill-informed, and irresponsible the Republican choice for that year was. Lamented one liberal Republican: "Every time Barry opened his mouth, he was campaigning for Lyndon!" In a campaign book entitled *Goldwater from A to Z*, Arthur Frommer presented 113 pages of Goldwater pronouncements on more than a hundred public issues that were in the main confused, contradictory, and, when it came to nuclear war, downright disturbing.[10]

As the campaign progressed, Goldwater began taking back some of the things he had said. He assured people he supported the U. N., didn't want war with Russia, accepted Ike's foreign policy, favored extending Social Security, thought the Civil Rights Act of 1964 should be conscientiously administered even though he had voted against it, and, under pressure from Eisenhower, said he didn't want the support of extremists. But by then it was too late. He was never able to correct the impression, conveyed by so many of his past utterances, that he was a drum-beating, sabre-rattling zealot who might get the country into a nuclear war if he became President. "Goldwater for Halloween," proclaimed Democratic stickers; "Vote for Goldwater and Go to War." TV spots sponsored by the Democrats portrayed Goldwater as a war-monger. One political commercial (repudiated by LBJ) showed a little girl plucking petals from a daisy while a nuclear countdown is going on, and after the screen erupts in an atomic explosion, the voice of Johnson is heard pleading for peace (and votes). Another commercial (also withdrawn) pictured a little girl with an ice cream cone; but the cone is poisoned with strontium-90, a voice in the background points out, because "there's a man who wants to be President of the United States" who voted against Kennedy's nuclear test-ban treaty with Russia in 1962.[11]

In the early weeks of the campaign LBJ devoted himself to being Chief Magistrate and got one headline after another out of his presidential peregrinations. Goldwater tried hard to focus attention on corruption in Washington, which he singled out, next to "socialism," as the major campaign issue. Ordinarily the most amiable of men, Goldwater was harsh in his comments on the Johnson administration. And he did something unusual for presidential candidates: attacked his opponent by name. Johnson, he said, was a "scheming wire-puller" who had by devious means amassed a fortune while in the Senate and who hobnobbed with men like Robert G. ("Bobby") Baker, Billie Sol Estes, and Matt McCloskey, all of whom had come under fire for their dishonest dealings. "To Lyndon Johnson," he cried, "running a country means . . . buying and bludgeoning votes. It means . . . building a private fortune. It means surrounding himself with companions" like Baker, Estes, McCloskey "and other interesting men. . . . It means craving and grasping for power—more and more, without end." [12]

LBJ eventually made public an audit of his holdings which satisfied many (but not all) voters. He also carefully dissociated himself from Bobby Baker, an old pal whose shady practices were then being investigated by a Senate committee. And he did a little name-calling of his own. "Extremism in the pursuit of the Presidency," he cried, "is an unpardonable vice." He also said "it takes a man who loves his country to build a house instead of a raving, ranting demagogue who wants to tear one down." His last statement produced outrage among Republicans and LBJ's press secretary assured reporters that the President had meant to say "raving ranting demagogues." But a little later he backtracked: LBJ had been talking about "a raving, ranting demagogue" after all. [13] Instead of a "me too" campaign, observed *Time*, it had become a "you're another" contest. Some people thought it was a fight between "a kook and a crook." [14]

"Some men are born to campaign," Lady Bird Johnson once remarked. "Lyndon was." At the end of September LBJ could restrain himself no longer. He simply had to take to the stump. For forty-two days he peregrinated the country, covering over 60,000 miles and making almost two hundred speeches promising peace and prosperity and warning against the threat to both by his opponent. He was in his glory as great mobs showed up wherever he went and cheered him on. He would halt his motorcade, make impromptu speeches through a handheld bullhorn, and then bound off his car to shake hands with people. Frequently his right hand was swollen and bleeding after hours of "pressing the flesh" and had to be bandaged. "Come on, folks, come on down to the speakin'," he would cry through a bullhorn as his limousine made its way down the street. "You don't have to dress. Just bring your children and dogs, anything you have with you. It won't take long. You'll be back in time to put the kids in bed." [15] And when people were assembled he would discuss his Great Society programs in homely language, talk about his family, reminisce about his life as a young man in Texas, and tell folksy and frequently funny stories about politics.

The crowds loved Johnson's corny style, even, to his joy, in New England. "I want to ask you just one question," he liked to cry; "Are you gonna vote Democratic in November?" "YES!" would come the roar. "I didn't hear you," Johnson would say. "Did you say *yes?*" "YES!" would be the response.[16] In more formal addresses, Johnson presented himself as a man of peace. "The only real issue in this campaign," he told an audience in Los Angeles, "the only one that you ought to be concerned about, is who can best keep the peace. In the nuclear age, the President doesn't get a second chance to make a second guess. If he mashes the button—that is that. . . . I tell you, as your Commander-in-Chief of the mightiest nation in the world, we can keep the peace, in the words of the Prophet Isaiah, by reasoning together, by responsibility, by negotiation." He repeatedly assured voters he did not intend to get involved in Vietnam. "Some are eager to enlarge the conflict," he said. "They call upon us to supply American boys to do the job that Asian boys should do. They ask us to take reckless action (such as bombing North Vietnam). . . . Such action would offer no solution at all to the real problems of Viet Nam." But after a brief encounter between U. S. warships and North Vietnam patrol craft in the Gulf of Tonkin he persuaded Congress to pass a resolution in August authorizing him to "take all necessary steps, including the use of armed force" to assist South Vietnam and "prevent aggression."[17]

LBJ wanted love as well as votes, but never quite got it. If Goldwater frightened people by his drum-beating, LJB put many people off by his reputation as a "Great Wheeler Dealer." Early in the campaign, the Very Reverend Francis B. Sayre, Jr., Dean of Washington's Episcopal Cathedral, deplored the fact that voters had to choose between "a man of dangerous ignorance and devastating uncertainty" on the one hand and, on the other, "a man whose public house is splendid in its every appearance, but whose private lack of ethic must inevitably introduce termites at the very foundation."[18] Not everyone was as hard on LBJ as Sayre was, but many people admitted they were more anti-Goldwater than pro-Johnson. "I think Goldwater is just beyond belief," said a Denver playwright, "I just don't think he represents the Republican party. Johnson leaves me very cold, but I am going to ring doorbells for him, and I am going to vote for him." "I don't think too much of President Johnson," said a Vermont Republican, "but I guess I'm really afraid of Senator Goldwater."[19] The majority of the nation's newspapers, including the Hearst press, supported the Democrats this time. So did many liberal Republicans, including onetime members of Eisenhower's cabinet. And scores of Republican leaders in business and finance joined the Independent Committee for Johnson and Humphrey.

Long before the campaign was over it was clear that Goldwater didn't have a chance. The polls were never in doubt. And on November 4, LBJ achieved his heart's desire: a landslide. He carried forty-four states and the District of Columbia (voting, by the 23rd Amendment, for the first time) with 486 electoral votes; Goldwater won only six states (Arizona plus five Southern states) with 52 votes. Johnson's popular plurality was over 16,000,000 (43,126,218 popular votes to Goldwater's 27,174,898), the largest up to that time. It was the most decisive victory since FDR overwhelmed Alf Landon in 1936. LBJ's percentage of the total vote cast was 61.1 (compared to 60.8 for FDR in 1936 and 60.4 for Harding in 1920), but his percentage of the total two-party vote was a bit less than FDR's and Harding's. This was something of a disappointment to LBJ who had wanted to break all the records. But he took satisfaction in the fact that forty Northern Democratic Congressmen were swept into office along with him and gave him the most comfortable working majority in Congress since FDR's 1936 landslide.

"It is a mandate for unity," exclaimed Johnson after the election.[20] Working with Congress, he was able to compile an impressive record in 1965 and put most of his Great Society programs into effect. But shortly after his inauguration he also began sending American troops to South Vietnam in an effort to prevent the North Vietnam Communists from taking over the country. And as the war in Vietnam escalated, the consensus LBJ had carefully constructed in 1964 gradually fell apart. By 1968 the Democratic party—and the nation as a whole—was rent by bitter dissension over American involvement in an apparently unwinnable war thousands of miles away on the Asian mainland.

Mr. Average Everyday American

In preparation for his campaign, LBJ decided to present himself to the people as "Mr. Average Everyday American." On the morning of April 11, he walked to the Southeast Gate of the White House and called over to people on the other side, "Would you like to take a walk with me before lunch?" The people outside were surprised but pleased and despite Secret Service objections Johnson had the gates opened and a crowd of about one hundred people admitted. "All right," he yelled, "all you ugly men go up there and all you pretty girls stay here with me." Then he walked around the White House grounds chatting informally with them. His performance received so much warm praise in the press that for several weeks afterward he went to the gate from time to time to shake hands with tourists, exchange remarks with them, and invite them to join him and reporters for walks around the White House. Sometimes Lady Bird joined him; sometimes the dogs, Him and Her, went along too.[21]

Economy

In the spring of 1964 LBJ announced at a news conference that he had asked Congress to appropriate $800,000 to provide staff help for an incoming President between his election and his inauguration. The Budget Director, he said, had told him, "My re-election would save $800,000." He added: "And you all know how strongly I feel about economy."[22]

Extremism

There was a storm of criticism over Goldwater's phrase—"extremism in the defense of liberty is no vice"—because it seemed to condone the views of such extreme-rightist groups as the John Birch Society and the Ku Klux Klan. Goldwater professed to be surprised by the clamor. He pointed out that the words were first used by Cicero when he was defending Rome against Catiline: "I must remind you, Lords, Senators, that extreme patriotism in the defense of freedom is no crime and let me respectfully remind you that pusillanimity in the pursuit of justice is no virtue in a Roman." The day after Goldwater's nomination Eisenhower invited him to the Fairmount Hotel to explain what he meant by the phrase. "Mr. President," said Goldwater, "when you landed your troops in Normandy, it was an exceedingly extreme action taken because you were committed to the defense of freedom." Ike caved in at once. "I guess you're right, Goldwater," he grinned. "I never thought of it that way."[23]

Countdown

Some Democrats found Goldwater's acceptance address so belligerent that their comment was: "10-9-8-7-6. . . ."[24]

All the Way with LBJ—and Isaiah

LBJ's slogan was, "Come, let us reason together," and in campaign speeches he liked to explain how he came to cherish the sentiment as a young man: "One time," he said, "I got into a fight with the head of a power company that wouldn't let me build a little REA [Rural Electrification Administration] line in my country district of Texas, and I said, 'As far as I am concerned, you can take a running jump and go straight to hell!' " Everybody applauded, said LBJ, but a former Senator who overheard him, took him aside and reminded him that "telling a man to go to hell and then making him go is two different propositions." Explaining, the ex-Senator said: "First of all, it is hot down there and the average fellow doesn't want to go, and when you tell him he has to go, he just bristles up and he is a lot less likely to go than if you hadn't told him anything. What you better do is get out the good book that your mama used to read to you and go back to the prophet Isaiah and read what he said. He said, 'Come now, let us reason together.' "[25]

Clarity

"Barry," Eisenhower told Goldwater, "you speak too quick and too loud."
Ike wasn't the only Republican who was dismayed by some of Goldwater's off-the-cuff remarks. "Don't quote what he says," a Goldwater supporter once shouted at reporters, "say what he means!" Observed *Editor and Publisher:* "What the Republican nominee for the President of the United States must bear in mind before he opens his mouth is that clarity begins at home."[26]

Pull My Ears

When LBJ pulled his two pet dogs by their ears onto their hind legs, dog-lovers protested violently, though he insisted it didn't hurt them. But in one campaign crowd he was delighted to see a pretty little girl holding up a big sign which read, "You can pull my ears anytime, Mr. President."[27]

At the Same Time

The good state of the economy helped LBJ with the rich; his war-on-poverty helped him with the poor. Sighed one Republican leader: "I can't remember a time when a President had prosperity and poverty going for him at the same time!"[28]

Improbable

Long before the campaign ended, the *Seattle Post-Intelligencer* declared: "It may be that Barry Goldwater will be elected. It may also be that Chase National will go broke, that Governor Wallace will get an honorary degree from Tuskegee, and that Mickey Spillane will win the Nobel Prize for literature."[29]

Midlash

Both Goldwater and Miller referred to vice-presidential candidate Humphrey by his full name, with special sarcastic emphasis on his middle name, Ho-ra-tio, so often that Humphrey finally exclaimed: "Senator Goldwater thinks he has found a real issue in my middle name. In the spirit of charity, however, I must warn him. The hidden middle-name vote—all those youngsters blessed by loving parents with a middle name they choose to convert to an initial—may rise against him. He should be aware of the midlash!"[30]

Friendly Faces

LBJ chortled so much about the "smiling, friendly faces" he encountered while on the stump that when one of his aides was asked how a campaign trip had gone he sighed: "Fifty thousand f---ing friendly faces!"[31]

Dirt

"Every time we ask an embarrassing question," said Goldwater, "Lyndon leaves town to dedicate a dam. Well, I want him to know, and you want to know, that we have more questions than he has dams." Johnson, Goldwater insisted, had so much power and wanted so much more that the Democrats didn't know whether to vote for him or plug him in. He also said there was so much dirt swept under the White House carpet that it could qualify for the soil bank.[32]

The Left

As his plane flew over Arizona, Goldwater made the first speech ever given by an airborne candidate. "This is Barry Goldwater talking to you . . . ," he announced as 750 Republicans at a $100-a-plate dinner in Phoenix listened intently. "We're at 39,000 feet. I can clearly see the lights of Phoenix down to the left. I hate to say 'the left' but that's where it is."[33]

Democratic Speech

In New Orleans LBJ boldly defended civil-rights legislation and then told a story about Texas Senator Joe Bailey who had been born and reared in Mississippi. One day, according to Johnson, Bailey was talking to young Congressman Sam Rayburn about the South's economic problems and about how it had a great future if it would develop its resources. "I wish I felt a little better, Sammy," Bailey told Rayburn. "I would like to go back to old Mississippi and make them one more Democratic speech. I feel like I have at least one more left in me." He paused and then said sadly: "Poor old Mississippi, they haven't heard a Democratic speech in thirty years. All they ever hear at election time is 'nigra, nigra, nigra'!" When LBJ finished, there were gasps and a moment of silence. Then people started applauding and stood up to give him an ovation.[34]

Dick Tuck

Dick Tuck got into the act again. A forty-year-old California Democrat with a penchant for practical jokes, he had discombobulated Nixon's campaign a couple of times in 1960: donned a trainman's cap and signaled the engineer to start the train just as Nixon was beginning a speech; switched signs on two campaign buses thus messing up Nixon's schedule. This time he sneaked Moira O'Connor aboard a Goldwater campaign train where she began distributing a news-letter, *The Whistle Stop*, to keep "you advised, informed, protected, and, with considerable assistance from the Senator himself, amused." En route, *The Whistle Stop* announced that "fluoride has not been added to the water on this train" and that as the train moved from EST into CST zone, Goldwater "has decided to use Washington time, George Washington, that is." The pair finally gave up in Toledo, Ohio, but not before distributing a final broadside: "We wish we could say that Goldwater's speeches speak for themselves, but they don't."[35]

Psychopolitics

Goldwater's sanity, like Bryan's in 1896 and T.R.'s in 1912, was partisanly called in question. The magazine *Fact* polled 12,356 psychiatrists on the question. "Is Barry Goldwater psychologically fit to be President of the United States?" Only 2,417 replied: 1,189 said "no," 657 said "yes," and 571 said they didn't know enough about it to answer. Both the American Psychiatric Association and the American Medical Association dismissed *Fact*'s poll as yellow journalism and criticized the editor for trying to pass off the personal political opinions of psychiatrists as therapeutic expertise.[36]

Racist Film

The Republicans produced a 28-minute documentary called "Choice," dwelling on the iniquities of the big city: girls in topless bathing suits, stripteasers, delinquent youths, pornographic book stores, and riots in black ghettoes. The film also contained contrasting bucolic rural scenes, a speeding, careening Lincoln sedan sequence (reminding viewers of LBJ's driving around his ranch with a beer can in his hand), and a portentous description by narrator Raymond Massey of Negro riots and looting. "People who were brought up in small towns and on the farms, especially in the Midwest, have a built-in prejudice against the city . . . ," explained the publicity-director for Citizens for Goldwater and Miller. "This film will obviously and frankly just play on their prejudices. . . . We want to just make them mad, make their stomachs turn . . . take this latent anger and concern . . . build it up, and subtly turn and focus it on the man who drives 90 miles an hour with a beer can in his hands." When Goldwater saw the film he was horrified and ordered it cancelled. "It is nothing but a racist film," he said. "If they show it, I will publicly repudiate it."[37]

Mine Eyes Have Seen

While cruising with Goldwater back from Wichita Falls to Washington, reporters (who liked Barry) turned out a parody to the tune of "The Battle Hymn of the Republic":

> Mine eyes have seen Goldwater at a million speaking dates,
> Mine ears have heard him give the lie to liberal candidates,
> And my head has quaked and trembled as he tells us of our fate
> If Lyndon should get in.
> Barry, Barry says he'll save us
> From A.D.A. which would enslave us,
> The curious crew that would deprave us
> He'll save us all from sin.[38]

Not Crazy Enough

Goldwater's running mate, William Miller, played bridge with the reporters while touring the country and he usually won. Toward the end of the campaign one reporter asked him if, as a sporting man, he would give him a chance to get even by betting on the outcome of the election. Miller replied that he might seem stupid, but he wasn't crazy enough to bet on the outcome of *this* election.[39]

CHAPTER FORTY-SIX

★ ★

1968
Nixon, Humphrey, and the
Vietnam War

For America 1968 was a sad and stormy year. On April 27, civil rights
leader Martin Luther King, Jr., was felled by an assassin in Memphis
and his death touched off an orgy of rioting in Washington, D.C., and
elsewhere that would have horrified that beloved apostle of non-vio-
lence. And on June 6, Senator Robert F. Kennedy of New York was
murdered in Los Angeles, just after he won the California presidential
primary, by a young Arab nationalist who resented his friendship for
Israel. Meanwhile the Vietnam War, which both King and Kennedy opposed, was bitterly dividing the nation. The hawks continued to support the Johnson administration's efforts to prevent a North Vietnam
takeover of South Vietnam, and the doves went on protesting involvement in a seemingly endless war thousands of miles away by means of
teach-ins, marches, sit-ins, demonstrations, and silent vigils. The Vietnam War dominated the presidential contest in 1968.

In the fall of 1967 Minnesota Senator Eugene McCarthy launched an
anti-war campaign for the Presidency which quickly attracted support
from dovish liberals throughout the country. College students were
particularly enthusiastic about McCarthy. To help him in New Hampshire, which held the first presidential primary, they cut their hair and
shaved their beards ("Clean for Gene") and began ringing doorbells on
his behalf. The "Children's Crusade" (as it was called) was surprisingly
effective. On March 12 the little-known Minnesotan won 42 percent of
the Democratic votes in the Granite State and twenty out of the state's
twenty-four delegates. A few days later Robert Kennedy entered the lists
as an anti-war candidate with the strong backing of many of his brother
JFK's former associates. It was clear that if Lyndon Johnson wanted to
run again he would have to fight for the nomination.

But on March 31, LBJ dropped a bombshell. In a telecast to the nation that evening he announced a reduction of American bombing in North Vietnam and invited North Vietnam leaders to join him in a "series of mutual moves toward peace." He then added: "I shall not seek and I will not accept the nomination of my party for another term." LBJ's "abdication" was followed by the launching of peace talks in Paris by representatives of North Vietnam and the United States. It also led Vice-President Hubert Humphrey to enter the presidential race with the backing of LBJ. In a strife-torn nation, though, Humphrey's speech announcing his candidacy was singularly maladroit: it dwelt on "the politics of joy." [1]

For the 1968 race Richard M. Nixon, now fifty-five, made an extraordinary comeback. After his defeat by JFK in 1960, the failure of his bid for the California governorship in 1962, and the stunning defeat of Barry Goldwater (whom he had loyally supported) in 1964, Nixon was regarded as something of a dead duck politically. But he never gave up hope. After 1964 he made the rounds, cementing his friendships with Republican party officials, spoke on behalf of Republican candidates in the mid-term elections of 1966, and, in the spring of 1968, entered several Republican primaries and did extremely well in all of them. By this time he had shucked his "loser's image"; he also convinced party leaders he could bring Goldwater conservatives and Rockefeller liberals back together again in a strongly united party. At the Republican convention in Miami Beach, Florida, early in August, Nixon easily staved off challenges from New York Governor Nelson Rockefeller and California Governor Ronald Reagan to win his party's nomination for President on the first ballot.

For second place Nixon picked Governor Spiro T. Agnew of Maryland, then largely unknown ("Spiro Who?"), but with an undoubted appeal to the border states and possibly to the states of the Deep South as well. The Republican platform demanded "a fair and equitable settlement" of the war in Vietnam and called for "progressive de-Americanization" and the gradual assumption of responsibility for the war by the South Vietnamese themselves. It also contained a long passage deploring the rise of crime and violence in the nation's cities and promising to restore law and order to the troubled nation.[2] Nixon's acceptance speech reiterated these themes and called for new leadership to implement them. And, in an obvious bid for support from middle-class Americans who were upset by the increasing stridency of both the civil-rights and anti-war demonstrators, he talked about the "forgotten Americans, the non-shouters, the non-demonstrators" who he said constituted the majority. "They're good people," he cried. "They're decent people. They work and they save and they pay their taxes and they care."[3]

The Miami Beach convention was largely languorous. The Democratic convention in Chicago in late August was the precise opposite.

Humphrey, it is true, received his party's nomination for President on the first ballot without much trouble; and his choice for second place, Senator Edmund Muskie of Maine, was also quickly approved by the delegates. But the convention was seriously divided between hawks and doves, the debates acrimonious at times, and the situation on the convention floor close to anarchy on occasion. There were bitter fights over procedures and credentials, followed by walk-outs, but the fight over the Vietnam plank was the fiercest of all. McCarthy and his followers demanded an unconditional halt to the bombings in Vietnam, followed by negotiations for the withdrawal of all foreign troops from South Vietnam. But Humphrey's supporters, following LBJ's instructions, pushed through a plank rejecting unilateral withdrawal, supporting the Paris talks, calling for an end to the bombing "when this action would not endanger the lives of our troops in the field," and specifying that any bombing halt "should take into account the response from Hanoi." When the majority plank was adopted, doves among the delegates and in the galleries put on black arm bands and began singing the civil-rights song, "We Shall Overcome."[4]

There were doves outside the amphitheatre as well as inside. Led by the National Mobilization Committee To End the War in Viet Nam, thousands of protesters, mainly young people, converged on Chicago during the convention to hold anti-war demonstrations: pacifists rejecting war in principle; anti-interventionists opposed to interference in the civil wars of other countries as contrary to America's national interest; radicals siding with North Vietnam in the belief that an efficient Communist dictatorship offered more hope for the people of South Vietnam than the corrupt authoritarian regime in Saigon; and a sizable group of hippies and yippies who regarded all political organizations as repressive and came to make fun of the system. Chicago's Mayor Richard Daley was prepared for the demonstrators. "No one," he vowed, "is going to take over the streets."[5] Not only did he order the city's entire police force, nearly 12,000 men, into twelve-hour shifts; he also arranged for thousands of Illinois National Guardsmen and army troops to be on the alert for possible reinforcement. Policemen were stationed everywhere: on every corner, in the middle of every block, inside buildings near the amphitheatre, and on top of buildings too.

City authorities took a tough line—prohibited a rally at Soldier Field, turned down the request of the yippies to camp in Lincoln Park, and forbade parades near the amphitheatre. All week there were minor, though at times bloody, clashes between the police and the demonstrators. To taunts ("pigs!") and missiles (bricks and bottles) the police responded with tear gas and occasional beatings. But the night the delegates gathered in the amphitheatre to nominate Humphrey for President, minor skirmishes turned into a major battle. Outraged when protesters lowered a U. S. flag during a rally in Grant Park, the police hurled tear gas into the crowd, and when the demonstrators, bent on marching to the amphitheatre, regrouped elsewhere, the police suddenly charged into the crowd with billy clubs, tear gas and Mace, and savagely attacked hippies, yippies, radicals, anti-war Democrats, reporters, photographers, and passers-by alike. As taped scenes of the bloody encounter appeared on television screens inside the amphitheatre, many delegates were horrified. "Gestapo tactics in the streets of Chicago!" cried Connecticut's Senator Abraham Ribicoff, who was on the podium; and when Mayor Daley and members of the Illinois delegation started shaking their fists, Ribicoff exclaimed: "How hard it is to accept the truth!" Cried a Wisconsin delegate: "Thousands of young people are being beaten on the streets of Chicago! I move this convention be adjourned for two weeks and moved to another city."[6]

The convention did not adjourn, but "Bloody Wednesday," as it was called, cast a pall over the rest of its proceedings and strongly dampened Humphrey's joy at receiving the party's nomination. Thursday night Daley filled the galleries with his supporters; and after a memorial film about Robert Kennedy was shown, they began chanting, "We love Mayor Daley!" In response, delegates on the convention floor started singing, "The Battle Hymn of the Republic." When Humphrey finally got around to his acceptance address, he expressed regret for what was going on in the city and promised to seek an end to the war in Vietnam. But about the time he was speaking, police were storming McCarthy's headquarters in the Conrad Hilton Hotel and beating up innocent people there. The "police riot," as a subsequent investigation termed it, hurt Humphrey's cause badly. "My wife and I went home heartbroken, battered and beaten," he said later on. "I told her I felt just like we had been in a shipwreck."[7]

Many Americans sympathized with the police. In a poll taken shortly after the Democratic convention, most blue-collar workers approved the way the Chicago police had handled the protesters; some of them, in fact, thought the police were "not tough enough" on them. Young people, in short, weren't the only angry Americans in 1968. What was called "Middle America" was angry too, particularly at permissive attitudes toward rambunctious young people. "It's beatniks," explained columnist James Reston. "It's hippies. It's draft card burners. It's demonstrators. It's blacks. It's high taxation. It's easy sex and dope and kids running away from home. It's uncertainty, fear, madness, murder—all these appearing day after day on the television and in the newspapers, adding up to a feeling that something is deeply wrong and must be changed."[8] There was a surge in Middle America toward Nixon and law and order.

The campaign began with Nixon far ahead of Humphrey in the polls and possessing everything that Humphrey lacked: a united party, an efficient campaign staff, careful scheduling, plenty of money, and the support of most newspapers. Confident of victory, Nixon played it cool: campaigned for the most part only in the crucial states, conserved his energy for major appearances, staged question-and-answer sessions on television in which he appeared wise, statesmanlike, and above-the-strife, skillfully turned down Humphrey's challenge to debate on TV, and spoke mainly in generalities about Vietnam and other issues. He assured voters that "new leadership will end the war" honorably, but refrained from specifics on the ground that he didn't want to jeopardize the negotiations in Paris.

Nixon made much of the law-and-order issue. He promised as President he would do something about rising crime rates, unsafe streets, and noisy demonstrations. He would, he said, "restore order and respect for law in this country."[9] Spiro Agnew was for a time a bit of a problem. While Nixon was trying to impress voters with the high level on which he was operating, Agnew was making one bad slip after another. He said Humphrey was "squishy soft on communism" and then apologized when Republican leaders in Congress came to Humphrey's defense. He called a Nisei reporter a "fat Jap", spoke of "Polacks," remarked that "if you've seen one city slum you've seen them all," and then had to issue more apologies, retractions, and explanations. "APOLOGIZE NOW, SPIRO," advised a big placard at one of his rallies. "IT WILL SAVE TIME LATER."[10]

George Wallace was a bigger problem for Nixon, however, than Agnew, who eventually learned to curb his tongue. Former Governor of Alabama, Wallace ran for President on the American Independence party ticket and posed a threat to Nixon in the South. On two issues he competed with Nixon for votes: integration and law and order. Wallace denounced the Supreme Court's 1954 decision outlawing racial segregation in the nation's public schools. Nixon accepted the decision, but objected to measures taken by the Johnson administration to encourage integration. On law and order, the two saw pretty much eye to eye, though Wallace spoke more crudely about it. "I was the first one to speak out on law and order," he complained at one point. "Now they usin' our phrase."[11] Nixon didn't think Wallace had a patent on it.

Wallace competed with Humphrey as well as Nixon. Campaigning in Northern industrial cities, he threatened to deprive the Minnesotan of the votes of blue-collar workers, normally Democratic, who were fed up with the noisy marches and demonstrations and vehement anti-American language of dissident white intellectuals, New Left college students, and militant blacks protesting the Vietnam War, racism, and poverty in the nation. Wallace delighted audiences in both North and South with sneers at "pointy-headed intellectuals," beatniks, the Supreme Court, school busing, liberals, and bureaucrats. He didn't expect to win the election, but hoped to win control of enough presidential electors to ensure that his policies "have some representation in the attitude of the new administration." [12] Wallace did very well at first and had both Republicans and Democrats worried about his raids on votes they were counting on. Then he began going downhill, partly because Northern labor began rallying to Humphrey's cause, and partly because his running mate, Air Force General Curtis LeMay ("Old Ironpants") began out-Agnewing Agnew when it came to outlandish remarks. In a press conference in Pittsburgh Wallace tried repeatedly to shut LeMay up as he rambled on blithely about using nuclear weapons in Vietnam and elsewhere whenever necessary. Afterward, someone told LeMay: "Keep yo' bowels open, and yo' mouth shut." [13]

Humphrey's campaign was in shambles at first: no money, no organization (until Lawrence O'Brien became chairman of the Democratic national committee), no campaign schedule, and a lag of eight to ten percentage points behind Nixon in the polls. Wherever the Vice-President went, moreover, he was tormented by hecklers, who associated him with LBJ's Vietnam policy and left Nixon for the most part alone. "He is stunned," noted one reporter, "standing there in mid-platform, to hear himself called a warmonger, a murderer and even . . . a racist, to see himself depicted on posters as an American Adolph Hitler. He tries reason and humor, eloquence and tough talk, gentle, paternal chiding and hard-eyed ridicule, but none of it works. They stand in the second-deck galleries, singly and in clusters and now in full groups, and scream, 'Stop the war! Stop the war!' and then, 'Dump the Hump, dump the Hump!' " At times Humphrey was reduced to tears as boos, chants, taunts, bullhorns, and obscenities drowned him out. "Why me?" he wailed at times. "What about Nixon?" [14] Like Humphrey's hecklers, Nixon of course made much of Humphrey's identification with the unpopular Johnson administration. "There's not a dime's worth of difference," he told audiences, "between the policies Hubert Humphrey offers America and the policies America has had for the last four years." [15] The New Leftists agreed.

It was not until Humphrey began asserting his independence of LBJ that his campaign started picking up steam. On September 25 he said that if he thought a bomb halt would de-escalate the war in Vietnam he would recommend it, and added: "The President has not made me his slave and I am not his humble servant." At Salt Lake City on September 30 he went even further. In a nationwide telecast which his backers managed to scrape up enough money to sponsor, he announced: "As President, I would stop the bombing of the North as an acceptable risk for peace because I believe it could lead to success in the negotiations and thereby shorten the war." [16] LBJ was insisting on a show of good faith by North Vietnam as a condition for a bombing halt; Humphrey proposed stopping the bombing first, hoping for a gesture of good faith and reserving the right to resume the bombing if it didn't come. The difference may have been slight but it was enough. Though Nixon charged that Humphrey's statement endangered prospects for a settlement in Paris (which chief U. S. negotiator Averell Harriman promptly denied), the reaction among anti-war Democrats was overwhelmingly favorable. Senator Edward Kennedy of Massachusetts sent a wire of congratulations, nineteen liberal Democrats in the House of Representatives announced they would support him, the national board of the Americans for Democratic Action voted to back him, and the *New York Times* endorsed him because he "has shown unmistakable signals that he intends, if elected, to move away from the errors of the past." [17] Even more: money began flowing into his campaign coffers and heckling declined precipitously. When he was in Nashville, young people carried signs saying: "Humphrey, if you mean it, we're with you." And in Detroit one big sign proclaimed: "HECKLERS FOR HUMPHREY—WE CAME BACK." [18]

After the Salt Lake City speech, Humphrey was like a new man; but it was really the old ebullient and energetic Humphrey finally getting on top of things at long last. He began tearing into Wallace for his appeal to racism, prejudice, and intolerance, reminded working people that Wallace's Alabama was a low-wage and anti-union state, and called Wallace and LeMay the "bombsy twins." He also began calling Nixon "Richard the Silent" and "Richard the Chickenhearted," for avoiding a frank discussion of the issues and refusing to debate him. "Give 'em hell!" cried one happy worker in Minneapolis. "What do you think I'm doing?" Humphrey shot back gleefully. [19] Organized labor finally went into action on his behalf. The major unions not only formally endorsed him; they also sponsored pro-Humphrey pamphlets, speeches, and door-to-door campaigning in Northern cities to persuade workers that a vote for Wallace was a vote for Nixon and that a vote for either of them was really an anti-labor vote. On the defensive for the first time, Nixon began hitting back with the law-and-order theme. "Hubert Humphrey," he cried, "defends the policies under which we have seen crime rising ten times as fast as the population. If you want your President to continue with the do-nothing policy toward crime, vote for Humphrey. If you want to fight crime, vote for Nixon." [20]

As election day approached Humphrey was rapidly becoming the "peace" candidate; even McCarthy finally endorsed him. He was also steadily gaining on Nixon in the polls. LBJ, moreover, was pressing hard for some kind of agreement in Paris that would enable him to halt the bombings in Vietnam and give Humphrey a major boost. By the middle of October he seemed to be getting close to his goal and, in foreign-policy briefings to all three candidates, mentioned a possible breakthrough in the Paris talks. On October 25, Nixon suddenly issued a remarkable statement. "In the last thirty-six hours," he declared, "I have been advised of a flurry of meetings in the White House and elsewhere on Vietnam. I am told that top officials in the Administration have been driving very hard for an agreement on a bombing halt, accompanied possibly by a cease-fire in the immediate future. I since learned that these reports are true. I am also told that this spurt of activity is a cynical, last-minute attempt by President Johnson to salvage the candidacy of Mr. Humphrey. This I do not believe." LBJ angrily accused Nixon of making "ugly and unfair" statements. But on October 31 he went on the air to announce that he had ordered a halt in the bombing of North Vietnam. "I have reached this decision," he said, "on the basis of developments in the Paris talks, and I have reached it in the belief that this action will lead to progress for a peaceful settlement of the Vietnam War."[21] Humphrey was elated. "I have been hoping for months that it would happen," he cried. "For months."[22]

The bombing halt probably helped Humphrey some, but came too late to carry him to victory. On November 5, more than 73 million people went to the polls and chose Richard Nixon as their next President. The popular vote was close: Nixon beat Humphrey by only 517,777 votes—31,783,783 (43.3 percent) to 31,266,006 (42.7 percent). In the Electoral College, however, the results were more decisive: Nixon carried 32 states with 302 electoral votes (he lost one, however, when a North Carolina elector cast his vote for Wallace), while Humphrey took only 14 states with 191 votes. Wallace did extremely well for a third-party candidate: 9,906,473 popular votes and 5 states with 45 electoral votes (plus one from North Carolina). The Republicans gained a few seats in Congress but the Democrats retained their control of both houses. Nixon was the first President in 120 years to begin his Presidency with the opposition party controlling both chambers.

"I saw many signs in this campaign," said Nixon in his victory statement. "Some of them were not friendly and some were very friendly. But the one that touched me the most was one that I saw in Deshler, Ohio, at the end of a long day of whistle-stopping—a little town, I suppose five times the population was there in the dusk—but a teen-ager held up a sign, 'Bring us Together.' And that will be the great objective of this administration at the outset, to bring the American people together. This will be an open administration, open to new ideas, open to men and women of both parties, open to the critics as well as those who support us. We want to bridge the generation gap. We want to bridge the gap between races. We want to bring America together. . . ."[23]

☆   ☆   ☆

Resurrection

After the New Hampshire primary on March 12, someone told Eugene McCarthy that three dead men had been voted in the third ward of

Manchester. "They were ours," quipped the witty Catholic Senator; "it was the Resurrection. They came back from the grave for this."[24]

A Little Yeats

McCarthy was speaking in Waukesha, Wisconsin, when the news came that LBJ was bowing out of the race. "He's not running!" someone in the crowd started yelling; "he's not running!" Reporters leaped on the stage to question McCarthy about it and he later said it was "like Orestes being smothered by the Eumenides." When he got back to his hotel he told his youthful supporters: "Come on, kids—relax." And as TV correspondents clamored outside the door for an interview he said calmly: "Just tell the TV stations to put on a little music until I get there. Or maybe they should read a little poetry. This is a night for reading poetry—maybe a little Yeats."[25]

Hubert the Happy

Irked by the loquacious Humphrey's call for "the politics of happiness and joy" when he threw his hat into the ring on April 27, New York writer Marya Mannes indicted some cruel lines:

> Hubert the Happy
> Goes yackety, yackety
> Yackety, yackety, yack,
> If anyone tells him for God's sake to knock it,
> He cheerfully yacketys back.
>
> If he stopped yacking, he couldn't go anywhere,
> Poor little Hubert, he couldn't go anywhere—
> That's why he always goes
> Hoppity, yackety
> Hoppity,
> Yackety
> Yack.[26]

Pledged

By 1968 all the TV networks had large research staffs busily at work ascertaining the loyalties of delegates to the national conventions so they could forecast presidential nominations. At the Republican convention a Reagan backer tried to switch a Nixon backer to Ronald Reagan. "But I can't switch," cried the delegate. "I'm already pledged." "To whom?" "I told CBS that I'm voting for Nixon. I'm pledged to CBS."[27]

Spiro Who?

When Nixon announced that Agnew was his choice for second place, there were headlines: "Spiro Agnew—Who's He?" The name, said one wag, rhymes with either "hero" or "zero." "I'm from Maryland," snorted one Nixon aide, "and even I have trouble remembering his name." But Nixon insisted: "This guy's got it." Said *Newsweek:* "Whatever that was remained something of a mystery . . . and would be revealed only in the months of campaigning ahead." In downtown Atlanta a reporter told pedestrians: "I'm going to mention two words to you. You tell me what they mean. The words are: Spiro Agnew." One man: "It's some kind of disease." Another: "It's some kind of egg." A third: "He's a Greek who owns that ship-building firm." Agnew himself was candid about it. "Spiro Agnew," he acknowledged, "is not a household word."[28]

The Compleat Delegate

In an item on "The Compleat Delegate," *Time* gave detailed instructions on what delegates should take with them to the Democratic convention in Chicago in August. "Embarking for the Balaklava of the Chicago stockyards," advised *Time,* "the foresighted Democratic delegate would ideally—and intelligently—go equipped with goggles (to protect the eyes from tear gas and Mace), cyclist's crash helmet (from billy clubs, bricks, etc.), flak jacket (from snipers), Vaseline (from Mace), Mace (from rioters), washcloth (from tear gas), bug bomb (to kill the flies that infect the amphitheatre from nearby stockyard dunghills), folding bicycle (there is a cab strike), roller skates (carpet tacks scattered on the streets by the demonstrators may de-commission the bike), wire cutters (in case delegate is trapped inside the amphitheatre, or outside because of pickpocketed credentials), all-purpose bail-bond credit card (if arrested), air mattress (in event of prolonged incarceration or inability to return to hotel because of transportation problems), bottled water (should yippies manage to turn on the Chicago water supply with a lacing of LSD or other hallucinogens), canned rations (one rumor has suggested that food in the hostelries where delegates are staying would be garnished with ground glass), ham radio (no phone service), walkie-talkie (if radio fails), chrysanthemums (for flower power if cornered by militant hippies), first-aid kit, gross of aspirins, and, finally, a *passe-partout,* collectively endorsed by A.D.A., Y.I.P., the Geneva Conference, Mayor Daley, the Black Panthers, and Interpol, certifying that the bearer is an accredited seeker of peace, racial harmony, revolution, law and order and legalized pot."[29]

Sheriff

Nixon, Humphrey, and Wallace all stressed the law-and-order issue so much in the campaign that San Francisco Mayor Joseph Alioto finally concluded: "None of the candidates is running for President. They're all running for sheriff."[30]

Trick and Treat

After LBJ announced a bombing halt on October 31, one reporter wrote: "President Johnson gave Richard M. Nixon a trick and Vice-President Humphrey a treat for Halloween. . . ."[31]

Hecklers

1968 was the year of the hecklers. Humphrey was main target though Wallace attracted catcalls too. Sometimes Humphrey was unable to go on speaking; other times he stayed in control. Once, when booed, he announced that "boo" meant "I'm for you" in the Sioux language, but added that "somehow I don't sense it that way today." Wallace enjoyed sassing back: "Get a haircut!"; "Watch out—We may convert you." Sometimes he even blew kisses toward hecklers and cried: "They got me a million votes!" He even pretended to enjoy heckling. "It's real difficult for me to speak to an orderly crowd," he once announced. "It really throws me, if you want to know the truth." But reverse heckling—satirical cries of "Kill commies!" and "Kill for peace!"—left him dumbfounded.

Muskie perhaps did the best with hecklers. When he spoke in Washington, Pennsylvania, about thirty anti-war college students made so much noise that he finally said, "I'll tell you what. I'll make a bargain with you." And he invited the ring-leader, the long-haired, sandaled Richard Brody, up to the platform to speak for ten minutes. People in the crowd were hostile, but Muskie persuaded them to give the lad a hearing. Cried Brody, when it was quiet, "You guys say we are dirty and unwashed. We are the true Americans. . . . We want America to stand for what the Constitution stands for, which is everyone is equal under the law. . . . The reason I am out here in the streets is because no one listened to us in Chicago. . . . You are going to hear a lot of stuff, a lot of platitudes, about apple pie, and motherhood. That's fine. But does it bring any sort of qualitative change?" When Muskie returned to the microphone, he admitted there were shortcomings in the American political system and praised young people for "jogging our institutions." Afterwards several youngsters clustered around him to ask questions and shake hands. "If they would do this more often," Brody said, "there wouldn't be all the really radical protests."[32]

Bombs Away

When his plane was en route to Hawaii, Agnew walked down the aisle, saw Gene Oishi, a Japanese-American reporter, taking a nap, and cried, "What's wrong with that fat Jap?" Later he apologized. But on the return flight, when the pilot announced over the loudspeaker, "And to your right you can see Pearl Harbor below," Oishi leaned forward and shouted into the ear of an Agnew staff man: "Bombs away!"[33]

Mrs. Chennault

When Johnson announced a halt to the bombing in Vietnam a few days before the election, Democratic hopes for victory soared. But when South Vietnam President Nguyen Van Thieu announced his government would not participate in the peace talks Johnson was proposing, it was clear there would be no settlement before election day after all. Robert Finch, a Nixon aide, told reporters that Johnson should not have announced a breakthrough on peace talks until "he had gotten all his ducks in a row." Finch's remark infuriated Johnson and he called Nixon to protest. "Who's this guy Fink?" he grumbled. "Why is he taking after me?" "Mr. President," said Nixon, "that's Finch, not Fink." But Johnson persisted in calling him Fink.

Some people thought Mrs. Anna Chennault, Chinese-born widow of wartime hero General Claire Chennault, played some part in Thieu's stand. An American citizen since 1950 and a strong Nixon backer, Mrs. Chennault was in close touch with South Vietnamese officials (as Johnson well knew since he had her telephone calls tapped) and was trying to convince them they would get a better break with Nixon as President. Eleven South Vietnamese officials even publicly announced their support for Nixon in the final days of the campaign.

When Nixon and his staff heard about Mrs. Chennault's activities they were dismayed. They knew if voters got the impression that the Republicans were trying to sabotage peace efforts for political reasons the reaction would be violent. For several days they were on pins and needles as they waited to see whether Humphrey would raise the issue. But when Humphrey learned what Mrs. Chennault was up to, he decided to do nothing, though some of his advisers wanted him to. He was convinced Nixon personally had nothing to do with Mrs. Chennault; he also thought bringing her behind-the-scenes activities into the campaign would wreck the effort to get Saigon to the peace table and make it impossible for Nixon, if elected, to govern.

After the election one Nixon aide concluded that the idea of a plot between Nixon and Mrs. Chennault had been too preposterous for Humphrey to accept. "Thieu and Ky were Mrs. Chennault's friends," he said, "but to suggest she alone could change Saigon policy was ridiculous. Theirs was a gut reaction. They resented the halt. They felt that Johnson was using them. They were aware how important what they were doing was politically. These fellows aren't fools." In the end neither Johnson nor Humphrey aired the story.[34]

More Fun

With victory assured, Nixon appeared in the ballroom of the Waldorf-Astoria to tell his supporters: "Having lost a close one eight years ago and having won a close one this year, I can say this—winning's a lot more fun."[35]

Nixon and the Press

Nixon's relations with the press tended to be strained, but his staff worked hard during the campaign to preserve correct though cool relations with reporters. Right after his victory, his aide John Ehrlichman gathered about twenty campaign workers together to congratulate them on their good public relations. Cried one of them, "Why don't we all get a member of the press and beat them up?"[36]

CHAPTER FORTY-SEVEN

★ ★

1972
Another Nixon Triumph

For the Republicans 1972 was what 1964 had been for the Democrats: a spectacular triumph. In his bid for re-election Richard M. Nixon reduced his challenger, Senator George S. McGovern of South Dakota, to mincemeat. Nixon regarded the 1972 contest as "probably the clearest choice between the candidates for President ever presented to the American people in the twentieth century." But he was swept by melancholy the night of victory. "To some extent the marring effects of Watergate may have played a part," he reflected, "to some extent our failure to win Congress, and to a greater extent the fact that we had not yet been able to end the war in Vietnam."[1]

Nixon was not the sanguineous type. In 1971 he was gloomy about things. His party had done poorly in the 1970 elections, the Vietnam War continued to drain the nation's energies and resources, anti-war demonstrations continued unabated, and his standing in the polls was not high. It "seemed possible," he recalled some years later, "that I might not even be nominated for re-election in 1972."[2] He knew that only a minority of the voters regarded themselves as Republicans and that a strong Democratic candidate might be unbeatable. He listed the possibilities: Edward M. ("Ted") Kennedy, Edmund G. Muskie, Hubert Humphrey.

By the spring of 1972 the possible became improbable. One by one, the candidates Nixon feared most dropped out of the running. Kennedy was the first to go. With a magic name and the kind of charm his older brothers had possessed, Kennedy long led Muskie and Humphrey in the polls. Then, one night in July 1969, Kennedy's automobile ran off a bridge in Chappaquiddick, Massachusetts, leading to the death of a young woman in the car, and his evasive behavior afterward evoked strong criticism. Chappaquiddick cast a blight on his political future and in January 1971 he announced he would not be a candidate. Muskie was the next to drop out. A splendid campaigner as Humphrey's running mate in 1968, he made a disappointing showing in the primaries in the spring of 1972 and ceased to be a viable candidate. That left Humphrey. The energetic Minnesotan worked hard for the Democratic nomination, but his poor showing in the California primary on June 6 killed his chance to run again. Meanwhile, George Wallace, a real threat to Nixon votes in the South if he ran again, was shot by a would-be assassin in a Maryland shopping center on May 15 and paralyzed from the waist down, and he withdrew from the campaign. That left George McGovern, who had entered the race in January 1971. Nixon's spirits rose; he regarded the South Dakota Senator as the weakest of all the Democratic challengers.

McGovern was a dark horse. Few people had heard of him when he first announced his candidacy and fewer still took him seriously as a presidential possibility. A former history professor who served as a minor official in the Kennedy administration and then entered the Senate in 1962, McGovern gradually emerged after 1971 as the leading spokesman for a variety of protest groups: anti-war activists, idealistic young people, black civil-rights workers, women's-rights advocates, and social-justice seekers. McGovern's main issue, though, was the Vietnam War, which since 1963 he had regarded as a "dreadful mistake." He made it clear from the outset that if he became President his first action would be to bring the boys home.

In seeking the nomination McGovern benefited from the reforms his party had adopted after the stormy convention of 1968. The new rules for selecting delegates (which McGovern himself helped frame) provided for greater representation of women, young people, and blacks, and drastically reduced the power of city bosses, union leaders, and professional politicians at Democratic conventions. They also produced an increase in the number of states holding primaries to select delegates to the national convention and to register presidential preferences. McGovern's strategy was to do well in the primaries, achieve the nomination with the help of his anti-war constituency, and then persuade party regulars to work for his election. He never really achieved his last objective.

McGovern arrived in Miami Beach, Florida, where his party's convention opened on July 10, with a majority of the delegates pledged to him and was nominated for President on the first ballot. But the convention's proceedings, telecast to the nation, irked party professionals and offended respectable people in every part of the country. Movie star Shirley MacLaine gleefully described her California delegation as looking like "a couple of high schools, a grape boycott, a Black Panther rally, and four or five politicians who walked in the wrong door."[3] Precisely. Televiewers got the impression that McGovern was the candidate of hippies, aggressive women, smart-aleck collegians, and militant blacks; they were also shocked to hear some of the delegates espouse homosexual rights, abortion, and amnesty for deserters. "I think we lost the election at Miami . . . ," lamented Congressman James O'Hara afterward. "The American people made an association between McGovern and gay liberation, and welfare rights and pot-smoking and black militants, and women's lib, and wise college kids."[4] McGovern's nominating convention was not really as far-out as some people thought. It did, to be sure, have more young people, blacks, and women than any previous party convention; and professionals (like Mayor Richard Daley) were conspicuous by their absence. Yet the delegates were for the most part earnest, dedicated, and hard-working and rejected the more extravagant demands offered for their consideration. They were also probably better behaved than delegates at most conventions and missed the rowdy fun that usually goes with such events.

But the platform the McGovernites approved went too far for many Democrats. Not only did it call for the immediate withdrawal of U. S. troops from Vietnam; it also favored amnesty for those who had refused to enter the service (once American troops and prisoners of war were safely home). In addition, it favored busing to achieve racial integration in the public schools, abolishing capital punishment, banning the sale of handguns, and, in the plank perhaps most outrageous to many people, announced: "Americans should be free to make their own choices of lifestyles and private habits without being subject to discrimination or prosecution."[5] McGovern's views were more moderate than those of many of the delegates supporting him and he made this clear in his acceptance address. But he didn't get around to delivering it until 3:00 a.m. and thus missed prime time on television. One reason for the delay was that the delegates, who had worked hard, decided to let off a little steam when it came to the vice-presidential nomination. They put up thirty-nine names, including Archie Bunker and Mao Zedong, though McGovern's choice, Senator Thomas Eagleton of Missouri, won easily on the first ballot.

Eagleton seemed an excellent choice for second place: an urban Catholic liberal, with strong labor backing, from a border state. Then came the upsetting news that he had experienced severe mental depression on several occasions in the past requiring hospitalization and electric-shock treatment. McGovern wanted to keep him on the ticket; he said he backed him "1000 per cent." But heavy pressure from his senior staff, party pros, and editorial writers in the nation's leading newspapers led him to do an about-face and ask Eagleton to resign. Then, after a frantic search, he turned to R. Sargent Shriver, former Peace Corps director and ambassador to France, who gladly agreed to take Eagleton's place. The Eagleton crisis hurt McGovern badly. Some of his supporters thought he should have stood firm; after all, Abraham Lincoln, they pointed out, had suffered from spells of deep depression without being incapacitated for high office. Others were contemptuous of McGovern for having wavered during the crisis. His behavior, said the *St. Louis Globe Democrat* sternly, "laid bare a lack of public honesty and political guts; it showed him as a blatant opportunist, who would dump his own choice for running mate in the interest of bald expediency."[6] But Eagleton's lack of candor about his background and his unwillingness to take the initiative in resigning put McGovern on the horns of a dilemma. He was damned if he did and damned if he didn't.

All of this was duck soup for Nixon and the Republicans. Nixon observed the Eagleton crisis and the split between McGovernites and regulars in the Democratic party with mounting confidence in his ability to win by a landslide. He planned to present himself to the voters in 1972 as an expert in foreign affairs and even as something of a peace candidate. The Vietnam War continued to drag on, despite his promises in 1968 to bring it to an end, but he had defused it as a major issue by bringing thousands of American troops home and turning more and more of the war effort over to the South Vietnamese themselves. In February, moreover, he had made headlines all over the world when he flew to Peking, hobnobbed with Communist leaders there, and took the first steps toward establishing relations between China and the United States (which he had once fiercely opposed). In May, furthermore, he had flown to Moscow, the first President to do so, and made a series of agreements with Russian leaders for expanding trade between the U. S. and the U. S. S. R., increasing cultural exchanges, and launching strategic arms-limitations talks (SALT). How all of this squared with the reason given for American intervention in Vietnam—to "contain" Chinese and Russian communism—it was hard to say. Nixon himself saw no contradiction in his policies.

Nixon's renomination by his party in Miami Beach late in August was practically a "coronation" and Spiro Agnew also received second place again without any difficulty. The Republican platform charged that the Democratic party "had been seized by a radical clique which scorns our nation's past and would blight our future" and Nixon himself seems to have believed this. He regarded McGovern as an extreme leftist and authorized the Committee to Re-Elect the President (CRP, or, CREEP, as McGovernites called it), an organization set up independently of the Republican national committee to seek funds and votes, to do whatever was necessary to discredit the Democratic candidate. McGovern was, in fact, clearly in the New Deal tradition and something of a "prairie populist" too. In one crucial respect, however, he did depart from tradition. Though he had served as a bomber pilot during World War II, supported the United Nations, and favored economic aid to the needy nations of the world, he seems to have been a sincere old-fashioned noninterventionist when it came to military policy. In accepting his party's nomination he asked the American people to "turn away from excessive preoccupation overseas to rebuilding our own nation" and reiterated the words, "come home, America," throughout his speech.[7] Nixon, by contrast, shared the view of Franklin Roosevelt and all the other Presidents since World War II: that the United States, with its vast wealth and power, bore major responsibility for the ordering of world affairs. Like FDR, Nixon insisted on the necessity for America's world leadership; he was convinced, too, that McGovern's apparent indifference to national aggrandizement would hurt him with voters who were anxious for the United States to be "number one." In his own acceptance speech he called for a "new majority" which would, among other things, sustain the "progress we have made in building a new structure of peace in the world."[8] During the campaign he and his supporters issued dire warnings about McGovern's "isolationism."

Nixon had an easy campaign. He remained mostly out of the battle, nourishing his image as a bold world leader and utilizing people on his staff, Congressmen, and cabinet members as "presidential surrogates" to push his cause. He called it "the most restrained campaign of his career."[9] Not until late in the campaign did he emerge from the White House to attack busing and permissiveness and criticize McGovern's foreign policy as dangerous to American security. His campaign organization was superb compared with McGovern's hastily improvised structure, and CRP had more money to spend than any party in American history. Nixon wasn't out merely to win; like LBJ in 1964, he wanted a landslide. For that reason, CRP, which concentrated on independent voters and anti-McGovern Democrats, focused its efforts on getting votes for the President and did little or nothing for other Republican candidates that year. Nixon's managers never succeeded in evoking much affection for their boss, but did manage to elicit considerable respect for him. They convinced people he was no longer "Tricky Dick," but a wise, self-assured, far-seeing, and courageous world leader who had brought great prestige to the United States.

Nixon's supporters portrayed McGovern as fuzzy-minded, impractical, and indecisive and the Democratic campaign was so poorly run that they succeeded in convincing many people this was so. The polls were cruel to McGovern throughout. In every age group, in every part of the country (especially among white voters in the South), at every educational level, among both Protestants and Catholics, and among women as well as men, Nixon stayed far ahead from the beginning to the end of the campaign. Even big labor deserted the Democrats. Though some unions endorsed McGovern, the AFL-CIO for the first time in years remained neutral; and AFL-CIO head George Meany said McGovern was not "good material" and charged that a "small elite of suburban types and students took over the apparatus of the Democratic party."[10]

Lyndon Johnson, Richard Daley, and other party leaders endorsed McGovern, but Democratic regulars for the most part sat on their hands during the campaign. But just to be sure the Republicans had things sewed up, Nixon announced his intention to end the draft and shift to a volunteer army in the near future and promised there would be no tax increases if he were given four more years in office. "We're really running scared," said one White House aide, "for about an inch." [11] "We aren't conceding anything," quipped Republican national committee chairman Robert Dole. "We aren't saying we'll win all 50 states, but we aren't conceding anything." [12] Sighed a dispirited McGovern staffer: "I'm not hoping for victory any more. I just hope we can avoid a debacle." [13]

But a debacle it was for the Democrats. On November 7, some 78 million Americans voted to give Nixon a huge popular plurality: close to 18,000,000 votes. Not only did the President win re-election by 60.7 percent (47,165,234) of the popular votes; he also carried forty-nine states with 521 electoral votes (though one Virginia elector withheld his vote from Nixon). McGovern ended up with only 37.5 percent (29,170,774) of the popular votes and carried only Massachusetts and the District of Columbia with seventeen electoral votes. In popular votes Nixon came close to the records set by FDR in 1936 (60.8 percent) and LBJ in 1964 (61.1 percent); electorally he was second only to FDR, who carried all but two states with eight electoral votes in 1936. McGovern had been identified with young people during the campaign, but on election day they gave him little help. Fewer than half of the 18-to-20-year-olds (enfranchised by the 26th Amendment, ratified in 1972) took the trouble to vote; and those who did split about evenly between the two candidates. The Democrats, however, remained in control of Congress.

Nixon interpreted his victory as an endorsement of his domestic and foreign policies and at his inaugural on January 20, 1973, promised even greater things for the future. Then his administration began to disintegrate. In October 1973, Vice-President Agnew, charged with income-tax evasion, was forced to resign; and, under the provisions of the 25th Amendment, Nixon picked Congressman Gerald R. Ford of Michigan as his replacement and Congress approved the choice. Then other members of his administration began facing charges connected with the break-in of the Democratic national headquarters in the Watergate complex in Washington on June 17, 1972. During the campaign McGovern and his supporters had tried to make the Watergate break-in, sponsored by CRP, a major campaign issue, but failed to rouse much interest. "Most people," McGovern discovered, "took the view that there was nothing exceptional about the Watergate incident except that the perpetrators were caught." [14] In 1973 and 1974, however, the efforts of grand juries, investigative reporters, and Congressional committees looking into the Watergate incident gradually unraveled an unsavory tale of intimidation, forgery, sabotage, bribery, and perjury running into the White House itself. In the end twenty members of Nixon's administration were convicted of various crimes related to the Watergate break-in and Nixon himself, facing impeachment by the House of Representatives, resigned as President on August 8, 1974. Gerald Ford, who stepped into his shoes, became the first Chief Executive who had not been elected either as President or as Vice-President. It was a strange sequel to a lustrous landslide.

☆　☆　☆

Acid, Abortion, Amnesty

McGovern didn't advocate legalizing marijuana; he favored decriminalizing its use and reducing punishment from imprisonment to a fine. Nor did he believe in abortion on demand; he simply took the position that the federal government should not interfere with existing state laws. Amnesty, moreover, was to come only with the end of the Vietnam War and then he wanted draft resisters given a blanket amnesty and deserters evaluated on a case-by-case basis. But his enemies called him "the candidate of the three A's: acid, abortion, amnesty" (or "grass, ass, and amnesty") and the charge hurt him with many people.

When McGovern campaigned in the Nebraska primary, Governor Frank Morrison tried to set the record straight for him. Introducing McGovern at a meeting held in a large Catholic high school in Omaha, he declared: "We have in our state tonight one of the finest young men in America. He is a great patriot, a highly decorated war hero who loves his country and wants to serve us as President. But he has been subjected to a vicious campaign of smears and innuendo." Then he got to the point: "They say that George McGovern is for the legalization of marijuana, but I say—" At this point there was a thunder of applause from the younger people in the audience which left Morrison puzzled, but when it died down, he ended his sentence, "I tell you that George McGovern does not advocate the legalization of marijuana." This produced cries of disappointment in the audience. Then Morrison continued: "They say George McGovern is for abortion on demand, but I tell you—" Again there was deafening applause, followed by sighs of regret when he finished the sentence: "But I say to you that George McGovern is *against* tampering with our state laws on abortion." And so it went. "George," said Morrison after the rally, "maybe I'm too old to understand this new generation. I'll get the oldsters for you, and you take care of the young ones as you think best." In the end McGovern won in the Nebraska primary.[15]

Eve and Adam

At one of the sessions of the Women's Caucus at the Democratic convention, Liz Carpenter, former press secretary for Lady Bird Johnson, introduced McGovern with the compliment, "We are all here because

of him." "The credit," said McGovern facetiously, "should go to Adam."
This produced hisses, so he pleaded, "Can I recover by saying Adam
and Eve?" Shouted one delegate, "Make it Eve and Adam!"[16]

What About Theirs?

Though most Democratic leaders pressed McGovern to drop Eagleton
because he had been treated for mental illness, a few McGovernites took
the issue lightly. "At least we know ours had treatment," said Georgia's
Julian Bond. "What about theirs?"[17]

Replacement

McGovern had so much trouble finding a replacement for Eagleton that
Senator Phil Hart of Michigan finally asked him: "Does the law require
that you have a Vice-President?" In the Senate the joke circulated that
he had posted a sign in the cloakroom: "Anybody willing to serve as my
vice-presidential candidate please call the following number." When
Sargent Shriver finally got the nod, he announced gamely: "I am not
embarrassed to be George McGovern's seventh choice for Vice President. We Democrats may be short of money but we're not short of talent. Pity Mr. Nixon—his first and only choice was Spiro Agnew." During the campaign, Shriver, a Kennedy-in-law, liked to tell audiences how
he tried to get his children to study harder by saying, "When Abraham
Lincoln was your age, he walked twelve miles back and forth to school
every day." "That's nothing," he reported one of his boys as retorting,
"When Uncle Jack was your age, he was President of the United States!"[18]

Best Line

When McGovern appeared in Battle Creek, Michigan, a young man
wearing a Nixon button heckled him so much that he finally leaned over
and whispered in his ear, "Listen, you son of a bitch, why don't you kiss
my ass?" Afterward a reporter asked the heckler what McGovern had
said and when he was told, he gleefully spread the words around. KMA
buttons soon began appearing in crowds at McGovern rallies. Several
years later Senator James Eastland of Mississippi, no McGovern-lover,
said, "George, I've wanted to ask you for a long time—did you really
tell that guy in '72 to kiss your ass?" When McGovern smiled and nodded, Eastland cried: "That was the best line in the campaign!"[19]

Sweeps D.C.

On election day Nixon's associates were so sure of victory that they tried
to guess how newspapers hostile to the President would handle his

triumph. Press secretary Ronald Ziegler's favorite suggestion was a *Washington Post* headline: "McGOVERN SWEEPS D.C.," with the sub-head, "Nixon Carries Nation."[20]

Worst Possible Way

When McGovern spoke to the Gridiron Club in Washington after his calamitous defeat, he told the journalists: "Last year we opened the doors of the Democratic party, as we promised we would, and twenty million Democrats stalked out." He added: "For years, I wanted to run for President in the worst possible way—and I'm sure I did!"[21]

★ ★

CHAPTER FORTY-EIGHT

1976
The Triumph of an Outsider:
Jimmy Carter

In 1976, the bicentennial year, the choice was between an "outsider" and an "insider." The outsider was James Earle Carter, or Jimmy Carter, as he insisted on being called. The insider was Gerald R. ("Jerry") Ford, who became President upon Nixon's resignation in August 1974.

Carter, fifty-two, was far out: a former peanut farmer, naval officer, and one-term Governor of Georgia with no experience in Washington. He was, in fact, so obscure when he entered the presidential race in December 1974 that people asked: "Jimmy who?" Even his mother was puzzled. When he told her he was running for President, she asked: "President of what?"[1] But Carter made a virtue out of being a dark horse. As far as Washington was concerned, he said, most Americans "are also outsiders."[2] He was determined to accomplish a turnabout: get the outsiders in and the insiders out. That way lay national salvation.

Ford, sixty-three, was the insider. He was an old Washington hand, first, Congressman from Michigan for many terms, then, minority leader in the House, and then, in quick succession, Vice-President and President. People liked Ford: he was "Mr. Nice Guy" with a reputation for decency. Still, there was the Nixon connection. Though Ford had not been involved in the Watergate scandal, he had, shortly after becoming President, given Nixon "a full, free and absolute pardon" for "any and all crimes." The reaction had been overwhelmingly hostile. Some people wondered whether it had been an "inside job." Ford insisted there had been no deal, but realized his pardon had roused suspicion and hurt him with many voters.[3] There was an emotional surge toward simple honesty in government in 1976 and Carter made the most of it.

Religion, as well as morals, played some part in America's bicentennial contest. George Gallup, Jr., called 1976 the "year of the evangelical."[4] For the first time in years both major candidates for the Presidency were evangelical Protestants. Carter was a born-again Southern Baptist who underwent conversion when he was about forty-three; and Ford, an Episcopalian, was something of an evangelical himself, having renewed his faith under the ministrations of the Reverend James Zeoli in the early 1960s. It was Carter, however, who was clearly the twice-born candidate. He had always taken religion seriously, according to his sister, evangelist Ruth Stapleton, but his conversion experience in 1966 was a profound one. After his awakening, Carter did missionary work in the Northeast for a while and made daily prayers and Bible-reading, as well as Sunday School teaching, regular parts of his life. Early in his campaign he referred to himself as a "born-again Christian Baptist Sunday School teacher deacon." He was, according to *Time,* the "most unabashed moralist" to seek the Presidency since William Jennings Bryan.[5]

Americans seem to like their Presidents to be religious, but not too religious. Some people, including Ford himself, were exasperated by Carter's religiosity. Others wondered about the extent to which his religion would alienate Catholics and Jews, normally Democratic, and attract evangelical Protestants, ordinarily Republican. Religion didn't play a major role in the 1976 campaign, but there was considerable discussion of it in the journals of opinions, religious and secular, especially at the outset of the campaign. Carter made it clear that, like John F. Kennedy, he was broadly tolerant when it came to religions other than his own. Unlike JFK, though, he felt continually obliged to prove that he was utterly human despite his religion.

The road to the Democratic nomination was long and hard and beset by perils. For close to two years Carter traveled around the country meeting people, shaking hands, delivering speeches, appearing on local television, and getting to know reporters and editors. His message was a simple one. He promised to eliminate the kind of secrecy in government and diplomacy that had produced the Vietnam War and the Watergate scandal and open government up to the average citizen. If he were President, he said, he would try to make his administration "as good and honest and decent and compassionate and filled with love as are the American people." He promised candor as well as compassion. "I'll never tell a lie," he vowed. "I'll never make a misleading statement."[6] An occasional Populist note crept into his pronouncements, as when he condemned government dominated by the rich and powerful, but for the most part he avoided specifics and took a vaguely centrist position.

But mere talk was not enough. Carter had to prove he was a vote-getter. Since 1972 there had been an increase in the number of states holding primaries for electing convention delegates and Carter realized he had to go the primary route to win the nomination. He did well in the Iowa caucuses in January 1976; and in February led the field in

New Hampshire, beating such Washington "insiders" as Birch Bayh of Indiana, Fred Harris of Oklahoma, and Morris Udall of Arizona, and proving, as he put it triumphantly, that "a progressive Southerner can win in the North." Television commentators, now the chief arbiters in interpreting primary elections, pronounced him the winner and before long his face was appearing on the covers of *Time* and *Newsweek.* Florida came next; after vigorous campaigning in the Everglade State Carter succeeded in beating George Wallace (who also campaigned against Washington) in a close race; he also defeated Wallace in Illinois and North Carolina. Late in April he defied an "anybody-but-Carter" movement in Pennsylvania and nosed out Senator Henry ("Scoop") Jackson of Washington, by a comfortable majority of the votes. He did not of course win all the primaries he entered; and from time to time new challengers, like Senator Frank Church of Idaho and Governor Jerry Brown of California, threatened his ascendancy. In the end, though, he won more than half of the thirty primaries he entered, maintained his percentage of the popular vote at close to 40 percent, and gradually moved up to top place as the preferred nominee in the opinion polls. After he won the Ohio primary on June 8, party leaders acknowledged he had the nomination in the bag. The Democratic convention, which met in New York City on July 12, was peaceful and harmonious, compared with those held in 1968 and 1972. The delegates picked Carter on the first ballot and then approved his choice for second place: Senator Walter F. Mondale of Minnesota, an experienced liberal Senator and, unlike Carter, an "insider."

The bicentennial Democratic convention contained several novelties. Carter was the first man from the Deep South since the Civil War (if we omit Woodrow Wilson, who resettled in the North) to receive the presidential nomination of a major party. A Congresswoman chaired the convention, a former astronaut delivered one of the keynote addresses, and a black Congressman from Georgia, Andrew Young, seconded Carter's nomination. "I'm ready to lay down the burden of race," exclaimed Young, "and Jimmy Carter comes from a part of the country that, whether you know it or not, has done just that."[7]

The Democratic platform stressed unemployment rather than inflation as the country's main problem; it also recommended cutting the defense budget, though maintaining parity with Russia on strategic weapons. In accepting the nomination, Carter began with the line he had used time and again during the primary contests: "My name is Jimmy Carter, and I'm running for President." He went on to offer the country "vigor and vision and aggressive leadership" and to blend liberal and conservative ideas in his proposals for the future. He called for a balanced budget, "minimal intrusion of government in our free economic system," and checking bureaucratic waste; but he also endorsed national health insurance, tax reform, and efforts to end discrimination on the basis of race and sex. "We can have an American government," he said, "that has turned away from scandal and corruption and official cynicism and is once again as decent and competent as our people."[8]

Carter wasn't the only "outsider" challenging the Washington establishment in 1976. From California came Ronald Reagan, popular two-term Governor, seeking to nose out President Ford in his quest for the Republican nomination that year. Reagan's entry into the race made Ford's road to the nomination as rocky as Carter's had been, despite his incumbency. Reagan had enormous assets: he had never held office in Washington and had no ties to the discredited Nixon administration; he was a former film-radio-television performer with great charm and skill as a public speaker; and he was a onetime New Deal Democrat turned ultra-conservative who had inherited Barry Goldwater's devoted following. Reagan declared his candidacy in November 1975; he said he wasn't running against either Ford or the Democrats but against "evil incarnate in the buddy system in Washington."[9]

For Ford, New Hampshire was as crucial as it was for Carter. To his delight he won a narrow victory over Reagan there in the February primary and hopefully called it a "great springboard" to success in the forthcoming national convention.[10] He went on to win primaries in Florida, Massachusetts, and Illinois; but Reagan's victory, first, in North Carolina, and then in Texas, put him behind the Californian in the number of delegates he had won. But Ford went on to win decisively in Michigan, his home state, and was neck and neck with Reagan on the eve of the convention. Then Reagan blundered: hoping to pick up delegates in the East, he announced his selection of a liberal Republican, Richard Schweiker of Pennsylvania, as his running mate. But the Schweiker choice alienated conservatives, especially in Mississippi, without picking up liberal support. The result was that Reagan lost narrowly to Ford at the Republican convention, which met in Kansas City on August 16, on the first ballot. Ford, a moderate, picked Senator Robert Dole of Kansas, a sharp-tongued conservative, as his running mate and, in his acceptance speech, defended his policies as President and criticized Congress (controlled by the Democrats) as well as Carter. In an effort to build up his image as a competent leader (which had been seriously damaged during the primary fight with Reagan), he also challenged Carter to a "face-to-face debate on the campaign's real issues."[11]

Ford needed something to boost his candidacy; he stood far behind Carter in the polls at the outset of the campaign. He was convinced that his experience as President, especially in foreign affairs (he had attended a summit meeting with Russian leaders in 1974) would assure his triumph over Carter in a confrontation on television and have the effect of elevating his standing with the voters. The first debate, on

September 23, did help him. He was calm and self-assured throughout and looked very much like a President; Carter was nervous and defensive at first and it took him a little time to get going. Before the debate, Carter had led Ford in the polls by 18 percent; afterwards his lead dropped to 8 percent.

In the second debate, October 6, Carter did better; he was surer of himself and made a good impression by his knowledge of the issues and his ability to articulate his point of view. But Ford himself did all right, too, at first. Then the *New York Times*'s Max Frankel asked him a question about the Soviet sphere of influence in Eastern Europe and Ford made a blunder that was to dog him for the rest of the campaign. There is "no Soviet domination of Eastern Europe," he told Frankel, "and there never will be under a Ford administration." "I'm sorry, could I just follow?" exclaimed Frankel in some bewilderment. "Did I understand you to say, sir, that the Russians are not using Eastern Europe as their own sphere of influence in occupying most of the countries there, and making sure with their own troops that it's a Communist Zone . . . ?" "I don't believe, Mr. Frankel," responded Ford, "that the Yugoslavians consider themselves dominated by the Soviet Union. I don't believe that the Rumanians consider themselves dominated by the Soviet Union. I don't believe that the Poles consider themselves dominated by the Soviet Union. . . . Each of those countries is independent, autonomous, it has its own territorial integrity and the United States does not concede that those countries are under the domination of the Soviet Union."[12]

Ford's supporters were appalled by what he had said. The headlines the next day were horrendous. Urged to issue a clarifying statement, Ford announced a few days later that "we are going to make certain to the best of our ability that any allegation of domination is not a fact." But this statement was murky and, pressed by his advisers, Ford finally issued another statement acknowledging there were Soviet military forces in Eastern Europe and "that is not what President Ford wants and that is not what the American people want." To the leaders of several Eastern European ethnic organizations whom he invited to the White House, Ford said frankly: "I did not express myself clearly—I admit." In the third debate, October 22, Ford held his own again. But he never really recovered from his image as "a mistake-prone, inept bumbler" which his gaffe during the second debate created.[13]

But Carter was having his troubles too. Before the campaign began, he had done a long interview with Robert Scheer, a free-lance journalist, for *Playboy*, in which he tried to convince people that although he was a devout Baptist he was no hard-nosed, narrow-minded, self-righteous fundamentalist. Carter discussed many issues with Scheer; but the passage which attracted the greatest attention when *Playboy* hit the stands in October had to do with sex. Referring to Jesus' statement that "anyone who looks on a woman with lust has in his heart already committed adultery," Carter said candidly, "I've looked on a lot of women with lust. I've committed adultery in my heart many times. This is something that God recognizes I will do—and I have done it—and God forgives me for it. But that doesn't mean that I condemn someone who not only looks on a woman with lust but who leaves his wife and shacks up with somebody out of wedlock." He pressed the point: "Christ says, Don't consider yourself better than someone else because one guy screws a whole bunch of women while the other guy is loyal to his wife. The guy who's loyal to his wife ought not to be condescending or proud because of the relative degree of sinfulness." [14] Carter's remarks on sex, like Ford's on Eastern Europe, were headline news for some time. "SEX, SIN, TEMPTATION—CARTER'S CANDID VIEW," announced the *Chicago Sun-Times*. The *Washington Star* put it this way: "CARTER ON SIN AND LUST; 'I'M HUMAN . . . I'M TEMPTED.' " [15] Religious liberals defended Carter; his view of sin, they said, was theologically unexceptionable; but many evangelicals who had been strong Carter supporters were deeply offended. The word "screw," an Atlanta clergyman explained, "is just not a good Baptist word." [16] But another remark during the *Playboy* interview, lumping Lyndon Johnson with Richard Nixon when it came to "lying, cheating and distorting the truth," also created a hubbub. Carter quickly backtracked and insisted his remark in the interview "distorted completely my feelings about President Johnson." [17] But when he campaigned later on in Texas, Lady Bird was on a vacation and her younger daughter, Luci, who did appear with Carter, treated him with icy reserve. Carter bitterly regretted the day he had agreed to the *Playboy* interview.

The bicentennial election was not, however, simply a comedy of errors. Issues did get discussed, points made, and views exchanged. But images rather than issues seemed to dominate the contest. Ford worked hard on "looking Presidential." For the first few weeks of the campaign he followed a "Rose Garden strategy": stayed close to the White House performing his executive duties and holding press conferences from time to time at which he showed he was on top of things. Meanwhile, television commercials sponsored by the President Ford Committee portrayed him as a good family man trying to do his best in difficult times and contrasted him with his unsophisticated, untutored, and inexperienced opponent. But Carter did all he could to shatter Ford's presidential image. Campaigning vigorously around the country, he called Ford "an appointed President," linked him to Nixon, insisted he lacked qualities of leadership, and asked audiences: "Can you think of a single program that he's put forth that's been accepted?" [18] His own image—the impression his media advisers tried to convey to the public—was one of complete candor, warm compassion, democratic simplicity, and quiet competence. "It's really come down to the character of the two men," remarked Ford's press secretary, Ron Nessen, toward the end of the campaign. "There's no really big issue moving people to vote one way or another. It's which man the voters feel more comfortable with."[19]

The voters, though, seemed largely turned-off. "The inability of President Ford and Jimmy Carter to excite, arouse, and mobilize the country," observed Jerald ter Horst, one of Ford's staffers, "can be ascribed to many reasons. The principal one is that vast numbers of voters have looked at the two men and see no practical differences. . . ."[20] Carter and Ford did not of course see it that way. Carter turned nasty about Ford on occasion, and Ford himself finally charged into the arena responding in kind. "Neither nominee," observed a *New York Times* writer, "appears able to decide whether he wants to be a good guy or a rabbit puncher."[21] Mishaps, moreover, continued to plague both candidates. Joint Chiefs of Staff Chairman General George S. Brown made anti-Israel remarks which Ford had to disavow; and Secretary of Agriculture Earl Butz told a racist joke during a plane trip that leaked to the press and obliged him to leave Ford's cabinet. Meanwhile, just before the election, a black clergyman from Americus, Georgia, showed up in Carter's hometown, Plains, applied for membership in Carter's segregated Baptist church, and was turned away. Pressed to withdraw his own membership in protest, Carter said he was "very sad" about what had happened but added: "I can't quit my lifetime of worship. . . . I'll do all I can to eliminate the last vestige of discrimination . . . but I'm not going to resign from the human race because it discriminates. My best opportunity is to stay in the church and try to change its attitude."[22] The President Ford Committee sent telegrams to 407 black ministers soliciting comments about the episode, but Carter's black supporters— Mrs. Coretta Scott King, Jesse Jackson, Andrew Young, and Martin Luther King, Sr.—rallied to his defense and he emerged unscathed.

As the campaign progressed, Ford rose steadily in the polls and by election eve Carter's 33-point summer lead had virtually melted away. Gallup called it "the greatest comeback in the history of public-opinion polling."[23] But Ford's advisers were not optimistic; many of them acknowledged that Carter would have to make a fatal error to lose the election. Carter played it cool and cautious toward the end. "I see the sun is rising on a beautiful new day," he said calmly just before election day.[24] His forecast was accurate. November 2 turned out to be beautiful for the born-again Georgian. The voters gave him 40,828,929 popular votes (50.1 percent) to Ford's 39,148,940 (48 percent), a margin of almost 1,700,000 votes; and saw to it that he won 297 electoral votes (twenty-three states plus the District of Columbia) to Ford's 240 (one Seattle elector voted for Reagan). It was a narrow victory; but it was greater than JFK's in 1960 and Nixon's in 1968. The Democrats swept Congress, establishing a two-thirds majority in the House and a 62-38 margin in the Senate.

Carter had campaigned as an "outsider," blaming the Washington establishment for the mess the country was in, but it was the traditional Democratic voters who put him in office: Democratic regulars, union families, ethnic minorities, and blacks. The Democratic national committee had worked hard to register voters and get them to the polls; so had the AFL-CIO, which had sat out the election four years before. Carter had a fairly folksy inauguration on January 20, 1977, and then began tackling the greatest establishment job in the nation.

☆ ☆ ☆

Olympian Will

Carter's sister Ruth C. Stapleton was struck by Jimmy's "Olympian will to win." "Honey," he once told her, "I can will myself to sleep until 10:30 a.m. when I've been up till 1:00 a.m., and get my ass beat, or I can will myself to get up at 6:00 a.m. and become President." Noted his sister: "He got up at 6:00 a.m."[25]

Not Knee-Jerks

When Ronald Reagan announced his choice of Richard S. Schweiker of Pennsylvania as his running mate if nominated for President, there was considerable dismay among Republican conservatives because of Schweiker's pro-labor record. But Reagan and Schweiker hit it off very nicely. "I'm not a knee-jerk liberal," Schweiker told Reagan. "And I'm not a knee-jerk conservative," said Reagan.[26]

Balance

"I'll never tell a lie," announced Carter repeatedly while campaigning in the primaries. Said one of his followers facetiously: "We're gonna lose the liar vote!" And "Miz Lillian," his seventy-seven-year-old mother, remarked: "Well, I lie all the time. I have to—to balance the family ticket."[27]

I See

"I see an America that has turned its back on scandals and shame . . ." announced Carter in a speech during the primary campaign. "I see an America that does not spy on its own citizens." Struck by the "I see" construction, William Safire recalled that in a speech he prepared for Nixon in 1968 he had written, "I see a day when Americans are once again proud of their flag. . . . I see a day when our nation is at peace. . . ." After Nixon's election, Safire reported, he told Judge Samuel Rosenman he had borrowed the construction from a speech Rosenman and Robert Sherwood had written for FDR in 1940: "I see an America where factory workers are not discarded after they reach their prime. I see an America where small business really has a chance to flourish and grow. . . ." Rosenman smiled and told Safire to look up the speeches of Robert Ingersoll. Safire did so and discovered that in a centennial oration in 1876 Ingersoll had declaimed: "I see a country filled with happy hopes. . . . I see a world where thrones have crumbled. . . . I see a world without a slave. . . ." Safire might have added that in 1952 Adlai Stevenson also made an "I see an America" speech.[28]

Uncollected

When Barry Jagoda, Carter's TV adviser, was in Detroit making arrangements to use the Sheraton Cadillac Hotel's ballroom for an election-night party after the Michigan primary, he told the hotel manager to send the bill to the Carter headquarters in Atlanta. But the manager demanded cash and when Jagoda tried to convince him he would eventually get paid the manager took him over to a file cabinet, extracted a folder marked, "uncollected," opened it and pulled out a bill, still unpaid, made out to the John F. Kennedy Campaign, 1960. Jagoda rounded up the cash.[29]

Football

To campaign against Reagan in the primaries, President Ford hired Don Penny, former TV writer, as a special consultant. Penny told Ford that, compared with Reagan, his wardrobe was too conservative, his speeches too long-winded, and he had no one-liners. "Governor Reagan and I do have one thing in common," Ford finally protested. "We both played football." Then he added after a pause: "I played for Michigan. He played for Warner Brothers."[30]

Voice of the People

Just before dropping out of the Democratic primary race, Arizona Congressman Morris Udall spoke to his supporters in New York and reminded them that he had campaigned for twenty months, traveled to every part of the country, and entered twenty-two primaries and lost them all. "The People have spoken," he concluded dolefully, and then added: "The bastards!"[31]

Well, Perhaps

Carter's vagueness on the issues produced several campaign jokes. In a bridge game, according to one of them, after an opponent has raised the contract to three spades, Jimmy says, "Well, then I'll bid four." "Four what?" he is asked. "I'll tell you after the convention," he replies. Another story had it that when Jimmy's father asked him if he had chopped down the family's beloved peach tree, the lad said: "Well, perhaps."[32]

Lust in His Heart

Carter's *Playboy* interview produced much mirth. In a *Los Angeles Times* cartoon, Paul Conrad showed Jimmy looking at a naked Statue of Liberty. "In his heart," proclaimed bumper stickers, "he knows your wife." At a Carter rally in New Orleans, a girl climbed on her boyfriend's shoulders waving a placard, "I lust after Jimmy Carter for President." The Ford people of course made the most of the *Playboy* incident. Toward the end of the campaign they placed advertisements in magazines and newspapers showing the *Playboy* cover, with its half-clad woman, plugging the Carter interview, side by side with a *Newsweek* cover featuring a lead story about Ford. "One good way to decide this election," said the caption. "Read last week's *Newsweek*. Read this month's *Playboy*."

One evening, to the tune of "Heart of My Heart," reporters serenaded Jimmy and Rosalyn:

> Lust in my heart, how I love adultery
> Lust in my heart, it's my theology
> When I was young, at the Plains First Baptist Church,
> I would preach and sermonize
> But oh how I would fantasize.

> Oh, lust in my heart, who cares if it's a sin.
> (It has never been)
> Leching's a noble art
> It's OK if you shack up
> 'Cause I won't get my back up
> I've got mine
> I've got lust in my heart.

> Lust in my heart, oh, it's bad politic'ly,
> Lust in my heart, but it brings publicity.
> When I grew up and ran for president,
> A bunch of women I did screw
> But in my head, so no one knew.

> Oh, lust in my heart,
> I said I'd never lie
> ('bout my roving eye)
> I should have played it smart
> But I'm no gay deceiver
> I'm a Christian eager beaver.

Said Carter ruefully during the third TV debate: "If I should ever decide in the future to discuss my deep Christian beliefs . . . I'll use another forum besides *Playboy*."[33]

Film Party

In Los Angeles, film star Warren Beatty threw a fund-raiser for Carter attended by celebrities from stage, screen, radio, and TV. Beatty remarked that coming to his party might help Carter blunt the religious issue with some of the people there, and Carter declared: "If I come to Warren Beatty's party, it should wipe out the issue." When someone in the audience asked Carter if this was his first trip to California, he said, "It's the first time anyone ever noticed I was here." Just before he left he announced: "It is a real thrill to meet the famous people here tonight. I hope I don't get to know too much about you!"[34]

No Accent

"Isn't it time," Carter asked in speeches in the South, "we had a President without an accent?"[35]

Embryonic

After outlining his views on abortion to six Roman Catholic bishops in Washington, Carter told them he hoped his relationship with them "will grow after this embryonic start."[36]

Only Sane One

"I got a mamma who joined the Peace Corps and went to India when she was sixty-eight," Carter's brother Billy told reporters. "I got one sister [Ruth] who's a Holy Roller preacher. I got another sister [Gloria] who wears a helmet and rides a motorcycle. And I got a brother who thinks he's going to be President. So that makes me the only sane person in the family."[37]

Blunders

Both Ford and Carter made slips of the tongue during the campaign and TV performer Johnny Carson finally announced: "I have a late score from the newsroom. Jimmy Carter is ahead of Gerald Ford, two blunders to one." Later on he remarked, "You know, the Carter-Ford election is going to be tough. It boils down to fear of the unknown versus fear of the known."[38]

Hiawatha

After Ford introduced S. I. Hayakawa, Republican candidate for Senator from California, as "Dr. Haya-kama," to the dismay of his campaign managers, one White House staffer said consolingly, "It was better than what he called Hayakawa in a private meeting. He called him 'Hiawatha' the first time."[39]

Dixieland Band

When making arrangements for the TV debates, Carter's TV adviser Barry Jagoda suggested that Ford stand in a hole to offset the fact he was taller than Carter and be addressed as "Mr. Ford" rather than "Mr. President," but he was laughed down by the Ford people. Then a Ford aide facetiously suggested the band play "Hail to the Chief" the moment Ford walked onto the stage. That was okay with him, said Jody Powell at once, so long as it "was played by a Dixieland band."[40]

Seems That Way

"Election day is not far off," announced Eric Sevareid toward the end of the campaign; "it just seems that way."[41]

★ ★

CHAPTER FORTY-NINE

1980
The Reagan Victory

In 1980, Ronald Reagan challenged Jimmy Carter and won by a landslide. But it was not a particularly gladsome event. Many people seemed to be taking comedienne Mae West's advice: if you have to choose between two evils, pick the one you haven't tried before. Negative votes abounded: anti-Carter rather than pro-Reagan, and anti-Reagan rather than pro-Carter. A public-opinion survey revealed an astonishingly weak attachment by voters to the man of their choice. Asked which candidate they were "personally interested in or excited about," only 11 percent of those polled picked Reagan while 9 percent named Carter.[1]

"We're talking big and not doing anything abroad," complained a young Pennsylvania industrial safety worker in mid-October. "We're losing credibility around the world. We're becoming a joke. And that just typifies Carter's ineffectiveness. . . . I think I'll vote for Reagan. . . . I think he'll act with more strength." Then he had second thoughts about Reagan. "I worry though," he added, "that he engages his mouth before his brain is in gear. I worry about that in a delicate foreign situation." He sighed and concluded: "What I'd really like is to have, along with the lines for the candidates, a 'no preference' line on the ballot."[2] The young man's misgivings were widespread in 1980 and both Carter and Reagan knew it. It was Carter's task to convince voters he was not as ineffective in the White House as he seemed to be and Reagan's to prove he was more qualified for the Presidency than he appeared to be.

Long before the Democratic convention Carter was worrying about renomination. By 1979 inflation was so high and his standing in the polls so low that Washingtonians joked he was the first President with poll ratings lower than the prime interest rate. Though he had performed creditably in some areas—won approval of the Panama Canal treaties, produced the Camp David accords between Israel and Egypt, developed a comprehensive policy for conserving energy—his general performance evoked little confidence, partly because of declining productivity, mounting prices, and rising unemployment, and partly because of his inability to work with Congress, his estrangement from Democratic party leaders, his abrupt changes of direction, and his periodic confessions of failure in public. In July 1979 he went on television to tell people that the nation was experiencing a "crisis of confidence" and asked for a renewal of faith "in the future of this nation."[3] Many people thought the crisis was Carter's, not the country's. His poll ratings continued to plummet. Party leaders yearned for an alternative in 1980.

For many Democrats the alternative was Senator Edward M. ("Ted") Kennedy of Massachusetts. He was relatively young, attractive, and energetic, and had never lost an election. The Kennedy name, too, was alluring; it evoked nostalgic memories of his murdered brothers, Jack and Bobby. In 1968, and in 1972 and 1976 too, liberals in his party had pressed him to seek the nomination, but he had held back. On Labor Day, 1979, however, he finally entered the race. By this time there were draft-Kennedy movements in several states and the polls put him far above Carter in popularity. The President professed to be unperturbed. "I'll whip his ass," he said calmly when told of Kennedy's challenge.[4]

An exogenous event, not Carter, finally whipped Kennedy. On November 4, exactly a year before the 1980 election, a band of student revolutionaries, protesting the entry of the recently deposed Shah of Iran, Mohammed Riza Pahlevi, into the United States for medical treatment, occupied the American embassy in Tehran, took all the Americans there hostage, and threatened to kill them or put them on trial if the United States did not return the Shah to Iran for punishment forthwith. Carter stood firm—let the Shah complete his treatment before leaving the country, froze Iranian assets in the United States, and appealed to the U. N. for intervention—and the American people rallied around him in an outpouring of patriotic fervor. For the first time in months his poll ratings climbed and interest in Kennedy as a presidential possibility dropped precipitously. But Kennedy hurt himself, too, while seeking to replace Carter as his party's nominee. In an interview with Roger Mudd for CBS in November he showed himself at his worst. His answers about the Chappaquiddick tragedy were awkward, rambling, and repetitive. He was even more incoherent, if anything, when asked, "Why do you want to be President?" He also aroused great hostility in a later interview when he called the Shah's "one of the most violent regimes in the history of mankind" and said he had stolen "umpteen billion dollars" from his people. The Iranians hailed him as "an American prophet," but the *New York Post*, in a typical superpatriotic reaction, reported his remarks with the headline, "Teddy Is the Toast of Teheran."[5]

But Kennedy hung in. He campaigned hard in Iowa, the first of the thirty-six states holding elections for delegates to the national conventions, but on January 21, the voters picked twice as many delegates for Carter as for Kennedy, "because," as one politico explained, "they thought . . . the patriotic thing to do is to support the President in time of national crisis."[6] The hostage crisis probably helped Carter win his party's nomination; in the ensuing state primaries and party caucuses he went on to win more delegates than Kennedy and more than enough to obtain a first-ballot nomination at the Democratic national convention. But the deadlock in negotiations with Iran for the release of the hostages hurt him badly. And the failure of the helicopter raid to rescue the hostages in April may well have dealt him a fatal blow. "The hostage crisis," said Hamilton Jordan, Carter's chief strategist, "had come to symbolize the collective frustration of the American people. And in that sense, the President's chances for re-election probably died on the desert of Iran with eight brave soldiers who gave their lives trying to free the American hostages."[7]

The Democratic convention, which met in New York in mid-August, was divided and unhappy. Kennedy refused to give up. He called for an "open" convention, that is, releasing delegates from the commitments they had made when they were elected. He was voted down and withdrew from the race; and Carter beat him handily on the first ballot. But Carter had to make concessions to Kennedy when it came to the party platform (he agreed to include a plank calling for wage-and-price controls), and Kennedy also stole the show the second day of the convention by making a rousing speech filled with sentiments to the left of the President's. Carter's acceptance speech was disappointing. It was apologetic: "I've learned that for a president, experience is the best guide to the right decisions. I'm wiser than I was four years ago." It was supplicatory: "Ted, your party needs—and I need—you." And it was clumsy: a paean to the late Hubert Horatio Humphrey came out "Hubert Horatio Hornblower . . . er, Humphrey."[8] Afterwards, Carter, Walter Mondale (renominated for second place), and other party leaders waited a long time on the podium for Kennedy to show up; and when he did, he shook hands with Carter, but refused to raise his hands in the traditional gesture of unity. Watching the proceedings on television, Reagan exclaimed: "If that's the best they can do in unity, they have a long way to go."[9]

Reagan had a long way to go himself. For years he had been eying the Republican nomination. First mentioned as a serious presidential possibility in 1968, he had come within 117 votes of wresting the nomination from President Ford in 1976. In 1980, however, he was determined not to fail; since 1977, he had been working zealously—traveling around the country, meeting people, giving speeches, raising money, organizing his staff—to capture the nomination. His message was sweet-sounding and simplistic: "get the government off our backs." He wanted lower taxes, reduced federal spending for social services, balanced budgets, and fewer governmental regulations. At the same time he favored a drastic increase in defense spending, a step-up of the arms race with Russia, and efforts to encourage the collapse of "communism" in the Soviet Union. How the U. S. government could be weak (at home) and strong (abroad) at the same time he did not make clear. It was enough for his devoted followers that he promised lower taxes and an end to inflation as well as primacy for the United States in the world of nations. Goldwater had failed when he took a similar message to the American people in 1964; Reagan was convinced he could win with it in 1980.

Reagan was not alone in the pre-convention race. Carter's vulnerability encouraged others to try for the Republican nomination: former Secretary of the Treasury John B. Connally, Senator Howard Baker of Tennessee, Senator Robert Dole of Kansas (Ford's running mate in 1976), ten-term Illinois Congressman John Anderson, and George Bush, wealthy oilman who had once been director of the Central Intelligence Agency, ambassador to the United Nations, special envoy to China, and chairman of the Republican national committee. One by one, all of Reagan's rivals dropped out of the running except Anderson and Bush. Anderson ended by running as an independent on a National Unity ticket and attracting attention (but not votes) by his intelligence and candor. Bush posed more of a threat. In January he beat Reagan in the precinct caucuses held in Iowa (where Reagan did not bother to campaign) and announced he had a "big mo" (momentum) going for him. But in February he was clobbered by Reagan in the New Hampshire primary (where Reagan did campaign vigorously) and the "big mo" ended in a "big no."

After New Hampshire it was clear sailing for Reagan. By the time of the Republican convention, which met in Detroit on July 14, he had swept most of the state primaries, conventions, and caucuses which picked delegates to the national convention and his nomination on the first ballot was a mere formality. So was acceptance of a platform setting forth his ultra-rightist views. The spirit of the convention was optimistic, confident, and good-spirited; Reaganites, joined by party moderates, were sure they could beat Carter in November. There was only one uncertainty: who would be Reagan's running mate? For a time former President Ford seemed to be a possibility. Many Republicans thought a Reagan-Ford combination would be a "dream ticket." Reagan approached Ford and Ford didn't say yes, but he didn't say no either. There was talk of increasing Ford's responsibilities if he agreed to run; and in an interview with Ford on CBS Walter Cronkite even used the word, co-presidency, to fit the situation. At this point both Reagan and Ford decided to call the whole thing off; and, since the convention was filled

with rumors about Ford, Reagan broke precedent and went to the convention hall himself to announce his choice: George Bush. Bush was
slightly more liberal than Reagan on some issues (he had called Reagan's views "voodoo economics") and conservative ideologues were disappointed by the choice. But Reagan's acceptance address the following
day left them pleased and happy. The Republican nominee criticized
Carter and the Democrats for their failures at home and abroad, promised to "bring our government back under control and make it acceptable to the people," and made the customary gesture to "lasting world
peace," but insisted the United States had "an obligation to its citizens
and to the people of the world never to let those who would destroy
freedom to dictate the future course of human life on this planet." He
also made a special point of calling for silent prayer at the end of his
speech.[10]

During the campaign Reagan categorically rejected Carter's notion that
there was a "crisis of confidence" in America. The American people were
as ingenious and energetic as ever, he insisted, and with new leadership
and fresh approaches they could solve the problems that had baffled
the Carter administration. He made much of his record as Governor of
California to prove he was an experienced executive who knew how to
cut taxes and spending (though he had done neither) and check the
metastasis of bureaucracy. He also indicted the federal government for
undue interference in the daily lives of citizens and said repeatedly: "It
is time to get *gummit* off our backs and get back to business." He ignored the primacy of the Pentagon in the life of the nation. "I used to
fantasize," he said, "what it would be like if everyone in government
would quietly slip away and close the doors and disappear. See how long
it would take the people of this country to miss them. I think that life
would go on, and the people would keep right on doing the things they
are doing, and we would get along a lot better than we think."[11] Reagan was an effective campaigner. His experience as a former film-radio-television performer stood him in good stead on the stump and he
was a master of timing. He was skillful, too, in turning aside hard questions, and came to be called "the Great Deflector." One of his advisers
called him "the greatest television candidate in history."[12]

But things were not entirely smooth for the Republican nominee. His
inclination to make offhand remarks to please his audiences produced
a series of minor crises. He said he favored restoring "official" relations
with Taiwan and thus angered China, whose good will Bush was in Peking trying to cultivate. He expressed doubts about evolution and suggested teaching "creationism" in the public schools, to the dismay of sci-
entists. He called Tuscumbia, Alabama, where Carter opened his
campaign, "the birthplace of the Ku Klux Klan," and had to apologize
for both the inaccuracy and the insult. He said the United States was
"energy rich" even though it was becoming dangerously dependent on

foreign oil. He blamed trees (not automobiles) for smog, leading students at one of his rallies to attach a sign to a tree saying, "Chop me down before I kill again." He also announced that air pollution had been "substantially controlled" and shortly afterwards his plane had to be diverted because Los Angeles was suffering one of the worst smog attacks in history. Reagan backtracked, apologized, and explained, after each blooper, but eventually the "gaffe game," as it was called, led his advisers to reduce his press conferences and put him under stricter supervision. One slip, though, Reagan turned to his advantage. When economists criticized him for calling the recession the economy was undergoing a "depression," he began telling audiences: "I'm told I can't use the word *depression*. Well, I'll tell you the definition. A recession is when your neighbor loses his job and a depression is when you lose your job. Recovery is when Jimmy Carter loses his!"[13]

Reagan's periodic tongue-slips were more than matched by Carter's verbal overkill. Carter did not spend much time defending his own record; his strategy was to emphasize his opponents' shortcomings. But he could be nasty; his mother once said he was "a beautiful cat with sharp claws."[14] By mid-September he was attracting severe criticism for the vehemence of his attacks. He was not satisfied to point out that Reagan opposed important social programs that most Americans favored; he also began suggesting that Reagan was both a racist and a warmonger and that if he took office "Americans might be separated, black from white, Jew from Christian, North from South, rural from urban." In Atlanta, he accused Reagan of injecting "hatred" and "racism" into the campaign and using such "code words" for segregation as "state's rights." In Los Angeles he insisted the election "will help to decide what kind of world we live in. It will help to decide whether we have war or peace. It's an awesome choice."[15]

Carter's portrayal of Reagan as a kind of "mad bomber" soon produced the "meanness issue": did Carter, generally regarded as honest, sincere, decent, and fair-minded, have a "mean side" to him that led him to do or say anything in order to win votes? "Mr. President," TV's Barbara Walters told him in an interview for ABC News on October 8, "in recent days you have been characterized as vindictive, hysterical, and on the point of desperation." Carter admitted he had "gotten carried away on a couple of occasions" and promised to speak "with more reticence in the future" and avoid name-calling.[16] "Well," said Reagan, when he heard what Carter had said, "I think that would be nice if he did . . . if he decided to straighten up and fly right, that'll be fine."[17] But Reagan also turned the war-or-peace issue against Carter, charging that "his foreign policy, his vacillation, his weakness, his allowing our allies throughout the world to no longer respect us" posed "a far greater danger of that unwanted, inadvertent war . . . than there is by someone in there who believes that the first thing we should do is rebuild our defense capability to the point that this country can keep the peace."[18]

Third-party candidate John Anderson thought Carter and Reagan were behaving "like two tarantulas in a bottle." Called a "spoiler," he cried: "What's to spoil? Spoil the chances of two men at least half the country doesn't want?" "I don't want to sound querulous," he said at one point, "but Reagan lacks balance; he's for giving everything to the oil companies; [he thinks] the Russians are behind everything." For Reagan's economic program he had nothing but scorn. "How do you balance the budget, cut taxes and increase defense spending?" he asked. "It's very simple. You do it with mirrors." Reagan, he said, was a product of "Eighteenth Century-Fox." But he was equally critical of the President. Carter, he said, "stands for a failed Presidency, and his campaign is nothing but a desperate attempt to cling to office."[19]

Anderson had launched his National Unity campaign in April, acquired former Democratic Governor of Wisconsin Patrick J. Lucey as his running mate in August, and issued a lengthy platform in September calling for gun control, a strategic arms limitation agreement with Russia, an Equal Rights Amendment, a tax of fifty cents a gallon on oil (to discourage overconsumption), and revitalization of the nation's mass transportation systems. Though a fiscal conservative, he was progressive enough on most issues to win the support of the Liberal party in New York and the endorsement of the *New Republic*. Eventually he got his name on the ballots of all fifty states and rose high enough in the public opinion polls to qualify for participation in the debates of presidential candidates sponsored by the League of Women Voters. But Carter refused to agree to a three-cornered debate; he was not willing by his presidential presence to advance Anderson's candidacy the way President Ford had helped Carter's cause by appearing with him on television in 1976. But Reagan agreed to debate Anderson; and on September 21 the two of them appeared together in Baltimore for questioning by a group of reporters. Anderson came off well enough, but Reagan did even better. He was relaxed, poised, articulate, and sure of himself; and any damage his earlier gaffes had done his candidacy was entirely dissipated that evening. His ratings in the polls went up after Baltimore. But Anderson's declined rapidly. It wasn't that people didn't admire the National Unity candidate. It was just that without party organization, adequate funding, and a solid economic or regional base for his candidacy, he really had nowhere to go and people knew it.

On October 28 Carter and Reagan met at long last to debate in Cleveland. Both had carefully prepared for the event, boning up on the issues and going through practice sessions with staff members beforehand. Carter was anxious to stress the war-or-peace issue; Reagan planned to pound away on Carter's failure to cope with the Great Inflation. Both were a bit on edge at first; but Reagan had the presence of mind to stride across the stage just before the debate (and right afterwards too) to shake hands with the President. The debate centered, as the contestants had planned, on economic policy and national security; and during the exchange the differences between the two candidates became crystal-clear to the 100,000,000 people who tuned in. Carter charged bellicosity; Reagan insisted military might meant peace. Carter emphasized the necessity of federal social programs for economic well-being; Reagan thought reduced government taxing and spending (except for the military bureaucracy) would produce prosperity. But differences in style as well as substance also came across clearly in the encounter. Reagan appeared as he had with Anderson: calm, reasonable, and self-assured, and quite capable of handling high responsibilities. And when he felt Carter was pressing him too hard, he simply shook his head, almost in sorrow, and sighed: "There you go again!" Carter seemed far less at ease and a bit solemn and preachy; and although obviously quite at home with the details of the issues being discussed, looked at times (as one of his advisers said later) as if he "was about to slug" Reagan.[20]

The only gaffe of the TV evening was Carter's. Discussing arms control toward the end of the debate, the President suddenly confided: "I had a discussion with my daughter Amy the other day, before I came here, to ask her what the most important issue was. She said she thought nuclear weapons and the control of nuclear arms."[21] The reference to little Amy took everyone by surprise and shocked Carter's advisers. By personalizing a serious issue, the President succeeded in trivializing it. He also opened himself to ridicule; after the debate scores of jokes began making the rounds. Carter's summation at the end of the debate was wise, thoughtful, and even eloquent, but Reagan's was masterful. In a nutshell, Reagan seemed to make clear what the campaign was all about. "Are you better off than you were four years ago?" he asked. "Is it easier for you to go and buy things in the stores than it was four years ago? Is there more or less employment in the country than there was four years ago? Is America as respected throughout the world as it was? Do you feel that our security is safe, that we're as strong as we were four years ago?" Then he declared: "If you answer all of these questions yes, why then I think your choice is very obvious as to who you'll vote for. If you don't agree, if you don't think that this course that we've been on for the last four years is what you would like to see us follow for the next four, then I could suggest another choice that you have." He probably won over many undecided voters by putting it this way.[22]

During the campaign the Reaganites worried about an "October surprise," that is, a last-minute breakthrough in Carter's negotiations with Iran for the release of the hostages which would give his candidacy a big and possibly decisive boost. But the breakthrough never came; the hostages were not freed, as it turned out, until inauguration day the following year. There was, though, a "November surprise." Most poll-sters had given Reagan a distinct edge over Carter from the outset, but none had foreseen the extent of his victory on election day. On November 4, Reagan swamped the President: his popular plurality was 8,300,000 votes (10 percent of the total). He won 43,899,248 votes (51 percent) to Carter's 35,481,435 (41 percent), while Anderson took only 5,719,437 (7 percent). He also took 489 electoral votes to Carter's 49, losing only Georgia, Minnesota, West Virginia, Rhode Island, Hawaii, and the District of Columbia. The Republicans also won control of the Senate and made substantial gains in the House. Carter's was the most stunning defeat for a presidential incumbent since Hoover's loss to Roosevelt almost a half-century earlier. The Great Depression had killed Hoover in 1932; the Great Inflation (and the hostage crisis) did Carter in. He was the first incumbent Democrat to fail of re-election since Cleveland in 1888. But nearly half of the eligible voters failed to go to the polls.

Asked afterwards why they had picked Reagan, many voters said it was "time for a change."[23] It was a change all right. Reagan made it clear he intended to be a kind of FDR of the right if elected and begin dismantling the welfare state inaugurated in the 1930s. It was, in a way, a "return to normalcy": Reagan, like Harding and Coolidge, favored lowering taxes on the rich to release the nation's productive energies. But Harding and Coolidge had sponsored disarmament, while Reagan favored accelerating the arms race. His election was a watershed, even a new departure, in American history.

☆   ☆   ☆

E, E and I

At first when asked about his intentions, Kennedy gave what his aides called his "E, E and I" answer: he *expected* Carter to be renominated, *expected* him to be re-elected, and *intended* to support him. But his lead over Carter in pre-convention polls encouraged him to enter the race himself. His disastrous interview with Roger Mudd, however, shown at the same time the shark movie, *Jaws*, appeared on television, hurt him badly. Afterward Republican Senator Dole commented: "seventy-five percent of the country watched *Jaws*, twenty-five percent watched Roger Mudd, and half of them couldn't tell the difference."[24]

The Weather

In speeches and interviews Kennedy talked so much about his concern for the sick, aged, blacks, and underprivileged, that a TV anchorman who went to Washington to do a story came back saying it was useless. "If I had asked him any question, he would have replied the same way," he sighed. "If I had asked him about the weather, he would have said, 'When I think about the weather, I think first about the sick, the black, the old people, the underprivileged."[25]

O and W

Right after the sixty-eight-year-old Reagan announced his candidacy Jack Kemp introduced him to a press conference in Washington as "the oldest and wisest candidate." Some of Reagan's advisers were dismayed; but the phrase caught on and reporters started calling the Californian "The Oldest and Wisest." And, in time, "the O and W." Nancy Reagan didn't like it, but Reagan accepted the designation good-naturedly.[26]

Ethnic

"How do you tell who the Polish fellow is at a cock fight?" asked Reagan when campaigning in New Hampshire. "He's the one with the duck. How do you tell who the Italian is at the cockfight? He's the one who bets on the duck. How do you know the Mafia was there? The duck wins." When newspapers reported the story, one of Reagan's aides, with Italian-American voters in mind, sighed: "There goes Connecticut!" Criticized for telling an ethnic joke, Reagan insisted he had told it as an example of the kind of stories politicians should never tell. "And from now on," he vowed, "I'm going to look over both shoulders and then I'm only going to tell stories about Irishmen, because I'm Irish."[27]

Deaf or Dumb

On NBC's *Today Show*, November 13, 1979, Reagan, sixty-eight, said he would be younger than most of the heads of state he'd be dealing with if he became President. "Giscard d'Estaing of France is younger than you," Tom Brokaw reminded him. "Who?" asked Reagan, as if he had never heard of him. "Giscard d'Estaing of France," repeated Brokaw. "Yes, possibly," said Reagan, who was fifteen years older than the French President, "not an awfully lot more." Reporters laughed at the exchange; many of them thought it showed Reagan didn't know who was President of France. But Reagan's press secretary, James Lake, said the reason Reagan had responded the way he did was that he hadn't heard what Brokaw said. "We could run a correction in the *Washington Post,*" reporter Lou Cannon told Lake. "We could say that the good news is that Ronald Reagan knows who the President of France is and that the bad news is that he can't hear." Lake laughed, shook his head and said: "We'd rather have you say he's too ignorant than too old!"[28]

Dream

When Reagan arrived in Detroit for the Republican convention, he told reporters: "I had a dream the other night. I dreamed that Jimmy Carter came to me and asked why I wanted his job. I told him I didn't want his job." He paused for a moment and then said: "I want to be President."[29]

Co-Presidency

After former President Ford talked with CBS's Walter Cronkite about a possible co-presidency, ABC News's Barbara Walters rushed over to the CBS booth as Ford came out and begged him to do another interview with her. "Mr. President," she cried, "you've got to talk to me, you've got to." "Well, Barbara," said Ford amiably, "I really have to go to this other meeting." "Oh, Mr. President," she persisted, "you've got to do it. . . . For old times's sake. . . ." "Okay, Barbara," Ford finally yielded. So he went into the ABC booth with her and she rushed to get ready for the interview. At one point a technician walked by, tripped over the cord from the tiny microphone pinned to her dress, and ripped the mike off as she let out a yell. "Now, Barbara," said Ford soothingly, as he leaned over and put his hand on her arm, "calm down, I'm not going anywhere." Walters got her interview but it was no sensation like Cronkite's. At a small luncheon the next day where both Cronkite and Walters were present Ford told some of the people there: "Don't shake my hand too hard. My shoulder's out of joint from Barbara twisting my arm to get me over to her booth."[30]

Prime Time

"My first thrill tonight," cried Reagan just before giving his acceptance address, "was to find myself, for the first time in a long time, in a movie in prime time."[31]

The Chair

When Carter refused to meet Reagan and Anderson in the debate set up by the League of Women Voters for September 21 in Baltimore, there was much criticism. "I see Anderson as primarily a creation of the press," said Carter firmly, but his critics said he was afraid to face Anderson. When League president Ruth Hinerfeld announced there "probably would be an empty chair in Carter's place," *Washington Star* cartoonist Oliphant pictured it as a baby's high chair to emphasize the President's petulance. Queried Johnny Carson: "What if the chair wins the debate?" In the end the idea of an empty chair was dropped.[32]

Bonzo

As a Hollywood performer, Reagan had once played in a film about a monkey named Bonzo (*Bedtime for Bonzo*, 1951), and in Battle Creek, Michigan, hecklers started yelling, "Bonzo! Bonzo!" at him. "Well," smiled Reagan, "they better watch out. Bonzo grew up to be King Kong."[33]

Trying

At a labor rally in Detroit, Kennedy substituted for the President who was absorbed in negotiations for the release of the hostages. In his speech, the Massachusetts Senator said that Carter had called him earlier in the day and asked him to fill in for him and he had replied: "I've been trying to do that for a year."[34]

Moral Majority

During the campaign, the Reverend Jerry Falwell, leader of the ultra-rightist Moral Majority, announced that he had had a conference with the President in the Oval Office and the latter had told him homosexuals needed representation in the White House and he had several on his staff. But it turned out there had been no such conversation; Falwell had never even been in the Oval Office. Confronted by reporters, the Moral Majority leader admitted he had "fabricated" the tale. But one of the "religious" TV spots continued to depict a mother telling her child that Carter was a bad man because he encouraged homosexuals.[35]

Forty-eight

When Carter spoke in Grand Rapids, Michigan, Jerry Ford's hometown, he called it Cedar Rapids, and Ford, campaigning for Reagan, made much of the fact that Carter "apparently . . . didn't even know that Michigan was one of the forty-eight states." Told there were fifty states, he quickly recovered. "I voted for Hawaii and Alaska," he said, "and I'm proud of it."[36]

Helpful

Asked why he quoted FDR and JFK so much, Reagan replied: "Show me a quotable recent Republican President." He added: "J.F.K.'s a hero, and helpful if you're going after the blue-collar votes—the same way Franklin Roosevelt is."[37]

Soap

"There's enough fat in the government in Washington," said Reagan in one speech, "that if it was rendered and made into soap, it would wash the world." [38]

Age

William Henry Harrison, who had been the oldest President, was sixty-eight when inaugurated in March 1841 and died a month later. Reagan turned sixty-nine in February 1980 and for a time age was an issue in the campaign. Reagan pointed out that Guiseppe Verdi composed *Falstaff* when he was eighty and Antonius Stradivarius made his best violins after sixty and was still making them in the year of his death at ninety-one. But he also handled the age issue with a series of one-liners. One of his favorites was a comment he said he had made after seeing a revival of his old film, *Knute Rockne—All American* (1948): "It's like seeing a younger son I never knew I had." He also liked to say: "Middle age is when you're faced with two temptations and you choose the one that will get you home at 9:30." At the annual Al Smith dinner in New York in mid-October he insisted "there is no foundation to the rumor that I am the only one here who was at the original Al Smith dinner" thirty-five years earlier. He also teased Carter (who was at the dinner too) about his Southern drawl. "Ronneh," he had the President asking him. "How can yew look younger every day when I see a new picture of yew ridin' horseback?" "Jimmeh," he supposedly replied, "I jes' keep ridin' older horses." In a speech attacking wage and price controls in Illinois, Reagan said they had never worked, even when the death penalty was used to enforce them, as under the Roman Emperor Diocletian. "And I'm one of the few persons," he added, "old enough to remember that!" [39]

Billygate

Republicans made much of Carter's "Billygate" (a word play on Nixon's Watergate), that is, the revelation that the President's good-ole-boy brother Billy had accepted $220,000 from the Libyan government for lobbying efforts in the United States. There was a Congressional investigation, Billy finally registered as the agent of a foreign government, and Carter defused the issue by admitting his "bad judgment" in asking his brother to seek the aid of Libyan officials in freeing the hostages in Iran. The difference between Carter and his brother, quipped comedian Bob Hope, a Reagan supporter, was that "Billy has a foreign policy." [40]

Factoids

Because Reagan liked to lace his speeches with horror stories, frequently exaggerated, about federal waste, Lou Cannon wrote in the *Washington Post* that Reagan had "never met a statistic he didn't like." Reagan's penchant for unchecked facts led reporters to call them "factoids."[41]

Ask Amy

Carter's reference in the TV debate to his little daughter Amy's concern about nuclear proliferation produced much mirth. "Ask Amy" signs began appearing at Republican rallies, and reporters suggested a new campaign book: *Prospects for Nuclear Disarmament,* by Amy Carter. When a crowd in Milwaukee started chanting, "Amy, Amy," Reagan responded: "I know he touched our hearts, all of us, the other night. I remember when Patty and Ron were little tiny kids, we used to talk about nuclear power." In another city he said, "Sorry I'm late, but I was busy starting a war." Former quarterback Roger Staubach, now a TV broadcaster, also got into the act. Covering a Dallas Cowboys–St. Louis Cardinals game and discussing the Cardinals' inability to throw the long pass successfully, he observed: "I was talking to my daughter Amy about it. She said St. Louis's biggest problem was the bomb."[42]

Just Begun

By 8:15 p.m., election night, the networks were announcing Reagan's victory and Carter decided to concede at once. He thought it would look ungracious if he waited until eleven; he didn't want people to think he was sulking in the White House. But his early concession—an hour before the polls closed on the West Coast—angered many Democrats. They thought it encouraged voters still lined up to vote to give up and go home and thus worked against local candidates. Reagan himself appeared with his wife on the stage of the Century Plaza Hotel in Los Angeles after Carter's concession to speak to the crowd there. "There's never been a more humbling moment in my life," he said. Then he quoted what Lincoln told newsmen when he knew he had won in 1860: "Well, boys, your troubles are over now; mine have just begun."[43]

What Hostages?

Just before the inauguration, when negotiations for the release of the hostages were still going on, Carter called Reagan to give him a detailed report on the matter. Afterwards, Hamilton Jordan asked: "What did he say, Mr. President?" Everyone in the Oval Office gathered around to hear. With a deadpan expression, Carter replied facetiously: "Well, I briefed him on what was happening to the hostages. He mostly listened. But when I finished, he said, 'What hostages?' "[44]

Debategate

From 1796 onward, billingsgate has been common in presidential elections. In 1972, though, came Nixon's "Watergate" and in 1976 Carter's "Billygate." And out of the 1980 contest came "Debategate."

In the summer of 1983 it came out that Reagan's campaign managers had gotten hold of President Carter's briefing book just before the Carter-Reagan television debate and that the advance knowledge was used to help Reagan in preparing for the encounter. Whether Reagan's advantage in the debate was crucial to the outcome of the election was not the question; the question, which both the Justice Department and a House subcommittee undertook to investigate, was whether the Carter material came to the Reagan people unsolicited or whether there was a "mole" in the White House. One Reagan aide said the Democrats were promoting a "pseudo-gate," but several members of the President's staff acknowledged seeing the pilfered campaign papers at the time, though they told conflicting stories about it. Reagan himself at first called it "much ado about nothing," but later promised to fire anyone proven guilty of wrongdoing. "I have a feeling," remarked one Republican party official, "they'll throw somebody to the wolves."

As the mole hunt went on some observers criticized the way journalists called the incident Briefinggate or Debategate. Said Columbia University Political Scientist Alan F. Westin: "I find myself just bored to tears by someone sticking 'gate' after every little foible." The briefing book affair, it was clear (and Billygate, too for that matter) did not remotely resemble Watergate.[45]

Willgate

About the time Debategate began making headlines it was revealed that the usually thoughtful conservative columnist George Will had coached Reagan just before the Carter-Reagan debate and then appeared on ABC's *Nightline* afterward and praised Reagan's "thoroughbred performance" without mentioning his own role as coach. Will, said the *New Republic* reprovingly, "posed as a referee without ever making it clear that he had been one of the seconds." "He impersonated a reporter," wrote Mary McGrory in her *Washington Post* column. "What he did was to work out in the gym with the challenger and then, without mentioning the fact to readers or reviewers, reviewed the fight on television." Will wrote a long column of his own in the *Post* defending what he had done, but admitting he would never do it again.[46]

★ ★ ★ ★ · ★ ★ ★ ★ ★ ★ ★ ★ ★ ★ ★ ★ ★ ★ ★ ★ ★ ★

CHAPTER FIFTY

1984
Another Reagan Sweep

The campaign of 1984 seemed interminable. This was partly because of the lengthy Democratic primary battle, which began with eight candidates early in the year, narrowed in the spring to three—Colorado Senator Gary Hart, Chicago civil-rights activist Rev. Jesse Jackson, and former Vice-President Walter F. ("Fritz") Mondale of Minnesota—and ended at long last in June with a victory for Mondale. But the campaign seemed tiresome, too, because it was almost a certainty by the time of the 56-year-old Mondale's nomination that, barring any unusual developments, Ronald Reagan (and George Bush) would win a comfortable victory in November. Even 1984's novelties—black leader Jackson's spirited bid for the Democratic nomination and Mondale's choice of a woman, New York Congresswoman Geraldine Ferraro, as his running mate—roused only passing interest for most voters. Complained Mondale himself at one point: "This campaign is *glacial.*"[1]

Themes, not issues, dominated the contest. The Republicans, meeting in Dallas in August to nominate the Reagan-Bush ticket for a second term, talked much of church, home, country, and morality; and some of the speakers seemed to think the Democrats no longer held these in esteem. But the Democratic convention in San Francisco in July also celebrated the ancient verities. Mondale's acceptance address was so eloquent about flag, faith, family, and fiscal restraint that after listening to it on television Reagan turned to his wife Nancy and exclaimed: "Didn't I write that?"[2] But in a stirring keynote speech in San Francisco New York Governor Mario Cuomo placed America's traditional values in a communal setting, thus reaffirming his party's commitment to justice for all since the 1930s.

During the campaign both Reagan and Mondale invoked the spirit of Harry Truman, America's newest folk hero. Mondale made use of

Truman quotations blasting the Republicans; he also reminded voters that all the experts thought Truman was a sure loser in 1948 and that just as Truman had won anyway, he, too, expected to sail on to victory despite predictions of defeat. But Reagan appropriated Truman too. In October he made a special point of retracing Truman's 1948 whistlestop campaign through Ohio, even using the same train, in an effort, apparently, to win over Democrats and make a clean sweep of all fifty states on election day. The President quoted Truman, too, and he also quoted Franklin Roosevelt and John F. Kennedy whenever he could. But he quipped as well as quoted. He charged that the Democrats had "gone so far left they have left the country," joked that the $200-billion deficit incurred by his administration was "big enough to take care of itself," and said he kept young by jogging three times a day around the portly Democratic Speaker of the House Thomas P. ("Tip") O'Neill.[3]

Reagan was doubtless young for his age; and in 1984, as in 1980, he enjoyed joking about it. At a party his wife threw to celebrate his seventy-third birthday in February, a young reporter told him, "I hope I'll be able to attend your 100th birthday," and Reagan exclaimed, "I don't see why not—you look in good health to me!" Later on he pointed out in one of his campaign speeches that Andrew Jackson "was actually 70 years old when he left the White House. Can you imagine that? And he felt pretty trim and vigorous when he left." Then, after a pause, he added: "I'm afraid the age factor may play a part in this election"; and, after the customary pause, completed the thought: "Our opponent's ideas are too old."[4]

Despite the quips, the "age issue" inevitably came up during the campaign. Dwight D. Eisenhower had been the oldest President to leave office, some observers noted, but he had been only seventy; Reagan, if re-elected, would turn seventy-eight shortly after ending his term of office. When news leaked out that Reagan occasionally dozed off while presiding at Cabinet meetings, White House officials issued embarrassed explanations and the Democrats began questioning his vigor. But Reagan made light of the matter. Visiting some campaign workers in Washington shortly after the disclosure, he told them: "Some of you here were up all night, I have found out, and working. I know the long hours that many of you have put in. And I can only tell you that, if I could manage it, I would schedule a Cabinet meeting so that we could all go over and take a nap together."[5]

As an issue Reagan's naps during Cabinet meetings roused little interest. But the President's faltering behavior in public on two occasions did elicit considerable comment and produced renewed speculation, even among people friendly to his candidacy, about his ability to withstand the rigors of four more years in the White House. In August, when a reporter asked him a question about arms-control agreements with the Russians, he seemed bewildered; then his wife whispered, "Doing everything we can," and he repeated the phrase. And in October, during the first of two television debates with Mondale, his mind seemed to go blank at one point and his summation of his position at the end of the program was rambling and inconclusive. The following day the *Wall Street Journal* had a front-page headline: "IS OLDEST U.S. PRESIDENT NOW SHOWING HIS AGE? REAGAN DEBATE PERFORMANCE INVITES OPEN SPECULATION ON HIS ABILITY TO SERVE." Reagan was disappointed by his performance, but he tried to laugh it off. "If I'd had as much make-up as [Mondale] had," he remarked, "I'd have looked younger too." But his aides explained that he had been given the wrong kind of coaching for the encounter. "We assumed Mondale would come in whining and strident," one of them revealed. "Instead, he was warm and knowledgeable. He out-Reaganed Reagan." In the second debate Reagan recovered lost ground, performed nicely, and even teased about the age issue again. "I will not make age an issue of this campaign," he said. "I'm not going to exploit for political purposes my opponent's youth and inexperience." In the end the energetic campaign he put on right up to Election Day helped kill the issue of age. So did his manifold activities as President in 1984: making a friendly visit to "so-called Communist China" (as he put it), opening the World's Fair in New Orleans and the Summer Olympics in Los Angeles, and attending a meeting of the industrial democracies in London.[6]

Religion, for a time, held the center of attention in 1984. Not only did such issues as abortion, prayer in the public schools, and tax credits for parents sending children to parochial schools produce heated arguments; the role of religion itself in American society also came in for discussion at one point. "The truth is, politics and morality are inseparable," declared Reagan at a prayer breakfast in Dallas on August 23. "And as morality's foundation is religion, religion and politics are necessarily related. We need religion for a guide." Reagan's statement was unexceptionable; most of his predecessors in the White House, even deists like Thomas Jefferson, from time to time made general references to religion in their public addresses. But Reagan went further than this: at times, to the delight of Christian fundamentalists (whose support he carefully cultivated), he blasted "modern-day secularism," gave the impression he thought the United States was a "Christian nation" rather than a land of many faiths, talked about Armageddon, and brought religion to bear on specific political issues. In Dallas he announced that opponents of organized prayer in the public schools were "intolerant of religion" and sought only "freedom against religion." His statement angered Mondale, a Methodist minister's son, who disagreed with him on the issue. "That's insulting!" he exclaimed. "He's calling me un-Christian." Against the advice of his associates (who didn't think it a "voting issue"), Mondale tried to make church-state separation a major issue of the campaign. Religious faith was a private matter, he insisted, and it was wrong for the President to "transform policy debates into theological disputes" and suggest that "political dissent from him is un-Christian." He failed, though, to generate much criticism of the President. Reagan soon backtracked and affirmed his support for church-state separation and the issue died a-borning. But Lee A. Iacocca, chairman of the Chrysler Corporation, grumbled: "I have heard a lot about Christianity and prayer in the schools, but these guys aren't running for Pope." He urged the candidates to talk about the serious economic problems facing the nation.[7]

The candidates did of course talk economics. Mondale made much of the Reagan administration's huge budget deficit and called frankly for a rise in taxes to meet the crisis. But Reagan strongly opposed raising taxes; he called instead for reduced spending on social programs (but not on the Pentagon) to bring down the deficit. He reiterated his belief, too, that economic growth, stimulated by lower taxes, would bring in more revenue and help balance the budget. Mondale's "program of high taxes, sugar-coated with compassionate rhetoric," he declared, "is a disaster in disguise that will destroy our economic expansion, increase unemployment, and re-ignite inflation." Mondale's belief that taking an unpopular position—calling for a tax hike—would impress voters with his candor and capacity for vigorous leadership turned out to be misguided. His recommendation produced antagonism, not admiration, and played right into the President's hands. In speech after speech Reagan gleefully depicted Mondale, and the Democrats generally, as big taxers and spenders who were saddling the country with debt when he took over in 1981. In a speech in Ohio charging that Mondale had distorted his record, Reagan quipped: "I was about to say to him very sternly, 'Mr. Mondale, you are taxing my patience.' And then I caught myself. Why should I give him another idea? That's the only tax he hasn't thought about."[8]

During the campaign Reagan mostly ignored the deficit. He dwelt instead on the improvement of the economy—particularly the end of the double-digit inflation of the Carter years—under his stewardship. "Our goal is an opportunity society," he told audiences, "giving everyone not only an equal chance but a greater chance to pursue that American dream. And we can build that future together if you elect people to Congress who will not vote for tax increases but vote for growth and economic progress." Mondale's emphasis on the economy's shortcomings Reagan dismissed as the whinings of a sour-faced pessimist. The Democratic party, he liked to say, was the party of gloom and doom; it was also a "blame-America-first" party when it came to foreign affairs, while his own was "America's party." Mondale's efforts to present a vision of an America that was better because it was fairer to all citizens evoked little interest among voters. Nor did his warnings about Reagan's hawkishness in foreign relations register with the voters. Reagan muted the war-peace issue by calling for negotiations with the Russians for arms control. Before long he was campaigning as the candidate of peace as well as of prosperity (and piety). "America's best days lie ahead," he exclaimed in the last days of the campaign, "and—you ain't seen nothin' yet!"[9]

On election day the Reagan-Bush ticket, as the polls had predicted all along, swept the nation. Reagan won 54,450,603 popular votes (59 percent) to Mondale's 37,573,671 (41 percent) and carried every state but Mondale's Minnesota and the District of Columbia (525 electoral votes to 13). His victory was something of a record. His popular-vote margin was second only to Nixon's in 1972; and the percentage of total votes cast which he won placed him with the top winners of the past: Harding in 1920, Roosevelt in 1936, Johnson in 1964, and Nixon in 1972. "Reagan is the most popular figure in the history of the United States," said Speaker "Tip" O'Neill after the election. "No candidate we put up would have been able to beat Reagan this year."[10]

O'Neill was probably right. Luck of course was with Reagan (as with all victors): inflation had slowed and voters thought they were better off than they had been in 1980. But Reagan himself, "the Great Communicator," unquestionably played a major role in his triumph. In an age shaped powerfully by television he was a masterful performer. During his first four years in office he had succeeded in projecting the image of bold and courageous leadership in the White House and in convincing millions of Americans that their beloved country still "stood tall" in the world despite all the disasters and upheavals of the past two decades: the Vietnam War, the rise of the counterculture, the student protest movement, the explosion of black militancy, Watergate, and the Iranian hostage crisis. Reagan himself "stood tall" too; and even people who disagreed with his position on specific issues liked the way he proclaimed himself an unabashed patriot and a champion of traditional manners and morals. The country was now profoundly conservative; Yippies had become Yuppies. The anti-Establishment agitations of the Johnson-Nixon years (which had bothered Middle America so much) seemed unthinkable in the Age of Reagan. In a sense Reagan's landslide victory meant that the eighties was somehow getting even with the sixties.

☆ ☆ ☆

Not So Stodgy After All

In February one day the crowds in the New Hampshire towns Mondale was visiting were unusually large and friendly. But he knew he wasn't the one they came to see. The big drawing card was film star Paul Newman, who was touring the state with him and giving short speeches on his behalf. At one place Mondale began a speech lambasting the Reagan administration while Newman sat perspiring on the stage behind him in the overheated room. After a while Newman loosened his tie and women in the audience murmured their approval; then he removed his jacket and they applauded loudly. Startled, Mondale turned, stared at the actor for a moment, and then said with a grin, "Are you finished yet?" And then, as Newman nodded, Mondale (whom some people considered stodgy) surprised everyone by suddenly removing his own jacket and tossing it over to Newman. His gesture brought down the house.[11]

Where's the Beef?

During the primaries, Gary Hart for a time posed a real threat to Mondale. He was especially appealing to the "Yuppies," that is, young upwardly mobile professionals, who liked the way he combined liberal Democratic policies with an emphasis on free-market economics and the need for economic growth. In his campaign for the Democratic nomination, Hart talked a great deal about "new ideas"; he had published a book about them in 1983 entitled *A New Democracy.* But in a debate in Atlanta in April, Mondale suddenly turned to him and exclaimed: "When I hear your new ideas, I'm reminded of the ad, 'Where's the beef?' " The phrase, taken from a TV commercial for Wendy's hamburgers, was soon ricocheting throughout the land. Hart later displayed his book between two buns, but he was never able to overcome the impression after Mondale's question that the ideas he was presenting were vague and unexciting.[12]

What the Dickens!

In his keynoter for the Democrats, Governor Mario Cuomo used the image of two cities, one rich and one poor, to describe Reagan's America and he borrowed the title of one of Charles Dickens's novels to press home his point: *A Tale of Two Cities.* Shortly afterward, Gerald B. H. Solomon, Republican Congressman from upstate New York, told the House of Representatives that Cuomo's knowledge of Dickens was as weak as his perception of President Reagan's record. Reagan, he said, had inherited a *Bleak House* from the Carter-Mondale administration, which had brought the nation *Hard Times,* but under Reagan the country had returned to its *Great Expectations.* "So go back and read your Charles Dickens, Mr. Cuomo," he advised. "You will have plenty of time after November, when Reagan will take your candidate, Mondale, and beat the dickens out of him (Charles Dickens, that is)."[13]

Do Our Best

After Governor Cuomo's riveting keynoter someone asked Joan Mondale, "Wasn't it wonderful?" "Yes, it was," agreed the Democratic candidate's wife, and added: "We're going to do our best to be that good." Then she turned to her husband's speech-writer and cried: "Won't we?"[14]

Oath

In 1984 Democrats worried about defections to the Reagan camp. When a delegate to the San Francisco convention came up and asked New York Mayor Edward I. Koch for his autograph, the Mayor said, "Raise your right hand. Do you solemnly swear that you will actually vote for Walter Mondale in November?" The delegate so swore and the Mayor signed his name.[15]

Etiquette

There was a great deal of discussion about etiquette after the Democrats picked the first co-educational ticket for a major party in American history. Mondale's staff issued precise instructions for his appearance on the stage with his running mate after the nominations: "WFM remains on the right side of the rostrum and applauds Ferraro as she comes on stage from left. They shake hands at rostrum and the two candidates wave together at rostrum without arms. No joined hands held aloft—now or at any time during demonstration." In St. Paul, a few weeks later, came the candidates' first joint appearance during the campaign. They circled each other a bit warily at first, as if they weren't sure how they should behave, and then exchanged greetings without shaking hands. Observed a Democratic campaign consultant: "He looked like a teen-ager on the first date with that 'how in the world do you pin the corsage on her' problem." Queried about his hands-off policy at a news conference afterward, Mondale explained: "Jimmy Carter never touched."

It wasn't only the behavior of the Mondale-Ferraro ticket that fascinated people; it was the language too. "A lot of stock phrases will have to be changed," advised one Democratic campaign consultant. "Mondale can never say we have a ticket with broad appeal." Other forbiddens: "clean skirts" and "intimate relationship." For the new "sexually integrated politics" the *New York Daily News*'s Joan Beck came up with some helpful hints:

> Neither the media nor other politicians should comment on a woman candidate's clothes or figure or hairstyle. The magazine that recently described Ferraro's calves as "ample" wouldn't have mentioned how Gary Hart's

waist measures or suggested Jesse Jackson be photographed in running
shorts more often because he has good legs.

A woman candidate shouldn't be called "Honey" or "Dear" or "Darling"
to her face or "the broad" or "that bitch" behind her back.

A man shouldn't take a woman candidate's elbow to help her up a step
or into a car or steer her through a crowd with an arm on her shoulder or
around her waist. It suggests to voters that she can't walk and talk at the
same time. . . .

Kissing should be left to family and intimate friends. It's too important
to be wasted on politicians, whether or not they're female, and it's no fun
if it's not well on target.[16]

Not a Yes-Man

George Bush had once dismissed Reagan's economic views as "voodoo
economics," but after becoming Vice-President he was one of the President's firmest supporters. "One thing about Bush—he's not a yes-man,"
went a 1984 joke. "If Ronald Reagan says, 'No,' he says, 'No!' too."[17]

Arms Across the Seas

In a voice test before a radio broadcast early in August President Reagan thought he would have a little fun. "My fellow Americans," he ad-
libbed, "I am pleased to tell you I just signed legislation which outlaws
Russia forever. The bombing begins in five minutes." His remarks were
overheard, carried in the press, and produced consternation in Europe
as well as in the United States. Nuclear destruction, observed the *New
York Times,* "is not something most people think of as a fit subject for
summer sport." Reagan quickly expressed regret for his remarks, but
also criticized the press for stirring up so much excitement about them.
A few days later, when the Republicans were meeting in Dallas, some
moderate Republicans put on a satirical little skit centering on a day in
the White House when war looms with Russia. The show opened with
Mrs. Reagan telling White House aides not to wake the President because "he needs his 16 hours, and besides we haven't had a holiday in
days." It ended with Reagan's going on television to inform the nation
that he has just pushed the button. "I am announcing an exchange program with the Soviet Union," he says genially. "It's my arms-across-the-
seas policy. Deficits will be a thing of the past. In fact, the past will be
a thing of the past."[18]

The President and the Doctor

In speeches President Reagan liked to include stories about Americans
who had risen high by pluck and diligence or who had acted bravely in
emergencies. One of his favorites was about a World War II bomber

pilot who went heroically down with his plane because his wounded gunner couldn't bail out. But when critics raised questions about witnesses to the event and film buffs pointed out that the episode had appeared in a 1944 movie, *A Wing and a Prayer*, Reagan dropped the story from his repertory. But during the campaign he found other tales to tell.

In September, Reagan singled out Dr. Joseph M. Giordono of the George Washington University Hospital for special praise. Giordono had attended the President right after the attempt to assassinate him in 1981 and Reagan credited him with saving his life. Reagan viewed Giordono's rise to prominence as a classic American success story: he was the son of an Italian immigrant who became a milkman and worked hard, struggled, and sacrificed to put his son through college and medical school. Unfortunately for Reagan, Dr. Giordono turned out to be a Democrat. He was pleased by the President's praise, Giordono told reporters, but he said that much of the credit for his success in life went to Federal social programs of the kind the President criticized: low-interest government loans to students and Federal funding for biomedical research.[19]

Typed Better

Mondale was admittedly better at face-to-face encounters than at making speeches on television. After one of his TV appearances, a supporter sighed: "The speech was *typed* better than it was read."[20]

Distance

During the campaign Reagan liked to tell baseball stories to make his point. "Our detractors would like to have you think we've made no progress," he declared in a speech in California in September. "You know, they remind me of a baseball rookie. He had a kind of know-it-all manager. And it was a crucial game in the pennant race and tied up in the bottom of the ninth. And they put him in as a pinch-hitter. And he boomed one way over right center field and clear over the bleachers into the street. And, of course, by the time he rounded third and headed for the plate, he had a broad grin on his face. Got to the dugout and that manager, that know-it-all manager, was waiting for him. And the first thing he said was, 'Your stance was all wrong. You were awkward up there. You held your arms too high.' And when he paused for breath in his criticism, the kid says, 'Yeah, but how was it for distance?' "[21]

★ ★

CHAPTER FIFTY-ONE

1988
Trivial Pursuit: Bush vs. Dukakis

In his speech accepting the Democratic nomination for President in
Atlanta in July 1988, Massachusetts Governor Michael S. Dukakis announced that the election was "not about ideology; it's about competence." He was wrong; the campaign of 1988 centered on neither ideology nor competence. Once the Republicans, meeting in New Orleans
in August, picked Vice-President George Bush as their candidate, the
campaign came quickly to center on social and cultural issues—the
Pledge of Allegiance, prisoner furloughs, capital punishment—which
had little or nothing to do with the big problems, domestic and foreign,
confronting American Presidents in the late 20th century. Long before
election day serious observers were deploring the trivialization of presidential politics in the 1988 race.[1]

The candidates did not, to be sure, completely ignore major issues.
With the Cold War ending, Dukakis proposed cutting military spending drastically and using the money saved on education, health care,
housing for the homeless, and other social programs. Bush, for his
part, promised to continue President Reagan's conservative economic
policies, called for a cut in the capital gains tax, and assured voters that
he would firmly resist efforts in Congress to levy new taxes ("Read my
lips, no new taxes"). But with the Republicans taking a vigorous offensive soon after the conventions adjourned, the campaign turned out to
be largely a negative one that ignored serious national questions. It was
also an exceptionally mean-spirited campaign. After it was all over, Lee
Atwater, one of the Vice-President's campaign managers, apologized
for the ferocity of the attacks on the Democratic candidate. "In 1988,"
he recalled (shortly before his death from a brain tumor in 1991),
"fighting Dukakis, I said that 'I would strip the bark off the little bastard' and 'make Willie Horton his running mate.' I am sorry for both

statements: the first for its naked cruelty, the second because it makes me sound racist, which I am not." [2]

Dukakis was slow to respond to the charge that he "coddled criminals" like Willie Horton (a black murderer who, on parole under a Massachusetts furlough program, raped a Maryland woman and terrorized her companion), and was, in general, "soft on crime." He also refused to take seriously at first Republican suggestions that he was lacking in patriotism because he vetoed a Massachusetts bill (which he regarded as unconstitutional) forcing schoolchildren to recite the Pledge of Allegiance in the classroom. And, in a major blunder, when asked during his second debate with Bush how he would react if someone raped and murdered his wife, he simply reiterated his well-known opposition to the death penalty instead of expressing outrage at the question. "I blew it," he admitted ruefully afterward. [3]

Bush's assault on Dukakis as being somehow out of the American mainstream laid to rest charges that he himself was something of a wimp and in the end brought a comfortable victory to him and his running mate, Indiana Senator Dan Quayle. On election day, with voter turnout the lowest since 1924, Bush won 54 percent of the popular votes and, when it came to electoral votes, overwhelmed Dukakis and his running mate, Texas Senator Lloyd Bentsen, with 426 votes to 112. About the only satisfaction the Democrats took from Bush's victory was his abandonment of his campaign pledge, "No new taxes," and his agreement with Congress in June 1990 to accept higher taxes after all in an effort to hold down the burgeoning national deficit.

☆ ☆ ☆

Not His Finest Hour

Arkansas Governor Bill Clinton's nominating speech for Michael Dukakis at the Atlanta convention was so long and dull that the biggest applause came when he reached the words, "In closing . . . ." Though Clinton said afterward that the Dukakis people gave him the speech and instructed him to deliver it exactly as written, he admitted it was "the biggest mistake of my life." He should have stopped, he later realized, when the TelePrompTer began flashing, "Your time is up," or when delegates began interrupting him with cries, "Duke! Duke! We Want Mike!," or when ABC and NBC cameras cut away from him to show a documentary film about Dukakis and interview delegates who were critical of Clinton's speech. Jokes abounded afterward, and Clinton, at first angered by them, finally calmed down, appeared on Johnny Carson's *The Tonight Show*, good-naturedly subjected himself to some teasing, and then took out his saxophone to play "a short number." "It wasn't my finest hour," he liked to say of his Atlanta speech. "It wasn't even my finest hour and a half." Four years later, when he appeared at the Democratic convention in New York to accept his own presidential nomination, he began by saying with a grin that he had come to Madison Square Garden to finish the speech he had made in 1988.[4]

Points of Light

For Bush's acceptance speech in New Orleans, speech-writer Peggy Noonan not only came up with the phrase "a kinder, gentler nation," which he used frequently during the campaign, but also with the phrase, "a thousand points of light," meaning volunteer and charity work as an alternative to government welfare programs. Dukakis said he was puzzled by the phrase, but went on to say he himself was for "240 million points of light," that is, for all the people in the United States. During the campaign Bush admitted he sympathized with people who weren't sure what the phrase meant, and he boggled it once himself, calling for "a thousand shining hills," and then hastily explained: "I can't do poetry." At a New York charity dinner, though, he joked about it. He said that he and his wife Barbara had gone to the movies the night before and asked an usher for help in finding a seat in the darkened theater. But the usher declined, he said, reminding him: "You're the one with the 1,000 points of light!" In the same speech Bush expressed amusement at *Washington Post* cartoonist Herblock's picture of a beer-drinking barfly telling a companion that he endorsed Bush's pledge of "one thousand pints of Lite." Weeks later, when Bush debated Dukakis in Los Angeles, his media consultant Roger Ailes paced nervously backstage while he and Bush's other campaign advisers watched the Bush-Dukakis encounter on television. Suddenly the hefty Ailes tripped over an electrical cord and brought a lamp crashing to the floor and shattering it into pieces. "Well," sighed Bush adviser Stuart Spencer, "that means there's only 999 points of light!"[5]

Willie Horton

In 1988 the Republicans made a black criminal named Willie Horton famous throughout the land. Horton, they learned early in the campaign, was a convicted murderer who raped a Maryland woman and stabbed her companion while he was on a weekend furlough from a Massachusetts prison while Dukakis was Governor. The Republicans, candidate Bush told voters, "don't let murderers out on vacation to terrorize innocent people. . . . Dukakis owes the people an explanation of why he supported this outrageous program." Bush's supporters went on to sponsor a TV commercial that showed menacing pictures of Horton, gave grisly details about his crime, and announced: "Dukakis not only opposes the death penalty, he allowed first-degree murderers to have weekend passes from prison." In Maryland the Republican party chairman went even further. He circulated a fund-raising letter which warned of the "Dukakis/Willie Horton" team and carried a picture of the convict next to one of the Governor, accompanied by the caption: "Is This Your Pro-Family Team for 1988?" The letter went on to warn: "You, your spouse, your children, and your friends can have the opportunity to receive a visit from someone like Willie Horton if Mike Dukakis becomes President."

The facts, as the Democrats belatedly made clear, were not so simple. The Massachusetts furlough program, it turned out, had been adopted during the administration of Francis Sargent, a Republican who was Dukakis's predecessor in the state house. Forty-two states, moreover, including California, had similar programs. While Ronald Reagan was Governor of California, the Democrats revealed, one criminal, on a 72-hour pass, murdered a Los Angeles police officer, and two other criminals, on 72-hour furloughs, murdered a woman in Orange County. The Democrats also pointed out that when Bush was Congressman from Texas, 1967–71, he helped found a chain of halfway houses for convicts in Houston (which included criminals who hadn't finished their sentences but were on parole), and, as Vice-President, he had spoken warmly of the good work being done by these houses. But, the Democrats noted, one of the parolees had committed murder. The Democrats eventually produced a TV commercial about the murder to counter the Republicans' Willie Horton ads. "In 1968," according to the Democratic ad, "George Bush helped an ex-convict fund a halfway house for early released felons in Houston, Texas. In 1982, one of those prisoners raped and murdered a minister's wife."

The Dukakis commercial came late and had little or no effect on the campaign. Willie Horton continued to be the campaign's celebrity. *Chicago Tribune* columnist Mike Royko found the situation ironic. "There must be some valid reason why it's O.K. for Bush to support a halfway house program that led to the murder of a minister's wife," he mused. "And for Reagan to support a furlough program that led to the murders of a woman and a cop. But it's wrong for Dukakis to have supported a furlough program (started, incidentally, by a Republican predecessor) that led to a rape." His conclusion: "The only thing I can figure is that maybe Bush's killer and Reagan's killer might have been Republicans."[6]

Passion

"Quiet on the set, everybody!" cried Dukakis sharply. "Quiet!" The TV crew was surprised; usually one of their people gave the order. But the cameras rolled and Tom Brokaw began interviewing the Democratic candidate in his hotel suite. Recalling that Dukakis had been called cold and unfeeling, Brokaw asked if the Massachusetts Governor thought the campaign was one without passion. "Or is that a misreading?" he wanted to know. "I think it's a misreading," said Dukakis solemnly. "I think there's an enormous amount of passion about this country's values, about whether we're going to respect the law and the Constitution and have a President who understands that and respects the law and respects the Constitution both here and abroad. I think there's great uncertainty about our economic future. Where are we going? What are we doing? How can we live with a federal budget deficit of 150 to 200 billion dollars a year, year after year after year. And that's why I think the next President has got to be somebody who is tested and brings very strong fiscal and economic leadership to the country." And on and on and on. With imperturbable calm, of course, throughout.[7]

The Light Touch

At an Alfred E. Smith Memorial Dinner in Manhattan the two candidates let their hair down a bit, and, for a change, tried teasing instead of taunting each other. It was a pleasant, though not especially memorable, interlude in a campaign marked by a notable lack of good spirits. The jests were mostly juvenile, the one-liners leaden, and the quips querulous. Americans like their leaders to have a sense of fun as well as a capacity for high seriousness, but there wasn't much mirth in the 1988 contest. The contestants seemed to be what novelist Sinclair Lewis once called "Men of Measured Merriment." The low voter turnout in November may well have come partly from the humorlessness that dominated 1988's "presidentiad."

Not that candidates didn't on occasion essay the light touch. At a luncheon for Democratic fund-raisers just before delivering his acceptance address, Michael Dukakis, known for his ponderousness, tried a bit of self-teasing. "As you all know," he said, "I'm a stem-winding orator." This produced polite laughter. Riding the wave, he went on to express trepidation over the fact that he was scheduled to follow two spellbinders at the Democratic convention: keynoter Ann Richards of Texas (whose remark that George Bush was "born with a silver foot in his mouth" brought down the house) and Jesse Jackson (eloquent black preacher who did well in the Democratic primaries and won many votes for President on the first ballot in the Democratic convention). He went on to joke about his supposed arrogance. "It's maybe the first time in my life that I have a small inferiority complex." This brought more polite laughter. Then, in a try for the big enchilada, he went on to say that his wife Kitty had asked for a look at his acceptance speech. "I said, 'O.K.,' and she went into the bedroom. When I went into the room myself to get my jacket, my wife was fast asleep on the bed, and the speech was beside her, half-read." Abraham Lincoln could have taught Dukakis something about gentle self-deprecation.

Bush didn't really do much better. His own self-teasing came largely from his efforts to recover from the campaign's most celebrated tongue-slip. "Forty-seven years ago," Bush told the American Legion convention on September 7, "we were hit and hit hard at Pearl Harbor." Then, as murmurs filled the hall, he exclaimed: "Did I say September 7? Sorry about that. It was December 7, 1941." He spent the next few days joking about his gaffe. "You ought to vote for me," he told one crowd. "I knew about Pearl Harbor three months before it happened." And when he was mistakenly introduced at one rally as President of the United States he said: "I don't feel so bad. Pearl Harbor was December 7, and this man's entitled to his opinion." Bush could have learned from Lincoln too.

But Bush's misdating of the Pearl Harbor attack wasn't the only gaffe of the 1988 campaign. There were plenty of *lapsi linguae,* in fact, on both sides and they surely helped to liven things up. But Dukakis, sad to say, didn't turn out to be much of a malapropist. He called for "modern musicians" instead of "modern munitions" in one speech, and in another speech criticizing Bush's support for arms sales to Iran he said: "I don't question Mr. Bush's terrorism," then laughed and corrected himself: "I don't question Mr. Bush's patriotism."

Bush was far better than Dukakis at this sort of thing. At one fundraiser he announced: "I see an America in the midst of the largest peacetime explosion [expansion?] ever." In another speech he called drug kingpins "ping-pins," and in still another assured people: "I'm going to be coming out here with my own drug problem." Elsewhere he exclaimed: "I stand for anti-bigotry, anti-Semitism, anti-racism," and then had to make it clear he opposed anti-Semitism. To one audience he insisted he would make sure that "everyone who has a job, wants a job," and to another he said he was "imposed to an independent Palestine state." And several times he also botched the phrase "thousand points of light," which he had used in his acceptance address in New Orleans.

But Bush-Speak, as the Republican candidate's speech habits came to be called, had its undoubted charm and surely added a bit of fun to an otherwise ill-natured campaign. And though Bush's campaign managers worked hard to keep him to his prepared script, he still managed to cut loose from time to time and come up with some glorious goofs. Asked about his experience as a fighter pilot during World War II, when he was shot down over the Pacific by Japanese gunners, he exclaimed: "What sustains you in times like that? Well, you go back to fundamental values. I thought about Mother and Dad and the strengths I got from them—and God and faith and the separation of church and state." There was something intriguing—if not hilarious—

about a young man pondering disestablishmentarianism at a time when his life was hanging in the balance.

Bush-watchers' favorite gaffe came at a Republican rally in Twin Falls, Idaho, where the Vice-President was discussing the closeness of his relationship with President Reagan. "I have worked alongside of him, and I'm proud to be his partner," said Bush solemnly. "We have had triumphs, we have made mistakes, we have had sex. . . ." There was a moment of stunned silence in the audience, and then Bush hastened to correct himself: "We have had setbacks." And as people roared with laughter he sighed: "I feel like a javelin thrower who won the coin toss and elected to receive."[8]

Flags

Campaign '88 was the most flag-bedecked campaign in U.S. history. Both candidates stood in front of flags when speaking, and their campaign workers saw to it that audiences received little flags to wave. But Bush was the flag-waver par excellence. He visited Findlay, Ohio, known as Flag City, during the campaign, and also a flag factory in New Jersey. "My friends," he announced, "American flags are doing well, and America is doing well." He went on to report that flag sales declined when Jimmy Carter was President but mounted steadily after Ronald Reagan took over the reins of office in 1981. Most of the flags at one rally, it turned out, were imported from Taiwan, but campaign workers carefully scratched out "Made in Taiwan" from the handles before distributing them to the voters. But even Lee Atwater thought New Jersey "was one flag factory too many."

"Where is George Bush?" asked Dukakis irritably during one of his TV appearances. "He's visiting a flag factory. Don't you think," he taunted his opponent, "it's about time you came out from behind the flag and told us what you intend to do to provide basic health insurance for thirty-seven million Americans?" But Dukakis realized he was in a bind. As Governor he had vetoed a bill mandating the recitation of the Pledge of Allegiance in the schools of his state because he knew the U.S. Supreme Court had outlawed the practice in a 1943 decision (devout believers like the Jehovah's Witnesses opposed the recitation as blasphemous) and because the Massachusetts Supreme Court justices had advised him the legislation was unconstitutional. But Dukakis's constitutional scruples did him no good. During the campaign Vice-President Bush made extensive use of Dukakis's veto to raise doubts about his patriotism. "I'll never understand," he cried, "when it came to his desk, why he vetoed a bill that called for the pledge of allegiance to be said in the schools of Massachusetts. I'll never understand it. We are one nation under God. Our kids should say the pledge of allegiance." Like many school kids, though, Bush occasionally garbled the words of the Pledge (written by a Christian socialist in 1892) when he introduced them into his pro-flag campaign speeches.⁹

Quayle and JFK

When Indiana Senator Dan Quayle faced Texas Senator Lloyd Bentsen at the vice-presidential debate in Omaha in October, there was some discussion of Quayle's youth (he was forty-one but looked younger) and inexperience, and Quayle earnestly defended himself. "It's not just age, it's accomplishments, it's experience," he declared. "I have far more experience than many others that sought the office of vice-president in this country. I have as much experience in the Congress as Jack Kennedy did when he sought the presidency. . . ." "Senator," rejoined Bentsen sharply, "I served with Jack Kennedy. I knew Jack Kennedy. Jack Kennedy was a friend of mine. Senator, you are no Jack Kennedy." Shattered by Bentsen's riposte, Quayle turned red and murmured, "That was really uncalled for, Senator," as the audience laughed and applauded.

Bentsen's remark lingered long after the campaign ended, and Quayle finally decided to turn it into a joke. A few months after becoming Vice-President, he appeared at a book party celebrating the publication of a book about the 1988 campaign by journalists Jack Germond and Jules Witcover and made a little speech. Reminding the audience of Theodore White's famous series of books on presidential campaigns beginning with *The Making of the President, 1960* (1961), he looked at Germond and Witcover and announced: "I knew Teddy White. Teddy White was a friend of mine. And believe me, you guys are no Teddy White!"¹⁰

Orchestra Pit

The media, said Roger Ailes, Bush's media adviser, in a panel discussion a few weeks after the election, were interested in three things: gaffes, attacks, and good visuals. "That's the one sure way of getting coverage," he declared. "You try to avoid as many mistakes as you can. You try to give them as many pictures as you can. And if you need coverage, you attack, and you will get coverage." He went on to say that he had "an orchestra pit" theory of politics. "If you have two guys on stage," he explained, "and one guy says, 'I have a solution to the Middle East problem,' and the other guy falls in the orchestra pit, who do you think is going to be on the evening news?" It was an error, he insisted, for a candidate to "get his head up too far on some new vision for America" because "the next thing that happens" is that the media people "run over" to his opponent and cry: "Tell me why you think this is an idiotic idea." Judy Woodruff *(The MacNeil/Lehrer NewsHour)* was appalled. Cried she: "So you're saying the notion of the candidate saying, 'I want to run for President because I want to do something for this country,' is crazy." Nodded Ailes: "Suicide."

Ailes may have been exaggerating, but it was generally agreed among political analysts that Campaign '88 was something less than edifying. "The process by which we choose our Presidential candidates," wrote the *New Yorker*'s Elizabeth Drew right after the primaries, "more resembles a demolition derby than a rational procedure." She found the general election following the primaries equally dismal. Even before it was over, 1988 was being known as an "issueless wonder." Reporters Jack Germond and Jules Witcover subtitled their book on the campaign (published in 1989) *The Trivial Pursuit of the Presidency* and came to the conclusion that it was "perhaps the most mean-spirited and negative campaign in modern-day American political history." Elizabeth Drew agreed. She thought the Bush-Dukakis contest "did something new to our Presidential elections. A degradation occurred which we may have to live with a long time. The Bush campaign broke the mold of modern Presidential politics. Negative campaigning of a new order of magnitude has now come to Presidential politics. And it worked." [11]

★ ★

CHAPTER FIFTY-TWO

1992
Clinton and the Call for Change

The campaign of 1992 was strewn with novelties. There were three major candidates, for one thing, and, for another, they were all from the South, with two of them coming from Texas: George Bush (Texas), William Jefferson Clinton (Arkansas), Ross Perot (Texas). The Democratic ticket, moreover, contained two candidates from the same region, the South, instead of being regionally balanced, as had long been the custom: Arkansas Governor Bill Clinton and Tennessee Senator Albert Gore, Jr. And the major independent candidate, Texas billionaire H. Ross Perot, in another novelty, was self-nominated as well as self-organized, self-promoted, self-scheduled, self-advertised, and self-financed. Perot's timing was his own, too, for he entered the contest in February, dropped out in July, offended by media attacks, and then plunged into the fray again in October.

Campaign '92 was unusual in procedures as well as in candidates. TV talk shows—hosted by Larry King, Phil Donahue, Arsenio Hall, Oprah Winfrey—played a major part in the struggle for votes. Perot launched his campaign on *Larry King Live;* Bill Clinton played the saxophone (as well as chatted) for Arsenio Hall; and President Bush, after initial doubts about what he called "weird talk shows," also decided to join the talk-show circuit to press for his own re-election. *New York Times* columnist Russell Baker concluded that presidential contests had, for good or ill, entered "the Larry King era" in 1992.[1]

On call-in talk shows the candidates could say pretty much what they pleased, for their hosts were amiable and indulgent; they were also able to field questions from the voters (in the audience or on the telephone) without the mediation of hard-nosed (and at times self-aggrandizing) reporters. There were formal TV debates, to be sure, in 1992, with panels of reporters pressing all three candidates hard, but for the second presidential debate, held at the University of Richmond in Virginia, there was only a moderator, Carole Simpson of ABC News, and she relayed questions to the three candidates directly from an audience of undecided (and at times skeptical) voters. Members of the Richmond audience made it clear from the outset that they were interested in issues, not personal attacks, and the Richmond debate underlined the seriousness with which voters took their responsibilities in 1992. The vice-presidential debate, in which Vice-President Dan Quayle tried to needle the rather stodgy Albert Gore the way an adolescent boy might do so on a high school debate team, embarrassed rather than amused most viewers.

Governor Clinton emphasized the economy in his speeches, interviews, and appearances on talk shows. His chief campaign adviser hung a reminder on the wall of the "war room" in Little Rock, Arkansas: "THE ECONOMY, STUPID!"[2] The recession into which the country had fallen in 1991 shaped much of his agenda. Rejecting the "trickle-down" approach of the Reagan-Bush years (according to which the benefits coming from government aid to business would eventually trickle down to the general populace), he proposed government action to revitalize the economy, develop fairer social and economic arrangements for people of all classes, and ensure that the American dream became a reality for future generations of Americans. Sometimes called a "policy wonk," Clinton came up with ambitious and detailed plans for reform which included devising a national health care system, rebuilding the nation's infrastructure, extending tuition loans to college students, reducing unemployment by public works, reforming the way campaigns were financed, and replacing welfare, where possible, with "workfare." Throughout the campaign, Clinton, as a New Democrat, took a centrist position, arguing that reinvigoration of the American economy would help everyone (especially the "forgotten middle class"), including blacks and Latinos. And since Ross Perot centered his campaign on the burgeoning federal deficit and the horrendous national debt (which moved from $1 trillion to $4 trillion during the Reagan-Bush years), Clinton added control of the deficit to his list of desiderata. "We've got to change this country," he insisted. There must be "courage to change."[3]

President Bush did not at first take the economic downturn seriously. He was, in any case, more interested in foreign than in domestic affairs, and prided himself on his experience on the world scene. Flushed by his enormous popularity after the Persian Gulf War (in which U.S. forces, under the aegis of the United Nations, repelled an Iraqui invasion of Kuwait), he took his re-election almost for granted and delayed launching his bid for a second term until early 1992. By this time things had turned sour for the President. Iraqui dictator Saddam Hussein remained in power, despite his defeat, and he continued to defy both the United States and the United Nations. Revelations of the Bush administration's coddling of the Iraqui dictator until the very eve of his invasion of Kuwait also cast doubts on the President's competency, even in his beloved field of foreign affairs. But the recession remained his primary problem. Bush at first took the traditional conservative view: if he followed a let-alone policy, the economy would eventually right itself. But as economic conditions worsened and middle-class Americans became increasingly jittery about the bleak future that seemed to lie ahead, the President's popularity plummeted and his advisers pressed him to throw himself into the campaign as soon as possible. At length he announced his concern for the state of the Union ("Message: I care"), launched his campaign for a second term, and asserted his determination to be "the Comeback Kid." He also reminded voters that Harry Truman had, like Bush, stood low in the polls during his 1948 campaign for re-election but had in the end fooled all the experts by defeating his challenger, Thomas E. Dewey, in November. But when Bush suggested that Truman would probably vote Republican if he were still living, the former President's daughter Margaret promptly intervened to reject Bush's suggestion with indignation and remind him that he was indeed no Harry Truman.[4]

In 1992, as in 1988, the campaign at times turned nasty. During the primaries, there were charges of marital infidelity against Clinton (and countercharges of the same nature, quickly laid to rest, against Bush), but this particular issue died after Clinton appeared on *60 Minutes* with his wife Hillary to acknowledge that their marriage had had difficulties in the past but was now going swimmingly. Republican efforts to denigrate Clinton as a draft-dodger (he had opposed the Vietnam War and participated in anti-war demonstrations when he was a student) also came to naught.[5] Most voters seemed to be put off by character assassination as a major theme in 1992. They shared the Clintonite priority: "THE ECONOMY, STUPID!"

Still, once President Bush was on the stump, he had a tendency to "go ballistic" (to use his own expression), and at times he came close to calling Clinton a subversive (as he had Michael Dukakis in 1988). Not only did he declare that Clinton lacked patriotism for opposing the Vietnam War; he also suggested that young Clinton's trip to Moscow as a student in 1969 had something sinister about it. At the same time some of his campaign aides delved into the State Department's passport files of both Clinton and his mother in the vain hope of digging up some kind of dirt to use against him in the campaign. In the final days of the contest, the President threw all dignity to the winds, dismissing Clinton and Gore as "bozos," referring to the latter, an environmentalist, as "Mr. Bozo," and announcing: "My dog Millie knows more about foreign affairs than these two bozos."[6] In the end, Clinton began responding in kind (he called the President "deceptive" and "untrustworthy"), and the campaign descended into an unseemly "battle of the negatives."[7] But last-minute revelations that Bush had been something less than candid when he said he was "out of the loop" as Vice-President during the Iran-contra arms-for-hostages scandal seemed to add weight to the doubts Clinton cast on Bush's integrity. In the final hours of the campaign, however, Clinton returned to the positive themes that had dominated his earlier appeals to the voters.

On election day, in the largest voter turnout since 1960, Governor Clinton won the election with 43 percent of the popular votes to Bush's 38 percent and Perot's 19 percent. His electoral victory was more impressive: 370 votes to Bush's 168. Perot won no electoral votes, but his share of the popular votes was the largest for an independent candidate since Theodore Roosevelt, running as a Progressive, took 27 percent of the popular votes in 1912. As Clinton, at forty-six, the first President to be born after World War II and the youngest since JFK, rode to victory, the Democrats retained control of both House and Senate, and there were hopes that the "gridlock" resulting from Republican Presidents confronting Democratic Congresses might at long last be broken.

The dolorous economy was primarily responsible for Bush's defeat; people who supported Clinton and Perot at the polls doubted the President's ability to cope with the crisis or even to understand the anxieties that ordinary Americans felt at the way things were going. The voters, observed Fred Steeper, Bush's pollster, "had not so much rewarded Clinton as punished Bush for their discontents of the recent past." *Newsweek* took the same view. Clinton, declared the newsweekly, "had been borne to the threshold of the White House not so much by faith as by a wave of anger at the way things were. He had four years to prove himself its master—or to join George Bush among its victims."[8] Clinton's future, it was clear, depended on whether his political foes were willing to accept the outcome of the election and give him a chance to try out his ideas and on whether the talk shows, which had been so helpful during the campaign, continued to be friendly to him.

☆ ☆ ☆

Voters and Reporters

Campaigning in the New Hampshire primary in February 1992, Bill Clinton was anxious to break away from the hordes of press, radio, and TV reporters covering the campaign and talk to the voters directly. Arriving in Manchester one cold morning with his wife Hillary, he headed for the home of one of his sponsors where he was to make a front-porch speech, only to run into more than 150 reporters waiting for him on the lawn, with their cameras, tape recorders, and boom microphones beside them. Somewhat taken aback, Clinton rolled down the window of his car and peered out to see if there were any voters around. When he finally spied a few Manchesterians he mused: "Those poor people don't have a chance!"[9]

Straight "A" Student

The first televised presidential debate of the New Hampshire primary campaign featured former Massachusetts Senator Paul Tsongas, Virginia Governor Douglas Wilder, and Arkansas Governor Bill Clinton (then scarcely known in the North Country). After the debates, Clinton regretted having gotten into a pointless argument with Wilder over negative advertising. As he returned to the hotel with his wife, media adviser Frank Greer tried to reassure him. Don't let Wilder get under your skin, especially on trivial matters, he urged, but stay cool and be presidential. "You're right, I blew it," moaned Clinton. "I *blew* it. I can't *believe* I let that happen." Mrs. Clinton then tried to raise his spirits, but he continued to reproach himself all the way to the hotel. Greer finally told him that the debate was a valuable learning experience and that, in any case, he hadn't done badly. "Look, Bill," he said, "it was a B-plus." "But Frank," wailed Clinton, "you don't understand. I've always had to get A's!"[10]

Faults

One day during the campaign Betsey Wright, Clinton's chief of staff, was scheduled to speak at a Little Rock elementary school. In her talk to the children she went on and on about how wonderful Clinton was and how smart he was and how many books he read and how important reading was, and then stopped to solicit questions. One little boy raised his hand and said hesitantly: "Well, what I want to know is whether Governor Clinton has any flaws." Wright thought for a moment and then conceded: "Well, yes, of course he does. He has allergies."[11]

The Ordeal of Bill Clinton

Was Bill Clinton merely a "pot-smoking, philandering draft-dodger," as one Bush campaign worker put it? Surely not. But in the early months of his bid for the Democratic nomination, he was forced to face one charge after another regarding his personal life that received far bigger headlines than the "New Covenant" which he was trying to promote for the betterment of the country. Sometimes skillfully, but sometimes clumsily, he responded to questions about his life style and at length succeeded in getting back to the public issues that he wanted to discuss with the voters.

Unquestionably Clinton handled the "pot" question poorly. Years before, when his running mate, Al Gore, was asked whether he had tried marijuana as a young man, he said shortly, "I smoked," and that was that. It's a pity Clinton didn't dispose of the question as forthrightly. His practice, when reporters broached the subject, was to say, "I never broke the laws of this country." Pressed on the matter, however, he finally acknowledged that he had tried marijuana a time or two when he was a student at Oxford, but "I didn't inhale it, and never tried it again." It was a maladroit way of putting it (though he assured his associates it was true), and it inspired jokes as well as doubts about his candor. Some people called him "Slick Willie," though a real "slicker" (as *Newsweek* columnist Joe Klein pointed out) would have had "a marijuana sound bite worked out in advance." In the end, Clinton turned his gaffe into a joke. Appearing on TV to play his saxophone, he told the host he took up the instrument because it didn't require inhaling: "You blow out."

Clinton handled the marital-infidelity question more thoughtfully. In January 1992, during the New Hampshire primary, when charges of adultery appeared in the *Star,* a supermarket scandal sheet, and were taken up by the mainline press, Clinton decided to accept the offer of Don Hewitt, producer of *60 Minutes,* to appear on the program with his wife Hillary to answer the charges. Twice, while the interview was being taped in a Boston hotel room, producer Hewitt, kneeling off camera, urged Clinton to confess to adultery ("It will be great television; I know; I know television"), but Clinton ignored him. Instead, he denied the specific charge made by the *Star,* and, though admitting there had been a crisis in his marriage at one time, he insisted that he and Hillary loved each other and their marriage was a good one. When the interviewer pressed for details, Clinton told him: "I think the American people, at least people that have been married for a long time, know what it means and know the whole range of things that it can mean. . . . I have acknowledged wrongdoing, I have acknowledged causing pain in my marriage. I have said things to you tonight and to the American people from the beginning that no American politician ever has. I think most Americans who are watching this tonight, they'll know what we're saying. They'll get it." When Steven Kroft, the interviewer, suggested that the Clintons had "reached some sort of understanding and an arrangement" in staying together, Clinton interrupted him. "Wait a minute, wait a minute, wait a minute," he exclaimed. "You're looking at two people who love each other. This is not an arrangement or understanding; this is a marriage. That's a very different thing." Mrs. Clinton heartily seconded her husband's sentiments. "You know," she said, "I'm not sitting here as some little woman standing by my man, like Tammy Wynette. I'm sitting here because I love him and I respect him and I honor what he's been through and what we've been through together. And, you know, if that's not enough for people, then, heck, don't vote for him." Mrs. Clinton's reference to Tammy Wynette offended the country-western singer, but, for the rest, the interview seems to have helped Clinton get back on track. In an ABC poll taken afterward, 79 percent of the people questioned said the press had no business poking into the private lives of the Clintons and 82 percent said they thought enough had been said about Clinton's personal life.

The pollees turned out to be wrong. Soon afterward, Clinton's foes accused him of having been a draft-dodger during the Vietnam War and diverted him once more from his effort to discuss public issues with the voters. Responding to the attacks, Clinton admitted that, like many college students in the 1960s, he had opposed American intervention in Vietnam and, though not a militant, had participated in some anti-war demonstrations when he was a student at Oxford on a Rhodes scholarship. To get a draft deferment, it turned out, he had briefly joined and then dropped out of ROTC, and his draft number subsequently turned up high in the lottery and he was never called up. When a letter he wrote in December 1969 (thanking the ROTC chief at the University of Arkansas for "saving me from the draft," which he couldn't otherwise have avoided without injuring his "political viability") came to light, it almost derailed his campaign in the New Hampshire primary.

Clinton, it must be said, unlike many of his contemporaries, was no "war wimp" (columnist Mike Royko's term for draft-age hawks who carefully avoided service in Vietnam), but neither was he a militant "peacenik." He seems to have had conflicting emotions about the military as a young man. He opposed the Vietnam War (like Arkansas Senator J. William Fulbright) but admired men like JFK (his boyhood idol) who served their country bravely in World War II, and he unquestionably would have done the same had circumstances been different. "I was in the draft before the lottery came in," he reminded Ted Koppel in an interview on *Nightline.* "I gave up the deferment. I got a high lottery number and I wasn't called. That's what the records reflect. A Republican member of my draft board has given an affidavit in the last couple of days saying that I got no special treatment and nothing in the letter changes that, although it is a true reflection of a just-turned-twenty-three-year-old young man." Two of Clinton's rivals in the New Hampshire primary took him at his word: former Massachusetts Senator Paul Tsongas and Nebraska Senator Bob Kerrey. Tsongas called the turmoil over Clinton's draft record "irrational," while Kerrey, a Vietnam War hero, said he was "tremendously sympathetic to Governor Clinton's dilemma" and insisted "the Vietnam War is not an issue in 1992 and should not be."

Clinton ended by coming out second to Tsongas in the New Hampshire primary, called himself the "Comeback Kid," and went on to do well in succeeding primaries and win the Democratic nomination in July.[12]

Chickens, Fish, and Ducks

When President Bush initially refused Clinton's challenge to meet him in debate, the Clintonians called him "chicken." In East Lansing, Michigan, where he was scheduled to speak, a young man suddenly appeared in the crowd dressed in a chicken outfit—yellow feathers, big beak, webbed feet—and flourished a sign, GEORGE BUSH IS A CHICKEN TO DEBATE. CHICKEN GEORGE. Soon Chicken Georges began turning up in crowds wherever the President appeared and some restaurants began listing "Chicken George" on their menus.

Bush was at first annoyed. Then he began tossing sarcastic remarks about Clinton to the Chicken Georges in the crowds and was soon enjoying himself immensely. Sometimes, before beginning a speech, he looked down into the crowd and cried: "Where's that chicken?" Then he might ask: "You talking about the draft-record chicken?" Or, recalling reports of pollution in the Arkansas River resulting from Arkansas' chicken-processing industry, he might exclaim: "Or are you talking about the chicken in the Arkansas River? Which ones are you talking about? Which one? Get out of here. Maybe it's the draft. Is that what's bothering you?" He also began telling fish jokes to the Chicken Georges in order to ridicule Clinton's environmental record. "It's so bad in Arkansas," he said, "the fish have to walk on water." Or: "The environment's so bad in Arkansas that the fish glow in the dark." And: "The baby fish can find the mama fish because they're glowing in the dark." When political consultant Mary Matalin warned Bush about the coverage the Chicken Georges were receiving on CNN, Bush simply laughed: "I love that chicken!"

Some of the Bushies turned to ducks to get even with the chickens. At one rally, where Clinton had lost his voice and his wife was about to fill in for him, the Republicans released a bunch of live ducks and then, prodding them with duck calls, sent them waddling and squawking across the stage. Furious at the insinuation that he had ducked the draft as a young man, Clinton saw to it that his campaign workers fanned out in the audience to restrain the duck-callers.

After more than a week of old-fashioned capers like these (unusual for a talk-show campaign), the Bush campaign gave in on the debates. Speaking at a rally in Clarksville, Tennessee, where Chicken Georges waved signs—READ MY BEAK: DON'T BE A CHICKEN. DE-

BATE—the President finally challenged Clinton to four debates on television. At that point the chickens, fish, and ducks dropped out of Campaign '92.[13]

Doubtful

Early in October 1992, when Larry King interviewed President Bush on location in San Antonio, a cranky caller from Tampa, Florida, called in to berate the President. "I am not happy with you," he wheezed. "For two years you did not recognize that people were hurting out there and we were in a recession. I feel like you have not come clean on Iran-Contra. And I'm tired of your party and you preaching to us about family values." Bush shrugged his shoulders and then said amiably: "I'll put you down as 'doubtful,' fellow."[14]

Perot's Infomercials

H. Ross Perot was America's first talk-show presidential candidate. He decided to run during an interview on *Larry King Live,* and he centered his campaign on "infomercials," that is, TV advertisements he paid for in which he explained his views. "I'm just going to sit down," he declared at the outset, "and talk to the American people." And he did just that, after picking retired Vice Admiral James Stockdale (who spent seven years as a prisoner of war in Vietnam) as his running mate. In "infomercials" lasting half an hour and more, he sat behind a desk in a TV studio with graphs and charts close by and, pointer in hand, explained his proposals for eliminating the deficit and reducing the national debt. Not until nine days before the campaign ended did he deign to appear in person at campaign rallies sponsored by members of his organization, United We Stand, America. He did bow to the conventionalities, however, in taking part in the presidential debates with President Bush and Governor Clinton.

Perot was in some ways the star of the first presidential debate, which took place in St. Louis on October 11. When moderator Jim Lehrer asked the candidates what distinguished them from their opponents, both Bush and Clinton emphasized their experience in public affairs. "Well, they've got a point," grinned Perot, when his turn came. "I don't have any experience in gridlock government, where nobody takes any responsibility for anything and everybody blames everybody else. I don't have any experience in creating the worst public school system in the industrialized world, the most violent, crime-ridden society in the industrialized world. But I do have a lot of experience in getting things done. . . . I've got a lot of experience in not taking ten years to solve a ten-minute problem."

Perot was undoubtedly a Great Simplifier. "I can solve the problem of the national debt without working up a sweat," he assured TV audiences. "It's just that simple." He put things in folksy (and seemingly forthright) terms. The federal government, he said, must learn to balance its accounts, just as "in your family, when you can't pay the bills, you either get a raise or start cutting back on the necessities." Asked in a TV interview what he stood for, he exclaimed: "I stand for the principles on which this country was founded." Was he trying to buy the election? "I'm buying it for the American people." What would he do if elected President? "In plain Texas talk, it's time to take out the trash and clean out the barns." The fact that major measures to reduce the deficit and pare down the national debt would necessarily have serious (and in some measure unintended) consequences for the nation's complex economy he seems never to have carefully taken into account.[16]

Fun

One day, just before Perot dropped out of the campaign temporarily, he sat talking with Ed Rollins, Republican political consultant, and he suddenly asked: "Is this ever gonna get fun again?" "Fun?" repeated Rollins, who had been working hard for Perot. "Yeah," said Perot. "When I started, this thing was fun." "Campaigns are never fun," Rollins told him. "It's like war. It's miserable. Running for office isn't fun. *Winning* is fun." Perot reflected for a moment and then asked: "What about the presidency? Is *that* fun?" Said Rollins sternly: "The only time the presidency is fun is the day you get inaugurated and the day you dedicate your library. If you're going to do what you're setting out to do, it isn't going to be fun."[17]

Perotxysms

During the 1992 campaign Ross Perot's name turned out to be eminently homonymic. When he dropped out of the campaign in July, critics called him "The Yellow Ross of Texas." When he re-entered in October, but complained of conspiracies against his family, some people called him paranoid and talked of "Perotnoia." On June 9, the *New York Times* pulled out all the stops in an editorial on "Perotxysms." If Perot were elected President, observed the editors, "he would offer economists . . . a new *Perotdigm.* Even if his Latin American policy made him sound like a *Perotnista,* his concern for global nuclear safety would remain *Perotmount.* In terms of domestic policy, he would surely be attentive to *Perotchial* schools. His concern for the handicapped would extend to *Perotplegics* and his health care reform would have to cover *Perotinitis* and *Perotdontia.* But his opponents can be depended on, before long, to ridicule any claim he's a *Perotgon* of virtue who could lead America to political *Perotdise.* They are more likely to prefer a sentence of life without *Perotle,* while the rest of us wish for, at least, no more name puns. While there's life there's hope, Caesar might have said. *Dum spiro sperot.*"[18]

Clinton Grammar and Bush-Speak

Grammar, as well as deportment, became one of the features of Campaign '92. When Bush asked, "Who do you trust?" a Florida schoolteacher indignantly corrected him—"*Whom* do you trust?"—and said she didn't trust anyone who "deliberately breaks the rule on pronoun case." *New York Times* speech maven William Safire, though, reminded her of "Safire's Law of Who/Whom," which dictates: "When *whom* is correct, recast the sentence." Bush would win back the purist vote, he suggested, if he said, "Which candidate do you trust?"

Safire also found Clinton grammatically (as well as politically) incorrect. When the Democratic candidate asked people to "give Al Gore and I a chance to bring America back," Safire read him a little lecture: "The word *I* is a subject, not an object; the word *me* is the pronoun to use in the objective case. Therefore . . . whatever he wants us to give, he should ask us to give to 'Al Gore and me.' " Safire overlooked Clinton's habit of converting normally intransitive verbs into transitives— "grow the economy," "explode the deficit"—possibly because a Republican President, Warren G. Harding, did the same thing ("We must prosper America"), or possibly because erudite academicians were busily converting nouns like access and privilege into verbs (empowering them?) and earning promotions by so doing. (Perhaps the fortysomethings really believed all parts of speech were created equal.)

President Bush, however, seems to have strayed from conventional grammatical paths oftener than his Democratic challenger. When making off-hand remarks in public, he tended to speak in a scattershot manner that sometimes left audiences bewitched, bothered, and bewildered. Journalists dubbed it "Bush-Speak," and the *New Republic,* a liberal weekly which gave Clinton its lukewarm support, began presenting examples of Bush's meanderings for the amusement of its readers. In October the editors published an 86-page paperbound collection of *Bushisms: President George Herbert Walker Bush in His Own Words.* Some of his words:

On religion (while campaigning in New Hampshire soon after returning from Japan where he became ill and threw up at a dinner in his honor in Tokyo): "Somebody said . . . we prayed for you over there. That was not just because I threw up on the prime minister of Japan either. Where was he when I needed him? But I said, Let me tell you something. And I say this—I don't know whether any ministers from the Episcopal Church are here. I hope so. But I said to him this. You're on to something here. You cannot be President of the United

States if you don't have faith. Remember Lincoln, going to his knees in times of trial of the Civil War and all that stuff? You can't be. And we are blessed. So don't feel sorry for—don't cry for me, Argentina!" (January 15, 1992).

On the economic slump (while campaigning in New Hampshire): "The guy over there at Pease—a woman, actually—she said something about a country-Western song, you know, about the train, a light at the end of the tunnel. I only hope it's not a train coming the other way. Well, I said to her, 'well, I'm a country-music fan. I love it, always have. Doesn't fit the mold of some of the columnists, I might add, but nevertheless—of what they think I ought to fit in, but I love it. . . . But nevertheless, I said to them you know there's another one the Nitty Ditty Nitty Gritty Great Bird [Nitty Gritty Dirt Band]—that they did. And it says if you want to see a rainbow you've got to stand a little rain. We've had little rain. New Hampshire has had too much rain. A lot of families are hurting" (January 18, 1992).

At a fund-raising lunch in Tampa, Florida: "Somebody—somebody asked me, what's it take to win? I said to them, I can't remember, what does it take to win the Super Bowl? Or maybe Steinbrenner, my friend George, will tell us what it takes for the Yanks to win—one run. But I went over to the Strawberry Festival this morning, and ate a piece of shortcake over there—able to enjoy it right away, and once I completed it, it didn't have to be approved by Congress—I just went ahead and ate it—and that leads me into what I want to talk to you about today" (March 4, 1992).

Not Available

In September 1992, when vice-presidential candidate Albert Gore appeared on CNN's *Larry King Live,* a woman called in from Asheville, North Carolina, and said coyly: "I know I probably shouldn't say this, but I think you're a very handsome man."

"Uh-oh," stammered Gore, not knowing what to say.

"Are you available for a date on Friday night?" asked the woman.

"No!" cried Gore, squirming in his seat.

"No!" echoed Larry King sternly, "he's not available. He's happily married."

"Come on!" persisted the woman.

"That's the answer," said Gore. "I'm not available."

"Not even for your wife?" teased the caller. Still puzzled, Gore murmured, "Yes, for my wife." Upon this, the caller started giggling and announced: "Hi, this is Tipper. I'm calling you from Asheville. You're doing great." Gore was stunned; he hadn't recognized his wife's voice. After the broadcast, Mrs. Gore got hold of a picture taken of her husband's baffled expression during their exchange, and saw to it that it was hanging prominently in the Gore house from then on.[20]

Till the Fat Lady Sings

During political contests, George Bush liked to quote the old reminder, "it ain't over till the fat lady sings," and in 1992 some of his opponents decided to use it against him. When he spoke in Detroit, a Clinton backer, dressed as an opera singer, turned up to flourish a sign, "The Fat Lady Is Singing. Hear the Music?" In Washington there was an even more ambitious fat-lady demonstration. Toward the end of October a group of hefty pro-Clinton women gathered one noon in Lafayette Park, across from the White House, for a sing-in. Among the tunes: "The Party's Over" and "So Long, Farewell." Among the singers: Jane O'Reilly, a self-described "fat lady" from New York who had helped organize the demonstration. "For once," she announced, "women of substance will be harbingers of change rather than objects of ridicule."[21]

The Price Is Right

In the final days of the campaign, when Clinton appeared at a town meeting in Winston-Salem, North Carolina (carried live on the CBS *Morning News*), Debbie Gilbert, mother of two and a part-time hospital worker, resolved to give him a little test before she decided how to vote. If he knew the prices of some basic consumer goods, she decided, he would get her vote. "Governor," she said, during the question period, "I just have a hard time believing that many politicians today, who claim that they want to help ease the burden on the average American, can really do that, because I don't believe that politicians know what it's like to be in the shoes of the average American family. I want to know if you know how much it costs to buy a pound of hamburger, a pair of blue jeans, a tank of gas and visit the doctor's office."

Clinton responded without hesitation. "Well, gasoline is about $1.20, depending on what kind of gasoline it is," he said. "Hamburger meat's a little over a dollar. A gallon of milk's two dollars. A loaf of bread's about a dollar now. . . ." When he next said he knew of "doctors that still do visits for fifteen dollars," and the audience started laughing, he quickly added, "I do, but not many." He went on: "Blue jeans run anywhere from $18 to $150, depending on what kind you get." At this point, Harry Smith, the host, interposed: "This is like *The Price is Right*. How did he do?" "Pretty good," admitted Mrs. Gilbert, noting that Clinton failed only on the ground beef, which was about $2 where she lived. But she would live up to her part of the bargain, she announced, and cast her vote for Clinton in November.[22]

Notes

Preface

1. Page Smith, *John Adams*, 2 vols. (Garden City, N.Y., 1962), II:1035.
2. Jules Abels, *The Degeneration of Our Presidential Election* (New York, 1968), 78; James Truslow Adams, "Our Whispering Campaigns," *Harper's*, CLXV (September 1932), 448.
3. William S. McFeely, *Grant: A Biography* (New York, 1981), 282.
4. Robert E. Carlson, "Pittsburgh Newspaper Reaction to James Buchanan and the Democratic Party in 1856," *Western Pennsylvania Historical Magazine*, XXXIX (1956), 71.
5. Elizabeth Drew, *Portrait of an Election: The 1980 Presidential Campaign* (New York, 1981), 263.
6. Carl Schurz, *Henry Clay*, 2 vols. (New York, 1915), II:187.
7. Arthur M. Schlesinger, Jr., ed., *A History of American Presidential Elections*, 4 vols. (New York, 1971), IV:3351; H. L. Mencken, *On Politics: A Carnival of Buncombe* (ed. Malcolm Moos, New York, 1960), 33.
8. *Major Campaign Speeches of Adlai E. Stevenson* (New York, 1953), 9–10.

CHAPTER ONE
1789—Starting Off: George Washington

1. Hamilton to Washington, September 1788, *The Papers of Alexander Hamilton*, 26 vols. (ed. Harold C. Syrett, New York, 1961–79), V:220.
2. *The Gazette of the United States* (New York), April 22–25, 1789, 3.
3. John Adams to Abigail Adams, December 19, 1793, *The Works of John Adams*, 10 vols. (ed. Charles Francis Adams, Boston, 1856), I:460.
4. Edward Stanwood, *A History of the Presidency, from 1788 to 1897* (Boston and New York, 1898), 28.
5. Rufus W. Griswold, *The Republican Court: American Society in the Days of Washington* (New York, 1854), 154.

CHAPTER TWO
1792—Washington Again

1. Personal Memorandum of James Madison, May 25, 1792, Arthur M. Schlesinger, Jr., ed., *A History of American Presidential Elections*, 4 vols. (New York, 1971), I:44.
2. Henry Cabot Lodge, *The Life of George Cabot* (Boston, 1877), 64n.
3. *The Gazette of the United States* (New York), November 24, 1792, p. 1.

CHAPTER THREE
1796—Federalist Succession: John Adams

1. Meade Minnigerode, *Presidential Years, 1787–1860* (New York, 1928), 37.
2. Donald H. Stewart, *The Opposition Press of the Federalist Period* (Albany, N.Y., 1969), 533.
3. George Gibbs, ed., *Memoirs of the Administrations of Washington and John Adams*, 2 vols. (New York, 1846), I:384–85.
4. Minnigerode, *Presidential Years*, 61.
5. Ibid., 65.
6. David Burner et al., *The American People* (St. James, N.Y., 1980), 124.
7. Minnigerode, *Presidential Years*, 74.
8. Page Smith, *John Adams*, 2 vols. (Garden City, N.Y., 1962), II:909; Merrill D. Peterson, *Thomas Jefferson and the New Nation* (New York, 1970), 545.
9. Edward Stanwood, *A History of Presidential Elections* (Boston and New York, 1888), 51.

CHAPTER FOUR
1800—Republican Takeover: Jefferson's Revolution

1. Page Smith, *John Adams*, 2 vols. (Garden City, N.Y., 1962), II:1002.
2. Henry S. Randall, *The Life of Thomas Jefferson*, 3 vols. (New York, 1858), II:544.
3. *Letter from Alexander Hamilton, Concerning the Public Conduct and Character of John Adams. . . .* (New York, October 24, 1800), in *The Papers of Alexander Hamilton*, 26 vols. (ed. Harold C. Syrett, New York, 1961–79), XXV:186, 190, 196.
4. Smith, *Adams*, II:1027–28.
5. Robert and Leona Train Rienow, *The Lonely Quest: The Evolution of Presidential Leadership* (Chicago, 1966), 36–37.
6. *A Short Address to the Voters of Delaware*, signed "A Christian Federalist" (September 21, 1800), 3.
7. *Connecticut Courant* (Hartford), September 15, 1800.
8. *The Duty of Americans, at the Present Crisis. . . .* (New Haven, 1798), 20–21.
9. John Mason, *The Voice of Warning, to Christians, on the Ensuing Election of a President of the United States* (New York, 1800), 22–23.
10. William Linn, *Serious Considerations on the Election of a President; Addressed to the Citizens of the United States* (New York, 1800), 4.

11. *Connecticut Courant,* September 29, 1800.
12. James Callender, *The Prospect Before Us,* 2 vols. (Richmond, 1800), I:30.
13. Smith, *Adams,* II:1034.
14. Meade Minnigerode, *Presidential Years, 1787–1860* (New York, 1928), 104.
15. Smith, *Adams,* II:1035.
16. Hamilton to Jay, May 7, 1800, *The Works of Alexander Hamilton,* 9 vols. (ed. Henry Cabot Lodge, New York, 1885–86), VII: 549–50.
17. Merrill D. Peterson, *Thomas Jefferson and the New Nation* (New York, 1970), 642.
18. Minnigerode, *Presidential Years,* 108.
19. Charles Warren, *Jacobin and Junto* (Cambridge, Mass., 1931), 158–59.
20. Randall, *Jefferson,* II:572.
21. John Bach McMaster, *A History of the People of the United States,* 6 vols. (New York, 1883–1924), II:525.
22. *Works of Hamilton,* VI:486, 521.
23. Minnigerode, *Presidential Years,* 87.
24. Sidney Warren, *The Battle for the Presidency* (Philadelphia, 1968), 48.
25. Minnigerode, *Presidential Years,* 117.
26. April 15, 1806, *The Anas of Thomas Jefferson* (ed. Franklin B. Sawvel, New York, 1970), 238–40; Morton Borden, "The Election of 1800: Charge and Countercharge," *Delaware History,* V (March 1952), 58–62.
27. Minnigerode, *Presidential Years,* 112.
28. Ibid.
29. Madison to Jefferson, February 28, 1801, *Letters and Other Writings of James Madison,* 2 vols. (Philadelphia, 1865), II:171.
30. Frank Van Der Linden, *The Turning Point: Jefferson's Battle for the Presidency* (Washington, 1962), 315.
31. Norman Risjord, *The Old Republicans: Southern Conservatism in the Age of Jefferson* (New York, 1965), 18.
32. "First Inaugural Address," March 4, 1801, James D. Richardson, *A Compilation of the Messages and Papers of the Presidents* (Bureau of National Literature and Art, New York, 1897), I:310.
33. Van Der Linden, *Turning Point,* 324.
34. Henry F. Reddall, *Scissors, or the Funny Side of Politics* (Boston, 1889), 99.
35. Warren, *Jacobin and Junto,* 7; *Connecticut Courant,* January 5, 1801; David H. Fisher, *The Revolution of American Conservatism: The Federalist Party in the Era of Jeffersonian Democracy* (New York, 1965), 31–32, 101, 134.
36. Martha J. Lamb, "Unsuccessful Candidates for the Presidency of the Nation," *Magazine of American History,* XII (November 1884), 390.

CHAPTER FIVE
1804—Jefferson's Landslide

1. Virginius Dabney, *The Jefferson Scandals* (New York, 1981), 10, 69, 74; Douglas Adair, *Fame and the Founding Fathers* (New York, 1974), 161.
2. February 8, 1805, *The Writings of Thomas Jefferson,* 20 vols. (ed. Albert E. Bergh, Washington, 1903), XI:62.

3. Merrill D. Peterson, *Thomas Jefferson and the New Nation* (New York, 1970), 800.
4. John Bach McMaster, *A History of the People of the United States,* 6 vols. (New York, 1883–1924), III:195–96.

CHAPTER SIX
1808—Madison and the Dambargo

1. William Cullen Bryant, *The Embargo* (Facsimile reproductions of the editions of 1808 and 1809, Gainesville, Florida, 1955), 22–23.
2. Henry Adams, *History of the United States of America,* 9 vols. (New York, 1917), IV:130.
3. John Bach McMaster, *A History of the People of the United States,* 6 vols. (New York, 1883–1924), III:291.
4. Walter W. Jennings, *The American Embargo, 1807–1809* (Iowa City, 1921), 128.
5. Henry F. Reddall, *Scissors, or, the Funny Side of Politics* (Boston, 1889), 65.
6. *A Political Sermon Addressed to the Electors of Middlesex* (n.p., 1808), 17n.; Jennings, *American Embargo,* 43–44; Irving Brant, *James Madison: Secretary of State, 1800–1809* (Indianapolis, 1953), 434.

CHAPTER SEVEN
1812—Madison's Wartime Re-election

1. Irving Brant, *James Madison: The President, 1809–1812* (Indianapolis, 1956), 458.
2. Irving Brant, *James Madison: Commander in Chief, 1812–1836* (Indianapolis, 1961), 102.
3. Glenn Tucker, *Poltroons and Patriots,* 2 vols. (Indianapolis, 1954), I:206.
4. Henry F. Reddall, *The Sunny Side of Politics* (St. Paul, 1892), 135–36.

CHAPTER EIGHT
1816—Monroe: Another Virginia Victory

1. Clement Eaton, *Henry Clay and the Art of American Politics* (Boston, 1957), 31.
2. Lynn W. Turner, "Elections of 1816 and 1820," Arthur M. Schlesinger, Jr., ed., *A History of American Presidential Elections,* 4 vols. (New York, 1971), I:301.
3. Rufus King to William King, April 22, 1818, Robert Ernst, *Rufus King: American Federalist* (Chapel Hill, N.C., 1968), 352; *Niles' Register,* XII (March 5, 1817), 20.
4. Edward Stanwood, *A History of the Presidency, from 1788 to 1897* (Boston and New York, 1898), 111.
5. To Christopher Gore, May 15, 1816, Ernst, *King,* 351.
6. Edward Stanwood, *A History of Presidential Elections* (Boston and New York, 1884), 68–69.

CHAPTER NINE
1820—Monroe's Quiet Re-Election

1. "The President," *Daily National Intelligencer* (Washington), October 17, 1820; Lynn W. Turner, "The Elections of 1816 and 1820," Arthur M. Schlesinger, Jr., ed., *A History of American Presidential Elections*, 4 vols. (New York, 1971), I:311–12.
2. Turner, "Elections of 1816 and 1820," 316.
3. William Plumer, Jr. to William Plumer, Washington, January 27, 1821, Everett S. Brown, ed., *The Missouri Compromises and Presidential Politics, 1820–1825* (New York, 1970), 62.
4. C. O. Paullin, "The Electoral Vote for John Quincy Adams in 1820," *American Historical Review*, XXI (January 1916), 318–19; Lynn W. Turner, "The Electoral Vote against Monroe in 1820—An American Legend," *Mississippi Valley Historical Review*, XLII (September 1955), 259.
5. Quoted, *Daily National Intelligencer*, November 7, 1820.
6. Edward Stanwood, *A History of Presidential Elections* (Boston and New York, 1884), 72–74.

CHAPTER TEN
1824—John Quincy Adams and the "Corrupt Bargain"

1. James F. Hopkins, "Election of 1824," Arthur M. Schlesinger, Jr., ed., *A History of American Presidential Elections*, 4 vols. (New York, 1971), I:360.
2. Ibid., 363.
3. Chase C. Mooney, *William H. Crawford, 1772–1834* (Lexington, Ky., 1974), 257–58.
4. Ibid., 250.
5. Eugene H. Roseboom, *A History of Presidential Elections* (New York, 1959), 82.
6. *Kentucky Reporter* (Lexington), November 25, 1822, in Paul C. Nagel, "The Election of 1824: A Reconsideration Based on Newspaper Opinion," *Journal of Southern History*, XXVI (August 1960), 325.
7. Hopkins, "Election of 1824," 362.
8. Ibid., 365.
9. Ibid., 399.
10. Mooney, *Crawford*, 287.
11. Clay to Francis Preston Blair, January 29, 1825, Schlesinger, *Presidential Elections*, I:407.
12. John T. Morse, *John Quincy Adams* (Boston and New York, 1882), 174.
13. John Bach McMaster, *A History of the People of the United States*, 6 vols. (1883–1924), V:489; Marquis James, *Andrew Jackson: Portrait of a President* (Indianapolis, 1937), 136.
14. Jackson to W. B. Lewis, February 14, 1825, *Correspondence of Andrew Jackson*, 7 vols. (ed. John Spencer Bassett, Washington, D.C., 1926–35), III:376.
15. Meade Minnigerode, *Presidential Years, 1789–1860* (New York, 1928), 151.
16. David Burner et al., *The American People* (St. James, N.Y., 1980), 172.
17. *Memoirs of John Quincy Adams*, 12 vols. (ed. Charles Francis Adams, Phila-

delphia, 1875), VI, 333; *Harrisburg Pennslyvanian,* May 4, 1824, Herman Hailpern, "Pro-Jackson Sentiment in Pennsylvania," *Pennsylvania Magazine of History and Biography,* L (1926), 203.

18. Benjamin Perley Poore, *Perley's Reminiscences of Sixty Years,* 2 vols. (New York, 1886), I:26.
19. John C. Fitzpatrick, ed., *The Autobiography of Martin Van Buren,* Vol. II of American Historical Association, *Annual Report for the Year 1918* (Washington, D.C., 1920), 150–52; John Spencer Bassett, *The Life of Andrew Jackson* (New York, 1916), 365; Margaret Bayard Smith, *The First Forty Years of Washington Society* (New York, 1906), 91.
20. *Perley's Reminiscences,* I:26; Bassett, *Jackson,* 365–66; S. G. Goodrich, *Recollections of a Lifetime,* 2 vols. (New York, 1856), II:403–4.
21. Thomas Hart Benton, *Thirty Years' View,* 2 vols. (New York, 1854), I:70–77; Nathan Sargent, *Public Men and Events,* 2 vols. (Philadelphia, 1875), I:123–24; William C. Bruce, *John Randolph of Roanoke, 1773–1833,* 2 vols. (New York, 1922), I:511–24.

CHAPTER ELEVEN
1828—Jackson vs. Adams

1. *Daily Albany Argus,* III (September 12, 1828), 2.
2. H. Shaw to Clay, January 9, 1829, Robert Remini, *Andrew Jackson and the Course of American Freedom* (New York, 1981), 147.
3. Robert Wickcliffe to Henry Clay, October 7, 1828, John Bach McMaster, *A History of the People of the United States,* 6 vols. (New York, 1883–1924), V:518.
4. Stefan Lorant, *The Glorious Burden: The American Presidency* (New York, 1968), 122.
5. David Burner et al., *The American People* (St. James, N.Y., 1980), 178.
6. John M. Blum et al., *The National Experience,* 2 vols. (New York, 1973), I:216.
7. August C. Buell, *History of Andrew Jackson,* 2 vols. (New York, 1904), II:181.
8. Ibid., 182.
9. Remini, *Jackson and Freedom,* 109.
10. *National Journal,* May 24, 1828, Remini, *Jackson and Freedom,* 131.
11. *New York American,* November 9, 1827, Remini, *Jackson and Freedom,* 148.
12. Lorant, *Glorious Burden,* 122.
13. Florence Weston, *The Presidential Election of 1828* (Washington, D.C., 1938), 55.
14. Remini, *Jackson and Freedom,* 134.
15. Weston, *Election of 1828,* 49.
16. Edwin Rozwenc and Thomas Bender, *The Making of American Society,* 2 vols. (New York, 1978), I:400.
17. Lorant, *Glorious Burden,* 124.
18. Weston, *Election of 1828,* 144–45; Robert Remini, *The Election of Andrew Jackson* (Phi adelphia, 1964), 154–56.
19. Buell, *Jackson,* II:195n.
20. [Charles Hammond], *View of General Jackson's Domestic Relations in reference to his fitness for the Presidency* (reprint from *Truth's Advocacy,* Cincinnati, Ohio, January 1828), 2; *The Correspondence of Andrew Jackson,* 7 vols. (Washington,

1926–35), III:427; Marquis James, *Andrew Jackson: Portrait of a President* (Indianapolis, 1937), 159.

21. [Hammond], *View of Jackson's Domestic Relations*, 3.

22. Buell, *Jackson*, II:204.

23. *United States Telegraph*, October 20, 1828; Remini, *Jackson and Freedom*, 145.

24. Buell, *Jackson*, II:199–200; James Parton, *Life of Andrew Jackson*, 3 vols. (New York, 1861), III:153.

25. Edmund P. Gaines to Jackson, November 22, 1828, Remini, *Jackson and Freedom*, 148.

26. Parton, *Jackson*, III:170.

27. John C. Fitzpatrick, ed., *The Autobiography of Martin Van Buren*, Vol. II of American Historical Association, *Annual Report for the Year 1918* (Washington, D.C., 1920), 240; Meade Minnigerode, *Presidential Years, 1789–1860* (New York, 1928), 163; Remini, *Election of Jackson*, 74.

28. Benjamin Perley Poore, *Perley's Reminiscences of Sixty Years*, 2 vols. (New York, 1886), I:89; James, *Portrait of President*, 159; Remini, *Election of Jackson*, 162.

29. Minnigerode, *Presidential Years*, 168–69; Remini, *Election of Jackson*, 171–80.

30. Jules Abels, *The Degeneration of Our Presidential Election* (New York, 1968), 170; Remini, *Election of Jackson*, 107.

31. *The Diary of Philip Hone, 1828–1851*, 2 vols. (ed. Allan Nevins, New York, 1927), I:97; Charles Francis Adams, ed., *Memoirs of John Quincy Adams*, 12 vols. (Philadelphia, 1874–77), VII:338; Remini, *Election of Jackson*, 122–23; Samuel Flagg Bemis, *John Quincy Adams and the Union* (New York, 1970), 101.

32. Remini, *Jackson and Freedom*, 132–33; Parton, *Jackson*, III:138; *Reminiscences of James A. Hamilton* (New York, 1869), 69–70.

33. John F. Parker, "*If Elected, I Promise . . .*" (Garden City, N.Y., 1960), 75.

34. Henry F. Reddall, *The Sunny Side of Politics* (St. Paul, 1892), 106–7.

35. Samuel Hopkins Adams, "Presidential Campaign Whispers," *Life*, XVII (October 2, 1944), 55; Herbert M. Baus and William B. Ross, *Politics Battle Plan* (New York, 1968), 351.

36. Abels, *Degeneration of Election*, 86; Remini, *Election of Jackson*, 117.

37. *U.S. Telegraph*, June 16, 1827; Jackson to Duff Green, August 13, 1827, James, *Portrait of President*, 157–58; Green to Jackson, July 8, 1827, *Correspondence of Andrew Jackson*, III:377.

38. *Perley's Reminiscences*, I:90.

39. Parton, *Jackson*, III:101–2; Sidney Warren, *The Battle for the Presidency* (Philadelphia, 1968), 70; Remini, *Election of Jackson*, 106.

CHAPTER TWELVE

1832—Jackson, Clay, and the Bank War

1. Samuel R. Gammon, *The Presidential Campaign of 1832* (Baltimore, 1922), 134.

2. Stefan Lorant, *The Glorious Burden: The American Presidency* (New York, 1968), 139; Robert Remini, "Election of 1832," Arthur M. Schlesinger, Jr., ed., *A History of American Presidential Elections*, 4 vols. (New York, 1971), I:510.

3. To A. J. Donelson, August 19, 1820, Gammon, *Presidential Campaign*, 105.

4. Remini, "Election of 1832," 498.

5. James Parton, *Life of Andrew Jackson*, 3 vols. (New York, 1861), III:420.

6. *The Journal of Frances Ann Butler, better known as Fanny Kemble* (reprint of 1835 edition), 2 vols. (Bronx, N.Y., 1970), I:176; Michael Chevalier, *Society, Manners, and Politics in the United States* (ed. John William Ward, Cornell University Press, 1961), 162.

7. James D. Richardson, *A Compilation of the Messages and Papers of the Presidents* (Bureau of National Literature and Art, New York), II (1907):590.

8. Remini, "Election of 1832," 509–10.

9. Edward Stanwood, *A History of the Presidency, from 1788 to 1897* (Boston and New York, 1898), 108.

10. Remini, "Election of 1832," 512.

11. Edward Stanwood, *A History of Presidential Elections* (Boston and New York, 1888), 160.

12. Lynn Marshall, "The Strange Stillbirth of the Whig Party," *American Historical Review*, LXXVII (January 1967), 446.

13. Remini, "Election of 1832," 512.

14. Ibid., 511–12.

15. Parton, *Jackson*, III:423–24; John Bach McMaster, *A History of the People of the United States*, 6 vols. (New York, 1883–1924), IV:147; Claude Bowers, *The Party Battles of the Jackson Period* (Boston, 1922), 241–42.

16. August C. Buell, *History of Andrew Jackson*, 2 vols. (New York, 1904), II:271.

17. Nathan Sargent, *Public Men and Events*, 2 vols. (Philadelphia, 1875), I:248.

18. Ibid., 248–49; Parton, *Jackson*, II:424–26.

19. Remini, "Election of 1832," 514.

20. Parton, *Jackson*, III:430.

21. Ibid., 310.

22. Remini, "Election of 1832," 516.

23. Robert Remini, *The Election of Andrew Jackson* (New York, 1963), 156.

24. *Works of Henry Clay*, 7 vols. (New York, 1897), V:576–77.

25. John P. Kennedy, *Memoirs of the Life of William Wirt*, 2 vols. (Philadelphia, 1849), II:382.

26. Claude Bowers, *The Party Battles of the Jacksonian Era* (Boston, 1922), 247.

27. Benjamin Perley Poore, *Perley's Reminiscences of Sixty Years*, 2 vols. (New York, 1886), I:144–45; Sargent, *Public Men*, I:224–25; Buell, *Jackson*, II:264–67.

28. Henry F. Reddall, *Scissors, or, the Funny Side of Politics* (Boston, 1889), 152–54.

29. Ibid., 60.

30. Buell, *Jackson*, II:272–86; Robert Remini, *Andrew Jackson and the Course of American Freedom* (New York, 1981), 388–89.

CHAPTER THIRTEEN
1836—Van Buren's Victory over Three Whigs

1. Nathan Sargent, *Public Men and Events*, 2 vols. (Philadelphia, 1875), I:297.

2. *Lexington Intelligencer*, June 2, 1836, Leland W. Meyer, *The Life and Times of Colonel Richard M. Johnson of Kentucky* (New York, 1931), 419.

3. Joel H. Silbey, "Election of 1836," Arthur M. Schlesinger, Jr., ed., *A History of American Presidential Elections*, 4 vols. (New York, 1971), I:585.

4. L. Paul Gresham, *The Public Career of Hugh Lawson White* (Nashville, Tenn., 1945), 23; Denis Tilden Lynch, *An Epoch and a Man: Martin Van Buren and His Times* (New York, 1929), 382–83; Sargent, *Public Men*, I:296–97.
5. Lynch, *Epoch and Man*, 383–84.
6. Thomas A. Bailey, *The American Pageant*, 2 vols. (Lexington, Mass., 1975), I:289–90.
7. Silbey, "Election of 1836," 578.
8. Ibid., 587–88; Eugene H. Roseboom, *A History of Presidential Elections* (New York, 1959), 112.
9. Holmes Alexander, *The American Talleyrand: The Career and Contemporaries of Martin Van Buren* (New York, 1935), 318.
10. Lynch, *Epoch and Man*, 395; Alexander, *American Talleyrand*, 326.
11. Schlesinger, *Presidential Elections*, I:596.
12. Dorothy B. Goebel, *William Henry Harrison: A Political Biography* (Indianapolis, 1926), 321.
13. John C. Fitzpatrick, ed., *The Autobiography of Martin Van Buren*, Vol. II of American Historical Association, *Annual Report for the Year 1918* (Washington, D.C., 1920), 196; Lynch, *Epoch and Man*, 385–86; David Crockett, *The Life of Martin Van Buren* (Philadelphia, 1837), 39, 81.
14. Sargent, *Public Men*, II, 16–17; Thurlow Weed, *The Life of Thurlow Weed*, 2 vols. (Boston, 1883), II:52; F. Byrdsall, *The History of the Loco-Foco or Equal Rights Party* (New York, 1842), 27, 29.
15. Meyer, *Johnson*, 129–33; Bernard Mayo, "The Man Who Killed Tecumseh," *American Mercury*, XIX (April 1930), 446–53; Henry A. Wise, *Seven Decades of the Union* (Philadelphia, 1872), 175; Richard Emmons, *Tecumseh: or, The Battle of the Thames, A National Drama in Five Acts* (New York, 1836).

CHAPTER FOURTEEN
1840—Tippecanoe and Tyler Too

1. Charles Francis Adams, ed., Memoirs of John Quincy Adams, 12 vols. (Philadelphia, 1874–77), X:351–52.
2. *United States Magazine and Democratic Review*, VII (June 1840), 486; ibid., VIII (September 1840), 198.
3. John Bach McMaster, *A History of the People of the United States*, 6 vols. (New York, 1883–1924), VI:562 and note; Richard Smith Elliott, *Notes Taken from Sixty Years* (St. Louis, 1883), 126.
4. Stefan Lorant, *The Glorious Burden: The American Presidency* (New York, 1968), 157.
5. Edward Stanwood, *A History of Presidential Elections* (Boston and New York, 1888), 131.
6. Ibid., 137; George Julian, *Political Recollections, 1840 to 1872* (Chicago, 1880), 20; George Templeton Strong, *The Diary of George Templeton Strong*, 4 vols. (ed. Allan Nevins and Milton Halsey Thomas, New York, 1952), I:151.
7. Julian, *Political Recollections*, 18–19; Thurlow Weed, *The Life of Thurlow Weed*, 2 vols. (Boston, 1883), I:490; Meade Minnigerode, *Presidential Years, 1789–1865* (New York, 1928), 190.

8. A. B. Norton, *The Great Revolution of 1840* (Mount Vernon, Ohio, 1888), 364; Sidney Warren, *The Battle for the Presidency* (New York, 1968), 90.
9. Stanwood, *Presidential Elections*, 129–30.
10. McMaster, *History*, VI:564–65.
11. Charles Ogle, *The Regal Splendor of the President's Palace*, April 18, 1840, House of Representatives, 3–7, 9, 26; Robert Gray Gunderson, "Ogle's Omnibus of Lies," *Pennsylvania Magazine of History and Biography*, LXXX (October 1956), 443–51.
12. McMaster, *History*, VI:584 and note; Minnegerode, *Presidential Years*, 189.
13. Robert Gray Gunderson, *The Log-Cabin Campaign* (The University Press of Kentucky, Lexington, Ky., 1957), 101.
14. Ibid., 101, 226; Dorothy B. Goebel, *William Henry Harrison: A Political Biography* (Indianapolis, 1926), 355–56; McMaster, *History*, VI:574n, 182; Norton, *Revolution*, 75.
15. Goebel, *Harrison*, 346.
16. *The Correspondence of Nicholas Biddle Dealing with National Affairs, 1807–1844* (Boston and New York, 1919), 256.
17. Gunderson, *Log-Cabin Campaign*, 222.
18. Freeman Cleaves, *Old Tippecanoe* (New York, 1939), 323.
19. Lorant, *Glorious Burden*, 163.
20. Ibid.
21. Gunderson, *Log-Cabin Campaign*, 257.
22. McMaster, *History*, VI:590.
23. Ibid., 592.
24. Minnegerode, *Presidential Years*, 205.
25. *Memoirs of Adams*, X:366.
26. Charles S. Todd and Benjamin Drake, *Sketches of the Civil and Military Services of William Henry Harrison* (Cincinnati, 1847), 208.
27. *The Diary of Philip Hone, 1828–1851*, 2 vols. (ed. Allan Nevins, New York, 1927), II:553.
28. Gunderson, *Log-Cabin Campaign*, 181; Norton, *Revolution*, 11, 233–34.
29. McMaster, *History*, VI:564–65; Gunderson, *Log-Cabin Campaign*, 127–28.
30. Julian, *Political Recollections*, 17; "American Bandwagon," *American Heritage*, XIX (October 1975), 19; McMaster, *History*, VI:564–65.
31. *Cleveland Axe*, May 28, 1840; Gunderson, *Log-Cabin Campaign*, 127, 135–39.
32. Henry F. Reddall, *Scissors, or, the Funny Side of Politics* (Boston, 1889), 153.
33. Malcolm P. Eiselen, "Campaign Ballads," *Review of Reviews*, XCIV (October 1936), 60; Gunderson, *Log-Cabin Campaign*, 235, 236–37.
34. Norton, *Revolution*, 365.
35. Carl Sandburg, *Abraham Lincoln: The Prairie Years*, 2 vols. (New York, 1926), I:236; Gunderson, *Log-Cabin Campaign*, 214; Jules Abels, *The Degeneration of Our Presidential Election* (New York, 1968), 184.
36. Allen Walker Read, "The Evidence on 'O.K.'," *Saturday Review of Literature*, XXIV (July 19, 1941), 3–10; Cleaves, *Old Tippecanoe*, 325; Gunderson, *Log-Cabin Campaign*, 234.
37. *Albany Rough-Hewer*, September 3, 1840, Gunderson, *Log-Cabin Campaign*, 129.

CHAPTER FIFTEEN
1844—Polk and Manifest Destiny

1. "Annexation," *United States Magazine and Democratic Review*, XVII (July 1845), 5.
2. *National Party Platforms*, 2 vols. (Urbana, Ill., 1978), I:4.
3. John Bach McMaster, *A History of the People of the United States*, 6 vols. (New York, 1883–1924), VI:359; Charles Sellers, *James K. Polk: Continentalist, 1843–1846*, 2 vols. (Princeton, N.J., 1957), II:101, 105, 139; James Phelan, *History of Tennessee: The Making of a State* (Boston and New York, 1888), 414.
4. Charles Sellers, "Election of 1844," Arthur M. Schlesinger, Jr., ed., *A History of American Presidential Elections*, 4 vols. (New York, 1971), I:785; Sellers, *Polk*, II:141.
5. Jules Abels, *The Degeneration of Our Presidential Election* (New York, 1968), 187.
6. Glyndon Van Deusen, *The Life of Henry Clay* (Boston, 1937), 371.
7. Schlesinger, *Presidential Elections*, I:791.
8. Sellers, *Polk*, II:149–50; McMaster, *History*, VII:384; Lyon G. Tyler, *The Letters and Times of the Tylers*, 2 vols. (Richmond, Va., 1885), II:352.
9. Sellers, "Election of 1844," 788.
10. Ibid., 790; Sellers, *Polk*, II:148.
11. Ibid.
12. Martha McBride Morrel, *"Young Hickory": The Life and Times of President James K. Polk* (E. P. Dutton, New York, 1949), 201.
13. Ibid., 211.
14. Sellers, *Polk*, II:152.
15. Phelan, *History of Tennessee*, 422.
16. Madeleine McDowell, "Recollections of Henry Clay," *Century Magazine*, L (September 1895), 768.
17. Carl Schurz, *Henry Clay*, 2 vols. (New York, 1915), II:267–68; Van Deusen, *Clay*, 376.
18. Abels, *Degeneration*, 140; Thomas A. Bailey, *A Diplomatic History of the American People* (New York, 1955), 233.

CHAPTER SIXTEEN
1848—Old Zach and the Michigander

1. Frank B. Woodford, *Lewis Cass* (Rutgers, 1950), 258–60.
2. John G. Nicolay and John Hay, eds., *The Complete Works of Abraham Lincoln*, 12 vols. (Harrogate, Tenn., 1894), II:63.
3. Brainerd Dyer, *Zachary Taylor* (Baton Rouge, 1946), 295.
4. Woodford, *Cass*, 266.
5. Holman Hamilton, *Zachary Taylor: Soldier in the White House* (Indianapolis, 1951), 118; Benjamin Perley Poore, *Perley's Reminiscences of Sixty Years*, 2 vols. (New York, 1886), I:345–46; A. K. McClure, *Our Presidents and How We Make Them* (New York, 1905), 106.
6. Henry B. Stanton, *Random Recollections* (New York, 1887), 162–63; Erwin

H. Price, "The Election of 1848 in Ohio," *Ohio Archaeological and Historical Publications*, XXXVI, 251–52.

7. *Works of Lincoln*, II:75–76.

CHAPTER SEVENTEEN
1852—Frank Pierce and Old Fuss and Feathers

1. Paul F. Boller, Jr., "Old Fuss and Feathers and the Fainting General," *Southwest Review*, XXVII (Spring 1952), 143–44.
2. Ibid., 146–47.
3. Ibid., 148.
4. John S. Wise, *Recollections of Thirteen Presidents* (New York, 1906), 47–48.
5. Charles W. Elliott, *Winfield Scott: The Soldier and the Man* (New York, 1937), 629.
6. Stefan Lorant, *The Glorious Burden: The American Presidency* (New York, 1968), 210.
7. *The Signal* (Washington), July 10, 1852, p. 23.

CHAPTER EIGHTEEN
1856—Buchanan and Bleeding Kansas

1. Allan Nevins, *Frémont: Pathmarker of the West* (New York, 1939), 505; Meade Minnigerode, "Presidential Campaigns: The Buchaneers, 1856," *Saturday Evening Post* (March 17, 1928), 158.
2. Stefan Lorant, *The Glorious Burden: The American Presidency* (New York, 1968), 224.
3. Robert E. Carlson, "Pittsburgh Newspaper Reaction to James Buchanan and the Democratic Party in 1856," *Western Pennsylvania Historical Magazine*, XXXIX (1956), 75.
4. Meade Minnigerode, *Presidential Years, 1789–1860* (New York, 1928), 321.
5. *National Party Platforms*, 2 vols. (compiled by Donald Bruce Johnson, Urbana, Ill., 1978), I:24–25.
6. Lorant, *Glorious Burden*, 224.
7. Roy F. Nichols, *The Disruption of American Democracy* (New York, 1948), 44.
8. Lorant, *Glorious Burden*, 225.
9. "A Song, Inscribed to the Fremont Clubs," *Poetical Works of John Greenleaf Whittier*, 4 vols. (Boston and New York, 1892), III:192.
10. "The Crime against Kansas," *The Works of Charles Sumner*, 15 vols. (Boston, 1873–1883), IV:137–256; Edward L. Pierce, *Memoir and Letters of Charles Sumner*, 4 vols. (Boston, 1893), III:441–524; Benjamin Perley Poore, *Perley's Reminiscences of Sixty Years*, 2 vols. (New York, 1886), I:462–63; David Donald, *Charles Sumner and the Coming of the Civil War* (New York, 1960), 278–327.
11. Henry F. Reddall, *Scissors, or, the Funny Side of Politics* (Boston, 1889), 103.
12. Ray Billington, *The Protestant Crusade* (New York, 1938), 418–19; *Remarks on the Majority and Minority Reports of the Select Committee on Secret Societies in*

the *Houses of Delegates in Maryland* (New York, 1856), 22–23; *American Union* (Boston), May 6, 1854; *The Pilot* (Boston), May 29, 1854.
13. Nevins, *Frémont*, 499–501; Ruhl J. Bartlett, *John C. Frémont and the Republican Party* (Columbus, Ohio, 1930), 68; Charles G. Hamilton, *Lincoln and the Know Nothing Movement* (Washington, D.C., 1954), 5.
14. Samuel Gilman Brown, *The Life of Rufus Choate* (Boston, 1879), 326.
15. Gerard Brady, "Buchanan's Lockjaw Campaign in Lancaster County," *Papers of the Lancaster County Historical Society*, LIII (1949), 125.

CHAPTER NINETEEN
1860—Lincoln and the Sectional Crisis

1. *The Works of James Buchanan*, 12 vols. (ed. John Bassett Moore, Philadelphia, 1910), X:97.
2. Emerson D. Fite, *The Presidential Campaign of 1860* (New York, 1911), 43.
3. William B. Hesseltine, ed., *Three against Lincoln: Murat Halstead Reports the Caucuses of 1860* (Baton Rouge, 1960), 54; James Ford Rhodes, *History of the United States from the Compromise of 1850*, 8 vols. (New York, 1892–1919), II:448.
4. Stefan Lorant, *The Glorious Burden: The American Presidency* (New York, 1968), 239.
5. Hesseltine, *Three against Lincoln*, 127.
6. Melvin L. Hayes, *Mr. Lincoln Runs for President* (Citadel Press, New York, 1960), 97.
7. Allen Johnson, *Stephen A. Douglas: A Study in American Politics* (New York, 1908), 432–33.
8. Fite, *Presidential Campaign of 1860*, 165.
9. Johnson, *Douglas*, 437.
10. Hayes, *Lincoln Runs for President*, 97.
11. Meade Minnigerode, *Presidential Years, 1789–1860* (New York, 1928), 386.
12. Sherman Day Wakefield, *How Lincoln Became President* (New York, 1936), 99; John G. Nicolay and John Hay, eds., *Complete Works of Abraham Lincoln*, 13 vols. (Harrogate, Tenn., 1894), V:286.
13. Isaac N. Arnold, *The Life of Abraham Lincoln* (Chicago, 1885), 162; William Eldon Baringer, "Campaign Technique in Illinois—1860," *Illinois State Historical Society. Transactions for the Year 1932* (Springfield, 1932), 223–25; Carl Sandburg, *Abraham Lincoln: The Prairie Years*, 2 vols. (New York, 1926), II: 331–32; Robert S. Harper, *Lincoln and the Press* (New York, 1951), 49–50.
14. Arnold, *Life of Lincoln*, 166; Hesseltine, *Three against Lincoln*, 155–56; Rhodes, *History*, II:463–64.
15. Henry C. Whitney, *Lincoln the Citizen*, 2 vols. (New York, 1908), I:289.
16. Arnold, *Life of Lincoln*, 169.
17. Osborn H. Oldroyd, *Lincoln's Campaign or the Political Revolution of 1860* (Chicago, 1896), 84.
18. Oldroyd, *Lincoln's Campaign*, 206.
19. Jules Abels, *The Degeneration of Our Presidential Election* (Macmillan Publishing Co., Inc., New York, 1968), 118, 224.
20. Hayes, *Lincoln Runs for President*, 120–21; Minnigerode, *Presidential Years*,

378; Fite, *Campaign of 1860*, 210–11; Sandburg, *Prairie Years*, II:367; Malcolm P. Eiselen, "Campaign Ballads," *Review of Reviews*, XCIV (October 1936), 61.

21. Helen Nicolay, "A Candidate in His Home Town," *Abraham Lincoln Quarterly* (Springfield, Ill.), I (September 1940), 137.
22. A. K. McClure, ed., *Lincoln's Own Yarns and Stories* (Chicago and Philadelphia, n.d.), 72.
23. Sandburg, *Prairie Years*, II:356–57; Andrew A. Freeman, *Abraham Lincoln Goes to New York* (New York, 1960), 25.
24. Oldroyd, *Lincoln's Campaign*, 198; Hayes, *Lincoln Runs for President*, 135, 173, 186, 192.
25. Rita McKenna Carey, *The First Campaigner: Stephen A. Douglas* (New York, 1964), 43, 69; Don Seitz, *The "Also Rans"* (New York, 1928), 187; Hayes, *Lincoln Runs for President*, 158.
26. Fite, *Campaign of 1860*, 194 and note.
27. Minnegerode, *Presidential Years*, 381, 386; Sandburg, *Prairie Years*, II:356; Reinhard H. Luthin, *The First Lincoln Campaign* (Cambridge, Mass., 1944), 174; Oldroyd, *Lincoln's Campaign*, 140; Julius G. Rathbun, "The 'Wide-Awakes,' the Great Political Organization of 1860," *Connecticut Quarterly*, I (October 1895), 327–35.
28. Thomas Dew, *Republican Song Book* (Boston, 1860).
29. George S. Hilton, *The Funny Side of Politics* (New York, 1899), 44.
30. McClure, *Lincoln's Own Yarns*, 300–301.
31. Eli Perkins, *Thirty Years of Wit* (New York, 1899), 271–72.
32. Hayes, *Lincoln Runs for President* (Citadel Press, New York, 1960), 173.
33. Paul M. Angle, *Lincoln in the Year 1860* (Springfield, Ill., 1927), 49.

CHAPTER TWENTY
1864—Lincoln and the War Crisis

1. Stefan Lorant, *The Glorious Burden: The American Presidency* (New York, 1968), 262.
2. John G. Nicolay and John Hay, eds., *Complete Works of Abraham Lincoln*, 13 vols. (Harrogate, Tenn., 1894), VIII:100–101.
3. Harold M. Dudley, "The Election of 1864," *Mississippi Valley Historical Review*, XVIII (March 1932), 509; Nathaniel Stephenson, *Abraham Lincoln* (Indianapolis, 1923), 240–41; Carl Sandburg, *Abraham Lincoln: The War Years*, 4 vols. (New York, 1939), III:98.
4. Sandburg, *War Years*, III:203; Lorant, *Glorious Presidency*, 264.
5. Dudley, "Election of 1864," *MVHR*, 502–5.
6. Clarence E. N. Macartney, *Little Mac: The Life of General George B. McClellan* (Philadelphia, 1940), 340.
7. William Starr Meyers, *A Study in Personality: General George Brinton McClellan* (New York, 1934), 457.
8. Arthur M. Schlesinger, Jr., ed., *The Coming to Power: Critical Elections in American History* (New York, 1981), 153.
9. Lorant, *Glorious Burden*, 265.
10. Sandburg, *War Years*, III:271.
11. Ibid., 100.

12. " 'Conservative' Ribaldry," *Harper's Weekly*, VIII (September 24, 1864), 610; Sandburg, *War Years*, III:389–90.
13. Macartney, *McClellan*, 348; *Lincoln and the Civil War in the Diaries and Letters of John Hay* (ed. Tyler Dennett, New York, 1939), 233.
14. W. R. Thayer, *Life and Letters of John Hay* (Boston, 1914), I:133–34; Alexander McClure, *Our Presidents and How We Make Them* (New York, 1905), 182.
15. *Albany Journal*, September 3, 1864, 2; J. G. Randall, *Lincoln the President* (New York, 1955), 225.
16. Lorant, *Glorious Burden*, 268.
17. Meyer, *McClellan*, 464.
18. *Private and Official Correspondence of Benjamin F. Butler*, 5 vols. (Norwood, Mass., 1917), V:336.
19. *Works of Lincoln*, X:263–64.
20. George S. Hilton, *The Funny Side of Politics* (New York, 1899), 236.
21. J. G. Randall, "The Unpopular Mr. Lincoln," *Abraham Lincoln Quarterly*, II (June 1943), 275.
22. Sandburg, *War Years*, III:569.
23. Hope Ridings Miller, *Scandals in the Highest Office* (New York, 1973), 137.
24. McClure, *Lincoln's Own Yarns*, 160–62; Ward Hill Lamon, *Recollections of Abraham Lincoln, 1847–1865* (Washington, 1911), 141–46; *Lincoln in Diaries of Hay*, 233.
25. "Mr. Lincoln Drawing His Salary in Gold," *The World* (New York), October 3, 1864, p. 4; "The Gold-Payment Slander," *New York Times*, October 20, 1864, p. 4. See also Sandburg, *War Years*, III: 196, 289–90.
26. McClure, *Lincoln's Own Yarns*, 220; Grant to Edwin Stanton, November 10, 1864, *Private and Official Correspondence of Benjamin F. Butler*, 5 vols. (Norwich, Mass., 1917), V:336.
27. *Miscegenation: The Theory of the Blending of the Races Applied to the American White Man and Negro* (New York, 1864), 1, 11, 18, 29–30; Sidney Kaplan, "The Miscegenation Issue in the Election of 1864," *Journal of Negro History*, XXXIV (July 1949), 274–343.
28. McClure, *Lincoln's Own Yarns*, 103.

CHAPTER TWENTY-ONE
1868—Grant and Reconstruction

1. Thomas A. Bailey, *The American Pageant*, 2 vols. (Lexington, Mass., 1975), I:506.
2. *National Party Platforms*, 2 vols. (compiled by Donald Bruce Johnson, Urbana, Ill., 1978), I:37.
3. William B. Hesseltine, *Ulysses S. Grant: Politician* (New York, 1935), 127.
4. John Hope Franklin, "Election of 1868," Arthur M. Schlesinger, Jr., *A History of American Presidential Elections*, 4 vols. (New York, 1971), II:1262.
5. Charles Coleman, *The Election of 1868* (New York, 1934), 268; *Nation*, XVII (July 23, 1868).
6. Franklin, "Election of 1868," 1280; Coleman, *Election of 1868*, 96–97.
7. William S. McFeely, *Grant: A Biography* (New York, 1981), 283.
8. Franklin, "Election of 1868," 1260.

9. J. L. Ringwalt, *Anecdotes of General Ulysses S. Grant* (Philadelphia, 1886), 69–70.

10. Ibid., 66; Dixon Wecter, *The Hero in America* (New York, 1941), 327; Ellis Paxson Oberholtzer, *A History of the United States Since the Civil War,* 5 vols. (New York, 1917–37), II:153n, 184n, 187; Louis A. Coolidge, *Ulysses S. Grant* (Boston and New York, 1917), 270–73; Hesseltine, *Grant,* 127.

11. Robert Werlich, *"Beast" Butler: The Incredible Career of Major General Benjamin Franklin Butler* (Washington, D.C., 1962), 139, 261; Stanley F. Horn, *Invisible Empire: The Story of the Ku Klux Klan, 1866–1871* (Boston, 1939), 150–51; Robert S. Holzman, *Stormy Ben Butler* (New York, 1954), 181.

CHAPTER TWENTY-TWO
1872—Grant and the Liberal Republicans

1. Dixon Wecter, *The Hero in America* (New York, 1941), 329.

2. Samuel Eliot Morison and Henry Steele Commager, *The Growth of the American Republic,* 2 vols. (New York, 1962), II:69.

3. Stefan Lorant, *The Glorious Burden: The American Presidency* (New York, 1968), 309.

4. Henry Watterson, "The Humor and Tragedy of the Greeley Campaign," *Century Magazine,* LXXXV (November 1912), 30.

5. Lurton D. Ingersoll, *The Life of Horace Greeley* (New York, 1873), 541–42.

6. Ellis Paxson Oberholtzer, *A History of the United States Since the Civil War,* 5 vols. (New York, 1917–37), III:28.

7. Ingersoll, *Greeley,* 540.

8. William Gillette, "Election of 1872," Arthur M. Schlesinger, Jr., *A History of American Presidential Elections,* 4 vols. New York, 1971), II:1318.

9. Lorant, *Glorious Burden,* 319.

10. Oberholtzer, *History,* III:48.

11. Eugene H. Roseboom and Alfred E. Eckes, Jr., *A History of Presidential Elections* (New York, 1979), 87.

12. Henry L. Stoddard, *Horace Greeley* (New York, 1946), 312–13.

13. Oberholtzer, *History,* III:57; A. B. Paine, *Thomas Nast* (New York, 1905), 41, 42, 44, 45, 47, 48, 49.

14. William Harlan Hale, *Horace Greeley: The Voice of the People* (New York, 1950), 343–44.

15. James Ford Rhodes, *History of the United States from the Compromise of 1850,* 8 vols. (New York, 1892–1919), VIII:64; O. J. Hollister, *The Life of Schuyler Colfax* (New York, 1880), 387n.

16. Stoddard, *Greeley,* 315; Hale, *Greeley,* 346–47.

17. *New York Tribune,* June 4, 1872, William B. Hesseltine, *Ulysses S. Grant: Politician* (New York, 1935), 277.

18. "The Week," *Nation,* XXV (July 4, 1872), 1.

19. Rhodes, *History,* VIII:54–55; *Nation,* XXV (August 8, 1872), 83.

20. Hale, *Greeley,* 345.

21. Ida Husted Harper, *Life and Work of Susan B. Anthony,* 2 vols. (Indianapolis, 1898), I:409–65; Rheta Childs Dorr, *Susan B. Anthony* (New York, 1928), 252–68; Katharine Anthony, *Susan B. Anthony* (Garden City, N.Y., 1954), 273–304.

CHAPTER TWENTY-THREE
1876—The Hayes-Tilden Disputed Election

1. Sidney I. Pomeratz, "Election of 1876," Arthur M. Schlesinger, Jr., ed., *A History of American Presidential Elections*, 4 vols. (New York, 1971), II:1876.
2. *National Party Platforms*, 2 vols. (compiled by Donald Bruce Johnson, Urbana, Ill., 1978), I:54.
3. Paul L. Haworth, *The Hayes-Tilden Disputed Presidential Election of 1876* (Cleveland, 1906), 34.
4. Ibid., 8–9.
5. Keith Ian Polakoff, *The Politics of Inertia: The Election of 1876 and the End of Reconstruction* (Baton Rouge, La., 1974), 145–46; Lloyd Robinson, *The Stolen Election: Hayes vs. Tilden—1876* (Garden City, N.Y., 1968), 113–14.
6. Robinson, *Stolen Election*, 115.
7. Haworth, *Disputed Election*, 46.
8. Robinson, *Stolen Election*, 126–30.
9. Ibid., 136.
10. Ibid., 206.
11. Haworth, *Disputed Election*, 169; Robinson, *Stolen Election*, 158.
12. Kenneth E. Davison, *The Presidency of Rutherford B. Hayes* (Westport, Conn., 1972), 43–44.
13. Robinson, *Stolen Election*, 217.
14. Ibid., 227.
15. James Ford Rhodes, *History of the United States from the Compromise of 1850*, 8 vols. (New York, 1892–1919), VII:266–76; Benjamin Perley Poore, *Perley's Reminiscences of Sixty Years*, 2 vols. (New York, 1886), II:318–20; Gail Hamilton, *Biography of James G. Blaine* (Norwich, Conn., 1895), 396.
16. Rhodes, *History*, VII:281; Dee Brown, *Year of the Century: 1876* (New York, 1966), 248–49; William P. Randel, *Centennial: American Life in 1876* (Philadelphia, 1969), 225.
17. A. B. Paine, *Thomas Nast: His Period and His Pictures* (New York, 1904), 459.
18. Robinson, *Stolen Election*, 178–81; Pomeratz, "Election of 1876," 207–8; Louis W. Koenig, "The Election That Got Away," *American Heritage*, XI (October 1960), 103.
19. H. J. Eckenrode, *Rutherford B. Hayes: Statesman of Reunion* (New York, 1930), 235.
20. A. B. Paine, *Thomas Nast* (New York, 1905), 348.
21. Robinson, *Stolen Election*, 221.
22. George S. Hilton, *The Funny Side of Politics* (New York, 1899), 238; Robinson, *Stolen Election*, 158–59.

CHAPTER TWENTY-FOUR
1880—The Triumph of "Boatman Jim" Garfield

1. Robert G. Caldwell, *James A. Garfield: Party Chieftain* (New York, 1931), 298.
2. J. B. McClure, *General Garfield from the Log Cabin to the White House* (Chicago, 1881), 226–28.

3. Herbert J. Clancy, *The Presidential Election of 1880* (Chicago, 1958), 210.

4. Theodore Clarke Smith, *The Life and Letters of James Abram Garfield*, 2 vols. (New Haven, Conn., 1925), II:1027; Margaret Leech and Harry J. Brown, *The Garfield Orbit* (New York, 1978), 218; Clancy, *Election of 1880*, 227–31.

5. David C. Whitney, *The American Presidents* (Garden City, N.Y., 1967), 180.

6. Claude Fuess, *Calvin Coolidge* (New York, 1940), 29.

7. F. M. Green, *A Royal Life, or the Eventful History of James A. Garfield* (Chicago, 1882), 344–45; "From Mentor to Elberon," *Century Magazine*, XXIII (January 1882), 434.

8. James Ford Rhodes, *A History of the United States from the Compromise of 1850*, 8 vols. (New York, 1892–1919), VIII:111, 131, 137; Leon Burr Richardson, *William E. Chandler: Republican* (New York, 1940), 261–63; Leech-Brown, *Garfield Orbit*, 220; Glenn Tucker, *Hancock the Superb* (Indianapolis, 1961), 304; Leonard Dinnerstein, "Election of 1880," Arthur M. Schlesinger, Jr., ed., *A History of American Presidential Elections*, 4 vols. (New York, 1971), II:1509–10.

CHAPTER TWENTY-FIVE
1884—The Cleveland-Blaine Contest

1. *Official Proceedings of the Convention* (Chicago, 1884), 3, 4; David S. Muzzey, *James G. Blaine: A Political Idol of Other Days* (New York, 1932), 277.

2. James Ford Rhodes, *History of the United States from the Compromise of 1850*, 8 vols. (New York, 1892–1919), VIII:219.

3. Allan Nevins, *Grover Cleveland: A Study in Courage* (New York, 1932), 166–67.

4. Ellis Paxson Oberholtzer, *A History of the United States Since the Civil War*, 5 vols. (New York, 1917–37), IV:174n. Muzzey, *Blaine*, 282.

5. Joseph B. Foraker, *Notes of a Busy Life*, 2 vols. (Cincinnati, 1916–17), I:167–68.

6. Nevins, *Cleveland*, 159.

7. Oberholtzer, *History*, IV:197n.

8. Horace S. Merrill, *Bourbon Leader: Grover Cleveland and the Democratic Party* (Boston, 1957), 54.

9. Frederic L. Paxson, *Recent History of the United States* (Boston, 1921), 91; Harrison Cook Thomas, *The Return of the Democratic Party to Power in 1884* (New York, 1919), 197, 203; Oberholtzer, *History*, IV:195.

10. Gamaliel Bradford, "James Gillespie Blaine," *Atlantic Monthly*, CXXVI (October 1920), 516–18; Herbert Eaton, *Presidential Timber: A History of Nominating Conventions* (New York, 1964), 47–50; Jules Abels, *The Degeneration of Our Presidential Election* (New York, 1968), 196–98.

11. Oberholtzer, *History*, IV:208–209; Marvin and Dorothy Rosenberg, "The Dirtiest Campaign," *American Heritage*, XIII (August 1962), 6; Muzzey, *Blaine*, 302–4; Thomas, *Return of Democratic Party*, 206.

12. Merrill, *Bourbon Leader*, 62–63; Rhodes, *History*, VIII:221–23; Nevins, *Cleveland*, 164–66.

13. Robert Bendiner, *White House Fever* (New York, 1960), 127 and note.

14. Oberholtzer, *History*, IV:193n.

15. Rhodes, *History*, VIII:223.
16. Nevins, *Cleveland*, 177; Abels, *Degeneration of Election*, 78.
17. William C. Hudson, *Random Recollections of an Old Political Reporter* (New York, 1911), 209–12; Rosenbergs, "Dirtiest Campaign," *American Heritage*, 100; *The World* (New York), October 30, 1884, p. 1.
18. Muzzey, *Blaine*, 324.
19. Mark D. Hirsch, "Election of 1884," Arthur M. Schlesinger, Jr., ed., *A History of American Presidential Elections*, 4 vols. (New York, 1971), II:1581.
20. Hope Ridings Miller, *Scandals in the Highest Office* (New York, 1973), 162; M. and D. Rosenberg, "Dirtiest Campaign," *American Heritage*, 100.
21. Henry Stoddard, *As I Knew Them: Presidents and Politics from Grant to Coolidge* (New York, 1927), 94; H. J. Eckenrode, *Rutherford B: Hayes: Statesman of Reunion* (New York, 1930), 116.
22. Robert McElroy, *Grover Cleveland: The Man and the Statesman*, 2 vols. (New York, 1923), I:86–88; Hudson, *Random Recollections*, 178–80.
23. M. and D. Rosenberg, "Dirtiest Campaign," *American Heritage*, 9, 97; McElroy, *Cleveland*, I:91; Nevins, *Cleveland*, 169; Hudson, *Random Recollections*, 186–90.
24. McElroy, *Cleveland*, I:92–94.
25. Oberholtzer, *History*, IV:169; Muzzey, *Blaine*, 276–77.
26. George S. Hilton, *The Funny Side of Politics* (New York, 1899), 302–3.
27. Henry Nash Smith, ed., *Mark Twain-William Dean Howells Letters*, 2 vols. (Harvard, 1960), II:501.
28. M. and D. Rosenberg, "Dirtiest Campaign," *American Heritage*, 4–9; Rexford G. Tugwell, *Grover Cleveland* (New York, 1968), 93; Nevins, *Cleveland*, 169; Abels, *Degeneration of Election*, 199–201; Bendiner, *White House Fever*, 127 and note.
29. Gail Hamilton, *Biography of James G. Blaine* (Norwich, Conn., 1895), 58.
30. Oberholtzer, *History*, IV:208 and note.
31. Hudson, *Random Recollections*, 221–22, 225.
32. Stoddard, *As I Knew Them*, 138.
33. M. L. Avary, *Dixie after the War* (New York, 1906), 286; Richard W. Gilder, *Grover Cleveland: A Record of Friendship* (New York, 1910), 218.

CHAPTER TWENTY-SIX
1888—Harrison, Cleveland, and the Tariff

1. Robert F. Wesser, "Election of 1888," Arthur M. Schlesinger, Jr., ed., *A History of Presidential Elections*, 4 vols. (New York, 1971), II:1620.
2. Harry J. Sievers, *Benjamin Harrison, Hoosier Statesman: 1865–1888* (New York, 1959), 392.
3. Robert McElroy, *Grover Cleveland: The Man and the Statesman*, 2 vols. (New York, 1923), I:286–8; Ellis Paxson Oberholtzer, *A History of the United States since the Civil War*, 5 vols. (New York, 1917–37), V:13.
4. Sievers, *Hoosier Statesman*, 379; Stefan Lorant, *The Glorious Burden: The American Presidency* (New York, 1968), 403.
5. Allan Nevins, *Grover Cleveland: A Study in Courage* (New York, 1932), 434.
6. McElroy, *Cleveland*, I:439; Nevins, *Cleveland*, 439.

7. Oberholtzer, *History*, V:60, 68; Nevins, *Cleveland*, 429–31; Sievers, *Hoosier Statesman*, 409–12.

8. R. C. Buley, "The Campaign of 1888 in Indiana," *Indiana Magazine of History*, X (1914), 47–50; "Letter from W. W. Dudley to a Local Republican Leader in Indiana," October 24, 1888, Schlesinger, *Presidential Elections*, II:1697–98; Robert Rienow and Leona Train Rienow, *The Lonely Quest* (Chicago, 1966), 126–27; Nevins, *Cleveland*, 436–37.

9. William Allen White, *Masks in a Pageant* (New York, 1939), 80; Sievers, *Hoosier Statesman*, 337n., 426–27; Jules Abels, *The Degeneration of Our Presidential Election* (New York, 1968), 158; Matthew Josephson, *The Politicos, 1865–1896* (New York, 1938), 433, 438.

CHAPTER TWENTY-SEVEN
1892—Cleveland's Return to Power

1. H. Wayne Morgan, "Election of 1892," Arthur M. Schlesinger, Jr., ed., *A History of American Presidential Elections*, 4 vols. (New York, 1971), II:1723.

2. Sherwin Lawrence Cook, *Torchlight Parade* (New York, 1929), 145.

3. A. K. McClure, *Our Presidents and How We Make Them* (New York, 1905), 341.

4. Ibid., 346.

5. Annie L. Diggs, *The Story of Jerry Simpson* (Wichita, Kansas, 1908), 84; Dale Kramer, *The Wild Jackasses: The American Farmer in Revolt* (New York, 1956), 105–6.

6. *National Party Platforms*, 2 vols. (compiled by Donald Bruce Johnson, Urbana, Ill., 1978), I:89.

7. John D. Hicks, *The Populist Revolt* (University of Minnesota, 1931), 244.

8. George H. Knoles, *The Presidential Campaign and Election of 1892* (Stanford, 1943), 187–89; Hicks, *Populist Revolt*, 244.

9. Leon Wolff, *Lockout: The Story of the Homestead Strike of 1892* (New York, 1965), 221.

10. Allan Nevins, *Grover Cleveland: A Study in Courage* (Dodd, Mead & Co., New York, 1932), 491.

11. Ellis Paxson Oberholtzer, *A History of the United States Since the Civil War*, 5 vols. (New York, 1917–1937), V:176–77; Cook, *Torchlight Parade*, 146; *The Autobiography of Thomas Collier Platt* (New York, 1926), 213, 215, 219, 247, 252; Samuel W. McCall, *The Life of Thomas Brackett Reed* (Boston, 1914), 188.

12. October 27, 1892, Elmer Ellis, ed., *Mr. Dooley's American* (New York, 1941), 46.

13. *Major Campaign Speeches of Adlai E. Stevenson, 1952* (New York, 1953), 83.

CHAPTER TWENTY-EIGHT
1896—McKinley, Bryan, and Free Silver

1. M. W. Werner, *William Jennings Bryan* (New York, 1929), 96.

2. Robert F. Durden, *The Climax of Populism: The Election of 1896* (Louisville, 1966), 136.

3. *National Party Platforms*, 2 vols. (compiled by Donald Bruce Johnson, Urbana, Ill., 1978), I:108.

4. Paxton Hibben, *The Peerless Leader: William Jennings Bryan* (New York, 1929), 189; Matthew Josephson, *The Politicos, 1865–1896* (New York, 1938), 680.

5. Werner, *Bryan*, 75–76; Hibben, *Peerless Leader*, 187.

6. Samuel Eliot Morison and Henry Steele Commager, *The Growth of the American Republic*, 2 vols. (New York, 1962), II:355.

7. Werner, *Bryan*, 85.

8. Josephson, *Politicos*, 684; Louis W. Koenig, *Bryan: A Political Biography of William Jennings Bryan* (New York, 1971), 214.

9. Josephson, *Politicos*, 692.

10. William J. Bryan, *The First Battle: A Story of the Campaign of 1896* (Chicago, 1896), 205.

11. Hibben, *Peerless Leader*, 191.

12. Koenig, *Bryan*, 218, 243; Charles E. Merriam, *Four American Party Leaders* (New York, 1926), 67–68; James A. Barnes, "Myths of the Bryan Campaign," *Mississippi Valley Historical Review*, XXXIV (December 1947), 395.

13. Koenig, *Bryan*, 231–32, 243.

14. Thomas A. Bailey, *The American Pageant: A History of the Republic*, 2 vols. (Lexington, Mass., 1975), II:641.

15. Koenig, *Bryan*, 228; Josephson, *Politicos*, 697.

16. Koenig, *Bryan*, 254.

17. Herbert Eaton, *Presidential Timber: A History of Nominating Conventions* (New York, 1964), 150; H. Wayne Morgan, *McKinley and His America* (Syracuse, N.Y., 1963), 228–29; Margaret Leech, *In the Days of McKinley* (New York, 1959), 69.

18. Koenig, *Bryan*, 211; Bryan, *The First Battle*, 219.

19. Paolo Coletta, *William Jennings Bryan: Political Evangelist, 1860–1908* (Lincoln, Nebraska, 1965), 167; Bascom N. Timmons, *Portrait of an American: Charles G. Dawes* (New York, 1953), 56; Koenig, *Bryan*, 232; Louis W. Koenig, "The First Hurrah," *American Heritage*, XXXI (April–May 1980), 8–9.

20. Werner, *Bryan*, 80; Paul W. Glad, *McKinley, Bryan, and the People* (Philadelphia, 1964), 173.

21. George S. Hilton, *The Funny Side of Politics* (New York, 1899), 138.

22. Coletta, *Bryan*, 180; Werner, *Bryan*, 86; John A. Garraty, *Henry Cabot Lodge* (New York, 1953), 174.

23. Hilton, *Funny Side of Politics*, 138.

24. Ibid., 138–39.

25. Glad, *McKinley, Bryan, and People*, 183.

26. Hilton, *Funny Side of Politics*, 140.

27. William J. Bryan, *First Battle*, 484–88; Charles W. Thompson, *Presidents I've Known* (Indianapolis, 1929), 102–3.

28. Coletta, *Bryan*, 175; Werner, *Bryan*, 96.

29. Koenig, "First Hurrah," *American Heritage*, 10; Koenig, *Bryan*, 241–42.

30. Werner, *Bryan*, 108–109; Jones, *Election of 1896*, 306.

31. Morgan, *McKinley*, 233–36; Leech, *Days of McKinley*, 88–94; Ellis Paxson Oberholtzer, *A History of the United States Since the Civil War*, 5 vols. (New York, 1917–1937), V:408–10; Sidney Warren, *The Battle for the Presidency* (New York, 1968), 169.

32. Leech, *Days of McKinley*; Jones, *Election of 1896*, 177.

33. William H. Harvey, *Coin's Financial School* (ed. Richard Hofstadter, Cam-

bridge Mass., 1963); Coletta, *Bryan*, 168, 180; Koenig, *Bryan*, 232; Matthew Josephson, *The Politicos, 1865–1896* (New York, 1938), 702–5.
34. Josephson, *Politicos*, 708; Werner, *Bryan*, 112.

CHAPTER TWENTY-NINE

1900—The McKinley-Roosevelt Triumph

1. Thomas A. Bailey, "Was the Presidential Election of 1900 a Mandate on Imperialism?" *Mississippi Valley Historical Review*, XXIV (June 1937), 44; Walter LaFeber, "Election of 1900," Arthur M. Schlesinger, Jr., ed., *A History of American Presidential Elections*, 4 vols. (New York, 1971), III:1911.
2. Stefan Lorant, *The Glorious Burden: The American Presidency* (New York, 1968), 454.
3. Margaret Leech, *In the Days of McKinley* (New York, 1959), 537, 542, 557.
4. Lorant, *Glorious Burden*, 467.
5. LaFeber, "Election of 1900," 1898.
6. Indianapolis, August 18, 1900, Ray Ginger, ed., *William Jennings Bryan: Selections* (Indianapolis, 1967), 66–67; "Mr. Bryan's Address on Imperialism," *Outlook*, LXV (August 18, 1900), 938–40.
7. Louis W. Koenig, *Bryan: A Political Biography* (New York, 1971), 344; Paolo E. Coletta, *William Jennings Bryan: Political Evangelist, 1860–1908* (Lincoln, Neb., 1965), 280.
8. H. Wayne Morgan, *William McKinley and His America* (Syracuse University Press, Syracuse, N.Y., 1963), 508.
9. *New York Evening Journal*, May 30, 1900; Leech, *Days of McKinley*, 548; W. A. Swanberg, *Citizen Hearst* (New York, 1961), 185–88.
10. Leech, *Days of McKinley* 535; Morgan, *McKinley*, 494.
11. Leech, *Days of McKinley*, 541; Morgan, *McKinley*, 498.
12. Cyrenus Cole, *I Remember, I Remember: A Book of Recollections* (Iowa City, Iowa, 1936), 293.
13. Morgan, *McKinley*, 502.

CHAPTER THIRTY

1904—T.R.'s Smashing Victory

1. Stefan Lorant, *The Glorious Burden: The American Presidency* (New York, 1968), 481.
2. *National Party Platforms*, 2 vols. (compiled by Donald Bruce Johnson, Urbana, Ill., 1978), I:134.
3. William H. Harbaugh, "Election of 1904," Arthur M. Schlesinger, Jr., ed., *A History of American Presidential Elections*, 4 vols., (New York, 1971), III:1976.
4. Stefan Lorant, *The Life and Times of Theodore Roosevelt* (Garden City, N.Y., 1959).
5. J. L. Heaton, *The Story of a Page* (New York, 1913), 206–7; Henry F. Pringle, *Theodore Roosevelt* (New York, 1931), 354–55.
6. Pringle, *Roosevelt*, 355–56.

7. John M. Blum, *The Republican Roosevelt* (Cambridge, Mass., 1954), 70.
8. Harbaugh, "Election of 1904," 1994.
9. Mark Sullivan, *Our Times: The United States, 1900–1925* (New York, 1927), II:460.
10. Lorant, *Glorious Burden,* 486.
11. Noel F. Busch, *T.R.: The Story of Theodore Roosevelt and His Influence* (New York, 1963), 185–86; Harold E. Davis, "The Citizenship of Jon Perdicaris," *Journal of Modern History,* XIII (1941), 517–26.
12. William Burlie Brown, *The People's Choice* (Baton Rouge, La., 1960), 135.
13. James Ford Rhodes, *The McKinley and Roosevelt Administrations* (New York, 1923), 294–95; Oscar King Davis, *Released for Publication* (Boston, 1925), 28–30.

CHAPTER THIRTY-ONE
1908—Taft's Big Victory over Bryan

1. Paxton Hibben, *The Peerless Leader: William Jennings Bryan* (New York, 1929), 281, 287.
2. Henry L. Stoddard, *As I Knew Them: Presidents and Politicis from Grant to Coolidge* (New York, 1927), 338–40; Henry F. Pringle, *The Life and Times of William Howard Taft,* 2 vols. (New York, 1939), I:352–53.
3. Paolo E. Coletta, *William Jennings Bryan: Political Evangelist, 1865–1908* (Lincoln, Neb., 1965), 407.
4. Louis W. Koenig, *Bryan: A Political Biography of William Jennings Bryan* (New York, 1971), 436.
5. Coletta, *Bryan,* I:411.
6. Pringle, *Taft,* I:359.
7. Koenig, *Bryan,* 452.
8. Coletta, *Bryan,* I:422.
9. Pringle, *Taft,* I:377.
10. Richard N. Current et al., *American History: A Survey,* 2 vols. (New York, 1975), II:589.
11. Judith Icke Anderson, *William Howard Taft: An Intimate History* (W. W. Norton & Co., Inc., New York, 1981), 109.
12. Nicholas Murray Butler, *Across the Busy Years,* 2 vols. (Charles Scribner's Sons, New York, 1939), I:325.
13. Anderson, *Taft,* 105–106; Pringle, *Taft,* I:376; William Burlie Brown, *The People's Choice* (Baton Rouge, La., 1960), 43.
14. Charles W. Thompson, *Presidents I've Known* (Indianapolis, 1929), 67.
15. Ibid.

CHAPTER THIRTY-TWO
1912—The High Tide of Progressivism: Wilson, Roosevelt, and Taft

1. Henry F. Pringle, *Theodore Roosevelt: A Biography* (New York, 1931), 556.
2. Ibid., 556, 560.
3. Ibid., 561.

4. Henry F. Pringle, *The Life and Times of William Howard Taft,* 2 vols. (New York, 1939), II:809.
5. William Henry Harbaugh, *Power and Responsibility: The Life and Times of Theodore Roosevelt* (New York, 1961), 442.
6. Harbaugh, *Roosevelt,* 443.
7. Samuel Eliot Morison and Henry Steele Commager, *The Growth of the American Republic,* 2 vols. (New York, 1962), II:514.
8. Sherwin Lawrence Cook, *Torchlight Parade* (New York, 1929), 173–74.
9. Arthur S. Link, *Wilson: The Road to the White House* (Princeton, 1947), 476.
10. Pringle, *Taft,* II:817–18.
11. Ibid., 834.
12. Stefan Lorant, *The Glorious Burden: The American Presidency* (New York, 1968), 523.
13. Harbaugh, *Power and Responsibility,* 431, 446.
14. Lorant, *Glorious Burden,* 529.
15. *New York Times,* October 15, 1912, 1, 2.
16. Lorant, *Glorious Burden,* 532.
17. Ibid.
18. Pringle, *Roosevelt,* 571.
19. "The Presidential Campaign: Third-Term Realities," *Outlook,* C (February 17, 1912), 338.
20. Charles W. Thompson, *Presidents I've Known* (Bobbs-Merrill Co., Inc., Indianapolis, 1929), 220–22; Harbaugh, *Power and Responsibility,* 430; Pringle, *Taft,* I:783.
21. Henry Stoddard, *As I Knew Them: Presidents and Politics from Grant to Coolidge* (New York, 1927), 410; Claude Bowers, *Beveridge and the Progressive Era* (Boston, 1932), 424.
22. Ray Stannard Baker, *Woodrow Wilson: Life and Letters,* 8 vols. (Garden City, N.Y., 1927–39), III:373; "The Counterpuncher," *Time,* XCII (September 20, 1968), 21.
23. Thompson, *Presidents I've Known,* 187.
24. Ibid., 144–46.
25. Stefan Lorant, *The Life and Times of Theodore Roosevelt* (Garden City, N.Y., 1959), 565; Pringle, *Roosevelt,* 562; Thompson, *Presidents I've Known,* 190–91.
26. Thompson, *Presidents I've Known,* 128–30.
27. Baker, *Wilson,* III:375.
28. Ibid., 276.
29. Thompson, *Presidents I've Known,* 288.

CHAPTER THIRTY-THREE
1916—Wilson and the Great War

1. Ray Stannard Baker, *Woodrow Wilson: Life and Letters,* 8 vols. (Garden City, N.Y., 1927–39), VI:250–53; S. D. Lovell, *The Presidential Election of 1916* (Carbondale, Ill., 1980), 55–56; Joseph P. Tumulty, *Woodrow Wilson as I Knew Him* (Garden City, N.Y., 1921), 185.
2. Baker, *Wilson,* VI:254, 257n.

3. Stefan Lorant, *The Glorious Burden: The American Presidency* (New York, 1968), 540.
4. Ibid.
5. Merlo J. Pusey, *Charles Evans Hughes*, 2 vols. (Macmillan Publishing Co., Inc., New York, 1951), I:336; Baker, *Wilson*, VI:247.
6. Lorant, *Glorious Burden*, 543.
7. Baker, *Wilson*, VI:275.
8. Pusey, *Hughes*, I:342–49; Lovell, *Election of 1916*, 142–45; Jules Abels, *The Degeneration of Our American Presidential Election* (New York, 1968), 142–45.
9. Arthur S. Link, *Wilson: Campaigns for Progressivism and Peace* (Princeton, 1965), 120; *New York Times*, October 22, 1916.
10. Link, *Wilson Campaigns*, 111; *New York Times*, November 4, 1916.
11. Link, *Wilson Campaigns*, 156; Edith Wilson, *My Memoir* (Indianapolis, 1938), 115.
12. Pusey, *Hughes*, I:361.
13. Link, *Wilson Campaigns*, 125; *New York Times*, October 14, 1916.
14. Link, *Wilson Campaigns*, 162; Stephen Gwynn, ed., *The Letters of Cecil Spring-Rice*, 2 vols. (Boston, 1929), II:354–55.
15. Pusey, *Hughes*, I:339; *New York Herald*, November 8, 1916.
16. Josephus Daniels, *The Wilson Era: The Years of Peace, 1910–1917* (Chapel Hill, N.C., 1944), 456–57.
17. Ibid., 462–66; Lovell, *Election of 1916*, 101.
18. Link, *Wilson Campaigns*, 18, 143–45; Hope Ridings Miller, *Scandals in the Highest Office* (New York, 1973), 166–99; Mary Allen Hulbert, *The Story of Mrs. Peck: An Autobiography* (New York, 1933), 158–79; 213–36.´
19. Pusey, *Hughes*, I:360; *New York Times*, November 8, 1916.
20. Ibid., 361–62; Link, *Wilson Campaigns*, 153–56.
21. Link, *Wilson Campaigns*, 160.
22. Pusey, *Hughes* (Macmillan Publishing Co., Inc., New York, 1951), I:364.

CHAPTER THIRTY-FOUR
1920—Harding, Nostrums, and Normalcy

1. "How Will You Vote," *Nation*, CXI (September 4, 1920), 260.
2. Francis Russell, *The Shadow of Blooming Grove: Warren G. Harding and His Times* (New York, 1968), 382; Samuel Hopkins Adams, *The Incredible Era* (Boston, 1939), 163; Clinton W. Gilbert, *The Mirrors of Washington* (New York, 1921), 5.
3. Wesley M. Bagby, *The Road to Normalcy* (Baltimore, 1968), 139; Adams, *Incredible Era*, 175–76.
4. Russell, *Blooming Grove*, 347 and note; Adams, *Incredible Era*, 116–17; Andrew Sinclair, *The Available Man: The Life Behind the Masks of Warren Gamaliel Harding* (New York, 1965), 162.
5. Adams, *Incredible Era*, 172.
6. Sinclair, *Available Man*, 174.
7. Bagby, *Road to Normalcy*, 160.
8. "Sees Harding as Compromise Choice," *New York Times*, February 21, 1920, p. 3; Russell, *Blooming Grove*, 342, 382–83, 395n, 402; Adams, *Incredible Era*,

130, 154–55; Bagby, *Road to Normalcy,* 42; Herbert Eaton, *Presidential Timber: A History of Nominating Conventions* (New York, 1964), 263–65.

9. Adams, *Incredible Era,* 185; William Safire, "Voice of Pop Sitpack," *New York Times Magazine,* December 19, 1982, p. 18.

10. Russell, *Blooming Grove,* 372, 404–5, 412–18; Adams, *Incredible Era,* 132–33, 179–85, 190–91; Sinclair, *Available Man,* 169–72; Hope Ridings Miller, *Scandals in the Highest Office* (New York, 1973), 207–9; Jules Abels, *The Degeneration of Our Presidential Election* (New York, 1968), 208–9.

CHAPTER THIRTY-FIVE
1924—Keeping Cool with Coolidge

1. Louis Untermeyer, *A Treasury of Laughter* (New York, 1946), 85; Boyce House, *Laugh Parade of States* (San Antonio, 1948), 138.

2. Robert K. Murray, *The 103rd Ballot: Democrats and Disaster in Madison Square Garden* (New York, 1976), 144.

3. Murray, *103rd Ballot,* 207, 221.

4. Belle Case and Fola LaFollette, *Robert M. LaFollette,* 2 vols. (New York, 1953), II:1112.

5. Murray, *103rd Ballot,* 252; Donald R. McCoy, *Calvin Coolidge: The Quiet President* (New York, 1967), 262–63.

6. Charles W. Thompson, *Presidents I've Known* (Indianapolis, 1929), 356.

7. John F. Parker, *"If Elected, I Promise. . . ."* (Garden City, N.Y., 1960), 46.

8. Murray, *103rd Ballot,* 119.

9. Ibid., 182.

10. H. L. Mencken, *On Politics: A Carnival of Buncombe* (ed. Malcolm Moos, New York, 1960), xiv.

11. Claude Fuess, *Calvin Coolidge* (New York, 1940), 352; Ishbel Ross, *Grace Coolidge and Her Era* (New York, 1962), 156; Donald R. McCoy, *Calvin Coolidge: The Quiet President* (New York, 1967), 295.

12. Bennett Cerf, *Shake Well Before Using* (New York, 1951), 9.

CHAPTER THIRTY-SIX
1928—Hoover, Smith, and the Catholic Issue

1. Stefan Lorant, *The Glorious Burden: The American Presidency* (New York, 1968), 575.

2. Lawrence H. Fuchs, "Election of 1928," Arthur M. Schlesinger, Jr., ed., *A History of American Presidential Elections,* 4 vols. (New York, 1971), 2595.

3. David Hinshaw, *Herbert Hoover: American Quaker* (New York, 1950), 201.

4. Alfred E. Smith, "Catholic and Patriot: Governor Smith Replies," *Atlantic Monthly,* CXXXIX (May 1927), 722.

5. Edmund A. Moore, *A Catholic Runs for President: The Campaign of 1928* (New York, 1956), 188–89n.

6. Thomas A. Bailey, *The American Pageant: A History of the Republic,* 2 vols. (Lexington, Mass., 1975), II:842–45; Moore, *Catholic Runs for President,* 168–78.

7. Moore, *Catholic Runs for President,* 136–37.

8. Ibid., 131.

9. *The Memoirs of Herbert Hoover: The Cabinet and the Presidency, 1920–1933* (New York, 1952), 192, 205–6.

10. Kent Schofield, "The Public Image of Herbert Hoover in the 1928 Campaign," *Mid-America* (Chicago), II (October 1969), 281, 282, 287, 288.

11. Matthew and Hannah Josephson, *Al Smith: Hero of the Cities* (Boston, 1969), 398.

12. Fuchs, "Election of 1928," 2603.

13. Jules Abels, *The Degeneration of Our Presidential Election* (New York, 1968), 93–94; Robert Bendiner, *White House Fever* (New York, 1960), 123.

14. "Great Sensation," *Time,* XII (September 10, 1928), 8.

15. "Yeah," *Time,* XII (July 16, 1928), 9; Frank Graham, *Al Smith, America: An Informal Biography* (New York, 1945), 204.

16. Samuel Hopkins Adams, "Presidential Campaign Slanders," *Life,* XVII (October 2, 1944), 6; "Three Whispers," *Time,* XII (September 17, 1928), 9; "The South-Splitters," ibid., XII (July 30, 1928), 8; Moore, *Catholic Runs for President,* 90, 105, 153.

17. Nicholas Murray Butler, *Across the Busy Years,* 2 vols. (Charles Scribner's Sons, New York, 1939), I:359–61.

18. "Gillett's 'Seed,'" *Time,* XII (July 30, 1928), 6; Moore, *Catholic Runs for President,* 158–62.

19. Butler, *Across Busy Years* (Charles Scribner's Sons, New York, 1939), I:361–62.

CHAPTER THIRTY-SEVEN
1932—Roosevelt, Hoover, and the Great Depression

1. Roy V. Peel and Thomas C. Donnelly, *The 1932 Campaign: An Analysis* (New York, 1935), 56; Sidney Warren, *The Battle for the Presidency* (Philadelphia, 1968), 220.

2. *The Memoirs of Herbert Hoover: The Great Depression, 1929–1941* (New York, 1952), 218.

3. David Hinshaw, *Herbert Hoover: American Quaker* (New York, 1950), xvii; Frank Freidel, *Franklin D. Roosevelt: The Triumph* (Boston, 1956), 324; Jordan A. Schwarz, *The Interregnum of Despair: Hoover, Congress, and the Depression* (Urbana, Illinois, 1970), 195.

4. Walter Lippmann, *Interpretations, 1931–1932* (New York, 1933), 287.

5. Frank Freidel, "Election of 1932," Arthur M. Schlesinger, Jr., ed., *The Coming to Power: Critical Presidential Elections in American History* (New York, 1981), 344.

6. James A. Farley, *Farley's Story* (New York, 1948), 25.

7. James McGregor Burns, *Roosevelt: The Lion and the Fox* (New York, 1956), 138.

8. H. L. Mencken, *On Politics: A Carnival of Buncombe* (ed. Malcolm Moos, New York, 1960), 262–66.

9. Lippmann, *Interpretations,* 261–62.

10. Freidel, *Roosevelt: Triumph,* 315; Ernest K. Lindley, *The Roosevelt Revolution*

(New York, 1933), 27; Samuel I. Rosenman, *Working with Roosevelt* (New York, 1952), 78.

11. Freidel, *Roosevelt: Triumph*, 329.
12. Stefan Lorant, *The Glorious Burden: The American Presidency* (New York, 1968), 594.
13. Sidney Warren, *The Battle for the Presidency* (New York, 1968), 229; Harris Gaylord Warren, *Herbert Hoover and the Great Depression* (New York, 1959), 267.
14. *The Public Papers and Addresses of Franklin D. Roosevelt*, 13 vols. (New York, 1938–50), I:745.
15. *Memoirs of Hoover*, 255; Lorant, *Glorious Burden*, 596.
16. Lorant, *Glorious Burden*, 597; Freidel, *Roosevelt: Triumph*, 339–40, 366.
17. William Starr Myers, ed., *The State Papers and Other Writings of Herbert Hoover*, 2 vols. (Garden City, N.Y., 1934), II:411, 418.
18. Lorant, *Glorious Burden*, 600.
19. Schwarz, *Interregnum*, 204.
20. Edward J. Flynn, *You're the Boss* (New York, 1947), 100; William Manchester, *The Glory and the Dream: A Narrative History of America* (Boston, 1974), 48; Arthur M. Schlesinger, Jr., *The Crisis of the Old Order* (Boston, 1957), 302–303.
21. "The Roosevelt Week," *Time*, XX (July 11, 1932), 10; Rosenman, *Working with Roosevelt*, 74; Warren, *Battle for Presidency*, 236, 245; Freidel, *Roosevelt: Triumph*, 312n.
22. James Roosevelt and Sidney Shalett, *Affectionately, F.D.R.* (New York, 1959), 225–26; Alfred B. Rollins, Jr., *Roosevelt and Howe* (New York, 1962), 347; Rosenman, *Working with Roosevelt*, 76–77; Freidel, *Roosevelt: Triumph*, 313–14, 315; Harold F. Gosnell, *Champion Campaigner: Franklin D. Roosevelt* (New York, 1952), 121.
23. Lindley, *Roosevelt Revolution*, 26n.; Rosenman, *Working with Roosevelt*, 81; John Gunther, *Roosevelt in Retrospect* (New York, 1950), 268–69.
24. *Memoirs of Hoover*, 225–32; Freidel, *Roosevelt: Triumph*, 326–27.
25. Charles Michelson, *The Ghost Talks* (G. P. Putnam's Sons, New York, 1944), 11–12, 51.
26. Joseph P. Lash, *Eleanor and Franklin* (New York, 1971), 462.
27. Jules Abels, *The Degeneration of Our Presidential Election* (Macmillan Publishing Co., Inc., New York, 1968), 271.
28. Freidel, *Roosevelt: Triumph*, 351.
29. Peel and Donnelly, *1932 Campaign*, 213.

CHAPTER THIRTY-EIGHT
1936—Roosevelt and the New Deal

1. James McGregor Burns, *Roosevelt: The Lion and the Fox* (New York, 1956), 271; Arthur M. Schlesinger, Jr., *The Politics of Upheaval* (Boston, 1960), 578.
2. "Warrior to War," *Time*, XXVII (February 3, 1936), 14.
3. "Outbursts Alarm Prof. Cerebellum," *New York Times*, June 27, 1936, p. 8; Stefan Lorant, *The Glorious Burden: The American Presidency* (New York, 1968), 616.
4. Robert Bendiner, *White House Fever* (New York, 1960), 94n.

5. *The Public Papers and Addresses of Franklin D. Roosevelt*, 13 vols. (New York, 1938–50), V:236.

6. "Topics of the Day," *Literary Digest*, CXXII (August 15, 1936), 4; "Merger of Malcontents," *Time*, XXVIII (July 27, 1936), 18.

7. "Strange Interlude," *Time*, XXVIII (September 14, 1936), 15.

8. "Red Issue," *Time*, XXVIII (September 28, 1936), 13; Donald McCoy, *Landon of Kansas* (Lincoln, Neb., 1968), 279; W. A. Swanberg, *Hearst* (New York, 1961), 477.

9. *Public Papers of Roosevelt*, V:389.

10. William E. Leuchtenburg, "Election of 1936," Arthur M. Schlesinger, Jr., ed., *A History of American Presidential Elections*, 4 vols. (New York, 1971), III:2820; McCoy, *Landon*, 295–96; Schlesinger, *Politics of Upheaval*, 635–36.

11. *Public Papers of Roosevelt*, V:569.

12. McCoy, *Landon*, 331–32.

13. Schlesinger, *Politics of Upheaval*, 640.

14. McCoy, *Landon*, 347–48.

15. Robert Bendiner, *White House Fever* (New York, 1960), 108; McCoy, *Landon*, 259.

16. "Democrats Hunt for 'Hoover Hay'," *New York Times*, June 23, 1936, p. 12.

17. McCoy, *Landon*, 271; Lorant, *Glorious Burden*, 620.

18. Leuchtenburg, "Election of 1936," 2833; George Creel, *Rebel at Large* (New York, 1947), 301–2; Burns, *Roosevelt*, 286–87.

19. Samuel I. Rosenman, *Working with Roosevelt* (Harper & Row Publishers, Inc., New York, 1952), 86–87; Frank Freidel, *Franklin D. Roosevelt: The Triumph* (Boston, 1956), 362n.

20. Schlesinger, *Politics of Upheaval*, 562.

21. Ibid., 583–84; Grace Tully, *F.D.R., My Boss* (New York, 1949), 202; Michael F. Reilly, *Reilly of the White House* (New York, 1947), 98–101.

22. Eric Goldman, *Rendezvous with Destiny* (New York, 1952), 345; William E. Leuchtenburg, *Franklin Roosevelt and the New Deal* (New York, 1963), 189.

23. Leuchtenburg, "Election of 1936," 2817; McCoy, *Landon*, 282.

24. "Strange Interlude," Time, XXVIII (September 14, 1936), 15; McCoy, *Landon*, 289; Leuchtenburg, "Election of 1936," 2836.

25. McCoy, *Landon*, 283; Leuchtenburg, "Election of 1936," 2820.

26. *Public Papers of Roosevelt*, V:362–63.

27. McCoy, *Landon*, 304; Schlesinger, *Politics of Upheaval*, 529.

28. *Literary Digest*, CXXII (August 22, 1936), 3; (September 5, 1936), 7; "Topics of the Day," for September 12, 19, 26, and October 3, 10, 17, 24, 31; "What Went Wrong with the Polls," November 14, 1936, p. 8.

29. Leuchtenburg, "Election of 1936," 2842–43; Lloyd Robinson, *The Hopefuls: Ten Presidential Campaigns* (Garden City, N.Y., 1966), 69; Schlesinger, *Politics of Upheaval*, 643.

CHAPTER THIRTY-NINE
1940—Roosevelt, Willkie, and the War in Europe

1. Ellsworth Barnard, *Wendell Willkie: Fighter for Freedom* (Northern Michigan University Press, 1966), 180; Herbert Parmet and Marie P. Hecht, *Never Again: A President Runs for a Third Term* (New York, 1968), 47.

2. Barnard, *Willkie*, 187.
3. "The Voice of the Convention," *Time*, XXXVI (July 29, 1940), 14; Warren Moscow, *Roosevelt and Willkie* (Englewood Cliffs, N.J., 1968), 118; Barnard, *Willkie*, 194.
4. Parmet and Hecht, *Never Again*, 190, 194; Moscow, *Roosevelt and Willkie*, 125–27.
5. Robert Sherwood, *Roosevelt and Hopkins: An Intimate History* (New York, 1948), 176; Barnard, *Willkie*, 210.
6. Moscow, *Roosevelt and Willkie*, 168; Barnard, *Willkie*, 229.
7. Barnard, *Willkie*, 231–33, 243, 250–51.
8. Sherwood, *Roosevelt and Hopkins*, 187–88.
9. Barnard, *Willkie*, 256.
10. Sherwood, *Roosevelt and Hopkins*, 190–91, 201.
11. "Can Willkie Happen Again?" *Newsweek*, LXXII (July 22, 1968), 18; Moscow, *Roosevelt and Willkie*, 70; Parmet and Hecht, *Never Again*, 108–9.
12. Frances Perkins, *The Roosevelt I Knew* (Viking Penguin, Inc., New York, 1946), 119. Copyright 1946 by Frances Perkins. Copyright renewed 1974 by Susanna W. Coggeshall. Reprinted by permission of Viking Penguin, Inc.
13. Herbert Eaton, *Presidential Timber: A History of Nominating Conventions* (New York, 1964), 392; Moscow, *Roosevelt and Willkie*, 122–23.
14. Irving Stone, *They Also Ran* (New York, 1945), 355; Jules Abels, *The Degeneration of Our Presidential Election* (New York, 1968), 128.
15. Henry O. Evjen, "The Willkie Campaign; An Unfortunate Chapter in Republican Leadership," *Journal of Politics*, XIV (May 1952), 248, 251; Barnard, *Willkie*, 198, 231; Moscow, *Roosevelt and Willkie*, 143, 148; Perkins, *Roosevelt*, 116–17. Reprinted by permission of Viking Penguin.
16. Perkins, *Roosevelt*, 115–16. Reprinted by permission of Viking Penguin.
17. Henry O. Evjen, "An Analysis of Some of the Propaganda Features of the Campaign of 1940," *Southwestern Social Science Quarterly*, XXVII (December 1946), 258.
18. Hugh A. Bone, *"Smear" Politics: An Analysis of 1940 Campaign Literature* (Washington, 1941), 35; Evjen, "Analysis of Propaganda," 258; Parmet and Hecht, *Never Again*, 240–42.
19. Sherwood, *Roosevelt and Hopkins*, 189–90; Barnard, *Willkie*, 256–57; Parmet and Hecht, *Never Again*, 260; Moscow, *Roosevelt and Willkie*, 156.

CHAPTER FORTY

1944—Roosevelt's Wartime Mandate

1. James McGregor Burns, *Roosevelt: The Soldier of Freedom* (New York, 1970), 497.
2. "Dewey Snaps GOP from Coma," *Newsweek*, XXIV (July 10, 1944), 36.
3. Barry K. Beyer, *Thomas E. Dewey, 1937–1947: A Study in Political Leadership* (New York, 1979), 230–31; "The Man They Loved," *Time*, XLIV (July 10, 1944), 18; "In the Wind," *Nation*, CLIX (July 29, 1944), 127; "The Pot Boils," *Time*, XLIV (October 2, 1944), 24; Stefan Lorant, *The Glorious Burden: The American Presidency* (New York, 1968), 655–56.
4. Lorant, *Glorious Burden*, 659.
5. Grace Tully, *F.D.R., My Boss* (New York, 1949), 275–76; Jim Bishop, *FDR's Last Year* (New York, 1974), 99–100, 107; Leon Friedman, "Election of 1944,"

Arthur M. Schlesinger, Jr., ed., *A History of American Presidential Elections*, 4 vols. (New York, 1971), IV:3015–17.

6. Jules Abels, *The Degeneration of Our Presidential Election* (New York, 1968), 212; "Clear Everything with Sidney," *Time*, XLIV (September 24, 1944), 14; Herbert Eaton, *Presidential Timber: A History of Nominating Conventions* (New York, 1964), 406–7; William D. Hassett, *Off the Record with F.D.R., 1942–1945* (New Brunswick, N.J., 1958), 288; Richard Norton Smith, *Thomas E. Dewey and His Times* (Simon & Schuster, Inc., New York, 1982), 409–10.

7. Friedman, "Election of 1944," 3028.

8. Bishop, *FDR's Last Year*, 10, 137, 157–58, 187, 189; Smith, *Dewey*, 432–33; Robert Sherwood, *Roosevelt and Hopkins: An Intimate History* (New York, 1948), 829.

8. Sherwood, *Roosevelt and Hopkins*, 820.

9. *The Public Papers and Addresses of Franklin D. Roosevelt*, 13 vols. (New York, 1938–50), XIII:284.

10. Ibid., 290; "The Old Magic," *Time*, XLIV (October 2, 1944), 21.

12. Smith, *Dewey*, 425.

13. "What Happened," *Time*, XLIV (November 13, 1944), 19.

14. Thomas A. Bailey, *The American Pageant: A History of the Republic*, 2 vols. (Lexington, Mass., 1975), II:935.

15. *New York Times*, November 8, 1944, p. 16.

16. "Pregnant Poem," *Time*, XLIV (September 25, 1944), 11–12.

17. Smith, *Dewey*, 437.

18. "For the Fourth Time," *Time*, XLIV (July 31, 1944), 9–10.

19. "Half a Horse," *Newsweek*, XXIV (August 14, 1944), 43.

20. Michael F. Reilly, *Reilly of the White House* (Simon & Schuster, Inc., New York, 1947), 196–7.

21. Smith, *Dewey*, 426–30; Sherwood, *Roosevelt and Hopkins*, 827; Jules Abels, *Out of the Jaws of Victory* (New York, 1959), 240.

22. James Roosevelt, *My Parents* (Playboy Press, New York, 1976), 277–84; Bishop, *FDR's Last Year*, 111.

23. Hassett, *Off the Record*, 291.

24. Smith, *Dewey*, 436; Bishop, *FDR's Last Year*, 195–96; Hassett, *Off the Record*, 294; "The Winner"; "The Loser," *Time*, XLIV (November 13, 1944), 20.

CHAPTER FORTY-ONE
1948—The Great Truman Surprise

1. Cabell Phillips, *The Truman Presidency: The History of a Triumphant Succession* (New York, 1966), 242, 245; Alfred Steinberg, *The Man from Missouri: The Life and Times of Harry S. Truman* (New York, 1962), 330; Stefan Lorant, *The Glorious Burden: The American Presidency* (New York, 1968), 726.

2. Jules Abels, *Out of the Jaws of Victory* (New York, 1959), 19; Steinberg, *Truman*, 314.

3. Abels, *Jaws*, 27.

4. Harold F. Gosnell, *Truman's Crises: A Political Biography of Harry S. Truman* (Westport, Conn., 1980), 386.

5. *National Party Platforms*, 2 vols. (compiled by Donald Bruce Johnson, Urbana, Ill., 1978), I:453.

6. Abels, *Jaws*, 41–45; Steinberg, *Truman*, 311–12.
7. Steinberg, *Truman*, 314.
8. Lawrence Lader, ". . . To Serve the World—Not to Dominate It," *American Heritage*, XXVII (December 1976), 48.
9. Steinberg, *Truman*, 317–18; Josephus Daniels, *The Man of Independence* (Philadelphia, 1950), 355–56; Gosnell, *Truman's Crises*, 380–81; Phillips, *Truman Presidency*, 222; Alonzo L. Hamby, *Beyond the New Deal: Harry Truman and American Liberalism* (New York, 1973), 244.
10. Lorant, *Glorious Burden*, 709.
11. Steinberg, *Truman*, 329, 323–24; Phillips, *Truman Presidency*, 236; Gosnell, *Truman's Crises*, 398–99.
12. "His Woman Have 'It'," *Newsweek*, XXXII (October 4, 1948), 22; Steinberg, *Truman*, 324–25; Gosnell, *Truman's Crises*, 396–97.
13. Abels, *Jaws*, 71; "Crucial Week," *Time*, XLIV (October 2, 1944), 24; Robert Shogan, "1948 Election," *American Heritage*, XIX (June 1968), 27; Lader, "To Serve the World," 47; David M. Kennedy, "The Model of Mugwumpery," *New Republic*, CLXXXIX (January 31, 1983), 35.
14. Robert A. Divine, "The Cold War and the Election of 1948," *Journal of American History*, LIX (June 1972), 91.
15. "Independence Day," *Time*, LII (November 8, 1948), 21; Lorant, *Glorious Presidency*, 726.
16. Harry Truman, *Memoirs: Years of Trial and Hope*, 2 vols. (Garden City, N.Y., 1956), II:222; Steinberg, *Truman*, 332; Abels, *Jaws*, 271–72; Shogan, "1948 Election," 111.
17. Irwin Ross, *The Loneliest Campaign: The Truman Victory of 1948* (New York, 1968), 246.
18. Lorant, *Glorious Burden*, 731–32.
19. Abel, *Jaws*, 290.
20. Ibid., 294.
21. Gosnell, *Truman's Crises*, 412.
22. Steinberg, *Truman*, 312–13; Shogan, "1948 Election," 30; Abels, *Jaws*, 46; "Whistle Slip," *Newsweek*, XXXI (June 28, 1948), 18; Jack Redding, *Inside the Democratic Party*, 178–80.
23. Steinberg, *Truman*, 314–17; Daniels, *Man of Independence*, 352–53; Abels, *Jaws*, 90–91; Margaret Truman, *Harry Truman* (New York, 1973), 13.
24. Richard Norton Smith, *Thomas E. Dewey and His Times* (New York, 1982), 532; "Confidence on Wheels," *Newsweek*, XXXII (October 25, 1948), 28; Steinberg, *Truman*, 327–28.
25. Jules Abels, *The Degeneration of Our Presidential Election* (New York, 1968), 289.
26. Smith, *Dewey*, 531; Abels, *Jaws*, 244.
27. Smith, *Dewey*, 509–10; Redding, *Inside Democratic Party*, 284–85.
28. Margaret Truman, *Truman*, 27; Steinberg, *Truman*, 325; Redding, *Inside Democratic Party*, 271.
29. Gosnell, *Truman's Crises*, 404–5; Margaret Truman, *Truman*, 28.
30. Phillips, *Truman Presidency*, 232–33; Redding, *Inside Democratic Party*, 279; Steinberg, *Truman*, 326.
31. Shogan, "1948 Election," 107; "Can Hubert Give 'Em Harry's Hell," *Newsweek*, LXXII (October 7, 1968), 29.

32. Morris L. Ernst and David Loth, *The People Know Best; The Ballots vs. the Polls* (Washington, 1949), 52, 54, 56, 57, 58, 60, 62, 65, 73, 76, 84, 85, 87.
33. Abel, *Jaws*, 270.
34. Smith, *Dewey*, 543.
35. Ibid., 545 (Simon and Schuster, Inc.).

CHAPTER FORTY-TWO
1952—The Eisenhower Landslide

1. *Major Campaign Speeches of Adlai E. Stevenson, 1952* (New York, 1953), 62, 103–5.
2. *National Party Platforms,* 2 vols. (compiled by Donald Bruce Johnson, Urbana, Ill., 1978), I:497, 505.
3. Ibid., I:499.
4. Stefan Lorant, *The Glorious Burden: The American Presidency* (New York, 1968), 748.
5. Sidney Warren, *The Battle for the Presidency* (Philadelphia, 1968), 272.
6. Herbert Eaton, *Presidential Timber: A History of Nominating Conventions* (New York, 1964), 469.
7. Warren, *Battle for Presidency,* 274.
8. Ibid., 275–76.
9. Sherman Adams, *Firsthand Report: The Story of the Eisenhower Administration* (Harper & Row Publishers, Inc., New York, 1961), 20.
10. Peter Lyons, *Eisenhower: Portrait of the Hero* (Boston, 1974), 463; Jules Abels, *The Degeneration of Our Presidential Election* (New York, 1968), 57–58.
11. John Bartlow Martin, *Adlai Stevenson of Illinois: The Life of Adlai Stevenson* (Garden City, N.Y., 1976), 675–77; *Campaign Speeches of Stevenson,* 126.
12. Barton J. Bernstein, "Election of 1952," Arthur M. Schlesinger, Jr., ed., *The Coming to Power: Critical Presidential Elections in American History* (New York, 1981), 415.
13. Adams, *Firsthand Report,* 30–33; Lyon, *Eisenhower,* 448–49, 451; Emmet John Hughes, *The Ordeal of Power: A Political Memoir of the Eisenhower Years* (New York, 1963), 41–43; Herbert S. Parmet, *Eisenhower and the American Crusade* (Macmillan Publishing Co., Inc., New York, 1972), 127–32, "The Campaign in Retrospect," *Newsweek,* XL (November 10, 1952), 24.
14. Martin, *Stevenson,* 713.
15. "The Trial," *Time,* LX (October 6, 1952), 19–22; Lyon, *Eisenhower,* 453–57; Parmet, *Eisenhower,* 134–41; Martin, *Stevenson,* 685–92.
16. Warren, *Battle for Presidency,* 280–81.
17. Martin, *Stevenson,* 641–42, 668, 673–74; "The Rapier Thrust," *Newsweek,* XL (September 8, 1952), 23; "The Crowds Appear," *Newsweek,* XL (October 20, 1952), 28; "Which One Is He?" *Time,* LX (October 6, 1952), 23.
18. *Campaign Speeches of Stevenson,* 225–26.
19. "I Shall Go to Korea," *Newsweek,* XL (November 3, 1952), 26.
20. Hughes, *Ordeal of Power,* 34–35; Lorant, *Glorious Burden,* 765; Adams, *Firsthand Report,* 44; Parmet, *Eisenhower,* 143.
21. Lorant, *Glorious Burden,* 773.
22. "A Good Loser," *Time,* LX (November 10, 1952), 25.

23. Parmet, *Eisenhower,* 57 (Macmillan Publishing Co., Inc.).
24. Lloyd Robinson, *The Hopefuls: Ten Presidential Campaigns* (Garden City, N.Y., 1966), 127.
25. Martin, *Stevenson,* 661–62.
26. De Los W. Lovelace, *"Ike" Eisenhower: Statesman and Soldier of Peace* (New York, 1961), 243.
27. Warren, *Battle for Presidency,* 411; Robert Bendiner, *White House Fever* (New York, 1960), 133.
28. "Eggheads," *Newsweek,* XLVIII (October 8, 1956), 53; Martin, *Stevenson,* 640, 647.
29. Richard M. Nixon, *Six Crises* (New York, 1962), 89, 93, 100, 109–23; Dwight D. Eisenhower, *Mandate for Change, 1953–1956* (New York, 1963), 67, 68; Lyon, *Eisenhower,* 457–62; Parmet, *Eisenhower,* 138–41; Garry Wills, *Nixon Agonistes: The Crisis of the Self-Made Man* (Boston, 1970), 91–114.
30. Bendiner, *White House Fever,* 147n.
31. Lorant, *Glorious Burden,* 772.
32. Adams, *Firsthand Report,* 44 (Harper & Row Publishers, Inc.).
33. *Campaign Speeches of Stevenson,* xii–xiii.

CHAPTER FORTY-THREE
1956—Another Eisenhower Landslide

1. Stefan Lorant, *The Glorious Burden: The American Presidency* (New York, 1968), 787.
2. Ibid., 788.
3. Adlai E. Stevenson, *The New America* (New York, 1957), xiii.
4. Ibid. 3–14.
5. Lorant, *Glorious Burden,* 793.
6. Ibid.
7. Stevenson, *New America,* 44–49, 64–66.
8. John Bartlow Martin, *Adlai Stevenson and the World* (New York, 1977), 385.
9. Ibid., 385–86.
10. Ibid., 393.
11. Lorant, *Glorious Burden,* 809.
12. Peter Lyon, *Eisenhower: Portrait of the Hero* (Boston, 1974), 671.
13. Martin, *Stevenson and the World,* 327.
14. Ibid., 322.
15. Theodore White, *America in Search of Itself: The Making of the President, 1956–1980* (New York, 1982), 81.
16. "Sunburned 'Preacher,' " *Newsweek,* XLVIII (October 8, 1956), 23; F. Hodge and Annie Laurie O'Neal, *Humor: The Politician's Tool* (New York, 1964), 153.
17. Arthur Larson, *Eisenhower: The President Nobody Knew* (New York, 1968), 21.
18. Richard Rovere, "Letter from Washington," *New Yorker,* XXXII (September 29, 1956), 140.
19. Martin, *Stevenson and the World,* 345.
20. Ibid., 392.

CHAPTER FORTY-FOUR
1960—Kennedy and the New Frontier

1. Kenneth P. O'Donnell and David F. Powers, *"Johnny, We Hardly Knew Ye"* (Little, Brown and Company, Publishers, Boston, 1970), 182; Theodore White, *The Making of the President 1960* (Atheneum Publishers, New York, 1961), 298–99n.
2. Arthur M. Schlesinger, Jr., *A Thousand Days: John F. Kennedy in the White House* (Boston, 1965), 57.
3. *New York Times,* July 16, 1960, p. 7.
4. Richard M. Nixon, *Six Crises* (New York, 1962), 319.
5. Ibid., 339; Henry D. Spalding, *The Nixon Nobody Knows* (Middle Village, N.Y., 1972), 408.
6. Stefan Lorant, *The Glorious Burden: The American Presidency* (New York, 1968), 830, 837.
7. Schlesinger, *Thousand Days,* 75–76.
8. Theodore C. Sorensen, *Kennedy* (Harper & Row Publishers, Inc., New York, 1965), 193.
9. Ibid., 195–206; Nixon, *Six Crises,* 336–55; Earl Mazo and Stephen Hess, *President Nixon: A Political Portrait* (London, 1968), 234–37; Lorant, *Glorious Burden,* 839; *New York Times,* September 28, 1960, p. 38; ibid., October 22, 1960, p. 8.
10. Spalding, *Nixon Nobody Knows,* 413–15; Schlesinger, *Thousand Days,* 73–74.
11. Sorensen, *Kennedy,* 193; Fawn Brodie, *Richard Nixon: The Shaping of His Character* (New York, 1981), 422–23.
12. Lorant, *Glorious Burden,* 840.
13. Mazo and Hess, *President Nixon,* 249.
14. Bill Adler, ed., *The Washington Wits* (New York, 1967), 109.
15. Sorensen, *Kennedy,* 119, 174.
16. O'Donnell and Powers, *"Johnny",* 177–78 (Little, Brown & Co.).
17. Sorensen, *Kennedy,* 197 (Harper & Row Publishers, Inc.).
18. Ibid., 151.
19. Schlesinger, *Thousand Days,* 38.
20. Sorensen, *Kennedy,* 167 (Harper & Row Publishers, Inc.).
21. F. Hodge and Annie Laurie O'Neal, *Humor: The Politician's Tool* (Vantage Press, Inc., New York, 1964), 181.
22. O'Donnell and Powers, *"Johnny,"* 235–36 (Little, Brown & Co.).
23. James D. Barber, *The Pulse of Politics* (New York, 1981), 75.
24. Sorensen, *Kennedy,* 177.
25. Brodie, *Nixon,* 422; Barber, *Pulse of Politics,* 76.
26. Sorensen, *Kennedy,* 179.
27. Ibid., 180.
28. Ibid., 208; Brodie, *Nixon,* 416; Barber, *Pulse of Politics,* 77.
29. Sorensen, *Kennedy,* 112–13 (Harper & Row Publishers, Inc.).
30. Ibid., 174 (Harper & Row Publishers, Inc.).
31. Alfred Steinberg, *The Man from Missouri* (New York, 1962), 428–29; Lorant, *Glorious Burden,* 31; "Morton Demands Kennedy Apologize for a Truman," *New York Times,* October 12, 1960, p. 1.
32. Sorensen, *Kennedy,* 183 (Harper & Row Publishers, Inc.).
33. Ibid., 188 (Harper & Row Publishers, Inc.).

34. Schlesinger, *Thousand Days*, 73.
35. Ibid., 71; Sorensen, *Kennedy*, 206.
36. White, *Making of President*, 220n.
37. Ibid., 266n. (Atheneum Publishers).
38. Ibid., 256.
39. Herbert M. Baus and William B. Ross, *Politics Battle Plan* (New York, 1968), 14.
40. Sorensen, *Kennedy*, 211; O'Donnell, *"Johnny"*, 257.

CHAPTER FORTY-FIVE

1964—Lyndon Johnson and the Great Society

1. James D. Barber, *The Pulse of Politics: Electing Presidents in the Media Age* (New York, 1980), 168.
2. Stefan Lorant, *The Glorious Burden: The American Presidency* (New York, 1968), 877.
3. John Bartlow Martin, "Election of 1954," Arthur M. Schlesinger, Jr., ed., *The Coming to Power: Critical Elections in American History* (New York, 1981), 462.
4. "The Late Late Show," *Time*, LXXXIV (July 24, 1964), 22; "Cow Palace Climacteric," *Newsweek*, LXIV (July 27, 1964), 21; Lorant, *Glorious Burden*, 888.
5. Sidney Warren, *The Battle for the Presidency* (New York, 1968), 356.
6. Lorant, *Glorious Burden*, 888.
7. Eric Goldman, *The Tragedy of Lyndon Johnson* (New York, 1969), 218.
8. Ibid., 231–32; Theodore H. White, *The Making of the President 1964* (New York, 1965), 335; Lyndon B. Johnson, *The Vantage Point: Perspectives of the Presidency* (New York, 1971), 102.
9. "The Fear & the Facts," *Time*, LXXXIV (September 25, 1964), 16; Johnson, *Vantage Point*, 102; Harold Faber, ed., *The Road to the White House* (New York Times Books, New York, 1965), 57; Barber, *Pulse of Politics*, 181.
10. Alfred Steinberg, *Sam Johnson's Boy* (New York, 1968), 676.
11. Barry M. Goldwater, *With No Apologies* (William Morrow & Company, Inc., Publishers, New York, 1980), 201–202; Milton C. Cummings, Jr., ed., *The National Election of 1964* (Washington, 1966), 61; "The Fear & the Facts," *Time*, LXXXIV (September 25, 1964), 15–16.
12. Cummings, *Election of 1964*, 48; "Marching through Dixie," *Time*, LXXXIV (September 25, 1964), 20.
13. "Promises & Punches," *Time*, LXXXIV (October 2, 1964), 41–42; Goldman, *Tragedy of Johnson*, 229; Faber, *Road to the White House*, 132.
14. Goldman, *Tragedy of Johnson*, 323–33; Steinberg, *Sam Johnson's Boy*, 686.
15. Goldman, *Tragedy of Johnson*, 229.
16. Steinberg, *Sam Johnson's Boy*, 686.
17. Ibid., 690; Goldman, *Tragedy of Johnson*, 235–37; Paul F. Boller, Jr., *Quotemanship: The Use and Abuse of Quotations for Polemical and Other Purposes* (Dallas, Texas, 1967), 422–23.
18. "From the Pulpit," *Newsweek*, LXIV (September 28, 1964), 27.
19. "The Itchy-Finger Image," *Time*, LXXXIV (September 25, 1964), 15.
20. Goldman, *Tragedy of Johnson*, 256.

21. Steinberg, *Sam Johnson's Boy*, 676; Faber, *Road to White House*, 47.
22. Faber, *Road to White House*, 45–46.
23. Goldwater, *No Apologies*, 194. (William Morrow & Co., Inc.).
24. "The Periscope," *Newsweek*, LXIV (October 5, 1964), 27.
25. Faber, *Road to White House*, 131–2; Steinberg, *Sam Johnson's Boy*, 690–91.
26. Goldwater, *No Apologies*, 168; Boller, *Quotemanship*, 374; Sidney Warren, *The Battle for the Presidency* (New York, 1968), 376.
27. Johnson, *Vantage Point*, 106.
28. Steinberg, *Sam Johnson's Boy*, 675.
29. Goldman, *Tragedy of Johnson*, 226.
30. Ibid., 231; Samuel Houston Johnson, *My Brother Lyndon* (New York, 1970), 172; Faber, *Road to White House*, 191.
31. Goldman, *Tragedy of Johnson*, 233.
32. Faber, *Road to White House*, 205; Theodore H. White, *The Making of the President 1964* (New York, 1965), 326.
33. Faber, *Road to White House*, 240; White, *Making of President*, 336.
34. Goldman, *Tragedy of Johnson*, 247–48; Johnson, *Vantage Point*, 110; Faber, *Road to White House*, 243.
35. "Tuck and Nip," *Newsweek*, LXIV (October 12, 1964), 34; Faber, *Road to White House*, 200–201.
36. Faber, *Road to White House*, 206.
37. "Morality Issue," *Newsweek*, LXIV (November 2, 1964), 25; Faber, *Road to White House*, 238–39.
38. Ibid., 240–41 (New York Times Books).
39. White, *Making of President*, 215n.

CHAPTER FORTY-SIX

1968—Nixon, Humphrey, and the Vietnam War

1. "The Once & Future Humphrey," *Time*, XCI (May 3, 1968), 19.
2. *National Party Platforms*, 2 vols. (compiled by Donald Bruce Johnson, Urbana, Ill., 1978), II:762.
3. "A Chance to Lead," *Time*, XCII (August 16, 1968), 10; Jules Witcover, *The Resurrection of Richard Nixon* (New York, 1970), 358.
4. "The Man Who Would Recapture Youth," *Time*, XCII (September 6, 1968), 19; Dan Cohen, *Undefeated: The Life of Hubert H. Humphrey* (Minneapolis, 1968), 328; David S. Broder, "Election of 1968," Arthur M. Schlesinger, Jr., ed., *A History of American Presidential Elections*, 4 vols. (New York, 1971), IV:3737.
5. Cohen, *Undefeated*, 319–20; "Daley City Under Siege," *Time*, XCII (August 30, 1968), 18.
6. "The Battle of Chicago," *Newsweek*, LXXII (September 9, 1968), "The Winner: How—and What—He Won," ibid., 30, 38–41; "Lots of Law, Little Order," *Time*, XCII (September 6, 1968), 20; Cohen, *Undefeated*, 329–32, 341; Eugene J. McCarthy, *The Year of the People* (New York, 1971), 218–22.
7. Cohen, *Undefeated*, 349; Theodore H. White, *The Making of the President 1968* (Atheneum Publishers, New York, 1969), 303.
8. "A Sense of Foreboding as Delegates Assemble," *New York Times*, August 26, 1968, 19.

9. Jules Witcover, *The Resurrection of Richard Nixon* (G. P. Putnam's Sons, New York, 1970), 359.

10. "The Sleeper and the Stumbler," *Time*, XCII (October 4, 1968), 19; Witcover, *Resurrection*, 386–91; *The Memoirs of Richard Nixon* (New York, 1978), 320–21.

11. "Neither Tweedledum nor Tweedledee," *Time*, XCII (September 20, 1968), 25.

12. Broder, "Election of 1968," 3716, 3743.

13. "Bomber on the Stump," *Time*, XCII (October 4, 1968), 21; "George's General," ibid. (October 18, 1968), 21; Lewis Chester et al., *An American Melodrama: The Presidential Campaign of 1968* (New York, 1969), 700; Witcover, *Resurrection*, 412–14.

14. Cohen, *Undefeated*, 368–71; White, *Making of President*, 336.

15. Witcover, *Resurrection*, 38.

16. Cohen, *Undefeated*, 314, 372–73; Albert Eisele, *Almost to the Presidency: A Biography of Two American Politicians* (Blue Earth, Minn., 1972), 378; "Some Forward Motion for H.H.H.," *Time*, XCII (October 11, 1968), 19.

17. Cohen, *Undefeated*, 373.

18. Ibid., 374; White, *Making of President*, 356; Eisele, *Almost to Presidency*, 379.

19. "Faint Echoes of '48," *Time*, XCII (October 4, 1968), 17.

20. "Fouls in the Final Rounds," *Time*, XCII (November 1, 1968), 15.

21. Witcover, *Resurrection*, 428–31, 435–36; *Memoirs of Nixon*, 327; "Auguries of a Breakthrough," *Time*, XCII (November 1, 1968), 14.

22. "Auguries of a Breakthrough," *Time*, XCII (November 1, 1968), 13–14.

23. Witcover, *Resurrection*, 455.

24. White, *Making of President*, 89.

25. Ibid., 125 (Atheneum Publishers).

26. Lewis Chester et al., *An American Melodrama: The Presidential Campaign of 1968* (Viking Press, Inc., New York, 1969), 146.

27. Theodore H. White, *America in Search of Itself: The Making of the President, 1956–1980* (Atheneum Publishers, New York, 1982), 185.

28. "Unlikely No. 2," *Time*, XCII (August 16, 1968), 19; "The Name Is Agnew," *Newsweek*, LXXII (August 19, 1968), 32; Stephen Shadegg, *Winning's a Lot More Fun* (New York, 1969), 212.

29. "The Compleat Delegate," *Time*, XCII (August 30, 1968), 19.

30. "Rising Voice of the Right," *Time*, XCII (September 13, 1968), 16.

31. *Memoirs of Nixon*, 328.

32. "Lurching off to a Shaky Start," *Time*, XCII (September 20, 1968), 18; "How to Handle the Hecklers," *Newsweek*, LXXII (October 7, 1968), 41; "The Sleeper vs. the Stumbler," *Time*, XCII (October 4, 1968), 19; "Avoiding the Dewey Syndrome," *Time*, XCII (October 25, 1968), 26; "The Jeering Section," *Time*, XCII (November 8, 1968), 31–32; "Problems of Dollars and Days," *Time*, XCII October 25, 1968), 28.

33. Witcover, *Resurrection*, 388–89.

34. Ibid., 440–42; Broder, "Election of 1968," 3752; *Memoirs of Nixon*, 328–29; Chester, *American Melodrama*, 734; White, *Making of President*, 380–83.

35. *Memoirs of Nixon*, 335.

36. Witcover, *Resurrection*, 456n. (G. P. Putnam's Sons).

CHAPTER FORTY-SEVEN
1972—Another Nixon Triumph

1. *The Memoirs of Richard Nixon* (New York, 1978), 77.
2. Eugene Roseboom and Alfred E. Eckes, Jr., *A History of Presidential Elections* (New York, 1979), 297.
3. Ibid., 305; Theodore H. White, *The Making of the President 1972* (New York, 1973), 188.
4. Roseboom and Eckes, *Presidential Elections,* 307; "The Battle for the Democratic Party," *Time,* C (July 17, 1972), 10–16.
5. *National Party Platforms,* 2 vols. (compiled by Donald Bruce Johnson, Urbana, Ill., 1978), II:791.
6. "McGovern's First Crisis: The Eagleton Affair," *Time,* C (August 7, 1972), 11–16; Gary W. Hart, *Right from the Start: A Chronicle of the McGovern Campaign* (New York, 1973), 250–56; Roseboom and Eckes, *Presidential Elections,* 308.
7. *New York Times,* July 14, 1972, p. 14.
8. Ibid., August 24, 1972, p. 47.
9. *Memoirs of Nixon,* 683.
10. Roseboom and Eckes, *Presidential Elections,* 307.
11. "The Coronation of King Richard," *Time,* C (August 21, 1972), 11.
12. Ibid.
13. "The Democrats Try to Get Organized," *Time,* C (September 11, 1972), 13.
14. Roseboom and Eckes, *Presidential Elections,* 312.
15. *Grassroots: The Autobiography of George McGovern* (Random House, Inc., New York, 1977), 162.
16. "Eve's Operatives," *Time,* C (July 24, 1972), 26.
17. "McGovern's First Crisis: The Eagleton Affair," *Time,* C (August 7, 1972), 12.
18. "George McGovern Finally Finds a Veep," *Time,* C (August 14, 1972), 15, 17, 18; "The Democrats Begin Again, *Time,* C (August 21, 1972), 1; "The New Nominee: No Longer 'Half a Kennedy'," *Time,* C (August 17, 1972), 17, 18.
19. McGovern, *Grassroots,* 246; White, *Making of President,* 339.
20. White, *Making of President,* 9.
21. McGovern, *Grassroots,* 256.

CHAPTER FORTY-EIGHT
1976—The Triumph of an Outsider: Jimmy Carter

1. Ruth C. Stapleton, *Brother Billy* (New York, 1978), 103.
2. Bill Adler, ed., *The Wit and Wisdom of Jimmy Carter* (Secaucus, N.J., 1977), 96.
3. "The Pardon That Brought No Peace," *Time,* CIV (September 16, 1974), 10.
4. "Counting Souls," *Time,* CVIII (October 4, 1976), 75.
5. Peter Goldman, "Sizing Up Carter," *Newsweek,* LXXXVIII (September 13, 1976), 23, 34, 36.

6. Theodore White, *America in Search of Itself: The Making of the President, 1956–1980* (New York, 1982), 189.

7. Eugene Roseboom and Alfred E. Eckes, Jr., *A History of Presidential Elections* (New York, 1979), 324; Kandy Stroud, *How Jimmy Won* (William Morrow & Co., Inc., New York, 1977), 170–76.

8. "The Jimmycrats," *Newsweek*, LXXXVIII (July 26, 1976), 23; *Jimmy Carter, A Government as Good as Its People* (New York, 1977), 125–34.

9. "Reagan: 'I Don't Want Another 1964,' " *Time*, CVIII (August 2, 1976), 10–11; Roseboom and Eckes, *Presidential Elections*, 327.

10. *A Time to Heal: The Autobiography of Gerald R. Ford* (New York, 1979), 367.

11. "Coming Out Swinging," *Time*, CVIII (August 30, 1976), 6.

12. Betty Glad, *Jimmy Carter: In Search of the Great White House* (New York, 1980), 390–91; Gerald R. Ford, *A Time to Heal* (New York, 1979), 422–25.

13. Ron Nessen, *It Sure Looks Different from the Inside* (New York, 1978), 269–7.

14. Nessen, *Sure Looks Different*, 300–302; Glad, *Carter*, 394; Adler, *Wit and Wisdom of Carter*, 59.

15. Glad, *Carter*, 383.

16. Ibid., 384.

17. Ibid., 386; Nessen, *Sure Looks Different*, 300–301; Stroud, *How Jimmy Won*, 397–98.

18. Jimmy Carter, *The Presidential Campaign, 1976*, 2 vols. (Washington, D.C., 1978), II:1107.

19. Stroud, *How Jimmy Won*, 394.

20. Glad, *Carter*, 398.

21. Ibid.

22. Ibid., 402; Glad, *Carter*, 396–98.

23. "Sputtering Down the Stretch," *Newsweek*, LXXXVIII (October 25, 1976), 26.

24. "The New Look," *Newsweek*, LXXXVIII (November 15, 1976), 26.

25. Stapleton, *Brother Billy*, 103.

26. Lou Cannon, *Reagan* (New York, 1982), 222n.

27. Martin Schramm, *Running for President: A Journal of the Carter Campaign* (New York, 1977), 31, 49; White, *America in Search of Itself*, 189.

28. William Safire, *Safire's Washington* (New York, 1980), 244; *Major Campaign Speeches of Adlai E. Stevenson, 1952* (New York, 1953), 311; "See?", *Newsweek*, LXXXVIII (June 14, 1976), 8.

29. Schramm, *Running for President*, 166.

30. Ford, *Time to Heal*, 377.

31. "Ol' Second-Place Mo," *Newsweek*, LXXXVII (June 7, 1976), 21; Richard Reeves, *Convention* (New York, 1977), 8–9.

32. Glad, *Carter*, 320.

33. Schramm, *Running for President*, 345–46; Stroud, *How Jimmy Won*, 381.

34. Stroud, *How Jimmy Won*, 339.

35. Ibid., 420.

36. Victor Lasky, *Jimmy Carter: Man and Myth* (New York, 1979), 274.

37. Jimmy Carter, *Keeping Faith: Memoirs of a President* (New York, 1982), 545; Schramm, *Running for President*, 131.

38. Lasky, *Carter*, 285n.

39. Schramm, *Running for President*, 178–79.

40. Nessen, *Sure Looks Different*, 259; Ford, *Time to Heal*, 414; Lasky, *Carter*, 293.
41. "Sputtering Down the Stretch," *Newsweek*, LXXXVIII (October 25, 1976), 28.

CHAPTER FORTY-NINE
1980—The Reagan Victory

1. John F. Stacks, *Watershed: The Campaign for the Presidency, 1980* (New York, 1981), 217–18.
2. Ibid., 238–39.
3. "Carter at the Crossroads," *Time*, CXIV (July 23, 1979), 20–29.
4. Stacks, *Watershed*, 33; Jack W. Germond and Jules Witcover, *Blue Smoke and Mirrors: How Reagan Won and Why Jimmy Carter Lost the Election of 1980* (New York, 1981), 52. Copyright © 1981 by Jack W. Germond and Jules Witcover. Reprinted by permission of Viking Penguin, Inc.
5. Germond and Witcover, *Blue Smoke and Mirrors*, 56–57, 87–88; Stacks, *Watershed*, 81–84, 88; Jeff Greenfield, *The Real Campaign: How the Media Missed the Story of the 1980 Campaign* (New York, 1982), 54, 61–65, 68.
6. Stacks, *Watershed*, 108.
7. Germond and Witcover, *Blue Smoke and Mirrors*, 160–61; Theodore White, *America in Search of Itself: The Making of the President, 1956–1980* (Harper & Row Publishers, Inc., New York, 1982), 21.
8. "Drawing the Battle Lines," *Time*, CXVI (August 25, 1980), 21; Stacks, *Watershed*, 208; Greenfield, *Real Campaign*, 190.
9. Germond and Witcover, *Blue Smoke and Mirrors*, 207.
10. "The G.O.P. Gets Its Act Together," *Time*, CXVI (July 28, 1980), 10–15; Greenfield, *Real Campaign*, 173–74; Peter Hannaford, *The Reagans: A Political Portrait* (New York, 1983), 281–82.
11. Stacks, *Watershed*, 48.
12. David Chagall, *The New Kingmakers* (New York, 1981), 293; Lou Cannon, *Reagan* (New York, 1982), 282.
13. Stacks, *Watershed*, 232, 234–45; Cannon, *Reagan*, 272–90; Greenfield, *Real Campaign*, 276–80, 290; Elizabeth Drew, *Portrait of an Election: The 1980 Presidential Campaign* (New York, 1981), 262, 268.
14. Drew, *Portrait of Election*, 307.
15. Stacks, *Watershed*, 228; Germond and Witcover, *Blue Smoke and Mirrors*, 256–57; Cannon, *Reagan*, 280–84.
16. Stacks, *Watershed*, 229; Hamilton Jordan, *Crisis: The Last Year of the Carter Presidency* (G. P. Putnam's Sons, New York, 1982), 350; Germond and Witcover, *Blue Smoke and Mirrors*, 262–63.
17. Germond and Witcover, *Blue Smoke and Mirrors*, 263.
18. Greenfield, *Real Campaign*, 100; Drew, *Portrait of Election*, 277, 278; Chagall, *New Kingmakers*, 178; Stacks, *Watershed*, 162.
19. Drew, *Portrait of Election*, 284.
20. Ibid., 324–25.
21. Greenfield, *Real Campaign*, 240; Jordan, *Crisis*, 356; Germond and Witcover, *Blue Smoke and Mirrors*, 280.
22. Germond and Witcover, *Blue Smoke and Mirrors*, 281.
23. Stacks, *Watershed*, 249.

24. Germond and Witcover, *Blue Smoke and Mirrors*, 49.

25. White, *America in Search*, 273. (Harper & Row Publishers, Inc.).

26. Cannon, *Reagan*, 244.

27. Ibid., 250–51; Germond and Witcover, *Blue Smoke and Mirrors*, 120.

28. Cannon, *Reagan*, 241–43 and note, 292n; Greenfield, *Real Campaign*, 85; Stacks, *Watershed*, 153.

29. Drew, *Portrait of Election*, 195.

30. Germond and Witcover, *Blue Smoke and Mirrors*, 184 and note (Viking Penguin, Inc.).

31. Drew, *Portrait of Election*, 217–18; Greenfield, *Real Campaign*, 172.

32. Greenfield, *Real Campaign*, 214–18, 225.

33. Germond and Witcover, *Blue Smoke and Mirrors*, 290.

34. Ibid., 17.

35. Jimmy Carter, *Keeping Faith: Memoirs of a President* (New York, 1982), 562.

36. Ibid., 563; Germond and Witcover, *Blue Smoke and Mirrors*, 290n.

37. Drew, *Portrait of an Election*, 264.

38. Ibid., 269.

39. Chagall, *New Kingmakers*, 253; Drew *Portrait of Election*, 269; Cannon, *Reagan*, 228; Greenfield, *Real Campaign*, 230.

40. Carter, *Keeping Faith*, 546–47; Chagall, *New Kingmakers*, 193–94; "Going after the Big Ones," *Time*, CXXI (March 28, 1983), 30; Cannon, *Reagan*, 269, 300.

41. Stacks, *Watershed*, 155; Cannon, *Reagan*, 260.

42. Germond and Witcover, *Blue Smoke and Mirrors*, 284–85; Cannon, *Reagan*, 295–96, 300; Hannaford, *The Reagans*, 297.

43. Jordan, *Crisis*, 373; Germond and Witcover, *Blue Smoke and Mirrors*, 314–15; Greenfield, *Real Campaign*, 299–300.

44. Jordan, *Crisis* (G. P. Putnam's Sons, New York, 1982), 399.

45. Howell Raines, " 'Pseudo-Gate or Not, Reagan Is in Trouble," *New York Times*, July 3, 1983, 2E; Ed Magnuson, "A Mole in the Garbage Can," *Time*, CXXII (July 18, 1983), 16; "I Never Knew There Was Such a Thing," *Time*, CXXII (July 11, 1983), 12.

46. Thomas Griffith, "The Danger of Hobknobbery Journalism," *Time*, CXXII (August 8, 1983), 57; "How Strait the Gate," *New Republic*, CLXXXIX (August 1, 1983), 8; "No Triumph of Will," *Nation*, CCXXXVII (July 23–30, 1983), 68.

CHAPTER FIFTY

1984—Another Reagan Sweep

1. *Newsweek Election Extra*, November/December 1984, 91.

2. Hugh Sidey, "A Conversation with Reagan," *Time*, CXXIV (September 3, 1984), 33.

3. "The Gipper Strikes Back," *Time*, CXXIV (August 16, 1984), 15; *New York Times*, March 28, 1984; November 12, 1984, 12.

4. *New York Post*, March 26, 1984, 33; *New York Times*, June 27, 1984, A23; September 14, 1984, 14.

5. *New York Times*, November 1, 1984, 22.

6. Ibid., August 15, 1984, A20; "Reagan and the Age Issue," *Newsweek,* CIV (October 22, 1984), 26; *New York Times,* October 14, 1984, E23; "Reagan Wins a Draw," *Newsweek,* CIV (October 29, 1984), 26.

7. *New York Times,* October 7, 1984, 12; Sidney Blumenthal, "The Righteous Empire," *The New Republic,* CXCI (October 22, 1984), 18–24; Elizabeth Drew, *Campaign Journal: The Political Events of 1983–1984* (New York, 1985), 607; "Politics and the Pulpit," *Newsweek,* CIV (September 17, 1984), 24, 26; *New York Times,* September 29, 1984, 9.

8. Drew, *Campaign Journal,* 701; "Reagan and the Age Issue," *Newsweek,* CIV (October 22, 1984), 28.

9. *New York Times,* September 27, 1984, 14; Drew, *Campaign Journal,* 755.

10. *Fort Worth Star-Telegram,* November 7, 1984, 2A.

11. *New York Times,* February 18, 1984, 9.

12. "Testing the Front-Runner Jinx," *Time,* CXXIII (April 2, 1984), 17.

13. *New York Times,* July 27, 1984, A12.

14. *Washington Post,* July 18, 1984, F3.

15. *New York Times,* July 20, 1984, A10.

16. *New York Times,* July 18, 1984, 1; July 21, 1984, 10; *New York Daily News,* August 2, 1984, 46.

17. *New York Post,* June 26, 1984, 29.

18. *New York Times,* August 13, 1984, A16; August 14, 1984, A22; August 21, 1984, A18.

19. "A View without Hills or Valleys," *Time,* CXXIII (February 6, 1984), 23; *New York Times,* September 19, 1984, 14; *Washington Post National Weekly Edition,* October 8, 1984, 26.

20. "God and the Ballot Box," *Time,* CXXIV (September 17, 1984), 26.

21. *New York Times,* September 13, 1984, 16.

CHAPTER FIFTY-ONE
1988—Trivial Pursuit: Bush vs. Dukakis

1. Jack W. Germond and Jules Witcover, *Whose Broad Stripes and Bright Stars? The Trivial Pursuit of the Presidency 1988* (New York, 1989), 354.

2. Thomas E. Patterson, *Out of Order* (New York, 1993), 50; *New York Times,* March 30, 1991, p. 1.

3. Germond and Witcover, *Whose Broad Stripes,* 6.

4. "Overheard," *Newsweek,* Aug. 1, 1988, 13.

5. "Bush's Line," *Fort Worth Star-Telegram,* Oct. 24, 1988, sec. I, p. 6.

6. T.R.B., *The New Republic,* July 11, 1988, 4; Elizabeth Drew, *Election Journal: Political Events of 1987—1988* (New York, 1989), 304–6; Roger Simon, *Road Show* (New York, 1990), 203–30; Sidney Blumenthal, *Pledging Allegiance: The Last Campaign of the Cold War* (New York, 1990), 224, 264, 296; "Campaign Trail," *New York Times,* Oct. 17, 1988, p. 10; "Inmate-Release Glitches Cross Party Lines," *Fort Worth Star-Telegram,* Oct. 10, 1988, sec. I, p. 17.

7. Simon, *Road Show,* 53–54.

8. Maureen Dowd, "Candidates Try Their Hand at Humor," *New York Times,*

Oct. 22, 1988, p. 7; "Dukakis Makes Pledge," *New York Times,* July 22, 1988, p. 9; "Campaign Trail," *New York Times,* May 12, 1988, p. 10; "Bush Hurls Lasers," *New York Times,* Sept. 17, 1988, p. 8; Germond and Witcover, *Whose Broad Stripes,* 406; Kitty Dukakis, *Now You Know* (New York, 1990), 217; "Campaign Trail," *New York Times,* Sept. 15, 1988, p. 15; Fred Barnes, "Mr. Congeniality," *The New Republic,* Oct. 3, 1988, p. 12; "Overheard," *Newsweek,* Sept. 19, 1988, p. 17; "Bloopers by Bush Balloon," *San Antonio Light,* Sept. 19, 1988, p. A-5; "Campaign Trail," *New York Times,* Sept. 13, 1988, p. 10; "Dukakis Makes Pledge of Competence," *New York Times,* July 22, 1988, p. 9; Molly Ivins, "Texas George," *MS,* May 1988, 24.

9. Germond and Witcover, *Whose Broad Stripes,* 161, 408; Drew, *Election Journal,* 266, 269.

10. Germond and Witcover, *Whose Broad Stripes,* 440; Germond and Witcover, *Mad as Hell: Revolt at the Ballot Box* (New York, 1993), 390.

11. David R. Runkel, *Campaign for President: The Managers Look at '88* (Dover, Mass., 1989), 136; Drew, *Election Journal,* 88, 262, 323; "The Keys to Election '88," *U.S. News & World Report,* Aug. 29–Sept. 5, 1988, p. 51; Germond and Witcover, *Whose Broad Stripes,* 458.

CHAPTER FIFTY-TWO
1992—Clinton and the Call for Change

1. Larry King, with Mark Stencel, *On the Line: The New Road to the White House* (New York, 1993), 15.

2. Michael Kelly, *New York Times,* Sept. 1, 1992, p. A10.

3. *Time,* Nov. 2, 1992, p. 27.

4. Margaret Truman, "Mr. President, I Knew Harry Truman," *Washington Post National Weekly Edition,* Aug. 21–Sept. 6, 1992, p. 28.

5. Peter Goldman et al., *Quest for the Presidency, 1992* (College Station, Texas, 1994), 97–98.

6. David Von Drehle, *Washington Post National Weekly Edition,* Nov. 9–15, 1992, p. 10.

7. "As Race Looks Tighter," *New York Times,* Oct. 29, 1992, p. 1.

8. "How He Won: The Untold Story of Bill Clinton's Triumph," *Newsweek,* Special Election Issue, Nov./Dec. 1992, p. 95.

9. Ken Auletta, "Loathe the Media," *Esquire,* Nov. 1992, p. 107.

10. Joe Klein, "Clinton: Survivor," *Newsweek,* July 20, 1992, p. 23.

11. David Gallen, *Bill Clinton: As They Know Him* (New York, 1994), 237.

12. Klein, "Clinton: Survivor," *Newsweek,* July 20, 1992, p. 23; Thomas E. Patterson, *Out of Order* (New York, 1993), 100–101; "Campaign Trail," *New York Times,* April 4, 1992, p. 10; *Newsweek,* Special Election Issue, Nov./Dec. 1992, pp. 34, 81; Tom Rosenthiel, *Strange Bedfellows* (New York, 1993), 80; King, *On the Line,* 64; Donnie Radcliffe, *Hillary Rodham Clinton: A First Lady for Our Time* (New York, 1993), 231; "How He Won," *Newsweek,* Nov./Dec. 1992, pp. 32–34; Jack W. Germond and Jules Witcover, *Mad as Hell: Revolt at the Ballot Box* (New York, 1993), 185, 187, 204, 207; Goldman et al., *Quest for the Presidency,* 113–14, 118, 124, 230, 497.

13. Mary Matalin and James Carville, *All's Fair: Love, War, and Running for President* (New York, 1994), 351–53; Germond and Witcover, *Mad as Hell,* 468–70.

14. King, *On the Line,* 88; "Democrats," *Fort Worth Star-Telegram,* Oct. 18, 1992, p. A-26.

15. "Sam to You," *Time,* Aug. 31, 1992, p. 13.

16. King, *On the Line,* 106, 122–23; Sean Wilentz, "Pop Populi," *New Republic,* Aug. 9, 1993, pp. 31, 34; John Hohenberg, *The Bill Clinton Story: Winning the Presidency* (Syracuse, N.Y., 1994), 165, 174; Goldman et al., *Quest for the Presidency,* 430, 536, 551–52; Germond and Witcover, *Mad as Hell,* 476.

17. *Newsweek,* Special Election Issue, Nov./Dec. 1992, 75–76; Goldman at al., *Quest for the Presidency,* 463.

18. "Perotxysms," *New York Times,* June 9, 1992, p. A12.

19. William Safire, "Who Trusts Whom?," *New York Times Magazine,* Oct. 4, 1992, pp. 13–14; *Bushisms: President George Herbert Walker Bush in His Own Words* (New York, 1992), 7, 18; "A Little Rain & Frogs," *Newsweek,* Jan. 27, 1992, p. 18; Goldman et al., *Quest for the Presidency,* 330.

20. King, *On the Line,* 84–85; "The 1992 Campaign," *New York Times,* Sept. 14, 1992, p. A14; Dirk Johnson, "A Political Spouse," *New York Times,* Oct. 10, 1992, p. A11.

21. Susan Feeny and Kathy Lewis, "Letter from the Road," *Dallas Morning News,* Oct. 27, 1992, p. 12A; "Campaign Trail," *New York Times,* Oct. 31, 1992, p. 8.

22. Feeny and Lewis, "Letter from the Road," p. 12A; Germond and Witcover, *Mad as Hell,* 17–18.

Index